SHIMODA
STORY

SHIMODA

University of Hawaii Press
Honolulu, Hawaii

STORY

Oliver Statler

下田物語

オリヴァー スタットラー

Library of Congress Cataloging in Publication Data

Statler, Oliver.
  Shimoda story.

  Reprint. Originally published: New York: Random House,
1969.
  Bibliography: p.
  Includes index.
  1. United States—Foreign relations—Japan. 2. Japan—
Foreign relations—United States. 3. Shimoda-shi (Japan)
4. Harris, Townsend, 1804–1878. I. Title.
[E183.8.J3S7 1986]   327.73052   85–29012
ISBN 0–8248–1059–7 (pbk.)

First published in 1969 by Random House, Inc.
and Random House of Canada
Paperback edition by University of Hawaii Press 1986

Designed by Anthea Lingeman
Chapter opening calligraphy by Charles Saito

Cover illustration courtesy Kurofunekan, Niigata, Japan

To the people of Shimoda,

then and now

CONTENTS

ILLUSTRATIONS

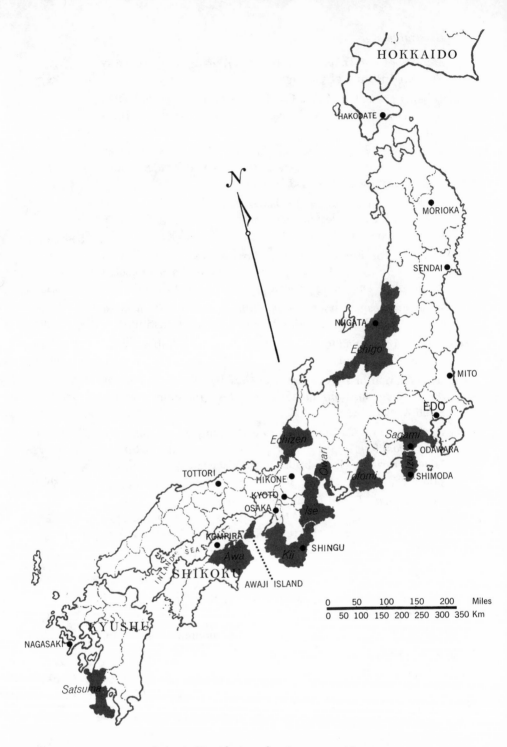

Japan in Harris's time, showing towns, cities,
provinces, and islands mentioned in this story.

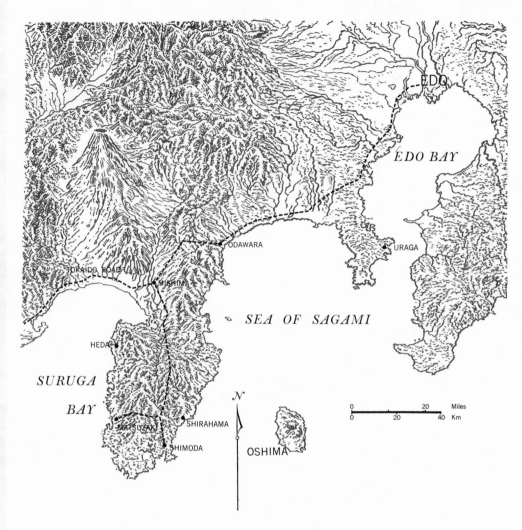

The Izu Peninsula and Edo, indicating
the mountainous terrain.

SHIMODA STORY

THE PRINCIPAL JAPANESE
IN THIS STORY

(Names are in the Japanese style, family name first; Japanese titles are
given in the index; the titles which Townsend Harris applied to
members of the Shimoda Governor's staff are shown in parenthesis.)

At Shimoda town

THE GOVERNORS AND THEIR STAFF

Governor Inoue Kiyonao, Lord of Shinano

Governor Okada Tadayoshi, Lord of Bingo

Governor Nakamura Tameya, Lord of Dewa

Executive Officer Wakana Miosaburō ("Vice-Governor")

Executive Officer Isa Shinjirō

Executive Officer Matsumura Chūshirō ("Vice-Governor")

Superintendent Wakiya Usaburō ("Third Governor," "Mayor of Kakisaki")

Superintendent Moriyama Einosuke (name changed later from Einosuke to Takichirō)

Vice-Superintendent Kikuna Sennojō ("Commissary of Shimoda")

Inspector Aihara Isaburō

Assistant Inspector Saitō Genzō

Assistant Inspector Uchino Ryūzō

Interpreter Namura Tsunenosuke

Interpreter Tateishi Tokojūrō

Physician and translator (on detached service from the Lord of Kii) Itō Kansai

PEOPLE OF THE TOWN

Headman: Hambei

Physician: Asaoka Kyōan °

Merchant: Wataya Kichibei °

Former town secretary: Hirai Heijirō °

Artist: Unshō

Girls of the entertainment quarter: Okichi, Ofuku

At Kakisaki village

PEOPLE OF THE VILLAGE

Headman: Yoheiji

Elders: Chūemon, Gennosuke, Kosaburō, Shinzaemon, Yahei, Kyūemon

Former headman, landowner: Heiemon

Buddhist priest of Gyokusenji temple: Bimō

Shugendō priest of Daijō-in temple: Buntatsu (later changed to Kentatsu)

His mother: Tami

Physician: Okamura Bunkei °

AT GYOKUSENJI

Attendants: Murayama Takizō, Nishiyama Sukezō

Servant: Kosuke

° Commoners were not permitted to use family names in this period. Exceptions were made for physicians and members of other highly respected professions. Wataya is not a family name: it is the "house name" or business name. In the case of Hirai Heijirō, this is the name by which this revered man of Shimoda is known today.

At Edo and on the national scene

MEMBERS OF THE GREAT COUNCIL
(AND, OF COURSE, INSIDE LORDS)

Hotta Masayoshi, daimyo of Sakura

Abe Masahiro, daimyo of Fukuyama

Matsudaira Tadakata, daimyo of Ueda

LORDS OF THE TOKUGAWA FAMILY

Tokugawa Nariaki, retired daimyo of Mito
(one of the Three Houses)

Hitotsubashi Keiki, his son, daimyo of
Hitotsubashi

Matsudaira Yoshinaga, daimyo of Echizen

INSIDE LORD

Ii Naosuke, daimyo of Hikone

OUTSIDE LORD

Shimazu Nariakira, daimyo of Satsuma

SHOGUNATE OFFICIALS

Kawaji Toshiakira, finance bureau and
committee on foreign trade

Mizuno Tadanori, finance bureau and committee on foreign trade

Tsutsui Masanori, *ometsuke* and committee on foreign trade

Hayashi Noboru, scholar

AT KYOTO

Ishikawa, steward to one of the nobles of
the Imperial court

A note on the pronunciation of Japanese names
(after Edward Seidensticker)

Consonants are pronounced approximately as in English, except that the "g" is always hard, as in Gilbert. Vowels are pronounced as in Italian and always pronounced separately, never in dipthongs. Also as in Italian, the final "e" is always pronounced. There is no heavy penultimate accent as in English; it is adequate to accent each syllable equally.

> Examples: Inoue—Ee-no-oo-weh
> Abe—Ah-beh

Marks to indicate long vowels are shown above and in the index and bibliography but not in the text.

A note on Japanese coinage

1 *ryo* = 4 *bu*, 1 *bu* = 1600 *mon*
(the rate of *mon* to *bu* fluctuated)

As this book begins, the exchange rate was one *bu* for one dollar. Under the terms of the Shimoda Convention of 1857, the rate was approximately three *bu* for one dollar.

3

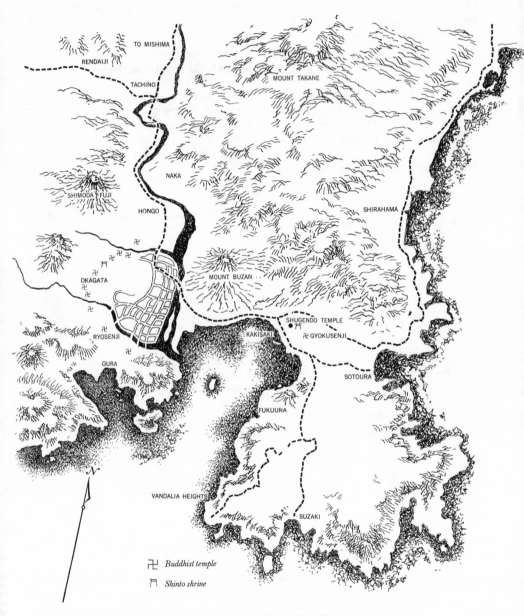

TO MISHIMA

RENDAIJI

TACHINO

MOUNT TAKANE

NAKA

SHIMODA FUJI

HONGO

SHIRAHAMA

OKAGATA

MOUNT BUZAN

RYOSENJI

SHUGENDO TEMPLE

OURA

KAKISAKI

GYOKUSENJI

SOTOURA

FUKUURA

N

VANDALIA HEIGHTS

SUZAKI

卍 *Buddhist temple*

鳥 *Shinto shrine*

Shimoda town and nearby villages.

Chapter 1

AUGUST 21, 1856

From Shimoda town one cannot watch the sun rise out of the sea. Mountains rim the harbor, and from Shimoda one looks out not to the open sea but across the harbor to the village of Kakisaki. The sun rises over the mountains behind Kakisaki and its glow hits first the mountains behind Shimoda. It touches the cone of Shimoda Fuji, local miniature of the great mountain. It caresses the rounded twin crowns Shimoda people call the Breasts. It slides down the ridges and tree-covered hollows until it burnishes the black tile roofs of the temples that stand in guardian line along the lower slopes. At last it washes over the town, warming the houses and flooding into the streets.

By that hour, on a morning something more than a century ago, the town was stirring from a summer night's sleep. The night watchmen had put away the clappers which had sounded reassurance through the dark hours. Now and again the stillness was broken by the racket of shutters' being opened. A few breakfast fires had been lighted and were sending tendrils of smoke into the pale sky. Crews of fishing boats were gathering their gear to go after bonito. Stonecutters were yawning and stretching. A farmer splashed cool water on his face; in those days there were paddy fields and a farming village between Shimoda and its row of temples.

But the center of the town, the area of shops and ships' inns, still seemed drained of life. The shutters of the pharmacy Nagasakiya were closed; above them sunlight slanted against the only Western letters to be seen in Shimoda: a sign advertising a Dutch remedy of great repute. The gate was barred to the house of Dr. Asaoka Kyoan, the town's most distinguished physician, who had studied not only Chinese but also Western medicine. The sprawling establishment of Wataya Kichibei—broker, shipowner, dealer in stone and charcoal—was quiet. No one stirred around the town office, the harbor master's office, or the Goyosho, the handsome new building from which this area was administered. In the willow-tree pleasure quarter a solitary roisterer, risen from a warm bed, moved unsteadily homeward past bars and restaurants closed and withdrawn against the dawn. He paused at one corner, braced himself against the cool stone wall of a shop, and while relieving himself, sang to the empty streets, only a little out of tune:

> "A long stay at Shimoda of Izu—
> Oh, give it up!
> For your striped purse will soon be empty."

It was an old song, and well worn, for of all Shimoda's products its most famous was feminine hospitality—more famous even than the stone from its quarries, much of which had gone to the Shogun's capital at Edo to form the massive ramparts and foundations of his great castle. Shimoda's hospitality was not for highway travelers: the town was cut off from the heart of the country by almost the full length of the long and mountainous Izu Peninsula. Shimoda's hospitality was for those who traveled the sea, for the crews of the hundreds of small unwieldy ships which kept the city folk of Edo—today called Tokyo—supplied with rice to eat, sake to drink, and lumber to rebuild after their frequent fires.

Once Japanese ships had ranged the China Sea and Indian Ocean. Then came the edicts of the early seventeenth century, and isolation. Foreigners were forbidden to enter Japan, except that a few Chinese and fewer Dutch were permitted a trickle of trade at Nagasaki because it suited the government at Edo to have a source of information about what was going on in the world. And by those same edicts Japanese were prohibited from going abroad. After that, the country had only coastal vessels. By dictate they were built with a flat bottom, an open stern to accommodate a great retractable rudder, and but one sail, rigged so they could go only before the wind. In bad weather they had to seek refuge in some harbor.

On the long run between Osaka and Edo, Shimoda was the most famous port of refuge. Furthermore, it once had been the checkpoint for all ships bound for Edo—a checkpoint, like the barrier-gates astride the highways, to guard against contraband weapons being smuggled into the capital. There were stories of times when the little ships were so densely moored that a man could walk clear across the harbor on their decks, a full mile, all the way from Kakisaki to Shimoda. And each ship paid the town a harbor tax, and its sailors spent their money ashore.

A Japanese ship (*a lithograph from a drawing by Meffert*)

Establishment of that checkpoint in 1616 climaxed a series of events which brought Shimoda its era of greatest prosperity. A few years earlier the government had begun to exploit a nearby lode of gold: mines were dug, a boom town mushroomed, and the gold had to be shipped out through Shimoda. Then came the decision to reconstruct Edo Castle on a scale hitherto undreamt of: Izu's quarries rang with the chisels of stone-cutters struggling to keep up with the demand, while three thousand vessels bore huge blocks from Shimoda to Edo. In one feverish decade Shimoda burgeoned from a nondescript village to a bustling town.

Shimoda people preferred, however, not to think about a year one century later—the black year 1720, when the checkpoint was shifted to Uraga, on the inner Bay of Edo and, in truth, a more logical location. Shimoda's prosperity went with it. Edo Castle was built, the quarries were no longer busy. And the gold mines had played out.

The town drifted somnolent through the next century and more. It came alive only in winter, when the rough seas and contrary winds around Izu might fill its harbor. Each ship had its designated inn. The ships of Awa Province, for example, had for generations made their headquarters at the ships' inn called Awaya, and ships from Ise, at the Iseya. Often it was the mistress and maids of the inn who rowed out to welcome the captain and crew. Their greeting set the tone: sailors called Shimoda "the harbor of women," "the harbor of song." And with many masts in view, the town would become cheerful again. Night-sounds of revelry would spill into the streets to mingle with the songs of strolling musicians, and graybeards would compare that winter with legendary ones when a man could cross the harbor on the decks of ships.

Sometimes the little ships were bottled up for weeks on end, but there is no recorded instance when Shimoda's hospitality ran out. And let it be said that the town knew how to entertain. At smaller ports the girls who did the honors were likely to be amateurs, home talent. But Shimoda had professional women: they could sing and dance and play the samisen, they followed the latest fads from Edo, and they knew very well how to please a man.

> In Shimoda of Izu
> You need no anchor:
> The samisen of the geisha
> Can tie up your ship.

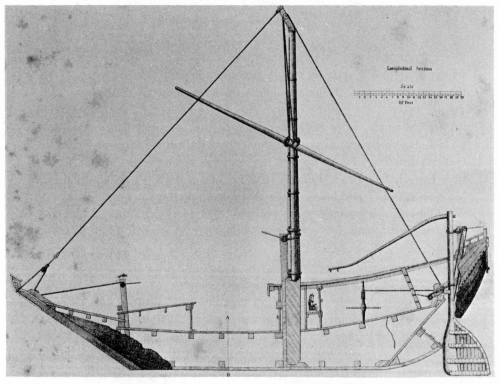

A Japanese ship (*a mechanical drawing by M. Kellogg*)

8

So there had been occasions when crews tarried longer than they needed to, past the times when they might have hoisted sail for home. As proof of Shimoda's hospitality, it was said that sometimes when sailors had emptied their purses to the girls of Shimoda, the girls then supported the sailors. For it could be lonely when the ships and their men had sailed away.

This particular morning—August 21, 1856, by the Gregorian calendar but quite another date to the Japanese—seemed routinely uneventful. In good time merchants opened their shops and children tramped off to school to learn their letters. The sky, which had been cloudless at dawn, became overcast.

Three weeks earlier farmers would have scanned a cloudy sky with desperate hope. The streams which fed the paddy fields were then drying up, and in the fields of millet and vegetables—the upland plots which were not irrigated—the earth was parched.

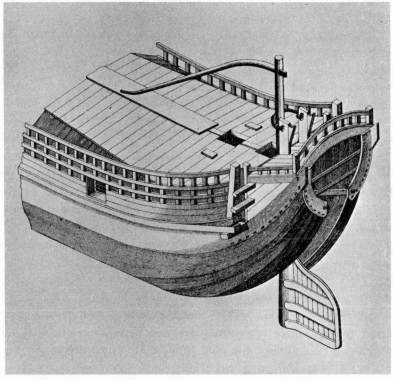

Stern and rudder of a Japanese ship (*a mechanical drawing by M. Kellogg*)

In Kakisaki almost every family—even those who were fishermen or keepers of ships' inns—did some farming, and the drought had brought the community together in emergency session. All agreed that serious measures were in order. The village officials had met at the headman's house with the priests of the village to make preparations. There was the priest of the Shinto shrine, who would invoke the deity of this village to succor his people. There was the priest of the Buddhist temple; though rainmaking was not really in his province, he too would offer prayers. Most important, there was the priest of the mountain religion called Shugendo, a faith which looked to the mountains as the Japanese have always done; water comes from the mountains and this priest would exert all the magic of his incantations, entreating the gods of the mountains to bring rain now. That evening all the villagers had assembled in the grounds of the shrine and the nearby Shugendo temple, and all night they were led in prayers and the ritual of fire.

They had been answered with reasonable promptness. Rain had come four days later, in just the quantity desired, and in the three weeks since, it had fallen in amounts sufficient to keep the fields green.

The people of Kakisaki probably should not get all the credit for the rain. No doubt the farmers of the many other villages roundabout held services too, because the rain, when it came, fell over a wide area. But the only existing record of those particular days is the diary of Yoheiji, the headman of Kakisaki, and we look to it for details.

Since the rain had come, Yoheiji had found few other items important enough to enter in his diary.—Government officials had got around to paying for some fishing boats they had requisitioned to use as harbor craft. Only yesterday they had demanded copies of all directives issued by the village. But a canny headman tried to be prepared for this kind of bureaucratic caprice: duplicates were ready and had been promptly forwarded, from as far back as 1781; Yoheiji thought that should satisfy them.

The headman also noted that the Governor on duty had inspected the villages around the harbor to the accompaniment of the usual formalities.

The Governor was one of a pair. Normally, as at present, one of them was stationed at Shimoda and the other at Edo. The man at the capital handled reports, accepted instructions, and kept himself posted on the government's policy while the man in Shimoda administered the district. Periodically they changed places. That was the government's way, to appoint such officers in tandem.

There were fewer than a dozen districts in Japan that had governors. The presence of governors meant that the capital had taken the area under its direct control, and that meant the area was a point of crisis. In the year 1856 crisis in Japan usually had to do with foreigners, and so it was with Shimoda.

Two years earlier Commodore Matthew C. Perry of the United States Navy had brought the full weight of his powerful personality and his powerful fleet to bear upon the Japanese government, and had succeeded in extracting a treaty which shattered the nation's two-century-old policy of seclusion.

By Perry's treaty the Japanese had agreed to open two ports where American ships might obtain provisions. This clause was especially designed to assist the whaling ships of New England which then roamed the North Pacific, but Perry was a man who looked to the future and he also had in mind the needs of the U. S. Navy and of transpacific steamers he envisioned as someday making the long haul between California and the China coast.

Choosing the ports to open had been a worrisome business for the Japanese, but finally they had offered Shimoda and Hakodate. Hakodate was on the northernmost of Japan's main islands, a distant outpost but fortunately convenient to whalers. Shimoda was much nearer the capital, Edo, but it seemed remote enough to be manageable, lying as it did near the tip of the fifty-mile-long peninsula of Izu. Most of Izu was wild and lonely, corrugated with mountains. It seemed a place where foreigners could be safely quarantined from the rest of the country. At least there was good precedent: Japanese rulers had been using Izu and its offshore islands as a place of exile for more than a thousand years. (For the same reasons, fugitives from the law had often disappeared there; a number of Shimoda's families could, if they wished, trace their ancestry to such men.)

And so the government had taken direct control of the town, which long had been administered as part of the province of Izu, and not only of the town but of the district for seventeen miles around, including some ninety villages, for that was the area opened to Americans by Perry's treaty. And it was only two years ago this past spring that Perry had brought his Black Ships to Shimoda, including the first steamships that the Japanese had seen.

The people had been thoroughly frightened at the prospect. It was well known that barbarian foreigners ate cattle and that their sexual habits were unspeakable. An old song reflected their fears:

> Through a black night of cloud and rain
> The Black Ships ply their way—
> Alien things of evil mien—
> Across the waters gray.

The government had offered no reassurance. In its notice announcing the visit, it stated:

> The foreigners will probably leave their ships and loiter about. It is ordered that all doors be closed, all merchandise be concealed, and the foreigners be kept away from houses. Those who possess cows are reminded to hide them from the foreigners' sight. It is particularly important that all women be kept indoors; they must never try to see the ships. This message is to be signed by the headman of each village and sent on to the next village as quickly as possible, day or night.

But the people of Shimoda survived the visits by Perry and his men and by the other foreigners who followed, and though there were those among the townsfolk who wanted to burn the bench in front of Wataya Kichibei's because foreigners had sat on it, others discovered compensations: the foreigners brought the Governors, and the Governors brought a large staff, and, together, the Governors and their staff and the foreigners brought prosperity—prosperity of all sorts:

> How grateful can one be!
> The honorable foreigner has
> paid eight coins for
> a one-coin harlot!

It had been a long time since prosperity had made itself at home in Shimoda.

The events that made August 21, 1856, special began about noon. From the lookout station high on Buzan hill, the roar of a cannon echoed around the harbor and up the valleys. It was the signal that a foreign ship was approaching. Farmers in their fields straightened for a moment, then bent again to their weeding. But Yoheiji, who had been putting his files in order after yesterday's fuss of pulling duplicates, set aside this chore and climbed to a spot behind his house where he could see the harbor's mouth. He was joined there by Gennosuke, one of the village elders and an innkeeper by trade. Together they watched for the ship.

She came into view soon enough, large, black, and trailing a cloud of smoke. Yoheiji asked Gennosuke to make certain that the required number of men reported to the guard station on the shore just below them, and then to go in person to government headquarters at the Goyosho to await any orders. He himself issued a call for all the seamen of the village to assemble. They would be needed for guard duty and to man harbor boats.

One of the first lads to report was put to work at once, picked by Gennosuke to scull him over to Shimoda; it would take too long to walk the shoreline. As Gennosuke moved across the bay, he watched the big ship. She had picked up one of the pilots that Commodore Perry had commissioned and was moving to the inner harbor. Gennosuke envied the pilot his chance to go aboard these foreign vessels; luckily, this pilot, Kyuhei, was a Kakisaki man—Gennosuke would talk with him later. He saw that the ship had no paddle wheels; she seemed to be propelled from the stern. This was something new; he must question Kyuhei about it.

A boatman (*a book illustration by Jichosai*)

Gennosuke's boat entered the river mouth, moved past the low sandy island where Shimoda's shipyards were clustered, and pushed up to the stone steps of the landing place. At that same moment the foreign ship dropped her anchor. Gennosuke climbed onto the quay and walked swiftly toward the Goyosho.

As he had expected, he was far from the first to arrive. Several villages were nearer than Kakisaki, and their officials were already on hand. Gennosuke reported with due formality at the back door: village functionaries were not expected to appear at the front entrance.

He could see that officials were already preparing to board the ship. He watched them leave and noted that the man in charge was Assistant Inspector Saito, an official of middling grade in the administrative department who had built an after-hours reputation for prowess with women of the gay quarter. Saito's usual responsibilities concerned real estate, but his superiors considered that his smooth manner and self-assurance—there were those who called it arrogance—qualified him for the reception of foreigners. Besides Saito there was a police official, an interpreter, and two censors, indispensable men who served both as recording secretaries and as part of the Governor's inspector-general department: reporting only to him, they were calculated to keep alert and honest any official whose performance they observed; it was a system the whole government found useful. Rain had begun to fall, and each man's servant held an umbrella over his master.

Saito and his party did not stay long on the ship. Within half an hour or so they had made their bows, climbed down into their boat, and were heading back to shore. As they were sculled along, the censors reviewed their record of the meeting, the interpreter mopped his brow and congratulated himself that it was over, and the laconic official of police reflected on the strange behavior of a host who did not even offer a cup of tea. Saito glowed with importance. He carried startling news, and he formed in his mind the phrases he would use to break it to his superiors.

The ship was an American warship, and she had brought to Shimoda a man that the Governors, their staff, and indeed the entire government, had been dreading to see: the Consul General of the United States for Japan.

When Perry was hammering out his treaty, the Japanese negotiators had fought hard against permitting an American official on their shores, but Perry had been adamant:

> There shall be appointed by the government of the United States consuls or agents to reside in Shimoda at any time after the expiration of eighteen months from the date of the signing of this treaty; provided that either of the two governments deem such arrangement necessary.

The Japanese government had been worrying ever since. Worry had reached a crescendo last year, when the eighteenth month—September, 1855—had rolled around. There was little doubt in anyone's mind that the United States would exercise its right, but there was great doubt as to the best way to handle the consul when he appeared.

Within the government there were those who thought that opening the country was inevitable, that foreign trade might even be desirable, and that the nation should face up to both and welcome a consul. There were others who believed that nothing more should be yielded to foreigners, that to allow them to take up residence would be but a prelude to more and greater trouble, that this was the point to take a stand, and that if war had to come, let it come. And there were views of every shade in between. The government acted characteristically: it appointed a committee to study the matter. The committee functioned characteristically: it was unable to reach a decision.

As the eighteenth month after treaty-signing came and then receded into the past, the sense of urgency in Edo diminished: there were plenty of other problems to be faced. But the Governors of Shimoda remained edgy, for Edo had shifted the problem to them. They were sent instructions which they must have regarded uneasily: if a consul appeared he was to be told that "due to some difficulties" the government could not permit him to stay, and he was to be persuaded to go away—peacefully. And the Governors were cautioned, in words heavy with implication for their careers, that this was a very important matter, to be handled with full awareness of their responsibility to their country.

Saito knew all this, and he anticipated with a pleasant tingle the excitement his news was bound to create. He was carrying three letters, two of them, he had been told, for the "Foreign Minister" in Edo, one for the Governor. And he had a couple of triumphs to report: he had parried all the foreign emissary's queries about a house to live in, and he had quashed a proposal by the Americans that they make a courtesy call on the Governor this afternoon. He had promised a reply later to the Consul General's added suggestion that he might land and call on the Governor tomorrow, if it was a fair day.

Saito was quite right in thinking he would create a stir. The senior officials on duty went into conference at once, and a report was dispatched to the Governor, who was at his residence and personal office a mile or so up the valley.

To his disappointment, Saito was not included in the second party to board the ship, though he drew some satisfaction from the fact that he was replaced by three men, all of higher rank. Now in charge was a trusted inspector named Aihara, and while the same two censors went out again, another interpreter was added to ease the strain. It was still raining when Aihara took his group out.

Aihara brought to his interview more age and more experience than Saito had done, and subtly he took charge of the conversation. The Consul General's purpose in coming to Japan was understood, he began. He offered sympathy for the difficulties of the long voyage and congratulations on safe arrival. Arrangements were being made to forward the two letters to Edo at once; the one addressed to the Governor was being translated and as soon as it could be read it would be answered. The Governor would receive the Americans tomorrow; men would be sent to the ship to conduct them to the meeting place. And finally he reiterated Saito's offer of supplies, whatever was available, to meet the ship's needs.

The Americans, who had before asked only for fresh water, now said they would like pears, watermelon, and oranges.

Aihara regretted that oranges, a winter fruit, were out of season, and pears and watermelon were not grown around Shimoda; however, he would try to order some. And thinking, no doubt, of the dinner to be prepared for the reception tomorrow, he asked how many men would land to meet the Governor.

The Consul General, his secretary-interpreter, and probably eleven or twelve of the ship's officers; Commodore Armstrong was not feeling well and would not join them. How many days, the American asked, did it take to reach Edo by land?

Five or six.

When would his letters reach the Foreign Minister?

In about five days.

And when would he receive an answer?

Ah, Aihara replied, that was impossible to say, for the letter would have to be discussed before an answer could be prepared. What was the commodore's condition?

He was a little feverish but he would recover soon.

Aihara hoped he would take enough rest.

The Americans had brought various kinds of seed, the Consul General announced, and would like to plant them for the Japanese.

Aihara was afraid they wouldn't grow.

Where were the Americans buried who had died while Perry's ships were in port?

They lay, said Aihara, at the temple of Gyokusenji in the village of Kakisaki.

The interview was closed. Aihara made his bows and left the ship.

Between the two visits to the ship, the Governors' office had dispatched an order to the headman of Kakisaki. It was about four o'clock when the messenger reached Yoheiji's house, where he sat talking with Chuemon. Like Gennosuke, who earlier had gone to Shimoda, Chuemon was one of the village elders. It followed that both were from old and respected families—there was no room for upstarts in village government—but while Gennosuke was an innkeeper, Chuemon was a farmer from the hills behind the temple.

Chuemon was a powerful man, tall and stout. In the past he had often been delegated to shepherd the village's tax payments on the long rough journey up the peninsula to the provincial magistrate's headquarters. That was before the Governors had been appointed; now taxes were paid locally.

But despite his brawn, Chuemon was a worrier. He had begun to worry when he heard the signal cannon, and his worries had multiplied since then. When he could bear it no longer, he had changed to kimono suitable for official business and set out to see whether the headman was also worrying.

He had been somewhat relieved to find Yoheiji going over old orders relating to foreigners. Together they read one issued three years earlier. Its topic was the government's very real concern that foreigner-hating elements of the population, especially drifters of the warrior class, might attack foreigners (though naturally the government was not so much solicitous of the foreigners' well-being as afraid of an international incident):

> Upon arrival of foreign vessels, strict restrictions shall be maintained. Should scoundrels or sinister persons be seen, they are to be apprehended immediately. If they cannot be arrested, they may be killed by swords or beaten to death . . . but this action may be taken only when arrest is impossible. If the scoundrels are in a group, it will be difficult to fight them unarmed; therefore, wooden staves should be on hand at all times for emergencies. Neighboring villages shall keep in touch with one another so that in emergencies they may assist each other . . .

Yoheiji was assuring Chuemon that Kakisaki had an adequate stockpile of quarterstaves when the messenger arrived from Shimoda. The headman signed for the order, and after lifting it to his forehead to show proper respect, unrolled and read it. No message in reply was called for, so he dismissed the man with a tip—making a mental note to add it to his expense account—and announced to Chuemon that the head priest of Gyokusenji was to report to the Governor's office at once.

Yoheiji could have sent for the priest, but he was a man who liked to keep in motion, so he suggested to Chuemon that they walk over to the temple and deliver the message themselves. They thought they knew what the summons meant. In the past two years Gyokusenji had been requisitioned so many times it was almost routine.

It had been used as a rest house by Perry's men, and again by Russians who came a few months later to negotiate a treaty of their own. The Russians' stay was prolonged by a tidal wave that smashed their ship and almost obliterated Shimoda (the town had been completely rebuilt in the past year and a half: the government had poured in men and material and money, lest the foreigners demand another port). Then the temple was turned over to some American traders who had sailed into Shimoda to do business; taken aback when they discovered that Perry's treaty didn't authorize trade, they had salvaged something from the situation by renting their ship to carry some of the Russians home, and while they waited for it to return they moved into Gyokusenji with their wives and children, the first American families to live in Japan. Kakisaki people still talked about the party they had held to celebrate a birthday; with Russian officers as guests and Russian bandsmen making cacophony, men and women had paired off and danced *with their arms around each other.*

Shimoda harbor from a hill behind Kakisaki: the Russian frigate
Diana at anchor, Japanese ships moored in Kakisaki inlet, the artist in the right
foreground (*a drawing by Aleksandr Mozhaiskii*)

The Americans had scarcely moved out after their ship's return when the temple was again taken over by foreigners, this time the supercargo and carpenter from a German vessel whose captain contracted to carry the remaining Russians to safety; since that ship and the Russians were captured by a British man-of-war (the Crimean War was in progress), the two men occupied Gyokusenji for six months, until the arrival of another merchant ship gave them a chance to leave.

As Yoheiji and Chuemon walked, Chuemon suggested that perhaps it had been a mistake to rebuild the temple eight years before; its newness apparently made it more desirable. But Yoheiji thought that, new or old, it was so ideally situated for the government's purposes—close to the harbor but away from Shimoda town—it was bound to be appropriated. They hoped that this ship's visit would be a brief one and that it would not be necessary, as it had been on each occasion in the past, to repaper all the sliding doors and re-cover all the tatami mats. Chuemon wished there were some way to get foreigners to take off their boots, like civilized people, before they walked on the mats.

They found Priest Bimo preparing for the evening service. He digested the news glumly, called an apprentice to read the sutras, and then was seized by stage fright. He had no idea how to behave in the Governors' office, he said. Where should he report? What should he say and do?

Yoheiji sympathized and Yoheiji had a solution: could Chuemon, he asked, accompany the priest to guide him through the formalities and save him from any embarrassment? Chuemon could, and the priest looked grateful.

Yoheiji and Chuemon sipped tea in the priest's quarters while the priest changed clothes, and then Yoheiji watched as they summoned a boat and started across the harbor. Pleased with himself for having thought of a job to keep Chuemon from fretting, he turned toward home.

It was after dark when Chuemon reappeared with the expected news. Gyokusenji was to be evacuated by noon tomorrow so it could be used as a resting place for the foreigners. Chuemon, who had given his pledge that everything would be ready as directed, said he would mobilize a group of farmers to clean the temple first thing in the morning, and then went home to a late supper.

The rain had ended and the sky was clearing. Yoheiji sat for a long time before the open doors of his house, watching the lights of the ship, wondering about it and the strange faraway place it came from.

Things were not so quiet within the white walls of the Governors' compound up the valley, built there after the tidal wave had demonstrated

Commodore Matthew C. Perry (*detail from a
scroll painting attributed to Takagawa Bunsen*)

that it was not always safe to be close to the sea. In their haste the builders
had not chosen the most attractive location available. They had requisitioned paddy land, flat and treeless, and they had scarred the hills behind
to get earth to fill in the irrigated fields. From caves in those hills thousands
of bats emerged each night. But bats were not distracting the men hard at
work this night.

Saito and Aihara had been questioned at length. The transcripts of
their interviews had been sifted. Not only the letter to the Governor but the
two letters addressed to Edo had been translated and studied. One depressing fact was clear: the Consul General authorized by Perry's treaty had
arrived to take up residence.

The conference agreed that the best hope seemed to lie in the ailing
commodore. Surely he must be this consul's superior: the Japanese remembered Perry, and after that experience they could not imagine that any
commodore of the United States Navy would be anything but in charge.
The fact that this commodore had not appeared today and apparently

would not land tomorrow seemed confirmation; Perry, too, had been aloof until it suited his purposes to show himself.

The first step, then, was to delay meeting the Consul General until the commodore was ready to accompany him. The Governor remembered his bad leg; a flare-up of that chronic ailment was in order: if the commodore could be ill, so could he.

That decided, the Governor dictated a report to the Great Council in Edo, to be dispatched by fast runner early in the morning. He described the ship and the circumstances of her arrival:

> On board are a Commodore, a Consul General who expects to be stationed in Japan, and others. They presented three letters written sideways. Two of them were written to the government and the other one to me. As copies of the letters to the government were not presented, I ordered those to be translated together with the other one, considering that they might help me when I receive the Americans. Each of the letters tells about sending a Consul General to Japan. I transmit the letters, with translations, and reports of the meetings on the ship. As you have ordered, I will do my best to prevent his residence in Japan.

The shipyard at Shimoda (*a woodcut from a drawing by Wilhelm Heine*)

The report finished, the staff bowed and took their leave, some to residences within the compound, others to quarters downtown, near the Goyosho. Saito decided not to go home; there was still time to join a party he knew was in progress at one of the restaurants. The Governor's servants saw the men off and then began to close the shutters of his office.

In Shimoda other shutters were being closed as the day ended. Fishermen's homes were quieter than usual, for most of the men who had gone to sea at dawn could not be expected back for another day or two. Ship carpenters lingered in little groups on benches in front of their houses, slapping at mosquitoes and discussing the American ship; arrival of a foreign ship always set off arguments: should the Japanese copy them or were the old ways best? And today's ship had introduced the propeller to Shimoda, another new idea to chew on. In the next block the town's greatest merchant, Wataya Kichibei, who had been designated as purveyor to foreign ships, speculated on the profits he might make from this one.

A block away the gay district lay clustered around a stream which purled between stone embankments lined with lanterns and willows. Light splashed from the houses, and the trees tossed sinuous shadows to a broken rhythm of song and shrill laughter. The fashionable new Edo-style restaurant Hamadaya stood on the edge of the quarter, part of it yet a little aloof; it was here that Saito joined the party. He was at once the center of attention. Friends poured him cup after cup of sake while they peppered him with questions about the American warship and what it brought. But when they seemed to be getting too serious, one of the women touched her samisen and made a ribald comment on the anatomy of foreign men. The party mood was restored. From the street below, a pair of strolling musicians sent up a bit of plaintive song:

> ". . . of last night's vows of love,
> of lately whispered tales of tears and sighs,
> of a dear lover from the past . . ."

It was from the ballad called "Raven at Dawn." Set in Edo's great gay quarter, the Yoshiwara, it was a sad tale of unlucky love between a courtesan and a merchant's son who had squandered on her all the tax money his father had entrusted to him. One of the girls present was famed for the way she sang it. There were demands for her, and a little flushed, a little unsteady, the girl pulled her knees together, smoothed her kimono, moved into the soft glow of the oil lamp, and took up the song:

". . . Silent the spring rain; dozing
and softly aroused, lost and disheveled
through love, the courtesan Urazato wonders:
'By what strange affinity
did I love him so from our first meeting?' "

Chapter 2

AUGUST 22–
SEPTEMBER 4, 1856

The American's name was Townsend Harris. He, too, kept a journal.

On the day after he arrived in Shimoda he recorded another visit by the Japanese:

Friday, August 22, 1856. The officers off again this morning to inquire after the Commodore's health; and, finding he was too unwell to go on shore today, they said the Governor begged to be excused from seeing me today, as he was unwell, etc. I said tomorrow would do as well. They asked if the Commodore would be well enough to go with me tomorrow. I answered I could not say, but that my visit was entirely independent of the Commodore; that, when he was well enough, he would himself call on the Governor. I found that it was their plan to delay my visit until the Commodore was well enough, so that they might afterwards deny having received me on my individual account, but solely as one of the Commodore's suite, and this was proved by their saying that when the Governor was well enough to see me he would send me word. I then said this was a matter concerning the dignity of my government, that the Governor should write to me excusing himself on account of illness, and that I would send that letter to my government, and leave it for its adjustment.

This proposition greatly embarrassed them.*

Inspector Aihara was the emissary again that morning, and he was indeed embarrassed. It was embarrassing that the American should see through their little device; it was even more embarrassing that he should be so tactless as to say that he did. But having been read a lesson in Western

---

* Quotations from Harris's journal throughout this book are in italic.

diplomatic etiquette, Aihara offered one in Japanese manners. "In Japan," he said, "it is more polite to deliver word by messenger than by letter."

Harris was adamant. He would have a letter and it must be from the Governor. Aihara was forced to accede.

Harris asked whether the consulate building was finished.

Aihara answered that he believed Saito had explained that yesterday. Year before last a tidal wave had struck this port. An uncounted number of lives had been lost. Every vessel in the harbor had been hopelessly damaged, including a Russian warship, the *Diana*. Most of the town had been washed away; only fourteen houses were left undamaged. Though reconstruction had been rushed, it was still not complete. So naturally a consulate had not been built.

Would Harris, he asked, give them copies of the letters addressed to Edo?—for evidently the Governor did not wish to admit that he had read

The tidal wave of December, 1854 (*a drawing by Aleksandr Mozhaiskii*)

them, and yet it might be inconvenient to pretend that he did not know their contents.

According to the Japanese record, Harris chose to lie. He had no copies, he said, and then made the lie unnecessary: he added that he saw no reason to disclose the contents to Shimoda officials.

Aihara did not show his anger. He delivered a gift of bonito and lobster for the ailing commodore, and some fruit in answer to yesterday's request, and took his leave.

By now the Japanese must have guessed that Harris was going to be difficult to deal with. Even in these preliminary skirmishes, these sound-ings-out, he seemed brusque, quick to anger, and very determined.

He was indeed determined. A few days earlier, after sighting the first outlying islands of Japan, he had written:

Monday, August 18, 1856. . . . Conflicting emotions caused by the sight of these Japanese possessions. My future brought vividly to mind. Mental and social isolation on the one hand, and on the other are important public duties which, if properly discharged, will redound to my credit. A people almost unknown to the world is to be examined and reported on in its social, moral and political state; the productions of the country—animal, vegetable and mineral—to be ascertained; the products of the industry of the country found out, and its capacity for commercial intercourse, what are its wants, and what it has to give in exchange. A new and difficult language to be learned; a history, which may throw some light on that of China and Korea, to be examined; and, finally, the various religious creeds of Japan are to be looked at. These various matters offer abundant oc-cupation for my mind, and will surely prevent anything like ennui being felt if only I give myself heartily to the work, and if that sine qua non of all earthly occupation—health—be vouchsafed to me by the Great Giver of all good. . . .

Tuesday, August 19, 1856. Rested badly—could not drive Japan and my duties, on which I am so soon to enter, from my mind. . . . I shall be the first recognized agent from a civilized power to reside in Japan. . . . I hope I may so conduct myself that I may have honorable mention in the histories which will be written on Japan and its future destiny.

These passages reflect more than a becoming modesty. Townsend Harris, as he approached Japan on the United States warship *San Jacinto,* carried with him anxiety and deep self-doubt.

Ten years earlier he had been a respected New York merchant, partner of his older brother John in a wholesale chinaware business. John spent most of his time in England, buying; Townsend's job, in New York, was selling.

Perhaps he found chinaware an uninspiring business. Certainly his interests ranged far wider. He was active in the Chamber of Commerce, he was a trustee of a savings bank and of a free clinic, he taught a Sunday School class. He was a member of the militia and a volunteer fireman. And he was active in politics—a liberal, a Democrat, a member of Tammany. The reward he had sought from his party organization was one that no one else wanted: he was president of the Board of Education. Self-taught, having started at fourteen as a clerk in his brother's shop, he was restricted to a business career because an education for the professions was beyond his reach; he felt inferior and he developed a passionate interest in education. At a time when not many of the city's children attended primary school, he conceived the idea that the city should establish a free academy for those who wanted to go beyond the grades. It was a radical idea, and he was attacked as a radical, but he campaigned successfully for his school and saw it established. It still exists—now known as City College.

It may be that his interests were too wide for the good of his business. His brother thought so. The once-prosperous firm was ailing. John thought he knew the answer, and it was not merely that competition had become stiffer. From London came a letter, a reproachful, accusing letter: it demanded that Townsend resign from the Board of Education.

Perhaps brother John was not very perceptive. It is true that Townsend was neglecting the business; true that though he had always been a temperate man, he was now drinking heavily. The reason was probably the death of his mother. Townsend Harris had never married, never had a romance we know of. His life had centered on his mother. She lived until she was eighty-three and he was forty-three, but when she died the fulcrum was gone from his world.

He did resign from the Board of Education; life seemed more pointless, and things became worse instead of better. There was another letter from John: he would return from London, dissolve the partnership, take over the business himself. Townsend Harris bought a half interest in a sailing ship, and in May, 1849, sailed on a trading expedition to Asia.

They say he was successful at first, but it did not last. He showed no more instinct for business in the Orient than he had in New York and he managed to fail in a period when American trade with China was doubling every year. Then came five years of wandering—the China coast, India, the East Indies, the Philippines, the South Pacific. He was a remittance man, living on funds from home, money which he said was due him from the partnership but which John called loans. It was money which added bitterness to the family quarrel.

But he made friends in Asia. He was an informed and traveled man. He could reminisce with the best of them about New York. He controlled his drinking. He was made welcome in clubs and in homes. He became more than once a godfather.

He began to campaign for a consular appointment in China. The Democrats were in power in Washington. The President was Franklin Pierce. His Secretary of State was William L. Marcy, an able man best remembered for his remark that "to the victor belong the spoils." Harris labored to persuade Marcy that he should apply that doctrine to the consular posts in China.

"I wish I could convince you," he wrote to Marcy in 1854, "that twenty years was quite long enough for one family of Whigs to hold the Canton Consulate, as in that case I might hope to see a change in it." He had the year before pointed out that the consuls and vice-consuls at both Canton and Shanghai were all partners in Russell & Company, adding that "The House of Russell & Company is now and has been for many years past engaged in the illicit traffic of *Opium, that great curse of China. . . .*" This was a serious charge and true enough (almost all the American firms in China were involved in the opium trade), but even so, it failed to dislodge those Whigs and open a post for him.

He tried to talk Perry into taking him along to Japan, and was again unsuccessful. Then, just when his Democratic friends back home were able to get him a minor consular post, at Ningpo, he shifted his sights: he wanted the job that Perry's treaty had opened in Japan. He began the long journey home, but slowly, for it was hard to go back as a failure. Meantime his friends in New York and Washington went to work again.

By the time he reached New York, in July, 1855, they had convinced Marcy, but President Pierce still had reservations, chiefly because he knew Harris's old weakness for the bottle. A couple of meetings with Harris won the President over. Harris was notified of his appointment on August 4, 1855.

During the next few weeks he assembled supplies for his isolated post, and now that his dignity was restored, he enjoyed the company of old friends in New York. He also sought the advice of Commodore Perry; "he is anxious for the success of my mission and has made a number of suggestions relating to my landing, reception, etc., etc., at Shimoda," Harris wrote to Secretary Marcy. It is probable that Perry visualized the mission in somewhat less grandiose terms than Harris did, for Perry believed it would be better to make haste slowly, that the Japanese should not be hurried into complicated commercial relationships until they were ready for them. Har-

Townsend Harris in 1855 (*a painting by James Bogle*)

ris had no such reservations, and he was burning to make a name for himself, something the commodore had achieved long before he went to Japan.

On one point, at least, Harris disregarded Perry's advice. The mission required an interpreter. Japanese interpreters were trained in Dutch; that would be the language of communication, and Harris did not speak it.* The commodore recommended the man who had been the Dutch interpreter for his expedition, Mr. A. L. C. Portman. Harris rejected him.

---

* The appointment to Japan had been offered first to John Romeyn Brodhead, a merchant-historian of Dutch extraction who could speak the language; Brodhead declined.

Perhaps Portman paraded his experience and his own ideas about how to deal with the Japanese. Perhaps he indicated that he would welcome the opportunity to improve his knowledge of Japanese women—a subject he had hotly pursued while he had the chance; to Harris, who considered Thackeray an unpleasant cynic, conversation on this topic would have been distasteful. For one reason or another, Harris passed up Portman and chose instead a personable young immigrant from Amsterdam named Henry Heusken.

They did not seem a well-matched pair. At fifty-one Harris had acquired an ample waistline to complement his flowing gray hair, wide brow, aquiline nose, and firm chin. His cheeks were whiskered and he wore a full mustache, but there was no reason to hide that chin—it was not weak.

During this brief stay in New York, just before he left for Japan, Harris sat for a portrait commissioned by the faculty and administration of the Free Academy he had founded. It is a revealing painting, showing the man as he was and as he saw himself. A magisterial air is unmistakable: it reflects pride in his new appointment, it evokes the years when he was important in the life of New York City, it sweeps aside those inglorious years on the China coast. It proclaims a man of substance: practical, experienced, strong-willed. (The gaze, the chin, and the jutting lower lip show that the strong will could flare into temper.)

Harris was fifty-one and seemed older. Henry Heusken was twenty-three and seemed exactly that: slender and lithe, spirited and romantic—twenty-three is an age at which everything seems possible.

We know little about him up to this point. He had attended a boarding school in Holland; at fifteen he had come home to learn the family business from his father, but before long his father died; for several years the boy had struggled unsuccessfully to manage the business, but finally it was liquidated to provide a small income for his mother, who was unwell. At twenty-one he had left for America, with high hopes of better luck there. Luck eluded him. Like Townsend Harris he seems to have had a distaste for business, and like Harris he lacked training for a professional career. Often he was without a job. Later he wrote of "days spent without dinner . . . black clothes shining with old age . . . shoes in which my heels and toes enjoyed perfect ventilation . . . trousers with holes worn in them." No wonder he sought the job as Harris's secretary and interpreter: it offered a salary of $1500 a year, escape from humdrum commerce, and a pass to "the enchanted palaces of the East, . . . the treasures of Lahore, . . . the mysteries of Japan."

Since the new Consul General was going to the Orient, the State

Department gave him another assignment, negotiation of a commercial treaty with Siam. It was arranged that the Navy's steam frigate *San Jacinto* would carry him to Siam and on to Shimoda. The *San Jacinto*, whose captain was Henry Bell, would also carry Commodore James Armstrong to assume command of the Navy's Asian squadron, Perry's old post.

But Harris preferred to travel the "overland route," by way of London, Paris, the Mediterranean, and then across the Isthmus of Suez to the Red Sea and the Indian Ocean. The *San Jacinto,* with Heusken and the heavy baggage (including the gifts for the Kings of Siam—there were two, brothers), would make the long voyage around Africa and they would meet in Penang. Harris sailed for London on October 17, 1855. On January 19, 1856, friends gave him warm welcome to Penang, warmer, he sensed, than on any of his previous six visits. *What a difference a title of office makes in this world of ours!* he told his journal. *Dear Penang! . . . primeval Paradise,* he called it, *the antipodes of New York.*

He was fortunate to be so far away. Five days after his arrival there Secretary Marcy wrote to General Prosper M. Wetmore of New York, Harris's chief advocate in the long campaign to get him the Japan consulate:

(Confidential)   Washington, January 24, 1856

My dear General:

I am overwhelmed by an avalanche of the most scandalous reports of our Friend Harris. It is said that his conduct was shameful on his way out, and is attributed to drunkenness. At Paris he has behaved, so reports say, like a fool. Has been strutting about in a gorgeous court dress, distributing cards of an Envoy Extraordinary and Minister Plenipotentiary, etc. Can these things be so? I tell you I have serious apprehensions on the subject.

I wish you could see the Captain of the vessel in which he crossed the Atlantic and get an account from him as to H's conduct while on the voyage out.

Will you be so kind as to send me a few bottles of Mrs. Miller [a stomachic] by the Express. I shall want an extra quantity to digest this matter of our common Friend Harris.

Yours truly

W. L. Marcy

It is true that Harris had been given diplomatic functions, in Siam and in Japan. (The distinction between consular and diplomatic duties was frequently blurred in those days, especially in Asia.) But that did not make

Harris an ambassador in either the President's eyes or Marcy's, and both were furious that he put on the airs of one. As if in answer to the charge that he had succumbed to his old weakness, Harris made an entry in his journal on Christmas Eve off Ceylon: *While in France I drank the delightful mild wine of the South, but after leaving Marseilles I came back to my old Asiatic habit—tea and cold water.*

We do not have General Wetmore's answer to Marcy's letter, but it must have refuted some of the charges against Harris, for Marcy's reply is noticeably calmer:

(Private)   Washington, January 26, 1856

My dear General:

I am somewhat relieved by your letter of yesterday in relation to our Friend Harris, yet I fear he is a little topheavy. I do not doubt he made a ridiculous display at Paris. What I am concerned in knowing is whether his conduct was the result of *sober* misjudgement. There were some officers of the Navy on board who seem to have taken sides with the Captain in the quarrel with H.

I thought of recalling him if a letter could reach him at Paris, but since I received yours I am inclined to change my mind. I shall write to him at Paris yet I believe he will have left before a letter can reach him.

I wish you would write to him. A little scolding will do him good. He thinks too well of himself and is not used to wearing an official garb. I shall write to him by the steamer which will leave Boston on Wednesday. It will be unfortunate if he has lingered in Paris.

Yours truly

W. L. Marcy

Marcy did write to Harris:

(Private and confidential)   Washington, January 27, 1856

My dear Sir:

I sincerely regret to be obliged to inform you that rumors have been received here in relation to your conduct while on your passage to Europe and at Paris which have given much pain to your friends, and to none more than to myself. In your misunderstanding with the Captain of the steamer, some of the passengers (and among them U.S. Officers) take sides with Captain Nye and speak disapprovingly of your deportment. Your conduct while at Paris is animadverted on with considerable severity. I regret that you had not passed on quietly and unostentatiously to your place of destination.

32

I hope you will excuse my frankness in saying to you that these things have been presented in such a light in a *certain quarter* as to awaken a suspicion that an objection to you which at one time prevailed here but was afterwards removed may not have had some foundation. I am not willing to yield to that suspicion, for if I did this would be a letter of recall. If the President should become satisfied that you have lost control of yourself, he would feel bound, however painful the step would be to him, to supersede you.

Should this reach you at Paris, where it will be directed, I take the liberty to suggest that you should make such explanation as may allay unpleasant apprehensions on the subject.

I am sincerely yours etc.

W. L. Marcy

Harris probably never received this letter, for Marcy indicated that it should not be forwarded from Paris. But General Wetmore surely conveyed Marcy's feelings in a letter that could not have made pleasant reading, even with paradisal Penang to soften the blow.

Much more agreeable were the letters received from China. One of his closest friends, merchant Sandwith Drinker, in whose house he had always lived when he was in Macao, sent congratulations and the typical American merchant's view of Perry's treaty:

> I . . . knew before you wrote of your appointment to Japan, and knew Marcy consulted Commodore Perry about it. I knew Perry's answer. So you see we are well posted up here. . . . Perry's treaty was not worth one damn and the Japanese know it, and will not let anyone reside on shore. . . . Several Americans have been to Japan to settle, and trade, and were driven out by the Japanese and not allowed to stop. . . . So you will have plenty of work when you get there.

One of his remarks may have made Harris wince: "I hope you have got a uniform rig, as with Eastern nations such talks."

Harris also heard from Dr. D. J. Macgowan, the medical missionary whom he had appointed to act in his stead at Ningpo:

> The last file [of newspapers] tells us that you are coming out not only with the powers of an envoy but in such state as is fit for one representing a Western power at these Oriental courts.

And Harris must have winced again. Perry's treaty pleased missionaries no more than merchants; their impatience frequently led the men of God to martial views:

Now that you are to have a steamer at your disposal I begin to hope that you will be able to get American affairs out of the imbroglio into which Commodore Perry plunged them at so much cost. Still it will be a hard task even if you have the whole East India Squadron at your disposal— indeed it would be no disgrace to fail now had one the whole force which that undiplomatic officer displayed.

Harris had two months to wait in his primeval paradise before the *San Jacinto* made her appearance: *Our men-of-war never hurry,* he wrote.

This was not fair. The *San Jacinto* was the first of the Navy's steamships with a propeller instead of paddle wheels. Both her design and her machinery were far from perfect and she trailed disaster throughout her career. On the cruise from New York, Commodore Armstrong had ordered the use of sail more often than steam, yet when she arrived at Penang her engines were ready for another ten days' repairs.

By the time Harris reached Siam, Harry Parkes, one of Britain's rising young diplomats, had been on the scene for about a month. Parkes was there to exchange ratifications of a treaty which Sir John Bowring, Her Majesty's Plenipotentiary in the Far East and Governor of Hong Kong, had negotiated the year before, and to work out an interpretation of some of the articles. *Mr. Parkes informs me,* Harris entered in his journal on April 19, *that I will meet a most friendly reception from the Siamese, but that I must be prepared for many and some very unreasonable delays which will greatly try my patience.*

This was good advice. The Siamese soon made it clear that they would deal with one nation at a time and that Harris would have to wait until they had finished with Parkes. In the meantime Siamese officials provided comfortable housing, along with lavish entertainment and sightseeing around Bangkok, a city he had somehow missed in his earlier travels. To this he responded by growing steadily more irritable. When his turn came, it took only about a week to make a treaty in line with his instructions from the State Department, but by this time he was writing that the proper way to negotiate with the Siamese was with men-of-war.

Now he was in a rush to reach Hong Kong before the month's mail ship left. The King of Siam asked him to delay his departure one day for an audience. Harris refused, but the King was the King and he had his way, probably more to give the bad-tempered American a lesson in manners than to have the pleasure of his company. Harris's outbursts in his journal make it impossible to believe that his behavior was gracious. His exit left a bad taste in everyone's mouth.

The hurry was all for nothing. The *San Jacinto,* after seven weeks of rest, was in no mood to work. *Something wrong about the machinery,* Harris fussed on June 1, *as we go only about four and three-quarters miles per hour.* And a week later: *At noon stop engines for repairs. No matter about this, as I find I cannot save the mail.*

He reached Hong Kong on June 12, and on Friday the thirteenth, made his first call on Sir John Bowring. Harris had been brought up to "fear God and hate the British" (his family had suffered in the War of 1812), and his state of mind was not eased by Sir John's strong interest in Japan and his announced intention to go treaty-making there himself as soon as affairs in China permitted. Yet the two men got along well, and several other meetings followed. For one thing, each had the pleasurable sensation of using the other.

To Harris, this was an opportunity to gather evidence of British schemes to assault Japan. Bowring made clear his conviction (shared by practically every foreigner on the China coast) that it was only by using at least the threat of force that Orientals could be brought to terms. Harris considered that this would be invaluable ammunition in persuading the Japanese to negotiate with him before the British came.

For his part, Bowring was quite aware of what Harris was up to and perfectly willing to cooperate. The British were nettled by United States policy in China, which was to let Britain fight the wars and then to step in and secure the same concessions. Many English considered it was high time the Americans pulled their weight in East Asia and were quite satisfied to let them bear the brunt of opening Japan.

Some ten days after their arrival in Hong Kong, Commodore Armstrong told Harris that it would take twelve to fifteen days more to make the *San Jacinto* ready for the voyage to Japan. Harris occupied the time chiefly in visiting Macao and his old friends the Drinkers. He also made business arrangements, did some shopping, hired five Chinese servants to take to Japan, and wrote letters and dispatches. One letter to Secretary Marcy concerns a subject which Harris always treated seriously—money—and the coy tone is certainly inadvertent:

(Private)   Hong Kong, June 16th, 1856

My dear Sir,

In a private communication which I had the honor to address to you when I was in Washington, I stated that I was willing to leave the question of my remuneration for my services in Siam to yourself.

I now beg to repeat that statement, and at the same time, to place before you something that may aid you in forming your opinion.

35

And first, I hope my reward will be of such a nature as will express your opinion of the *value* of the Treaty I have made, so that my remuneration may not *depreciate* my services in the opinion of the World.

Secondly.—I beg you to observe that had I been charged solely with the Consulate in Japan, I should not have waited for the *San Jacinto,* but would have left the United States on the 17th of last September, and could have arrived in Japan on or before the 15th of December, 1855. I cannot expect to arrive at Shimoda before the 15th of July, 1856, thus making a difference of full seven months in a salary of $5,000 per annum.

I know how difficult it is for a man to convince the world that he is disinterested in a matter where his pecuniary interests are involved; but Sir, you have placed a large confidence in me, larger even than I could have expected; if I have up to this time justified that confidence, I pray you to believe that I look to the amount of my remuneration more as a mark of *your* appreciation of the value of my services, than the mere matter of dollars and cents.

I remain my dear Sir

Gratefully and Sincerely Yours

Townsend Harris

Thursday, July 10, 1856. The San Jacinto got under way at five A.M. but after running one mile came to a dead stop. Cause—the propeller has lost the keys that confine it on the shaft—has slipped down so far that it overlaps the outer stern post to which it gave several blows that shook the whole ship. It has been determined to put the ship into dock at Whampoa* *for repairs. . . .*

A trying delay for me. I am losing some fourteen dollars per day besides the wages of my servants, some sixty dollars per month.

On August 12 the *San Jacinto* at last began her journey to Shimoda.

Harris had spent two months on the China coast with little to do. It is unfortunate that he never found an opportunity to talk with one man there, very possibly the one man in the world best equipped to advise him on his mission to Japan, Samuel Wells Williams.

Williams had come to China in 1833 to take charge of the missionary press. In the years since, he had become a notable student of that country and its language, and had written a vast amount of material which is still valuable.

In 1837 he had been one of those who sailed to Japan on the merchant ship *Morrison.* Their aim, as Williams wrote, "was to return to their homes

* The deep-water port for Canton.

Samuel Wells Williams (*detail from a scroll painting attributed to Takagawa Bunsen*)

seven shipwrecked Japanese, and by so doing endeavor to open some communication with that people. . . . The voyage . . . had for its ultimate object the extension of civilization and Christianity." They tried twice, in the Bay of Edo off Uraga, and in the south, off Satsuma. Both times they were fired on and driven off, and they gave up.

The cruise was not without its rewards, however. Williams set about to learn Japanese from the exiled sailors, with the result that when Perry arrived in China in 1853 he summoned Williams to be the expedition's interpreter in Japanese, as Mr. Portman was its interpreter in Dutch.

Williams was with Perry on both his trips to Japan—the brief voyage in 1853, when Perry contented himself with announcing his purpose to the Japanese, and the longer visit in 1854, when, backed by a formidable fleet of nine ships including three steamers, he succeeded in making his treaty of friendship.

The treaty made, Perry had inspected the ports where American ships would be able to obtain supplies, and so Williams spent about six weeks at

37

Hakodate and almost two months at Shimoda. He was the most acute and sensitive observer with the expedition. His knowledge of the language enabled him to communicate with the people. Especially at Shimoda he took long walks and made many friends among both the farmers and the townspeople. He could have given Harris a different view of the Japanese, a more intimate and a more sympathetic one. But Harris never sought him out, though it would be surprising if Perry had not suggested that he do so.

There is no question of the commodore's admiration for his former interpreter. It was partly because of Perry's enthusiastic recommendation that Williams had been offered the position of secretary and interpreter to the American legation in China, succeeding the man who had been raised to Commissioner, medical missionary Dr. Peter Parker. Williams was still undecided as to whether to accept the appointment, but in the meantime he was performing the duties. Most of the old China hands believed Williams far abler than his chief. Sandwith Drinker, in one of his letters to Harris, had summed up the general estimate of Dr. Parker: "the old stupid fool."

The *San Jacinto*'s voyage to Japan was eventful. She followed in the wake of a typhoon, picked up the survivor of one wreck from a raft, and came across several disabled Chinese junks. From one of them the crew was taken on board, to be delivered to Shanghai when the ship returned there. Others were given what they needed—a compass, a spar and topsail, water. The *San Jacinto* herself established something of a record: she made it all the way to Shimoda with only one mishap, a broken air pump, which slowed but did not stop her.

As they neared Japan, Harris's excitement and anxiety grew. He was strong in his faith in his God and his country, but not so sure of himself. His past weighed on him. He could not forget the disintegration of a flourishing career and the aimless years that had followed. He had been jarred by the clear indication that the President's and Secretary Marcy's confidence in him was anything but complete. Townsend Harris was a proud man. He wanted his name to live. He believed that Japan was his last chance to make it live.

Now he was in his second day in Shimoda harbor. The visit from Aihara that morning had made it obvious that though the Japanese were most civil they were not welcoming him. Nothing had happened so far to allay his anxieties.

After Inspector Aihara left the ship Harris made his first trip ashore, taking with him Henry Heusken and some of the ship's officers. He went not to Shimoda but to Kakisaki. He wanted to see the graves of those members of Perry's expedition who had died here.

He crossed the beach. Before him stood the red torii gateway to the village Shinto shrine. On his left a sheer rough cliff of soft stratified stone curved from the hills almost to the sea. Set far back, almost lost in the shadows of ancient trees, was a simple building of weathered wood, the shrine itself.

Far more imposing was another structure nearby. Neither Shinto shrine nor Buddhist temple, this was yet a center for religious services which affected the whole life of the village. Here lived the priest of the mountain religion. Pregnant women came to him before seeking a midwife. He was

The American graves at Gyokusenji (*a woodcut from a drawing by Wilhelm Heine*)

called upon to rid a house of the defilement death had brought to it, and to exorcise the malevolence of epidemic. It was this priest the village had turned to when it needed rain.

To the right of these shady precincts a road curved upward. Harris followed it as it narrowed between closely built houses, now opened to the breeze and to his gaze. And so he came to Gyokusenji, mounted its worn stone steps, passed through its gate. The cemetery stretched up the hill beside and beyond the temple. On a slope close by the main hall he found the graves he was seeking, *four neat tombs and prettily fenced in.*

He took a look at the temple. *The rooms are spacious and very neat and clean,* he noted (Chuemon and his crew had done a creditable job that morning), *and a person might stay here for a few weeks in tolerable comfort.*

An earlier visitor had expressed a more poetic reaction. Samuel Wells Williams had brought with him a Chinese scholar named Lo to assist with the written language, since the Japanese had borrowed their way of writing from China. Lo had visited Gyokusenji, which he identified as "The Temple of 'Great Repose.' " There he had sipped tea with its priests while they silently conversed, as Lo put it, "by means of the pencil." To commemorate the occasion he had been asked for some calligraphy, and "struck by the scenery around," he had brushed the characters reading "encircling peaks, girdling waters." Priest Bimo in turn had written a poem for Lo:

> Here in our little cells we sit,
> Round our inkstones the white clouds meet.
> Mere dust to us is gold so rare,
> The future gives us not a care.

Bimo was a poor prophet; the future bore him malice. The regulations negotiated by Perry to supplement his treaty designated Gyokusenji, along with Ryosenji in Shimoda, as "resting-places for persons in their walks, until public houses and inns are erected for their convenience." What with American sailors, Russian sailors, American traders, and German traders, Bimo and his subordinates had had little repose since then.

Now Harris had his eye out for a place to live; Aihara had convinced him that the Japanese had built no consulate. But sight unseen, Ryosenji across the harbor seemed more appealing; Perry had used it and described it glowingly. Harris thought: *perhaps I may have to reside in it until a house can be prepared for me.*

Kakisaki is a small and poor fishing village, but the people are clean in person and civil in manner. You see none of the squalor which usually attends poverty in all parts of the world. Their houses are as clean as need be. Every inch of ground is cultivated. . . . Headman Yoheiji would have been taken aback to hear Kakisaki described as poverty-stricken. The villagers considered themselves not rich but secure. Of course, there has never been any such thing as a satisfied farmer, or fisherman either for that matter, and it is bad luck to talk about prosperity, especially if the tax collector gets wind of it, but "poverty-stricken"—they would have bristled. True, there was Tobei, who was unlucky, or shiftless, or anyway too fond of drink, and certainly his family had fallen on evil times, but on the other hand, there was Heiemon, farmer and landowner, really a very wealthy man, with a big house and a storehouse bulging with treasures. Anyone, even the headman, would tell you that Heiemon was the most important man in the village. Until a few years ago Heiemon was headman himself, but he had grown bored with the ceremony and detail of the job and the elders had elected Yoheiji, no doubt with Heiemon's blessing. Yoheiji appears to have been the logical choice, for he was the only man in the village who owned *two* boats, and his boats were used to carry condemned criminals to exile on the outlying islands, giving him a certain official status (giving him, too, exemption from the fishing-boat tax, though he had to pay the usual dragnet tax). Everybody knew that Yoheiji was an independent man, with a strong sense of duty, but of course he did not often do anything he thought would offend Heiemon.

As for the people being *clean in person and civil in manner,* Yoheiji would have retorted that indeed they were, a good deal cleaner and more civil than foreigners. Most of those who had come to Shimoda reeked of the animal flesh they ate, bathed infrequently, and seemed to have no manners at all.

But Yoheiji could not know what Harris was writing in his journal, and anyway he was kept busy that day. The Goyosho sent five separate officials to give orders and to check on progress. They wanted men sent to clean the "washing place" at Fukuura, the isolated little valley down the coast which was cut by a clear stream and which had been set aside ever since Perry's visit as a place for foreign sailors to do their laundry. It was also the clandestine burying place for the unwanted mixed-blood babies that had been born after the visits by the American and Russian fleets: there was a cluster of little gravestones a few yards from the stream.

The officials seemed satisfied that Gyokusenji was presentable, but they were so insistent on the village's responsibility to keep it that way that Yoheiji felt it necessary to set up a roster of village functionaries to go on guard duty, two each night. And the villagers were told to redouble their efforts to "maintain public security," which was another way of saying that they should keep one eye on the foreigners and the other cocked for any strangers who might drift in to make trouble.

As a matter of fact, Yoheiji was so busy that he didn't even notice the visit by Harris and his party. He did make note of a couple of officers who landed and strolled off toward Suzaki, the village on the tip of the little peninsula which forms Shimoda harbor.

A good many of the *San Jacinto*'s men were roaming Shimoda. Some discovered the town's bars, others found a good supply of coal waiting for steamships like theirs. The most popular spot for the officers was the bazaar established exclusively for foreign visitors, built around a pebble-paved courtyard at the rear of the Goyosho. Dr. William Maxwell Wood, the *San Jacinto*'s physician, described it at length, for he was improving his leisure by writing a book. "This place was our principal resort during our stay in Shimoda, not only for the purpose of purchasing, but on account of the beauty of the display and the comforts and conveniences of the establishment." There were rooms to rest and relax, where tea and tobacco were served:

> Indeed, every ordinary want and necessity was neatly and commodiously provided for by these Japanese; . . . The whole was new and fresh, the timber was soft and satiny white pine, covered with black paint where exposed to the weather, and roofed with dark blue and white tiles with ornamental edges. All was neat, quiet, clean, fresh and toy like.

Of course, the greatest attraction was the open-fronted shops, ranged around the courtyard and filled with lacquerware:

> black and gold, black and inlaid scarlet maroon, gilded and inlaid boxes and cabinets . . . in value from fifty cents up to two hundred dollars. Lacquered cups, bowls, and waiters, of various sizes, shapes, and colors; maroon, scarlet, green, and gold predominating. There was also a small collection of silks and of porcelain. . . . Up to the last day of our stay in Shimoda, a lively excitement of purchasing Japanese lacquer-ware was kept up; almost every boat-load of officers on leave made their way to the Goyosho, and every returning boat was piled with boxes, the result of their bargains, while in the evening our apartment was brilliant in the exhibition and comparison of the results of the day's work.

Harris, the former merchant, did not call them bargains. *The sales in the bazaar cannot be much under two thousand dollars. The prices are most exorbitant. They appear to raise them at each new arrival of a ship here.*

Later that Friday afternoon Aihara made another call on the ship. Harris now decided to be aloof: he would not appear, and Heusken carried messages back and forth between the parties. It was a trick used by Commodore Perry, who may have suggested it to Harris. (Perry, a consummate actor, had used it more astutely, refusing to be seen from the very first until his subordinates had set the scene to his satisfaction.)

Aihara told Heusken that the doctors considered that the Governor would be well enough to receive the Consul General day after tomorrow, and since the delay was so short no letter was considered necessary.

Harris gave in. He wanted to oblige the Governor, he replied; however, since the day after tomorrow was Sunday, and *no visits could be paid on Sunday or any business transacted that day*, he would postpone his visit till Monday.

Unfortunately, the effect of Harris's inaccessibility was lost when Commodore Armstrong chose this occasion to make his first appearance. Aihara was delighted to see him. Would the commodore explain, he asked, the difference between the positions of commodore and Consul General?

The commodore gave Harris valiant support. A Consul General was concerned with diplomatic relations, he said, stretching the facts to fit the American view of the situation: since Perry's treaty provided for only a consul, that consul would be the only man on hand to conduct diplomatic negotiations. Mr. Harris was therefore a very important person, while he himself was "only a commodore who belongs to the U. S. Navy." He would ask for an interview with the Governor after the Consul General had been received.

Aihara persisted. Their understanding, he said, was that the commodore was ordered to bring the Consul General and to negotiate with the Japanese about his being stationed here. Therefore, they believed they should first receive the commodore and discuss matters with him.

The commodore demurred. He was only providing transportation.

Well, anyway, said Aihara, the Governor recognized that the Americans must be weary after their long voyage—he was especially concerned to learn that the commodore had been ill—and he wanted to place at their disposal the temple Gyokusenji, to use as a resting place. The commodore thanked him and the meeting ended.

The next day, Saturday, Harris paid his first visit to Shimoda.

"At the landing place is a small shrine under a large pine, and near it a hillside covered with trees invites one to explore its grassy slopes," Samuel Wells Williams had written, but Harris did not sense the invitation nor did he set down any impressions of the town he had come to live in.

43

The landing place at Shimoda (*a woodcut from a drawing by Wilhelm Heine*)

Perry's report describes Shimoda as it was before the tidal wave; however, the town had been rebuilt with few changes:

> [It] is situated . . . on a plain at the opening of a fertile valley. Its name is probably derived from its low position, *Shimoda* meaning *Low field*. . . . [It] is compactly built, and regularly laid out. . . . The streets are about twenty feet in width, and are partly macadamized and partly paved. . . . A few of the houses of the better classes are of stone . . .

But whether of stone or of plaster on a wooden frame, the walls of most buildings were covered by black tiles, more than a foot square, laid diagonally and then framed in a heavy molding of white plaster. These handsome black and white walls pleased the people of Shimoda, and moreover they were resistant to fire and tight against the cold west wind of winter; Commodore Perry thought they gave the town "a curious pie-bald look."

With Heusken and Captain Bell, Harris walked the streets of Shimoda, seeing for the first time its houses and its people. Since he was house-hunting, he made for Ryosenji, the temple which two years earlier had been set aside for Commodore Perry's use. Perry had enjoyed himself at Ryosenji, and he had described it with some warmth:

> It is situated on the south side of the town, and has quite a picturesque aspect, with a precipitous rock of over a hundred feet on one

side, and a burial ground on the other, extending up the acclivity of a thickly wooded hill. Connected with the temple is a kitchen garden, which supplies the priests with vegetables, and pleasure grounds with beds of flowers, tanks containing gold fish, and various plants and trees. A small bridge, neatly constructed, leads from the gardens to a flight of steps, by which the hill in the rear is ascended. Adjoining the ecclesiastical part of the establishment there is a room used for lodgers, which is so constructed with sliding doors that it may be separated into several rooms for the accommodation of many persons, or left as one large apartment.

Perhaps Commodore Perry had suggested that Harris might take up residence there if no consulate had been built for him, but Harris saw Ryosenji with different eyes: *It is badly placed for hot weather, being at the foot of a steep hill that shuts out the S. W. wind entirely, and is surrounded by stagnant pools and other disagreeables.*

We afterwards visited six or seven other temples. They are all built after one pattern; some a little larger and in better order than others, and having more agreeable situations, but beyond this they are exactly alike. We afterwards walked up the valley some two miles. Saw a large enclosure containing some twenty detached buildings—all new, and in fact some were not

Namako-kabe: the tile and plaster walls of a
Shimoda house (*a print by Kitaoka Fumio*)

yet completed. I learn this is the residence of the Governor. In the after-noon I went again to Kakisaki. I find the temple there has been cleaned out, apparently to prepare it for my reception. I have thought much about my accepting this temple for my residence. The building is as good [as], if not better than any of the others, but it is isolated, and the approach is through the narrow and crooked alleys of a very poor fishing village. I should here be unseen and unknown to the <u>people</u>, and to go to market my servants in bad weather could not cross in a boat, and the road to go and return would be nearly five miles.* Again,—the Treaty says, and my commission says, I am to reside in Shimoda. Now, Kakisaki is not Shimoda. I, therefore, think I shall refuse this temple as my place of residence.

Weather delightful. Barometer, 30.10. The air is like that of the United States, full of oxygen.

On this day Yoheiji spotted Harris's visit and noted it in his diary: "Around four in the evening, two foreigners came from the direction of Shimoda and visited Gyokusenji; after a survey, they took a boat back to their ship."

It had been another busy day in Kakisaki. Saito came in his capacity as a real estate officer, bringing with him a master carpenter; with the help of some laborers hastily rounded up by Yoheiji a fence was built around Gyokusenji. Yoheiji sent another four men ("it is our understanding," he wrote, "that the authorities will pay for these men") to repair the wall around the well and to clean the American tombs—Harris had seen nothing to complain about the day before but Saito saw room for improvement. Officials from all the villages around Shimoda were summoned to the Goyosho, and Gennosuke was sent to represent Kakisaki; he received fur-ther instructions about "tightening public safety control" in view of the arrival of the foreign ship. The number of men sent for duty to the various guard stations was doubled (government officers manned the stations but the village had to supply handymen and runners—one of these popped up to say that his post needed a bottle of sake, a bottle of soy sauce, and a dish of salt; Yoheiji's wife remarked that clearly they were laying in for a siege, and produced the items from her own kitchen).

The next day was a little quieter, but still there were more inspections of Gyokusenji, messages to be relayed from one guard station to another, a stream of patrol officers. And about eleven at night Yoheiji was wakened from a sound sleep to receive notice that Lord Okubo of Odawara—a

---

* Actually, the distance by road from Gyokusenji to the center of Shimoda is about one and a quarter miles.

daimyo whose fief centered on the old castle town of Odawara and thus straddled the Tokaido Road—was on his way with a contingent of his soldiers. The news was not unexpected. The government had given Lord Okubo prime responsibility for the defense of Izu, and he appeared whenever a foreign ship put in. Yoheiji, after mentally ticking off preparations to be made tomorrow, went back to sleep.

Things had been quieter that day on the *San Jacinto* too: *Sunday, August 24, 1856. Do not leave the ship. In the afternoon the Japanese come off and desire to see me; I decline to see them or to hear their message, for the reason that it is Sunday. They urge me at least to hear their message, saying it is very important and from the Governor. They also say that when Commodore Perry was here, he made no difference for Sunday, etc., etc. I adhere to my previous determination, telling them (through Mr. Heusken) that they can come off to-morrow morning as early as they please and then state their message.*

Aihara was not happy about Harris's refusal to see him but he left his message with Heusken: the Governor would receive them at ten tomorrow morning. He learned from Heusken that the landing party would consist of about a dozen officers but that the commodore, though feeling better, would not be among them. He asked, too, the size of the ship, and Heusken told him: she was 218 feet long and 48 feet wide; in the very first interview Harris had for some reason refused to give this information to Saito, and that had rankled ever since; Aihara felt a little better as he left the ship.

The next morning Yoheiji found time to note an occurrence not directly concerning his bailiwick: "Around ten in the morning, several foreigners left in four boats from the American ship and landed in Shimoda. The cannon were fired ten times when the four boats were being lowered to the sea."

Harris would have been piqued by this account, for Yoheiji had short-changed him. Harris could be depended upon to record salutes with accuracy: *. . . go on shore accompanied by Captain Bell and some ten others. I go in the Commodore's boat, having my secretary with me. The three boats preceded me so that the officers could land and form in order before I landed. When my boat had pulled well off from the ship a salute of thirteen guns was fired, waking up the grandest echoes among the hills. On landing I found the streets thronged with persons collected to see us pass. I was conducted to a new building nearly in the center of the town. As I shall hereafter have both time and better knowledge of this building and of the manners and dress of the people, I shall not now describe anything beyond my interview with the Governor. . . .*

Harris never did get around to a description of the Goyosho; but fortunately, Dr. Wood had a good eye for such things: "We entered the council house by a hall, covered with fine white matting, almost too neat and white for the tread of our boots." (Any Japanese would have struck out the "almost," but those who had to deal with foreigners had learned to steel themselves against this particular barbarism.)

One side of the upper end of this hall was screened off by a folded screen of gilded paper, and to the left of this we entered a light and airy room, almost toy-like in its delicate structure, and the superlative of Japanese nicety. The peculiar, soft, white wood used for the posts, ceiling joists, and window-frames, smoothly worked, was fresh and unpainted. Whenever bolt-heads came through, they were covered with neatly chased hexagonal brass nuts. The floor joists over head were exceedingly delicate—not thicker than the wrist. Light window-frames, covered with a silky, white, semi-transparent paper, formed the windows, but these were now freely opened to admit the air. The dead wall of the room was covered by a delicate light-colored, figured paper. Down the centre of the room were two lines of benches, with a red serge framed tightly over them. In front of one row of these benches were low tables, and upon each table a black lacquered tray, upon which lay two new, long-stemmed, brass pipes, a porcelain cup with fire, another for ashes, and a small lacquered box of tobacco.

The benches provided with tables and smoking equipment were for the Americans; politely ushered to them, they seated themselves (as a Japanese would have put it) with their legs dangling to the floor. The Japanese placed themselves (as Dr. Wood put it) "with their limbs bent under them" on the benches opposite.

Harris and Governor Okada faced each other at the upper ends of the benches. Next to Harris was Captain Bell, then Mr. Heusken, and then the officers from the *San Jacinto,* according to rank.

The Governor's staff was similarly arranged: back of the front row was a second bench of officers, and behind them a number of men knelt on the floor; Harris counted seven scribes among them. All this gave Harris a chance to see the hierarchy of the office he was dealing with; he might have noticed, though he did not remark upon it in his journal, that none of the men he had so far encountered were seated in the front row: Aihara headed the second bench, Saito was considerably below him. In a unique position, at the upper end of the space between the Japanese and Americans, on his own raised platform, was another new man; it was he who now handled the

Japanese half of the interpreting, bent toward the Governor as the Governor spoke, making a deeper bow when the Governor concluded, and then turning to Heusken as he put the Japanese into Dutch, which Heusken put into English. Replies from the American side traveled back the same slow route. It was a system which did not lend itself to quick and easy banter— nor to complete understanding.

I was politely received by the Governor and Vice-Governor. Asked after my health, when I left the United States, etc., etc. In fact, Governor Okada opened with a polite inquiry about the health of the President, and courteously worked his way down to Mr. Heusken, with special thanks to him for his "effort in interpreting." It was then the turn of the man seated next to the Governor to introduce himself: he was Wakana Miosaburo, one of the executive officers at Shimoda, he said, and since his was the responsibility for day-to-day management with respect to foreigners, he expected to see Harris often; Harris labeled him the "Vice-Governor."

By this time servants had brought tea and with it sponge cake and sugar candies; the Governor urged his guests to enjoy them. Gifts of lacquerware were brought to Harris, Captain Bell, and Heusken, and the Governor explained that as he did not know the number of officers who would attend he had not been able to prepare anything for them; his presents for them would be delivered later to the ship. And then he excused himself while the Americans took their tea and sweets; his legs ached, he explained, and so he could not sit long: it was the malady which had prevented his receiving the Consul General earlier.

When he returned, the Governor remarked that it had been pleasant to hear the ship's guns; he had not heard that sound in a long time.

They asked in whose honor the salute was fired and were told that it was in mine, when I perceived that I instantly rose in their estimation. The Governor said he should like to see such guns fired, whereupon Captain Bell invited him to visit the ship on Saturday next, as they are now painting on board and he feared they might soil their clothes.

Wakana now introduced the man who was interpreting today. His name was Moriyama, a member of the Governor's staff; they would rely on him, Wakana said, for liaison.

I asked the Governor when I could see him on business. He said I could enter on business then if I pleased. I replied that it would not be good breeding to enter on business on a visit of ceremony. He then said the Vice-Governor would attend me the next day, at the same hour and place, and that the Vice-Governor could act as well as [he] himself, etc., etc.

Harris tried to end the meeting then, in consideration of the Governor's aching legs. The Governor would have none of it. Sake was about to be served, he said, and it was—two kinds, one of them a special health-giving wine in which a viper had been steeped (it is perhaps as well that the Americans did not know this)—and with it a number of appetizers, individually served in handsome dishes: raw bonito with shredded radish, broiled eel with a tiny yam and ginger, shrimp with a garnish of vegetable mousse.

Harris complimented the food, and the Governor apologized for it: they had had so little time to prepare, he said. They chatted about the weather at Shimoda—in winter the wind blew very hard, the Governor said—and Harris tried once more to leave.

The Governor protested—dinner was about to be served. There followed grilled sea bass, simmered duckling, broiled lobster, vinegared abalone, and marinated trout (each with its own flower-like accompaniment of vegetables), three kinds of soup, and, of course, rice and pickles and fruit and tea.

The cooking was excellent and served up with extreme neatness and cleanliness. I am much prepossessed in favor of their cooking.

The Americans ate with gusto: it was a great change from the diet on the *San Jacinto*. And Japanese and Americans talked through Moriyama and Heusken: of drill on the ship, of the Japanese seeds which Commodore Perry had taken back to America (some were growing splendidly, Harris reported), and of the cultivation of rice (Harris, like the man who took coals to Newcastle, had brought rice to Japan; it had been grown in dry fields, he said, and the Governor made no effort to repress his disdain for that kind of rice).

Our visit lasted nearly two hours, and we were all much pleased with the appearance and manners of the Japanese. I repeat, they are superior to any people east of the Cape of Good Hope. The sake and the food had worked well on Harris. This was the first mellow comment in his journal since he had arrived.

The officers hurried the boats back to the *San Jacinto*. They wanted to see the gifts the Governor had sent them. To each of them had been delivered a pair of chickens in a wicker basket.

One thing was certain after this meeting: the Americans were impressed by Moriyama. Other interpreters had been nervous. *The interpreters were in constant trepidation and fear,* Harris had written after the first day's interviews, *and large drops of perspiration stood on their foreheads.* . . . Moriyama was cool, assured, yet gracious. Moriyama occupied a raised seat. Moriyama obviously commanded respect.

Moriyama Einosuke and interpreter Tateishi Tokujuro (*a daguerreotype by Eliphalet Brown*)

To Dr. Wood, Moriyama "appeared to be a gentleman of rank . . .
intelligent, polished, and courteous." Harris forgot to mention him as he set
down the day's events, but he rectified that mistake the next day. *I omitted
yesterday to state that a superior interpreter appeared at my interview. He
is attached to the office of the Ministry of Foreign Affairs; a good interpreter, of most agreeable manners and a true courtier.*

51

Having been told that Moriyama was one of the Governors' staff, but that sometimes he was called to Edo, Harris concluded that he was attached to the Ministry of Foreign Affairs: *the person from Edo, who evidently has come down since our arrival was reported there, although they say the journey cannot be made under five days from here to Edo.*

Wood reflects much the same opinion. Because they were impressed by Moriyama, the Americans—ever ready to believe that they were being lied to—deduced that he had been rushed to Shimoda after their arrival. And having deduced that, they further deduced that it did not take nearly as long as the Japanese said—five or six days—to travel between the two points. They were wrong on both counts (though of course a relay of fast runners could deliver a message in much less time). Moriyama had been in Shimoda all along, held in the background until the right moment.

Obviously Harris had not placed Moriyama, though Commodore Perry had certainly spoken of him. And therefore Harris did not realize—for some time at least—that here was a man who understood English, who knew what was being said on the American side whether it was intended for Japanese ears or not.

Moriyama had been a key figure during Perry's negotiations. On his first appearance, Samuel Wells Williams had called him a

> new and superior interpreter . . . recently returned from Nagasaki, whence he arrived in twenty-five days and hurried on at that. He speaks English well enough to render any other interpreter unnecessary, and thus will assist our intercourse greatly. He inquired for the captain and officers of the *Preble*, and asked if Ranald MacDonald was well, or if we knew him. He examined the machinery and at last sat down at dinner in the ward room, giving us all a good impression of his education and breeding.

In asking about Ranald MacDonald, Moriyama was asking about the young man who had been his tutor in English.

MacDonald deserves more than a footnote in any account of America's early relations with Japan. He was born in 1824 in the Oregon Territory. His father was an agent of the Hudson Bay Company, and his mother, who died a few days after Ranald's birth, was a princess of the Chinook tribe of Indians.

The boy was about ten years old when he first heard of Japan. Three Japanese seamen were tossed up on the shores of British Columbia. Seventeen months earlier their little ship had been disabled in a storm off Japan while carrying crockery to Edo, and then, caught in the Black Current, had drifted helpless all across the North Pacific. Those three sailors were the survivors of that seventeen-month ordeal.

As if they hadn't been through enough, they were first captured by Indians and then rescued by the Hudson Bay Company before starting back on the long voyage home, via London. Before they left, young MacDonald saw them and heard all the talk about them. He became convinced that the Japanese were the same race as his mother's people and this fired a determination to go to Japan.

When he grew up he became a sailor, and after knocking about the world a good bit looking for the right chance, he signed on with a whaler in the Hawaiian Islands, making a bargain with the captain that he would be put off in a boat near Japan whenever he requested, a bargain the captain made only because he thought MacDonald would never go through with it. But MacDonald did. In June, 1848, he left his ship, and in a small boat, made it to the northern tip of Japan's northern island, Hokkaido. He was promptly picked up by the authorities.

Nagasaki was the only port open to foreign ships, and so the Japanese sent shipwrecked foreigners there for repatriation. At Nagasaki, MacDonald met Moriyama:

> Of this young man a few special words are called for.
>
> He was, by far, the most intelligent person I met in Japan.
>
> He had a pale cast of thought, piercing black eyes which seemed to search into the very soul, and read its every emotion. He spoke English pretty fluently, and even grammatically. His pronunciation was peculiar, but it was surprisingly in command of combinations of letters and syllables foreign to the Japanese tongue.
>
> He was my daily companion—a lovable one—ever afterwards, during my sojourn in Japan. When with me he always had books in Dutch, and a Dutch and English dictionary. The Dutch factor at Nagasaki, John Levyssohn, told me that Moriyama spoke Dutch better than himself. The books were on different subjects, but principally on the commerce and customs of European nations.
>
> I asked him whether he, Moriyama, had ever been out of the country, to which he replied in the negative. He told me that he had a large library; and also, that he was studying Latin and French.

At Nagasaki, MacDonald was interrogated at length, with Moriyama most often as interpreter. He was frequently asked about his religion. He had been brought up an Episcopalian, and on one occasion he answered by beginning to recite the Apostles' Creed, "but when I had said, 'And in

Jesus Christ, His only Son, born of the Virgin Mary,' Moriyama suddenly stopped me, saying, quickly, in whisper, 'That will do! that will do!'" MacDonald's answer as Moriyama interpreted it was: "There are no gods nor Buddhas. I merely cultivate mind and will and reverence heaven in order to obtain clear understanding and to secure happiness. I have nothing else to declare." "In that," MacDonald said, "he was my friend, indeed!"

Moriyama had learned his English from dictionaries and rough sailors. Now he was one of fourteen, all hereditary official interpreters at Nagasaki, who became MacDonald's students. "They were all very quick, and receptive. It was a pleasure to teach them." But Moriyama was his star pupil and best friend.

In April, 1849, the United States warship *Preble* arrived to pick up thirteen American seamen, ostensibly the victims of shipwreck, actually mutineers and deserters. MacDonald was sent home with them. He was never able to return to Japan, but he never forgot Moriyama (nor Moriyama him). Summing up his adventure, listing the Japanese to whom he was grateful, he wrote:

> . . . the dearest to me in every regard, and most esteemed, and ever loved—was the brilliant Moriyama Einosuke, of medium height among his people, say five feet six inches; of delicate and finely cut features; with signs of great intelligence; eyes intensely black, brilliant, and penetrating, yet with an expression mild and loving—truly magnetic; of very light complexion—like the white of the Southern States of America, lighter much than the average Japanese. His countenance, when in repose, had the air of mild dignity, such as is observable in our clergy, as a class. When speaking to me before officials it was always with a smile, as if to give me encouragement and confidence. He showed a great desire to learn English, and displayed much aptitude in doing so. He was fluent in Dutch, for he was one of the official interpreters of that language; and I take it for granted that he was well grounded in the history and musty traditions of his country: of which, however, he never spoke to me; nor did I ever ask him. His general appearance was that of a studious and earnest scholar, and a refined gentleman.
>
> He was my favorite.

Some five years after MacDonald's departure Moriyama was exercising his English with Perry's men. He quickly took charge. In the following months he occasionally exhibited a streak of temperament, or skill at bureaucratic infighting, but these were human traits. At a crucial point Williams wrote: "All the management of the Treaty seems to have been transferred to his hands by the commissioners . . . In all these consultations Einosuke seems to possess decisive authority, and he is pretty well fitted for it."—And Williams had a better sense of what was happening than any other member of the expedition.

Moriyama was assigned to the staff of the Shimoda Governors now, for Shimoda was a critical spot. Crisis having erupted, things were stirring in Edo, as shown by an order dated the same day as Harris's reception, August 25:

> AN ORDER OF THE GREAT COUNCIL TO INOUE, LORD OF SHINANO, THE SHIMODA GOVERNOR STATIONED IN EDO. CONCERNING HIS OFFICIAL TOUR TO SHIMODA.
>
> As you were previously informed verbally, you will proceed to Shimoda to handle the problem of the American ship, with the assistance of Okada, Lord of Bingo.

And so Inoue, the senior of the two Governors of Shimoda, was preparing to leave his family and his friends and the excitement of the capital, and to make the tiring journey to Shimoda.

Others, as we know, were converging on the little port. "The party of Lord Okubo of Odawara was due to arrive today," Headman Yoheiji recorded, "and we sent Gennosuke and Rokubei out along the road to greet them as they approached." Yoheiji was busy, for this little army would be billeted in his village. Every home would have its soldier-guests. Heiemon's house would become Lord Okubo's. Yoheiji climbed the hill to break the news; Heiemon took it very well, and his womenfolk and all the servants began at once to clean house and to air the bedding. There was a sudden flurry of housecleaning all over Kakisaki.

Nor was the village forgotten by the Goyosho. At least two patrols appeared during the afternoon. Predictably, even monotonously, they ordered Yoheiji to "tighten public safety control."

Around five that evening the advance party arrived from Odawara; meeting at the headman's house, they went down Yoheiji's list of the houses in the village and the capabilities of each, and made the assignment of quarters. From eight to nine o'clock that night the force streamed over the hill from the coastal road, their lanterns and their banners making it seem like a festival procession. The men had to be shown to their assigned houses, a kitchen had to be set up, the baggage had to be stowed. Two hundred porters had borne that baggage; they had to be fed, but no one worried about putting a roof over their heads; they were rough men, used to sleeping in the open, and it was a warm, fair night.

Baths and supper over, there were conferences to be held and plans to be made and the American ship to be scouted from the shore—there was little sleep in Kakisaki that night. And just before dawn the five ships of the party, carrying its rice and the fuel to cook it, arrived, and no one got any sleep after that. The curious thing is that apparently all this activity went quite unnoticed on the *San Jacinto,* for not one of the several diaries being kept on board mentions that an armed force of three or four hundred men had moved in upon them.

Yoheiji mobilized twenty men to unload the Odawara ships and to stow the rice in the village storehouse. The farmers' group on the hilltop put all available hands at the job of hulling some of that rice for the soldiers. Both the elderly and the very young could work at this, pounding the rice with mallets in mortars hollowed in the ends of logs until the hulls came free of the grain and could be sifted out. They worked far into the night, but they cleaned more than a hundred bushels of rice, pounding to the rhythm of songs like this one, a favorite of old grannies and young blades:

> I'm just seventeen, and it's the barley-hulling season.
> I went out to the beach for a look and
> the sailor of a boat just in
> has grabbed me and won't let go.
> "Let go my sleeve, let go my dress—
> I am someone's maidservant and have work to do!"
> *Ton-ton* the falling pestle sounds: my poor mistress,
> pounding barley in my place. Oh, if I could
> but get away from this rough fellow!

This was the day Townsend Harris began serious talks. For the first time he was faced with hard evidence that the Japanese did not want him. The euphoria of the previous day evaporated.

To-day ashore at ten with Mr. Heusken. Met the Vice-Governor and the person from Edo. . . . My interview was long and far from satisfactory. To sum it is all I shall attempt. They did not expect the arrival of a Consul, —a Consul was only to be sent when some difficulty arose, and no such thing had taken place. That Shimoda was a poor place and had been recently desolated by an earthquake; that they had no residence prepared for me; that I had better go away and return in about a year, when they hoped to have a house ready. The Treaty said that a Consul was to come if both nations wished it; that it was not left to the simple will of the United States Government.

Harris was not being unfair in this summary. And it is as accurate as should be expected, for one must remember the cumbersome double interpretation which was taking place. Subtleties and implications died in that tortuous process; misunderstandings grew like weeds.

For most of these conversations we have at least two versions: the summary which Harris put in his journal, and the report—generally including a transcript of the conversation made by the several scribes present—sent by the Governors' office to the government in Edo. It ought to be kept in mind that both versions were written to be read. Neither was disinterested. Each was colored by a point of view. Each sought to make a case. Naturally there are differences between them, sometimes of fact, sometimes of understanding, sometimes of judgment.

In this particular case the differences between Harris's summary and the Japanese report are not enormous but they are there. For example, the Japanese record includes no suggestion that Harris "go away and return in about a year, when they hoped to have a house ready"; Wakana did suggest that Harris go away, and in another context he said, in answer to a question from Harris, that to build a house as fine as the Goyosho would take about a year, but he did not offer to build such a house or indicate that Harris would be welcome a year hence.

Wakana's position was that the treaty authorized stationing a consul only if both nations agreed it was necessary. But the Governors and their men had little confidence in this argument, and faced with a man who was evidently determined to remain in Japan, they were trying for a reprieve. Stay as a private individual if you must stay, Wakana urged, and let us discuss later whether you are to be recognized as a consul.

What the Japanese were fighting against was a foreign official's being stationed on their soil. They knew that Perry's treaty obligated them to accept him; their arguments to the contrary were clumsy, and they knew it. But they were desperately trying to forestall a situation they dreaded.

They revealed their fear to Harris, but because he did not, could not, know what was going on in Japan, he did not understand them. After telling him of the tidal wave that had nearly wiped out Shimoda, and the even more recent earthquake that had ravaged Edo, Wakana added: "The public feeling is uneasy, too. In a situation like this, we believe that receiving an official from abroad will unwisely arouse the emotions of the people. . . . Please consider our viewpoint, and put off your residence here."

Wakana was disclosing raw nerve-ends. He was admitting that in the face of bitter anti-foreign feeling, the government was worried and insecure.

Harris's reply shows how little had reached him of what Wakana was saying. He answered: "We shall live in any house until you build a consulate, and of course we will pay rent for the temporary house."

Wakana could only suggest, with obvious frustration, that the interpreters had not conveyed his meaning, but he did not pursue the subject: it was dangerous ground.

They adjourned until the next day. The next day was worse.

Wednesday, August 27, 1856. On shore at ten A.M. *by appointment, to meet the Governor or Vice-Governor, but neither of them made his appearance. Ten persons were present including the Edo official.* (Among the others were Aihara and Saito.) *They said the Governor was very ill the previous night with a violent headache, so they were unable to consult with him.*

> HARRIS: How is the Governor's health?
>
> MORIYAMA: He has been suffering from a severe headache since yesterday, and is in bed today too.
>
> HARRIS: I hope he will recover soon.
>
> MORIYAMA: Every request you placed yesterday was repeated to the Governor. He sent us today to tell you his answer. I attend the meeting with you today as a personal messenger from the Governor. I will listen to your requests and tell you ours, one by one, making each attendant here understand it clearly. It must take time, but please permit me to do so.
>
> HARRIS: Yes, I will.

How did Harris get the idea that the Governor had *not* been consulted? Was it misinterpretation? Is the Japanese transcript in error? Or in his subsequent anger did Harris forget exactly what he had been told?

Moriyama then amplified on the previous day's argument. If the United States had sent a mission to discuss assigning a consul, Japan would not have agreed. No mission having appeared, Japan was not expecting a consul nor had she made any preparations to receive one, and now the emergency needs for reconstruction at Shimoda and Edo took all the government's energy. But as Harris had come all the way from America, it was regrettable that trouble should arise because of lapses on both sides. The Japanese had no intention of acting contrary to the treaty, but they asked Harris to understand their position and to accept Gyokusenji as a temporary residence until the whole question of his official status could be negotiated.

At this point Harris lost his temper. Since Vice-Governor Wakana had not appeared, and Moriyama had only repeated yesterday's proposition, there was, he said, no room for further discussion. He would return to the ship and consult with Commodore Armstrong about whether to sail to Edo.

Any threat to go to Edo agitated the Japanese, as Perry had learned and Harris well knew. Moriyama was nettled. He protested that the Governor had told Harris that the problem would be handled at Shimoda, and also that he might send Wakana or Moriyama for discussions in his place. Harris had not objected then, why did he now? Was it because of Moriyama's rank?

Harris repeated that he considered the discussion closed, that he would talk only with the Governor or Vice-Governor.

The Officer from Edo said he was of higher rank than the Governor and asked why I should object to negotiate with him.

There is ample indication in the Japanese record that Moriyama was angered by Harris's refusal to talk with him and by the implied disparagement of his rank, but there is not the slightest suggestion that Moriyama advanced the preposterous notion that his own rank was higher than the Governor's. Was it misinterpretation? Is the Japanese transcript in error? Or in his anger did Harris forget what was said?

Harris demanded a letter from the Governor by the next morning giving a firm answer as to whether he would be accepted at Shimoda as Consul General.

The meeting broke up on a Japanese note. Moriyama said: "Please help yourself to tea and cakes."

The record of the next day's negotiations suggests that the fog begot by double interpretation may have had its advantages after all. *Thursday, August 28, 1856. The Vice-Governor, the high person from Edo and a large suite came off this morning. The Vice-Governor explained his absence yesterday, by saying that the individual from Edo was of higher rank than [he] himself and had full powers from the government to act in my matters. He then said that he was ready to receive me with all the honors due to my high place, and to assign me the only place that was habitable for my residence—the Temple of Gyokusenji at Kakisaki; . . .*

According to the Japanese record, Wakana said something quite different. All that he said about Moriyama's rank was:

He is an official of the government, and as he understands Dutch he can talk with you without an interpreter. So the Governor ordered him to meet you for negotiations. I think you were told by the Governor that he and I might be sent to conduct negotiations with you. I don't want you to think of him as an ordinary interpreter.

And concerning Harris's reception:

We cannot decide without careful discussions whether or not we will permit your being stationed in Japan formally as Consul General, because there is a difference between Japan and the United States in understanding the treaty. The Japanese government still believes that there must be preliminary negotiations between the two countries about your being stationed here. But as you have come to Japan, you may land and reside at Kakisaki temporarily.

But what did it matter that the Japanese had not budged from their original position when by happy misunderstanding Harris believed that they had capitulated? He now opened bargaining about a house. He believed he should not live at Gyokusenji because Gyokusenji was in Kakisaki and not in Shimoda. The best building he had seen was the Goyosho. He would, he said, move in there.

Wakana was aghast. That was out of the question, he said. That building was the local headquarters of the government; the whole area was administered from it. It was a building of great importance; even officials could not enter unless their duties required it, and no one lived in it—no, they could not let Harris use even a part of it. Kakisaki was a part of Shimoda, no matter what Harris thought; it lay at the heart of the area designated by the treaty. And Gyokusenji was the only temple available: because it had been used so much as a residence for foreigners, many of the priests who once lived there had left; it could be requisitioned with less disturbance to the community than any other temple.

Gyokusenji, Harris said, was damp, and as he was getting old, the dampness would be bad for his health.

They would do their best to recondition the temple, Wakana said, and with genuine feeling he assured Harris that the Japanese held great respect for old age.

Harris thought he could never reach agreement at Shimoda; he would go to Edo and open direct talks.

Then, said Wakana, he would have to follow Harris to Edo and continue the discussion there; for, as dealing with the Consul General was the Shimoda Governors' responsibility, only Shimoda officials could talk with him. And he said flatly that Gyokusenji was the only temple the Governors would make available: if Harris refused it, they could do nothing more for him.

The morning slipped away as each side repeated its pleas and arguments in every conceivable form. Harris finally wearied of the game; perhaps it was lunchtime. He announced that he would think it over.

He sent his answer some two hours later: *I instructed Mr. Heusken to say to the Governor that I was most anxious to avoid any difficulties; and, although I feared my Government might blame me for accepting a residence at Kakisaki instead of Shimoda, I would accept it with the full understanding that a suitable house was to be prepared for me as soon as possible, and that I must have a boat and men constantly at my command for my use while there.* It is worth noting that he was to be charged no rent for the temple; the Japanese would house their unwelcome visitor free of charge.

There were left only details to haggle over.

Harris had two days earlier ordered two spars to make a flagstaff, a heavy lower one of fifty feet and a lighter extension of thirty feet. On this afternoon the thirty-foot spar was delivered; *price five dollars; and word was sent that to get the spar fifty feet long, they must go to the mountains to cut it and would require three or four days to get it, and that would cost eighty dollars. Sent the carpenter on shore to select the best one he could find, even if short of the fifty feet.*

Friday, August 29, 1856. Mr. Heusken goes on shore with the carpenter to aid him in selecting a spar, etc., and afterwards to go over to Kakisaki to indicate what alterations, etc., are required in the temple to fit it for my residence, etc.

The Governor informs me that three rooms in my house will be required for Jananese officers who are to be with me night and day "to await my pleasure." I return a message that I require all the rooms, and that under no circumstances would I permit any Japanese (except servants) to be in my house, or even to enter it without my permission. The carpenter comes off at three P.M. saying he cannot find a stick that will answer for my flagstaff. Mr. Heusken at six P.M. informs me that the Japanese say they have cut three trees that will answer, but they cannot be got to the ship before Monday morning. The authorities have agreed to give me all my rooms, and to withdraw their threatened police force.

The argument over Gyokusenji had concerned the priest's quarters (Harris and Heusken would live in the temple itself), which the Japanese thought would be ideal for the guards they intended to provide. But Harris, who had lived long enough on the China coast to develop some ideas on how foreigners should live in an Oriental country, had brought from Hong Kong a butler, a cook "and his mate," a tailor, and a laundryman. He intended that they should lodge in the priest's apartment. The Japanese understood. They relinquished the rooms for use as kitchen, tailor shop, laundry, and noisy home for the Chinese. But they did not *withdraw their threatened police force*; they merely moved it to the barracks beside the temple's gate which previously had housed itinerant monks.

The dispossessed priest, who was unmarried, moved just outside the temple wall into a small house which had been used by his apprentices. They in turn moved to the two hillside chapels, in one of which the altar and sacred images were installed. The priest could conduct his prayers there, and since the parishioners never gathered for "Sunday services" a large hall was not essential.

The assistant priest went back to live with his family. That young man came from an old and respected house whose chief occupation was farming. He had entered the priesthood at fourteen as the result of falling out of a tree. Climbing after wild berries, he had slipped, fallen on a child below, and killed him. Under the circumstances it seemed fitting that he should become a priest to pray for the repose of the dead boy's soul.

The village school had to be moved too: it was taught by Priest Bimo and had been held in his quarters; tuition consisted of gifts, first on entering and then on festival days. Somehow room was found in the little house for the dozen or so low tables at which the boys, who ranged from six to twelve or thirteen years old, sat on the matted floor (in a village like Kakisaki it was considered that what a girl needed to know she should learn at home from her mother). Hours were from eight to eleven in the morning and then from noon to four o'clock, by which time the scholars' hands, faces, and even legs and feet were liberally smeared with charcoal ink.

Reading, writing, and the arithmetic of keeping accounts were the basic subjects. The older boys studied geography, which they had been learning informally from the ships and sailors and cargoes which came to their harbor from distant provinces. They were taught manners and morals, too, copying maxims which were accepted as good to live by, such as: "They that do good in secret shall be rewarded openly," and "When you visit a country, learn its ways." Of course, to the young scholars "country" meant another province of Japan, but the idea could have been recommended to the new residents of Gyokusenji.

All these arrangements for priest and school could be made, and were made, now that Gyokusenji was requisitioned again, but that does not mean that the people of Kakisaki were content with them. Their temple was a meaningful part of their lives, and many of them, especially the older folk, were unhappy without it.

Governor Okada, who had not made an appearance since his first interview with Harris and Captain Bell, now sent word that his doctor would not permit him to visit the ship on Saturday, but invited Harris and the commodore to visit him at the Goyosho on Monday. Harris thought it was a ruse to get the commodore to make a courtesy call before the Governor came to the ship. If he was right, the Japanese must have been relieved when the commodore (not Harris, though Harris in his journal says *I told them*) informed them that etiquette required a visiting ship's commander to make the first call. They happily accepted an invitation to visit the ship on Tuesday, and it was agreed that Harris would move ashore on Wednesday.

While all of this was going on, Yoheiji had his hands full. There was, first, the little army the Americans hadn't noticed. After a day of rest the two hundred porters left for home, and that was a relief; porters were ruffians practically by definition, and Yoheiji was glad to see the last of them. The village now had to guard the Odawara ships; five men in two boats patrolled around the clock. (Lord Okubo paid these men in rice—two rations for a day's work, which was not munificent but was welcome.) Rice had to be hulled daily for Lord Okubo's soldiers. These duties were in addition to the previous demands for men to be sent each day to the guard stations and to Gyokusenji. And special requirements multiplied. On Friday, when Heusken met with Aihara and his retinue at Gyokusenji to discuss alterations to the temple, Yoheiji sent two men to serve tea and provide smoking utensils. Then when carpenters appeared from Shimoda, two responsible men always had to be on hand to supervise them, and the carpenters worked late each night. What with one duty and another, the strain on Kakisaki's manpower was great—fields had to be cultivated, and fish caught—and Yoheiji negotiated with the neighboring hamlet of So-toura, which was a semi-independent sub-village of Kakisaki, to provide two men each day.

Advance word had been circulated to all the villages that Governor Inoue would arrive from Edo on Saturday. Although the Governor was traveling the road down the middle of the peninsula and therefore would not pass through Kakisaki, the village had to send a man to greet him. Yoheiji nominated Chuemon, who set off on Friday with the reception committee from Shimoda and other villages roundabout to meet the Governor early the next morning, as he began the last day of his journey, and to escort him into Shimoda. And on Saturday morning innkeeper and village elder Kosaburo set out to augment the escort as the party neared Shimoda. The Governor was a very important person, and it was unthinkable to stint in showing the deference due him.

Harris caught wind of the Governor's arrival. On Saturday evening he noted: *Learn that some great personage has arrived at the residence of the Governor, as a long procession was seen by some of our officers, preceded by heralds bearing the coat-of-arms, then a number of norimono* [palanquins], *one very large—a led horse—servants bearing luggage, etc., etc.*

Harris spent a quiet Sunday writing letters. He turned out nineteen. True to his principles, he dated them all Monday.

He wrote to Commodore Perry and to General Wetmore. He wrote to Sir John Bowring and to the United States consuls in Hong Kong, Shanghai, Penang, and Calcutta. He wrote to friends in China, including the Drinkers and D. J. Macgowan. These were personal letters; he did not put copies in his letter books and none of them seem to have survived.

He did keep copies of his business letters. One was to his London bankers, Baring Brothers and Company. (He had chosen a substantial firm; Richelieu had said, "There are six great powers in Europe: England, France, Russia, Austria, Prussia, and the Baring Brothers.") He had designated them to draw his salary from the State Department, and he informed them that he had entered upon his duties at Shimoda as of August 21: that was the date his salary of five thousand dollars a year began. He asked Russell & Company in Shanghai if they would negotiate his bills against his credit with Baring Brothers, because it was one thing to have credit in London and quite another to have cash in the Far East. To Armstrong & Lawrence in Hong Kong, another American firm, he was a little more chatty. He had found, he said, "an excellent climate and picturesque country," but aware that trade with Japan was on the minds of the merchants in China, he added:

> Shimoda is not now, nor can it ever be, a place of any large business. It is situated at the extremity of a narrow and mountainous cape, without roads, or being the port of any considerable place in the interior. The harbor is rather a roadstead than a harbor; it is quite insecure in a blow from S.S.E. to S.W., besides, the inner harbor would not have room for four ships like the *San Jacinto*. In fact, Shimoda is simply a fishing village without resources for any commerce in the shape of manufacture or other articles of import or export.

Going on to business, he asked them to pay for the waffle iron that his Chinese butler, Assam, had bought from DeSilver & Company for $1.50 but forgot to pay for; asked them to reimburse Purser Bradford of the *San Jacinto* for a box of candles purchased from the ship; and enclosed an order for items evidently overlooked when shopping in Hong Kong: oil for lamps, and sixty pounds of Fuchau bacon, "provided it is fresh and in good order, or failing Chinese bacon, send forty pounds of English bacon, in the smallest tin you can procure."

On Monday morning Harris and Heusken went ashore with the commodore and a suite of officers, including Dr. Wood, to meet the Governor. They found not one Governor but two.

More upsetting, the new Governor seemed disposed to start once more at the beginning: *They then run over all the old objections, and civilly ask me to go away; and, on my declining to do so, they asked the Commodore if he had no power to take me away.*

He replied, "None at all" [Dr. Wood takes up the story]; he commanded the military, and had received orders to bring Mr. Harris to Shimoda, and, he added emphatically, "leave him there." They then inquired of the Commodore if he knew any reasons why Mr. Harris had been sent there? He answered, none other than the provisions of the treaty. He was next asked if he did not think it would be better to receive a statement of their reasons for not receiving Mr. Harris, and take him away until some future time when more urgent reasons might exist. The Commodore replied that he had no discretion but to obey his orders. They asked if he would take a communication from them to the United States government. He would, he said, take anything, but it must come through Mr. Harris.

Tea had been served, of course, with sweets to be eaten and sweets to be carried away. Dinner had followed, equal to that of the first reception, and the Japanese had delighted in instructing a new set of officers in the technique of chopsticks.

Before dinner, lacquerware had been presented to the commodore, Harris, and Heusken, and again the officers had been told that their gifts would be delivered to the ship. Disillusioned by the chickens a week earlier, the officers did not let their hopes run high. It was just as well: this time each was presented with half a fish; it was *tai*, a fish the Japanese prize so highly they often use it as a gift of ceremony, but the officers could not know this and they were not flattered. Neither a pair of chickens nor half a fish could be carried home to be displayed on the parlor table.

During the dinner Governor Okada tactfully turned the conversation away from the troublesome negotiations at hand. He asked the commodore about the recently ended Crimean War, how peace had been made, and the terms. "I think," he commented, "that many people died."

"Yes," replied the commodore, "on both sides, about half a million, including those who died from sickness."

Where would the commodore go after he left Japan?

To China. And he told them how in sailing to Japan they had followed in the wake of a great typhoon, and given relief to many battered junks. He added that if the Governors had any business in China he would gladly do it for them.

And here the Japanese record includes one of its rare parenthetical remarks: "The Governors were impressed by his words, thinking that the commodore spoke as if the five continents were in his hands, he uttered those words so casually."

After the Japanese found that, in Dr. Wood's words:

> no diversion in their favor could be expected from the Commodore, they apologized for having detained him so long, and suggested that he and the officers might at their pleasure take their leave, but would be glad if Mr. Harris and his secretary would remain and continue the negotiation. This was assented to. Mr. Harris requested me to remain over with him. The remainder of our party took their leave, accompanied by attendants, carrying their bundles of confectionery. After we had resumed our seats and refilled our pipes, the conversation was resumed . . .
>
> [The Japanese seemed] like men who had an appointed task, and were anxious to rid themselves of it. They would frequently, before putting a question or proposition, read from a paper, which one of them kept before him; and during what appeared to us must be to them the most earnest and interesting part of the discussion, they would converse in a pleasant, smiling manner with each other, and the most earnest arguments passed through Moriyama, without in the least disturbing the placidity of his countenance or ruffling the courtesy of his demeanor.

Dr. Wood thought he could explain this placidity:

> Minute, earnest, exacting in carrying out the wishes or instructions of the government, a British or an American statesman would patriotically identify himself with his cause, but the Japanese, his business being over, has no personal interest in the matter. This enables them to be cool and equable during the most interesting and important discussions.

The doctor misread the men before him—despite their composure they had deep convictions about what was good for their country—but he did not exaggerate their cool urbanity. He had, of course, a striking contrast before him. He had seen enough of Townsend Harris, in Siam and here again in Japan, to know that he was an irascible man. The self-control of the Japanese stood out all the more.

"They now said they would receive Mr. Harris temporarily"—showing that Dr. Wood understood the Japanese position, though Harris indicated that he was being accepted without qualification—". . . but they would in the meantime forward their objections to our government . . ."

I was then asked would I forward a letter from the Japanese Government to the American Government? I answered I would if it was written by the Minister of Foreign Affairs. Would not the Governor of Shimoda do as well? He had full powers to treat with me; therefore it was the same thing. I replied that it might be the same thing to them, but it was not in our eyes. Would I write to my Government asking for my own removal? This was declined.

The Japanese asked about Harris's letter to the Minister of Foreign Affairs. It contained the disquieting statement that "the President has given me directions to make from time to time such new arrangements as may tend to increase the intercourse between the people of the two countries." The Japanese were certainly not seeking to "increase the intercourse." What did Mr. Harris have in mind?

"Here," commented Dr. Wood, "was the secret of their perseverance in asking what were the reasons of Mr. Harris's coming, and showed their dread of new business and demands being thrust upon them. . . ."

Harris used a diplomat's license to dodge. He had a long list of proposals in mind, but he chose not to bring them up now. He replied that he had made in his letter merely a general allusion to such business as might arise in the future, and had in view no definite point at the present time. The Japanese did not seem convinced.

> During all this long, triply-translated discussion [according to the doctor] there were as many changes of clouds and sunshine as mark an April day; but as the business drew toward a close, and difficulties gradually disappeared, the sunshine of cheerfulness and good humor rested abidingly upon us all. The Japanese felt the satisfaction of men who had done their duty, and the Consul General had done his, and accomplished his ends. I, having nothing to do but look on, had smoked comfortable pipes of mild tobacco, and drank small cups of sweet sake, and kept as calm and placid as Moriyama himself.

The sunshine of cheerfulness did not warm Harris entirely: *I do not like the looks of the new Governor; he has a dark, sullen look, like a bandog, and I fear I shall have trouble with him. I much regret the change.*

Back at the *San Jacinto,* boats from Shimoda were waiting to carry ashore the Americans' baggage. *All of the supplies—furniture and some heavy luggage—was sent off, and all in pretty good order except a hat in a leather box, which was destroyed.* And then Harris sat down and wrote a letter to Commodore Armstrong, to thank him for his support.

Carpenters were still at work in Gyokusenji, officials from the Governors' office made frequent appearances to inspect, and, just as often, the men of Kakisaki served them tea and tobacco. "Around three in the afternoon," Yoheiji recorded, "we offered twenty men, who, while officials stood witness, carried the baggage of the foreigners into Gyokusenji. This was completed by eight at night, and the officials left for home about an hour later. So we named five, including village officials, to keep vigilance at Gyokusenji."

Harris and Heusken went ashore the next morning, taking some of the officers and the Chinese servants. "About nine in the morning," again according to Yoheiji, "some ten foreigners came in two boats and proceeded to Gyokusenji. After inspecting here and there, five Americans went back to the ship but five Chinese remained. At lunchtime, the government officials wanted us to offer them some dishes, and we served thirty-five large sardines seasoned with soy sauce and brown sugar, plus eggplant mixed with bean paste. Around noon the cannon on the foreign ship were fired several times." Evidently Yoheiji felt this called for some action on his part, for "We then served the foreigners at Gyokusenji two platefuls of tobacco."

The salute was part of the commodore's reception for the Japanese, and it gratified Governor Okada's wish to see the guns fired. *Men were exercised at the guns and went through all the maneuvers of an action. Marines put through the manual and marching, etc., and a salute was fired.* Both Governors came aboard with a party of about thirty, including their executive officers, Moriyama, "attendants, sword-bearers and all." To Dr. Wood it seemed a successful party:

> They partook freely and with great zest of the entertainment set before them; ate ham, tongue, cold chicken, lobster-salad, hard bread, soft bread and cake; drank ale, white wine, champagne, brandy; laughed, talked merrily, jested and played practical jokes. Mustard and sweet oil seemed curiosities to them, but they used them freely. I mention these things to show that their natural appetites do not confine them to rice alone, and that they are glad to throw off official stiffness and reserve. The feast being ended, they drew from the folds of their

fine silks, squares of paper, in which, after asking permission, they wrapped up fragmentary specimens of their entertainment. They partook of our viands with a complimentary vigor which chopsticks alone would not supply; and though they left us gentlemanly and proper in deportment, their gleaming eyes and rubicund noses were inconsistent with the supposition of totally abstinent principles.

(Unlike the local people, the sophisticated officials from Edo were not averse to eating meat—when it was served at foreigners' banquets.)

Harris's account of the same party is sour, and he ends: *The new Governor was cold and rude; not even the raw brandy which he and others drank seemed to warm his heart, or thaw him towards us.*

. . . The spar for my lower flagstaff only reached the ship at one P.M. *The carpenter says it shall be done tomorrow.*

Wednesday, September 3, 1856. Go on shore and select spot for flagstaff to stand. Return and write letter to Secretary of State, twelve foolscap pages. . . . leave the ship at five P.M., *having taken a kind leave of all. As I left the ship the men manned the rigging and gave me three hearty cheers. The men in my boat responded, and a counter cheer of two more came from the ship, and then the band on the quarter deck struck up "Hail, Columbia." I was both flattered and touched by this mark of attention.*

It showed at least that I had so conducted myself while on board the San Jacinto *(off and on five months) that I had secured the good will of all on board*—he could not forget Secretary Marcy's stinging rebuke for his conduct on another ship, crossing the Atlantic. *On reaching my temple, I found the Vice-Governor and a suite of officials awaiting my arrival to welcome me, which they did in very good terms, at the same time showing me a present of fowls, eggs and lobsters from the Governor. . . . We were up until after midnight in getting copies made of my dispatches. The spar came on shore just at dusk, too late to put up my staff.*

Today [Yoheiji recorded] we delivered Gyokusenji, all cleaned, to the foreigners. The government officials moved to the barracks in front of Gyokusenji, and to clean the barracks we mobilized three men. The foreigners' light baggage was unloaded, and five men carried it to Gyokusenji. The foreigners brought a large pillar to the beach in a boat. Four of the men carrying things to Gyokusenji were ordered to unload the pillar. It was too big for the four, however, so, on order from the officers present, we mobilized twenty men, and all tried to carry the pillar from the beach but in vain. Soon night fell, and we reported the situation to the officials in charge and had the operation postponed till tomorrow.

The next morning the Goyosho sent a large group of common laborers from Shimoda to handle the spar. Even they had trouble, and Yoheiji sent ten Kakisaki men to help. By ten o'clock they had succeeded in carrying it across the beach and up the road between the houses and through the gate of Gyokusenji.

Gyokusenji as the consulate (*drawing by Heusken from his journal*)

Thursday, September 4, 1856. Slept very little from excitement and mosquitoes, —the latter enormous in size. At seven A.M. *men came on shore to put up my flagstaff. Heavy job. Slow work. Spar falls; break cross trees; fortunately no one hurt. At last get a reinforcement from the ship. Flagstaff erected; men form a ring about it, and, at two and a half* P.M. *of this day, I hoist the "First Consular Flag" ever seen in this Empire. Grim reflections —ominous of change—undoubted beginning of the end. Query, —if for the real good of Japan?*

The sailors went back to the *San Jacinto*, the Japanese returned to their homes, and the new folks at Gyokusenji began to borrow from their neighbors. "The foreigners wanted a large kettle," Yoheiji recorded, "and we arranged with the priest of Gyokusenji to lend it to them. We hope the foreigners will consider paying for it."

The men of the *San Jacinto* hurried to make her ready to steam out.

Curiosity about these preparations, and realization that this was their last chance to see the ship, got seven Japanese sailors in trouble. Their little freighter was moored at Kakisaki; boating across the harbor to Shimoda they sculled close to the big steamer and gaped at it. When they reached Shimoda they found irate police officials waiting to seize them: scrutinizing foreign ships was reserved to government officials.

The San Jacinto left at five o'clock, saluting me by dipping her flag which was answered by me, and then she left me "alone in my glory," not feeling very sad, for in fact I was too busy in opening boxes, searching out eatables and mosquito nets, to think of being downhearted. Go to bed at eight P.M. *and sleep well.* No doubt he was comforted by Commodore Armstrong's assurance that he would send a ship to Shimoda early next spring.

Young Henry Heusken recorded the *San Jacinto*'s departure differently. He, too, was keeping a diary, and it reflected literary ambitions. When his sensibilities were aroused he was very apt to break into poetry, either his own or someone else's. Now he remembered an exile king from the age of the Crusades, and he wrote:

> From atop a hill I had seen disappear the last object that still linked me to the civilized world and I sang out with more reason to do so than Lusignan, who at least was King of Cyprus, the famous lines:
>
> > "Wretched exile upon a foreign strand,
> > How he mourns for his beloved land!"

Chapter 3

SEPTEMBER 5–30, 1856

A REPORT BY THE GOVERNORS OF SHIMODA TO THE GREAT COUNCIL: DATED THE SEVENTH DAY OF THE EIGHTH MONTH OF THE YEAR OF THE DRAGON [corresponding to September 5, 1856].

The American steamship which sailed in to this port on the twenty-first day of last month left port about five o'clock yesterday. It was reported by the watch station on Mount Buzan that the ship sailed south by southeast and soon disappeared. The Consul General landed day before yesterday and is temporarily staying at Gyokusenji in Kakisaki with an interpreter and five servants. We sent some of our own officials to manage them, replacing the guards provided by Lord Okubo.

INOUE, LORD OF SHINANO

OKADA, LORD OF BINGO

In Shimoda the townspeople relaxed a little, relieved to see no foreign ship in the familiar panorama of their harbor. Those fortunate merchants who were authorized to sell to foreigners—to be ship chandlers and to operate shops in the bazaar—repossessed the shady lounging rooms which lately had been full of souvenir-hungry Americans, and lingered over tea as underlings put the shops in order. It was pleasant to reflect on the profits of the past two weeks and to contemplate those of the future—for, surely, the American official's staying at Gyokusenji would mean more foreign ships coming to this port.

These merchants were privileged men. In theory there was a gulf of class distinction between them and the samurai governing class, but with their airs and arrogance they had more in common with the samurai than with the poor shopkeepers down the street, and they were well aware of the extent to which the Governors' men leaned on them. Most government officials were realists, and it was established policy never to interfere in local affairs as long as they were being satisfactorily tended by local people. So much was policy: it was not policy for officials to mix socially with businessmen, but for all their samurai rank and official status most of the Governors' staff were poor men, caught in a grinding squeeze between the fixed income of their stipends and the rising level of prices. If the merchants of Shimoda liked to entertain their betters, and occasionally even to provide a loan, why should those merchants be denied such unselfish pleasures?

Across the bay in Kakisaki, Headman Yoheiji set down this day's events as seen from his village:

> The officials on duty at the guard station withdrew and the men we had been sending there were relieved of duty. Replying to a summons from the regular patrol officer, Kosaburo, as a village official, and Toemon, the innkeeper for the sailors who were arrested yesterday for approaching the American ship, reported to the harbor master's office at Shimoda at ten in the morning and were told that the affair was settled and the sailors released.

On another hillside in Kakisaki the new occupant of Gyokusenji recorded the activities of his day: *Friday, September 5, 1856. Busy all day in opening packages, arranging contents, ordering various articles from the Japanese. Get an old belfry made into a nice pigeon house in which I installed my four pairs of pigeons. Clear all day.*

It took more work to make the people comfortable than it had the pigeons, but Gyokusenji converted easily to residence. A large central room contained the altar and paraphernalia of worship; behind it, against the hillside, was a room which held a library of sutras and the ancestral tablets for most of Kakisaki's families; along each side were two smaller rooms, set off by sliding doors.

The middle room in the rear was cleared of its sutras and ancestral tablets and turned into a storeroom. The corner rooms in back became bedrooms. Harris chose the one on the west; on an August day it was the cooler and more private, shaded by a ridge which rose sharply to the level spot where the American sailors lay buried. Heusken drew the east room, facing a bit of garden hidden from public gaze by the gallery which connected the priest's quarters and the temple. In the garden was a pool which was home to two golden carp and countless droning insects.

The room in front of Harris's bedroom became his library and office, so that the whole west side of the building was his. The large central room, stripped of its altar, and the room in front of Heusken's bedroom were thrown together to become the reception and dining room. Across the front of the temple and along Heusken's side there ran a wood-floored gallery with two sets of outer doors, paper and wooden. When the solid wooden doors were slid shut they might conceivably keep out the cold winds of winter; they would also shut out all daylight. Harris's side had both paper and wooden doors but no gallery.

Heusken's bedroom at Gyokusenji (*a drawing by Heusken from his journal*)

Now there was unpacking and arranging and putting away to be done. There were clothes for a long stay, including the uniform Harris had purchased in Paris: a single-breasted blue coat lined with white silk, the straight-standing collar, cuffs, and buttonholes embroidered in gold; "white cassimere breeches" with gold knee buckles; white silk stockings; gold shoe buckles; a cocked hat with a black cockade and a gold eagle; a sword. He had worn these at the court in Bangkok and he hoped to wear them at the court in Edo.

There were household supplies and office supplies. There were his books: atlases and general references, works on the duties and responsibilities of consuls (after all, he was new to the profession), volumes on Japan. He had brought many of the available books on Japan, starting with those by Dutchmen who had lived at Nagasaki and had set down what they had seen and heard. Their accounts were basic; in 1856 people who wanted to learn something about Japan still looked to Dr. Englebert Kaempfer's

74

fascinating narrative of his experiences from 1690 to 1692, as well as to the reports of men who came later to the Dutch entrepot.

Shelves had to be built for his books, closets devised for his clothes. And though he had brought some furniture, he decided that he needed more. He plagued the Japanese officials with requests for objects quite unfamiliar to them and to Japanese workmen, and like any other house-holder engaged in a remodeling project, thought the carpenters maddeningly slow: *Get on very slowly in fitting up the house with shelves, closets, tables, etc., etc. Every carpenter that comes to do anything is attended by an officer. It may be to keep him from stealing, but more likely to prevent any communication between us.*

Just how he thought he might communicate with the carpenters he does not make clear. Yoheiji records one such futile attempt: "At noon a foreigner came out of Gyokusenji and strolled on the beach, where he came across the stonemasons at work. He spoke to them but failed to make himself understood, so he returned to Gyokusenji." The stonemasons were building a jetty to serve the consulate.

Yoheiji might not have had time to notice so trivial an incident except that things were relatively quiet again in Kakisaki: Lord Okubo and his soldiers had packed up and gone home. They left behind a satisfying sum of money for the owners of the warehouses taken over for rice storage; for Heiemon, who had moved his considerable household into the kitchen so that Lord Okubo might enjoy the rest of the house; and, as Yoheiji mentions almost as an afterthought, for the village officials, to compensate them for their trouble. It could have been worse, Yoheiji realized: when the lord had come down at the time of Perry's visit, he had brought along one of his mistresses, a pampered lady who had caused a great deal of extra work.

Even before Okubo and his men left, there arrived the first of a long line of visitors which Harris's presence would occasion. A retainer of the Lord of Sendai arrived to have a look around. The Lord of Sendai had no position in the government, but he was the most powerful daimyo in northern Japan (with a fief at least five times larger than Okubo's) and any opinion of his would be listened to with respect in Edo. Unfortunately, the lord and his advisors found it difficult to arrive at an opinion. When polled on what to do about Perry, they had urged rejection of his demands but had stressed that the situation must be settled peacefully. This seemed like a happy solution, but it had not turned out to be a workable one.

The Sendai man had come to Shimoda to observe and to report back to his fief headquarters, and he had to be treated with deference. Kakisaki had the responsibility of guiding the party on the last leg of their journey along the coast and into Shimoda, and Yoheiji nominated six elders for the mission, drawing them from the officials of the neighboring villages of Suzaki and Sotoura as well as from Kakisaki. His efforts were not unrewarded: Kosaburo answered a summons from the visitor next day, taking with him three bottles of sake as a gift from the three villages, and brought back a gold coin for each of the three headmen and a silver coin for each of the elders. Recognition of that kind made a man feel appreciated.

On the second day after the *San Jacinto* sailed out of Shimoda harbor, the Governors sent Moriyama, with Saito, an interpreter, and a couple of censors, to begin the delicate adjustments necessary to getting along with the American official. (Since Moriyama would converse in Dutch, the interpreter was there to keep Saito and the censors informed of what was being said.)

Harris in his journal dismisses the interview as unimportant: *Moriyama, the Edo official, visited me to-day on a mere visit of friendship, as he said. Gave him "cakes and champagne."*

But Moriyama dealt with at least one of the several demands that Harris had placed, as the Japanese record shows:

> MORIYAMA: We were informed by the official in attendance that you want milk. In Japan, milk is never used for food. Cattle are kept by peasants only to work the fields and to transport heavy loads. Their number does not increase and milk is used only to feed calves. We must refuse your request.
>
> HARRIS: Thank you for telling me the reason. I want to keep a cow here then. I will milk it myself.
>
> MORIYAMA: As I told you, cattle are used only for farming and transport. To the peasants they are important property and one cannot be spared for you.
>
> HARRIS: Then I shall give it up. But as we gradually find lacking things that are necessary for us, please try to provide them.
>
> MORIYAMA: We will do our best.
>
> HARRIS: Are there goats here?
>
> MORIYAMA: No, there are none in Japan.
>
> HARRIS: If I order one from Hong Kong, will it be possible for me to keep it here?
>
> MORIYAMA: Yes, but you may not let it roam free in the pasture lands.
>
> HARRIS: Can I keep it within the temple grounds?
>
> MORIYAMA: As it will be like a dog, you may keep it within the temple compound. But you must not put it out to pasture.

Moriyama was no farmer. He came from a long line of officials, but he did not have to be briefed on one of the government's cardinal policies: that the peasant was the foundation of the state, and that one did not lightly interfere with his capacity to grow rice. Certainly one did not commandeer one of his most important assets (such as a cow), and one did not tamper with the grass lands jealously held as common property by each farming village.

Perhaps Moriyama had convinced Harris that the subject of milk lacked dignity. Perhaps that is why Harris did not mention it in his journal, which he was still filling with domestic problems: *Same employment as yesterday. Am getting things to look a little more comfortable. . . .*

Hear a curious insect of the cricket tribe to-night. Sound was precisely like a miniature locomotive at great speed. Bats in rooms. See enormous tête de mort spider; the legs extended five and a half inches as the insect stood. Unpleasant discovery of large rats in numbers, running about the house. To add to these creatures, he had brought ashore cockroaches from the *San Jacinto;* they thrived.

He had imported some inanimate irritants too: *The sealing wax sent me from the Department is so bad it will not run or even drop. It appears to be composed of rosin and tallow, no wax or shellac in it. When a stick is lighted it will burn to the end like a pitch pine splinter.* A couple of days later: *Much trouble with the lock of the iron chest. Procure mechanics to open it; and, after removing a load of mortar placed over the lock, find it cannot be repaired. Caution: Never buy an iron chest with a patent lock of Mr. Gaylor's or any other man's make, especially if you are going to a semi-civilized country. I can close and bolt the chest, but not lock it. It is a protection from fire (soi disant), but not from thieves.* And on his first Sunday at Kakisaki he ran up the flag, only the second time it had been flown, and recorded an unpleasant discovery: *My flag badly made, the wind has whipped out the end hem and frayed the bunting in many places three inches—so badly is all government contract work done.*

The flag was to be flown *on Sundays, holidays—Japanese ditto—and when foreign ships are here. The Japanese were much pleased when I told them I would hoist my flag in honor of their holidays, and gave me a list for six months.* The list included the first and fifteenth days of every month, which were nominally holidays even if most people kept right on working. Harris would learn that the Japanese, who did not rest on the seventh day, actually took few holidays.

As headman of the bailiwick, Yoheiji of course was involved in Harris's domestic arrangements. There was a steady stream of orders from the Governors' men stationed at the temple. One concerned water. Harris did not like the water from Gyokusenji's well. After sampling various waters he settled on that from Chuemon's well, which was on the hilltop half a mile away, and so Yoheiji had to appoint a water carrier.

The village would also have a hand in supplying Harris's larder. Fish were sent straight from the sea to the kitchen: mackerel one day, a fine yellowtail another, sometimes lobster. As for vegetables, carrots were in season and carrots were what Gyokusenji got.

Evidently Harris never considered that his five Chinese servants were enough to take care of himself, Heusken, and the small temple. One of the early requests he placed on the Japanese was for two houseboys. A few days later he expressed irritation that they were not immediately forthcoming, that the Governors *must write to Edo about them.* The next day Moriyama (again with Saito, the interpreter, and censors) once more called at Gyokusenji, and from the Japanese record we learned that Harris had asked for more than two boys.

> MORIYAMA: You recently requested permission to employ a cook. Are you having inconvenience in cooking?
>
> HARRIS: As I have a Chinese cook, there is no inconvenience now, but I will return him to his country in the near future. So I want a Japanese who will learn European cooking.
>
> MORIYAMA: You also requested permission to employ a washerman. Are you having inconvenience in that, too?
>
> HARRIS: Not now, because I have a Chinese who does that work. But I shall be inconvenienced if ships of my country arrive. To prepare for such occasions, I want to employ some Japanese and teach them how to launder.
>
> MORIYAMA: You also requested two young men who are to work beside you. The Governors are now considering this request, but they cannot decide without asking Edo. Therefore we cannot answer you now.
>
> HARRIS: I urgently need personal servants. The Chinese are busy with cooking and washing, as I told you. Since I am without a person to clean my rooms and do minor private work, I have been doing this myself since I landed. Look at my hands.
>
> (He held out his hands, which were scratched, presumably as the result of his labor.)
>
> I am in too high a position to clean my room myself. Please arrange for me to be able to employ houseboys.

MORIYAMA: We understand your request. But as I told you, the Governors must consult the government and consider your requests carefully before they make a decision. Especially the request for house-boys. Please wait until they get an answer from Edo.

HARRIS: I was told that all problems here at Shimoda were entrusted to the Governors. I should think they could easily decide whether I might employ just two persons. I cannot understand why they must think it over. It is unreasonable.

MORIYAMA: Almost all of the young men of Shimoda are working in offices or shops or are craftsmen. It is hard to find two to work for you privately.

HARRIS: I cannot believe that, considering the number of people living in Shimoda. If you can't find two young men here you can find them in Edo or some other place. I requested this before I landed.

MORIYAMA: All problems here must be carefully considered. You cannot expect straight and quick answers. Please remember that not all your requests can be handled just as you wish.

HARRIS: I want an answer within a week.

After two days of consideration, during which the Consul General steadily grew more irritable (. . . *Had a flare-up with the officials, who told me some egregious lies in answer to some requests I made. . . .*), the Japanese had reached a decision: it was that Executive Officer Wakana had better try his hand at coping with the American.

Friday, September 12, 1856. . . . The Vice-Governor and Moriyama, with the usual suite.

The object of the visit was my demand for two boys as house servants. It was a rare scene of Japanese deceit, falsehood, flattery and politeness.

The Japanese record:

WAKANA: As this is the first time for us to receive a Consul General, I think that you must be experiencing many inconveniences. Please tell me anything you care to.

HARRIS: I am troubled by delays on every problem. For example, though I asked to employ two young men the other day, I haven't been answered yet. Today is the fourteenth day and I am being seriously inconvenienced.

WAKANA: We are not neglecting your request, but we must consider all the ramifications of our decision. We cannot treat people as we do things. Please tell me if there are any things you need.

HARRIS: When are the boys to be sent to me?

MORIYAMA: As I told you day before yesterday, the Governor is considering your request but he cannot decide so quickly. You requested an answer within seven days. I cannot understand why you say today is the fourteenth day.

HARRIS: I am sorry. It was my mistake. Will they be here within the seven days?

WAKANA: What do you wish them to do?

HARRIS: They will take care of my room and look after me.

WAKANA: No one is permitted to meet foreigners except officials. The sailors assigned to you work under the direction of Japanese officers. This problem of houseboys cannot be decided as easily as you may think.

HARRIS: Superintendents of the Dutch house at Nagasaki have been using Japanese houseboys for the past two hundred years, though the superintendent's position is lower than mine. Why can't I be permitted to employ them?

WAKANA: Foreign ships have been calling at Nagasaki for two hundred years and everything necessary for them is available there. Shimoda is new and cannot be compared with Nagasaki. We cannot rush decisions.

HARRIS: It is written in the treaty that Japan and the United States are friendly powers. But when I consider your treatment of me, I cannot help thinking that you treat me as an enemy.

WAKANA: Because our countries are friendly we have been discussing many problems with you. If your country and ours were not friendly, we would not give you a chance to talk with us. It is the custom of the Japanese government to consider and discuss problems carefully, even when they are trifling. But we understand that you are having difficulties and we will do our best to fulfill your requests.

HARRIS: Thank you, I expect a favorable answer.

WAKANA: We hear that you want to employ young boys. We would like to confirm this.

HARRIS: I want boys from fifteen to seventeen years old.

WAKANA: Can they return to their homes at night?

HARRIS: No, I want them to live with me.

WAKANA: They will not want to live with you. If they cannot go home at night, at least for a while, no boys will want to work for you.

HARRIS: How about your servants? Do they go home at night? Besides, you told me that you could not find such boys around here. If they come from a distance, how can they go home each night and return the next morning?

WAKANA: Even when we Japanese employ servants we permit them to go home at night for the first few months, as they wish. Young boys are difficult to handle, and since working beside you will be very different from ordinary apprenticeship, they will certainly have problems. If you concede this point, we think we can find boys around here.

HARRIS: It is natural for boys to wish to return home sometimes. I have no intention to keep them by me all the time. They need not stay at my side if they are within the sound of my bell, and they may go home if there is no work to be done.

WAKANA: We cannot force anything on the people. We cannot do as you wish immediately, but we will inform the Governors and give you an answer later. . . .

HARRIS: It seems you have no intention of acting promptly on any of my requests. You always say first that there is no such thing, even if it is within eyesight, and only after my repeated insistence do you act. It seems, too, that there are many lies in the words of officials. Yesterday I asked the official on duty here to send me a swordsmith, and he answered that there was no such person in Shimoda. But when I insisted, a man was sent. Don't you think that I was lied to? I hope it never happens again.

WAKANA: Because our languages are so different, there are bound to be difficulties between us. We hate lies as much as you, and our officials have never lied to you. It is true that there is no swordsmith in Shimoda. When you insisted, we sent you a mirror polisher.* You seem to have misunderstood what we tried to tell you. We have ordered a dining table, ashtrays, and so forth, as you have requested, but it will take time to have them made. If you are troubled by lack of these things, we would like to lend you some of ours until yours are made.

HARRIS: I would be very glad if you could arrange to do so.

WAKANA: You requested birds. What kind of birds do you wish?

HARRIS: Ones with beautiful voices.

WAKANA: Would you like canaries?

HARRIS: Yes, but I would also like some native Japanese birds.

WAKANA: We do not keep them on hand. We will arrange to have them sent from other districts, but it will take time.

HARRIS: Yes, I am sure it will.

One can almost hear his sigh.

Clearly the Governors were not overeager to oblige Harris. He was not welcome. He had been received on a temporary basis and they did not want to make him so comfortable that he would not consider leaving.

Furthermore, every request granted would establish a precedent, and that was not something to be undertaken lightly. And every request was suspected of being a wedge toward another demand more formidable.

Nevertheless, the Governors were not waiting passively for Harris to

* In Japan at this time mirrors were made of metal.

raise problems, though he was raising a great many. They were trying to anticipate disagreements and to resolve them in advance. Here is a letter that they had already sent to the Great Council. Evidently there was an attached sheet, now lost, with a number of questions, but the question considered most critical was emphasized in the letter, along with an almost plaintive request for a reply more swift than the Governors were used to getting:

> We request instructions concerning the Americans who have recently come. Our questions are written on an enclosure. Since we have permitted the Americans to stay, though only temporarily, we must study conditions in foreign countries and consider the prices of things. When we received them the other day, we promised that during their residence here necessities will be sold to them at the same prices charged the people of Shimoda. But we have been ordered to tax their purchases. If we add taxes, they will have to pay more, and if they discover this it will make negotiations very difficult. Therefore, we think that we should not tax them. Please answer us as soon as possible. We ask that at least you give us an answer to the above question.

There is no indication that at this early date Harris was aware that his purchases were being taxed. But he was very aware of another problem concerning money, a problem which had plagued Perry and which the State Department was concerned about. The Japanese insisted on evaluating their silver coin, the *bu,* as equal to the American silver dollar, though the dollar weighed three times more. This affected Harris's budget: as he noted in his journal, it tripled the price of everything.

Perhaps the conversation with Wakana left Harris less sure of himself than he indicated (*I at last got them cornered . . . I was firm and carried my point*); the Japanese must have seemed most adept at this kind of verbal fencing. At any rate, he changed tactics: he might make more headway with written communication. Next morning he wrote a letter to Governor Inoue, including a request designed to raise the conversion issue. "I have to request Your Excellency to give orders to the proper officer to receive from my Secretary, Mr. Heusken, five hundred dollars in silver coins and to give him in exchange the same weight of Japanese silver coin." *I am sure he will refuse . . . But this must have an end, and I am fully instructed by my Government to insist on our money being taken at its proper value.*

He took up another topic also:

> I have been requested by Captain Bell, Commander of the U.S. Steam Frigate *San Jacinto,* to inform Your Excellency that the coals

recently supplied to that ship were of an inferior kind; that quite one half of the weight was merely coaldust, which not only is of no value as fuel, but it injures the burning of the coals with which it is mixed; the remaining part of the coals were in very small pieces and of a poor quality.

Captain Bell desires Your Excellency to order further supplies of coal, to be delivered free from any dust, and in pieces not weighing less than one catty, and as much larger as may be procurable.

Captain Bell suggests that the future supplies of coal should be taken from the deepest part of the mines and he is of the opinion that the coals recently supplied to the *San Jacinto* were surface coals, which are always inferior in quality.

By curious coincidence, on exactly the same day that this peremptory letter went to the Governors, the senior engineer of the *San Jacinto*, in the port of Shanghai, was submitting a report to Commodore Armstrong concerning the Japanese coal. He noted that it had been "but the outcropping or surface coal," but after citing technical comparisons of the various coals used during the voyage, he concluded that "In the furnaces the Japanese coal ignited readily, came quickly to steady action, and burned freely . . . the Japanese coal stands in the first class of steam generating coals."

Harris having finished his letter, Heusken put it into Dutch and took a boat to carry it across the harbor to the Goyosho. No doubt he was glad to escape from housework, but he must have been especially eager to go to Shimoda that day. The town's festival was in progress.

Harris knew about it: *To-day is the anniversary of the Patron Saint of Shimoda, and is one of their greatest holidays; but as my house is not in order, I remain at home arranging books, etc., and trying to eradicate the cockroaches, which I have brought from the San Jacinto by thousands.*

Less than a month earlier he had written that he wanted to look at *the various religious creeds of Japan;* this festival was one of those creeds in action, a once-in-a-year occasion, but he devoted the day to books and cockroaches.

There were many Shinto shrines in Shimoda—shrines of families, of streets, of fishermen, of farmers, of shopkeepers, of craftsmen—but there was one which was the shrine of all the town. Its god was the god of this place, this port, these streets and houses, these people—to be thanked in prosperity, turned to in adversity, honored daily, and celebrated annually in a great rough cavalcade that carried the presence of the god into every corner of his town, to be honored, to be regaled, and in turn to purify, to bless, to give heart—sometimes to punish.

There had been months of preparation. At last, two days ago, everything was ready—streets decorated, carts polished, drummers and flutists rehearsed—and daily work was laid aside.

That night, in each block of the town, the elders gathered to check final arrangements, and the young men gathered in another house "to wait the day." They waited noisily, with sake and food and song, and geisha, to pass the hours. Some of them left with sake and fish to pay a ceremonial visit to a "sister block"; those who remained received similar delegations, and each man drank with each guest and the parties became noisier. They spilled into the streets. Drum-carts were hauled out for a last trial run and drummers sent the rhythms of the festival booming into the night. Old men listened critically, and youngsters crept from their beds to peer wide-eyed from open-fronted houses. There were bristling encounters when groups that were not friendly met and, taunting each other, had to pass in the streets.

In one such wrangle, close to the quay, the son of a shopkeeper flung an old insult at a band from a fisherman's block: "To kill a fisherman doesn't take a knife—ten days' west wind will do it." Everyone in Shimoda knew this slur; it meant that fishermen were so poor, so improvident, so near the edge of starvation, that ten days' forced inactivity could starve them. It was not safe for fishing boats to go out of Shimoda harbor in a west wind. (And what made the cut deeper this night, the wind had been two days from the west.)

A son of a fisherman punched the son of a shopkeeper and a brawl erupted. Festival lanterns, bearing their block's crest, rolled in the dust; one caught fire, and in its flash the fury mounted. Older men plunged in and separated the youths, but coldly refused to speak to their opposites. Word sped around the town that a feud was on between the fishermen's block and the shopkeepers' block, and even that night the long, complicated formalities of reconciliation were begun. A festival was hardly a festival without them.

The next morning, at a measured pace, the festival ceremonies were begun. The town officials gathered at the shrine, which, like the Buddhist temples, lay at the back of the town, against the hills. The priest, in his high robes, received them in the shrine office, and there they took sake made from rice grown in the shrine's own paddy fields, and officially declared the festival open. Outside, the beat and murmur were already building.

Down the tree-lined approach to the shrine the first of the neighborhood drum-carts rumbled, drawn by the toddlers of its block, wide-eyed, bright-kimonoed, holding tight to the long thick pull-rope, helped by only a few solicitous uncles. The creaking high-wheeled cart behind them shone in

The shrine at Shimoda (*a lithograph from a drawing by Wilhelm Heine*)

the sunlight. Over it rose a red torii, the gateway symbol of Shinto. From the torii, heavy silk rope, tied and looped and tasseled, held the deep-voiced drum. Above the torii loomed this block's symbol: the figure of a renowned calligrapher at a crisis in his life, dejected, disheartened, drenched by rain, idly watching a frog struggling to save itself; the frog, nearly swept away by the downpour, leaping again and again toward safety, failing and failing, yet trying and trying, and then, impossibly, succeeding—and the calligrapher takes heart: a legendary lesson fit for a place familiar with earthquake, tidal wave, typhoon, fire. Beside and behind came youths of the block, strutting, swaggering; drummers, light-footed, peppering the drum rim, slugging the drumhead, arms and hands and sticks striking great drum, small drum, bell; flutists, embroidering flighty airs on tricky rhythms; geisha, slim in workmen's tights, workmen's jackets, workmen's head towels, strumming samisen, yelping encouragement.

And behind this cart, other carts, alike but for the figures rising from the torii perches: the Empress Jingo, who conquered Korea while carrying a stone in her obi sash to delay the birth of a child; a dancing monkey, symbol of all festivals, protector against fire, sacred messenger; a great falcon, wings stretched, diving on prey, commemorating the gift to its block of a stuffed falcon, once a favorite of the lord of the province of Kii—given because the captains and crews of Kii's many ships had, since memory ran, found hospitality in the ships' inns of this block.

These first four carts represented the blocks that this year were managing the festival, for the responsibility rotated, and none but the largest of the neighborhoods could afford to stage the ceremonies single-handed. For three years these four blocks had been raising money to insure success. Now they came proudly first, over the hump of the arched bridge, through the great torii, down the long approach to the shrine itself, out and around but not through the massive tile-roofed gate, passing in review before the elders of the town, falling back in line along the approach-way.

The carts were manned by youths. The men of these blocks, those in the prime of life, had greater responsibility. They would bear the sacred vehicle and the emblems that went before it. Days earlier they had withdrawn from their homes and their wives. They had congregated in a lodging apart, to purge their minds and bodies by abstinence and ritual. Finally they had cleansed themselves in the sea.

They waited now, each with a towel around his head against the sweat that would be flowing. They stood in three groups, divided by height, groups that would spell each other in shouldering the vehicle of the god. And each group was a score or more of strong men, for the vehicle was heavy and no harm must come to it.

Other carts trundled in now. Golden dragon of the block of fishermen, the dragon being the god of the sea, who, when he chooses, grants abundant catches and protection from shipwreck. Lion dancers for the farmers on the other side of town. The boy born from a peach. A badger who turns himself into a teakettle, caught in the very act of transformation. The first Emperor. The sixteenth Emperor, revered for the concern he manifested for his subjects, shown as he peered from a tower, looking for smoke rising from his people's houses, sign that they had food to cook and eat. The angel who, lured to swim by the beauty of Miho beach, hung her feathered robe on a pine tree and had to dance before a fisherman to get it back.

Townsend Harris might have learned something about Shimoda and something about Japan had he not remained at home. Someone, perhaps Moriyama, might have told him the history of this festival: how a couple of centuries earlier—early in the rule of the Tokugawa house, when Shimoda, designated a Shogunate port, suddenly grew from a village to a town —the Governor of that day had redesigned the simple village festival to commemorate the fall of Osaka Castle, the victory which assured Tokugawa supremacy, and to commemorate the way Tokugawa troops had marched into the fallen castle to the beat of great drums.

But more than likely no one, not even Moriyama, would have told him that, for government officials were not aiming to plant in his mind any doubts about the legitimacy of the Tokugawa regime. There had always been some Japanese who nurtured such doubts, and lately there were more of them, even after two and a half centuries of peace and stable government; all the more reason to keep such dangerous ideas from foreigners.

And though the drum-carts and their figures might have caught Harris's fancy, what would he have thought of the tumultuous procession?

Probably he would have been charmed by the vanguard, for that belonged to the children: little boys in *happi* jackets, carrying banners; little girls who slipped their *happi* off one shoulder, the better to show their kimono (tinkling bells in the sleeves), their hair done up butterfly-style, carrying staves with jingling rings; older boys bearing "devil-destroying bows."

But surely he would have been appalled when, a long lull after the last child had marched out, the god's convoy erupted from the shrine precincts.

The priest had led the way to the shrine, had opened the high inner doors, had revealed the vehicle of the god, glowing black and gold in the dim interior. And the priest had prostrated himself and cried to the god to leave his residence in the heavens and return, if briefly, to his town that his people might do him honor and offer him entertainment. And when it was considered that the god was present among them, he was offered sake, fish from the sea, rice, fruits, and vegetables from the fields and hills.

And the priest had reaffirmed to the god his people's gratitude for his protection in the past, and had begged that his strength continue to guard them in the future. And the town officials had stood in silent pledge, grave gray men against the deep red of their shrine against the green mountain.

Then those stalwarts who would bear the god and his accouterments had pressed forward while the priest waved over them a sacred wand, exorcising any evil that might still cling to them. And out of the turmoil two men had marched, and they had dipped green branches into buckets filled from the sea and had dashed a purifying spray of salt water on the way before them. And behind them men had struck wooden clappers in a sharp staccato beat, commanding attention. And there had come two trees, sacred *sakaki* trees, in heavy frames slung on the shoulders of young men, and something primitive had taken hold, and the trees had quivered in wild dance.

Halberds had cut the air, and four guardian deities had made their way, symbolized on tall poles by green dragon, white tiger, red bird, and black turtle, mounted in frames like the trees, carried by men still young, and the deities had dipped and staggered after the trees.

And men strong in their maturity had tightened the towels about their heads and moved into the shrine, and slowly the vehicle had risen in the air, slowly had emerged, slowly had descended the shrine steps, slowly had passed through the gate. And gathering life from the men beneath it, the vehicle had begun to lift and to sway, and the men had sent up a rhythmic chant, and the vehicle had jostled the drum-carts and, turning, had swept into the crowds, and the chant had grown swifter, and there had been a cry and the vehicle had thrust skyward, and again, and again, and the golden phoenix atop its roof had trembled toward flight. And the vehicle had shuddered back to its men's shoulders, and a new crew had slipped beneath the heavy shafts, and the chanting and the dance, slowly beginning, had driven again to a climax, and the third crew had taken over, and all the time the tempo had increased, inexorably, and then the vehicle had swept through the torii over the humpbacked bridge and was free in the streets of its town.

Ahead of it the sacred trees separated and then rushed back together in combat, and the pole-high deities flung themselves upon each other, struggled, broke apart, warily proceeded, struggled again. And the vehicle was a thing alive, dancing in the street to the guttural chant of the men beneath it, and every golden ornament upon it shook and shimmered.

And behind it the drum-carts lumbered into line, crashing out the beat of this festival. For more than a mile the procession stretched through the town, beginning the circuit that would thrust through every street. People followed, pressing as close as they dared—their god was a boisterous creature, unruly in his joy, surging roughly from side to side, backward, forward.

And so his train convulsively moved and stopped, thrust forward, paused, thrust forward again, as a committee of shrine officials tried to guide and pace it. At shops and houses of unquestioned dignity, whose families were old in Shimoda, it took sake and food to give it strength through the long hot afternoon. As darkness fell the emblematic figures were lifted from the drum-carts and carried to their neighborhood homes, and in their place were strung crested lanterns to glow in the night. At last, nearly spent, the procession reached the halfway point, an open place where men had built a temporary shelter, and under the shelter the god's vehicle was placed on a platform, and the protective deities and weapons and sacred trees were arrayed around it, and the drum-carts passed before it and turned back each to its own block, and the god rested in the heart of his resting town. A collection box was set before the vehicle and men and women came forward to toss in a coin, clap hands to beg attention, and whisper a prayer. And the god took these prayers under advisement.

The old man who had carried the collection box all day took up his post to stand guard all night. He was a scrawny old man whose ancestors had been Shinto priests to a great daimyo in the age of wars. For generations his family had served this shrine and been close to it in a way that important men of the town could never be, and if sometimes the old man's talk seemed addled, nobody took heed. These were his great days, these and the days at New Year's when people called him into their houses to mutter a chant that would exorcise the evil of the old, dead year. He would not sleep tonight, nor tomorrow, until the festival was finished.

The next morning it began again. The bearers put on clothes chill and rancid with sweat, yet soon their bodies were hot again and the procession took on new urgency, for this was the last day. And on this day, as he continued his rounds, the god three times came upon houses that angered him. They were the houses of merchants who had been rapacious, who had raised the price of rice when people could least afford it, who had refused credit, who had turned away the poor. And the god sensed out these houses and scourged them. He sent his vehicle crashing into them. He shattered doors and spilled goods upon the ground.

The Governors had sent police officials to keep order during the festival, but they managed not to be near when these things happened, and by the time they reached the scene it had been tidied up and they could see no reason for action. Accidents, they agreed among themselves. They were bound to happen in a festival as rough as this one and were nothing the town officials could not handle; it was best to let the local people manage.

The afternoon was waning when the procession traversed the farthest street in the town and bent at last to make its return to the shrine. All along its length it slackened and came to a halt.

Youngsters were plucked from the long pull-ropes and carried home, where anxious mothers tried to get some supper into them. The vehicle of the god settled squarely before the house of the town's greatest merchant, Wataya Kichibei, and servants of that house at once appeared with trays of food and bottles of sake. Sweat-streaked bearers, squatting in the shadows under the eaves, filled their bellies and pulled hard at the sake. Back among the drum-carts the precious figures again were taken down and lanterns put up. Drummers and flutists disappeared but small boys gathered to imitate them and made the big drums yield hollow thumps. The town took a long breath.

When the sun dropped behind the hills the respite ended. The long train stirred and buzzed, an ungainly animal rousing to action. The bearers got to their feet, shouting slurs on each other's strength and masculinity, grabbed for the sake bottles as they passed from hand to hand, threw back their heads to take long draughts. The drummers and the flutists were back at it, faces flushed. The shrine committee reappeared, looking official and purposeful: we will now, they seemed to say, bring this festival to a speedy and a dignified conclusion—but who can take charge of a god?

The youngsters in front moved out, and they at least marched with a sense of order. But the sacred trees, the guardian deities, and the god himself, braced in his vehicle, showed no inclination to behave. Tossed and jostled while the chanting grew—*Ho-ra! Ho-ra!*—whirling and swerving in the narrow street, they tore back the way they had come, back toward the drum-carts, away from the shrine and the finish of this festival.

Now the committee went to work. They shouted, they waved lanterns, they coaxed and commanded this unruly monster. But every rush forward brought a rush back—*Ho-ra! Ho-ra! Ho-ra!*—every side street meant a dart to escape.

What the committee ordered, the drum-carts seduced. The first drummer, nearly naked—kimono flung off his shoulders, caught up to free his legs—lunged with brute strength. From first cart to last, drums throbbed syncopated fever, flutes skirled hot melody. Cohorts chattered wild tattoos on drum frames, carts, bells, bottles frequently upended.

It was hours before the officials could maneuver the vehicle back through the town and trap it in the street that led to the shrine. No more side streets to dart into, no more escape. Confined, the fury mounted.

The sacred trees were in shreds, stripped of leaves, bruised and battered. Now they and the deities rushed together. Their frames locked end to end, and with a great cry they pushed up to form an arch. *Ho-ra! Ho-ra!* Another cry and the arch fell as each section raced away, only to fling back upon the others and again strain upward from reaching hands. *Ho-ra! Ho-ra! Ho-ra!* Again and again they hooked and broke away, joined and scattered, but slowly they were pushed down the road, toward the humped bridge. Again and again they shied away, at last swept over it, through the torii gate. Their men sagged to the cool earth.

The humped stone bridge to the shrine
(*a lithograph from a drawing by Wilhelm Heine*)

Now it was the vehicle.

The smell was sweat, the din a pounding rhythm. The vehicle heaved and staggered—*Ho-ra!*—tossed toward the sky—*Ho-ra!*—dipped crazily, caromed between houses. *Ho-ra! Ho-ra!* The crowd swept with it, screaming, falling back as it careened toward them.

Shrine officials before and behind it, shouting, waving lanterns, urging it over the bridge, back to the shrine. With a push it charged the bridge, balked, roared back. *Ho-ra! Ho-ra! Ho-ra!* Again it charged, again balked. *Ho-ra! Ho-ra!* Over the frenzied bearers, splashes and flicks of water, arching from branches dipped in buckets.

No teams now. Bearers felt a surge of strength and slipped under the heavy shafts. Others weakened, fell away, gulped air, gulped sake, plunged in again. Men tossed buckets of water, and dazed men, drenched, shook themselves, fought back.

Bearers, officials, glistening vehicle on long shafts were one machine, a living thing caught in elemental rhythm. Convulsively it thrust, pulled back along the street, thrust toward the arch of the bridge, pulled back, thrust toward the torii gateway, pulled back, working to a wild pulse—*Ho-ra! Ho-ra! Ho-ra!*—pounding in the night.

Closer to the bridge, closer, up its rounded arch, higher, thrusting, withdrawing. The crowd shouted the count—twenty! thirty!—the rushes shorter, the pulse faster—forty!—to the top of the arch—fifty!—again, again, raging to climax—*Ho-ra!*—over! and through the torii.

From the town, from the men beneath the vehicle—from the god?—a great moan, a great sigh; then release, almost quiet. Steady now, on the shoulders of men dazed and spent, the vehicle glided under the arching trees, withdrawing from the town.

The crowd sagged, began to drift away into darkness. The drum-carts moved again, through the street now cleared, still beating the rhythms, sounding the airs of that long-ago triumph in battle. Up to the arching bridge they came, and one by one turned back to their own blocks.

Drained men guided the vehicle up the shrine steps, into the dark enclosure, settled it in place. The priest came forward, closed the tall doors. The presence of the god slipped away.

The night was far advanced. It was deep into Townsend Harris's Sabbath, and he had been long abed.

The next day, Monday, September 15, Harris wrote in his journal that he expected a visit from the Governor in response to his request to exchange money. He was still looking for quick action from the Japanese, though Moriyama and Wakana had told him not to expect it.

He did have visitors that day, but not to discuss money. In the afternoon a delegation appeared, headed by Moriyama and Superintendent Wakiya Usaburo. Wakiya was the official who, to his own regret, had been placed in charge of Gyokusenji. He had been dubbed "the Third Governor" by Harris (he was one step lower in the hierarchy than Wakana, "the Vice-Governor"); later, with less logic, Harris would start calling him "the Mayor of Kakisaki."

Moriyama and Wakiya were answering one of Harris's requests by bringing two boys to Gyokusenji. They were aged fifteen and sixteen and their names were Sukezo and Takizo.

A few months earlier the boys had entered the Shogun's service as *ashigaru*, foot soldiers. The Governors' office was almost always seeking such recruits. The Shogunate was a military government and all its men held military rank, but as is well known, an army of all officers and no privates is most unsatisfactory. Despite the fact that the appointment put a young man in the samurai class, entitled to wear two swords and to use a family name (as his parents might not), there were not many applicants, for the appointment was temporary and often amounted to becoming an officer's orderly.

Applicants were invariably the younger sons in a family. The first son stood to inherit the estate. A younger brother, unless he was adopted into a family which had no son and heir, had to cast about for a way to make a living.

It is not surprising to find that most of the *ashigaru* at Shimoda came from Naka. This was the village a large part of whose paddy land had been appropriated for the Governors' compound and a new jail. Many of Naka's farmers were left without land to grow rice, their most valuable crop. To make matters worse, the Goyosho had paid only half the modest price agreed on for the land they took and then had pronounced the treasury dry. For a while the men of Naka had been kept busy constructing the new buildings in their village and helping to rebuild Shimoda, but such work was running out. Naka was a poor place now and its young men had to search for jobs.

Takizo and Sukezo were farmers' sons from Naka. They had been carefully coached, freshly barbered, scrubbed until they glowed, and inserted into new kimono. Now they pressed their foreheads to the mats at Gyokusenji and entered the service of the foreigners.

> WAKIYA (introducing them): They have never worked for foreigners and are very young. They may be a trouble to you, but please forgive them because of their inexperience.

Harris thanked him for making the arrangements.

> WAKIYA: We ask you to let them sleep in the barracks with the Japanese officials, for they are young and anxious about working for you. And we must tell you that they will be allowed to return to their homes if they become sick, or if their parents become sick, or if their parents need them.

> HARRIS: They may sleep in the barracks, and when I need them I will

call them. I will let them return to their homes when it is necessary. I will treat them with sincerity and generosity.

Being the senior, Takizo became Harris's servant; Sukezo was assigned to Heusken.

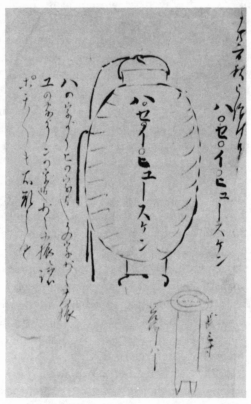

Design for Heusken's lantern, with instructions
(*a sketch from the Shimoda journal of town affairs*)

Wakiya had brought something else, in answer to another request from the consulate: two paper lanterns. One bore Harris's name and title, the other, Heusken's, formed in strange characters, jet ink brushed on white paper. Harris had seen that Japanese officials traveling at night were heralded by such lanterns and had promptly placed an order. "If you don't like them," said Wakiya, "we will have them remade." But Harris did like them and he liked the thought of their official glow in the dark.

WAKIYA: We hope you don't intend to walk out at night.
HARRIS: Not as a rule—only if some urgent business should come up.

WAKIYA: If that happens, we would like you to tell the officials who are attending you. One of them will go with you. We are anxious about lower people causing you trouble, for they cannot read the characters written on the lantern.

Harris agreed to notify the attending officials if he had to go out at night.

Moriyama had a complaint. Harris had requested that the pillars across the front of Gyokusenji be painted white, as they would have been at home. Moriyama had vetoed the suggestion forthwith, his sensibilities wounded. The temple's altars and images might be removed; the hall of worship might be turned into a foreigner's parlor; these things could be undone. But to paint the pillars carefully chosen for the beauty of their grain would be to destroy them in Japanese eyes. "We thought you understood," he said now, "and we agreed to repaint the plaster walls. But two days ago you placed the same request again. Why did you do so?"

No serious reason, said Harris. "I only thought it would be beautiful."

Moriyama scolded him. "We think that misunderstandings are unavoidable," he said, "because our languages are different. But it can only cause difficulties when you renew requests which have already been disposed of." Harris promised that he would not again ask for paint on the pillars.

He had a complaint of his own, however, and as usual his complaint found its way into his journal, as Moriyama's did not. Yesterday, Sunday, some of his Chinese servants had gone for a walk, followed, of course, by three of the guards posted at Gyokusenji. The servants complained about the way they had been treated. *They offered to purchase some fruit, but were refused, and finally, on asking for a drink of water from a man who was by a well, he refused, and ran away with the drinking vessel. . . . I remonstrated sharply against such conduct as disgraceful, inhospitable, etc., etc. . . .* Wakiya said: "We will investigate the matter and report it to the Governor." Harris answered, somewhat mollified: "If any of my servants should behave rudely to your officials in such a case, please let me know."

Harris tried to coax a little information from his guests, with only partial success. He produced Kaempfer's volumes on Japan and showed Wakiya their map of Edo. . . . *he at once pointed out the place of his and Moriyama's house in Edo, showing the general correctness of the plan of that city. I tried in various ways to get at the population of Edo from them, but without any success. They said it was a large place; that there was such a large number of persons going and coming daily, that it was out of their power to state the population, etc., etc.*

While Harris was ferreting for information about Edo, the Great Council, in Edo, was ferreting for policy regarding Harris. They had before them not only the formal reports from the Governors of Shimoda but also a number of informal and secret letters, in which the writers could speak with more candor and less formality. One of these, though it is unsigned, almost certainly came from a man quite high on the Shimoda Governors' staff who was doubling as a secret informant of the central inspector-general's department. The wording of the letter seems to point to Superintendent Wakiya, who had just brought the houseboys and now was parrying Harris's questions about the capital. It reads:

> We had been secretly ordered to do our best to make the American return to his own country, but when he said he would sail directly to Edo Bay to confront officials of the government we could only agree to let him use Gyokusenji as a temporary house. . . . Everything follows the tendency of the times, and we realize with regret that we can do nothing to prevent it. I was pleased that I was not appointed one of those who had to receive him when he arrived, but then I was appointed as a manager for Gyokusenji. Things don't always go as one wishes.
>
> Since the Americans know conditions in the Netherlands establishment at Nagasaki, they trouble us with their willful actions and requests. . . . However, though the Consul General has placed a number of requests, he has not shown a selfish attitude, and has shut himself up in his residence, not even going for a walk. But we are afraid that gradually he will make more important requests which will be unacceptable and a source of great harm to Japan. . . .
>
> I accompanied the Governors to the American ship, where I saw their firing of cannon and muskets and their skill at using swords and spears in defense. The guns were excellent great machines, but their use of swords and spears was not as masterly as we had expected. Those who came this time looked to us weaker mentally and physically than those who came with Commodore Perry.

Men in Edo drew what comfort they could from this, but they knew that the Americans would not choose to fight with swords and spears.

The government had before it the list of questions from the Shimoda Governors, including the urgent one about taxing the Consul General's purchases, but they were wrestling a more basic problem. On the same day the houseboys were delivered, the Great Council ordered those officials charged with maritime defense to study whether or not Harris's stay should be formally authorized.

Harris would have been upset to find that this question was still up for discussion. He would have been surprised to learn that a committee for maritime defense was the closest thing the Japanese had to a foreign ministry. As far as most Japanese were concerned, foreign relations was synonymous with coastal defense: the problem concerning foreigners was how to keep them out of the country.

The committee, however, consisted chiefly of men whom Harris would have called progressive, as their reply indicated. There was an alternative to receiving the Consul General, they pointed out, and that was to negotiate directly with the United States government. But they could find no precedent in Japanese history for sending a mission abroad, and they rejected that idea as improper. As for negotiation by letters, that seemed hopeless. So, since Harris was already here and nothing could be done about it, it would be best to authorize his stay formally and to negotiate with him as the need arose—and if antagonism to the treaty grew, there might be such need. Anyway, it was better to grant formal authorization than to try to hedge with temporary permission, for, as the Shimoda Governors had pointed out, the latter would make it more difficult to manage Harris and would cause ill feeling which would lead to more trouble later. As far as his residence was concerned, however, the Shimoda Governors should be ordered to make no concessions—it must remain Gyokusenji.

And though, as Wakana had told Harris, it was the custom of the Japanese government to consider and discuss even trifling problems carefully, the Great Council had not too much difficulty acting on these recommendations—possibly because they were faced with a *fait accompli* and because the chief of the Great Council, Lord Hotta, had taken charge of foreign affairs and generally saw eye-to-eye with the men in the committee for maritime defense (which is not surprising, since he had been instrumental in placing many of them there).

And so, on September 22, the Great Council sent an order to the Governors of Shimoda:

> As we told you last year, we object to American officials staying in Japan, and we instructed you to negotiate with this in mind.
>
> But since you have allowed the official to land temporarily, if you spend more days without granting him permission to stay, no one can tell how he may complain and brew great difficulties for our country. Therefore, as you have suggested, it is better that you allow him to stay.
>
> You are to take care that no heretical religion is propagated in this country. His stay must also be considered in the light of our treaty with

Russia, and of the fact that Britain and France will also seek entry for their envoys. Therefore, you are to be attentive to details: his residence must be kept as small as possible and everything he does held to the most modest scale. You are to oversee all that he does.

The Governors never told Harris that his stay was approved. He thought it had been done three weeks earlier, and they judged, no doubt correctly, that to tell him differently now would only vex him.

The order above was sent to Shimoda, but because the Great Council had reason to be concerned about political repercussions, it was not made public. The public order implied that no decision had been made:

Lord Hotta Masayoshi (*a painting by an unknown artist*)

AN ORDER TO THE GOVERNORS OF SHIMODA.

Without deep consideration we cannot decide whether or not to permit the American official to stay in Shimoda, for the decision will greatly affect the honor of Japan. We are therefore sending Iwase Shuri to Shimoda immediately. On his arrival you will consult with him to resolve all problems concerning treatment of the American official.

It was a canny move to send Iwase as troubleshooter. He was one of that brain trust that councillors like Lord Hotta had created in recent years by plucking men of marked ability from the lower echelons and elevating them to positions of responsibility. The method was unorthodox; it created jealousies and strains within the tradition-ridden administration; but it brought to the fore men like Iwase and Inoue and Inoue's older brother, Kawaji (both Inoue and Kawaji had been adopted and hence bore different names). Iwase's ability was important in the present situation, but equally important was the fact that his ability was respected by the men likely to cause trouble, those powerful lords most bitterly opposed to foreign inroads on Japan.

Iwase (*a drawing by Kobayashi Donge*)

The order to Iwase reiterated the worries manifest in the secret order to the Governors, and concluded:

> You and the Governors of Shimoda must do your best to prevent the spread of Christianity and of foreign habits among the people of Shimoda. Together you must try to minimize the American's demands, which will begin with the problems of his residence and household

Launching the Russian schooner (*a painting by an unknown artist*)

affairs. You must see to it that nothing related to him becomes fatal to Japan. We are waiting for your prompt report.

We hope, however, that your travel to Shimoda will be done carefully in order not to trouble the villages along the way. And as we have many problems facing us here at Edo, you must return as quickly as possible after completing your investigation there.

The passage of an official of Iwase's stature could of course be troublesome to those villages obliged to provide bearers, escorts, and all the other requisites of travel, but in this case the problem was avoided. Someone ordered that Iwase be carried on one of the Shogunate's new foreign-style ships, which was about to sail on a shakedown cruise.

These ships were a result of the tidal wave at Shimoda, as if to bolster the philosophy that finds good in everything. For when the Russians' ship was sunk, they set about to build a new one at the port of Heda, not far from Shimoda but, they judged, much safer. The shipwrights of Heda were drafted to help build the ship, and in building it, they learned how foreign

ships were made. The Japanese government promptly ordered some for themselves. Now the Shogunate had several sleek, new two-masted schooners, called Kimizawa ships because Heda lay in the Kimizawa district.

The journey that by land would have taken Iwase six days, or four if he had exhausted himself by rushing, now took but one. He left Shinagawa harbor at Edo in the darkness of early morning on September 22, and that afternoon he was at Shimoda. It was an exhilarating experience and he wrote a poem about it. He called it "Verse Hummed to Oneself Aboard the Kimizawa Ship."

> The sails cut through the sea-spray
> > like flying wings,
> The ship skims the vast moonlit
> > Bay of Sagami—
> This is one of the joys of living;
> Leaving Shinagawa in the morning,
> > reaching Shimoda by evening.

The ship delivered Iwase and slipped out to sea again. It was raining and her officers may have noticed that Shimoda harbor was filling with little freighters; their weather-wise captains were fearing a blow.

Back in Edo, the Great Council set about to mend its fences. The decision to authorize Harris's stay would have to be defended. They began to draft a note to the Imperial court in Kyoto, explaining, justifying, reassuring. And lest Kyoto accuse them of being soft on foreigners, they issued orders that the Lords of Kii and Awa provinces build warships to defend that area; a month earlier they had ordered batteries constructed there.

As finally sent, their message to Kyoto read:

> Since we have permitted American ships to sail into the ports of Shimoda and Hakodate, we must also, by the terms of the treaty,* permit an American official to be stationed in Japan. Further, we need someone who understands how to manage the American ships. The United States government believes that such an official is necessary, and has requested authorization from us. We know that it is most undesirable to permit foreigners to stay in Japan. But we must consider that we cannot foresee what kind of persons will come on foreign ships or what problems they will raise. Reflecting on this we have decided to permit the American official to stay at Shimoda, so that we can handle such problems through him.
>
> We have fixed it deeply in our minds to prevent the spread of Christianity. We will regulate all things and keep his house as small as possible. We are dispatching Iwase Shuri to Shimoda to resolve with the Governors of Shimoda all problems relating to this American official.
>
> We know that rumors concerning this have been spread about, and they might be causing the Emperor to worry. So we are telling you the situation and the steps we are taking to meet it.

Harris would have been surprised had he seen this letter. The West knew of the Emperor's existence but commonly thought of him as a kind of pope, without temporal authority. He was in fact the source of temporal authority. In controlling the country the Shogun was acting as his deputy.

The Shogunate was nothing new in Japan. It was a system hallowed by age. Very few emperors of the hundred and twenty-one who were said to have reigned over Japan since the dawn of history had personally held power. Power had a way of slipping away from them, either to prime ministers or to Shoguns, who then established their own dynasties. But sooner or later these dynasties of power had all been toppled, and new

* The Emperor had approved the Perry treaty.

strong men had turned again to an emperor, asking not that he govern but that he sanction their governing.

But Harris did not see the Great Council's letter to the Imperial court. He had no reason to doubt that he was dealing with the ultimate authority in Japan. He had no way of knowing that the Tokugawa Shogunate—for over two centuries so powerful that it need answer to no one—now felt obliged to defend and justify its actions.

The Great Council, Lord Hotta presiding, addressed itself to another problem, too. The treaty that Commodore Perry had made was little more than a pact of friendship and a pledge that American mariners shipwrecked on Japanese shores would be treated with kindness until they could be repatriated. But the Japanese knew perfectly well that the aim of the Americans, and of the Russians and the British and the French, was trade. They knew perfectly well that Harris was there to raise that issue. It was an idea that most Japanese found appalling.

When Wells Williams's Chinese teacher Lo was in Japan with Perry's expedition, he and a Japanese official exchanged long letters. Lo told of the turmoil and misery in China. The Japanese had commiserated and given a samurai's analysis, all very Confucianist:

> The essential evil of such a state may be described in a single phrase —it is the desire of gain. Now, the desire of gain is common to all men, and is the pregnant womb of all evil. Confucius seldom spoke of gain, wishing to check the lust of it in its source. This, also, was the reason why my ancestors cut off all intercourse of foreign nations with Japan, because the desire of gain led astray the ignorant . . . till filial duty, modesty, and the sense of shame were all forgotten. . . .

The writer could see blessings in commerce "by which people exchange the commodities which they have abundantly, for those which they have not, and one nation succors the distresses of another; . . . Yet if gain—gain —be what is sought for by it, it will only develop the lusts and angry passions of men, and there will be a melancholy termination to what may be begun under good auspices."

It is true that others of his class had fewer reservations. They argued that foreign trade could make Japan richer and stronger. Some advocated that Japan build its own merchant fleet. They cited the example of another island nation, England, which had prospered by sending her ships all over the world. But unlike the English, most of these men thought of trade as a government monopoly. They could not see how the government could profit otherwise. Private trade would enrich only the merchants—who were too rich already—and it would weaken the position of their own class—which was certainly too poor.

Earlier in the month, while the *San Jacinto* was still in Shimoda harbor, Lord Hotta had sent an order to all officials of the government who had a hand in formulating policy toward foreigners:

> Once before you expressed your opinions about concluding a trade treaty with Britain, the British government's desire having been presented through the captain of the Dutch steamer. But this is so important a problem that we cannot decide easily, though we must decide.
>
> If once Japan expresses her willingness to open trade, not only Russia, America, Britain, and France but all other countries will want to trade with us. If we should be driven to this, it would be impossible to trade with one country and not with others.
>
> As we are in difficulty already, it may be better for us to change the law of seclusion and to carry on trade ourselves and thus to strive for national prosperity. But however hard we try, it will be several years before we can sail all over the world, trading with different countries. In the meantime, we shall have to answer the limitless requests of foreign countries with surplus goods produced within Japan.
>
> Japan has been exporting copper to the Netherlands. But the amount of copper mined is decreasing year by year, and at present it is required to arm Japan. Casting of temple bells has already been prohibited and the government is trying to decrease the amount of copper exported to the Netherlands. If we open trade with European countries, the main thing they will want is copper. We must consider how we can trade with them and at the same time prevent the decline of our country.
>
> Whether or not Japan should open trade with foreign countries must be decided after considering the above points. Especially those officials who are stationed at Nagasaki, Shimoda, and Hakodate must think them over carefully. We are waiting for your opinions.
>
> The above was written at midnight, as it is a secret of the government and very important.

A view so unpopular had to be kept secret. In public Lord Hotta put on a different face. The Shogunate had convoked an assembly of scholars, mobilizing all the intellectuals at its disposal. And to them Lord Hotta posed the same question in even graver fashion:

> Trade with foreign countries can never benefit Japan. If we allow foreigners to engage in trade with Japan, this country will become impoverished. But if we do not permit trade, foreign countries will act

in unison, and threatening us with their forces, will force us to grant permission. How should we deal with them?

To make profits is the primary objective of commerce. Today, when this country is suffering from many troubles and successive natural disasters, the samurai class will become gradually impoverished, while merchants will reap profits. In the end those now of high social standing will lose their influence, and those now of low standing will become influential. What policy is to be adopted to correct this trend?

These were dilemmas that would have to be solved if Japan as these men knew it could continue to exist.

The valley above Shimoda, a small Shinto shrine in the foreground
(*a woodcut from a drawing by Wilhelm Heine*)

Harris was not aware of Iwase's arrival. He may have noticed the schooner putting into port, but he could not know that it carried an official sent to cope with him. Besides, he was ill.

A few days earlier he had finally felt free to take a walk with Heusken, accompanied, of course, by some of the Japanese detachment posted to Gyokusenji.

A fine bright morning. Sky as blue as sapphire. Wind light from the northwest. Thermometer, 76° at eight A.M. At eleven o'clock go out for a walk. The paths lead over towards Edo Bay, and the views were enchant-

ing. Sky clear—water blue—whitecaps cresting the waves. High lands on the opposite side of Edo Bay (northeast side) dimly seen. Japanese junks with their large square sail scudding merrily before the wind. . . . I never saw such fine crops of rice, or rice of so good a quality as here. . . . We pursued our pleasant walk until we reached the highest hill in this vicinity, —say some 2,800 feet; and from that we could just see the top of the celebrated Fuji Yama, the highest mountain in Japan, which is 12,500 feet high and not many miles from Edo.

Harris had climbed Mount Takane. In a simple shelter on its crest, he must have seen and dismissed the stone statue of the god Jizo, compassionate Buddhist helper of those in trouble. This image, crudely but powerfully carved, was venerated by seafaring men from one end of Japan to the other.

From the sea Mount Takane can be distinguished for more than fifty miles, all across the Bay of Edo, all across Suruga Bay. It was a sailor's landmark. When it was visible in clear weather they felt safe and assured. When it disappeared in storm clouds they called upon its Jizo for protection. Many were the stories of guiding lights sent through dark and storm-tossed seas to sailors and fishermen who in grave danger called upon the Jizo of Takane.

It is said that this Jizo, made of a hard stone not native to Izu, was found long ago buried at the foot of the mountain where a temple now stands. The priest who found it had it carried to the top of the mountain and built its chapel there. Years later another priest of the temple decided that the statue was too ugly to be an object of worship. He had a new one made of bronze, put it on the mountain and brought the old one down. Thereafter his sleep was haunted by dreams in which the old Jizo appeared, crying: "The reason I am ugly is that I protect the children of this place against smallpox, taking it upon myself, making my face ugly. Why did you remove me from the mountain which is my home?" Finally the priest carried the old Jizo back to the mountaintop and brought the new one down to the garden of the temple, where it still sits, pretty, plump, and ignored.

When he came down from Mount Takane, Harris used the path worn by countless worshippers, its eighteen stone markers brought by sailors from ports up and down the coast; and when he crossed the grassy lower slopes he was walking where most of the cattle of this area were hidden on the occasion of Commodore Perry's visit to Shimoda. *We reached home at three P.M. much pleased with our walk. Our distance out [and] in was about eight miles.*

His walk must have been good for him (though he remained cantankerous: *Our poultry has been taken with some disease during the last few days and is dying off rapidly . . . I charge the Japanese with selecting all the sick fowls they have and bringing them to me. They deny it, and say the poultry all around is dying off in the same manner*), but on the following day he stepped on a large nail, probably from the debris of his packing cases. The wound was deep and painful and became infected; he could scarcely walk. With that, and the case of nerves and upset stomach he had already developed in his continuing skirmishes with the Japanese, he was quite ill.

And so on the rainy day that Iwase arrived he did not feel well enough to see Inspector Aihara when he called at Gyokusenji. When that official and his entourage approached the temple gate under bobbing yellow umbrellas, Harris told Heusken to receive the visitors.

He had called, Aihara told Heusken, in answer to the Consul General's letter. They would do their best to provide large lumps of coal without dust, and they would forward the suggestions about digging it from deep pits. But, he added, coal had to be shipped to Shimoda from the southernmost island; they could not insure that the persons in charge of mining would heed the suggestions, or that the coal, when it arrived, would meet Harris's specifications; and they had a large quantity on hand which they would have to use up—there was no way to exchange it, for the Japanese did not use coal. So he asked for understanding.

He also asked about coke; he had heard, he said, that preburned coal produced more heat. But Heusken seemed to know even less about this than the Japanese.

As to the exchange of money, said Aihara, the Consul General's request was rejected. It was forbidden by Japanese law, and besides, it was quite unnecessary: the Americans could get everything they needed by the means established in the treaty. (The treaty was explicit. Americans could obtain goods for their own gold and silver coins or by exchange of other goods, and the supplementary regulations stated: "Whenever goods are selected in the shops, they shall be marked with the name of the purchaser and the price agreed upon, and then be sent to the Goyosho, or government office, where the money is to be paid to Japanese officers, and the articles delivered by them.")

Heusken said he was certain that Mr. Harris would resubmit his request after thinking it over, and he thanked Aihara for coming out in the rain, and saw him out of the temple.

Even though Harris was so ill that he was making almost no entries in his journal, he did keep up his record of the weather. Four times a day he set down his observations. Before he had sailed for Japan he had applied to the Navy Department and then to the Smithsonian Institution for meteorological instruments. Both had turned him down, and so at Shimoda he was reduced to recording the temperature, the direction of the wind, and general conditions. This he did faithfully. That evening after Aihara left he found himself making some extra observations. He was recording a typhoon.

It had rained most of the day, with light winds from the northeast and east. At four o'clock there were heavy squalls of wind and rain from the northeast, and then the wind increased and hauled to the southward. This was the signal that the storm was a typhoon, one of those violent cyclonic storms that originate in the Pacific and whirl northward, as hurricanes move northward in the Atlantic. In the next few hours the gale boxed the compass. About eight o'clock it raged from the south-southeast. It increased in fury and swung to the south-southwest. At midnight it was from the west-northwest. Then at last it began to moderate.

I was under much apprehension that my house would be blown down, as it shook in every post and beam, and swayed to and fro as the heavy gusts struck it. My kitchen was partly unroofed. Flagstaff blown over so as to stand at an angle of 65°. In the harbor every junk was cast ashore and many lives lost and much property destroyed. In Kakisaki, full one half the houses were blown down and some persons killed. The landing jetty and breakwater at Kakisaki are totally destroyed.

At Shimoda, the bazaar part of Goyosho is totally destroyed, and a large amount of beautiful lacquer and inlaid ware lost. One hundred houses blown down and twenty lives lost. The Japanese say it was the severest storm ever known at this place. (They did not tell him that some people blamed it on the anger of the gods at his being there.)

One wishes that one could turn to Yoheiji's account of what the typhoon did to his village, or to the diary kept by Headman Hambei of Shimoda. (One thing the storm blew away was the feud between the fishermen and the shopkeepers, the one which had broken out on the eve of the festival; the ceremonies of reconciliation had been taking place ever since: intermediaries had met, conferred seriously and at length, and managed to consume large quantities of sake—but there was no time for that now.) Unfortunately, these records have disappeared. Henry Heusken's is the only other eyewitness report of the damage:

> A frightful hurricane laid waste the coast of Japan. All the junks in the Bay were cast against the shore. Almost a third of the town of Shimoda was destroyed. When, the next morning, I sighted the destruc-

tion of the night, the masts scattered on the beach, the debris of ships and houses, I was astonished at the behavior of the Japanese. Not a cry was heard. Despair? What! Not even sorrow was visible on their faces. On the contrary, they seemed quite indifferent to the typhoon and everyone was already busy repairing the damage caused by the tempest.

The people of Kakisaki would have been puzzled by the young foreigner's astonishment. What were they to do? They lived with a history of disaster: it was less than two years since a tidal wave had smashed over them. Once again they were surrounded by the litter of wrecked homes, scattered possessions, broken ships. There were injured to be cared for, dead to be buried. Tears were shed that morning, but privately. In Kakisaki and Shimoda they had learned long ago that tears blur the eyes for work.

There was another pressure on the men who were on the beach that morning, working among shattered masts and battered hulls. Part of their village lay in ruins behind them, but before them lay a chance for profit which could wipe out their losses. For a seacoast village like Kakisaki or a town like Shimoda, the salvage of wrecked ships was not only a responsibility laid on by the government but a source of important income.

In the past, one is pained to learn, there had been some wicked people along this Izu coast (although not, of course, at Shimoda or Kakisaki). In a bad storm they lighted fires along the shore to lure some hapless vessel onto the rocks, and then when the storm passed they looted the wreck. They appropriated the cargo and the gear, and the ship's timbers turned up as beams and walls in their houses. It was a business with low overhead and high profit. It gave rise to a cryptic New Year's greeting. "Come on, storm," the first party would say. And the second would answer, "Let's celebrate with old nails."

When the Tokugawa regime brought peace and order to Japan, ending the long age of war and brutality, this sort of wickedness naturally ceased. The people's character improved and, besides, punishment became swift, ruthless, and inevitable.

Storms continued to lash the coast, and vessels continued to be wrecked, even without encouragement from shore, but now the government had the power to reaffirm and enforce ancient regulations: seacoast villages were enjoined to give all possible aid to vessels in distress, and in case of shipwreck, to assist in the salvage of ship and cargo, and suitable rewards were prescribed. Villagers got ten per cent of cargo sunk, five per cent of cargo floating on the water, and three per cent of cargo still on board the ship. The reward was handled through the fishermen's association of the village, for the prime responsibility for rescue and salvage operations fell on the local seamen, who were mostly fishermen. The rewards were always presented with suitable ceremony in the presence of village officials, who were given a share for their trouble, and a little gift was made to the port officials—"sake money"—and then the balance was divided according to a long-established formula. Such money flowing into a village was important in keeping it solvent.

But that was only the beginning. Even if the cargo was unhurt, wages could be charged for carrying it ashore from a damaged ship. And usually the cargo had to be sold locally. If, for example, rice had become wet, it could not be reloaded and carried farther; there was nothing for the owner to do but get what he could for it. It was put up for the local merchants to bid on, and the result was cheap rice for the townsfolk. Even before the bidding, there were negotiations between the village officials and the cargo owners which always ended with a share being set aside for the local poor, as well as several bags being given to the headman and the elders, to the ship's innkeeper, and to the broker who acted as a local business agent.

It can be seen that to seacoast villages there was profit in shipwreck, and on the morning after the typhoon, with every ship in the harbor driven ashore, there was a great deal of profit in prospect. Since the fiercest winds had come from the south-southwest, most of the ships had ended on the beaches of Kakisaki rather than of Shimoda, and the men of Kakisaki were hard at work making the best of that.

Yoheiji sent the necessary report to the Goyosho, including the fact that twenty-five ships had been cast on the beaches of his village, and later in the day the Governors' office sent two officials to inspect. The havoc was obvious, and they could see no alternative but to direct the village to press forward with the salvage operations they had started.

The trouble began the next day. The men of Kakisaki, working hard along their beaches, were startled by the arrival of an imposing delegation from Shimoda, led by Headman Hambei and including several of the important shipping agents and owners of ships' inns.

Yoheiji hurried to meet them. There were the usual civilities, somewhat perfunctory on this occasion, and then the Shimoda group announced the reason for their visit. They had come, they said, to take over disposal of the wrecked ships and their cargoes, for since the wrecks occurred within the port of Shimoda, it was clearly the responsibility of Shimoda town to conduct the salvage operations.

Yoheiji was outranked. He represented a small village. Against him were arrayed the strength and prestige of a town of considerable importance. A lesser man might have crumpled, but Yoheiji was tough. Quite coolly he refuted the Shimoda contention.

There could be no objection, he said, to the town of Shimoda's having control over the port of Shimoda. But Shimoda bay included not only the port of Shimoda but also the port of Kakisaki. Kakisaki was an independent village which paid taxes directly to the Shogunate because it did business independently. The ships were cast on the beaches of Kakisaki and therefore the people of Kakisaki were dutybound to dispose of the wrecks.

Harsh words were traded before the Shimoda delegation withdrew, but Yoheiji did not budge. From then on, there were meetings and arguments daily. The dispute was carried to the Goyosho, and the Governors' men, too, split on the issue. Those officials who hailed from Edo sided with Kakisaki, but those who previously had been assigned to the Governors' office at the port of Uraga supported Shimoda.

Uraga and Shimoda had been closely related for well over a century. When the Tokugawa Shogunate had made Shimoda a checkpoint, sixty-three of the town's families, those of samurai descent and ancient lineage, had been given the hereditary right to conduct the inspection of ships. When the checkpoint had been shifted to Uraga, the sixty-three families were saved from disaster by being permitted to continue to function at Uraga, though they maintained their homes at Shimoda and it was four or five days' travel between the two towns.

Because of this travel back and forth, and because the harbor master at Shimoda was appointed by and reported to the Governors of Uraga, there had been a long association between Uraga officials and Shimoda townsmen. When Governors were again appointed at Shimoda, to cope with the foreigners, it was natural that many of the staff were shifted from Uraga, for they were familiar with Shimoda, and it was natural that they should be sympathetic to the Shimoda point of view. To the men from Edo, on the other hand, logic seemed all on Yoheiji's side.

The stakes were high and the quarrel was bitter. And though the physical work of salvage went forward, the shipowners and cargo owners found that no disposition could be made of their property, and the crews sat in idleness. There was not much for them to do but to get acquainted with the local girls, and this they proceeded to do.

News travels swiftly, and the girls of Kakisaki, who were quite unable to handle all the attention showered on them, were soon reinforced by *yamagoshi*, girls from villages "over the mountain," who ordinarily appeared only for the winter refuge season but now responded to the emergency. They moved in with the families they were accustomed to stay with, and the sailors moved in with them. It was all family-style.

Shimoda had its professional women, and if a man wanted night life, and could pay for it, he crossed the harbor. Some of the captains, who had money, or perhaps credit established on previous visits, found their way into the new expensive restaurants. Some of the old-timers grumbled that the influx of Edo officials had made things so fancy that a seafaring man no longer felt at home.

Not all Shimoda women were expensive, of course. There were, for example, the waitresses in certain noodle houses, which, contrary to general practice, were divided into cubicles for privacy. For cheap, quick satisfaction of basic appetites, a man went to one of these houses.

Townsend Harris was as unaware of all this as he was of the quarrel that had erupted between Kakisaki and Shimoda on the littered beach below his temple (he would have been interested in Yoheiji's argument, because it would have bolstered his position that he was living not in Shimoda but in a separate village, contrary to the provisions of the treaty).

He seems to have been unaware also that courtesy and diplomatic good form required that he send a message of sympathy to the Governors on the disaster that had struck the area. Such a message would have been appreciated by the Japanese, themselves quick to commiserate. Instead he began to draft a peevish response to the answers delivered by Aihara. When Heusken delivered this letter to the Goyosho on September 25, three days after the typhoon, some of the officials there must have supposed it to be an expression of sympathy, and they must have been shocked to find in it no reference to the death and destruction all about them.

> Consulate General of the
> United States of America
> Shimoda, September 25th, 1856

To His Excellency the Governor of Shimoda:

I have received through a messenger a verbal reply to the letter I had the honor to address to Your Excellency on the 13th inst.

I have to request that in the future Your Excellency will favor me with written answers to my letters, and for reasons that must be obvious to you, and therefore need not be repeated here.

The precedent of giving written answers will be found in the letters written by the High Nobles, Hayashi, Ido, Isawa, Udono, and others, who frequently wrote to Commodore Perry.

The answer to my application for Japanese money in exchange for silver dollars may be stated under two heads:

1. By the Treaty all supplies for Americans are to be procured by the Government officials and payment made to them.

2. That the Laws of Japan forbid the giving any of the coins of the country to an American.

I answer, it is true that by the Treaty all Americans coming to Japan for supplies of food, etc., etc., are to procure them only through the intervention of Government officers, but this clause does not in any respect apply to the Consul General, who is here as the representative of his country, and as such has privileges which cannot be taken away from him without a violation of the "Laws of Nations" as admitted throughout the civilized world.

Among those privileges are the inviolability of his person, of his house, and of his servants.

For such supplies as are required by him, he has full liberty to procure them in the freest manner, in person, by his servants or any other persons he may appoint, and in no case can be restrained by any regulations made to control private persons.

I have acquiesced in the having my supplies obtained up to this time by Government officers solely because I was not prepared to employ other means, but I fully notified the Vice-Governor, on the 3rd inst., that this must be considered only a *temporary arrangement,* and I now repeat that as soon as my residence is put in order, and the various mechanics have left, I shall dispense with the attendance of any persons, except those actually employed and paid by me.

To the statement that Japanese coin cannot be given to Americans, I reply that no such regulations can apply to the Consul General, for the reasons before written.

I am informed that Japanese copper coin was sometimes given at the Goyosho to the officers of the Frigate *San Jacinto,* in making change, so that the law is not even enforced by the Japanese officers themselves.

I add that so long as the value of the dollar is unknown to the Japanese generally, I cannot obtain my proper supplies unless I have the coin of Japan to purchase with.

Another point, connected with these questions, remains to be stated; heretofore at Shimoda the dollar has only been allowed as the value of one *ichibu,** while it weighs nearly as much as three *ichibus.*

At Hakodate the dollar was taken at its true value, i.e., three *ichibus.†*

I am directed by my Government to call the attention of the Japanese

---

* *Ichibu* means "one bu"; foreigners at this time usually referred to the *bu* as *ichibu,* though the redundancy now is obvious.

† This slip by the Governors of Hakodate was speedily corrected on orders from Edo.

authorities to this fact, and so convinced is my Government of the *justice* and *rectitude* of the Government of Japan, that it has no doubt but that this wrong will be immediately rectified.

I was assured by Your Excellency that all supplies I should want should be furnished at *the same price as would be paid by the Japanese.*

I now request Your Excellency to redeem this pledge; for so long as "one dollar" only passes for one *ichibu,* instead of paying the *same* prices as the Japanese I am required to pay *three times* as much for every article I purchase.

I beg Your Excellency to consider that by making treaties with foreign nations, the Government of Japan has assumed the responsibilities under the "Laws of Nations" that naturally grow out of treaty arrangements, and in reference to some of your laws, which were made long since and under a state of things very different from the present, I would quote from a letter written by the Japanese Commissioners to Commodore Perry; they wisely say: "For us to continue attached to the ancient laws seems to misunderstand the spirit of the age."

I avail myself of this opportunity to renew to Your Excellency the assurance of my distinguished consideration.

Harris was here propounding an aggressive doctrine which the Governors had heard before. More than a year earlier, Lieutenant John Rodgers had commanded a U.S. naval expedition which surveyed much of Japan's coastline, despite indignant protests from the Japanese. At Shimoda he had found those Americans who were living at Gyokusenji while their ship carried some of the Russians home; he had found those would-be traders under pressure from the Japanese to leave as soon as their ship returned, and he had taken up cudgels in their behalf.

Writing to the Governors, Rodgers had stated: "When a treaty gives a thing, it gives every thing which is necessary to the enjoyment of the thing given." Now Harris was saying much the same thing. In signing a treaty, the Japanese had committed themselves to conform to the "Laws of Nations."

It was this kind of argument that made the Japanese so apprehensive. Every demand granted to foreigners seemed a basis for greater demands. There appeared to be no end.

Harris was leaning heavily on the "Laws of Nations." What did he have in mind?

He had on his shelves a book titled *The Law of Nations,* which he had purchased on the way to Japan. He had inscribed the flyleaf—

Townsend Harris
London
October 13/55

It was written by G. F. von Martens, Professor of Public Law in the University of Göttingen, who had subtitled it, "The Science of National Law, Covenants, Power, Etc., Founded upon the Treaties and Customs of Modern Nations in Europe."

Professor Martens, unfortunately, was no great help to Harris. It would never have done, for example, to quote him on the subject of coinage:

> But, the right of coining extending no further than the territory of the state, no sovereign is obliged to admit foreign money into his dominions; and, if he admit it, he has an indisputable right to fix the value of it, without respect to that which it bore in the country where it was coined.

On the rights of consuls, the professor was scarcely more encouraging. He wrote "Of the Inviolability and Independence of Ministers," but when he came to consuls he asserted that "they are far from enjoying the advantages that custom allows to ministers." Harris could explain that he was a Consul General sent to do the work of a minister, but this was not an argument the Japanese could be expected to accept: the treaty authorized only a consul, and a consul was clearly what Perry and the Japanese had in mind when they wrote it.

There must have been times when Harris was just as irritated with Professor Martens as he was with the Japanese.

On the same day that Harris sent his letter to the Goyosho, Sir John Bowring, at Hong Kong, was writing to Harris, in answer to a letter Harris had sent by the *San Jacinto*. It would be a long time before Harris received this letter but the delay was not important, for Sir John's urbane chaffing would have done nothing to cool Harris's impatience.

Hong Kong
(Private) 25 September 1856
My dear Sir:

> I am much obliged to you for your letter from Shimoda of 1st inst. I am glad that the charms of change and of climate will be some recompense for annoyances necessarily associated with your position. One does not always see how, but we may be quite certain events will bring about great alterations in the nature of our intercourse with Japan. And it is a comfort to think that a little delay counts as nothing in the great history of progress. Nay! the delay is sometimes most beneficial to the interests of those who *insist* and those who *cede*.

I did not anticipate any satisfaction on your part with your location at Shimoda, which would not have been chosen had there been adequate information as to the capabilities of different ports and places. But you may be able from your adjacency to the Capital to gather useful political *pabulum*.

Thanks for your kind offer. I had rather welcome you becomingly in Edo than worship at your temple at Shimoda. You may be very useful in making straight the path for future negociators,—and useful *as* a negociator if you can persuade the Japanese that there may be *doings* behind your *sayings*. Everything confirms the statements that the people are well disposed—they out of love may do what their rulers would only cede to fear. But the more we know the better we shall do.

I hope the settlement of the European questions will untie the hands of the Treaty Powers,° and permit them to think a little more about the farthest east—to an American one should probably say the farthest west. But of this you may be assured—that we cannot long remain in our present position as regards Japan. If I go [to Japan] I shall certainly go reasonably *determined*,—but *determined* in my reasonableness— with olive branches in both hands—but behind me—a becoming accompaniment.

Ever very faithfully yours

John Bowring

I send you a Chinese translation of *our* Siamese treaty.

Sir John knew Harris well enough to know how to needle him.

Iwase, who had arrived from Edo just in time for the typhoon, now found most of the Governors' staff too busy with the aftermath of the storm to work on anything else, and he may have been glad of the chance for a few days' quiet investigation on his own.

The attitudes and ideas that he brought to Shimoda can be made out from a memorial submitted to the Great Council at this juncture by Iwase's associates on the committee for maritime defense (among them, Governor Inoue's brother, Kawaji). The timing of this document makes it look as though it was intended to make Iwase's task easier.

Its main theme was the familiar one which had been emphasized again and again by these men. Times had changed, they wrote:

> Once Japan was the strongest nation in the world, and we Japanese were accustomed to treat foreign nations as inferiors. Present circum-

° The Crimean War being over, Britain and France were free for larger action in Asia.

Kawaji (*a drawing by Kobayashi Donge*)

stances are different but we seem unable to discard our old practices; and yet we must, for there are vicissitudes in the destiny of any country, and we have to change our attitudes in accordance with them. . . .

The important thing is that we not stickle over trifles because they are not provided for in a treaty. Intolerance may invite national disaster. We do not know what demands other countries may make as a result of accumulated indignation. The best way for us to deal with foreign countries is to grant their requests generously as long as they are within the limits of the treaty. Of course you will be criticized for such a policy, but it is the only way you will be able to bequeath a peaceful Japan to our posterity. . . .

Everything depends on how you look at it. We consider it advisable to permit the American official to have a courtesan and to let him keep a cow. We dare say these things worry you as they do us. But the Dutch at Nagasaki must be considered government officials, and the American can point out that they are allowed to go to the licensed quarters there. Moreover, he can ask why a cow cannot be provided for him if it is used to obtain a kind of medicine, while we Japanese can, in emergency, obtain pills made from human liver. . . .

It is natural that since our conventions have been violated by unrefined foreigners, there are people who think ill of foreigners. It is natural that there are people who, indignant because of foreigners' past practices, denounce them over even trifling matters. These people are worthy Japanese, but present circumstances do not permit such an attitude. It will lead to greater difficulty, perhaps even conflict. . . .

It is hard to find words to compose this kind of letter when we would like to write something heroic and valiant. But our nation faces trouble and we write out of sheer necessity. We ask that you endure for a while, that you avoid giving offense, and that you use the time gained to rebuild our national strength. . . .

We have all conferred, and together we sigh out the above.

Iwase had come to Shimoda prepared to advocate greater lenience toward some of Harris's demands. And it would seem that those demands included a mistress, for it is doubtful that the Edo officials would have volunteered their recommendation if the issue had not arisen.

It is quite understandable that if Harris had requested women for himself and Heusken, he would not have written about it in his journal; he did not mention milk or the cook or the laundryman either. It is equally understandable that the Governors would have reported such a request to Edo secretly, perhaps verbally, for they were as loath as Harris to let the public in on such a matter. And so it is not surprising to find no chronicle of this proposition, if it was made.

But looking back at the record of this, Harris's first month in Japan, it does seem that his performance is more easily explained if there was some deeper frustration than those he mentions. We know that he was hot-tempered: when General Wetmore was campaigning to secure Harris's appointment, he admitted to Secretary Marcy that "He is impetuous—prompt to act—at times perhaps inclined to be irritable . . ." But even allowing for his hot temper, his agitation this first month seems to have been greater than called for by the circumstances.

On the last day of September the flag would have been run up at Gyokusenji, except that the flagstaff was still canted at the crazy angle the typhoon had left it. The first foreign ship since the *San Jacinto* arrived at Shimoda. It was the Dutch steam frigate *Medusa,* on her way back to Nagasaki after a visit to Hakodate. Heusken, especially, was happy to see her and some of his countrymen.

Chapter 4

OCTOBER, 1856

Twelve days after the typhoon an unidentifiable body washed ashore at Suzaki village. It was generally believed that the man had been one of the crew aboard a ship that was lost off Suzaki during the storm. She had been loaded with lumber from Owari Province, and the lumber, having been requisitioned by the government, was a matter of official concern, though the body was not. The Edo office of the Lord of Owari sent two retainers (each of whom brought a retainer of his own) to Suzaki. They initiated a circular directed to all the coastal villages around Suruga Bay: any lumber found floating in the sea or washed ashore was to be reported to shipping agent Shichiemon of Shimoda; if a village had found none, it was to so certify before passing the circular to the next village.

Another circular originated in the Goyosho but appeared, as such orders sometimes did, over the seal and signature of the headman of Shimoda: all the villages within the Governors' area were to report to the government construction office the quantities of building materials and the number of men used in reconstruction. It was hard to tell whether such a report would eventually lead to a rehabilitation grant from the government or merely end in Edo as a statistic. (They had problems of their own in Edo, for the typhoon had also struck there.)

As for the quarrel between Kakisaki and Shimoda over the ships wrecked in the harbor, it grew more bitter daily. The strain was severe in little Kakisaki, and Yoheiji spent much of his time rallying his forces, trying to convince the worried elders of his village that they could win against the big town if they held firm, and that winning was important.

A little way up the valley, the village of Naka, being somewhat sheltered by the hills, had not been hit as hard as the coastal villages. Since the Governors' residences were there, and since the rice ships due in Shimoda had been either wrecked or delayed, the Goyosho turned to Naka for a supply of rice. The village officials sensed an opportunity:

> We are filled with distress that you are suffering from a shortage of rice. We express our gratitude for your kindness in nominating us to supply rice and other commodities to your office in our village.
> We shall spare no effort, and you will suffer no inconvenience.
> It would be highly appreciated if you would permit us to supply rice and water to vessels in Shimoda harbor. If we could have sole right to this business we would be able to collect commodities over a wide area and fill all needs in good order. Please give us this right in accordance with our application now pending in your office.

It was a bold scheme—a poor village trying to put half the merchants in Shimoda out of business. But like so many of Naka's petitions, it was ignored. The men of that village were addicted to petitions, and though they often had good cause, they deafened the ears of government officials. Excessive petitioning and a bent toward litigation were regarded as flaws in the character of the lower classes.

The typhoon had dominated almost everyone's thoughts since it struck. Naturally it came into the conversation when Captain Fabius of the Dutch frigate *Medusa* called at the damaged Goyosho to present his compliments. The captain told Iwase and Governors Inoue and Okada that his ship had been pounded by the storm on her way from Nagasaki to Hakodate. Governor Okada told the captain that the coal he had ordered would be loaded quickly, as he had requested (for seeing how the typhoon had struck Shimoda harbor made the captain nervous for his ship), but that, regrettably, since the typhoon had delayed shipments to Shimoda, they could not provide all the rice he wanted, and the quantity available was very expensive.

The Japanese were eager to hear about the training program at Nagasaki. At Edo's request the Dutch had brought more than twenty engineers and technicians to Nagasaki to teach a carefully selected group of Japanese students the intricacies of the steam engine and the operation, maintenance, and navigation of steamships. Fabius was able to answer that the Japanese were quick to learn and were making remarkable progress.

They talked for a while about foreign trade. Did Dutch merchant ships belong to the government, Iwase wanted to know, or were they private? And if they were private, were they taxed? They were private and they were taxed, Fabius answered, but these laws were complicated and he thought he had better give the details in a letter.

Okada asked why the Dutch wanted copper from Japan, and Fabius answered that Holland had no copper whereas Japan had a surplus; such situations were the basis of all trade. Japan was running out of copper, Okada replied, but Fabius said he thought the country had plenty of the metal; the problem was to find it and mine it properly. His ship had carried a number of mining engineers from Holland and he hoped the Shogunate would grant them permission to search for minerals and show the Japanese how to develop their mines. (This was a view shared by Harris. Foreigners generally were convinced that with all those mountains, Japan must be rich in minerals waiting to be unearthed by modern technology. As a matter of fact, Japan's mineral resources were scanty, and since she had been mining very efficiently for a couple of centuries, Governor Okada's pessimism was justified.)

But the three officials spent most of the session pumping the captain on the care and treatment of consuls. Was it possible, Inoue wanted to know, for a consul to insist that he was above the provisions of a treaty? Not at all, said Fabius, a consul must act according to the treaty and the laws of the country where he was stationed; in return, the host government must treat him in accordance with his position. A consul, Fabius thought, ranked about equal to himself, the captain of a ship, but a Consul General, like Harris, should be treated as equal to a commodore.

This led to the question of salutes. Was there any significance, Okada asked, in the number of times the guns were fired? Indeed there was, the captain assured them. For example, the Dutch saluted their king with a hundred and one rounds; the crown prince rated thirty-three, a commodore, thirteen.

Okada wanted to know who was responsible for building a consulate, and Fabius told him that usually it was built by the country which sent the consul; if the country receiving the consul undertook to provide a consulate, it should be constructed with the greatest care, to show proper respect for the other nation.

And the captain took the occasion to deliver a little lecture on the subject of foreigners. Twelve years earlier, he reminded them, the King of Holland had sent a letter to the Shogun. "The future of Japan causes us much anxiety," the King had written. "May we succeed in averting imminent disaster by our good counsel." The letter went on to point out the disasters that had overtaken China in her relations with Western powers, and continued: "The intercourse between the different nations of the earth is increasing with great rapidity. An irresistible power is drawing them together. Through the invention of steamships distances have become shorter. A nation preferring to remain in isolation at this time of increasing relationships could not avoid hostility with many others. . . .

"This, Allpowerful Emperor," the King told the Shogun, "is our friendly advice: ameliorate the laws against the foreigners, lest happy Japan be destroyed by war."

Unfortunately, said Captain Fabius, the Japanese government had ignored this good advice, and now was driven into the difficulties it had been warned of. Britain, France, and Russia were poised. If Japan refused to trade she would be faced with battleships. He had talked with Bowring at Hong Kong; the Englishman could be expected to lead an expedition to Japan within two months.

Leaving his hosts to chew on this, the captain excused himself. The wind was rising, he said, and he must return to his ship. They could talk further when the Governors visited the *Medusa* next day.

When the Japanese came aboard, they wanted, as always, to see the cannon fired, and then they settled down to talk more of foreign trade.

Could Japanese ships visit foreign ports, they asked, and receive fuel and supplies? They had but to pay for them, the captain answered. Could the Japanese rent Dutch ships? The captain quoted the price. As to what they might export, he told them that their lacquerware and porcelain were unique in their high quality, but very expensive; tea was also too expensive to be a big item; it came down, it seemed, to copper.

Townsend Harris also visited the *Medusa*. He wrote that he *was kindly received by Captain Fabius, who gave me a salute of eleven guns on leaving.* (Had the captain forgotten that he had called the Consul General equal in rank to a commodore, and consequently entitled to thirteen guns? One may be sure the Japanese were counting.)

On board, Harris learned of the instructors at Nagasaki, and that *two steam vessels are now being constructed in Holland for the Japanese.* He also caught up with some twelve-year-old news: *The King of Holland has, as it is said, written a letter to the Emperor of Japan, strongly urging him to open his kingdom to the commerce of all nations.*

The *Medusa's* arrival had set Harris to writing letters, for he thought this was a chance to get out some mail: the first drafts against his salary, and an order to Armstrong & Lawrence, Hong Kong, for—

> About 50# of lard, let it be clean
> sweet and good

> 30# butter
> 10 dozen pale ale if good and cheap
> 5 gallons molasses American if possible
> An aneroid barometer in good order
> and not at an extravagant price

—with a note that "I am well and much pleased with climate, country and people." Then he discovered that the ship was going only as far as Nagasaki, and he held his letters.

It was Henry Heusken who most enjoyed the *Medusa's* visit and most regretted seeing her go:

> Having seen the destruction of the last hurricane, and that the harbor provided no sanctuary, Captain Fabius hurried to leave Shimoda, and so after a three-day visit, the flag of my native country disappeared. The officers of the ship had received me most warmly; we had been able to speak of subjects dear to my memory, and the departure of the ship left a great void in my heart.

It might have been pleasant if Captain Fabius had chosen to stay another day or so; then Townsend Harris might have had a proper birthday party. The day after the *Medusa* sailed he wrote: *Saturday, October 4, 1856. I am fifty-two years old to-day. God grant that the short remainder of my life may be more usefully and honorably spent than the preceding and larger portion of it.*

As it was, Harris and Heusken dined alone, which was no novelty, and the celebration was mild at best. Heusken was dejected over seeing the *Medusa* sail away and Harris seems to have spent the day nursing his sore foot, brooding over the failures of his earlier years and assessing the possibility of failure at Shimoda—for if John Bowring were to appear soon with a sizable fleet, as Captain Fabius thought he might, he certainly could accomplish what Harris hoped to and sail away with all the glory.

Harris does not mention what he and Heusken ate at his birthday dinner, a sure indication that nothing on the menu seemed notable. Shoping lists have survived but they give no clue. They include fire tongs, shovel, and charcoal brazier for the kitchen; canary cages against the day the Japanese might deliver some songbirds; and opium. Some of the Chinese servants craved the stuff but Harris did his best to keep it from them; this order was for himself. Like many other foreigners on the China coast he had acquired the habit of smoking a little opium when he felt ill. It did nothing to cure the illness but it brought a euphoria which blotted out the symptoms.

It is a pity that Harris could not get out and wander through the countryside. The days were warm and sparkling, and the landscape, except where the typhoon had ravaged it, was at its most beguiling. The rice stood golden in the dry paddy fields, heads drooping with the weight of ripening grain. It was almost time for harvest.

Harvest time was tax time. All over Japan most of the basic taxes were computed and paid in rice. They were the lord's share of the yield. Most of every daimyo's income was in rice; his wealth and power were measured by the rice his lands produced; his retainers were paid in rice, or by an allotment of land judged to grow so much rice.

All this was true as well for the Shogun, the greatest daimyo of them all. His domains dwarfed those of any other lord, but his responsibilities were correspondingly great. It was rice from his lands that paid for the government at Edo, that paid for the army of administrators and scholars and clerks and policemen who ran it and its outposts at places like Nagasaki, Hakodate, and Shimoda, that paid for the soldiers and guns and ships which were supposed to be the country's first line of defense, and that paid for the vast extravagant court within the walls of Edo Castle. Shimoda and the villages nearby were part of the Shogun's lands. They paid their taxes into the Shogun's treasury.

The assessments were fixed, but there was machinery for adjusting them annually. At this time of year, just before the harvest, the Shogun's stewards all over his domains went into the fields to inspect the crop. As they watched, a little rice was cut, threshed, winnowed, and measured, and based on this the crop was assessed. If it was poor, if bad weather or disease had blighted it, the stewards had power to decrease the taxes, and sometimes they did.

In the old days, before the Shimoda Governors and their men were on the spot, the provincial magistrate had journeyed the length of Izu to make these inspections, and they were occasions of no little ceremony.

They began with a circular which read like this:

> Since the Magistrate will soon be coming to inspect the rice crop, your records concerning the crop, field by field, should be made ready for submission. Notice boards should be erected in each field, showing the owner and the number of the field as it appears in the tax records. And when the Magistrate is conducted through the fields, no field shall be left unexamined.
>
> There is to be no special, out-of-the-ordinary entertainment for the Magistrate and his party when they stop overnight. They will pay for

their firewood and rice, and will take only one soup and one other dish, prepared from any foods which happen to be handy. Nothing more elaborate shall be served, for it would mean unnecessary expenditure on the part of the village.

There are to be no gifts of any kind to officials or attendants, and most emphatically no gold or silver, and should any of these people become overbearing or drop hints about a present, it is to be reported promptly to the Magistrate.

This occasion puts each village to some expense, which should never be increased by village officials' entertaining themselves with sake and fish before or after the inspection, as has sometimes happened in the past. In view of all the orders prohibiting it, such behavior is outrageous. In accordance with government notices, you should work to keep local expenditures down and at the same time try your best to complete the tax collection on time.

All the above shall be carefully studied, and transmitted to the farmers as well. All necessary tools to cut, thresh, and winnow the grain shall be ready at the edge of the field but no unnecessary workmen shall be hired.

The headman of each village shall affix his signature and seal to this circular, and the last village shall return it to the sender.

The remarkable thing about this document is that it meant what it said. The request for a simple meal could have been a suggestion that a banquet was in order, but it was not. The injunction against gifts could have been a hint that an expression of appreciation, preferably negotiable, could ease the strain of inspection, but it was not.

The people of Izu were fortunate in having a magistrate who was both honest and able. When he toured southern Izu, he always stopped overnight at Shimoda. Entertaining him was a challenge—when a high official limited the menu to one dish, that dish had to be a triumph. The responsibility was laid on the town's richest men. Each year the chief of the merchants' association was summoned and told that "he should take care of all things, as he had customarily done in the past." "Take care of" included paying for.

The town officials packed their formal clothes, name cards, and a lunch of rice balls stuffed with pickled plums (provided by the merchants), and journeyed up the peninsula to greet the magistrate as he entered the town where he would stay the night before reaching Shimoda.

For years they had carried with them a keg of sake as a gift, but the austerity-minded magistrate had put a stop to this, and after that they only presented themselves at the entrance of his quarters to inquire after his health, repeated their greeting next door where his staff was staying, and the following day escorted the party into Shimoda.

The inspection itself must have been largely ceremonial, confirming a decision reached well beforehand in quiet conversations in one of those inns where village representatives and lesser government officials found it convenient to meet, quite unofficially, over a few bottles of sake. For of course the magistrate could not examine every paddy field. But the ceremony of the occasion was important: the visit symbolized the concern of the Shogun for the well-being of his farmers, and each year town officials carefully reviewed the details of the necessary arrangements as they had been recorded by the man who had been town secretary for more than fifty years, until his death in 1843. It is this man that we must thank for most of our knowledge of what Shimoda was like in the old days.

The story goes that one day in the late eighteenth century a Shimoda official named Hirai, on his way to visit the provincial magistrate's branch office in Naka village, came across a boy at the side of the road writing Japanese and Chinese characters in the sand. On being questioned, the little fellow replied that he did not care for the games other children played but that he loved to write. Hirai was so attracted by this talented child that he arranged to adopt him. The boy became Hirai Heijiro, and when he grew up he was appointed town secretary.

Very quickly after he assumed the office, the young man came to realize that because of all the disasters Shimoda had experienced, the town had very little in the way of records. In a society so conscious of history and sustained by precedent, this was a serious lack and Heijiro spent his life remedying it.

When he had finished he had compiled eighty-seven volumes containing everything he had learned about town affairs. He had made a complete record of annual events from the first day of the year to the last—the ceremonies of each festival, the preparation of each report, the collection and payment of each tax. He tells us how the town functioned as a port, about its ships' inns, its brokers, its hereditary inspectors of cargo. He explains how the fishermen, the merchants, the shipbuilders, the carpenters, the stonecutters, the plasterers, the paperers, the blacksmiths, and all the other craftsmen were organized and controlled. He covers everything from floods and the repair of riverbanks to the regulation of hairdressers, pawnbrokers, itinerant entertainers, and the outcast classes; from the administration of shrines and temples to lawsuits and the punishment of crimes like double suicide and gambling.

Hirai Heijiro *(a painting by Unsho)*

Along the way he tells us something of himself. "How is it that I have been able to hold this post of secretary for over fifty years without mishap? I cannot do anything in a keen manner. I am not sure that I am thick-headed but I know that I am stolid and cannot do much beyond providing for my parents. I have been placed in charge of various town affairs and I have devoted myself solely to them."

Today there is a monument to Hirai Heijiro in the grounds of the shrine. It pays tribute to him as "the venerable library of Shimoda."

We also have a portrait of him painted by one of his contemporaries, a Shimoda artist named Unsho. Unsho survived Heijiro by several years and was still painting when Harris was at Gyokusenji. When Perry's fleet was in port, the Chinese scholar Lo learned of one of Unsho's eccentricities (as an artist he was entitled to several and he took full advantage of that fact) and sought him out: "Having heard that in Shimoda there was one . . . famous for his skill in writing with his mouth, I went to him and got him to draw and inscribe for me about a dozen pictures."

It is pleasant to hear of this reciprocity, for everywhere that Lo went he was asked to brush a little something. "While I was at [Shimoda] I am sure I inscribed more than a thousand fans," he wrote. "The Governor and the various officers conducting the intercourse with the Americans, all requested my services in this matter."

As for Unsho, he was versatile. He could hold the brush not only with his teeth but also in his hand, and with even better results. He painted his portrait of Heijiro in the conventional manner.

Of course, after the Governors had taken over from the provincial magistrate, the ceremony of crop inspection was minimal. The examinations were made by Goyosho officials who were stationed in Shimoda. They could observe the paddy fields almost continually.

This year, despite the typhoon damage, they judged the crop up to standard. They duly noted that certain low-lying fields near the shore had been flooded with sea water and consequently produced nothing at all, but these were marginal fields, newly developed; any yield from them was a welcome bonus but failure could not be regarded as critical. If the crop was less than had been hoped for, it was still, in their opinion, good enough to afford the Shogun his accustomed levy; if belts had to be tightened, the villagers would tighten theirs.

With that in mind the Governors' men wholly approved the pledge made by the headmen of the twenty-four local villages. Meeting at an inn on the outskirts of Shimoda to ponder the misfortunes the typhoon had wrought, they agreed on these countermeasures:

1. To be very watchful against fires.

2. To refrain from parties and the exchange of gifts on festive occasions.

3. To refrain from pilgrimages to sacred mountains (a blow to the priests of the mountain religion).

4. To economize in funeral services (a blow to the Buddhist priests).

5. To refrain from giving alms to beggars or offering accommodations to travelers (if word of this got around, beggars and wanderers might avoid the area).

For its part, the Goyosho twice postponed and finally canceled the formal visit that all village officials were obliged to pay the Governors on the Crysanthemum Festival, the ninth day of the Ninth Month (which this year fell on October 7 by Harris's calendar; he had made a note to fly the consulate's flag on that day, but his flagpole was still broken). At such a time the villagers were expected to bring gifts, and tokens would be given in return, but there was little heart for the festival this year. Of course, a few well-off families celebrated quietly at home, eating rice boiled with chestnuts and drinking sake flavored with crysanthemums.

The day after Harris's birthday the American merchant schooner *General Pierce* (named for the President) arrived from Hakodate—it began to look as though there would be considerable traffic at Shimoda. The *General Pierce* would next sail to China, and again Harris set himself to letter-writing. He wrote a number of personal notes: to the Drinkers in China, to Captain Bell of the *San Jacinto,* to General Wetmore, and to his clerk of New York days, Nathaniel Dougherty. None of these has survived, but we can read his optimistic dispatch to the Secretary of State:

. . . I have been living in much harmony with the Japanese officials, and I flatter myself that I have secured their confidence and good will.

I have opened the subject of the value placed on American coin, and although it is still pending, I have strong hopes of bringing it to a favorable issue.

After this point is settled, I shall then bring forward the other matters contained in my instructions.

From all I can see and learn, I am of the opinion that the making of a full commercial treaty with this country is only a question of time, and that if the business is prudently conducted, not a very long period will elapse before it will be completed.

A severe typhoon visited Shimoda on the 22d ult. and destroyed many lives and much property. All the junks in the harbour were driven ashore, and had there been any American ships here at the time they would doubtless have shared the same fate.

This occurrence fully proves the great insecurity of the harbour, to which I referred in my [dispatch] No. 15. Various strong reasons exist why this harbour should be exchanged for another, and I shall bring the subject forward when I enter fully on the business with which I am charged.

If Harris's optimism was genuine it must have been based largely on a meeting held with the Governors and Iwase at the Goyosho on the day of the Crysanthemum Festival. Harris makes no mention of this meeting in his journal, and there is nothing in the record to show that he was aware of the identity or importance of the new man, Iwase.

The Japanese sent three separate letters to Edo as a result of the conference, each dealing with one of the topics discussed.

> Mr. Harris asked us to provide him with a *norimono* [palanquin] because his foot pained him so that he could hardly walk. We agreed, thinking we could lend him one of ours when he needs it, and then he said he wanted it specially built, like ours in appearance but six and a half feet long with width and height in proportion. This cannot be made in Shimoda, so we will order it from Edo.

(*Norimono* were made to sit in on crossed legs; Harris wanted to stretch out in his.)

A *norimono*

He also asked for a horse in order to take exercise. As we officials ride often, we cannot deny this to him. We tried to persuade him to furnish his own harness,* and he said he would order one but that it would take a long time to get it. Seeing a Japanese harness, he said he would like one. We will buy a horse at a proper price from a landlord around

---

*A harness was considered military equipment, and by government regulation should not have been furnished to Harris.

Shimoda, and a harness from a merchant who comes to Shimoda often. We will tell him he must not ride farther than seven *ri* from Shimoda.

(The area opened by the treaty was that within a seven-Japanese-*ri*, or about seventeen-mile, radius from an island in the center of Shimoda harbor.)

In his journal Harris gives a different reason for his requests: *To-day a horse was brought to me to examine the saddle, bridle, etc. They are queer affairs, but I have ordered a horse and trappings to be sent to me from Edo, —not only for actual use, but to give me increased importance in the eye of the natives. For the same reason I have ordered a norimono.*

The other two reports to Edo dealt with more critical matters. One took up the thorny question of money exchange. Harris had brushed aside the Japanese argument that a coin had value over and above the gold or silver it contained, that it was something special because it bore the government's

Man alighting from a *kago* (*detail from a print by Masanobu*)

mark (it would take several decades for the other governments of the world to come around to this point of view). Coins should be exchanged on the basis of weight, he maintained, but Japanese coins contained more alloy than American coins and therefore should be discounted.

The Japanese were surprised to find that the United States government had made an analysis of coins that Perry had taken home. But they knew perfectly well that their government had a long history of debasing its currency,* and they were uncomfortable arguing from this position. They proposed, instead, that exchange should be made not by weight but coin for coin.

As they understood it, Harris consented, and agreed that the Japanese should be entitled to a six-per-cent discount to cover the cost of reminting foreign coins. Consequently they wrote:

> We think this proposal is not unfavorable to Japan, and we recommend acceptance. As we would like to answer him quickly, please give your instructions as soon as possible. Iwase Shuri will give you all necessary details on his return to Edo.

Language had again proved a stumbling block, for Harris's understanding, as expressed in a letter to the Governors two days after the conference, was something else. He had proposed, he said, exchanging coins "weight for weight, gold for gold, or silver for silver, allowing the government of Japan 5 per cent for the loss in remelting and recoinage." But since the Governors had said they preferred to exchange on the basis of coins rather than weight, he had promised to examine whether this could be done. His examination showed him that three *bu* weighed five and a half per cent less than one dollar. This involved a loss of one half of one per cent more than his proposal of five per cent, "yet so anxious am I to meet all your wishes, that for the present I am willing that three silver *ichibus* be given in exchange for one silver dollar (without any deduction)."

For the present, that was how matters stood, and though the two parties were not as close as each seemed to think, Harris's optimism seemed warranted: the Japanese were quite willing to discuss terms of exchange on the basis of three for one.

The third letter that went up to Edo reflected the Japanese shock when Harris told them he was no longer interested in having a consulate built at Shimoda. Surprised, they pressed him for his reasons, and were told that he

* The gold content of the *ryo* had dropped to forty-two per cent of what it had been in 1601, and the slide was becoming a tumble; within four years it would be down to about twelve per cent. Silver coins like the *bu* were similarly debased. All this was part of the Shogunate's economic malaise.

did not consider Shimoda a suitable port and would request that it be changed for another; ultimately, he said, he would request that ten ports be opened to Americans.

He had already jolted his audience, but he went on to say that he knew Bowring and he knew the British intentions, but that these were matters he would discuss only at Edo.

The Japanese admitted to their government that Harris had surprised them with "these deep-laid plans." Iwase would furnish details; the Governors could only promise to be alert and to do their best in negotiating with Harris.

In the meantime Mr. F. A. Lühdorf of the *General Pierce* was making no headway in business. This was not Lühdorf's first visit to Shimoda: he was that German trader who had lived in Gyokusenji for six months after the brig on which he was supercargo was chartered by the Russians to carry them to one of their ports on the Sea of Okhotsk and was captured by the British in the attempt. He must have been amazed by the changes Harris had wrought at Gyokusenji. Lühdorf and his carpenter companion had camped there, servantless, doing their own cooking, and suspending their food from the ceiling to outwit the rats. (Harris had acquired a cat.)

Lühdorf had spent most of that six months trying to sell his cargo, which had been unloaded before the ship left with the Russians. The Japanese were chiefly interested in rifles and were unhappy that he had only old-fashioned flintlocks. Sales were exasperatingly slow until he was about to leave (the *General Pierce* had sailed in and Lühdorf had bought her)—then suddenly the Japanese offered to buy all that were left. Irked by their tactics, Lühdorf raised his price and made a handsome profit. Now he was back with more obsolete flintlocks, hoping to repeat. This time he was not so lucky. "The ship sold nothing at all," reported Heusken, "and bought only a few lacquered cabinets."

Lühdorf did accomplish one thing. He reinforced Harris's hand, very likely at Harris's suggestion. While chatting at the Goyosho the merchant told Japanese officials that it was common knowledge that if Bowring did not succeed in his negotiations when he came to Nagasaki he would bring his ships to the Bay of Edo. This was Perry treatment, and the Japanese did not relish the prospect of another such experience.

The *General Pierce* sailed from Shimoda on October 9, carrying Harris's letters and leaving Heusken to "the monotonous life I lead here."

Yoheiji's life at this time was anything but monotonous. The day before, he and Kosaburo had been summoned to the Governors' office at Naka. Two officials confronted them. "Yoheiji," they demanded, "on what grounds do you say that Kakisaki is entitled to dispose of ships wrecked in the port of Shimoda, a matter which has always been undertaken by the shipping agents of Shimoda? If you fail to produce sufficient grounds for your contention, you will have to face punishment." The punishment they had in mind was all too evident, for ropes and whips were conspicuously on hand.

But if they thought to settle the dispute by intimidating Yoheiji, they misjudged their man. The headman was ready to cite decisions reaching all the way back to 1590, and that was the beginning of the law as far as these officials were concerned, for it was in 1590 that the Tokugawa had taken control of Izu. The land survey of that year, and the subsequent assessment of rice taxes, recognized that the village was unable to support itself by agriculture alone. Hence its people, from the beginning of Tokugawa rule, had been authorized to fish (and were taxed for the privilege), to offer their homes as inns for seamen (more taxes), and to salvage ships. There had been other disputes over this matter in the past, and Yoheiji rattled off old decisions which supported Kakisaki's claims.

If there was an effective rebuttal, nobody could think of it, and the frustrated officials ended their embarrassment by hasty adjournment. Yoheiji and Kosaburo celebrated on the way home with a couple of bottles of sake at an inn.

Harris's "Vice-Governor," Executive Officer Wakana, now felt that things had gone far enough. The case would have to go to Edo for a once-and-for-all decision, he thought, but in the meantime it was necessary to get the job of salvage done so that shipowners and seamen would not be inconvenienced any further. He issued an appeal to reason: Shimoda and Kakisaki should work together, and he appointed police officials Namiki and Arakawa as supervisors.

Yoheiji was not pleased by the appointments. Namiki, he noted, was the second son of an official of some importance; second sons, raised in an atmosphere of power but cut off from inheriting it, were likely to be flighty. This Namiki was well versed in the martial arts of a samurai and was also good at calligraphy, which was a mark of a cultured man, but he was overbearing and a heavy drinker. The merchants of Shimoda had for a long time been satisfying his thirst, and Yoheiji could see trouble ahead.

Trouble came a couple of days later when the two officials summoned the headman to appear at the headquarters of the Shimoda association of ships' inns, an unlikely place for an impartial hearing. Kosaburo answered the summons but soon came hurrying back with word that the room was filled with glowering Shimoda shipping agents and that Namiki, who obviously had been drinking, was furious at the headman's failure to appear in person. Yoheiji crossed the harbor as quickly as he could.

As he feared, Namiki had made use of the interval to drink some more. His face was flushed and his voice strident. Sharply he demanded to know why the headman had not appeared the first time.

"Certainly you summoned me," Yoheiji answered, "but other officials had ordered me to do certain things for the foreigners at Gyokusenji, and so I could only send Kosaburo. However, since you insisted on my appearance, I left my other duties to appear."

"You defied our orders and came late," Namiki shouted, and he was so visibly intoxicated that Arakawa was embarrassed and tried to calm him. Yoheiji judged it was best to say nothing, and he remained silent until Namiki threw a pertinent question at him. "Yoheiji, you are disputing with Shimoda about salvaging wrecked ships. But the shipwrecks occurred in Shimoda bay. Obviously, the responsibility belongs to Shimoda."

As Yoheiji recalled it later he laughed at the maladroit question, but he probably was not so rash as to laugh aloud. "The sea outside the bay is called the Sea of Sagami," he answered, "but when a wreck occurs there we don't wait for officials to come down from Sagami Province. It is well established that the responsibility falls on the local authorities. The wrecks now in question took place in Shimoda bay but within Kakisaki port. The local authority is Kakisaki. The responsibility is ours."

Namiki was furious but nonplused, and Arakawa hastily adjourned the session. Once again Yoheiji had stood his ground.

Next day it occurred to someone in the Governors' office that it might be well to check on the authority that Yoheiji kept citing, and they sent an inspector to his home to examine the document.

Yoheiji produced it. It dated from the 1660's and was yellowed and creased, but it was legible and unquestionably legitimate and its intent was clear. The inspector examined it, nodded, and departed. He appeared satisfied, but his visit had unnerved Yoheiji's wife.

"I am only a woman," she told her husband, "and I cannot help feeling anxious. In Kakisaki there are only four or five to stand with you, and some of them may drop out. How can you fight alone? You know the rumors that Shimoda shipping agents and innkeepers are getting ready to take matters into their own hands. If it comes to violence, how can you protect yourself? These days you often have to go to the Goyosho at night, and I worry about what may happen to you. You have to serve as headman for these five or six years, but you have to consider the rest of your life too."

And Yoheiji answered: "I appreciate your concern, and I know that others in this village are concerned for me. But this case is a serious one. If I do not defend our position, who will? I am ready to fight even at the price of my life because the survival of all our villagers is at stake. I am a mere farmer now, but I am descended from the warrior who in a faraway province was the Lord of Kakisaki Castle, and who came here and gave his name to this place." To Yoheiji, this reminder of his samurai ancestry was sufficient to end the discussion.

His wife could argue no further, but she did what she could. She again climbed the steep hill to the old shrine on the summit, to pray for her husband's safety and success as she had been doing every day since the dispute began. Yoheiji watched her go and sighed. She was really not strong enough for that sort of thing. He sighed again when word came that another body, long in the sea, had washed ashore at Suzaki.

Iwase's visit was drawing to a close. There was a final conference, and of course a final party, and, if talk around Shimoda may be believed, one of the girls summoned to help entertain him was seventeen-year-old Okichi, whom he remembered from previous visits. It was she who was noted for singing that ballad "Raven at Dawn."

> . . . Each meeting
> must have its parting. The raven
> is not so hateful: it's
> the cock's cry at dawn that
> may not be taken lightly—sometimes
> too early, sometimes too late; which,
> depends on whom a courtesan is sleeping with.

And they say that at this final party Iwase wrote a poem and gave it to the girl:

> Last year I had leisure
> to enjoy your songs.
> This year, how different!
> No time for pleasure—
> so many worries.

On the twelfth or thirteenth of October the Governors said goodbye, and Iwase was escorted to the harbor, where one of the Kimizawa ships had put in to take him back to Edo. He was carrying to the Great Council a translation of Harris's letter on the currency question, and a great deal of firsthand information on the situation in Shimoda.

He had brought about no sweeping changes in the treatment of Harris, but a certain mellowing of mood can be detected.

On the thirteenth, for example, a circular went out to all the villages in the area:

> If the foreigners who are staying at Gyokusenji in Kakisaki ask for tea or sweets when they go for a walk, they are to be given such things freely. If they pay for them, the foreign money is to be handed to the accompanying officials, and at the end of the month the Goyosho will issue Japanese coins in return.

At about this time, too, Harris began to receive meat of the wild boar, and Iwase has been given credit for this, though it may have been simply that the hunting season for boar had opened. (Lühdorf had been given boar meat too, and been told that the Japanese hunted the animal only for its hide, to make leather.) At any rate, Harris was pleased. He at first judged it to be the "hog deer of India": *The flesh is peculiar. It is very tender, juicy and of an excellent flavor. The taste is something between delicate veal and the tenderloins of pork. I am promised a full supply during the cold weather, which will be a great relief to my housekeeping.* Later he realized it was boar, but that did not spoil his appetite. *It is,* he declared, *the best flesh meat in the world!!*

As to some of his demands, he was to get the horse he wanted, but no cow. And if those demands included a mistress, he was again turned down.

Did the Governors convince Iwase that this man had to be dealt with cautiously? Did Harris himself arouse misgivings? In any case, Iwase carried back to Edo serious apprehensions concerning this American. One of the first orders emanating from the Great Council after his return was addressed to one of their own number in the name of the Shogun. This councillor was to be prepared to go to Shimoda at any moment to handle the American if he refused to obey the Governors. "Arrange matters as you think fit, but amicably, if possible."

Another order from the Great Council reflected Iwase's worrisome news concerning the British, plus a report from Nagasaki that a British warship had put into the harbor, and that its men, defying the Governor, had first visited the Dutch depot and then toured the town. The Japanese had been worrying about the British for a long time, and it looked as though things were coming to a head. The order told Iwase and his colleagues that if the English should appear at Nagasaki for talks, a team of negotiators was to rush there; if they should sail into Edo Bay, then the team would go to Shimoda, to try to divert the British to that port.

Though the Japanese did not know it yet, on the same day that the British vessel had entered Nagasaki an incident had occurred at Canton which would grow into another war between China and Britain, a war which would intensify Japanese worries about Britain but would at the same time keep the British busy and away from Japan.

A small vessel named *Arrow* was lying in the river at Canton when Chinese authorities boarded her, seized some of her crew as pirates, and hauled down her flag. The flag was the British ensign, for though the *Arrow* was owned by a Chinese and all her crew, except her young Irish master, were Chinese, she was registered at Hong Kong as a British vessel.

The Chinese said the *Arrow* was Chinese and no business of the British. The British said that she was British and that the Chinese had violated the treaty and insulted their flag. Relations between the two countries were already at the breaking point over the way the Chinese had been treating foreigners at Canton, and the *Arrow* was enough to start the two sides shooting at each other.

Americans became quickly involved, beginning with the classic maneuver of landing the Marines to protect American property. The British attack on Canton was joined by the American Consul for Hong Kong; indeed, he may have led it: it was widely reported that he was first over the walls—bearing Old Glory—gloriously drunk. These acts made President Pierce and Secretary Marcy unhappy when they heard of them, but they were applauded along the China coast, for, as Captain Bell wrote to Harris, "the entire American population was as enthusiastically for the war as the British themselves . . . Dr. P. himself shared the same feeling." [*]

And so war came again to China, and the Japanese were provided yet another lesson on how not to handle foreigners.

Within a day or two after his return to Edo, Iwase was sent by the Great Council to visit the man who was their greatest trial. What made the gall more bitter was that the man was a Tokugawa, prince of one of the family's three most prominent branches—the "Three Houses," all descended from younger sons of the first Shogun, Ieyasu. The Three Houses had an

[*] Dr. Parker was, if anything, more belligerent than Commodore Armstrong. Like Commodore Perry and Townsend Harris, he advocated wresting Formosa from China in one way or another, and when, shortly after he presented himself as Commissioner, he considered Chinese actions insulting, he wanted to take a warship to demand redress: the *San Jacinto*, acting in character, thwarted him by breaking down.

anomalous position: they were granted enormous deference and no authority. Ieyasu had survived too many family fights to put relatives in positions of power. The branch houses had the function of supplying an heir should the main line run out, but they were effectively excluded from the government.

The man Iwase went to see was Tokugawa Nariaki, head of the house based at Mito (he was retired but no one doubted who pulled the strings at Mito). Of the Three Houses, Mito held a special position: it was ineligible to provide an heir but by tradition its lord was "advisor" to the Shogun and his government—who were in no way obligated to accept the advice. This was another avenue to frustration, and Nariaki was a frustrated man. Unquestionably he was dominant among the branch houses. Attractive and aggressive, he was a born leader denied a position of leadership.

Opinions of him ran the gamut.

Most of Iwase's colleagues had great respect for him; true, he was virulently anti-foreign and they were not, but in internal politics he seemed to them to represent a breath of fresh air and new hope for a battered government.

Lord Hotta had little use for him. To the other member of the Great Council who was about equally important, Lord Abe, he was the key to the situation: sympathetic to the government, he might save it; estranged, he might bring it down.

Lord Abe was particularly astute in his handling of Nariaki. A year or two earlier, for example, Mito had undertaken to build a warship as a contribution to the defense effort. It was a massive vessel, 180 feet long and 40 feet wide, but it turned out to be unseaworthy: it had no balance. Mito named her *The Rising Sun,* but others called her *The Nuisance.*

When word of *The Nuisance*'s shortcomings reached the Great Council, most of the councillors were in favor of ordering a stop to her construction. Lord Abe alone disagreed.

"What is your opinion of the Elderly Lord?" Abe asked his colleagues (at the ripe age of fifty-six Nariaki was dubbed the Elderly Lord; Hotta was forty-five; Abe, thirty-seven), and then he answered his own question: "He is courageous and talented, and one of the most respected men of our day. It is fortunate that he is closely related to the Shogun. He happens to be the kind of man who finds it impossible to be doing nothing. When he is entrusted with a mission he works at it night and day; he thinks of nothing else until it is completed. He can endure things that make others give up.

"I hear," Lord Abe continued, "that there is a beast called the lion. The lion is so strong that none can rule it. When the lion is angered it dashes about, roars, and hurts many people. There is only one way to stop it. If you throw it a ball, which is round and rolls endlessly, the lion kicks, bites, and scratches it; then, finding there is no use fighting the ball, the lion calms down and plays with it all day long without doing harm to anyone.

Lord Abe Masahiro (*a painting by Goseda Horyu*)

"If I may say so, to entrust the Elderly Lord with supervision of building the battleship is to give him something to kill his anger." And when Abe said further that it was more important to keep the Elderly Lord content than to save money, none of his colleagues disagreed with him. Nor did they disagree when Abe called him courageous, talented, and respected. The question was how he was using his talents.

He was a Tokugawa and deeply concerned that the Shogunate be preserved, yet he was from Mito, and the Mito house nurtured a reverence for the Emperor that threatened the Shogunate. Nariaki was full of contradictions, torn by divided loyalties. It is debatable whether he was a complicated man or a confused one.

In 1844, for alleged anti-Shogunate activities, he had been forced to retire as head of his house, disgraced and confined to his Edo mansion. The next year Lord Abe had come to power and had begun a long process of reconciliation. At last in 1853, when the nation was faced with the threat of Perry, Abe succeeded in having Nariaki appointed as military advisor. Within a year Nariaki's programs had aroused such antagonism within the government that when he threatened to resign over the Perry treaty, Abe had no choice but to accept his resignation. Nariaki departed, leaving the suggestion that the officials who had negotiated with Perry should atone by committing suicide.

Just last year Abe had succeeded in bringing him back as advisor, an appointment made—a ball thrown to him—with assorted hopes: hope that he would bolster the government's prestige in certain quarters; hope that he would support essential reforms within the government; hope that better acquaintance with the government's problems would modify his anti-foreign stand; hope that being closer to the government might curb some of his activities against it.

One of the reasons Iwase had been sent to Shimoda was to placate Nariaki. Nariaki trusted Iwase, and might listen to what he had to report. The Elderly Lord needed placating, as shown by this outburst to the Great Council when he learned that they had approved Harris's stay as Consul General.

> After three nights of worry, I write this letter under the lamp. In my opinion, things have come to this sorry pass simply because you lacked courage and foresight. Now that you have agreed to the stationing of the American official, you have only to do the same for other countries and Shimoda will become a nest of foreign aggressors. Hakodate will be the same. Now that things have come to this, the only thing you can do, and urgently, is to have all daimyo, not to mention the central authority, properly armed with warships and cannon so that you can take determined action when necessary. If you hesitate to start war against them, they will only become more unruly, even to taking control of the castle itself.

His imagination raced on in an even more melodramatic postscript:

> Once they control Edo Castle, they will naturally attempt to take control of the Imperial Palace in Kyoto also, and may go so far as to seek

nuptial ties with the Imperial family. You must not remain idle. If the worst comes, and you are compelled to go to war against them, they will ally with each other and the situation will be grave. If you permit the stationing of foreign officials, it is certain that the vicious religion will also spread among our people, and not a few may eventually take sides with them.

Now that Iwase was back in the capital, the Great Council wasted no time in having him report to their overwrought advisor. With Iwase went two of his associates on the committee for maritime defense, Inoue's brother Kawaji and another official, Mizuno. Nariaki respected the abilities of all three.

A year earlier Kawaji had tried to allay Nariaki's fears by describing government policy in these terms: "We keep the treaties but we try to reduce their contents to make foreigners feel helpless when they come here; meanwhile we bolster our defenses." Nariaki knew that defenses were not being bolstered in any significant way and now he was told that Harris was acting in a manner which seemed anything but helpless. In addition, his three visitors had the mission of persuading him that recent developments made it essential to open foreign trade.

They failed. Had Nariaki's two most trusted advisors still been alive, things might have been different, but both had been killed the year before in Edo's earthquake, struck by falling beams as they were helping their lord out of his mansion. Now the Elderly Lord was unable to produce a clear recommendation one way or the other. He only fretted that foreign trade would surely raise prices at home, and then reverted to his old theme: the country should be roused to defensive preparations. Everything seemed to be going wrong, he lamented: "I fear that the rule of the Tokugawa has not much longer to live. It is closer to sunset than five o'clock." It was this depressing thought that the three officials carried away with them.

As soon as they had left, Nariaki began a flurry of letter-writing, and this was one of his activities that pleased the government least.

One of his letters went to another member of the Shogun's sprawling family, the powerful Lord of Echizen, Matsudaira Yoshinaga. (Matsudaira was the family name before the first Shogun, Ieyasu, decided to change his name to Tokugawa. It was still used by those houses which were not closely enough related to be eligible to provide a Shogun. And over the years it had been bestowed as a mark of special favor on several families who were not related at all. In consequence, there were a great many Matsudaira in Japan.)

To Yoshinaga, Nariaki raced through the obligatory comment on the weather and wish for good health to complain that the Great Council never asked for his opinion any more (forgetting that it had just been asked for): no doubt this was the result of a plot, and no doubt Buddhist priests were involved in it. (The old gentleman hated Buddhism almost as much as he did Christianity—they were both foreign religions; one of his projects was melting temple bells to make cannon, and another was breaking up Buddhist stone images to build roads.)

Lord Matsudaira Yoshinaga (*left, a painting by Hahakabe Kinshu*) and Lord Tokugawa Nariaki (*a painting by an unknown artist*)

It has become increasingly cold but I am happy to hear that you are keeping in good health.

No doubt due largely to the slanderous tongues of evil men and priests, I have not visited Edo Castle since the first month of the year, and I had heard nothing concerning foreign ships. Recently, however, the Great Council informed me that the Americans had made their way into the country, bringing their official to Shimoda, and that the government had given him permission to take up residence there.

Following this I received no further word until three officials paid me a sudden visit, and Iwase, who had just returned from Shimoda, told me a number of things.

During his stay there, a Dutch vessel called at the port and when

Iwase met with the Dutch he was told that the British who recently came to Nagasaki asserted that if Japan refused to accede to their demands they would declare war. Such conduct is unpardonable.

In the meantime the American, notwithstanding the treaty which states that Americans may travel no farther than seventeen miles, now insists that officials should be excepted from this ruling and that he should be allowed to travel freely beyond that limit. And when the Governors told him that this could never be approved, he closed his eyes and shook his head and said it would happen before long.

He also said that Shimoda is not a suitable port and he wishes to exchange it for another. And when the Governors told him that this could not be done, he again closed his eyes and shook his head, and said that before long we would be compelled to grant that too.

On being told that we would erect a residence for him at Shimoda, he replied that he would not be there long and would put up with inconveniences in the meantime.

Yet when asked if he knew when the Britisher Bowring would arrive, he once more closed his eyes and shook his head and said that he could not answer.

Taking all this into consideration, it seems clear that not only the Americans, the British, and the Russians, but even the French, the Germans, and the Dutch all share the same den.

To my way of thinking, the Russians, after suffering defeat at the hands of the British [in the Crimean War], gave certain Russian possessions in America to the British in order to become reconciled with them. The Russians then proceeded to flatter the British, telling them that no nation is superior to them in military power, and stirring them up by persuading them that it would be an easy matter to conquer Japan, hoping that thereby northern Japan would fall to Russia. If war should break out, there is no doubt that Russia would seize our northern regions at the earliest opportunity.

I am of the opinion that this coming of American and British foreigners to our shores is part of a great Russian stratagem. The foreign nations have conspired together and have already agreed among themselves that Nagasaki, for example, is to belong to so-and-so, Edo to so-and-so, Osaka to so-and-so, and so on, and consequently, once things begin to happen all around us, we will be utterly helpless.

Needless to say, in the old days [A.D. 1281], when a vast army consisting of the combined forces of Mongolia and Korea invaded us but were repelled by a fierce storm and a united country, we had to cope with only a single foreign enemy, but now we are confronted by several powerful foreign nations.

He might have added that in 1281 Japan was a martial land with a strong army, which was not the case in 1856.

To another of Nariaki's letters the government could have no objection, for it was addressed to Lord Abe and dealt with a topic clearly within the Elderly Lord's province as military advisor:

What if they send their forces to Osaka? It would be virtually impossible to drive them away even if the men under arms in Osaka Castle and all others in neighboring territories join forces. In such an eventuality, where can His Majesty go for safety? Osaka Castle is no longer impregnable, and Kyoto Castle is even less safe. Suppose His Majesty takes shelter on Mount Hiei [a Buddhist stronghold outside Kyoto]. In the first place, it is not fortified. It is a mountain hard for us to climb, but foreigners are as nimble as wild monkeys. Moreover, the priests are almighty there, and His Majesty could never live a pleasant life in such a place. Kofu Castle [a Shogunate castle deep in the central mountains] is strongly guarded, but it would be better for His Majesty to come to Edo Castle than to go as far as Kofu. Then he could move to Kofu together with the Shogun, because in that event many daimyo would also move there, accompanying the Shogun, and they could protect His Majesty too. Shizuoka Castle is not a good place, for it is too close to the sea.

It was perfectly clear to Lord Abe what Nariaki was driving at. The daimyo responsible for safeguarding the Emperor was Lord Ii Naosuke, the Shogun's most powerful liege. And Lord Abe could be pardoned for wondering what Nariaki was most interested in: demonstrating his perennial concern for the Emperor or disparaging Lord Ii.

Lord Ii Naosuke and Lord Tokugawa Nariaki nurtured an intense dislike of each other. It did not make the Great Council's work easier.

More than two and half centuries earlier Lord Ii's ancestor had been the good right hand of the first Shogun, and had been rewarded with power and responsibility: a fief more than twice as large as any other vassal, at a critical location next to Kyoto, with the duty of protecting the Emperor. That power and responsibility were still intact. By tradition no Lord Ii could be a member of the Great Council—he would overshadow all other members—though in time of crisis he might be made Chief Councillor, the highest office in the government. The position of Chief Councillor was not filled now, and Ii Naosuke was not an active member of the administration. But by heredity he had that avenue to power.

Both Naosuke and Nariaki loomed large in the calculations of the

Great Council. Hotta and Abe must sometimes have felt caught between two millstones as they tried to appease both Naosuke and Nariaki.

The letter that Nariaki had written to Matsudaira Yoshinaga probably had little effect, for Yoshinaga was well informed; he had a good head and some exceptionally able scholars as advisors. The letter to Lord Abe was probably shrugged off. But Nariaki knew that he would have a rapt audience for his next letter, which he addressed to Kyoto. The courtiers of Kyoto were, for the most part, badly informed and not overly brilliant: for two and a half centuries the court had been sealed off from the rest of the country, knowing little of what went on, inbreeding and dabbling with poetry. Now the gentlemen of Kyoto were breaking their bounds, but they were singularly unprepared to cope with the problems of the day. Nariaki knew how to play on them.

His letter went to a man named Ishikawa, who was steward to one of the court nobility and had access to others, and thus was an excellent channel for clandestine communication:

> When Ieyoshi [the previous Shogun] was Shogun, he was so worried by the visits of foreign ships that he called his senior aides to a midnight conference. This time the Shogun shows no concern, as if nothing were happening. Whatever hard study officials give to countermeasures, it is as though they are planning a war without a commander, and there can be no victory in such a war. The Tokugawa administration is degraded, and Edo is losing face to Kyoto.

This was music to Kyoto's ears, and Nariaki knew it. But when he wrote of "war without a commander," he had a point. Hotta and Abe were intelligent and reasonable men but they did not seem to be the decisive leaders that the times cried for; there is little doubt that Nariaki yearned to be summoned to command. Further, the Shogun was mentally and physically incompetent—although just how incompetent was shielded behind a veil of inaccessibility. Since he was childless and likely to remain so, it was necessary to choose an heir: Nariaki had a candidate, who happened to be his own son.

Nariaki's letter to Ishikawa continued, working on Kyoto's fear of foreigners:

> We are anxious to strengthen the defense of Kyoto, but events are not running in that direction. I would rather die than permit what now seems all too possible. If we do not use force to hold back the Americans, there will be more and more foreign aggressors to follow—Russian, British, French, Turk, and German, all ready to prey on a weak Japan.

May I take advantage of this occasion to tell you this in confidence: I learned from Iwase the other day that the American official says his government possesses three hundred million guns and forty million cannon, not counting those in private hands. I suppose such is also the case with other countries, although their possessions of arms may be smaller.

(It seems doubtful that Harris would have been so carried away as to assert that the United States had more than ten guns and one and a third cannon for every man, woman, and child of its population, "not counting those in private hands." It appears that the figures had got out of hand during translation, since the Japanese sometimes confuse "million" with their word *man*, meaning 10,000.)

The American official further says that it is inconceivable that Japan, an island nation, is so poorly armed for defense. He says his country is ready to provide three or four thousand cannon at any time, if we need them. In this respect, he is kind enough to point out the danger we invite by our unpreparedness.

I further learned that America earns as much as $500 million a year from shipping.

(This must be another case of mistranslation. What Harris might have said with reasonable accuracy is that the combined total imports and exports of the United States were running about $500 million annually.)

And all these earnings are spent on ships and cannon. The more ships they possess, the more they trade and the more money they make. And the more money they make, the more ships and cannon they manufacture. Thus they grow strong enough to invade and conquer lands overseas.

To them, Japan is a country easy to absorb. We are in desperate need of strengthening our defenses. To try to wage war against them now, when we are still poorly armed, would be like prescribing poison for one seriously ill, so we had better remain passive in dealing with them for the time being. But this course alone will only mean falling prey to them, so while we deal with them thus, we must hasten our rearming. In spite of these facts, no instructions are likely to be issued by the supreme authorities, and I am afraid that the Americans will gain the upper hand while we dillydally.

These are not mere rumors but facts I learned directly from Kawaji, Mizuno, and Iwase. This is all secret information, but I dare pass it to you because I am so deeply concerned about the security of Kyoto.

Clearly the government had reason to worry that rumors were being spread, and that they might cause the Emperor concern. When Nariaki passed secrets to Ishikawa it was with neither hope nor expectation that they would remain secrets. It took very little time for this letter to reach Ishikawa's master, and for him to call in other nobles to read it, in strictest confidence, and for them to decide that it should be shown to His Majesty the Emperor, in greatest secrecy.

With all this secrecy it was natural that everybody in the court should hear what Nariaki wanted them to hear, and inevitable that the government should learn what was going on. Governor Inoue's brother Kawaji was delegated to apply the brakes. He journeyed to Kyoto to try to check the whispered stories, but it was too late. Nariaki's little campaign was complete, and the Kyoto court was more than ever convinced that among other things Nariaki was their greatest friend and Townsend Harris was a devil.

The devil in question, fortunately for his peace of mind, knew nothing of all this. He was, in fact, beginning to feel better. The wound in his foot was healed and Shimoda's mild October weather raised his spirits. He had been, he wrote, suffering *from a total loss of appetite, want of sleep and depression of spirits.* He attributed these to: *first, inability to take exercise in the open air; and second, smoking too much. The latter I must break off. As I am now much better, I shall begin to go out for exercise and hope to be in robust health again. The climate here is delightful.*

And always sensitive to the bill of fare, he noted gratefully not only the wild boar, which was being delivered regularly, but *a great variety of the persimmon, some as large as a pippin and all of good quality. Chestnuts have also been sent to me.* All the grapes, he wrote regretfully, had been destroyed by the typhoon.

It was too early on Izu for tangerines, but farther south and west, in the province of Kii, the first of this fruit was being picked and the race was on to get the first cargo to Edo. The citizens of Edo were always ready to pay a handsome premium for the first of any new crop—the first eggplant, the first bonito, the first tangerines—and the sailors of Kii were ready to brave high winds and rough seas for the bonus awarded the winners. There was a popular song that went:

> I see white sails on a dark ocean;
> Those must be the tangerine vessels of Kii.

The fishermen of Shimoda were delighted when one of these tangerine boats sailed close, for its crew would invariably call out to ask if they were the first to pass by, and the fishermen would invariably answer yes, even if the truth was no, and the happy Kii sailors would toss them some fruit as a reward for the good news, and sail on toward Edo, ringing bells and drumming on the anchor and looking very dashing with red headbands and red loincloths against bronzed bodies.

Across the village from Gyokusenji, Yoheiji's wife still climbed the steep path several times each day to pray at the shrine of the god Fudo, begging divine aid and protection. When violence seemed imminent and Yoheiji's life seemed at stake, she even prayed that she could die for him. Then one night the figure of Fudo appeared at the head of her bed and told her: "You say that you are ready to die for your husband, but this is impossible. It is predestined that your husband will live more than eighty years, but you are short-lived. However, because of your devotion to your husband I will give you a life span of fifty years. And I assure you that your husband will succeed in his work."

She was greatly relieved, but she continued to worship Fudo with even increased piety. And since her age was then thirty-six she looked forward to years more at her husband's side.

As the god had prophesied, the bitter dispute came to an end. Isa Shinjiro, of rank equal to Wakana (there were three executive officers, though only Wakana had much to do with Harris's day-to-day problems), conducted an investigation of his own and then stepped in. Calling the headmen of Shimoda and Kakisaki to his office, he told them: "It is a matter of great regret that the dispute over salvage rights remains unsettled. In view of the hardships which the owners and seamen of the wrecked ships are suffering because of the protracted dispute, I hereby declare that Shimoda and Kakisaki are to cooperate, handling this case as a joint project, and that Suzaki village is to serve as witness, keeping all necessary details on record. I order you to make this decision known to all your men responsible for this salvage operation." And that was that.

Yoheiji gratefully accepted the arrangement; it was really a victory, for the little village had won equal footing with the big town. He was glad to have an end to the quarrel, and perhaps even glad to share the responsibility for getting the job done. The operation was proving too big for Kakisaki, especially when Shimoda offered nothing but obstruction.

Shimoda people were not so happy. They made one last attempt to have their way. Next day Namiki and Arakawa issued a call for representatives from Shimoda, Kakisaki, and Suzaki to come sign and seal a document which set forth the settlement ordered by Isa. Gennosuke answered for Kakisaki, and despite the glowering Namiki he took time to peruse the document. He found that it named Shimoda as sole party to undertake the salvage, with both Kakisaki and Suzaki as mere recorders. Gennosuke thereupon refused to affix his seal. Arakawa took the document, saw what had been written, and had a new and correct one made. Perhaps someone thought that Gennosuke would not be able to read.

On that same morning twelve seamen and their captain pulled into the harbor in a small boat. Their ship, loaded with rice and tiles from the town that is today a part of Kobe, had been wrecked in a storm two days earlier. The Shimoda shipping agent representing the cargo-owner sent the usual circular to the headmen of all the villages along the coast: if they found any wreckage of the ship or any of its cargo, they were to report at once. Even in the absence of typhoons, the sea took its toll.

Harris, as he had resolved, began to take long walks. *The country is very beautiful—is broken up in steep volcanic cones, but every possible spot is terraced and cultivated like a garden. . . . * Hills looked *like the steps of a giant staircase . . . running over the rich fields of the valley and terminating with a glimpse of the blue water of the sea . . . The labor expended in cutting down the rock to form some of these terraces is something wonderful. My walk led me first to Vandalia Point* [the name given by Commodore Perry to the cliff near Suzaki], *the most southeastern part of the land. From this I had a view of the vast Pacific, and it was a curious thought that, looking due south, there was no land between me and Australia, some five thousand miles!*

Oshima from the south-southwest
(*detail from a map prepared by Perry's expedition*)

Turning more to the eastward I saw the Island of Oshima, with its volcano smoking on its summit. The day is almost calm, so the smoke arose like a mighty pillar for thousands of feet. It then spread out forming a vast white cloud.

Oshima and its volcano excited Harris, as it had Perry before him. Perry had wanted to visit it, never had. Now Harris wanted to. The Japanese insisted it was farther than seven Japanese *ri*, or seventeen miles, and therefore outside the area opened to Americans. To Harris this was preposterous. There were times, especially in early morning or at dusk, when the island seemed almost close enough to touch. Any claim that it lay more than seventeen miles distant was patently false: it was one of the lies they kept telling him. In point of fact, Oshima was over twenty-three miles away.

Another of his walks took him to the top of Buzan hill and the watch station that signaled the arrival of foreign ships. *Walked to the top of the hill that overlooks the harbor, about one thousand feet high; has a wooden cannon, about twelve pounder, bore. It is strongly bound with bamboo hoops from end to end, the hoops are close together. Here also are two old iron guns, nine pounders, bearing the shield of the Dutch East India Company. These guns are only for signals. A lookout house is erected here and a guard is always here from daylight to dark. It commands a vast range of vision, and a ship could, in clear weather, be seen some twenty miles off.*

On my return I met a mountain-priest,—one of a class whose vow binds him to ascend all mountains he can meet with. He bears a staff surmounted with a circle of iron; within is a trident like that of Shiva, four loose rings are attached to the circle, two on each side. These make a jingling noise when the priest shakes his staff.

I get 4,800 of the small copper coin of Japan for one dollar. Ten of these given to the priest produced a long prayer and a great jingling of his rings.

The priest was of good pleasant countenance and very robust in appearance.

Harris does not seem to have realized it, but in giving him 4800 copper *mon* for one dollar the Japanese had really conceded the argument over currency exchange; for one *bu* converted to 1600 *mon*, and the officials had therefore given him the equivalent of three *bu* for one dollar—no fee, no discount. It seems strange that he did not seize on this and pursue it with his relentless logic; he still had faith in logic. Perhaps the individual coppers seemed so nearly worthless—even when strung together in hundreds as the Japanese did to keep them straight—that he could not use one as a basis for argument.

Wherever he went he noticed the trees and plants. *I saw to-day cherry, peach, pear and persimmon trees, grapevines, ivy, althea,—the last just putting out new leaves. Blue privet—very pretty; many ferns; pine trees in variety; cedar, spruce, fir and camphor trees. Camellia Japonica forms the jungle here and is cut for fuel.*

I saw a few bushes of the common rose, but no flowers were on them. Among the flowers whose names I know I found: blue bell, Canterbury ditto, Scotch thistle—the first I ever saw in the East—heart's-ease, yellow shamrock, daisy and others whose forms are familiar but whose names I do not know, and then many that were strange to me. How much I wish I was a botanist.

He wrote at length on the crops: rice, cotton, and hemp . . . *some maize, millet, a little wheat, barley and buckwheat . . . a great variety of pulse and lentils . . . many oleaginous seeds . . . the taro of the South Seas. . . .*

I was much moved to-day on finding in the woods a bachelor's button. This humble flower, with its sweet perfume, brought up so many home associations that I was inclined to be homesick,—i.e., miserable for the space of an hour.

He also commented: *There are deer, wolves, hares and wild monkeys among the hills of this place.*

But he never made note of his neighbors. He alluded to them sometimes, as in speaking of the labor it had taken to terrace the hillsides. The kind of people who had made those terraces lived all about him. They were before his eyes whenever he stepped out of Gyokusenji—in their fields, their shops, and their homes, working and resting—but he left little evidence that he saw them at all.

Samuel Wells Williams and his friend James Morrow, the botanist with Perry's expedition, made more friends around Shimoda in less than two months than Harris ever did. Both their journals are full of human encounters. As the expedition was preparing to sail away, Williams was able to write of the townsmen: "I have found some pleasant people among these shop people," and of the farmers in the villages: "All official business being over, Morrow and I took a last walk up the valley, over the hill into the upper part of it, and around by the side of the river, walking nine or ten miles and finding many old faces and acquaintances along the road, most of whom, especially at Hongo, seemed really pleased to see us."

One will hunt in vain for any similar passages in Harris's journal. He wrote, during this month of October, *I hope when I have made some further progress in the language I shall find some pleasure in the society of the upper classes here.* But he made no effort to know his neighbors or the ordinary people he encountered in his walks.

Not that this displeased the Japanese officials; most of them were distressed by the free and easy informality of Westerners. When, two years earlier, Kawaji was in Shimoda to negotiate with Admiral Putiatin, he recorded his mortification when a Russian he met on the street tipped his hat and said good morning. Such familiarity appalled punctilious samurai, and Harris's snobbery was not only more to their taste, it made him easier to manage—there was no telling what disturbing notions he might pick up if he hobnobbed with the commoners.

But if he had known the people better he would not have made such gross misjudgments as the one he set down after visiting the jail. He learned that it was used only for detention until judgment was passed, and that punishment for crimes tried locally generally consisted of either whipping or death. No one told him about the great prisons at Edo to which men were sentenced, and so he noted: *The Japanese cannot understand our imprisonment for punishment. They say for a man to be in a good house and have enough of food and clothing cannot be a punishment to a large portion of men, who only care for their animal wants and have no self-respect; and, as they never walk for pleasure, they cannot think it hard to be deprived of wandering about.* This was nonsense, but evidently he could not believe that a people without the twin benefits of Christianity and democracy could be quite human.

But in at least some of his sightseeing he was looking for people. Like every other foreign visitor to Japan he peered into the public baths. This ogling was a must for all tourists—missionaries, merchants, and naval persons—and the books and letters they wrote for the folks at home were spiced with titillating accounts of the nakedness they saw and their delightfully scandalized reactions.

Townsend Harris found it necessary to edge into the topic with a remark on his own bathing habits: *The Japanese are much surprised to see me bathing in cold water, and particularly when the thermometer stands at 56°, as it does this morning.*

The Japanese are a clean people. Everyone bathes every day. The mechanic, day laborer, all male and female, old and young, bathe every day after their labor is completed. There are many public bath-houses in Shimoda. The charge is six seni [mon], or the eighth part of one cent! The wealthy people have their baths in their own houses, but the working classes all, of both sexes, old and young, enter the same bathroom and there perform their ablutions in a state of perfect nudity. I cannot account for so indelicate a proceeding on the part of a people so generally correct.

I am assured, however, that it is not considered as dangerous to the chastity of their females; on the contrary, they urge that this very exposure lessens the desire that owes much of its power to mystery and difficulty.

But visiting Shimoda and its public baths did not dampen his appetite for bigger things. He was still digging for information about Edo. Tateishi

Tokujuro, one of the interpreters who accompanied Harris on his walks (Harris never mastered the man's family name, so he broke his given name in half and called him Toko Juro), told him *that Edo contains more than a million of houses, and that the city is twenty-four Japanese ri in circumference. This is more than fifty-eight miles, English measure.* Harris was not sure he ought to believe that, but it whetted his desire to see for himself.

He was feeling much better and the Japanese officials were *daily becoming more and more friendly and more open in their communications with me.* It seemed time to start pushing negotiations.

He decided to announce that he would visit Edo.

Consulate General of the
United States of America
Shimoda, October 25th, 1856

To His Excellency, the Minister of Foreign
Affairs for the Empire of Japan:

I have the honor to inform Your Excellency that I am charged by my Government with some highly important matters, which greatly concern the interests of Japan, and I have been directed to communicate the same to the Government of His Imperial Majesty.

The President of the United States has written a letter to His Imperial Majesty, the Emperor of Japan, and has directed me to deliver the same.

In all matters concerning the interests of two great nations, it is best that all transactions should be entrusted to those of the highest authority, and that the persons so entrusted should by the means of personal interviews enter into full, frank and free communications with each other on all the points in question, as they can thereby directly discover the best course to be adopted.

On the other hand, to attempt to conduct such a business by means of letters would be most unfortunate; great delays would arise, and many misunderstandings grow out of a wrong construction of some word or phrase. To avoid this or similar misfortunes, I have concluded to go to Edo for the purpose of communicating directly with the High Officers of His Imperial Majesty.

I have preferred to wait a few weeks after my arrival at Shimoda before making this communication to Your Excellency, thinking it would be better to go quietly to Edo, instead of proceeding there in a Frigate, which might have caused some uneasiness among the ignorant people. As I am now situated, I shall only be attended by my Secretary and my servants.

I shall feel greatly obliged by Your Excellency's giving orders for my proper accommodation on the road from this [town] to Edo, and having me informed when such arrangements have been completed.

I transmit herewith a translation into the Dutch language of a Commercial Treaty which I had the honor to make with the two Kings of Siam, as I was on my way from the United States to Japan, and I would respectfully request Your Excellency to inform yourself of its provisions.

Sir John Bowring, Governor of Hong Kong, has given me full information of the wishes and intentions of the English Government as it regards the Empire of Japan, and I will communicate the same to Your Excellency, when I shall arrive at Edo.

I have the honor to renew to Your Excellency the assurance of my most distinguished and respectful consideration.

There it was, out in the open. He wanted to make a commercial treaty —that was really all the President's letter asked for. He wanted to go to Edo to negotiate directly with the Shogun's ministers. And to sugar the pill, he offered to reveal the British plans.

On the day that Heusken finished the translation into Dutch, Executive Officer Wakana visited Gyokusenji and the letter was handed to him. Wakana tried to find out what it was about, and was told it did not concern the Shimoda Governors. But Harris did identify the Siam treaty, which came along with the letter. This led to a discussion of treaties in general, and Harris offered to lend one of his books, *Treaties of the United States with Foreign Nations.* Wakana carried it back to Naka compound with him, as Harris noted, *for the purpose of having it translated. It will be a heavy work for them, as they will have to do it by means of a dictionary in English and Dutch.*

The Governors lost no time in forwarding Harris's letter to the Great Council:

> In accordance with our orders, we asked him about the contents. He said they were secret and had no relation to us. If, after you have the letter translated, you find something in it that we should know, please send us a copy.

As for the book of treaties, the Governors agreed that it would be heavy work, but they told the Great Council they thought it should be done:

> . . . We think that a translation would be very useful, and if you agree we will have Moriyama, Ito Kansai, and others work on it. However, it will take about two years to complete, so we will ask them to pick out the important parts and do them first.
>
> We would like to have your opinion.

155

The Great Council endorsed the letter: "Approved. You may present documents to us as soon as they are translated."

The Governors also asked for approval of something they had already done:

> The American official Harris requested Japanese coins so that he can make offerings to the Shinto shrines and Buddhist temples he visits when he takes walks, and can give alms to mendicant priests and beggars along the way. We refused his request, saying that we could not issue Japanese coins to foreigners.
>
> But he insisted, saying he wanted money only for offerings and alms, and adding that he knew we were giving gold coins to the Dutch at Nagasaki.
>
> We thought it over: the Americans are here formally, not just as temporary visitors; and the head of the Dutch house is given money for the same purpose. We could think of no further reasons to refuse, and so we agreed, although we think that money should be given only to officials.
>
> We should like to know your opinion.

As October drew to a close, Harris remarked again and again on the delightful weather. It meant even more to the local people. They were still cleaning up after the typhoon. They were still hustling from village to village official inquiries concerning ships lost that stormy night. They were worrying about the damage done to their crops.

True, there were some things to be grateful for. The dispute between Kakisaki and Shimoda was finished. Certificates were issued so that new boats could be built to replace the ones lost. And if a man was one of that lucky few who had money, there was more money to be made as the rice cargoes of wrecked ships were released to local bidders; officials made half-hearted attempts to keep the price up so the owners would make a little something (". . . Unreasonably low bids or attempts to connive at the price will be thoroughly investigated and severely punished, and bidders are hereby exhorted not to resort to such irregularities. . . ."), but there was just too much rice on the market.

Harris was still walking daily—except Sunday, of course. *These rambles over this broken country, climbing the steepest of possible hills, descending on a similar plane, is improving my health very much. My appetite improves and I begin to sleep better, though not as well as I could wish.*

Certainly a more genial climate than that of Shimoda, so far, is not to be found in the world. All that is wanted to make me quite happy is society.

I hope when I have made some further progress in the language I shall find some pleasure in the society of the upper classes here.

As it happened, the upper classes were moving to make themselves available. The Governors had decided to visit him. Probably Iwase had urged them to get better acquainted with this foreigner: the better they knew him the better they could negotiate with him.

Harris's first note that the Governors were to call shows no excitement. But then Moriyama went to work, and Harris wrote: *By a law of Japan no high officer can invite me to his house. He may make friendly visits to me, but he can only see me in return at the Goyosho, a sort of "Hôtel de Ville" or City Hall.* The Governors did not want Harris dropping in on them.

It also seemed advisable to impress Harris with the importance of the Governors, lest he be inclined to take them too lightly. Moriyama had a flair for this sort of thing. After his indoctrination, Harris commented: *These Governors are of the highest rank of any men in Japan after the vassal princes, being no-kami,*—i.e., men so learned that nothing can be taught them, and so sublimated in goodness that they rank in name—Kami —with the demi-gods or saints of Japan. This word—kami—has a variety of meanings.—e.g., demi-god, noble, paper and hair.*

If Moriyama was responsible for this little essay on the language, he must be faulted as a teacher: it was not a case of one word having several meanings but of several words, written with different characters, sounding alike—homonyms.

As to the Governors' having "the highest rank of any men in Japan after the vassal princes," that was true enough except that there was a world of difference between the two—all the difference between being a lord and being a retainer; between having a hereditary title and one issued at the pleasure of the government and not transmittable to one's heir; between being a noble and being a bureaucrat.

Moriyama had already created a flurry of excitement at Gyokusenji, but he had not finished. He invented a new law: it was not only illegal for a foreigner to visit the Governors, it was illegal for them to visit him; this last law the Governors were sweeping away. And so Townsend Harris wrote: *This will be remembered hereafter as an important day in the history of Japan. The laws forbidding the Imperial Governor of a city to visit any*

---

* These words *no-kami* are usually translated "Lord of"; Inoue was Shinano-no-kami, Lord of Shinano; Okada was Bingo-no-kami, Lord of Bingo. (Such titles are not to be taken literally: Inoue was not lord of a place called Shinano, nor was Okada of Bingo.) Harris sometimes referred to the Governors as Princes, which is too grand a word for men in the middle ranks of the bureaucracy.

foreigner at his residence is to-day to be broken, and I am to receive the two Governors, with the Vice-Governor, in a friendly and informal way.

They arrived about noon with a large suite, but only four came into my private apartments with the two Governors and Vice-Governor.

This last was particularly gratifying to Harris because he had been complaining about the troupe of officials always present at meetings. As the Governors put it in a letter to Edo:

> The American official has told us that though he wishes to talk with us in a frank and friendly way, it is extremely difficult with so many officials present. . . . Moreover, he objects to our taking notes on everything that is said, and seems to feel that we do it because we do not feel secure. He has complained often about this, and the atmosphere of past meetings could not be called comfortable. . . . His opinion seems reasonable to us, and, besides, the attendance of many officials costs a great deal. . . .

This was one of the problems that Iwase had helped iron out while he was at Shimoda. Lord Hotta accepted the recommendation, but added a note of caution:

> Bear in mind that when an executive officer or lower official visits the temple, a censor must accompany him. It seems the Americans work without formality, while we naturally differ. Taking this into consideration, you should act prudently.

As Governor Okada entered Gyokusenji, his eyes lit on "a ceramic picture of a child joining his hands in prayer," and he asked about it.

It was a child praying, as he prayed every night before he went to bed, Harris answered, but he artfully dodged a discussion of Christianity. He had no intention of giving his guests an excuse to send him home on grounds that he had tried to propagate the faith.

Governor Okada asked about fortifications at foreign ports. Harris told him that Western nations always fortified their ports, not only against enemy nations but against pirates.

The Governor then confided that they planned to build a fort at Shimoda. Harris deprecated the project; it was not very important to do that, he replied, but Edo, Osaka, and Uraga certainly should be protected.

Finally the Governors got around to the topic that was bothering them most.

The Governors were very anxious on the subject of coast surveys, and inquired where Lieutenant Rodgers was, whether he would return here to survey; whether the American Government had given orders for any new expedition to survey the coasts, etc., and if I knew what the English intended doing in the matter of surveys, etc., etc.

I told them that Lieutenant Rodgers had returned to the United States, and that I did not know of any intended expedition here for a similar purpose, and that the English had no such squadron out here at present. They wished me to promise to order off any vessels that might come here for such a purpose, but I told them that would be out of my power.

THE JAPANESE: There is no article in the treaty which permits surveying.

HARRIS: There is no article which prohibits it.

MORIYAMA: Not to permit it means that we refuse it. The whole country opposes surveying. We have been aroused about it for two years. If a ship should come for this purpose again, I would offer my life to prevent it.

HARRIS: It is said that faith will move a mountain. . . .

But Harris did go on to promise, according to the Japanese record, that additional surveys would not be attempted for a while, and that if his government ordered him to request permission to survey he would discuss the problem fully with the Japanese, and handle it so as not to cause them difficulty. The United States and Japan were friendly powers, he assured them, and his country would never act in such a way as to hurt a friendly power.

("We know that it is very hard to fathom the true intentions of foreigners," the Governors reported later to Edo, "but he promised that he would try not to place Japan at a disadvantage, even if ordered to by his government.")

I then informed them that the United States Government and all the other Governments of the world expended large sums in surveying their coasts and harbors, and that those surveys were published with charts so that any nation in the world could have them; that the whole world was surveyed except Japan; that these surveys made many books, and that all shipmasters purchased these books (for they were sold freely to all) before they went on any voyage to a part of the world that was new to them; that all this was done for the security of ships, it being the great object of all civilized nations to encourage commerce, which next to agriculture was the great spring of prosperity of nations; that, for the same reasons, both America and England (as well as other nations) had hundreds of light-

houses on their coasts, and the channels leading into their harbors were carefully marked out with buoys, etc., etc. All of this astonished them much, and appeared to remove some of their anxiety, although at the beginning they told me that it was a matter of life and death to them, as they must perform the hara-kiri, *or "happy dispatch" (suicide), if the surveys went on.*

Moriyama has been fasting for some fifty days on this account, but he was so much consoled by what I said that he ate flesh most heartily. He thanked me warmly for my friendly deportment towards them, and got down on his knees and prayed fervently for my welfare.

The Governors were less volatile than Moriyama, but Okada was moved to remark on the inconveniences the Consul General must be suffering in this temporary residence, and again offered to have a consulate built. Harris declined; these temporary quarters would be quite sufficient "for the time being."

The business session was followed by a jolly party.

My company partook of my refreshments (which were prepared in our manner) without any hesitation, and by their eating showed their approval. They drank punch, brandy, whiskey, cherry bounce, champagne and cordials, but the punch and champagne were their favorite drinks.

All this, and relief over the survey question, thawed even Governor Inoue: *The last Governor warmed entirely and showed himself (like the other Japanese) of a most genial temper.*

And Harris was able to write with a straight face: *They did not eat or drink to excess in any respect, and their conduct during the whole visit was that of well-bred persons.*

I made the second Governor a present of a Colt's pistol of five discharges, with which he was much pleased.

He made other gifts, too: to Governor Inoue, a sword cane of bamboo and a small covered salt dish; to Wakana, a picture; to Superintendent Wakiya and his lieutenant, Kikuna, who were directly responsible for Gyokusenji, wooden canes; to Moriyama, a rattan cane; and to Ito Kansai, a highly respected physician whose skill at the Dutch language had brought him to Shimoda in a double capacity—as translator and as personal physician to the top officials—a fan.

After staying about four hours they took their leave with abundant thanks for my hospitality. This P.M. *they brought me a leg of* real venison. *It is excellent, tender, juicy and well flavored.*

Chapter 5

NOVEMBER, 1856

For anyone as interested as Harris in the antics of the physical world around him, Shimoda was a likely place. In two and a half months he had experienced a typhoon, heard much about the most recent tidal wave, and had been through a small, but sharp, earthquake. He had not been aware of the latter, for it hit while he was aboard the *San Jacinto,* and he was left to wonder for a time how it felt when the earth shook.

Tuesday, November 4, 1856. Yesterday it rained steadily all day and only cleared up at daylight this morning. At eight A.M. *we had an earthquake. It seemed like a heavy blow, which shook the house as though some ponderous thing had fallen, and was accompanied with a corresponding sound. Two or three light vibrations followed the great shock.* The noise and motion, he noted, seemed to come from the direction of Oshima but the island's volcano did not show any increased activity. He could not see Oshima from Gyokusenji, so he must have scrambled to the top of the high hill behind the temple; it is doubtful that he would have trusted young Heusken to make such an observation.

The tremor had startled him but it had done no damage, and after concluding that there would be no sequel, he and Heusken settled down to a project brought on by the rain and chill of the day before. Clearly winter was coming on, and it was time to set up the stove brought from America on the *San Jacinto.* Common sense dictated that they place it on the wooden floor of the gallery rather than on the straw-matted floor of an interior room. They set it in front of Harris's office-library and they must have partitioned off that portion of the gallery just in front of this room, for even on a November day that was merely chilly, it was obvious that it would be impossible to warm more than one room.

The hole for the stovepipe had already been cut in the wall. With the questionable help of Takizo, Sukezo, and Assam the butler the stove was put together. It was another disappointment. *It is a poor affair; it will not draw. The plates warped and cracked the first time a fire was kindled, atlhough only a handful of charcoal was put in. . . . The stove appears to be a patent one and made by Abbot & Lawrence of Philadelphia. So miserable is it that bituminous coals go out even when the blower is up. Let me avoid all the works of Abbot & Lawrence as I would those of the evil one. . . . I have now a smoky house, but luckily no scolding wife.*

He had in mind an old proverb: "A smoky chimney and a scolding wife are bad companions." There was a variant on this saying which seems to fit him even more aptly: "Better travel than stay at home with a scolding wife, crying children, and a smoky chimney."

Townsend Harris had traveled and he had shied away from matrimony. He enjoyed being gallant to his friends' wives and playing honorary uncle to their daughters, but on the whole he found the female sex defective.

He kept a commonplace book in which he copied pithy sayings, bad jokes, curious facts, and useful information. He put in it several epigrams aimed at the frailties of women, most of them gleaned from the Chinese, who are eloquent on the subject. "The minds of women are quicksilver, their hearts are wax." "The happiest mother of daughters is she who has only sons." And this allusion to the practice of binding the feet: "The tongues of women increase by all they take from their feet." Townsend Harris was a confirmed bachelor.

His aggravation over his faulty stove, which he could not blame on the Japanese, was somewhat relieved by a delivery of fresh meat: *A fine wild boar brought to me to-day.* And the officials who delivered it gave him an opportunity to send a message back to the Governors: with regard to his letter addressed to the Minister of Foreign Affairs (the one about going to Edo), he would like an answer within ten days. The Governors dashed off a note to the Great Council, passing on this request.

Though he does not say so, Harris's thoughts must have turned homeward on this November 4, for it was election day in the United States, and he was concerned over the outcome.

Since President Pierce had alienated most of the North by his pro-Southern policy on the question of whether slavery was to be permitted in Kansas, the Democrats had dumped him to nominate James Buchanan. Harris, of course, wished to see the Democrat elected. When he had stopped in London on his way to Japan he called on Buchanan, then minister to Great Britain: *I told him that I had no doubt he would be the next President.* This must have pleased Buchanan, who for a long time had wanted the office.

On the explosive issue of slavery, Buchanan stood, as the Democrats stood, as Harris stood, for sensible compromise. Harris was no abolitionist (some of his friends grew hot on the subject of those "stump orators . . . tobacco-eating, greedy abolitionists").

Democrats liked to believe that the slavery question had been settled by a set of compromises in 1850, if only people would let these measures work. When Harris finally learned that Buchanan had been elected, he wrote: *I am glad to hear it, and trust that under his administration peace and quiet will settle on the land. . . .* Peace and quiet would be a long time coming. Kansas was aflame with terror. North and South alike were past wanting compromise.

Though the Democrats elected their man in 1856, the results showed that their party was shattering on the issue of slavery; it would not elect another President until 1884—Grover Cleveland. Yet in foreign policy the Democrats had successfully mirrored the mood of the country, which was expansionist. As Pierce had put it in his inaugural address, "the policy of my administration will not be controlled by any timid forebodings of evil from expansion." He had an eye on Cuba, but even as he spoke Perry was moving on Japan.

Perry came not to take territory—whatever the fears of men like Nariaki—but he and Harris after him certainly meant to change Japan. And they were quite certain that the change would benefit the Japanese as well as the rest of the world.

Perry and Harris and their fellow Americans had a sense of mission and a sense of destiny. Perry believed that it was altogether appropriate that the United States should open Japan to the world, for when Columbus set out on his great voyage, inspired by the maps of Marco Polo, it was Japan he hoped to reach:

> But though not destined himself to find and open Japan to Christendom, it has so happened, in the order of Providence, that on the continent which he discovered, and which barred his way to the land he sought, has grown up a nation which has . . . fulfilled a portion, at least, of the plan which lured him westward; . . . a nation which has, as it were, taken the end of the thread which, on the shores of America, broke in the hands of Columbus, and fastening it again to the ball of destiny, has rolled it onward. . . .

It was Manifest Destiny. This was one of the great periods of American expansion. America's westward thrust did not stop at California's coastline. Captain Bell of the *San Jacinto* was writing to Harris: "Shanghai proved to be quite an interesting place, for China, and is destined (that or Woosung) to be a vast commercial city, under the influence of American enterprise and the 'Pacific Rail Road.'" It was commonly believed that with a transpacific steamship line and completion of the transcontinental railroad not only America's but all of Europe's commerce would flow across the Pacific and across America. In Chicago, an orator speaking of that great railroad project cried: "This, sir, is the road to India!"

Americans of the 1850's were set to grasp "the magnificent purse of the commerce of the Pacific." But commerce was not merely making money. It was part of God's plan. There were no misgivings concerning "the desire of gain." A Secretary of the Treasury wrote that in Asia "commerce must be the precursor of Christianity—commerce which teaches peace and intercourse between nations." Commerce was "the handmaid of the Gospel." The *New York Journal of Commerce* said that "commerce and religion . . . go hand in hand as pioneers of an enlightened civilization."

There was a widespread conviction that civilization would reach its peak in America and then spread throughout the world. It was said that Americans were "in charge of the final theatre and the final problems of history." The *New York Daily News* declared:

> Our hearts beat for an oppressed world. Our object is the greatest good of all men. We believe that our Government is best calculated to make men happy, and that it can be extended over a continent or a world . . . What hinders, we ask, a Government like this from extending over the world and making it politically happy?

Townsend Harris was in perfect accord with this. He would have been utterly astounded had he known that some Japanese were thinking similar thoughts about their own country's destiny. Tokugawa Nariaki and Ii Naosuke both entertained such ideas. Lord Hotta looked into the future, and invoking "divine law and human sense" he saw a great opportunity:

> Once we have laid the foundations of national wealth and strength, . . . it will be by no means impossible for us to accomplish thereafter the great task of uniting all the world . . . and so gradually subject the foreigners to our influence until in the end all the countries of the world know the blessings of perfect tranquillity and our hegemony is acknowledged throughout the globe.

Harris would have found this incomprehensible. How could the people of this "semi-civilized" land talk of bringing the world perfect tranquillity, of exercising hegemony throughout the globe? He was bringing civilization to Japan. He would do it by opening the country to commerce. Christianity would follow commerce and democracy would follow Christianity, for as another American said: "What, indeed, is Democracy but Christianity in its earthly aspect?" This was in the back of Harris's mind when he wrote, on a Sunday in this November: *I regularly read the service of the Protestant Episcopal Church of the United States every Sunday. I am probably the first resident of Japan who ever used that service. How long will it be before that same service will be used in Japan in consecrated churches?*

Harris had observed that the day of the earthquake brought clearing weather after a siege of cold rain. The signs also seemed favorable to Seihachi, captain of one of the small ships of Shimoda, and he decided to load and sail for Edo. The fish merchant Yamasa had a cargo of *katsuobushi* which he was eager to send to the city; he had heard that stocks were low there because of the recent typhoon, and that prices were high.

Katsuobushi can be defined as dried bonito, or *katsuo*, the Japanese name for this useful fish, but that hardly tells the story. It looks like a dark brown board and is just as hard. Its production at Shimoda was the reason the fishermen of that place were able to make a living. In winter their main catch was tuna, which in the cold weather could be rushed fresh to Edo in fast boats, but in summer they caught mostly bonito, which could be preserved only by turning them into *katsuobushi*. It is an essential in a Japanese kitchen. Thin shavings of *katsuobushi* flavor many dishes and make the stock for almost all Japanese soups, and scarcely any Japanese meal is complete without at least one soup.

Making *katsuobushi* was, and is, a slow process. A bonito fresh from the sea is split and its spine plucked out. The halves are cooked in unsalted water, the small bones and skin are removed, and for half a month the fish is smoked over a wood fire an hour each day. When that is finished, a filet which was two feet long will have shrunk to about fifteen inches, it will have lost four fifths of its weight, and it will have become hard and brown. It is dried in the sun for a day, scraped clean with a sharp curved knife, and put away in a wooden chest for two weeks. When taken out, it is covered with mold. It is sunned for a day to kill the mold, scraped clean, and put into another chest. Five times it is stored, becomes moldy, is sunned and cleaned; the dry hard brown board is given a final polishing—and it is ready for market.

As fish merchant Yamasa and Captain Seihachi viewed the situation, if the people of Edo were running out of *katsuobushi*, it would be both profitable and humanitarian to relieve their distress. Seihachi set out from Shimoda the evening of the fourth, carrying not only Yamasa's *katsuobushi* but also some dried seaweed and bundles of charcoal. With fine weather and a good breeze he had gambled by overloading, and his vessel lay low in the water. The crew rowed out of the harbor, then hoisted their single sail, and Seihachi set a course northward along the Izu coast. He intended to stay close to land as far as possible, rather than cut across the open Sea of Sagami.

All went well the first few hours. By the middle of the night they had run more than thirty miles and were ready to cross the narrowed sea toward Edo Bay. Then things went wrong. The wind rose, the sea roughened, and their heavily loaded little ship started to take water. They fought back, bailing furiously, but then the rigging failed—Seihachi cursed his decision to use the old lines a little longer. Without a sail they wallowed in the waves, clearly about to capsize. The crew pleaded, then threatened, and finally Seihachi gave the word: they tossed overboard all the *katsuobushi*, seaweed, and charcoal intended for the kitchens of Edo. Their boat rode higher then, and by bailing they were able to stay afloat. Next morning they drifted ashore at a village on upper Izu. The brief storm of the night had passed. It was a beautiful day, with a fair breeze for Edo.

As the disconsolate captain and crew were taken into custody and the usual investigation set in motion, as the provincial magistrate for Izu was appointing an officer to make certain that these sailors had not feigned distress and hijacked their cargo, as a circular was initiated to notify villages along the coast about possible drifting cargo (none was ever reported), Townsend Harris was setting out for a walk.

Wednesday, November 5, 1856. . . . Walked to-day about five miles up the Valley of Shimoda and nearly all the way by the banks of Shimoda River, or creek, as we would call it in America. . . . The hamlets are almost continuous. You are never out of sight of a temple.

He marveled at the weather of this late autumn. *A lovely day, superior to the American Indian summer, the sky clear and blue and the air balmy.*

It was harvest time. In field after field families were working together under a warm sun. He could hear bursts of laughter, sometimes of song. It is doubtful that the pastoral life had ever looked more appealing to him, and he was moved to observe that *In no part of the world are the laboring classes better off than at Shimoda. . . . they live comfortably, are well fed according to their wants, and are abundantly clad, and their houses are clean, dry, and comfortable.*

He stopped to watch. There was nothing new in the way men held the grain erect and cut it close to the ground with sickles, but their one mechanical contrivance interested him: *Rice is cleaned from the straw by a machine exactly like the hetchel used for cleaning flax with us. This is done by the women and children. They take a small number of rice straws (not over thirty), draw them through the iron teeth which stand upright on a board. They are six inches long and they are usually some twelve in number. The straw is drawn once or twice through these iron teeth, which effectually strips every grain of paddy from the straw.*

The process is a slow one, but the straw is of more value than time; and, as the former is uninjured by this process, it is not likely the Japanese would adopt a more rapid process, if the straw would be injured thereby. . . .

Visited a hot sulphur spring about three miles from Shimoda. A tank about twelve feet square, paved and lined with stone, contains the water which bubbles out between the interstices of the stone. The water is beautifully clear, about three feet deep, and is about 150° Fahrenheit in temperature. Some few bubbles of gas arise to the surface. The whole tank is covered with a building, and is a favorite bath for the Shimodeans. No charge is made for its use. It is held in high repute for its medical properties in cutaneous and rheumatic affections.

The fine weather held, and on the sixth and seventh Harris continued his walks, with time out for *dirty work with my wretched stove. Happily I cannot make it worse by any experiments I may try with it, and some lucky hit may improve it.* Wherever he went he reveled in the beauty of the countryside. *What a field for an artist! Every half mile gives a new view well worth drawing.*

But on the eighth there was something more exciting, the arrival of two ships of the Russian Navy.

Harris at once called for the boat which Yoheiji kept available for him and went out to greet the visitors. He was a little miffed at not receiving a salute, but even so he was pleased to see them. He was prepared to like the Russians, if for no other reason than that they had been fighting his favorite villains, the British.

He was greeted by the ranking officers, Captains Constantine Possiet and Woyin Rimsky-Korsacoff (the latter had a younger brother, Nicolai, who was in his first year at the naval academy in St. Petersburg, and was

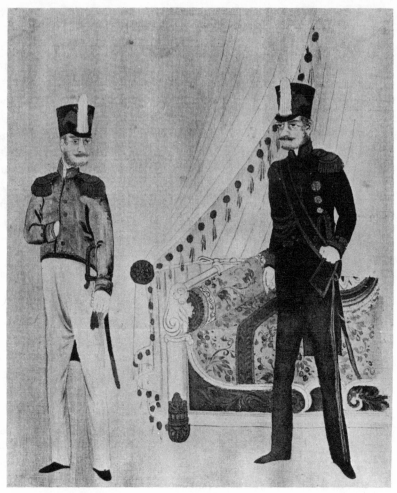

Captain Possiet and Admiral Putiatin *(a painting by an unknown artist)*

beginning to fall out of love with the sea and in love with music). Possiet was not making his first visit to Shimoda: he had been aboard the *Diana* in 1854 when Admiral Putiatin came, a few months after Perry, to negotiate a Russian treaty with Japan. He had survived the tidal wave and the loss of the *Diana* and now was back to exchange ratifications of the treaty.

Harris warmed to the two Russians at once, found them *very agreeable persons and very friendly,* and was delighted to learn that they would probably remain several weeks. Before their first meeting was over, Captain Possiet promised Harris a copy of the Russian treaty, and Harris in return had promised Possiet copies of three treaties: the American treaty with

Japan, the treaty he had negotiated with Siam, and the recent Dutch treaty with Japan, a draft of which he had picked up in Hong Kong. And within a few days Possiet pleased Harris by waiving formality between them: *He desires that our visits should be without ceremony, and as between friends; that I should make myself at home with him, and he will do the same with me.*

Harris was not impressed by the larger of the Russian ships: *The corvette is a poor affair, old in age and older in model . . . armed with old-fashioned carronades.* But he approved of the schooner: *She has a pretty cabin, very handsomely furnished; has oilcloth on the floor, tables of fine woods, and the hangings are of mazarine blue velvet.* She had been *built by the Russians at the River Amur for the Japanese, and is a present, as I understand.* He added that she looked very much like a Japanese schooner he had seen (no doubt when Iwase arrived or when he left). This is not surprising since it seems a very good guess that she was the original Kimizawa ship, built by the Russians with Japanese help at Heda. We know that the Russians did return her, and this appears to have been their only opportunity to do so. If so, she was not built at the Amur but refitted there.

At any rate, she promptly disappears from our chronicles, never to be mentioned again. It is likely that she was almost immediately turned over to the Japanese, who sailed her away.

Despite the return of the schooner, news of the Russians' arrival was received with no great joy in Edo, though the time had passed when the arrival of a foreign warship could make the whole government tremble. As a matter of fact, things were so quiet it was agreed that the Emperor need not continue the special services which had been scheduled to solicit the protection of the gods.

Within the Emperor's court, however, things were not so calm. There was a rumor abroad that the British were preparing to sail on Osaka, and Nariaki made sure the Kyoto courtiers heard it. On the same day that the Russians arrived at Shimoda, Nariaki was writing to his correspondent Ishikawa to transmit his suspicions:

As I see it, Russia is pulling the strings behind other countries' sending their ships to Japan. First Russia arranged that America would send its ships to Edo, while it awaited developments by sending its own ships to Nagasaki in an ostensibly law-abiding manner. In this light, we can surmise that Russia is behind Britain sending her ships this time. Russia has already sent ships to Osaka and knows the geography there.

Nariaki wanted to be placed in charge of the defense of Kyoto. Yet he knew that many in the government considered his loyalty suspect and that any such suggestion from him would more likely lead to another period of house arrest than to command of a great army. It would be gratifying if the Emperor made a request for his appointment, but he knew he would be suspected of having engineered it. He felt utterly frustrated:

> I cannot but wonder if the Shogun is aware that the British are coming. Or if he is told, that he will understand what it means. Of the senior officials, Lord Abe is the sole capable man and if he goes to Kyoto there will be none in Edo to take care of things properly. On the other hand, if there are words from Kyoto to Edo recommending me as the right man they will certainly suspect that I am pulling the strings in the background. Today even patriotism to the Throne backfires. Woe the day! At any rate, the defense of Kyoto must be strengthened. However many courtiers are on hand, they are no help in strategic planning. If the worst comes, the sacred mission of "expelling the foreigners" will collapse. This prospect frightens me.

These indirect but unsubtle attacks must by now have convinced many of the courtiers that they could not rely on the man designated to defend Kyoto and protect the Emperor, Lord Ii Naosuke.

In other quarters, Nariaki's slurs did not always go unchecked. When he maligned Naosuke in another letter to Matsudaira Yoshinaga, Yoshinaga sent a trusted retainer to Kyoto to investigate. That man sent back a reassuring report. There was no doubt, he wrote, that Naosuke considered protection of the Emperor his paramount duty: three generations ago the head of the house of Ii had sworn to carry the Emperor to safety on his back if necessary, and indubitably the present lord had the same spirit.

This report probably satisfied Yoshinaga but Nariaki would have scorned it. And in his castle at Hikone, Lord Ii Naosuke was well aware of Nariaki's campaign of defamation. The enmity between the two grew steadily more bitter.

There is no question that Ii Naosuke's loyalty to the Emperor was as deep as Nariaki's, and it was not tainted with opportunism. Nariaki's endless machinations sprang from frustration: to an ambitious, frustrated man the end may justify any means. It is impossible to question his devotion to the Emperor, but to him the Emperor was also a means—to rally the country against foreigners, to reconstruct the Shogunate, to make his own son the next Shogun.

Both Ii Naosuke and Tokugawa Nariaki were loyal to the Shogunate and wanted to preserve it as the government of Japan, but Naosuke wanted it kept as it was, with power secure in the hands of the hereditary liege lords of the Tokugawa—like himself—and Nariaki wanted it remodeled so that power would be shared with those who had always been cast in the role of outsiders—like himself.

Both disliked and distrusted the foreigners who were pressing in upon Japan and both wanted to make the country strong enough to stand against those foreigners. But Naosuke was convinced that to make a stand now would be suicide, while Nariaki was just as certain that Japan must make a stand or lose her soul—that faced by a dynamic, unified Japan (one led by himself), the foreigners would cease their assault or could be turned back.

Their differences were less in goals than in tactics, but they were none the less irreconcilable. These two men who should have been pillars of strength to the Shogunate were pitted against each other.

For a time it seemed that Nariaki was winning: after a year on the sidelines he had been reappointed as military advisor, and he had persuaded Abe to dismiss two members of the Great Council who were of Naosuke's camp. But it was not that easy to dismiss the power of Ii's faction. Two months later Abe found it necessary to reverse himself: he drafted Lord Hotta for the Great Council. Not only was Hotta aligned with Ii, but in ticking off the candidates Nariaki had labeled him out of the question, "crazy over Dutch learning." Yet the appointment was made, and what is more, Abe demoted himself and gave Hotta first seat in the Council.

It might not have happened as suddenly except for the earthquake that ravaged Edo in November, 1855, one of a series of disasters—among them the earthquake and tidal wave that leveled Shimoda and a fire that destroyed the Emperor's palace in Kyoto—that left the Shogunate nearly bankrupt. This earthquake not only cost the lives of Nariaki's best advisors but also scuttled most of the plans that he and Abe had worked out for rearming the country. Funds earmarked for defense had to be diverted to rebuild Edo. Abe felt tired and defeated. He was willing to relinquish leadership. He yielded to the pressure from the lords headed by Ii.

When Ii Naosuke was born in 1815, no one could have foreseen his future. He was his father's fourteenth son and the likelihood was remote that a fourteenth son would inherit the fief.

When his father died the oldest son succeeded him, and he, having no sons, designated the second son as his heir. Suitable adoptions into other daimyo families were arranged for all the other sons down to Naosuke. He and his one younger brother were installed in a small house with a small stipend, for it was a family law that excess sons should be treated as ordinary retainers.

When Naosuke was nineteen he and his brother were summoned to Edo. There the head of the family, their oldest brother, was able to place the youngest boy as heir to a sizable fief, but Naosuke was rejected by the only family that had shown any interest in him, and he was obliged to return to Hikone. He moved back into his cottage, and what he expected from life can be judged by the name he gave it, "The House of Oblivion." He resigned himself to genteel poverty but not to idleness. With a burning, sustained determination he applied himself to the arts and skills of a samurai, while cultivating the virtues which the samurai code finds in frugality.

He continued his military training: the physical skills of fencing, archery, horsemanship, and gunnery; the mental exercises of tactics and strategy. He studied Western military science too, from specialists who had been brought from Nagasaki to Hikone. The one who influenced him most was an outspoken critic of Japan's policy of isolation.

He studied Zen Buddhism with the abbot of a nearby temple, and would gladly have accepted the priest's offer to adopt him had not his eldest brother forbidden it as beneath the dignity of the family. He studied the classics and wrote poetry. He found joy and release in the tea ceremony, and wrote a series of essays about it which have put his name among the masters. One point he emphasized was that in the ceremony social barriers are leveled and rank forgotten; all that matters is the taste and accomplishment the participant brings to the teahouse. One of his regular guests was a plasterer.

For fifteen years he lived this life of denial. Those were the years that changed him from a stolid, stubby, overweight, and unattractive youth to a man toughened by disappointment and disciplined by rigorous training.

He was thirty-one when he was told that his older brother, the heir to the fief, was dangerously ill, and then that he had died. Suddenly Naosuke was catapulted from his life of oblivion. The only unadopted son in the family, he was now its heir. Five years later, in 1850, his eldest brother died and Naosuke was Lord Ii of Hikone, the Shogunate's most powerful direct vassal.

When the storm broke with the arrival of Perry, he was aligned with those few who advocated changing the old laws and undertaking trade, though not by permitting foreigners into Japan: he would put an end to "imprisoning ourselves"; he would forestall the foreigners by sending Japanese ships out to Western markets:

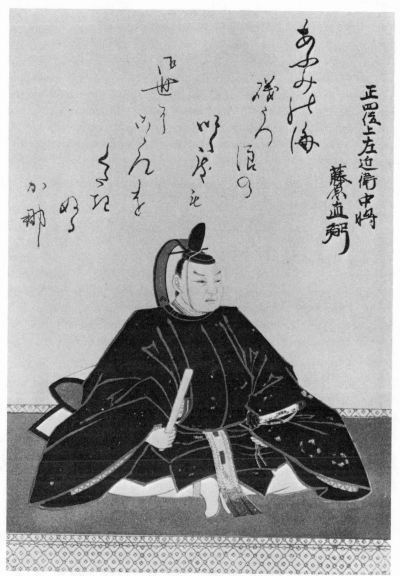

Lord Ii Naosuke: the poem across the top is one of Naosuke's; it refers to
waves beating ceaselessly against the shore, an allusion to the foreigners' beating
against Japan, and stresses Naosuke's concern over the future of his country
(*a painting by Kano Eigaku*)

Openly these will be called merchant vessels, but they will in fact have the secret purpose of training a navy. As we increase the number of ships and our mastery of technique, Japanese will be able to sail the oceans freely and gain direct knowledge of conditions abroad without relying on the secret reports of the Dutch. Thus we will eventually complete the organization of a navy. Moreover, we must shake off the panic and apprehensions that have beset us and abandon our habits of luxury and wasteful spending. Our defenses thus strengthened, and all being arranged at home, we can act so as to make our courage and prestige resound beyond the seas.

Thus Naosuke put himself squarely in opposition to Nariaki, who bluntly advocated war:

When we consider the respective advantages and disadvantages of war and peace, we find that if we put our trust in war the whole country's morale will be increased and even if we sustain an initial defeat we will in the end expel the foreigner; while if we put our trust in peace, even though things may seem tranquil for a time, the morale of the country will be greatly lowered and we will come in the end to complete collapse. This has been amply demonstrated in the history of China and is a fact that men of intelligence, both past and present, have always known.

The Shogunate had followed neither course—it no longer had the necessary power. It could neither force the daimyo to prepare for war nor force them to accept trade. It had granted Perry the least he would accept, and given the same to the Russians who followed. It had tried to buy time.

Yet the course of events, the unremitting pressure from the foreigners, had pushed it in the direction that Naosuke, not Nariaki, advocated. Abe had stepped down, Hotta had taken over.

At Hikone Castle, Naosuke received a steady stream of intelligence. He was kept informed by the Great Council. He regularly received copies of the reports submitted by the Governors of Shimoda. Notice of Harris's arrival had been rushed to him, as was word of the Russians' appearance. Almost simultaneously he learned that Lord Hotta had been named to take charge of foreign affairs and to direct a committee set up to investigate the possibility of foreign trade. A few days later he learned that the Great Council was considering the idea of sending students to Europe to learn Western seamanship; inviting the Dutch instructors to Nagasaki was too small a step, "for we know that in the near future we will have to begin trading with other countries."

All these moves Naosuke approved; it seemed to him that at last the government was moving in the right direction.

Just how swiftly the government would move was, of course, a matter of intense concern at Shimoda. Harris wrote that the Russians were holding constant conversations *with the Japanese on the subject of finally and fully opening Japan to the commerce of the world. All agree that it is only a question of time, and Moriyama Einosuke goes so far as to place it less than three years distant.*

All these things will help to prepare the way for me in my attempt to make a treaty which shall at once open Japan (at different dates for different ports) to our commerce.

Moriyama's remark had been repeated to Harris at dinner aboard the Russian corvette. The foreigners at Shimoda were trading entertainment almost every day. This particular party had begun auspiciously: the Russians had given Harris a satisfying salute of thirteen guns, *although by the rules of the Russian service a consul general is saluted with eleven guns. Captain Possiet told me that he gave me thirteen guns so that I should not receive less than he gave the Japanese Governor of Shimoda.*

The conversation had been to Harris's liking too. In addition to making cheerful remarks about the prospects of trade with Japan, the freshly defeated Russians had reminisced about the Crimean War in terms most likely to please their guest. *They speak in high terms of French generals and soldiers. They say the first have skill equal to any in the world, and the last are unsurpassed in military courage and enthusiasm. The English, on the contrary, they put directly opposite: generals without skill, and men without one of the prerequisites for a soldier, except mere bulldog courage; that to deprive an English army of its full supply of food and comfortable quarters is to demoralize it; that an English soldier dreads an attack on his belly more than a blow aimed at his head. A current remark at Sebastopol during the siege was that A or B had been out on so many occasions of sorties; the question was instantly asked against which force? If against the English, the querist would shrug his shoulders and say, "That was nothing"; but if against the French, he would say, "Oh! then [he] had something to do."*

And Harris must have relished the dinner as much as the conversation, for he confessed in his thank-you note the next day that he had a headache from overindulgence. In token of his appreciation he sent along a few pounds of coffee, a Siamese sarong ("when I next shall have the pleasure of seeing you, I will show you how it is worn"), and some Siamese silver coins for Captains Possiet and Rimsky-Korsacoff.

The Russians had given *him* some spirits of turpentine and a big bag of potatoes from Hakodate. They had sent a party of seamen to repair his flagstaff, which had stood broken since the typhoon. They had offered him one of the *Diana's* boats (declined with thanks because it was too heavy; Yoheiji would continue to supply both a boat and the men to scull it). They had promised to lend him a barometer, which he could turn over to the Russian consul expected to arrive next spring. (This was good news: *I am told the Russian Consul for Japan speaks English very well, and that he is very friendly to the Americans. I am inclined to think he will bring a family with him*—there were prospects of again becoming an honorary uncle.)

No wonder that Harris had written in his journal, as he sent off the coffee and souvenirs of Siam, *I am glad to find anything I can present to the Russians as a small return for their favors to me.* Up till then he had been able to offer the two captains only the services of his laundryman, explaining that *the Japanese do not know how to wash. I also said that I was sorry I could not offer the same compliment to all of the officers, but my washman had no assistance.*

Of course, Harris had entertained at dinner, too. *I never passed a more agreeable evening. The Russians behaved like polished men of the world, and at my table they did not merit the charge so often brought against them of being hard drinkers. They ate with good appetites (and my dinner was both good and abundant), and took their wine in moderation. I do think the same number of American or English officers would have drunk twice the quantity of wine the Russians did.*

It was at this dinner that Possiet told him that the Japanese had refused for the present any payment for the supplies they had furnished to his ship, saying *that the American Consul General had made a demand on the Government to have a just value put on the dollar, and that they expected a favorable answer in a few days.*

This was encouraging, but Harris thought it best not to relax. On the seventeenth of the month he wrote to the Governors, pressing for a reply on the currency question—a reply in writing, he was careful to specify. On the next day the Goyosho forwarded a translation of his letter to the Great Council. "As we indicated earlier," said the Governors in their accompanying note, "we think that this problem should be settled as quickly as possible. It also affects our relations with Russia, and lack of a decision will be inconvenient."

Harris's relations with the Japanese had been, like the weather, sunny of late, probably because the visiting Russians had kept him in such good humor. Moreover, the Japanese had been sending him presents. Among them were two small spaniels—*very fine ones*. He named the male "Edo" and the female "Miyako"—another name for Kyoto—which may have amused some of the officials, and in looking at them he realized that the stone statues of dogs he had seen so often in front of temples were not so far removed from nature as he had supposed.

Japanese dogs (*a woodcut from a drawing by Wilhelm Heine*)

The Governors also sent him a pheasant, *the finest specimen of a male golden pheasant I ever saw*. He thought at once to invite Captains Possiet and Rimsky-Korsacoff to dinner, with four of their officers, and he hoped Possiet would bring those who had not already dined at Gyokusenji:

> I regret that my domestic arrangements are so limited that I cannot invite more than six persons to dinner at one time.
>
> I cannot promise you much in the way of a dinner, but we will try for some mock turtle soup, wild boar steaks, and roasted pheasant, with a hearty and sincere welcome.

Still another gift from the Japanese were some marine growths which he found both new and beautiful, and in addition he was informed that *the Governor has sent special word to the village of Sotoura that all should go to work to procure me specimens of the marsupial fish, which is said to be found there*.

There are no marsupial fish in Edo bay or anywhere else. The Japanese were probably talking about certain fish called ovoviviparous, or "live-bearing": the female hatches her eggs within her body. Such confusion over terms was mild considering what was possible in double interpretation.

We have no way of knowing whether the fishermen of Sotoura ever delivered such a fish to Harris, for he never mentions the subject again. Perhaps "marsupial fish" were filed away in that bulging category in his mind labeled "Japanese lies."

Certainly the men of Sotoura, and the men of Kakisaki on the other side of the hill, were busy enough without such special assignments. They had to harvest the rice, and while good weather held they ranged far out to sea for bonito and dragged nets along the shore for sardines, useful both for supper and for bait. Sometimes the nets brought in a real prize, a fat pink *tai;* it would likely go to the owner of the net, or if it was a beauty it might be wrapped in seaweed and rushed to the Governors' compound as a gift.

The nets, like the boats, belonged to households well-off by Kakisaki standards, but it took more than one family to handle a net. Folks worked on shares, the women helping alongside the men, though by village logic a woman got only half a share when it came time to divide the catch.

It was customary for village officials, including of course the chief fisherman, to designate certain days for dragnetting since so many people were involved and the village was taxed for the privilege. Yoheiji's diary mentions two or three occasions during this period. The catches, he noted, were disappointing.

It was unfortunate that just at this time it was necessary to collect the dragnet tax. This was part of the annual "business tax," which the village paid in money, in contrast to the much larger land tax paid in rice.

Both taxes were billed to the village in a lump sum. It was up to the village officials to distribute the levy among their people, and this was probably their most onerous responsibility. This year they set the dragnet tax at two hundred copper coins from each household that owned a net. As the elders collected it they also collected grumbling about empty nets. The grousing was beside the point, as everyone knew. Even if the villagers never wet the nets they would still have to pay the tax on their use, for the Shogunate shared with most other governments in history a reluctance to rescind any tax once levied. Kakisaki and its neighboring villages were still paying a salt-making tax, for example, though it had been a couple of centuries since people around Shimoda made their own salt—coastal freighters brought it in from the southwest too cheaply. They also paid a tax on deer tails, which those who had studied such matters said stemmed from an ancient right to hunt deer in the Shogun's forests; nowadays deer were scarce and it had become illegal for the common people to kill them—only the tax survived.

There was still another kind of tax: the requisitioning of labor. In many ways this was the most irksome levy of all. It might be planting time or harvest time or fish might be running, but when a call came men had to stop work and assist some samurai along the road from here to there.

Shimoda and the nearby villages lay fifty mountainous miles off the Tokaido Road. Yet the post town of Mishima had authority to reach that fifty miles whenever it needed men and horses for an out-of-the-ordinary requirement—the passage of major daimyo or of emissaries from the Emperor on their way from Kyoto to Edo or home again. Over the years an arrangement had been worked out. Now, though Mishima still worded its demands in terms of men and horses, it was taken for granted that the villages would send money to hire substitutes.

But closer to home it was not possible to buy out. And these days, in addition to all the chores to be done for the foreigners and officials at Gyokusenji, Yoheiji was receiving a steady stream of requisitions: three men to help load a ship the Goyosho was sending to Edo; a man and a horse to meet an official up the coast and bring him, his retainer, and their baggage into Shimoda; two men and a *kago* (a palanquin similar to a *norimono* but less elaborate) to carry an official on the first leg of his journey home to Uraga; five men and two *kago* for another party.

It was especially trying to Yoheiji that busy as the village was, some of its members found time to misbehave. There was a summons from the Goyosho for Otokichi, the carpenter; he was to appear for questioning in the company of a village official. The summons didn't say what Otokichi was suspected of and he stoutly denied the slightest wrongdoing, but knowing his tendencies the headman guessed that gambling would be involved.

Gennosuke went to represent the village, since Otokichi's house was near his, and he and the carpenter were able to convince the police that on the day in question, when there had indeed been a raid on some gamblers, most of whom had got away, Otokichi had been hard at work on a casket for a recently deceased man of Sotoura. In his heart, however, Gennosuke did not have the same faith in Otokichi's story that he had manifested before the police, and he upbraided the carpenter all the way home and then marched him up to Yoheiji for further tongue-lashing. It was an embarrassing reflection on the village administration when the Governors' police had to step in.

Another case reached into the past and was more disturbing. There was a small chapel called Mida-do on the hill above Gyokusenji; the chapel and its apprentice priest were supervised by the priest of Gyokusenji. Late one November evening Kosaburo called on Yoheiji with distressing news: he had received a tip that the young priest was a fugitive from the law.

Despite the hour, Yoheiji summoned Priest Bimo. To the startled priest Kosaburo unfolded his story. In the aftermath of the typhoon the captain of a wrecked rice-ship from northern Japan had lived for some time at Kosaburo's house, a seamen's inn. With little to do he had become well acquainted with the villagers and had often wandered over the hills.

When the drawn-out salvage operations had been completed and the captain was ready to leave, he had taken Kosaburo aside to talk privately. He had several times encountered the young priest, he told the innkeeper, and from the first had been struck by a sense of having seen him before. At last, the captain said, the elusive memory had come to him: the man who was now the priest of Mida-do was the son of a well-to-do rice merchant in the captain's home town in the north. The young man had had an affair with a servant-girl in his father's house and the two had fallen deeply in love. When the boy's father had discovered the affair, partly as a result of his son's reluctance to marry the daughter of another merchant—an unattractive girl but one who would bring a sizable dowry—he had ordered the maidservant returned to her parents in disgrace and his son married to the merchant's daughter without delay. The lovers had determined on the classical solution to their plight, double suicide. They had fled to a lonely place and exchanged last vows of love. The young man had killed the girl, but when he turned his sword upon himself something had gone amiss. Perhaps he fainted before he could finish the deed, but his own wound was not fatal. The pair had been discovered, the girl dead, the boy unconscious. In such a case the law decreed that the survivor be handed over to the *eta*, to live out his life as one of those lowest of pariahs, but the merchant had used his money and his influence to spirit his son out of town to a place where he could be nursed back to health and then had given him some money and bid him goodbye forever.

For some minutes Priest Bimo sat silent and downcast, for he wanted to disbelieve what he had heard. At last he raised his eyes and admitted that the date of the young man's arrival at Gyokusenji seemed to fit the story that Kosaburo had told, that the young man's speech betrayed his north-country origin, and that he himself had seen a scar on the young man's body. Speaking very slowly he told how the youth had appeared at Gyokusenji and applied to become a priest. He had questioned him carefully, Bimo said, for there was always the possibility that a fugitive would seek to enter the priesthood. But the young man's story had been convincing, and his intelligence and sincerity had erased misgivings. He had been quick to learn and devout in his duties, as Yoheiji and Kosaburo and all the village knew. The old priest stopped there, letting his plea go understood but unspoken.

Yoheiji cleared his throat. It would be necessary, he said, for all the village elders to confer. They parted for the night, but each lay awake with his thoughts.

The elders convened early the next morning, not only the current officials but those retired, like wealthy landlord Heiemon. Kosaburo again told his story, adding that the captain had said that he himself would never reveal the young priest's identity to anyone else. They talked for a long time that morning. It was illegal, of course, to harbor a fugitive, but they all knew that for centuries Izu, because of its isolation, had been a haven for men with a secret to hide. Perhaps some of them remembered an ancestor of his own; they all knew of several Shimoda families whose prosperity was due to the vigor and intelligence of some man who had mysteriously appeared, whose abilities had recommended him as a son-in-law, and who had been taken into the family without too much probing into his past. This was an old story to the people around Shimoda. They were likely to boast of such forebears. Some said that it was this heritage which accounted for the strong streak of independence, even perversity, in Shimoda people—and they boasted of that too.

When Priest Bimo judged that the time was right, he begged that this matter be forgotten. He would warn the young man that his past had come to light, but he asked that public knowledge stop with those in the room. The young priest of Mida-do was living out his life in repentance, and his fate as an *eta* was too dreadful to contemplate.

There were many more cups of tea drunk that long morning, but in the end the men who ran the village agreed that Bimo was right. Each pledged himself to secrecy (and because each now was guilty of complicity the secret was kept). The case was closed, and each man went home to ponder in his own way the follies of this transient world.

The day after Harris wrote to the Governors to dun them for a reply on the currency question, he had callers, Executive Officer Wakana and Moriyama. The latter might have been pleased to find that Harris was referring to him in his journal as "my old friend." *They apologized for their long absence saying the arrival of the Russians had kept them much occupied, etc., etc. They brought me a cage containing six pretty tame pigeons, a*

*present from the Governor, and they told me that he had written to Edo
expressly for them, as they are scarce in Japan.* This was thoughtful of the
Governor, for about a month earlier Harris's cat had spent an orgiastic
night in the belfry and that was the end of the pigeons that had traveled to
Japan on the *San Jacinto.*

*I knew the visit of ceremony and the present were all a pretence, and
that something else was behind, and a short time brought it out.*

*They (as if casually) said my letter of yesterday to the Governor had
been at once forwarded to Edo by a "Special Post"; and that, as soon as an
answer was received, the Governor would let me know it.*

He was convinced that this was the reason for the visit and the pigeons
from Edo—to avoid writing him a letter, even though there was nothing to
say except that they had received his and sent it on to Edo. So he read them
another lecture on diplomatic courtesy. *I told them I was happy to see them
at all times, but I could not consent to receive verbal answers to, or notices
of, my written communications.* He "knew" the government had been
writing to the Dutch and the Russians and he *could not consent to be
treated with less formality.* . . . The Japanese went home, but they did not
write to confirm receipt of his letter.

Harris was neglecting his walks these days. Despite the lesson of a few
weeks earlier he was taking little exercise. The Russians brought an opportunity to get out some mail and so he was spending most of his time in the
chilly temple writing letters: there was no certainty of another ship until
the one Commodore Armstrong had promised to send next spring.

Harris was of course unaware of events in China and Armstrong's deep
involvement there. After landing the Marines the commodore had had
second thoughts. "A little reflection and consultation" had brought him to
think, correctly as it turned out, that his government in Washington might
consider him overzealous, and so he decided to withdraw his force from
Canton "lest his neutrality should be compromised." Unfortunately, as some
of his ships were proceeding upriver on November 15 to do this, the Barrier
Forts along the river fired on them, and the commodore promptly ordered
the forts destroyed. This operation took only three days, for as Captain Bell
later wrote to Harris, "God smiled upon us at every step." Both Americans
and British cheered.

Harris would have cheered too, but, unknowing, he was occupied with
less stirring affairs. He first disposed of some routine reports, and then
started a letter which must have given him genuine pleasure. It was
addressed to Macao, to his favorite among the Drinkers' children, their
eldest, fifteen-year-old Catherine Ann:

U. S. Consulate General
Shimoda Japan, November 21st, 1856

My dear Kate

I sit down for the purpose of redeeming the promise I made of writing to you after I had got quietly settled here—

It was a long chatty letter, with excerpts from his journal about his walks and the beauty of the countryside. He praised the climate and he praised the people: "The Japanese are a fine race of men; genial in their temper, and cleanly in their persons and houses—they are possessed of so much graceful, natural politeness that they might be called the French of Asia." All his acquaintances knew that from Townsend Harris this was a high compliment.

Writing to a fifteen-year-old girl, he did not belabor the facts of life: "Every Japanese of all ranks, all ages and all sexes, bathe, after the labour of the day is over," but he did not say that the sexes bathed together. He said: "I am living on cordial terms with the authorities here, and no restraint is placed on me, or on my movements," and found it unnecessary to mention his "flare-ups" and their "falsehoods." But this is consistent with the face he always put on when writing abroad; it is as though he wanted no one to think that his well-known temper was hampering this mission.

He described his temple-consulate, beginning: "As you enter the house you open into a large room, neatly matted in Japanese style, and furnished with couches, chairs, tables, side board, clock &c &c in Western style." And he itemized his animals: pigs and chickens to supply his table, in pigpen and poultry house "vis-à-vis to the kitchen"; the belfry again occupied, by "six of the prettiest tame pigeons you ever saw" (he does not mention his cat, but in spite of her transgressions he must have kept her to cope with the rats and mice); the "little fish pond with some *real live fishes in it!*"; his two dogs, "Edo" and "Miyako," with their "large protuberant eyes of a very soft expression."

Nor was this all. "My pet fowls are beauties! Some of the cocks are very beautiful, and I have two darling little hens, that are just laying a nest of eggs, which I mean to have hatched—In the house, I have five cages of birds, of which canaries and bull finches are the only ones I recognise; they are all singing birds."

The birds had arrived only the day before he began this letter, but since this was an expurgated account he did not mention the irritation he recorded in his journal on receiving this gift. *The Japanese sent me yesterday some singing birds which I asked for about the 10th of September—so*

*long does it take them to determine whether any new demand of mine shall
be granted or refused. . . . As the cages are too small I ordered new ones
made. To-day I am told that three of the four cages wanted must be
procured from Edo, as they cannot be made in Shimoda. I ordered some
four quires of a soft cheap paper for waste, blotting, etc., etc., and to-day I
am told that the paper must be ordered from Edo, as the quantity desired
cannot be had in Shimoda!!!*

*Whether this is an untruth, or that the place is so deplorably anti-com-
mercial that four quires of common paper cannot be furnished, I cannot
say. Nor can I see any object they have in telling a falsehood about it, as it
is to be furnished.*

He could not understand that what might be common paper in New
York or even in Hong Kong might not be common at all in Japan, simply
because the Japanese had no use for it. But none of his spleen is displayed
in his letter to Kate:

> For the life I lead—I rise early, feed pets. Bathe and dress, then read
> prayer—and breakfast at ½ past ten—perhaps a little work may have
> been done before breakfast in the way of writing journal and studying
> Japanese. . . . I am getting along slowly with Japanese; I have two Boys,
> and can now give them all orders about the house, table, my bed room,
> dress &c &c in Japanese. . . .
>
> For my occupations beyond my official duties—they consist of read-
> ing, writing—study—walk for exercise—looking up shells and objects of
> natural history—receiving and paying visits—entertaining company at
> dinner &c &c—Of course, all these things are not done on the same day
> —I should remark that the thermometer and the barometer are noted
> four times a day—the weather observed and record made of that and of
> the winds— This letter will be taken to Macao by the Russian Corvette
> Olivuzza and I have given Commodore Possiet and Captain Korsacoff
> letters of introduction to your Mamma—they have been very kind to
> me, and are worthy of attentions on your part, as they are most
> estimable persons, and I hope you will like all the young officers— Some
> of them are very good looking, and you know all Russians dance well—
> Nothing has been offered me in the way of Japanese productions that I
> think nice enough for you. So I do not send you anything but this letter.
> But do not despair my dear Kate, for *I shall go to Edo one of these days*
> and then I shall see what I can get for you— By the way don't let these
> young Russians steal away your heart from me.—

He sent "all kinds of kind messages to all in your house" and to friends
at Macao; "my kindest regards to the French legation; that is as comprehen-
sive as I can make it." And he closed:

You do not know how I long to hear from you all—it seems a year since we parted—and yet months, long months must pass before I can hear from you— I wish you a merry Xmas and happy New Year and many happy returns of the seasons in the enjoyment of health, love and happiness . . .

Affectionately yours,

Townsend Harris

Harris was working hard at his letters but there were interruptions.

Monday, November 24, 1856. The Goyosho people came to inform me that my cook and tailor went to the apothecaries' shops in Shimoda yesterday, and asked for opium, and were told they had none; but, the Chinese characters being on the drawers, they discovered it and demanded it in my name and with a show of violence. They took the whole they found in two shops, which was all the opium there was in Shimoda.

Superintendent Wakiya's assistant, Kikuna, was charged with "miscellaneous affairs" relating to the Americans. This opium business unfortunately fell into that category, and Kikuna girded for a visit to Gyokusenji. He took an aide, an interpreter (Tateishi Tokujuro), and two censors (for he was not of high enough rank to visit the American without witnesses).

He arrived before ten in the morning, and perhaps because of the early hour (he preferred to think it was that rather than his rank) it was Heusken who received him. Kikuna was determined to be reasonable, and all he asked was that at least half of the opium be returned for use in treating the sick. Heusken excused himself to inform the Consul General.

I gave orders that the whole should be taken from them [the Chinese]. *Mr. Heusken got a lump of some six ounces from the tailor, but the cook had dissolved his in water to refine it in the Chinese way, so as to make it fit for smoking, and refused to give it up. I went to him myself; he was very surly, and after some time brought me a dish containing a small quantity of sediment and water. I demanded the filtered liquid, and it was not until I had given him his choice between a prison and the surrender of the drug that he gave it up.*

When Heusken returned, Kikuna learned with relief that he had the Consul General on his side. Heusken delivered the lump and displayed the solution, and then threw away the latter.

The sale of opium, the young man said, was prohibited in the United States. Addiction to the stuff was a vicious habit, most difficult to cure. Mr. Harris requested that the Japanese forbid the sale of opium—and sake and other intoxicants as well—to his Chinese servants.

Kikuna agreed with alacrity, and added that he hoped the servants would be warned against causing trouble in the shops. What did Mr. Heusken propose regarding the opium which had been dissolved and thrown away?

"If you tell us the cost," Heusken answered, "we will have the Chinese pay for it." And by eleven o'clock Kikuna was on his way back to the Goyosho with a pleasant feeling of accomplishment and a markedly higher opinion of the American official.

But this could not be the end of the matter for Harris. The tailor had been a troublemaker from the beginning. Hired at Hong Kong on the fifth of July for fourteen dollars a month, he had begun intruding into Harris's journal as soon as departure for Japan became imminent.

Wednesday, August 6, 1856. . . . My tailor has been gambling, lost all his money, and now impudently demands one month's wages. I, having already advanced him three months, refused. Soon afterwards he sent the butler to inform me that he had not only lost his money, but had pawned all his clothes and even his sleeping mat and blanket, and asked for five dollars to redeem them. I again refused, but will take them out of pawn to-morrow and keep them until I get him on board ship.

Saturday, August 9, 1856. . . . My tailor has absconded—sent to every gambling place and other disreputable place, but he cannot be found.

Sunday, August 10, 1856. . . . Called on the security of my tailor for the forty-two dollars I had advanced him,—when he went out and in twenty minutes brought the man to me tied hand and foot. I ordered him to be sent on board and wrote to Captain Bell, requesting him to receive the tailor and not permit him to leave the ship without my permission.

Monday, August 11, 1856. The tailor did not go on board yesterday. Had him sought for again and at last got him on board.

To charge him three dollars for absence at Macao and one dollar for the same reason at Hong Kong.

And only two days after taking up residence at Gyokusenji—

Saturday, September 6, 1856. . . . My tailor is proving to be a desperate character. He will not work and says he does not care how much I cut his wages. He is the first Chinese I ever saw who was indifferent on this point.

I gave him a serious lecture. Told him if he expected to eat that he must work; that I had the power of putting him in jail and causing him to be fed on very spare diet, and also might order him to be whipped every day; that I would give him until Monday to reflect which he would take,—work, wages and good food,—or prison, hunger and whipping.

Now, with the cook, he had forcibly seized opium. And while this morning it was the cook who had been more obstreperous, Harris no doubt believed that the tailor was the ringleader. Anyway, the tailor was dispensable and the cook was not. Harris made up his mind to ask Captain Possiet—whom he was now calling Commodore—to carry the offender back to China.

Matsuzaki (*a painting by Ryusai*)

He may have mentioned the subject when Possiet called next day to tell about the long walk he had taken last Friday, across the peninsula to its west coast and the village of Matsuzaki. The captain was retracing a road he had walked two years earlier; Heda, where the Russians had built their schooner, was on the west coast, farther up the peninsula, and the officers had traveled frequently between Heda and Shimoda.

He speaks in such high terms of the beauty of the road that I shall take the same walk, as soon as the Russians leave here. (Harris knew he was neglecting his exercise.) Further, Possiet had stayed in Matsuzaki all night, which made the trip an adventure, doubly exhilarating because the Japanese immediately protested. Harris thoroughly approved the captain's reply: *that he would give orders to his officers that if any of them went to a greater distance than seven ri, then they must not sleep there, but that, within the distance of seven ri, he claimed the right for himself and all other Russians to sleep on shore as often as it suited their convenience.*

To-day finish a letter of fifteen sheets to my friend General Wetmore (a letter which has not survived).

The next day his letter-writing caught up with him.

Wednesday, November 26, 1856. I have taken a violent cold; have pains in my head, bones; and some little fever. Take some Brandreth's pills, and diet.

I do not give up to it, but employ myself in writing letters to go by the Olivuzza.

On this same date he reported a visit from Moriyama, who wanted to make sure the Consul General did not think the Governors had forgotten about getting him a horse. *Three horses have been offered, but none suits the Japanese; one is too old and clumsy, one too young and vicious, the third is too ill-looking for me. The Governor is a good judge of a horse and has promised to select one that will suit. He says he is responsible for my personal safety to both the American and Japanese Governments, and if I should be killed by a vicious horse, he would have to perform the hara-kiri.*

And he also recorded an encounter which Heusken must have reported to him: *Commodore Possiet and Mr. Heusken took a walk southwest from Shimoda, and were followed by a Gobanyosi* [a police official from the Goyosho]. *The Commodore, in a decided and stern manner, ordered him to go about his business and not to follow him; and the man left them. But soon afterwards he reappeared and pertinaciously kept with them. The Commodore then seized the man and gave him a thorough shaking, and when he was released, the Gobanyosi started off running like a deer and no more appeared.*

There is not much doubt from the tone in which Harris set this down that he approved of Possiet's action. Foreigners were always irritated when they were followed on their walks. Yet Possiet's action was a bad example to Heusken, and Harris's approval made it worse. The young man was impressionable.

Three days later the cold seemed to have run its course. Harris wrote that he had *quite recovered* and he sent Possiet some of his books on Japan.

He was, of course, still occupied with his letters, *of which I have five to write to the State Department, and one of them explaining my action in trying to get to Edo is of necessity a long one.*

It was a long one because he had not been instructed to go to the capital. That was his own idea and he had to justify it.

In China, as Harris very well knew, one of the great struggles was over the Western powers' insistence on their right to send envoys to Peking and to negotiate there, rather than with commissioners at the treaty ports. Washington, London, and Paris were sensitive to this issue. Envoys like John Bowring and Peter Parker were embroiled in it. Bowring had told Harris that when he came to Japan he would parley at no place but Edo. Harris knew that it would be a triumph for himself and the United States if he got there first. He also knew that the President and the Secretary of State considered him a Consul General whose post was Shimoda. They had been angered by reports that in Paris he had "strutted about" like an "Envoy Extraordinary and Minister Plenipotentiary," and he had to allay any suspicions that he was again becoming, to use Marcy's word, "topheavy."

He began by assuring Secretary Marcy that relations between the Japanese and himself had steadily grown friendlier, and that this had enabled him "to learn some interesting facts" (the kind of thing John Bowring called "political pabulum").

In all of this we can detect the tutoring of his "old friend," Moriyama Einosuke. Moriyama was the only Japanese in Shimoda who was permitted to talk alone with Harris—he was the only one who could, who spoke enough English. No doubt Moriyama liked to exercise his English, though having been trained in a rigid bureaucracy he was a little uneasy about the freedom he was being granted. But the Governors—Inoue especially—knew their man and were content to let him talk. And so it was gossipy, ebullient, sharp-witted Moriyama, probably the one Japanese who really enjoyed talking to Harris, who took upon himself the task of teaching this often difficult American something about Japan.

He had early discovered, Harris told the Secretary, that "the people" were eager that their country be opened to foreigners; then he had learned

that the officials entertained similar opinions; . . . but matters of more importance subsequently came to my knowledge. I was informed that a large, influential, and increasing Party in favor of changing the old policy of the country existed in Edo, and that even some members of the Regency or Council of State were members of it. The importance of this last statement will better appear when it is considered that the Emperors, as foreigners term the Mikado * and Shogun, are mere cyphers; "they reign but do not govern," the whole power of the state being absorbed by a hereditary council, which enacts, amends, or repeals laws at pleasure.

This was a highly colored description of the harassed Council in Edo which was seeking so desperately for solvency and some acceptable course for the nation, but it was like Moriyama to romanticize his superiors.

Harris went on to cite evidence of an awakening Japan—the Kimizawa ships, the steamers ordered from Holland, the Dutch instructors at Nagasaki:

> It is clearly the object of the Japanese . . . to resume the place they occupied in the early part of the sixteenth century as bold and skillful mariners and navigators. In familiar conversation with the officials, I have playfully proposed that they should go in one of the American ships and visit the United States, that they might see the country, its agriculture, manufactures, cities, ships, steamers, railways, &c &c, to which they invariably reply, "The time will soon come when we will build ships like yours, and then we can visit the United States in a proper manner."

Everything he had learned, he continued, induced him to believe that the time had come to open negotiations for a new treaty, and therefore on the twenty-fifth of October he had sent a letter to the Minister of Foreign Affairs proposing broad discussions. And he outlined to Marcy the strategy of the campaign he intended to conduct.

Once he got to Edo, he explained, he could recite the advantages of "free intercourse" and point out to the Japanese government that they could not hope to "long remain on their present footing."

> I shall, of course, enlarge on the benefits that must enure to the government and people from Japan taking a place among the commercial nations of the world, and the vast encouragement it would give to the skill and industry of the masses in Japan. The easy mode of raising a revenue from customs duties will, as I think, have much weight with the government.

But most important, "I shall fully explain to them the intentions of the English government . . ." John Bowring, unsolicited, had given him permission "to communicate to the Japanese Government all that he had said to me"—that he would come with a fleet larger than Perry's and that he

* The Emperor, in Kyoto.

would accept nothing short of the complete opening of Japan to the English and their commerce, "concluding by saying that Japan should be brought into the great family of commercial nations peaceably or forcibly, at her own choosing."

Sir John's demands would not be moderate, but if he found on his arrival that a treaty opening Japan to foreign trade had been made, if the Japanese could say, "We have opened our country to the Americans and you shall have the same terms as have satisfied them," then he might well be induced to accept those terms.

> I shall call their attention to the fact that by making a treaty with me they would save the point of honor that must arise from their apparently yielding to the force that backs the plenipotentiary and not to the justice of his demands. I shall particularly urge on them another consideration: supposing hostilities ensue, the English would seize on the island of Jesso [Hokkaido], which they no doubt covet, for with that island in their possession they could effectually watch the movements of the Russians, whose establishments at the Amur River and in the island of Sakhalin have aroused their suspicions that Russia intends striking a blow at China, adding that the discovery of coals near Hakodate immensely enhances the importance and value of the island in a naval point of view.

This was to be Harris's case and campaign. And if it seems based less on the "justice of his demands" than on the presumed villainy of the British, it must be remembered that Harris's faith in that justice was just as strong as his faith in British villainy.

He did not want Secretary Marcy to think that in going off to Edo he would neglect his consular duties, for "Should any American vessels arrive at Shimoda during my absence at Edo, I shall immediately return to attend to their business."

To all this optimism, to all this confidence of a treaty soon, Harris added a small reservation: "I should not under any circumstances expect an early reply to my letter, and I feel quite assured that I shall not receive one until after the departure of the Russian corvette."

But word was on the way. As he was drafting these lines, a courier was on the highway, bearing an order from the Great Council to the Governors of Shimoda. Enclosed with it was a translation of Harris's letter, the one that he had said did not concern the Governors.

In the Japanese way, the Great Council's order was brief:

TO THE GOVERNORS OF SHIMODA:

We received a translation of the American official's letter. In it we could see his wish to come up to Edo and talk directly to the Great Council. But to talk with the Governors is to talk with the government. If he talks to the Great Council over the heads of the Governors, the stationing of the Governors will be meaningless. Since the Governors should deal with any problem, we will not answer his letter. After studying the letter thoroughly and after careful consideration, explain to him that you are entrusted with all problems and that he should talk with you frankly.

At Shimoda, winter was beginning to close in. On November 27 a ship from Owari on its way to Edo was swept by great waves, became water-logged, and took shelter in the harbor. On the last day of the month a ship from Totomi was wrecked in the offing. Its crew was rescued by another ship and brought to Shimoda. The usual investigation was ordered in each case.

Chapter 6

DECEMBER, 1856

Kosuke could not be called a pillar of the community. His was not one of the old patriarchal families who controlled shrine and village affairs, but he had his place in Kakisaki and he was respected for the way he filled it.

Like most of his neighbors he was half farmer and half fisherman. He grew rice on a small paddy field about a mile from his house, and vegetables on another little plot, higher in the hills and without irrigation. He was one of the crew of Zenemon's boat, which went to sea after bonito in the summertime, and on dragnet days he and his wife and his widowed mother helped to handle Zenemon's net; if luck was with them they carried home a nice mess of sardines.

He lived close to the beach below Gyokusenji, in a house that was small but new. He took no pleasure in its newness. He had liked the old house, where he and his father and his grandfather had been born, but it had been smashed two years earlier by the tidal wave. To pay for the new house he had had to borrow from Heiemon, pledging his paddy land as security. It would not be easy to repay that loan, and if he lost the rice field his family's cherished independence would be lost, and they would sink to the level of day laborers. The new house threatened him. It jeopardized his place in the community. He could not feel comfortable in it.

The chief of his neighborhood group knew this, and Yoheiji knew it, and both of them knew that Kosuke was a quiet, steady man and not a troublemaker. Because of all this they selected him, and because of his worrisome debt he accepted. On the fourth day of the Eleventh Month of the Year of the Dragon he went to work for the foreigners at Gyokusenji. By Harris's calendar it was the first day of the twelfth month.

Monday, December 1, 1856. Engage another servant, Kooski. His duty will be to scrub floors, sweep the compound, bring coals and do all the coarse heavy work about the house; is to come at sunrise, eat his food (which he is to furnish himself) here, and leave after sunset; wages 400 seni per diem.

Harris was not being overcharged. He was paying the prevailing rate for common labor around Shimoda. But four hundred copper coins a day, coming regularly, would make it possible for Kosuke to repay his debt to Heiemon. He would have to give up his place in Zenemon's boat, and his wife and mother would have to carry the full burden of the farming, but working together they would manage.

The astonishing thing is that Kosuke was added to the staff at Gyoku-senji with so little fuss. Harris's journal contains no blow-by-blow account of battles to get him, no malediction on officials determined to thwart a reasonable request. It makes one suspect that all the negotiations were handled by Heusken. Of course, a precedent had been established when Sukezo and Takizo were hired, and since they were young they were no doubt eager to testify that they were overworked. But after the battle to put those two on the payroll, the casual way that Kosuke is announced is startling.

It must be pointed out, however, that at this point the journal has been bowdlerized. While the manuscript was still in the possession of the Harris family, his niece, Miss Bessie A. Harris, a self-appointed editor with all the wrong instincts, made a copy, perhaps with a view to publication. "In her copy," wrote Dr. Mario E. Cosenza, who later prepared the original for publication, "Miss Harris did not hesitate to correct words misspelled in the original, to change 'would' to 'should,' etc., to recast entire sentences, and to delete remarks that were somewhat too uncomplimentary or that, in her opinion, were for various reasons to be suppressed!"

Unfortunately, Miss Harris went further. She cut from the original one entire page, which ran from mid-passage in the entry for November 29 to mid-passage in the entry for December 1, and then pasted in a new page bearing her own much briefer text. The quotation above, therefore, is not from the original journal but from Miss Harris's revision. We have no way of knowing what she deleted. It may have related to the hiring of Kosuke. It may have concerned something entirely different. Whatever it was about, Miss Harris judged it offensive and it is lost.

Having appeared in the journal, Kosuke will now disappear. Like Sukezo and Takizo, he will sink into anonymity; Harris will discuss the foibles of his canaries, but not of his Japanese servants.

No matter how little attention was paid to Kosuke as he worked daily

Three villagers: a young woman, an old woman,
and a boy (*a drawing by Aleksandr Mozhaiskii*)

around the temple or in the garden, he was a link between Harris and the people of Kakisaki. On the rare occasions he could be persuaded to talk, he was a source of fascinating information concerning the foreigners, though his neighbors never believed him when he told them that the old man took a *cold* bath every morning.

Some of the villagers were still frightened by foreigners. A few still practiced safeguards which had been general when the place was overrun by brawling, drunken sailors from Perry's or Putiatin's expeditions: a family so cautious slept in the loft of their house, a place intended only for storage, and they pulled up the ladder after them. Kosuke convinced most of his neighbors that there was no reason to be afraid.

His eight-year-old daughter, Asa, was even more persuasive. After Kosuke began to feel at ease around Gyokusenji, he sometimes took his daughter there with him. Harris always had been susceptible to little girls, and though his conversations with Asa were limited, he conquered her shyness with rock candy, patted her on the head, gave her little presents. Sometimes he gave Kosuke a handful of candy to take home to his family or to the children of the neighborhood. It came, Asa always announced, from "the kind old uncle." Townsend Harris had made it again.

Kosuke gave Harris one more reason to be concerned about the rate of exchange. At the old rate, a dollar equal to one silver *bu,* the new servant's four hundred copper coins a day would be equal to twenty-five cents a day or more than ninety dollars a year; at the rate Harris wanted, a dollar equal to three silver *bu,* Kosuke would cost only eight and one third cents a day, a bit over thirty dollars a year.

Harris considered it vital that the Russians join him in taking a firm stand on this issue. He and Possiet kept each other informed. Only a couple of days earlier, before going off to confer with the Japanese, Possiet had sent a hasty note asking Harris if he had held any recent talks with the Japanese on this subject. Harris replied that he had not, assuring the captain that he would share any information concerning his negotiations "at all times and with perfect frankness . . . for I consider my knowledge of all transactions in Japan as belonging to the whole of the civilized world." He added: "I am quite recovered from my cold."

By this first day of December either that cold had taken a turn for the worse or he had acquired a new one, but despite it he went out to the corvette. As a gift to the officers he took three bottles of oil from India; he had discovered that the Russians were *using common Japanese oil for table purposes.* Perhaps he intended to discuss the currency problem; if so, he had no chance: *am soon interrupted by a lot of Japanese officials who come to see the Commodore on the subject of boat landings. Commodore Perry's Additional Articles provided that certain landing places should be provided at Shimoda and Hakodate, and the Japanese now wish to confine us to landing at these places alone. I resist the propositions, as does the Commodore.*

Perhaps because of his cold, Harris retreated to Gyokusenji while Possiet and the Japanese were still arguing. But he told his boatmen to wait, and sent them back to the ship with a packet of letters which he had forgotten to take with him, letters of introduction for the Russians to present to his friends in China.

My dear Mrs. Drinker,

This will be presented to you by Commodore Possiet of the Imperial Russian Navy, who will visit Macao on his way back to Russia.

Commodore Possiet has seen more of the Japanese than many men of the present day, and he can give you a lively description of my residence, the country and people, their manners, customs, etc.

I know that you need no urging to induce you to be attentive and kind to all strangers of respectability who visit China, yet I beg to bespeak your particular attention to Commodore Possiet and his officers, and I am sure you will cause them to remember their visit to Macao with the greatest pleasure.

Commodore Possiet speaks English with great fluency, which will render your intercourse still more agreeable.

There was another letter for Possiet to present to Patrick Stewart in Macao, and similar letters for Rimsky-Korsacoff. The latter acknowledged them at once, explaining that Captain Possiet was occupied, "as the Japanese still continue their assault," and speaking for them both, thanked Harris for his "affability" and "readiness to oblige us." This last was a reference to a different matter: the Russians were running short of cash. Several days earlier Harris had written that *Captain Korsacoff visited me. Wants me to cash some bills for them. This I cannot do, but offer to lend him $1,000 to be returned at Hong Kong on the corvette's reaching that place, to my agents Armstrong & Lawrence.*

This was the second sizable loan he had made since arriving in Japan. He had lent Purser Bradford of the *San Jacinto* $1000 before that ship sailed.

It seems curious that both ships needed loans. One would like to believe that both American and Russian naval officers were sufficiently bright to anticipate their normal requirements of cash. Probably the emergencies arose because the men of both the *San Jacinto* and the *Olivuzza* drew unusually large amounts against their salaries in order to buy souvenirs at the bazaar. The conclusion is that the merchants of Shimoda were doing very well.

The loan to the Russians would leave Harris with not much cash on hand. But he must have believed that what he had left would last until the arrival of the ship which Commodore Armstrong had promised for next spring. That ship would surely bring repayment of both loans.

When the Japanese officials, having concluded their "assault" on Captain Possiet, returned to their offices, some at the Goyosho and some at

Naka compound, they learned that a directive concerning Harris had been received from the Great Council. The Governors and their chief lieutenants were now studying the order and the enclosed translation of Harris's letter. Their reactions were varied: indignation that Harris had gone over their heads; gratification that the matter had been returned for them to handle; disappointment that the Great Council had furnished no guidelines for dealing with the man and, in particular, had not even mentioned the thorny question of currency conversion, despite the Governors' several pleas for a quick decision. There was agreement on one thing: that Harris would be angered to learn how his letter had been handled. No one volunteered to rush over to Gyokusenji with the news.

Elsewhere on this busy first of December, there was one more item of importance: in Shimoda town and all the villages nearby, headmen received their tax bills.

There were no surprises. Yoheiji, opening his with the customary formality, knew in advance that it would call for forty-four *koku*, seven *to*, eight *sho*, and nine *go* of rice, or about 229 bushels.* He also knew that it would call for the usual amounts of cash, equivalent to several dollars: gold and silver coins, wrapped in fine paper, most of which were earmarked for repair of roads, bridges, and riverbanks, and for upkeep of the Emperor's palace in Kyoto. There were also a few silver coins, separately wrapped, to make up for any rice that might be lost or eaten by rats before it reached the storehouses in Edo: the Shogun was entitled to his full share.

It was not an exorbitant share, and Yoheiji knew how very fortunate his village was to pay its taxes directly into the Shogun's coffers. For that he could thank the fact that Shimoda was a Shogunate port, and that therefore the town and the surrounding villages had been kept under the Shogunate's direct control.

Elsewhere, much of Izu had been parceled out to the Shogun's retainers, men like Inoue and Okada, Kawaji and Iwase. These men were not landed barons. They were the Shogun's own men, his personal staff, the soldiers and administrators who manned his government. The rice from the land they were allotted constituted their salaries.

Generations ago these salaries had been adequate, though not much more than that, for the first Shogun had believed that one could not buy a man's loyalty, and had also attributed great virtue to austerity. But since that time there had been crucial changes in the economy. Now the rice which was a samurai's income was cheap and everything he had to buy was

---

* A *koku* is about 5.12 bushels. There are ten *to* in a *koku*, ten *sho* in a *to*, and ten *go* in a *sho*.

dear. Many of the Shogun's men were desperately poor, helplessly in debt to the merchants they despised. The retainers of the daimyo were in the same fix. Most of the daimyo and the Shogun himself were insolvent.

Edo never ceased to wrestle the problem, but never solved it. Its best brains groped for answers. Just about this time, for example, one of its staff, an old gentleman who had held a variety of important posts, was preparing another of his verbose memorandums to the Great Council. He began, of course, by lamenting his incompetence, "but to maintain silence in an attempt to hide one's own shortcomings is a great disloyalty" and so he begged to offer his "foolish views."

He reviewed the tribulations. There had been droughts, earthquakes, and storms which not only reduced the crops but compelled great expenditures for relief; both the Shogun's castle and the Emperor's palace had been ravaged by fire and had to be rebuilt; worst of all, the foreign threat demanded that vast sums be spent to build up the nation's defenses. Not only the government but the daimyo were hard-pressed.

But as always, he went on, it was the lower ranks of samurai who felt the greatest distress. In some cases their stipends had been cut by their harassed lords. Many led a hand-to-mouth existence, in want of food and clothing. Under the circumstances it was impossible for them to carry out their duties. How could they attend military drill or lectures at the academy when they could not afford the clothes to be presentable or the extra cost of lunches away from home, lanterns for travel in the darkness of early morning or nightfall, umbrellas or raincoats for bad weather? How could a man maintain martial spirit when he was so beset? How could his loyalty not be strained?

Only the merchant classes flourished—in the streets of Edo they seemed to flaunt their prosperity—but there were few merchants who would grant more loans to samurai. And so in the realms of both the Shogun and the daimyo, many retainers who held tenures of land were exacting extra taxes from their farmers, leading to bitterness and anger and sometimes to violence and revolt.

"It is indeed," this old man was writing, "a time of sore trouble." He offered a remedy, another manipulation of the already debased currency. His scheme was not tried. It would not have helped.

In the meantime, a town like Shimoda and a village like Kakisaki were lucky, and they knew it. At Matsuzaki, just across the peninsula, there was a depressing illustration of what the old man was talking about. The Shogun's man to whom these lands were allotted was squeezed for money, and in turn he squeezed his farmers. He demanded advance payment of taxes. In order to pay, the farmers were forced to borrow. There was a local merchant, a dealer in liquor and charcoal, who was ready to lend if he was given a mortgage on the land. Few of the farmers could repay their loans. Most of them lost their lands to the merchant. The farmers around Matsuzaki were angry and bitter.

Yoheiji knew that situation and he knew how fortunate Kakisaki was to pay its taxes directly to the government. The Shogunate was as hopelessly bankrupt as its retainer at Matsuzaki, but far from calling for taxes in advance, it had postponed collections in the Shimoda area for the year of the tidal wave and for the grim year that followed. Payment for both years had been made only this past May.

Yoheiji had set it down in his diary: "Today we carried our tax rice to the warehouse in Hongo village, mobilizing our village labor for the service."

There had been two stacks, the usual forty-four *koku* for year before last and forty for last year, which had brought such a poor harvest that the government had cut ten per cent off the taxes. Together there had been eighty-four bales of rice, bagged in woven straw and trussed with rice straw rope. Most of the able-bodied men of the village had helped transport it. Doubtless there had been some showing off. A man who could handle a bale by himself could attract an audience of small boys any day.

Among the many achievements of the Tokugawa regime, one approaches the magnitude of a miracle, and governments today might well look into it: somehow the payment of taxes was made into a festive occasion.

For one thing, that ugly little word "tax" was avoided. The rice brought to the lord's warehouse was an "offering." It was good rice, no broken kernels. There was pride at stake, for every bale carried a wooden tag showing what village had delivered it, and the names of the headman, the inspector, and the measurer.

As an offering it was handled with respect. It was almost sacred. It was unthinkable to sit on a bag of the Shogun's rice. Around fishing towns like Shimoda, where people often had racks of fish out drying in the sun (a handy way to preserve them but naturally smelly and a magnet to flies), no such thing was permitted along the streets the Shogun's rice would travel. And when the rice reached the warehouse, the matters of delivery, inspection, and acceptance were handled with grave ceremony.

Last May, when the men of Kakisaki had deposited their rice at the collection point, Goyosho officials had picked at random three bales from each of the two years' payments. Yoheiji had recorded with pride that each bale had been found to contain more than the required amount. Kakisaki could not be accused of slighting the Shogun's interests.

The same could not be said for the villages of Hongo and Okagata, Yoheiji implied, for when their payments for year before last had been examined, the bales were found short. In this mortifying situation they could only request permission to take that year's bales home again, check them all, and bring them back the next day. Their request had been granted.

With all of Kakisaki's officials standing witness, the village's rice had been placed in the warehouse, and then the whole party, functionaries and laborers together, had moved to a nearby inn to take "the lunch time rest." The tab had been paid from the village treasury. The austere magistrate for Izu might label this outrageous and issue stern orders against it but he could not stop it. It was part of the day's ceremony.

The government had moved swiftly to convert some of its rice to cash. In the afternoon it had auctioned two hundred *koku* to local merchants. The men of Kakisaki had had the satisfaction of seeing their rice bring a good price. They had gone home with the glow of men who have performed worthily.

Not that the ceremonies were finished. Two days later Yoheiji had paid courtesy calls on the two Goyosho officials who had accepted the rice for the government, and also had dropped in on the headmen of Hongo and Okagata, who had been responsible for the warehousing. Both headmen had treated him with sake. He had not alluded to the unfortunate shortages in their payments.

Two weeks later Yoheiji and Chuemon had joined a pair of officials from each of the other villages and together they had called at the quarters of the Governor's chief lieutenants. They had not gone in, of course, but at the entry hall they had expressed their gratitude to the officers for having accepted their taxes.

A couple of days later Yoheiji had taken advantage of one more opportunity to compliment the officials who had overseen the delivery, and then at last he was able to feel that those particular taxes had been properly paid. The only thing lacking was a receipt; on such matters the government moved slowly, but one could be expected within a year or so.

Now, on this first of December, Yoheiji received the tax bill for the current year and the whole business was to begin again. He anticipated no problems.

The second of December found Harris still writing letters. He was interrupted by a visit from the man he called "the Third Governor," Superintendent Wakiya Usaburo, who was saddled with much of the responsibility for Gyokusenji. Wakiya, though certain his luck had run out when he was put on this job, was doing his best to keep the American content.

His visit is on the important subject of the oil furnished for my lamps . . . on some days we have a capital article sent; then will follow some that will not burn for two hours. Told . . . [him] it was wanted for my lamps and not for eating.

He promises a full supply of what I want now [that] they fully understand my wishes. I told the Governor that it was high time the jetty or boat landing of Kakisaki was repaired; that it was destroyed on the 22nd of September, more than seventy days ago, that all the materials for its repair were still there, and that it was a great neglect to leave it so long. He promised it should be immediately attended to.

In order to have a clear understanding about the orders I give, I have procured a book in which I write every order, and there are columns left in which to enter the name of the interpreter to whom the order was given, with the date of it, and another column for the date at which it was executed. By this means I shall know whether my orders have been given by Mr. Heusken, or forgotten by him, and also whether the interpreter neglects them after he has received them. So far it works to a charm, and I have had more done in the last two days than in the previous fortnight.

This record book is evidence of a situation that had been building for some time. Harris and Heusken were getting on each other's nerves.

Harris's irritation with his young secretary and interpreter becomes more evident the next day. Recording that the cold he had "quite recovered from" on Saturday had come back with a vengeance on Sunday, he draws a picture of two men under lamplight in a little paper-walled room, sitting out the long evenings with resentment smoldering between them like the fire in their balky Philadelphia stove.

Still occupied with my letters.

I have had a very bad cold and sore throat for the last four days. This arises from the habit Mr. Heusken has of never putting any fuel on the fire. During the day I attend to the fire myself and it is well kept up, but in the evening I get busy, and, as Mr. Heusken is on the side of the fire, I neglect it; and, being made with charcoal, it soon goes out, and with our paper windows and loose joints of the house, it soon becomes like sitting out of doors. I believe that Mr. Heusken only remembers when to eat, drink, and sleep,—any other affairs rest very lightly on his memory. Busy to-day in writing letters.

There is nothing like a cold to make a man feel abused. It was easy for Harris to forget his neglect of exercise and his overindulgence at table with the Russians while he dwelled on Heusken's negligence.

Colds were going around in Kakisaki. The priest's records show that on this day Tokugoro died in his house near Gyokusenji, and that three days later death took Tomokichi of the farmers' hamlet on the hill behind the temple. There is no word of this in Harris's journal, but on two days in quick succession the somber ceremony of burial took place outside his paper doors.

There in his chilly temple, funeral sounds in the air, beset by sore throat and nasal congestion, it would be surprising if Harris did not take the view that Heusken was spending too much time with the Russian officers. Heusken himself writes: "I spent many a happy day with them in the cabin." He was also sightseeing, shopping, and perhaps wenching with them, for surely the Japanese made available some entertainment less formal than banquets at the Goyosho. At the very least, Heusken must have joined the Russians in some bath-watching.

Harris may also have been irritated by Heusken's growing intimacy with the Japanese. In the course of his work, Heusken was with the Japanese much more than Harris was. He was learning more of their language and was slipping into an easier relationship with them. And their talks together must occasionally have strayed from business. In any very lengthy conversation with, for example, a man like Saito, whose duties involved real estate and whose hobby was philandering, the subject of women was bound to come up. This was a matter uppermost in Heusken's mind, too, since he was at that age when the itch is strongest. Had junior officials like Saito perhaps begun to invite him to some of their parties at Shimoda restaurants? Harris would not have been pleased.

Even if these guesses are wide of the mark, it is clear that the relationship between Harris and Heusken was becoming strained. The tension between them was likely to increase after the Russians left them alone.

And the Russians' stay was drawing to a close. Exchange of ratifications with the Japanese was to take place on the coming Sunday, December 7, and after that there would be little reason for Possiet to linger.

The Russian commander invited Harris to assist at the ceremonies.

I much regret that I cannot attend. I am suffering from a severe cold and great hoarseness; but the most important reason is that I cannot con-

sistently "assist" in any such matter on a Sunday. From the time of my arrival I have refused to attend to any kind of business on that day, and after a short time the Japanese ceased to ask it of me. Should I now join the Russians, I shall contradict all my previous acts on this account, and lose my character for consistency*, a point that cannot be too carefully watched in dealing with people like the Japanese. They delight to convict a man of inconsistency.*

As it turned out, he was too ill to attend.

Sunday, December 7, 1856. About eight last night we had several distant, but very heavy claps of thunder with some vivid lightning, which preceded violent squalls from the west, and heavy rain succeeded, which continued through the night. The barometer fell from 30.50 to 29.72. (Harris may not have noticed the omens of this storm, but weather-wise Japanese sailors had, and all day Saturday little coastal freighters had scudded into the harbor. Among them was a ship from Edo carrying condemned criminals to exile on the Izu islands; here in port they would be tantalized by the nearness of the shore and thoughts of escape.) *About the same time I had a violent exacerbation of bile; severe vomiting for two hours, and purging which lasted all night.*

Sunday—*a bright clear morning, with a true old-fashioned American northwester, blowing a gale*—found dozens of Japanese ships in the anchorages of the bay, clustered like courtiers around the big Russian corvette. It was as though they had come to help solemnize the ratification.

With the wooden doors of Gyokusenji's west wall closed, though rattling in their grooves, Harris was able to stay warm. He was still weak and unwell, but he kept tab on the ceremonies. He noted the salutes fired as Possiet left his ship and again as ratifications were exchanged; the Russian, American, and Japanese flags flown from the *Olivuzza's* three masts; the transfer of the *Diana's* guns. *The guns have been neatly furbished up and a double guard of honor composed of Russians and Japanese were mounted over them. The guns were then formally presented to the Japanese.*

At this point Governors Inoue and Okada were embarrassed. They had no gifts to present in return. Some nest of bureaucrats in Edo had pondered the matter and had decided that something of a martial nature was in order. In return, then, for fifty-two cannon, they selected one suit of armor lacquered with flecks of gold, along with a bookcase lacquered in gold, an inkstone in a case lacquered in gold, a vase, and twenty rolls of silk. Unfortunately, the Great Council advised, these gifts could not be made ready in time. The Governors were reduced to handing Captain Possiet a list of the gifts he might expect to receive when next he called at Shimoda.

The captain thanked them and invited them to the *Olivuzza, where they received a salute and a dinner,* and thus the ceremonies were completed.

The next day Harris was diverted by a visit from Wakiya and Moriyama. *After kind messages and inquiries on behalf of the Governors, they said they had been ordered to inform me of the exchange of ratifications, etc., etc. Moriyama was quite communicative and oracular; said that a great change was impending in Japanese affairs (as it relates to foreign intercourse), and that it would surprise all, when it took place, from its suddenness, etc., etc.*

This was encouraging, but pending that great day there were a few details to be arranged. Harris worked at one of these the following morning, the day appointed for Possiet to settle his accounts with the Japanese.

Tuesday, December 9, 1856. Up at seven A.M. to go on board the corvette to see the Commodore before he meets the Japanese to-day on the subject of the currency. I got him to agree that he would refuse to pay, except on the basis I had named,—viz., one dollar to pass for three ichibus; that he would pay that amount to them; and, if they were dissatisfied, he would place the difference in my hands (until the arrival of a Russian Consul) to await the final settlement of the question. I am much pleased with this, as it will greatly strengthen my demands for the adjustment of the question.

This is not exactly as he reported it to Secretary of State Marcy. Apparently he did not want the Secretary to think that he was twisting any arms, Russian or Japanese, and so he gave the impression that Possiet had taken a firm stand without any urging from him. "Believing the action of the Russians to be just," he wrote, "and calculated to aid in bringing the question to a more speedy settlement, I consented to receive the trust . . ."

Since his optimistic earlier reports had forecast a settlement before this, it may have surprised Marcy to learn that the matter was still under consideration:

> The Japanese excuse this delay by saying that in Japan all things must be most deliberately considered, and that they must not be expected to act with the same promptitude as is looked for in Western governments.
>
> I feel called upon to exercise all possible patience towards them, in consideration of the anomalous position they have occupied for more than two centuries.

Am told the corvette will leave on Friday next, and am invited to dine with them for the last time on Thursday next. . . . The Commodore is anxious to get away, as this strong northwester, which still blows, causes the ship to drag, and she is so situated that she cannot "cut and run." The strong northwester kept the harbor full: the little Japanese ships were waiting it out.

Harris had a fat packet of letters to finish up. One was addressed to America's great pioneer in meteorology and oceanography, Lieutenant Matthew Fontaine Maury, at the Hydrographical Bureau in Washington, outlining the weather observations he had made at Shimoda and begging more instruments and instructions.

Another, to Captain Bell of the *San Jacinto,* sent news of recent developments and ended with praise of the Russian officers, which altered Bell's opinions not a bit. When Bell had a chance to reply he made clear what he thought, expressing the views of most of the Navy, including Commodore Perry. He was certain that the Russians, eager to extend their influence in Asia, would support the Chinese in their expanding war with the British, and he feared the consequences:

> It is dreadful to contemplate the extension of Russian influence in opposition to the free and enlightened sway of the British; the one gloomy, dark, and inscrutable, treads its certain pace with an iron heel; the other, free, enlightened, and commercial, spreading her wings to the breezes and the vivifying rays of the sun, invites social intercourse and interchange, making glad the hearts of men with trade, traffick, abundance, and increased happiness.
>
> It has been said, and is generally believed, that Russian despotism and American democracy are to be the two great contending principles in the world; and the two seem to be marching onward to their goal as if unconscious of the approaching shock of arms: Russia towards India and China, and America with the speed of the iron horse in the same direction on to the shores of the Pacific. The one with the tread of conscious power; the other with the dash and speed of enthusiasm directed by genius and courage. Where and when will the conflict be?

Harris, knowing nothing of the war in China, also had a long and chatty letter for Sir John Bowring, closing as follows:

> The Japanese are quite anxious to know when you will come here, and what are your intentions, whether you will go to Nagasaki, or come to Shimoda, etc., etc. I have declined giving them any satisfaction on this point, telling them that what I had to say would only be communicated to the Minister of Foreign Affairs at Edo. A short time since, I wrote to the Minister that . . . I had concluded to proceed to Edo. . . .

Knowing their dire anxiety on your account, and availing myself of your kind permission to repeat to the Japanese what you said to me at Hong Kong, I wrote to the Minister that I was fully informed of your intentions and that I would communicate them to him in person when I should see him in Edo.

Throughout my letter, I put my visit on my undoubted right and did not for a moment ask any permission from the Japanese. Time will show in what light they will regard this.

When you come to Japan I hope you will run in to Shimoda; it will not detain you six hours. I need not say how happy I shall be to see you, nor that I will communicate to you in the fullest manner any and all information I may possess.

By now Harris had three letters addressed to his Hong Kong agents, Armstrong & Lawrence, with some news and several instructions. As in most of his other letters he gave a glowing report of the climate: "The weather here is truly delightful. . . . the barometer is always high, producing a fine stimulus to the nervous system." He added a prophecy which in later years would come true: "From what I have seen of this climate, I think it the true sanitarium for all Europeans who have become deranged in health by too long a residence in the tropics."

He ordered more supplies, including a rain gauge, champagne, sherry, and a list of seasonings, written in Chinese by Assam:

May I beg of you to strongly enjoin your comprador not to send any opium or other intoxicating drug to any of my servants. I have had much trouble on this point, and have been compelled to send away my tailor by the Russian corvette for his incorrigible misconduct on this and similar points. I pray you to pardon this trouble but you can hardly conceive its importance to me.

The third of his letters to Armstrong & Lawrence concerned repayment of his loan to the Russians.

I have advanced to Captain Korsacoff of the Russian corvette *Olivuzza* the sum of one thousand dollars. This sum is to be paid into your hands for me in unchopped Mexican dollars.

I shall be obliged to you if you will have the coin carefully examined to see that it is according to the description noted.

Please have this sum carefully sealed up in a bag by itself, so that it may not be mixed with any other coin, and transmit it to me by the first safe opportunity.

On Wednesday, Harris sent aboard a double coop containing two pairs of pet fowls, a gift to Mrs. Patrick Stewart of Macao, with feed and gravel and a note to Captain Korsacoff thanking him for his "kind offer to take this troublesome present."

Sometime during the night the four-day gale fell off to a gentle breeze and Gyokusenji's shutters stopped their rattling. When Harris rose on Thursday morning the Japanese ships were filing out of the harbor. Among the first to leave was the one bound for the outlying islands. Its cargo of condemned men was still intact.

The weather is the most lovely ever seen at this season of the year in a similar latitude. The sky is as blue as a sapphire, and a light air from the west raises the thermometer to 53°. . . .

My black pet hen commenced to incubate on the 9th inst., therefore I shall look for some chicks from her about New Year's Day.

Fine as the day was, Harris found a way to improve it. *Send my tailor on board the Russian corvette. He had the impudence to ask me to give him a good character! Who can ever hope to fathom the want of moral principle in a Chinese?*

With the tailor went another note to Rimsky-Korsacoff.

My dear Captain Korsacoff,

With this note my rascally tailor will come on board your ship. He brings with him ample food for 25 days, as well as his bed, therefore all he will need on board your ship will simply be fire and water. I have supplied him with his requisite cooking pot. I would recommend you to search his boxes before he lands at Macao. Although he is deeply in my debt, yet I have given him $3, which will be ample to support him at Macao for one month, and also to pay his passage to Hong Kong or to Canton, at both of which places he has relations.

I pray you to keep him at work. He will plead sea-sickness, but that will be untrue, as he never is seasick.

I cannot sufficiently thank you for your kindness in relieving me from this *domestic pest.*

Believe me dear Captain Korsacoff

Yours most sincerely
Townsend Harris

P.S. I send by my boy Skezo your washclothes. I hope the clothes of yourself and Commodore Possiet have always been properly returned to you.

The Russians' departure was delayed a day, and the farewell dinner on board the corvette was held on Friday, the twelfth. *After dinner see the process of lacquering performed on some boxes of Commodore Possiet.*

There was a final flurry as the Japanese added up their accounts. For provisions, the use of boats in the harbor, and pilot services they submitted a bill totaling 4,732,199 copper coins.

Possiet wrote to Harris that he was paying this according to his and Harris's evaluation of the ruble and the dollar, giving the Japanese one third of the silver they considered themselves entitled to. The other two thirds, about $1835, would be paid to Armstrong & Lawrence for credit to Harris's account at Hong Kong.

Saturday, December 13, 1856. Go on board the corvette to see her off, but the wind being so unfavorable she could not get out of the harbor. Not feeling well, I bid adieu to all and go on shore.

Next morning the Japanese mobilized dozens of fishing boats from Shimoda and Kakisaki, and the wind having shifted, they were able to tow the *Olivuzza* out of the harbor. She set sail and soon passed from sight.

She left a sick man at Gyokusenji. *I am quite ill. I find my complaint to be "Saint Anthony's Fire." Face and forehead much swollen, and burning hot and itching.*

Saint Anthony's fire is erysipelas, an infectious disease of the skin and subcutaneous tissues which can be severe, even fatal. Since Harris was able to make a diagnosis, it seems likely he had suffered the same affliction before. In Siam he had suffered a painful attack of boils. All this suggests a predisposition to skin infection. Harris would have benefited more from the hot springs he had visited at Rendaiji village than from the Spartan cold baths he was so proud of taking.

It is difficult to say whether Harris or Heusken was sorrier to see the Russians leave. Neither was delighted to be left in the company of the other.

Harris felt all the more alone because he was ill. While the Russians had been here, the ship's doctor was at hand; Possiet had offered his services. Harris does not indicate that he consulted him, but at least he was available.

Heusken felt himself marooned with a cranky, sick old man. He must have been eager to escape from the temple whenever he could, but the more he was away the more Harris resented it. Heusken was writing very little in his journal these months, but he noted the Russians' departure with "most sincere regrets."

It is doubtful that Yoheiji, on the other side of the village, was at all sorry to see the last of the *Olivuzza*. Her sailing meant less work and less worry. With the Russians gone, he turned his attention to an order from the

Goyosho that the villages were to pick up their allotments of Dutch sweet potato plants. Potatoes were not new in Japan. Perry had brought some as a gift, thinking what a pleasant change from rice the Japanese would find them. He found instead that the Japanese were quite familiar with potatoes, and not enthusiastic about them. When they called them "Dutch" they meant "foreign," and when they labeled them "foreign" they meant they would rather eat something else. But since the government was insistent, the plants would be set out and tended, and eventually someone would eat potatoes. Yoheiji hoped it would not be he.

At the Goyosho and at Naka compound, there may have been those who were sorry to see the Russians leave, sensing that now Harris would become more difficult. A nervous letter had already gone off from the Governors to the Great Council, dispatched on Saturday, when they expected the *Olivuzza* to sail.

> During the Ninth Month we asked for your instructions concerning the conversion rates for foreign gold and silver, and we also asked for permission to give Japanese money to the American official. As yet we have received no answer.
>
> He has pressed us for a reply to these requests, and when we sent an executive officer to see him recently, he asked about them again. He complains that three months have passed without an answer, and that all his requests encounter delays.
>
> The Russian ship will leave port today. We intend to open negotiations with the American as instructed by your most recent letter, but it will be impossible to negotiate with him without giving him an answer to these two questions, because when he is dissatisfied he will never listen to what we have to say. This is a common attitude among foreigners.
>
> So please give your directions on these two issues.

The Japanese sound like men bracing for trouble. They got it.

On Thursday, December 18, five days after the Russians sailed, Executive Officer Wakana appeared at Gyokusenji on a courtesy visit to inquire about the Consul General's illness. He learned that recovery was slow (*Have drenched myself with purgative medicines,* Harris wrote on this date, *but my complaint is but little relieved*). He also learned that sickness did not improve the American's disposition. He received a volley of complaints and demands.

I demanded the immediate removal of the people who have been in my compound from the day of my arrival. . . . I complained that the shopkeepers of Shimoda would not sell anything to my people or even give the prices. I added that I had before complained of this and had been promised redress, but things went on just as they did before. I also demanded ten silver ichibus to make presents to my Japanese servants on Christmas Day according to the custom of the country. (Evidently he was including his boatmen, though he did not pay their wages.)

The executive officer bowed himself out, promising to take action concerning the complaint and to confer with the Governors concerning the demands. Harris probably felt a little better for having vented his anger.

Wakana went back to the Goyosho to work on drafting another letter for the Governors to send to the Great Council. Harris still had not been informed that his letter to the government had been returned to Shimoda. Quite clearly, no one relished the prospect of telling him. The Shimoda staff felt they were being put on the spot, and there was no agreement on how to escape it. As the letter was finally dispatched, four or five days later, it read like the product of several dissonant conferences.

It reflected the bruised feelings left by Harris's attempt to deal directly with the Great Council: "It means a disregard for our position and dignity." It reveals little confidence: "We know it will be very difficult for us to persuade him to tell us the matters which he wished to tell the government directly." It indicates only one new approach:

> Considering his letter and his firm attitude, we think it will be useless to conduct negotiations as we have been doing. So at the next meeting only the two of us will attend. Many of our officials have been attending the past meetings, for we considered that he was not an ordinary foreigner and that he must be treated with the utmost politeness and respect. But this treatment seems to irritate him, and at the latest meeting he complained about our sending an executive officer in our place.

It was a long and inconclusive letter and it told the Great Council nothing new. It ended with a weak query as to whether the Governors should carry out the order previously given them to press negotiations at Shimoda—a query amounting to a request for reconsideration.

It took Lord Hotta very little time to answer this letter when it reached him. He dictated a brief endorsement: "You may follow my former order."

In the meantime, one day at Gyokusenji was somewhat brighter than the others. *Saturday, December 20, 1856. At last my horse has arrived. It is not a high mettled racer, but will answer my purpose.* The problem now was for Harris to get well enough to ride.

He calculated that the horse cost him twenty-six dollars, while the

Straw horseshoes *(a print by Hiroshige)*

saddle and bridle, *real curiosities*, cost forty-two dollars, *or about 60 per cent. more than the horse!* With another exclamation point implied, he wrote that the horse was *shod with straw sandals, which last about an hour on the road.*

The animal was stabled at the government guard post at Kakisaki. *The groom . . . costs me seven ichibus per month, about one dollar [and] seventy-five cents* (a remark which indicates that Harris's illness had affected his arithmetic; at the rate of three *bu* to one dollar, which he was struggling for, seven *bu* would have been two dollars and thirty-three cents).

After the arrival of the horse, things seemed to go downhill at Gyokusenji.

Moriyama called on Christmas Eve, but though he usually brought cheer, this visit was brief and unpleasant. It was his duty to announce that Harris would not get the ten *bu* he wanted to give to his Japanese servants on Christmas. "But as your wish to tip your servants on a festival day is a thoughtful one, we ask you to tell them the amount that you are giving them, and we will pay them the money."

This set off a wrangle. Harris said he knew the Dutch were given money, so why not he?—he was being treated like a prisoner. And that reminded him that the guards were still posted at the temple. How long must he endure these annoyances? Why was he being treated so rudely?

To these old complaints Moriyama gave his old answers. The Japanese were inexperienced in these affairs, Shimoda was newly opened, decisions could not be made quickly. The government had ordered that the Consul General be treated respectfully, but he must realize that some matters take time.

Harris suggested that though he had no wish to force anything upon the Japanese, he thought he must consult with his government "to reconsider our method of negotiation." Then, pointing to one of Moriyama's party, he asked, "Who is this man?"

Moriyama admitted that he was a censor, and Harris announced that from now on he must refuse a censor's presence during negotiation; he had been wishing for some time to say this.

Moriyama said he could promise nothing but he would report the Consul General's words to the Governors. Harris made no reply and the interview was over. Some time passes before we learn that the Goyosho did in fact present one *bu* to each of the Japanese servants as a holiday gift from Harris.

As for the censors, it gave Harris satisfaction to write: *I have given notice that I will not allow any spies to come into my presence or even on my premises; that, when they wish to see me, I will only receive the principals and interpreters, excluding spies and secretaries. The Japanese term for spy is "a looker across."*

He was in a semantic tangle, and since this is a recurring theme, it may be well to try to unsnarl it. He was objecting to the officials called *metsuke*, whose department, as indicated earlier, constituted a kind of inspector general's branch which ran through the entire government. They were appointed openly and functioned openly. The word "spy" is not appropriate.

There was an entirely separate group of officials called *ometsuke*, who had entirely different functions. Their primary assignment was to exercise surveillance over the daimyo, who within their own realms had a great degree of independence. This was a job which necessarily required undercover agents. It may sometimes have been true, as Engelbert Kaempfer wrote in the late seventeenth century, that some of a daimyo's

> Stewards, or Chancellors, . . . attend their Princes rather as Spies than in any other capacity. For this purpose they are taken out from among the Emperor's [he meant Shogun's] own and most faithful Domesticks, and their business is to have a watchful eye over the actions and whole conduct of the Prince to whom they are sent, and to give notice to the court of Jedo of every thing that happens at their court.

The *ometsuke* thus maintained for the Shogunate a kind of external security, while the *metsuke* kept their watchful eyes on the internal functioning of the Shogun's own government.

The *metsuke* also used secret informants. As we have seen, Wakiya Usaburo may have been one of their agents at Shimoda. But a man officially designated as belonging to the *metsuke* staff, a man who, like the censor that accompanied Moriyama to Gyokusenji on Christmas Eve, sat openly as an observer of another official's conduct, could not reasonably have been considered a spy.

There could have been a secret informant for the *metsuke* in Moriyama's party that day, but if there was, Moriyama did not know it, and the censor did not know it, and Harris could not know it. Harris might exclude the censors but he could not exclude the spies.

Perhaps he believed that these grave unspeaking men constrained the negotiators, who might otherwise have been more frank or more flexible. Perhaps he was tired of being so outmanned, of confronting so many solemn-faced gentlemen of Japan at every parley. Perhaps he grudged serving refreshments to a crowd.

Thursday, December 25, 1856. Merry Christmas! How happy are those who live in lands where these joyous greetings can be exchanged! As for me, I am sick and solitary, living as one may say in a prison—a large one it is true—but still a prison. I will here note where I have been on Christmas Day for the last eight years:

Christmas, 1849, at sea in the North Pacific Ocean
* "   1850   " Manila*
* "   1851   " Pulo Penang*
* "   1852   " Singapore*
* "   1853   " Hong Kong*
* "   1854   " Calcutta*
* "   1855   " Ceylon*
* "   1856 in Japan*

The weather here is as fine as one could desire. The fields are very green with wheat which has been largely planted or "sowed," and the camellias begin to appear.

There is no doubt that Townsend Harris was sick. His severe colds, his stomach disorders, his erysipelas testify to that. When he calls himself solitary he is recording a frame of mind: Heusken has been relegated from companion to employee, and like the servants does not count; the scores of neighbors do not exist; the many officials, including his "old friend" Moriyama, are antagonists. And when he calls himself a prisoner he is merely adding evidence that he is sick.

In the summer of 1855, while he was trying to obtain this post, he had written to President Pierce: "I have a perfect knowledge of the social banishment I must endure while in Japan, and the mental isolation in which I must live, and am prepared to meet it." If he remembered those words now, after only four months in Japan, they must have seemed to mock him.

Commodore Perry, back in New York, must be credited with a fair degree of prescience, for at just this point he was writing to Harris:

> The only apprehension I have of your failure is from the *ennui* which may be produced by the isolation from European society which must necessarily be imposed upon you. You may possibly become restless and dissatisfied. This is doubtless what the Japanese would like, for though they will unquestionably perform their part of the treaty they will not for some time come fully and cheerfully into the idea that the U.S. and other powers have [not] some unfair design to take advantage of them, and it will be for you by management and tact to disabuse them of such a suspicion—in fact, I hope you will bring them rather to court than to avoid our friendship. A full share of patience will therefore enable you to accomplish all that you or the country can desire. . . . I know that you were, in part, selected for the responsible situation you now hold . . . [because of] your well known bachelor habits and love of Eastern travel, and I have great confidence in the hope that you will be satisfied

with your residence in a country into which European travelers would give their best to be admitted. Therefore patience, perseverance and firmness. . . . Please remember me very kindly to my friends amongst the Japanese and say to them that I shall never forget my agreeable intercourse with them. . . .

Unfortunately, it would be a long time before this letter reached Shimoda.

Friday, December 26, 1856. Moriyama Einosuke has gone to Edo to see about the currency question and to try to hurry a decision. . . .

When Harris was ill and distraught his journal suffered. It did in this period. He recorded Moriyama's visit as coming on the twenty-second; it occurred on the twenty-fourth. He recorded an adventure of Heusken's as of the twenty-third; it did not occur until mid-January. And now he wrote that Moriyama had already left for Edo; he (in the company of the third executive officer, Matsumura Chushiro) would not leave until the thirtieth. Discrepancies like this show that Harris did not always keep his journal current. Often he wrote it later from notes or an unreliable memory.

More accurate records were being kept by the ex-resident of Gyoku-senji, Priest Bimo. On the twenty-sixth he registered the death of another farmer of the hilltop community. For the third time this month the priest led a cortege to the temple cemetery, and Harris, behind his paper doors, listened, whether he would or not, to the chanting of the burial service. His illness, the somber mood of early winter, and the funerals around him must have deepened his mood of depression.

When Matsumura and Moriyama left in the darkness of early morning on the thirtieth, they carried with them not only Moriyama's memory of his recent unpleasant interview with Harris but a copy of a freshly dispatched letter from the Governors to the Great Council which recounted the fuss over the ten *bu*. "We doubt whether it is profitable for us to persist in our refusal," the letter said.

> We know that it is still forbidden to provide foreigners with our currency. But the daily personal expenses of the Americans are not large, and since money given them would be by conversion of their coins, we think we need not be concerned over a decrease of gold and silver in Japan. We believe that the small amount of Japanese currency needed to cover their personal expenses had better be handed to them by conversion of their currency whenever they request it. We ask your directive concerning this opinion of ours.

Wednesday, December 31, 1856. The last day of the year. How many events of great importance to me have occurred during this year! I am very low spirited from ill health and from the very slow progress I am making with the Japanese. However, I must keep up my spirits and hope for the best. My pet hen has presented me with five chicks,—the merest mites of chickens ever seen. The weather this month has been very fine. The thermometer was as follows: mean for the month, 48 9/10; highest, 69°; lowest, 36°. First white frost, December 12th. Rain on no days, showers on four days, clear twenty-seven days.

Chapter 7

七

JANUARY, 1857

January 1, 1857. Happy New Year! What a busy day in dear old New York, what universal joy appears on the faces that throng the streets,—each hurrying along to get through "his list of calls." It is a good custom and one that I hope will never be given up. How many friendships are then renewed which, without the occurrence of this day of "oblivion of neglect," would otherwise die a natural death. I pass the day in calling, in my imagination, on my friends; but, as to Japan, not a soul has darkened my door. I could only exchange greetings with Mr. Heusken, and present my Chinese servants with the expected cumshaw. . . .

Harris had ended the old year depressed. He began the new one bitter: *not a soul has darkened my door.* He wrote that he had invited the Governors to dine with him and that they had refused, *making a flimsy excuse.* It is not hard to guess why they declined his invitation. Harris was obviously unwell and certainly ill-tempered; perhaps just as important, particularly since relations were strained, was the fact that Moriyama was not available to interpret, having been sent off to Edo. The Governors always felt more at ease when they could lean on Moriyama to lubricate the conversation.

Though Harris spoke only of New York, his thoughts must also have turned to his friends in China. He craved news of them. Eventually he would get some in a long letter from Sandwith Drinker: the Drinkers had a new daughter, born in October, "the prettiest little blue-eyed thing you ever saw"; poor Mrs. Stewart was scarcely able to enjoy the pet fowls that Harris had sent her, for her health was failing fast; and so on through a catalogue of intimates and acquaintances.

Drinker would provide news, too, of Harris's new friends, the Russian officers, and of the immediate success they had scored at Macao. The *Olivuzza* needed an overhaul, but, as Drinker put it, Possiet "would not bring his vessel into Hong Kong owing to the present war with China," there being "every prospect of an outbreak or an attack on the place by the Chinese"; "he did not wish to get involved," but "had the Chinese made an attack he would have considered himself bound with the other men-of-war to assist. So he stayed out of the port." (The Russians, like the Americans, were generally foxy in China, inclined to let the British do the fighting, and then, as Drinker wrote of his own countrymen, "taking advantage without cost of the exertions of others.")

So the men of the *Olivuzza* had improvised repair facilities at an island near Macao, and Rimsky-Korsacoff had been left in charge while Possiet exercised a commander's prerogative and gave himself some shore leave, at Hong Kong no doubt.

"You have my best thanks for your kind letters and introduction of Capt. Korsacoff," Drinker would write, for through Harris's letters he had secured the Russians' business. Evidently he had given "entire satisfaction," for the captain had given him "a most handsome letter addressed to any Russian ships which might arrive hereafter" and had even announced that

> he intends to try and get me appointed Russian Consul. . . . He certainly is a noble fellow. . . .
>
> I paid a lot of money over to Armstrong & Lawrence for your account at the request of Captain Korsacoff. Lawrence handed over to me your order for sundries. . . . You shall have them at cost from us, much below our present war prices. I see you want quite a quantity of champagne. My impression is you wish it for the Japanese, not sure. I have determined to send you part a cheap article, well up and foamy and sweet, which will suit them equally well; and also some really good for your own use.

Rimsky-Korsacoff had seen much of the Drinkers. "Our steamers to and from Macao"—Drinker's firm operated three ships, the *Thistle,* the *Queen,* and the *Lilly,* which plied between Macao, Hong Kong, and Canton—"stopped every day at his vessel," and when he and his officers were in the city they lived with the Drinkers. "All his officers enjoyed themselves very much. We gave them numerous parties. Capt. Korsacoff was much with us . . . Kate was particularly pleased with him and I think he liked her much. What a perfect gentleman he is."

There must have been parties especially at New Year's, dancing on New Year's Eve, dinners and calls upon friends the next day. No doubt spirits were somewhat subdued by the fact that only two days earlier

Drinker's steamer *Thistle* had been captured between Canton and Hong Kong by Chinese, who beheaded the eleven Europeans on board. But the sense of danger added a flush of excitement. Against the background of war, young people danced and flirted, friends traded greetings and hopefully toasted a better year to come—in sharp contrast to the solitary, joyless day at Gyokusenji.

It was not yet, of course, New Year's for the Japanese, but they were already into the Twelfth Month, and as the year's greatest holiday approached, the tempo of things quickened. This was a time to settle affairs, to pay debts, to clean house, to put things right for a fresh start—and then, with farm work at a midwinter standstill, to take time out for the only extensive holidays of the year.

The first installment of tax rice from the new crop had to be paid. As soon as it was delivered from the villages, the Goyosho auctioned off seven hundred bales to realize cash. It also sent out orders that village headmen should report to receive the rice due them as a perquisite of office (Yoheiji brought home more than three bushels), as well as the wage rice for the *ashigaru* (like Takizo and Sukezo) appointed from their villages.

These were routine affairs for the closing month of any Japanese year. In Edo greater events were in progress. The Shogun was to be married.

In a matter of such importance to the state, the wishes of the principals were of little concern. In some quarters it was considered doubtful that the Shogun had any. Opinions of him vary according to the political stripe of the writer, but if he was not daft as well as impotent, he certainly was not robust in mind or body. The bride was not consulted. Probably she never expected to be.

For the wife of a Shogun she had a most unusual family background. She came from the family of one of the Outside Lords, from one of those fiefs who had fought against Ieyasu, the first Shogun, when he was wresting control of the country. Ieyasu had branded those lords "not to be trusted" and had excluded them from any place in his government. Two and a half centuries later they were still so branded and so excluded.

The bride was from the Shimazu family of Satsuma. There was no doubt that the Shimazu were a great family, powerful and respected. Its head was on the best of terms with the Shogunate. Still he was an Outside Lord. It had taken considerable doing to make this girl the future wife of the Shogun. It had been accomplished because she was part of a plan.

The head of the Shimazu was Nariakira, a name distressingly close to Nariaki when trying to keep this cast of characters straight in one's mind.

Lord Shimazu Nariakira was in fact allied with Lords Tokugawa Nariaki
and Matsudaira Yoshinaga and Abe in the scheme to make Nariaki's son
Keiki the heir of the present Shogun, who, married or not, was unlikely to
produce a son. It was Nariakira's idea that the bride-to-be, once she was the
Shogun's wife, could help influence him to adopt Keiki.

Lord Shimazu Nariakira (*a photograph taken
by a retainer at Nariakira's direction because of
his interest in photography*)

The plan hinged on a series of adoptions. In the first place, the bride
was not Nariakira's daughter but was from a lesser branch of the Shimazu
family. When Nariakira had conceived his plan he had adopted her to
increase her importance (she had already been betrothed but that engagement was broken). Then he had sent her up to his mansion in Edo, to be
more conveniently at hand. That had been three years ago.

First the marriage had been delayed by the fire which destroyed the
Imperial palace in Kyoto, and then by the earthquake in Edo, catastrophes
which precluded an immediate marriage of state. And in addition there had
been fierce opposition to the Shogun's marrying a Shimazu, so that finally

Lord Tokugawa Keiki *(a drawing by Artillery Captain Brunet, French Army)*

Lord Abe had advised Nariakira that the only way to arrange things would be to have the girl adopted into another family. Earlier this year she had become the daughter of Konoe, one of the ancient Kyoto nobility and the Emperor's Minister of the Right. At last it was possible to announce the engagement.

It had taken one more maneuver to make the whole plan feasible. As a son of Nariaki, Keiki was ineligible to become Shogun. Some say that the first Shogun, on his deathbed, had directed that the Mito house should be forever excluded from succession; this is difficult to prove or disprove (though it is quite in character). At any rate, there was a firm tradition that the lords of Mito could not provide an heir but should instead act as advisors. To get around this, Lord Abe managed to have Keiki appointed head of a branch house of the Tokugawa which *was* eligible to provide a Shogun if the direct line failed.

Finally the stage was set. And why had all this been done? It was because Abe and Nariaki and Yoshinaga and Nariakira were leaders of a group who believed that the Shogunate must be reconstructed, "reformed" as they put it. The old distinction between Inside Lords, who were permitted to hold office, and Outside Lords, who were excluded, must be abolished. If Japan was to survive the crises she now faced—a domestic economy close to collapse and a foreign threat to her very existence—then, these men earnestly believed, the Tokugawa Shogunate must share its power and authority with all the daimyo. Keiki, an able young man of twenty, held the same view. With him as Shogun, such a reconstruction of the government could be pushed through.

It is true that Lord Abe had cracked the old system when, faced with Commodore Perry's demands, he solicited the opinions of all the daimyo, not just the Inside Lords. Abe had been attacked for that, but that act was minor compared to the reconstruction now envisaged.

Of course, such a scheme engendered bitter opposition.

There were first of all the Inside Lords—Ii Naosuke, for example—who would lose their monopoly of power. They would cease to be the sole custodians of the government.

On the other flank there were certain Outside Lords who had for two and a half centuries nurtured their hatred of the Tokugawa. Unlike Nariakira, a moderate and reasonable man who was trying to promote reform, not revolution, they wanted to see the Shogunate not reconstructed but destroyed.

Yet, curiously, now that all the roadblocks to the marriage had been removed, the man baying most loudly against it was Nariaki, whose son it was designed to make Shogun. He could not suppress his feelings as a Tokugawa. It was truly shameless, he said, to make a daughter of the "enemy" the wife of the Shogun, and to force the Shogun's mother and the other women of the castle, daughters of the Tokugawa's hereditary retainers, to bow before her.

His objections were disregarded, as they so frequently were these days. The Emperor in Kyoto had given his ritual approval of the marriage, and at that point the young lady, who had borne the artless name of Sumiko, became the Princess Atsu. Last month the daimyo had been informed of the approaching marriage, with the word that in view of the national emergency, the ceremonies would not be elaborate. And Princess Atsu had already entered the castle. She had moved from Nariakira's mansion along a route where traffic was stopped and each lord put out emblems of respect. Injunctions to simplicity notwithstanding, Nariakira had made it a spectacular procession—with a seemingly endless train of porters bearing, in chest after chest after chest, an enormous wardrobe and the costliest of furnishings for her apartment.

On January 6 the betrothal took place. Lord Abe was in charge and it was he who delivered to the princess the Shogun's gifts of seven wadded silk kimono, seven obi sashes, and ten scroll paintings, in addition to the ceremonial fish and sake. After which the Shogun personally thanked him and gave him the customary gift of abalone and dried sea-ear, and all the officials on duty at the castle and all the women of the Shogun's inner court were served food and sake.

The marriage took place on January 13 (the eighteenth day of the Twelfth Month to the Japanese). Food and sake again were served to those at the castle, and everybody of any rank was received in audience. The next day—after, one hopes, the Shogun had summoned up the energy to consummate the marriage—gifts were delivered to the Konoe as the bride's family: seven chests of rich fabrics and five hundred and eighty rice cakes. Two days later the daimyo were invited to a program of felicitous Noh plays and dances.

Now the Shogun had a bride, if he was interested, and the bride was being initiated into a new life. Now she was surrounded by the implacable females of the Shogun's private court—his mother, the women who had reared him, the dozens of girls available to him as concubines. They knew why she was there and they were determined to keep her from succeeding: if it were necessary to adopt an heir, he should be a manageable child and not a grown man with radical ideas of change. To show Atsu where she stood, they had all her ornate furniture taken away. It was too ostentatious, they said. It looked like an attempt to overshadow the Shogun.

In the excitement of the Shogun's marriage it would be easy to overlook a lesser event. On January 11 foreign affairs specialist Iwase was promoted. He was raised to the same rank as men like Inoue and Okada, with whom he had conferred at Shimoda. He was given the right of audience with the Shogun. He was given a title: Iga-no-kami, the Lord of Iga. It was an example of one of the reforms advocated by Abe and Nariaki and their group: promoting men of ability regardless of the station to which they had been born.

While Iwase was celebrating his promotion, while Princess Atsu was settling into imprisonment behind the stone walls of Edo Castle, the man who thought of himself as a prisoner at Shimoda was ill in his temple.

He knew that he was ill. He brooded over it and imagined the worst. On January 3 he had appointed Heusken his vice-consul so that there would be someone to carry on if he could not.

Harris tells us often enough during this month that he is ill. If other evidence were needed, the state of his journal provides it. In chronology it is a shambles, as a comparison with Japanese sources shows.

On January 6 he had met with the Governors at his request. He tells us nothing of this meeting, but we have the Japanese record.

He complained again that the boat landing at Kakisaki had not yet been repaired, and the Governors told him that winter was a most unsuitable time for such work and that it would be done in early spring.

He complained that he had received no answer concerning currency conversion. It was such a simple matter, he said, that the Governors should have been able to give him an immediate answer, yet he had already waited four months.

It might seem a simple matter to him, the Governors answered, but to their government it was a complex one and any decision would have wide-ranging effects. They could not give a quick answer.

Harris said he was sure he would get a quick answer if he had some battleships to back him up.

Not so, said the Governors, but because they knew he was in a hurry they had sent Executive Officer Matsumura and Moriyama to Edo to press for a decision. They hoped for an answer in the near future.

And, finally, Harris announced that he had some secret information he wanted to give directly to the ministers in Edo. He would write a letter, and he asked the Governors to arrange for its speedy delivery.

Since they were discussing secret matters, the Governors dismissed all their attendants but the interpreter. Harris remarked that he hoped all future meetings could be conducted in such privacy. Regulations prohibited that, the Governors replied, but on important and secret matters they would talk alone.

When, Harris wanted to know, was he going to get an answer to his last letter to the government (the one announcing his intention of going to Edo).

This was a question the Governors had been dreading. The answer had been in their office for more than a month while they waited for a good moment to break the news. This did not look like that moment. But they did not lie. They had something to tell him on that topic, they said, but they wanted to wait until Moriyama was back from Edo, for he was their best interpreter and they wanted no possibility of misunderstanding.

Harris repeated that he wanted quick delivery of the new letter he was about to write.

They would arrange it, they told him, but he must understand that they were stationed in Shimoda to handle all matters. Even if he wrote to Edo, the subject would be referred back to them, and he could not expect an answer direct from Edo.

Harris must have realized then that this was essentially what he was to be told when Moriyama returned, and his temper flared. The information he had for their government could not possibly be discussed in Shimoda, he said. If the Governors' dignity and importance were so negligible that they could not on their own decide so trifling a matter as currency conversion, he certainly could not discuss with them a grave matter affecting the future of Japan. He was a high official of the United States, and he must be answered directly by their government.

They, too, were high officials, the Governors replied, and he needn't expect to make progress by slighting them.

And on that congenial note the meeting ended.

Back at Gyokusenji, feeling miserable, bundled up next to his Philadelphia stove, Harris drafted another letter to Edo. It might have made him feel better to know that in Hong Kong on that same day he was being elected a corresponding member of the China Branch of the Royal Asiatic Society. His certificate of membership was signed by its president, John Bowring, who no doubt had proposed him. Harris's latest letter, carried on the *Olivuzza,* was fresh in Sir John's mind. He had just answered it, assuring Harris that he hoped to come to Japan during this present year, adding that the large fleet on its way to deal with the Chinese "may perhaps prepare the way for placing our relations with Japan on a satisfactory foundation." This was a passage Harris would have loved to quote: it might have caused some tremors in Edo, but the letter was still lying in Hong Kong, awaiting a ship bound for Shimoda.

This calm, confident letter to Harris and the business-as-usual proceedings of the Royal Asiatic Society were indications of John Bowring's energy and optimism. In point of fact, the war with the Chinese was not going well.

The capture of the *Thistle* and the massacre of its passengers were not the only reverses. Two weeks earlier the Chinese had retaliated against the British attacks on Canton by burning much of the European quarter of the city—homes, offices, and warehouses. Most of the residents had already left, but a nephew of Sir John's, whom he had made consular assistant at Canton, lost his life. Samuel Wells Williams was away, but all his household goods and printing equipment, including the valuable Chinese type, were destroyed. He doubted that the mission board would ever provide the money to replace it, and he finally decided to accept the position as secretary and interpreter to the American Legation. Earlier he had written: "I wait for God to direct me, and cannot doubt his wisdom." Now God seemed to have directed.

Judging that there was not much left at Canton to protect, Commodore Armstrong had pulled his ships back: first to Canton's deep-water port of Whampoa, and then all the way to Hong Kong. What followed, and the wrath of the American merchants, was summed up in Sandwith Drinker's letter to Harris:

> . . . old Armstrong, after getting us involved, abandoned Whampoa against the strong protest of all the Americans. . . . The English Admiral had only one frigate to spare to protect the Whampoa docks, and this, with Armstrong's ships, would have preserved all those fine docks until the Admiral could get a larger force out. . . . The Admiral could not risk his one frigate and was obliged to leave also; immediately after leaving, every thing was destroyed. Armstrong is an old fool. He did well in giving the Chinese fits at the Barrier,* but having got us involved he was bound to protect Whampoa, as you well know the large amount of American property that was always there. . . . All Whampoa docks are destroyed. . . . the Chinese burnt everything up. Endicott lost $180,000 clear. . . . You never saw such desolation, both there and at Canton. Armstrong has very much failed since you saw him, and he should be at home and [a] younger man in his place. Bell and all the other officers of the fleet are completely disgusted. . . . we must have a better man than old Armstrong here, his day has gone by.

There was fear that the Chinese might attack Hong Kong itself, and a week after Sir John wrote his letter they did, in a completely unexpected way. An attempt was made to poison the entire foreign population of the colony by mixing arsenic in the one bakery's bread. Fortunately for the community, the poisoners were overzealous: they put in a dose so large that

* That is, in destroying the Barrier Forts along the river.

it caused vomiting and saved the victims' lives. But many were severely ill. "I suffered much, lost most of my fingernails," wrote Drinker, and Lady Bowring's death the following year was due to aftereffects.

But Harris knew none of this as he sat in his chilly temple by his smoky stove, drafting his letter to the "Minister of Foreign Affairs."

He opened with another lesson in etiquette, chastising the Japanese for the verbal answer offered to his letter of October 25, and the implied slight to the President and himself. "Courtesy and politeness both require that a letter comprising such important matters should be answered by the person to whom it was addressed."

Then he went on:

> Japan is at this moment threatened with great calamities; these calamities are close at hand; they threaten equally her national honor and the welfare of her people. They do not emanate from the United States but from other governments.
>
> I am convinced in my own mind that I can point out to Your Excellency a safe and honorable remedy against these threatened evils, which will not only save the honor of Japan but greatly promote the prosperity and the happiness of the Empire; but to make these measures of any avail, no time must be lost. It may even now be too late, but I hope with prompt action that you still may be in time. . . .
>
> I would therefore urge Your Excellency to order arrangements to be made for my visit to Edo without delay.

Heusken put it into Dutch and carried it to the Goyosho, where no doubt he chatted awhile before leaving to let Tateishi Tokujuro begin translating it into Japanese.

It would have been natural for Heusken to tarry in Shimoda, strolling the streets or looking into a bathhouse. This might have been the day he walked to the hot springs at Rendaiji and found there, as he told Harris, who was sufficiently titillated to record it in his journal, *three men, entirely naked, lying in the tank; while he was looking on, a young female some fourteen years of age came in, coolly stripped herself to her "birthday suit" and lay down in the bath in close proximity to a young fellow of some twenty years of age.*

Harris later discussed this matter with Wakana: *I asked the Vice-Governor if this promiscuous bathing was not rather injurious to the chastity of their females. He said it sometimes did so happen. I then inquired what a man did when he married a female who was supposed to be a virgin, but on consummation he found she was not one. "Nothing," replied the Governor.*

228

"*What can he do?*" and then naïvely added, "*I was once served in that way myself, but what could I do? It was not my fault.*" Wakana was probably referring to one of his "second wives," but knowing that would scarcely have lessened the shock to the Victorian from America.

Or on this particular day, after delivering Harris's letter, Heusken might have called on one of his Shimoda acquaintances—he had made friends in town, though we don't know who they were.

Perhaps one was Kyuhachi, a playboy who found foreigners amusing. When Perry was at Shimoda, Kyuhachi had arranged at least one party for some of the officers, no doubt at the Goyosho's instigation. It is said that he called in four of Shimoda's party girls without telling them who the guests were to be; and when the Americans appeared, the girls had to be forcibly kept from fleeing. However, after a few bottles of sake the mood mellowed. The girls were able to overcome their aversion to mustached men, and were delighted when the officers repaid entertainment with entertainment by singing and dancing themselves. Surely a veteran party-giver like Kyuhachi was an acquaintance of Heusken's.

Could it have been at Kyuhachi's that the young Dutchman had the experience which Harris recorded? *Mr. Heusken reports some queer examples of Japanese manners. To-day he entered the house of a respectable Japanese, who received him quite cordially, gave him tea, etc., etc.* Conversation was a problem on such occasions, though Heusken's Japanese was improving steadily. Shimoda people, on the other hand, were always eager to learn some English, as was Heusken's host that day. *He then began to inquire the names of various things in English—parts of persons—hand—arm—eye. I should have noted that there was present the mother, wife and daughter of the man, who gathered around so as to see and hear all.*

After asking many names of things, the man opened his dress and taking his privities in his hand—in sight of all the females—asked the names of the various parts in English! Heusken gave him the information requested.

When Tateishi Tokujuro finished his translation of Harris's letter, Dr. Ito Kansai checked it and certified that he found no mistakes. Then the Governors and their chief advisors studied it and prepared a letter of transmittal to the Great Council.

Though Harris's etiquette lesson would perhaps make some impression in Edo, it was lost on the Governors. This letter, they wrote, was little different from the earlier one he had written. The negotiations with Harris that they had been directed to pursue had been delayed, they explained,

first by Harris's illness and then by the emergency requiring that Matsumura and Moriyama be sent to Edo: it was difficult to parley without
Moriyama. (This was a rather neat way of saying that the delay was the
Great Council's fault, for the emergency had followed from the Council's
failure to issue the instructions which the Governors had requested so
many times.) As soon as Moriyama returned, they would persuade Harris
to tell all at Shimoda, "explaining that our law requires this."

While many of the events which Harris misdates in his journal can be
correctly dated from Japanese records, it is not so easy to plot his fever
chart.

There seems no way of knowing when it was he was cheerful enough
to write about flowers and wheat fields—

*There is a fine show of a bulbous flower around my house. It has but
little scent, is of a pale yellow, and is, as I think, a species of jonquil. It
gives a cheerful look to everything. The camellias are increasing in number
and the wheat fields are as green as emeralds.*

—or when he was so depressed that he could only write: *Ill, ill, ill. I
have cured the "Saint Anthony's Fire," but I am constantly wasting away in
flesh.*

*I have a relax that takes me every four or five days, and continues
about the same time. I am most careful in my diet, but all is of no avail.*

There seems no way of knowing for certain when it was that he was
exercising within Gyokusenji's compound, *walking from five to six miles
every day,* tramping back and forth in front of the temple, between the
Russian graves on the hillock past his servants' quarters and the parishioners' cemetery spread on the hill beyond and above his bedroom and office.

Or what day was he venturesome enough to hike to "Vandalia Point,"
toward Suzaki village along the path that followed the high spine of the
little peninsula that enveloped Shimoda harbor? It was too much for him:
*climbing the steep hills knocks me up. I have no wind. I must continue my
exercise in the compound.*

He did not know what was wrong with him: *My liver acts well, and
what it is that ails me I cannot say. I left Penang on the 2nd of April last,
and am now forty pounds lighter than I then was.*

He could see nothing wrong with his diet: *We are well supplied with
wild boars' hams, some venison, plenty of fine golden pheasants, and large
and good hares.* Whatever ailed him, meat could not cure.

Though Harris talks much about his illnesses, it is impossible today to
make a sure diagnosis.

He may have had intestinal parasites acquired during his years in the

Orient. Most Westerners who lived in that area then did pick up such infestations at one time or another.

It seems almost certain that he had peptic ulcers. The mental strain he suffered from isolation and fear of failure, his constant complaints of "acid indigestion," a later occasion when he vomited fresh blood, and despite all this his ability to continue work and strenuous exercise, all point to ulcers. His diet, as he describes it at this point, was not helping him. He wanted milk but could not get it. He ate heavily of meat, and no doubt his Chinese cook leaned heavily on oil and his skillets.

Another question must probably remain unanswered: Did he, in these black days, sometimes turn to alcohol as he had in New York? Many years later Sukezo testified that though his master normally drank little or nothing, he would sometimes go on a solitary binge, retiring to his room and draining one bottle after another. If he did, he only aggravated his tormented stomach.

But if, like Harris himself, we cannot make a diagnosis, we at least know how he felt. This entry, which appears in his journal under the date of January 18 but which might belong to almost any other day of the month, is the despairing cry of a man who is losing his grip.

First snow seen on the hilltops. I cannot sleep nor can I study. I have laid aside the Japanese entirely, my reading is unsatisfactory; I have a craving for something I cannot define.

Harris's health and state of mind must have distressed Heusken, now vice-consul. No doubt he tried to be helpful, but he must have worried about eventualities: What if Harris should die, or lose his mind? There is nothing of this in the young man's journal—indeed the month of January is a blank; it is too discreet a record, for Heusken, like Harris, was writing to be read.

As far as Harris's disposition is concerned, the Japanese could have drawn an accurate chart of that. He began the month bad-tempered and became progressively more difficult.

Wakana called at the temple on January 12 to talk about the year-end settlement of accounts. He ran into a hornet's nest. This day the Consul General was not only sick and lonely but frightened. On the day before, Heusken had taken a walk *alone and unarmed. On the road he met a Japanese wearing a coat-of-arms on his sleeve. As soon as he saw Mr. Heusken, he flourished a long stick he had in a threatening manner and then drew his sword, which was also flourished. Mr. Heusken at first halted and then, being unarmed, turned back. [I] directed him never to go out unarmed again.*

Wakana got the story in a rush, and was taken by surprise. It was, he said, the first he had heard of it. The man could not, he thought, be from this area. He must have been a traveler, either mad or a scoundrel.

Such an incident, stormed Harris, arose from "your prejudice and hatred against foreigners. We cannot relax even among the villagers here. We will carry weapons whenever we go out for walks in the future."

Wakana must have been alarmed. It was the kind of occurrence the Governors' men lived in dread of. He tried to be reassuring, but he granted it might be a good idea for Harris and Heusken to carry a gun when going out alone.

The Governors' police certainly launched an investigation as soon as Wakana reported, but as far as we know they never found the assailant. It seems doubtful that it was a *ronin* who had slipped through the guardposts, because Harris described the man to Wakana as wearing one short sword; a samurai would have carried both a long and a short sword.

The encounter took place near Tachino village, a little upriver from Naka village and the Governors' compound. Some of the villagers there had their own ideas of what happened. According to them, Heusken habitually visited their public bath in the afternoon, when the village women gathered there. Some of the girls were so annoyed that they changed their time for bathing. But one young woman who particularly attracted Heusken held to her regular bath hour, flaunting her curves before Heusken as though she enjoyed teasing him. Perhaps she did, but she also reported what was going on to her lover, who happened to be the local gambling boss. It was he who decided to frighten Heusken out of his afternoon visits—the villagers were sure of it, but they were not about to inform against a gangster.

When Wakana managed, that morning at Gyokusenji, to open the subject he had come to discuss, he ran into more trouble. He had not come to collect from Harris, for that was in abeyance until the conversion rate was settled, but he wanted Harris to know that it was the custom to settle all accounts at year-end, and that the Goyosho would be paying those merchants who had furnished supplies to the consulate.

Harris announced that he was convinced his bills were padded. Wakana stoutly denied that the prices charged Harris were higher than those to anyone else, avoiding an outright lie: the prices generally were the same—it was the special tax that raised Harris's bills. Harris said he was going to investigate.

How about the wages for Takizo and Sukezo, Wakana asked, for this question was still unsettled. What did Harris intend to pay them?

What did the Japanese officials pay their servants?

There were many grades of servants, Wakana answered. These young men were not like ordinary sailors or handymen; they were personal servants to an official of high position, and therefore had to dress formally and wear a sword; they had been selected on that basis.

Harris said he thought one *ryo* (about $1.35) a month was enough.

How much did Harris pay his Chinese servants?

That situation was entirely different, said Harris. They had reluctantly left their homes and families in China, and they spoke English.

Takizo and Sukezo had also been persuaded to serve him against their will, Wakana replied, and they could not be satisfied with the pay of ordinary servants. They ought to receive three or four *ryo* a month.

Quite impossible, said Harris; they would talk about it later. Changing the subject, he wanted to know why the peddlers of fish and vegetables never called at Gyokusenji. Had they been forbidden to sell to him?

They had not, Wakana answered, reminding Harris that when he moved in he had announced that no one could enter the consulate precincts without his permission, and on that basis peddlers had been told to stay away. They could be a nuisance, and Wakana advised that they be kept out.

No, he wanted them to call, said Harris, and his people would deal with them directly; he wanted no interference from Japanese officials. Which reminded him that he had repeatedly requested that the guards be removed. What about that?

They were there to protect Harris, the executive officer said, a matter which greatly concerned the Governors.

Harris didn't think they offered much protection. They seemed to sleep all night and were hardly prepared for an emergency. Anyway, burglars couldn't come very often, while the "thief of high prices" seemed to rob him every day.

This angered Wakana. He would not permit such a remark, he said. Was it misinterpreted?

It was a joke, said Harris lamely and he apologized.

One more thing, said Wakana. He had heard that Heusken wished to make an excursion to Mount Amagi and to stay there overnight. That was impossible. If he could not walk back the same day, the officials would hire a *kago* to carry him home.

That set off a wrangle about the seven-*ri* limit established by Perry's agreement. Like the matter of the two boys' wages, it could not be resolved and was put off to another day. The mutually unsatisfactory meeting ended. It would be surprising if Wakana did not go back to his office seething inwardly, and no doubt he left Harris in a temper.

Four days later, on the sixteenth, Wakana was back. Since he brought with him a *kachi-metsuke,* an official in charge of *ashigaru* like Takizo and Sukezo, he probably meant to discuss the boys' wages.

He was given no chance. The *kachi-metsuke* was refused admittance. Moreover, Harris insisted that the interpreters sit on the floor. They sat on the floor at the Goyosho, said Harris, yet at Gyokusenji they insolently took chairs. He would no longer permit it.

There was a significant difference between the tatami floor at the Goyosho and that at Gyokusenji. At the Goyosho no one walked on the mats in footgear which had been worn outside (save, of course, Harris and Heusken in their occasional visits, and one may believe the floor was meticulously cleaned after they left). At Gyokusenji, Harris, Heusken, and probably the Chinese wore the same shoes indoors and out. Gyokusenji's floor was, in Japanese eyes, a dirty floor.

Wakana protested both pronouncements: he could not accept them for the future but in order that this meeting might continue he would accede today. He might better have picked up and gone home.

He had come, Harris wrote, *to say that orders have been given to all the shopkeepers to give prices or sell anything my people may ask for. I asked when those orders were given?* *He said they had been frequently given but were specially renewed eight days ago.* He added that any difficulties must have arisen because some Shimoda merchants were unaccustomed to dealing with foreigners (he might more accurately have put it that they disliked foreigners; they also disliked waiting to collect their money from the Goyosho, but many of them would have been just as hostile if Harris's Chinese, who did almost all the buying, had entered with cash in hand; incidents like the seizure of opium left a bad taste). Wakana asked a little understanding of the situation.

He got a tirade. Harris accused him of lying, said it was clear the shopkeepers had been told not to sell to him or his people. He cited the case of Assam, who the day before had tried to buy some sweet bean-cakes, and had been refused until he went to the Goyosho and got a man to accompany him to the bakery. The Japanese were breaking the treaty, trying to drive him away.

Wakana said that if they were trying to break the treaty they would not do it over a matter of bean-cakes.

There were many other examples, Harris steamed: the unwelcome guards at the temple, the failure to permit him Japanese money, the outrage against Heusken. It was all part of a plan to drive him from Japan. After reporting his ill-treatment to Washington, he would leave as soon as possible. War would follow and it would be Japan's fault. The United States would trounce her.

The poor Vice-Governor shook in every joint, and the perspiration streamed from his forehead and that of the interpreter.

That was no doubt true, but not because, as Harris thought, Wakana was confounded and confuted. He was enraged. He had been subjected to provocation and insult far greater than any samurai would give another unless he intended to kill. His natural instinct was to slash out with his sword, but he had to sit and take it, with his interpreter watching. He sweat, and his inferior sweat for him and for himself.

Wakana's experience demanded action by the Governors. That same afternoon they sent a request that Harris meet them at the Goyosho the next morning. *Although quite ill I consented.*

Attempting to calm Harris, the Governors told him that they had that morning issued another order that shopkeepers must sell whatever he or his people wanted to buy. They thought he would not again be inconvenienced and they asked to be notified at once if he was. The people of Shimoda were temperamental, they went on. Shopkeepers sometimes gave trouble even to the Governors themselves. If he lived in Shimoda a few years, he would understand.

Harris said their explanations were puerile.

He demanded that they remove the guards from Gyokusenji. *They . . . begged me to wait until they could write to Edo . . .*

In reply I told them . . . that I would not consent to the delay of one day longer as to the guard; that more than three months had elapsed since I had requested their removal; and finally, so long as they remained, I declared I should consider myself a prisoner and would not leave the compound, and that I would write to my Government the manner in which they had treated me. The trouble of the Governors increased. Finally they told me the officers should be removed. "When?" said I. "Very soon," was the reply. "How many days?" They hesitated. I repeated firmly that, now [that] I had so strongly brought the matter up and that they had consented to the removal of the guards, every day they remained was a new outrage, and they must abide the consequences. They then said that the officers should be removed to-morrow. Knowing their duplicity, I told them the removal must be real and not nominal; they must not post them near, or even in sight of my house; that, if they made any such attempt, I should consider it as an aggravation of the wrong already done me.

They assented to the justice of my remarks and said the officers should be brought back to the Goyosho. . . .

I then inquired about the currency question and received the old reply, "Waiting for decision from Edo." I told them that it had the appearance of a determination on their part to postpone the question indefinitely. They eagerly assured me that it was their wish to close the matter as speedily as possible. . . .

As for the censors and other officials, the Governors said, they must be present at their meetings by government regulation. Harris said they could follow that regulation when they met at the Goyosho but not at his residence. Then, said the Governors, all meetings must be held at the Goyosho, and they thought that would be inconvenient for him. No, it would not, Harris answered; there would be no more meetings at the temple.

"We wanted to take exception to some of the official's remarks," the Governors reported, "but we could not, for he seemed very angry and began to shout at the *kachi-metsuke* who attended the meeting. He also by gesture refused to accept tea when the servant brought it into the room. As he had lost his temper, we concluded the meeting."

So, after four hours of stormy debate, I went home, where I was agreeably surprised to find the officers and guard packing up to leave, and, in effect, they did leave in the evening. So much for showing them a bold face.

The temple-consulate would from now on be unguarded. Takizo and Sukezo would have the barracks to themselves. There is no reason to suppose they were any happier for being left alone.

The Governors and their advisors, meanwhile, had gone into conference. Clearly, Harris was becoming violent. Reason told them that his threats of war were irrational, that his displays of temper were those of a sick man, but they did not know foreigners well enough to be confident in this judgment.

At any rate, Edo must be informed that the situation here seemed about to explode. Some decisions had to be wrested from the government, however reluctant it was to move. And the Great Council had to be told of, and persuaded to confirm, the concessions hastily granted this afternoon.

This was a large order. Executive Officer Matsumura, with Moriyama, was already in Edo, but even given all the facts, he had not the rank to get quick decisions.

One of the Governors had to go. Okada was the logical choice. He was the junior and therefore most likely to get an onerous errand. He had been longer away from Edo and his family. And pretty clearly it was he who had advocated the concessions; now let him defend them.

His party was quickly organized. A runner set out with advance notice. Reports of Wakana's meeting yesterday and the Governors' meeting today were hastily drawn up and dispatched by another runner. The Great Council would have a little time to digest the news before the Governor arrived.

The call went out for bearers for the first leg of the journey. The roster for that sort of thing having been checked, it was determined that Kakisaki should furnish four men, and Shirahama, up the coast, fifty. Possibly Okada chose to use the coastal road through Shirahama instead of the route up the middle of the peninsula and over Mount Amagi, where snow and ice would surely slow him. Certainly he intended to waste no time: the trip which normally took five or six days, he would try to do in four.

Yoheiji named the four men from his village. They were to report at Hongo village at two o'clock the next morning. They, and an elder to shepherd them, prepared to lose a night's sleep.

Harris heard about it quickly enough. *Bingo-no-kami, one of the Governors, goes to Edo to-day. I suppose in consequence of the flare-up of yesterday. I am determined to take firm ground with the Japanese. I will cordially meet any real offers of amity, but words will not do. They are the greatest liars on earth.*

Harris had been told that one reason he was selected for his post was his "knowledge of Eastern character." That knowledge was one of his greatest handicaps. The China hands of his day "knew" the "Eastern character": it was unreliable, devious, and mendacious. After five years on the China coast, Harris shared these prejudices with a vengeance. He brought them full-blown to Japan. They perverted his whole relationship with the Japanese.

The greatest liars on earth?—the compliment was undeserved.

They had said the guards were at Gyokusenji to protect Harris, and this was true. They knew it would not be difficult for some fanatic *ronin* to creep into the unguarded temple and slaughter the foreigners. (Quite apart from international relations, they worried for themselves: woe to the Governors and their staff if this American should be killed.)

They had said that Harris had no right to have Japanese money or to make purchases except through the Goyosho, and under the terms of Perry's treaty they were quite right. It was Harris, not they, who wanted to contravene the treaty.

They had said that the people of Shimoda had a wide streak of independence and perversity. This was notoriously true.

In one particular they had lied. They had told Harris the prices charged him were not padded, and they were, by the government tax. (On the same day as the stormy meeting at the Goyosho, they had sent out a circular restating the taxes, from ten per cent on daily necessities to thirty per cent on lacquerware, porcelains, and other souvenir items.) In their defense, it can be said that as yet Harris had not been asked to pay for anything he had purchased in nearly five months at Shimoda, that the Governors were doing their best to have Harris exempted from those taxes, and that they probably thought they would succeed.

But when it came to lying, Harris had a few blemishes on his own record. Most notably, he must have known perfectly well that he was bluffing and blustering and threatening war in a manner that would never have been supported by his government. It was one thing to insist that the Japanese live up to the treaty. It was quite another to demand rights and privileges which the treaty did not grant and was never intended to.

It is fortunate that he did not have the Navy at hand to back him up. And with the fleet involved as it was in China, there was little likelihood of its appearing soon.

Perhaps having stirred things up so, having had the satisfaction of seeing Okada packing off to Edo, and having rid himself of his guards, Harris relaxed a bit.

One hopes that on January 20 especially he was well enough and cheerful enough to brighten the atmosphere at Gyokusenji, and that the Chinese prepared a good dinner that day. It was Heusken's twenty-fifth birthday, though neither Harris nor Heusken mentions the fact in his journal.

As far as the people of Kakisaki were concerned, the state of Harris's health meant little. He was too aloof for them to be much aware of it.

The new servant Kosuke carried out his duties of sweeping and carrying; the boatmen sculled the Consul General across the bay when he wished. They had learned not to expect small talk from him. He did not banter with them or ask about their families. Perhaps they noticed that sometimes he did not appear well, but with foreigners it was hard to tell.

Anyway, they had other things on their minds. The old year was drawing to a close and they were busy with preparations to greet the new.

The roster for the New Year, under which officials from eighteen local villages would take their turns of duty at the Goyosho, had already been drawn up. Yoheiji had represented Kakisaki at the meeting. As always, the negotiations had been tedious, for the schedule had to be adjusted around the festivals and special days of each village, and each headman was on guard lest he and his elders be imposed on. It had been past midnight when the roster was completed.

As Wakana had told Harris, it was a time to settle accounts. Bills must be collected, debts paid. In difficult cases, a man's community might rally to aid him: Yoheiji and the elders made extraordinary efforts to help a Kakisaki farmer who was mired in debt, and when they succeeded in negotiating a settlement with his creditors, Gennosuke and Kosaburo went with him to the Goyosho to stand as witnesses to the settlement.

It was not only business that had to be cleaned up, but homes.

First came the job of clearing the soot from under the roof. Since houses had no chimneys, smoke from the open hearth and the cooking fire-pots found its way out through openings under the peak of the roof, leaving a deposit of soot. Around Shimoda, the thirteenth day of the Twelfth Month was the established one for clearing soot, unless it fell on the day of the Ox. There was an old belief that the Ox disliked fire and anything to do with it was avoided on one of his days. There was no problem this year: the thirteenth day was the day of the Monkey.

As for the regular turn-the-place-inside-out housecleaning which every housewife considered obligatory, there were no regular days for that, though there were certain taboos. Around Kakisaki, women would not clean house on the twentieth day, because that day had come to be the established one for cleaning prisons, nor would they clean on the day of the Hare, because the Hare was especially associated with the New Year and it seemed disrespectful.

It was to know such things—the zodiacal signs for each day, the days which were lucky and those which were unlucky, the days for sowing and the days for reaping—that every family had to have a calendar. This was true as well for Harris's Chinese, who ran their lives by the same zodiacal calculations as the Japanese. The fact that Assam bought a calendar at Shimoda for forty-eight copper coins was duly reported to the Goyosho by Hambei.

This year a dispute raged around the calendar business. For as long as anyone could remember, a calendar-maker of Mishima town, and his ancestors before him, had held the sole privilege of selling calendars in Izu Province. But in recent years someone connected with the great shrines of Ise had been encroaching on this territory, offering calendars along with the shrines' talismans against evil, a bargain which was hard to resist. The Mishima calendars were being driven off the market. This year nothing could be done, but a time-honored monopoly was not lightly surrendered and the Mishima man was appealing to the Izu provincial magistrate. The case would have to go all the way to Edo, to the governor for shrines and temples and finally to a member of the Great Council, but the calendar-maker of Mishima would win his case. This was the last year that Ise calendars would go on sale in Izu.

A calendar maker (*a book illustration by Jichosai*)

In the midst of these busy days, a ship limped into port, with its cargo of rice wet from the rough seas it had weathered. The rice belonged to the Lord of Tottori, who had come into his position by adoption, for he was the fifth son of Tokugawa Nariaki. For this reason, as well as the fact that Tottori was a powerful fief, the cargo was handled with special care. A large group of men was drafted from Shimoda, Kakisaki, and Suzaki to unload and safeguard the rice, and officials from all three places were on hand as supervisors.

On the last days of the month almost everyone was frantically busy. Food had to be prepared for the holidays, for no cooking would be done on the first three days of the New Year. Most important were the rice cakes called *mochi*, made by steaming glutenous rice and then pounding it in a big mortar to make a thick dough which was shaped into cakes. *Mochi* would be the treat and staple of the holidays, toasted in the hearth or boiled with greens to make a rich soup called *zoni*.

Making *mochi*, with everybody taking a hand in the pounding, was a gay prelude to the holiday. (When the Japanese look at the moon they see not the face of a man but a hare pounding *mochi*.) Usually it was made on the thirtieth day of the month, the last day of the year. This year, however, the thirtieth was a day of the Ox, which precluded making a fire to steam the rice, as the town clerk of Shimoda duly reminded the head of each block. And in Kakisaki, there was a prejudice against making *mochi* on the twenty-ninth, because twenty-nine in Japanese is *niju-ku*, and *ku* can also mean "pain" and "affliction," and who could relish a New Year's dish with such associations? So most of Harris's neighbors made their *mochi* on the twenty-eighth day. They brought from the mountains special wood, which burned with a fine crackling, and carefully placed three rice straws under the mortar—though no one quite remembered why—before they started pounding.

On each of the little freighters anchored in the harbor for the holiday the crew made their own *mochi*, using a full bag of rice, and as they pounded they thought of the parties to come, when they would bring their *mochi* to their inn, and there would be girls and sake and song.

Throughout Japan there is probably no food as closely linked to the New Year's holidays as *mochi*, yet there are always exceptions. There was a village just upriver from Shimoda which was such an exception. In Tachino —where, if you want to believe that story, Heusken liked to peek at the girls in the bath and had his encounter with a jealous lover—*mochi* was never made or eaten at New Year's, for the people believed that their tutelary god hated it and would take revenge with fire or worse if his taboo were violated. From hazy memories they would cite proof: cases of houses that burned and people who died. They would tell of a shrine priest of some uncertain age long ago. Of all people, he should have known better, for he was the intermediary between his village and its god, yet one New Year's he ate *mochi*. He choked to death on it.

On the last two days of the year townsfolk and villagers tramped to the mountains to cut branches of pine and bamboo poles for decoration. They decorated the gates of their houses, and within their houses, those places most primal to life: the shelves where the deity of the kitchen and the deity of good harvest resided, the well, and the toilet. Those fortunate enough to own a horse or an ox decorated the stable. A boatowner decorated the prow.

Every Kakisaki family also brought down from the forest an old tree stump, which, burning slowly, would furnish the fire for the first three days of the New Year. There would be no breath blown on this fire to fan it, for it was, like the flame of a candle at an altar, a sacred flame, not to be defiled by human breath.

The last day was the most frantic—the final rush to pay old debts (sometimes by borrowing to create new ones), the stream of town and village officials into the Goyosho to complete the year's business, the cleaning and cooking and decorating. It was a long, exhausting day, with a late meal of noodles, auspicious because their length suggested long life, and a hot bath with a good scrub so that one could greet the New Year clean. For the men there was a visit to the barber, who had to remain open until well past dawn to dress his customers' hair and shave their crowns as well as their faces.

As darkness fell in Shimoda the old man who at festival time guarded the temporary shrine in all-night vigil began an all-night tour of the town streets, from door to door, chanting: "In the year to come the god of prosperity will visit this house. The god of poverty will disappear over the Western Sea." The people of the house thanked him and pressed coins into his hand.

In Kakisaki the priest of the temple of the mountain religion spoke his ancient formulae to rid his village of old evils and bring good fortune.

At midnight the Year of the Dragon slipped into the past and the Year of the Serpent came into being. The crisp air pulsed to the tolling of temple bells. Except that at Kakisaki there were only echoes across the harbor, for Gyokusenji was in the hands of foreigners and its bell was strangely silent.

Some folk slept a little. Many stayed up all night waiting for the dawn, then climbed a mountain to watch the sun rise on the New Year. Returning, the head of the family ritually drew the first fresh water from the well, and the family ate their first breakfast, *mochi* and *zoni*.

In Shimoda the officials gathered early—the headman, the elders, the chief fisherman, the chief merchant, the chief innkeeper, and all the others —each wearing *kamishimo,* his most formal clothing, with stiff flaring shoulders and bearing his crest. And on this greatest of days, each wore his sword. They went first to the shrine, offering rice and sake, and then to Headman Hambei's house for congratulatory sake and breakfast. While they were there a messenger brought the Governors' New Year greeting. Hambei read it aloud and then started it on its round to the villages. Having been fortified by spirits and food, these men of Shimoda completed the day's official duties by visiting the Goyosho and the harbor master's office, leaving gifts of fans at both places. They separated then, each to his own family. Visits of greeting today would be limited to relatives.

Kamishimo (detail from a print by Kiyonaga)

In Kakisaki, likewise, the headman and elders brought sake and rice to the god of their shrine, and then adjourned to Yoheiji's. By village custom the heads of all families gathered before the headman's house to offer their congratulations.

At Gyokusenji, Townsend Harris had the American flag run up in honor of the holiday. *Monday, Tuesday, Wednesday, January 26, 27, 28, 1857. Festival of the Japanese New Year. Everyone released from labor; all*

*in their best clothes; faces shining with sake and everybody paying visits
of ceremony to everybody. Persons of rank put on their* <u>kamishimo</u> *or dress
of ceremony on these occasions. I went out on Thursday to see the decorations of the houses. Evergreens, rice in the straw, oranges, radishes, etc.,
etc., were festooned about the front of every house. Before each house was
a pine or cypress branch planted in the ground to represent a tree, while
at the base of the tree a quantity of firewood some fourteen inches long was
set on end, forming a bulk of some seven feet in circumference. The fuel
was kept in its place by straw ropes. At some houses wheat straw was neatly
twisted into the form of a cornucopia, in others the universal shoe of
Japan,—i.e., a straw sandal,—was hung up. Everyone appeared under the
influence of sake, while but few were intoxicated and none quarrelsome.*

Since by his own account Harris did not go out during the first three
days, what he wrote of the festive atmosphere must have been what
Heusken told him, with perhaps a few details from Assam, who certainly
joined the celebration. As Hambei recorded in his diary, the butler bought,
on the second day, two sweet bean-cakes from a confectioner of Number
Three Block. Perhaps he was a little tipsy, for he left a silver dollar, a
payment roughly six hundred times the price of the cakes. The Goyosho
straightened things out.

It must have been Harris's curious sense of aloofness from the Japanese
people that made him shut himself up during the three greatest days of this
greatest holiday. It is hard to believe that he did it out of consideration for
the Japanese, though truthfully, they might not have enjoyed seeing the
foreigner in their midst.

There were some Japanese who stayed at home for just such reasons.
Buddhist priests kept out of sight these first three days. Since their chief
function was to bury the dead and pray for their salvation, the priests knew
that to most people they brought depressing thoughts.

And in Shimoda, that class of outcasts who were hereditarily watchmen, a kind of volunteer police who patrolled the streets, manned the jail,
conducted tortures and similar unpleasant chores, and lived partly by
payment from the town and partly by begging—these people were forced
to stay at home. In the past they had gone out to beg from the happy
crowds, but, as the town records put it, they were "a repugnant sight to look
upon" (though neither Harris nor Heusken could have distinguished them
from other Japanese), and for more than forty years they had been forbidden to appear on the streets during the first three days of the year. To
compensate, each family was given two *bu*, the necessary money being
collected without demur by a property tax on the householders of Shimoda.

A holiday is not, of course, exempt from distressing events. As a reminder that the sea could be cruel, a circular was received on the first day that a ship had been wrecked in high winds off the coast a few miles from Shimoda while trying to run for the safety of the harbor; the crew were saved but the cargo and rigging were lost.

A street watchman (*a book illustration by Jichosai*)

The second day was the day for symbolically beginning the work of the New Year. Farmers conducted a simple ceremony in the fields, woods-men in the mountains. Women did a few stitches of needlework; boys and girls left off play for a few strokes of calligraphy. A boatowner and his crew boarded their craft. At Kakisaki the owner asked the priest of the mountain religion to purify his boat by prayer and exorcism. Then the crew were invited to the owner's house for entertainment, and were given towels when they left. If a sailor was not invited, it meant he was being dropped from the crew. This did not happen often, but when it did it was a blow.

It was on the second day, too, that Hambei made discreet inquiry as to when it would be most convenient for Governor Inoue to accept the greetings of the town and villages under his jurisdiction. The answer, as the headman wrote in a circular for immediate transmittal, was that the Governor would receive on the sixth day, as in the past.

The third day was a day of rest. People needed it after the hard work of preparing for the holiday and then two strenuous days of enjoying it. But since on the fourth day people would remove the decorations from their gates, Shimoda's town clerk initiated the annual circular reminding everyone that the bamboo cut for decoration was not to be destroyed, but gathered where it would be convenient if it were needed, as it usually was, to repair breakwaters and riverbanks at flood time.

On the fourth day the Buddhist priests made their first appearance, visiting their parishioners to distribute talismans against evil, and it was the day when the headman and elders of Shimoda, in ceremonial exercise of futility, issued their annual stricture against gambling, "even a children's lottery."

On the sixth day, as scheduled, the officials of Shimoda and of all the villages again put on their most formal clothes and in a body called at the Governors' compound at Naka village to offer their respects.

The sixth day was to Harris the thirty-first of January. He wrote his usual monthly summary: *Saturday, January 31, 1857. To-day closes the first month of the year. I wish I could say that my health and spirits were as good as the weather is fine* . . .

Chapter 8

FEBRUARY, 1857

The New Year festivities were far from over.

What was February 1 to Harris was the seventh day of the First Month to the Japanese, and another holiday: the Festival of the Seven Herbs. The flag was flown at the consulate.

The day had its official aspects, of course. In Shimoda the town officials gathered and made the usual round of ceremonial visits before settling down at the headman's home for a feast; fish and side dishes and soups, with plenty of sake ("Those weak at drinking," Hirai Heijiro had stated in his chronicle of annual events, "may be served sweeter dishes with tea and cakes"). But the featured dish of the day, at the headman's as at most other houses, was rice gruel prepared with the seven herbs of the season.

Families had gone to the fields and woodlands the afternoon before to gather the herbs: parsley, shepherd's-purse, cudweed, chickweed, henbit, Chinese rape, and radish. Those who guarded tradition had pounded the herbs on a willow block with a branch of privet; they were careful to beat the parsley at the hour of the Cock (sunset), the shepherd's-purse at the hour of the Dog (about eight P.M.*), the cudweed at the hour of the Boar (about ten P.M.*), and the chickweed at the hour of the Rat (midnight). Then they could go to bed, for no hours were specified for the henbit and the Chinese rape. But the radish had to be beaten and all the herbs compounded at the hour of the Dragon (call it eight A.M.), mixing them with water drawn from a well to the east, which would be "the water of youth." There was, naturally, a song to go with all of this:

---

* One must say "about" eight P.M. and "about" ten P.M. because Japanese hours changed length with the seasons: the equivalent of six P.M. always came at sunset and the equivalent of six A.M. at dawn, so that in the winter the daylight hours were short and the night hours long, and in the summer the opposite was true.

The seven young herbs are delicious,
the shepherd's-purse is the best!
Let us pound it, let's enjoy it,
before we welcome the birds from the south,
or the winter birds leave for the north!

When the gruel was made, it was first offered to the gods and then enjoyed by the family. It was not only tasty, but it would ward off spring fever, the complaints of summer, dysentery in autumn, and jaundice in winter. It was particularly efficacious against depression of spirits. Townsend Harris could have used some.

The eleventh day of the New Year was the day appointed for the first conference of Shimoda town officials. As the town clerk invariably pointed out when he sent out the notices, it was the day for celebrating armor and poetry at Edo Castle, but in Shimoda discussion centered on mundane matters like preparing the reports of the market prices of rice and oil during the past year. But as the book of annual events made clear, the business session was to end as soon as dinner was ready.

There were usually some new faces at this first meeting, for it was the time of year when officials grown old retired from public office. This year the leaders of three blocks had retired. Their replacements were on hand to be toasted.

The officials of Kakisaki had already held their first conference of the year. Then on the twelfth day they convened the first general meeting of the villagers, which is to say, the heads of all households. Yoheiji reminded them of the necessity to keep a close watch on the foreigners in their midst, especially since the guards had been withdrawn from the temple, and he had some good news: their village treasury was richer today, for yesterday he and Kosaburo had been summoned to the Goyosho along with officials from Suzaki and Shimoda, and there each village and the town had received a heavy, handsome coin worth one thousand coppers as a reward for their help last month to the disabled rice-ship of the Lord of Tottori.

Then everyone settled down to the annual reading of the laws which molded their lives. They had heard this code before and they would hear it many times again. There may have been some whose attention drifted to other things.

The first and most important law was the one which bound all families into groups, most often of five families, neighbors who were jointly responsible for each other's conduct. This group was the basic unit of the village and the foundation of the Shogun's rule. It was an ingenious device for maintaining peace and order, for inculcating the proper point of view, for collecting taxes—and for making the people do all this themselves. There was only one household in Kakisaki which did not belong to such a group, the new one at Gyokusenji.

> If any member of a group, whether farmer, fisherman, innkeeper, or merchant, is lazy and does not attend properly to his business, the group leader will advise him, warn him, and lead him into better ways. If the person does not listen to this advice, and becomes angry and obstinate, he is to be reported to the village elders. As fathers, sons, members of families, relatives, and fellow-villagers, we will endeavor to live in peaceful and kindly relations; as members of a group, we will cultivate friendly feeling even more than with our relatives, and will promote each other's happiness as well as share each other's griefs. If there is an unprincipled and lawless person in a group, we will all share the responsibility for him.

Then came the familiar precepts:
—the injunctions to filial piety, hard work, and frugality;
—the interdiction against Christianity;
—the prohibition against selling one's land, the restrictions on mortgaging it, and the limitations on dividing it among one's sons (to prevent farms from becoming too small to support a family);
—the ban against gambling;
—the warning against quarrelsomeness and litigation, for "villages given to law suits are always poor."
—the necessity, as a seacoast village, to look out for ships in distress and give them assistance, and to investigate for possible fraud if a ship reported that it had jettisoned its cargo;
—the rules about adoption, which should be within the family if possible, and about disinheriting a first son who proved worthless in favor of a younger son who was worthy;
—the assertion of communal responsibility to report wrongdoing, prevent fires, and catch robbers, to keep a wary eye on strangers, and to keep out of the village heretical priests, prostitutes, and boys used for sodomy;
—the obligation to provide necessary services to travelers on official business;
—the restrictions on travel by villagers;
—the recourse available in case of unjust taxation or corrupt officials;
—and so on and so on and so on.

When the droning voice reached the edicts on paying taxes, the minds which had been wandering returned, for this important matter meant that the end of the reading was near. When it came, these men of the village filed forward, in an order of precedence long established, to sign and seal the document, and the meeting was over. Then most of them went home to preside at the ceremonial first-opening-of-the-year of the storehouse which held whatever treasures their family had been able to accumulate.

Midmonth, with its full moon, brought a new peak of celebration. On the fourteenth day the New Year's decorations inside and outside the house came down, and each neighborhood group collected these and the gate decorations (which had been removed on the fourth day) to make a big fire. Everyone gathered about it, bringing *mochi*, for it was said that eating *mochi* toasted in this fire would ward off sickness.

To replace the burned decorations, people made "fourteenth-day dumplings" of rice flour. They molded them into lucky symbols like *tai* fish, or gold coins, or the cocoons of the silkworm, and they hung them on branches of willow placed where the New Year's pine had been.

The fifteenth day was "Little New Year's." Townsend Harris had the flag run up. In the houses around him people breakfasted on rice cooked with red beans, supped on the dumplings they had made the day before, and in between passed the day in a holiday mood. There was only one thing that really had to be done on this day: those who had fruit trees went out and struck them with willow wands while invoking them to bear fruit heavily and "Make me a millionaire."

The sixteenth day was the traditional apprentices' holiday. Apprentices, servants, and young wives got one of their rare days off to return to their parents' home. If Takizo and Sukezo were lucky, Harris followed the custom and let them go back to Naka village.

It was also the day for the year's first visit to one's temple, though it was mostly the old women who honored this custom. At Kakisaki they crowded the chapel where Gyokusenji's altar had been set up, chanting over and over again the name of the Buddha.

A young wife returning to her husband's home the next morning traditionally brought a gift of tea from her parents to his, and then settled down to another year as her mother-in-law's slavey. Takizo and Sukezo had no obligation to bring anything. As a matter of fact they may not have been sure they were Harris's employees. The issue of their wages remaining unsettled, they had received none. Of course, they still received their stipends as *ashigaru*.

The New Year's celebrations were about over now, but there was still New Year's business to be done.

On the seventeenth day Shimoda and the associated villages held a conference at Rendaiji to make plans for meeting the year's calls from

Mishima for men and horses, or cash in lieu, to help move official travelers along the Tokaido Road. To underline the problem, there was on hand at the moment an order to provide assistance to the Lord of Owari on his way to Edo. The Lord of Owari was a Tokugawa. His house, like Nariaki's, was one of the Three Houses, the senior branches of the Shogun's family. His train would be enormous, and the demands from Mishima were heavy.

On the twentieth day, the keepers of ships' inns at Kakisaki met to plan projects like clearing the harbor of sharp rocks that cut ships' ropes, and sinking poles to serve as mooring points. This work was their responsibility. There was an old saying they liked to quote:

> As a boat depends on its sail,
> and a sail depends on its rudder,
> so a port depends on its inns.

They also discussed how they would care for sailors who became ill or died in port; the ship's captain had his obligations but most of the burden fell on the innkeeper. If a sailor died far from home there could be no waiting until his family was told. It was his innkeeper who arranged for a proper Buddhist funeral, and other inkeepers who attended as mourners. It was his innkeeper, and his innkeeper's family in generations after, who would care for his grave and pray for the repose of his spirit.

The Goyosho called for the annual installment in repayment of the loans granted after the tidal wave, along with a demand for a report that must have caused some qualms: a list of those who were in arrears. A not very subtle threat accompanied this order: cases of default, town officials were told, would be dealt with by the Governors *personally*. The Shogunate had been generous in making loans, but now it was making it clear that those loans were not to be considered gifts.

Interspersed with these activities were some which had no connection with its being a new year, such as the arrival of a new construction superintendent for the Goyosho.

There was enough work to keep the new superintendent busy. The Goyosho itself was still under repair after the damage suffered in last September's typhoon. The Governors wanted a new storehouse in their compound at Naka, presumably to store the rapidly accumulating records of their negotiations with Harris. A rest house for foreigners was being built in front of the temples at the back of the town.

This rest house was one of the projects that Commodore Perry had strongly advocated, with the support of Wells Williams. They had argued that a comfortable place for the boys to get drunk would keep them off the streets and out of more serious trouble. Female companionship was implied. The Japanese had been reluctant, but now it was being built.

Also for the foreigners, a shed was being put up at Fukuura, where the crews of foreign ships could do their laundry. The guardhouse at Kakisaki was being enlarged now that the guards had been removed from Gyokusenji. And when milder weather came, there was Harris's jetty to be rebuilt. (These last three projects were in Kakisaki, and it must have annoyed Yoheiji that Shimoda men were appointed to oversee the work.)

All this activity and a new construction superintendent meant a rash of inspections, each of which required that the Shimoda town office provide guides and boats.

As a matter of fact, Governor Inoue himself made an inspection of all the sites. The tour carried him right past Gyokusenji, but he did not go in. As far as the irascible foreigner was concerned, the Governor and his staff were lying low. Until the men who had gone to Edo brought back some decisions, they were avoiding Harris as much as possible. Perhaps they hoped that a cooling-off period would help.

These tactics were probably well considered. The lack of contact with Japanese officials gave Harris no occasion to get excited, and getting rid of the guards and compelling one of the Governors to hustle off to Edo gave him a feeling of accomplishment. Besides, that book of his in which he entered his orders was evidently working, for there are numerous Japanese records of goods and services provided: clothing and shoes repaired, a gun polished, a brass kitchen pan mended, a mattress made to order—the kind of routine chores whose completion brings a sense of order to one's life. As a result, the tone of his journal indicates that his health and attitude were noticeably improved, despite the fact that, as usual, February brought the worst weather of the year.

Gray unruly skies threatened rain or snow and the wind blustered out of the northwest, from the great cold mass of Siberia, cutting to one's bones. This was the wind against which Shimoda townsfolk built their homes with walls of stone and overlaid them with black tile and white plaster. Behind those walls old men sat with their legs bundled under a padded quilt thrown over a charcoal brazier, cackling to each other about their town's fame for biting winds and shrewish women while their women brought them hot tea.

This was the wind which kept the harbor filled with little freighters from central and western Japan. Most of them were homeward bound. They could make it to Edo with a west wind behind them, and a break in the weather might let them return as far as Shimoda, but there the blasts of winter were likely to bottle them up. If the wind turned easterly the harbor would quickly empty, but often the same ships would soon fill it again. Some of them might have made it almost home, only to be blown back when the wind shifted.

To kill the long days the crews sometimes staged sumo wrestling on the beach. Sumo was the country's great sport: schoolboys grappled when classes let out and the professional champions were national heroes (when Perry was at Shimoda some of his men challenged the local lads; the Japanese won every match).

Since the dim recesses of Japanese history sumo had been presented as an offering to the gods and a petition for their favor. Nor was it merely sport at Kakisaki. It was called "fair weather sumo." As in every sumo tournament, the wrestlers were divided into two camps, the East and the West. A victory for the East was considered to augur an east wind which would carry the ships safely home. A victory for the West meant they would be longer harborbound.

But mostly what the crews had on their minds was women and sake. Practically every ship had a souvenir pillow, a long round bolster with the ship's name embroidered on it along with the names of the girls of a home-port brothel. It was a gift to say "forget-me-not," but home and those girls were a long way off and Shimoda was the harbor of women, the harbor of song.

In villages like Suzaki and Kakisaki, sailors and girls flirted and made love as sailors and girls have always done, the girls of the villages reinforced by girls from over the mountain. Some lucky fellow might find a home with a daughter just nubile, and chances are he could bring her to bed with him for a bag of rice stolen from his ship. Rice to feed the family through the winter: that was fair exchange for a daughter's virginity.

Across the harbor Shimoda's gay quarter beckoned as darkness fell to veil its daytime tawdriness. Along the willow-lined street, lanterns were hung before each bar and restaurant to glow an invitation. Men would be drawn here and would call for company, and answering summons, the women with white-powdered faces would bundle against the cold and scurry to respond. Yet like other Shimoda folk they prided themselves on their independence, in their case the right to reject an offensive customer. Very possibly some girl would desert a man who displeased her, someone would praise or damn the obstinacy of Shimoda geisha, and someone would remember the legendary Oko.

Again and again Oko had laughed at the ship's captain who was obsessed by her. "Bring me a chest with a thousand pieces of gold," she taunted, and driven by desire he stole such a chest from the merchant he sailed for, was caught and exiled for life to one of the Izu islands. Years later Oko learned of it, and she bribed a boatman to take her to the island. She found the man near death, but she nursed him and gave him a kind of triumph in his last days, and then carried his ashes to his home. Oko was the model for Shimoda geisha: spirited, capricious, mettlesome.

The insistent lover (*a print by Sugimura Jihei*)

These were traits which made the game more exciting. Like hot sake they warmed the blood. Then shadows met on papered windows while the wind outside tossed the willows and the lanterns, swirled dust along the street, caught up and flung away the night sounds of this place: from one house giddy laughter, from another, acerb strum of samisen and bittersweet ballad—

> . . . silently they embrace, both
> lost in tears, holding each other tightly.
> Tears falling, flutter.
> "But to go on like this—there is no
> termination to our love: the longer
> that I stay, the greater is our peril . . ."

Given the slightest chance by the weather, the fishermen of Shimoda went out where the sailors of the freighters dared not go. They ranged far from home after tuna, or at night went after squid, hanging a blazing basket of fire from their prow, so that the sea sparkled with dozens of fires, drawing the squid close to the boats where they could be hooked. In their open boats the fishermen of Shimoda wagered their toughness and their courage, wagered and sometimes lost.

Against the wind, Gyokusenji had no walls of stone or tile, only of thin wood and plaster. The wind rattled and whistled through. It was a struggle to keep the Philadelphia stove stoked, to make even one small circle of warmth where a man could sit and read.

But even in February there were a few sunny days. *Friday, February 6, 1857. I made an effort to-day and walked some seven miles up the valley of Shimoda, as it is level ground. This was in part a new walk to me, never having gone so far before in that direction. The vegetation improves as you recede from the seacoast, and I found the bamboo quite green in many places. Hamlet succeeds hamlet in quick succession; the houses, temples and cultivation all of the same character as at Shimoda.*

On the tenth he had a relapse: *A violent attack of cholera morbus,*[*]*— being the third I have had since last December, and it has so happened that I ate potage à la purée on each of those days. I shall, therefore, with great regret give it up. First snow on the level ground to-day, about one inch, but it soon melted and by eleven o'clock was all gone.*

But two days later he felt well enough, as we learn from Hambei's diary, to be strolling around Shimoda with Heusken. Four sumo wrestlers from Edo were working out in front of the town shrine. No doubt they attracted a crowd, and Harris and Heusken stopped to watch; Harris indicated that he would enjoy seeing some matches. Word of all this took very little time to reach the Goyosho, and in even less time a patrol officer rushed over, stopped everything, and sent the sumo men packing out of town.

It is difficult to tell from Hambei's account whether the officials were exasperated because sumo was being staged, even though informally, without a proper permit (strictly against Shogunate regulations), or because the foreigners had happened upon it, or both. But the chief priest of the shrine and the three Shimoda men who had "offered convenience" to the wrestlers were in trouble. They had to undergo a four-day investigation, during which they were several times summoned to the Goyosho to be quizzed, lectured, and reprimanded, and in the end they were required to endorse the official report of the investigation and to submit written apologies. Of course, Harris was quite unaware of the fracas.

---

[*] Despite its ominous name, cholera morbus is non-infectious and rarely fatal; Harris seems to have used the term for any attack of diarrhea and cramps.

On the same day this case was being wound up, a Goyosho messenger delivered a package to Gyokusenji. *Monday, February 16, 1857. Bingo-no-kami, now at Edo, sends me from thence a present of English walnuts and dried persimmons. They call the latter figs and, indeed, the best quality of them is very like a good dried fig. I am daily expecting his return here, when I hope I shall be able to bring our pending matters to an amicable conclusion.*

Actually, Okada, with Matsumura and Moriyama, was already on the road back to Shimoda. Their mission to Edo has to be called a success, though the Governor may not have accomplished all that he had wished to.

He was carrying back a letter from the Great Council which absolved Inoue and himself from blame for capitulating to Harris following his "flare-up":

—withdrawal of the guards from Gyokusenji was approved, "but you must be careful in managing the foreigners and their residence";

—*metsuke* need not attend conferences between the Governors and Harris;

—Harris might be permitted gold and silver coins if the amounts he requested were "moderate" (if they became large he was to be given paper money);

—the seven-*ri* boundary was to be considered flexible, for there was no critical installation on Mount Amagi (an evident reference to the jaunt Heusken wanted to make to the mountain);

—when it was unavoidable, the officials might be permitted to stay elsewhere overnight, but only at a temple and only as approved by the Governors (again referring to the long walks Harris and Heusken had discussed);

—it was all right to exchange presents with Harris "if there is no way to avoid it";

—the Governors were granted some freedom with their budget if the amount was not large and the need was urgent;

—the Governors might make decisions at Shimoda and need not consult the government on everything (but Okada knew very well that questions of importance still had to be referred back to Edo).

So much Okada and his men had gained. But the ten-per-cent tax was to be kept on Harris's purchases, contrary to his and Inoue's recommendations, and whatever guidance the Governor had been able to get about negotiating a new rate for currency exchange was apparently too vague to be reduced to writing. (There are indications that at least some men of the finance bureau were resisting a rate of three *bu* to one dollar, while no doubt others in the government considered it inevitable; this disagreement would be enough to account for the government's inability to issue firm instructions.)

Okada was also carrying another letter, this one from the Great Council to Harris. It was designed as an answer to both his letters—his announcements that he was the bearer of a letter from the President, that he wished to come to Edo for direct discussions with the Shogun's ministers, and that he had vital information concerning the British threat to Japan— but it said only: please handle all problems with the Governors of Shimoda.

It was an achievement to get this letter, for there were many in the government who opposed writing to Harris. Whether Okada had any confidence that it would help the situation at Shimoda, we have no way of knowing.

Another letter from the Great Council to the Governors gives us our first information concerning a positive step taken by the residents of Gyokusenji toward warmer relations with the Japanese: they had offered to give English lessons to some of the Japanese officials. The instructions from the Great Council show how much the offer was appreciated. Dr. Ito Kansai and interpreter Tateishi Tokujuro were permitted to attend, along with the sons of some of the Goyosho officials; some other officials would be sent from Edo to take advantage of the opportunity; all "must realize their position and obligation." Clearly, the Japanese were grateful, but the fact that there is so little about these lessons in Harris's journal—no mention at all until some months after this—could mean that the initiative came from Heusken, not Harris, and that it was Heusken who would do most of the teaching.

In short, Okada, who was even now making the cold journey back to his post, can be credited with accomplishing a good deal in Edo. It may be that he had accomplished too much for his own good, that he had got decisions going beyond those that his senior, Inoue, favored, and that in pushing his rather liberal ideas on how to handle Harris he had offended certain men in the government. Okada was not a tactful advocate. He was scornful of thinking he considered flaccid, unrealistic, or outdated. He certainly antagonized those whose opinions were close to Nariaki's, and those as well who believed in the line that Lord Abe had laid down for dealing with Commodore Perry: "Our policy shall be to evade any definite answer to their requests, while at the same time maintaining a peaceful demeanor."

To Lord Hotta, on the other hand, such a policy of procrastination was no longer workable, and he was now in charge of foreign relations. It was Hotta's directives that Okada was carrying to Shimoda, but they were by no means pleasing to all in the government.

In addition to wresting decisions from a reluctant bureaucracy, Okada must be given credit for stimulating debate on the whole issue of foreign relations in general, and on how to handle Harris in particular. Staff papers were flooding the channels of government. It was Hotta who called for them, but there is no doubt that Okada's brief, disturbing visit had accelerated the process of decision-making, always painful when the decisions mean a break with the past.

The Governors of Nagasaki and Hakodate were of course consulted. Their joint reply rather vaguely recommended "friendly treatment" and became specific only when they urged letting Harris have coins so he could buy directly what he needed in Shimoda. On the other hand, eager to reinforce the dignity of their colleagues at Shimoda, they argued against the Great Council's writing a letter to Harris—let the Shimoda Governors tell him the government's answer.

A standing council of senior officials, the Tribunal, made it clear they opposed any concessions to Harris at this time. Certainly he should not be permitted to come to Edo now. Permission could not be refused indefinitely, they admitted. "But almost all of his demands are unfavorable to Japan," they argued, "and if he is permitted to come to Edo and see the highest officials of the government he will undoubtedly place many difficult requests and behave rudely. This could lead to war. So permission to come should be deferred as long as possible and granted only after preparations for war are complete."

But it is likely that Hotta leaned most heavily on the advice of the committee he had appointed to advise him on foreign trade. His directive to the Shimoda Governors followed closely their recommendations. The trouble was that these recommendations had been wrung from the committee under pressure, and its two factions promptly forwarded papers dissenting in one way or another.

Hotta's committee consisted of men from the finance bureau, the *ometsuke*, and the *metsuke*. The committee had almost immediately split. And it might have jolted Harris to learn that it was the *ometsuke* and *metsuke*, whom he had been conditioned to despise, who were by far the more liberal according to his way of thinking.

The *ometsuke* and *metsuke*, including men like Iwase, were already on record as favoring Harris's trip to Edo. They had voiced this recommendation as soon as Harris had made his first request. Now they repeated it, expressing doubt that the Consul General would be persuaded by the Great Council's telling him to deal with the Governors. They pointed out that the Dutch had been permitted to visit Edo for two hundred years, though they were only merchants conducting a limited trade. "Once we have signed a friendship treaty with a country," they wrote, "it is a matter of course that we must permit officials of that country to visit our capital." To refuse Harris would make him think the government was afraid of him, and that would make him even more stubborn and arrogant, and would certainly increase the difficulties with him and with other nations in the future. "In our negotiations with foreign nations we have often persisted in our stand even when we knew that what they said was reasonable and what we advocated was quite unjustifiable: if we have no confidence in our position, we can never reach a satisfactory solution."

In contrast, the men of the finance bureau, including Mizuno and Inoue's brother, Kawaji, were much more cautious. It was true, they wrote, that the Dutch had been permitted to visit Edo, but those visits now had been stopped because they were troublesome; if the American was permitted to come, the Dutch would feel aggrieved. Clearly, the American would be demanding, and whatever was done for him would establish precedents for all other nations in the future. "Of course," they went on, "we cannot refuse him flatly—that would lead to disaster—but we should postpone any invitation until the government has had time to chart a safe course, and in the meantime we should ask him to be reasonable and follow our procedures by dealing with the Shimoda Governors."

Taking up the matter of the tax on Harris's purchases, which as finance people they considered within their province, they insisted it should be retained. They made no distinction between merchants who sailed into Shimoda to trade and Harris, who was stationed there as an official. Their argument ran like this: "The goods, like lacquerware, sold to foreigners are luxuries, not necessities. The merchants of Shimoda have sold such goods at about triple the domestic price, making enormous profits. It must be assumed that foreigners make the same kind of profits when they sell to us. Considering the profits made by Shimoda merchants, a thirty-per-cent tax is not unreasonable and it helps to offset the vast cost of opening the port. If the foreigners consider the prices excessive, they will not buy"—and the finance chiefs figuratively shrugged "so what?"—"but to tell the truth, the merchants of Shimoda are excessively greedy, and we think the right to sell to foreigners should be taken out of their hands and given to reliable merchants of Edo, Kyoto, and Osaka, such as the Mitsui company. Then the tax might be reduced to ten per cent." (Had the merchants of Shimoda been able to read this, they must have shivered, but it is doubtful that they would have altered their prices—except perhaps up, on the theory that they had better get while the getting was good.)

Both the finance and the *metsuke* groups were unhappy that they had been unable to agree. The *ometsuke* and *metsuke* submitted another paper to Lord Hotta and the Great Council which revealed this discouragement. All the officials of the government had been discussing the best way to deal with the American, they wrote, trying in vain to reach accord. "We think it is almost impossible for us to agree. Our disagreement has driven us into difficulties. We must ask you to give us your decision."

There were stories going the rounds in Edo that Hotta was vexed by this failure of his staff to produce a sound plan. He was reported to have said that the mediocrity of officials was the reason that the prestige of the Shogunate was fading.

Despite the contradictory advice which he received, Lord Hotta did come to some conclusions, and he announced them in a brief directive:

> We have sent a letter to the American official and told him to talk with the Shimoda Governors on all matters. However, we think that we must permit him to make an official trip to Edo in the near future, and we had better make preparations. He is of high position and cannot be treated as the Dutch were. We must consider most carefully his route, reception, accommodations, etc. You must study these matters and give us your opinions as soon as possible.

Of course, the American official in question had no way of knowing about this.

The day after Harris received his gift of walnuts and dried persimmons, Hambei began receiving advance notices of the arrival of Okada, Matsumura, and Moriyama. Word was sped to the villages, for naturally their representatives would join the town officials in greeting the party.

Also, sixteen new padded quilts had been ordered from Wataya Kichibei for Okada's residence. The merchant was notified that delivery must be made before the Governor arrived.

In addition, it was learned that Moriyama had received a significant promotion in Edo. In accordance with custom he had taken a new name to mark the occasion: he was now Takichiro, no longer Einosuke. With his step up went all the emoluments: more status (he was now equal in grade to Superintendent Wakiya), more salary, more servants, and better quarters. Evidently his new accommodations were not ready, for it was decided that temporarily he would be put up at an inn. While the inn's best rooms were considered adequate for a short stay, its food was not, and Hambei was notified that the town would be responsible for boarding him. Arrangements were made for one of the best restaurants to send in his meals.

While Okada and his party were still on the road, the twenty-fourth day of the First Month (February 18 to Harris) brought the festival of the Jizo of Mount Takane. The sailors of every ship in the harbor joined the seafaring men of Shimoda in a trek to the top of the mountain, each crew carrying a banner from their boat attached to an offering of rice. They and the many others who were attracted to this festival also carried kegs of sake and boxes of food. One needed sake and food against the cold, and this Jizo liked to see his people enjoy themselves. He aided mariners and protected children from smallpox, and in other matters he was considered a complaisant god:

> The Jizo of Takane
> is of lax character:
> for sex and gambling
> he's the one to pray to!

The police never climbed Takane to check on this midwinter spree. Gambling was open and in the woods lovers found a way to keep warm.

February 19, 1857. Rain, sleet and snow. . . .

In this storm the Governor's party arrived and were greeted by a chilled and dripping local delegation.

But the storm had hit after most of Shimoda's fishermen had gone to sea after tuna. Perversely, fish were plentiful, and with fishermen's stubbornness the crews refused to go in, though many a man among them murmured a prayer to the Jizo of Takane. One boat the Jizo could not help. It capsized and its men were thrown into the icy water.

Because of the storm the other crews did not see the accident. Only one man, swimming blindly, came near enough to one of the other boats so that his cries were heard. The men of that boat seized their oars and put about in what they judged was his direction. After minutes that seemed like hours they spotted him. By an old rule they gave no sign. They believed that if they hailed a man in the water so that he knew he had been sighted, all the strength would go out of him and he might drown before their eyes. Fighting to keep their own boat afloat, maneuvering in the wind and waves, they at last came close enough to toss him a rope, and then they shouted encouragement. He grabbed it with numb hands, held on, and they pulled him in more dead than alive.

That boat and the others scoured the area. They found no one else, though they stayed out long after dark, while anxious families ashore prayed at their fishermen's shrine or walked the hundred-times-pilgrimage between this shrine and the big shrine of the town. The boats went out again the next morning. They found no man, living or dead.

That same morning, losing no time, Matsumura and Moriyama called on Harris. And now another journal becomes available, for beginning with this date Moriyama's diary has come down to us. It is a valuable addition to the record, for though Harris was inclined to undervalue Moriyama, no man was more important in the negotiations, no man on either side deserves more credit when they went well, no other man taught Harris as much about Japan. It was because Harris was, to use Secretary Marcy's word, "top-heavy," that he insisted on negotiating only with the Governors. Obviously, he never realized how much they leaned on Moriyama.

The visit by the executive officer and Moriyama rated only one sentence in Harris's journal, but Moriyama tells us what happened.

The atmosphere was friendly, he reports, which certainly means that Harris broke out the liquor. He could scarcely avoid it, for Matsumura and Moriyama had brought both him and Heusken gifts of sake from Edo.

They had much to chat about, for the two Japanese had been away almost eight weeks. When they got down to business they arranged for Governor Okada to pay a call the next morning, and they planned the salute which Harris had requested in honor of Washington's birthday (since it fell on Sunday, the salute was to be fired on Monday).

Word that the Governor was to "inspect" Gyokusenji was flashed to Hambei, for of course town officials were expected to greet him and provide an escort. Okada arrived about eleven o'clock, with Matsumura, Moriyama, and interpreter Tateishi Tokujuro.

After the usual compliments, as Harris put it, the Governor called for his gifts to be brought in: a salted salmon, three rolls of silk crepe (two for Harris and one for Heusken), and a sword. The salmon, he announced, had been given to him by the Governor of Hakodate. He was presenting it to Harris because he had heard of his fondness for salmon.

Finally the sword was laid before Harris, who was sufficiently appreciative to use two exclamation marks in recording the fact. *He told me the blade was one he had worn for some years; that it was by the first sword-maker of Japan, etc., etc.; that, having procured another blade, he had shifted the scabbard and mountings to it, and therefore presented me with the blade; that no foreigner had ever before obtained such a blade, etc., etc.; and to all this I made the required replies. The blade is really a superb one and has the "shark teeth mark" the whole length of it. This, I am told, is not a mere surface mark, but extends through the metal like the pamom in some Malay krisses.*

Obviously, Harris was impressed, yet Okada had done him the honor of supposing he could appreciate the blade for itself alone, and this was not entirely true. *It was in a common, white wood scabbard, and had a handle to slip on of the same. In fact, was simply a packing case.* Harris had an eye for the ornamental.

Having taken full advantage of the Great Council's permission to exchange gifts with the American "if there was no way to avoid it," Okada now tried subtly to indicate that Heusken might make that trip to Mount Amagi. Supposing the young man were to go there, he said, would it be possible, as he had heard, to measure the mountain's height with a thermometer?

Nothing to it, replied Harris. If a thermometer were put in boiling water at sea level it would register 212°. In boiling water at 12,000 feet it would register 180°. It was thus a simple matter to measure any mountain. But neither foreigner seems to have got the point Okada had tried to make.

The Governor had one more surprise, an invitation to Naka compound. Harris was so unprepared for this that at first he turned it down, understanding it to be a request for a Goyosho meeting to resume negotiations. He was busy just now, he said, perhaps in a few days: evidently he had decided not to appear too eager. But when Moriyama made the invitation clear, he accepted with alacrity for the following Tuesday.

Okada said that dinner would be served. Would Harris prefer Japanese or European food?

Harris sensibly chose Japanese.

Okada was delighted, and would Harris please save his appetite by not breakfasting that morning.

So I am at last to see the inside of their residence.

The next morning Hambei was informed of the party and given his responsibilities. The dinner was to be prepared by the chefs of the town's two best restaurants, Hamadaya and Mangetsuan. A couple of men were sent to Suzaki to buy shrimp and *tai* fish. And Rihei, who usually took charge of such matters, was summoned and told to arrange for two *kago* and eight bearers to transport the guests.

On the same day the fishermen of Shimoda, having abandoned all hope, gave their valediction to the men whose boat had capsized three days earlier. No bodies had been recovered, but the neighbors of the bereaved families, who as always took charge of funeral arrangements, provided coffins as for a regular burial, and in each coffin they placed a small figure made of straw. From the stricken homes close to the harbor the cortege wound across the town toward the hills and to Kaisenji, since all of the men had belonged to that temple. The last coffin in the procession was that of the captain of the crew, to show that in death as in life he was watching after his men.

Suzaki (*a painting by Ryusai*)

After the burials, the mourners turned back toward the sea, carrying now the wooden tablets on which the men's posthumous Buddhist names had been brushed. Again, the tablet of the captain came last. They crossed the river to the rocky beach beyond. There an altar had been erected facing the sea. There all the fishing families of the town were gathered: no fishing boats would go out on this day. There the priests of all the temples were waiting.

The altar bore dishes heaped with boiled rice and white candy, because surely men drowned in the cold sea would be hungry. The memorial tablets were placed upon the altar. The priests chanted from the sutras. And everyone there knew that any fisherman might end this way.

When the service was finished, the rice was thrown into the sea and the candy given to the children, and the people drifted back to their homes. It was agreed that all that was earned in the next two days of fishing would be divided among the families who had lost men.

The next day was Monday, February 23, so the Goyosho sent over to the beach below Gyokusenji *two handsome brass howitzers* for a twenty-one-gun salute to honor Washington's birthday.

Harris and Heusken came down to observe the firing. The cannon, wrote Harris, were *exactly copied in every respect from one Commodore Perry gave them; every appointment about the gun, down to the smallest particular, was exactly copied: percussion locks, drag ropes, powder or cartridge holder and all. . . . The Japanese say they have made 1,000 howitzers like those used at the salute!! But they are great liars, consequently you do not know when to believe them.* (Whether the Japanese had a thousand howitzers of exactly this design, or whether they even claimed they had, is doubtful; but it is very possible that they had a thousand howitzers.)

Heusken commented: "The gunners served their artillery pieces in the most remarkable manner, and with utmost accuracy." Harris, as usual, found a way to meld compliment and insult: *The firing was good, quite as good as I have seen among civilized persons.*

Early the next morning twelve men were sent to help Moriyama move to his new quarters in the compound at Naka. Somewhat later Rihei reported to Gyokusenji with the two *kago* and the bearers, who spent the next two hours gossiping and smoking in the barracks by the gate.

Tuesday, February 24, 1857. Norimono were sent at nine this morning, but I did not leave until eleven, when I proceeded with quite a train of attendants. The norimono is a horrible affair. The only position you can assume is to sit on your heels, Japanese fashion, or else cross-legged. For the two foreigners, with their tight trousers and their inelastic muscles, the two-mile trip was torture. Harris, like Heusken, must have "expressed thanks to Heaven" when he was jogged through the gate of the white-walled compound and freed from his little cage.

—So this was where the Governors and the chief members of their staff lived. "Each has a small house of his own where he lives with his servants," wrote Heusken. There were, in Harris's words, *some twenty to thirty buildings in one grand enclosure . . . The houses are all of wood covered with tile roofs. The sides of each room are a series of paper windows some six feet high, and have sliding shutters to close them in during storms or cold weather. The houses are very open and are only warmed by charcoal braziers.*

From Moriyama we learn that the guests were entertained not in the house of one of the Governors but in their reception and office building. Lined up to greet them, in ascending order of importance, were two of the Governors' attendants, then Inspector Aihara, Moriyama, and finally the two executive officers who dealt with the foreigners, Matsumura and Wakana, all formally dressed in *kamishimo*. Dr. Ito Kansai and Tateishi Tokujuro joined the party for dinner.

I was received with all formality by the two Governors in an ante-room. I was then conducted to an inner apartment furnished with seats, braziers, etc., etc. After drinking a cup of tea and smoking three whiffs of tobacco, I was again conducted to the room of my entertainment. This room, out of compliment to me, was furnished with seats and tables. On the table before me were pipes, tobacco, a brazier, etc., etc. My seat was on the left of the Governor and close to the toko, or sacred place, and consequently the seat of honor. He meant the *tokonoma*, the recess where the room's painting was hung. It was probably a good one, carefully chosen in his honor. According to Moriyama, Harris took a close look at this scroll and gave his views on it. No doubt he complimented it and no doubt he was insincere: his private description was *paper hangings, with trees, flowers, storks, etc., drawn on them. . . .*

On a table placed across the foot of the room was a dwarfed cedar tree, decorated with storks cut out of radish and neatly colored. These were fastened to the tree by springs of twisted wire, which continued any motion for a long time. Flowers also, both real and artificial, were used to decorate the dishes of cakes, bon-bons, etc., etc., which were also placed on this table. I was told the storks were a wish for my longevity, and that the various flowers had a complimentary meaning in them. . . .

The meal consisted of fish cooked in every possible Japanese way, and fish raw; the latter cut from a large fish which was brought to me to see. It was in a large dish, decorated with a mast and sail, the colors of the latter indicating welcome. Of course, *sashimi*, raw fish, was served, for this was a Japanese dinner in high style, but Heusken's memory was probably more accurate when he wrote that this particular fish was cooked.

A pâté made of lobster was very nice; sweet potatoes and radishes served up in various forms were the vegetables. There were also, as Heusken noted, soups, poultry, oysters, and a few dishes he may have had trouble identifying, which went under the heading, "etc., etc." *Some ten courses were served, all brought to me in wooden cups brightly lacquered.* Like many a foreigner since, Harris kept wondering when the rice would appear: *Contrary to my expectations, neither rice nor bread was served with the dishes.* (Why he thought bread might be served is a mystery.)

"At the same time," Heusken wrote, "we are served in small porcelain cups hot sake, a drink distilled from rice." Harris and Heusken shared a hearty dislike for sake, which means that the gifts brought to them from Edo by Matsumura and Moriyama were wasted.

Harris had an excuse: *I plead ill health and only drank tea.* But poor Heusken was obviously in the pink.

> The first Governor wishes to drink to my health. He does that drinking sake, the Japanese wine, from a small porcelain cup. I do the same thing, keeping a pleasant countenance, although the drink is detestable. Then I am told that the porcelain cup is mine and I must take it along with me. I then go through the same ceremonies with the second Governor and the Vice-Governors which makes me the proud owner of a number of cups of the beautiful Japanese porcelain. But at the same time my palate suffers unbearable tortures in the transferring of the awful liquor from the cups to my stomach.

After all the fish dishes were done, rice was served without salt or any other condiment—no sauce, no seasonings, no raisins and nutmeg; not fried in oil with onion and herbs and egg as his Chinese cooks prepared it—and to this dish he could not plead ill health.

Let Heusken continue the account:

> The first Governor now explains through his interpreter, Moriyama Takichiro, that if persons of distinguished rank want to pay a great compliment to other persons equally distinguished who happen to be at their homes, they make them some tea with their own hands, and the first Governor wishes to pay that compliment to His Excellency and close friend, the Consul General. A Japanese dignitary brings a box from which the noble Governor takes a small brazier, a cute little teapot, and other necessities. He explains, with all the pride of an amateur, the different phases of the process to which he submits the aromatic herb. He warms the tea and places it in the teapot. He boils the water, pours it over the tea and presents the tea to the Consul while making him a

present of the box and all the objects he used to prepare the tea for him.

The conversation now took the usual Japanese turn. The lubricity of these people passes belief. The moment business is over, the one and only subject on which they dare converse comes up. I was asked a hundred different questions about American females, as whether single women dressed differently from the married ones, etc., etc.; but I will not soil my paper with the greater part of them, but I clearly perceived that there are particulars which enter into Japanese marriage contracts that are disgusting beyond belief. Bingo-no-kami informed me that one of the Vice Governors was specially charged with the duty of supplying me with female society, and said if I fancied any woman the Vice-Governor would procure her for me, etc., etc., etc.

I was asked if their people could receive some instruction in beating the drum when the next man-of-war came. I replied I had no doubt the commander would be willing to gratify them on that point. They said they had brass drums copied from the Dutch. They asked me about the various signals given by beat of drum, which I answered as well as I could. Then— oh, shame! They asked me if we had not a beat of the drum as a signal to our soldiers to go to the houses of ill fame, and I emphatically replied no. They evidently did not believe me; for, said they, "We know the Dutch do so at Nagasaki,* and all your armies are much the same." I gladly took my leave at three P.M. and reached home quite jaded out.

Dismissing the *kago*, he gave Rihei two silver dollars to tip the bearers and the cooks who had prepared the dinner. Rihei turned the dollars in to the Goyosho and received two *bu* in return.

One topic had been discussed at Naka which Harris did not mention. Okada had said that he and Inoue would like to reopen talks, and Harris had agreed to meet them at noon the next day.

For a while, at least, Harris had had quite enough of *kago*. Next morning, despite a cold north wind, he went by boat to Shimoda.

The session that day at the Goyosho marked the resumption of negotiations after a lapse of four and a half months. There had been no discussion of serious issues—as distinguished from Harris's stream of complaints about the way he was being treated—since the meeting of October 7 when Iwase was present on his mission from Edo. At this point, therefore, it may be well to read Heusken's review of the situation: it constitutes a better apologia for Harris's course than anything Harris wrote himself.

* The Dutch, isolated on their little island, were periodically permitted, under escort, to visit the city's gay quarter.

We are beginning today our official interviews with the two Governors. While we have been here we have already won quite a few points from the Japanese. These may seem trifling, but they really are of great importance to a people so isolated from the rest of the world, and whose suspicious diplomacy had caused the failure of all efforts at the time of Commodore Perry's arrival in these parts two years ago. At the beginning, I couldn't take a step outside the consulate without having a *gobangoshi*, or police officer, dogging my steps, and following me like my own shadow. If I raised my cane, the man disappeared, but he was sure to reappear again behind another tree or house. When we complained of it to the government, we were told that these people were for our own protection against the populace, and were a sort of guard of honor. Poor populace of Japan, whom they tried to make appear to us as so impressive and so fearsome! These poor people's hands were tied to such an extent that they did not dare look at us. And then the inhabitants of Shimoda had received the most rigorous orders not to communicate with us. If I appeared in the street, they would usually close their doors and windows. Women especially fled at a gallop at our approach. The young girls particularly ran as though the very enemy of mankind was at their heels; and if we were lucky enough to see a woman marching boldly towards us, it was a wrinkled octogenarian whose weakened sight did not enable her to distinguish those foreign devils from her beloved countrymen. Beasts of burden, usually quite indolent in Japan, came out of their lethargic state when we arrived, made pirouettes and somersaults and even though carrying a heavy burden they ran away at a gallop. Dogs, who had forgotten how to bark except at the moon, seemed to mistake us for that heavenly orb, for when they saw us they raised a frightful racket and a concert of all the dogs of the town, gathered together by the sound of the alarm gun, followed us to the limit of the city where they relinquished their privilege to howl to the dogs of the countryside. Only the cats did not seem to submit to the rigorous laws of Japan against foreigners, and watched us with indifference. And I had fallen so low as to call these aloof animals models of hospitality.

Secondly, the little house in the consulate yard inside the entrance gate was always occupied by two officers and soldiers who were relieved regularly every day.

Thirdly, if an officer came to visit us, he was always accompanied by half a dozen secretaries who wrote down every word uttered.

Fourthly, there were in Shimoda three imperial spies, accredited by the government. These spies were empowered to enter the Governors' house at any moment, even in the night, and to attend all the conferences which the government held with us. These worthy people are supposed to report to their masters in Edo all that goes on here. If Japanese dignitaries came to see us, the spy was sure to appear later if he did not come with them. Spies stood apart from the other officers and observed all that went on between us.

Fifthly, all the letters the Consul-General addressed to the Governors were never answered by another letter. The reply was always verbal. Every time the Consul-General complained of these indignities he received evasive answers, either that such was the custom in Japan, or that these measures were only taken in order to protect us, etc.

The Consul was aware that he had to change his attitude towards the Japanese, that his gentle and courteous remonstrances were of no avail. One fine day, he boldly addressed the Governors and told them that his government would never stand such outrages against the person of its representative, that the sacred character of a diplomatic agent was recognized by all civilized nations of the world, that when the Japanese had concluded treaties with foreign nations they had consequently subjected themselves to the general laws that rule all nations and that he could not be responsible for the reprisals and the indignation of all civilized nations which the government of Japan was about to draw upon itself by these outrages against the law of nations.

"I demand," he said, "that the guards posted at the door of the consulate and who treat like a prisoner a representative of the United States be immediately removed or I shall declare myself a prisoner and you will have to take the consequences." That speech seemed to make an impression, for when we returned to the consulate the guards were already packing and by sunset no one was left except those people directly attached to the consulate.

The Consul also said that if a Japanese dignitary wanted to visit him he would always be glad to receive him, but he did not want to see them hereafter flanked by secretaries who insulted him by writing down everything that went on and that the first time he sees a spy appear at his house he will eject him. Since that day spies and secretaries have ceased to come here, and even when we have interviews at the Government House they are absent. I do not doubt that during conferences at the *Goyosho* there are secretaries hidden behind the thin partitions of the chamber because with their usual tenacity they will conform to the ancient laws of the Empire as long as possible. I have no doubt either that there are among the Japanese officers secret spies who report all that goes on. In a word, every Japanese spies on another, and it is only by that system of mutual spying that the government can maintain itself in power. But, at any rate, appearances are saved and I do not doubt that communications established between the Japanese and civilized nations will gradually destroy this system of absurd, obsolete, and absolute laws that weigh heavily upon the Empire.

Now, when we walk the streets police agents do not dare any more to follow us; I enter the houses freely; I speak with the common people without anybody daring to oppose it. Young girls are getting to be less shy when they see us and do not run away from us anymore; beasts of burden, formerly so imbued with Japanese doctrines against foreigners, can't distinguish them anymore from their lords and masters. The dogs alone remain faithful to their principles and bark just as loud and show their teeth just as fiercely as they did the day we arrived.

Now the Governors reply to us by letters.

This may be accepted as what it was intended to be: a report of progress and a justification of tactics. Yet surely even Heusken would have admitted that many of the changes he chronicled had resulted simply from the passage of time. After six months the people of Shimoda were getting used to the two foreigners.

On the morning of the twenty-fifth the Governors were suitably escorted to the Goyosho by their own attendants and staff, a Shimoda town elder, and several block leaders. Harris and Heusken had learned by now to counter with the best escort they could muster: Takizo and Sukezo. Presumably, from boat landing to Goyosho they were also accompanied by barking dogs.

Wednesday, February 25, 1857. Met the Governors at the Goyosho at noon to-day. They brought in, with great ceremony, a box which was reverentially placed before me. Then a Vice-Governor [it was Matsumura] *opened the box,—*

Said Okada: "This is a gift from the government. It is a silk called *rinzu*. Only persons of high position can wear it."

—which I found to contain five pieces of a very poor satin damask, which I was told was from five members of the Regency [the Great Council, which was not a regency] *at Edo,—one piece from each person. This over, another box was brought which, as I was told, contained an answer to my two letters to Edo,—*

Again it was Matsumura who brought the box, and it was Okada who opened it and handed the letter to Harris.

—and at last they mustered courage to open it and unfold a sheet of paper about five feet long by eighteen inches wide, written quite full and bearing the seals and signatures of the . . . members of the Regency . . . with a Dutch translation of the same which they [it was Moriyama] *placed in Mr. Heusken's hands.*

I directed Mr. Heusken to put the letter and translation in the box and close it. The Governors wished me to have it translated into English at once. This I declined, saying I should prefer having it done at leisure, and that in the meantime I should like to hear their answer on the currency question. Now ensued a scene quite Japanese, which occupied two full hours. The substance of it was that they admitted the justice of my demand in part, but said my offer (five per cent.) to pay for the recoining was not sufficient; that they should lose by it, and they therefore begged me to reconsider it and make them an increased offer. I asked them what was the cost of coining money in Japan? They gravely replied twenty-five per cent.!! Twenty-five per cent. I told them it was simply impossible; that the cost in Europe and America for such labor was not one per cent.; that I would bring competent moneyers from the United States who would do the whole work for five per cent., or even less. They said the laws of Japan forbade the employment of foreigners about their coinage.

I endeavored to solicit a direct offer from them, but without success. Among other statements made by them was this: that gold and silver before coinage had no value; that it was the mint stamp that gave it its value, etc., etc. I told them their Government had an undoubted right to deal with the precious metals produced in Japan as they pleased, but they had no such right over a foreigner, and that to attempt to exercise such a right over him would in effect be a confiscation of his property; that they might stamp pieces of paper or leather, and compel their own subjects to take them in lieu of gold and silver, but they could not expect the foreigner to take them in exchange for his merchandise, or to have his coin measured by the intrinsic value of such worthless tokens.

In his arguments Harris was conveniently forgetting that no trade treaty existed between Japan and the United States, so that the question of what kind of Japanese money an American took in exchange for his goods was quite beside the point. He was also forgetting that irritating sentence in that aggravating book by Professor Martens on *The Law of Nations*—". . . the right of coining extending no further than the territory of a state, no sovereign is obliged to admit foreign money into his dominions; and, if he admit it, he has an indisputable right to fix the value of it, without respect to that which it bore in the country where it was coined . . ."

This ground was traveled over and over again, the Japanese always reasoning in a circle and trying to gain their point by simple pertinacity. I passed four weary hours and left at four P.M., appointing the next day to meet again.

It was snowing. Should it be raining tomorrow, he said, would the Japanese please send *kago*.

On reaching home, Mr. Heusken translated the Dutch copy of the letter, and found it to be a simple announcement that all business was to be transacted with the Governors of Shimoda or Hakodate, and not one word in reference to the President's letter to the Emperor of Japan, of which I told them I was the bearer.

What it actually said, as Heusken translated it into warped English from Moriyama's Dutch, was:

We have duly perused both the letter of the Ninth Month of last year concerning the order of His Majesty the President and other circumstances, and to communicate to us, in person, an important matter relating to the Japanese Empire and the United States, and the later written communication of the Twelfth Month. But, since the opening of the harbors of Shimoda and Hakodate, Governors have been appointed for both places, and all the affairs of both countries have been confided to their management, therefore to communicate anything, however important, to the Governors of the above mentioned places, is the same as if it had been done to us in person, so it will be well to deliberate faithfully with the Governors, which we bring to your knowledge.

It was not a tranquil evening at Gyokusenji.

Next morning it did rain. Harris and Heusken folded themselves into *kago* dispatched from the Goyosho.

Thursday, February 26, 1857. On reaching the Goyosho to-day, the Governors asked me if I had perused the letter from the Regency, etc., etc., and said they had something to add, which was that they had full powers to receive from me any propositions I had to make, and to treat on all the matters referred to in my two letters to the Minister of Foreign Affairs, and then began to question me as to certain matters contained therein. I told them I was not yet ready to answer, but rather to ask questions, and that I wished to know the nature of their powers. Could they give me answers at once on all matters I might propose without waiting to hear from Edo? They assured me in the most solemn manner that they could. I then asked could they make a new treaty without such reference? Their answer soon proved what I before suspected,—that, in any minor matter, they could decide, but, on any important one, they could only hear and report. As the Governors put it, that was, after all, the way their government functioned.

The way the Japanese government functioned was just what irritated Harris. As for the Great Council's letter, he said it sounded like instructions issued to a merchant; did the Japanese realize that the Consul General ranked much higher than the Dutch "Kapitan" at Nagasaki? (This was another of Harris's misconceptions, for the government of the Netherlands had taken over from the Dutch East India Company, and Donker Curtius as Commissioner outranked Harris.) Not only was the Great Council's language wanting in respect, but their letter failed to show proper consideration for the President's message and it denied Harris's right to present himself at the capital.

The Governors protested. The letter was not at all the sort sent to a merchant. The language was not impolite, it was simply the terse official style. And it was a singular honor that it had been written at all: only twice before had the Great Council written to a foreigner, first to the King of the Netherlands and second to the Prime Minister of Russia. Harris's complaints were due to misunderstanding.

Ordinarily, Harris went on, a Consul General restricted himself to seeing that his own countrymen obeyed existing treaty provisions and that their rights were not infringed. He did not become involved in such weighty matters as negotiating a new treaty or—probing a tender spot—a trade agreement. But he himself was specially empowered for such negotiations, having been designated a plenipotentiary.

The Governors said that they, too, were plenipotentiaries and ready to negotiate any matter. Fortunately, they added blandly, they and the Consul General were on friendly terms.

Indeed they were on friendly terms, said Harris, and he was ready to negotiate with them, but not at Shimoda. In all other countries, negotiations on important matters were conducted at the capital. He would be happy to negotiate with the Governors at Edo, where, he was certain, matters could be successfully concluded in five or ten days. Should he, however, agree to negotiate at any place but Edo, and the President heard of it, he would at once be relieved of duty and recalled.

This was not true. Harris's instructions do state that—

A principal motive of the President in selecting you as Consul General for Japan was the hope that, by your knowledge of eastern character, and your general intelligence and experience in business, you would make such an impression upon the Japanese as would in time induce them to enter into a commercial treaty with us. As it is possible that a juncture favorable for making an overture for this purpose might arise before you could communicate with the Department, upon the subject, after your arrival at Shimoda, you are now furnished with a full power to negotiate and conclude such a Treaty.

—but they nowhere suggest that Harris should attempt to visit the capital, either to negotiate or to deliver the President's letter. There is no reason to suppose that the President or the Secretary of State would have objected to these goals, but there is good reason—Marcy's indignation at Harris's conduct in Paris, for example—to assume that they would have objected to his tactics.

The Governors were not easily convinced. How about Perry and the Russian commodore, they asked. They negotiated elsewhere than at the capital.

Entirely different; they were opening treaty relations and they could not leave the naval forces they commanded. But he was the representative of a country with whom Japan had signed a treaty. He was qualified to live in the capital city, he asserted, and he could not understand why he was not permitted to do so. For the important matters at issue, he had been directed by the President to proceed to Edo, but since it seemed the Japanese were not ready to permit that, he would report the situation to his government by the next homeward-bound ship that called here. He trusted that the President would issue new orders.

There was no need to tell them that, the Governors answered, because that was strictly his own affair. The President himself had said that the United States had no intention of interfering with the political affairs of another nation. Would Harris please keep this in mind?

He could not discuss important matters at Shimoda, Harris reiterated, but—*I then said, "I have some matters under the Treaty which properly come under your jurisdiction, and will now proceed to open them." They wished to renew the discussion of the currency, but I told them, unless they had some new matter, or a distinct proposition to make, I should prefer leaving that for the present.*

Harris placed four demands that afternoon.

I then stated that the Port of Nagasaki had been opened to the Russians as a place where their ships could obtain necessary supplies and coals for steamers, and I demanded the same rights for the Americans.

The Japanese raised no objections to opening Nagasaki to the Americans; they never had. Okada, however, did inquire why it was being asked for now, since Perry had stated that the port was quite unacceptable. Harris replied that Perry had asked for two other ports on the assumption that the Russians would ask for Nagasaki, and thus the Americans would get it anyway under the most-favored nation clause. This was probably an erroneous answer (Perry said he refused Nagasaki on the grounds "that its inhabitants and authorities, having been so long accustomed to the servility of the Dutch, would doubtless exact more from the Americans than they would be inclined to submit to, and serious consequences might follow"). It was certainly an unfortunate answer, for it reinforced the Japanese belief that all foreigners were in collusion against her.

My next was, that American ships in want of supplies and not having money, that goods should be taken in payment. They said this was already granted by our Treaty. I told them, if that was the case, of course they could have no objection to reaffirming it, and this was agreed to.

The Governors were quite correct: Perry's treaty already provided that American ships "shall be permitted to exchange gold and silver coin and articles of goods for other articles of goods . . ." This was the gateway to trade, and Secretary Marcy had emphasized that it should be guarded zealously. There seems to have been no good reason to tamper with it.

My next was that Americans committing offenses in Japan should be tried by the Consul and punished if guilty according to Japanese laws.* To my great and agreeable surprise this was agreed to without demur.

Harris need not have been so agreeably surprised. The Japanese had already yielded extraterritoriality to the Russians in their 1855 treaty, a copy of which Possiet had given Harris, and ratifications of which had been exchanged under Harris's aloof observation only last December. The same right was written into the Netherlands convention of 1855, and Harris had a copy of that too.

To the Japanese, the system no doubt seemed the simplest solution to a sticky problem, and none of the foreign negotiators ever pointed out to them that in granting it they were relinquishing some of their sovereignty. Perry's treaty contained no such provision. Credit for this is sometimes given to S. Wells Williams, who had had ample opportunity (as had Harris) to see the evils of extraterritoriality in China. Consuls were ill-fitted to act as judge and jury; and somehow burglary, rape, or murder when the victims were yellow-skinned heathen did not seem to call for punishment as severe as the same crimes did at home. American justice was faultiest of all, for Congress had made no provision for jails: if the British or French were unable to provide accommodations in their prisons, which were often full, even convicted murderers were perforce turned free. Williams no doubt argued against extraterritoriality, but the decision was Perry's and it stands to his credit.

I next told them that I demanded the right for Americans to lease ground, buy, build, repair, or alter . . . buildings at their pleasure, and that they should be supplied with materials and labor for such purposes when-

---

* This was a slip of the pen. Harris meant to write "according to American laws."

ever they might require it. I told them I founded this claim on the 12th and 13th Articles made with the Dutch at Nagasaki on the 9th of November, 1855, by which all the ground at Deshima was leased to the Dutch and the buildings sold to them; and that they also had the right to build, alter or repair, etc., etc.; that I claimed those same privileges under the 9th Article of the Treaty of Kanagawa.

To Harris, it was all quite clear. Since these rights—amounting to the right of residence, which he was determined to fight for—had been granted to the Dutch subsequent to Perry's treaty with its most-favored-nation clause, the same rights accrued to the United States.

From the moment that Harris raised this proposition the Governors stoutly resisted it. *The Governors were amazed. They never heard of any such convention. It did not, it could not, exist. When, where and by whom was it made? I told them. It was not known to the Government at Edo; had never been ratified, and therefore had never gone into effect. . . .*

Now, will it be believed that during all this time (more than one hour) the Governors had an authentic copy of that very Convention lying before them in a dispatch box? It was so; and all this barefaced falsehood was a fair specimen of Japanese diplomacy.

Perhaps a calmer man might have reasoned more carefully. The Governors did not deny that the convention had been written, they said it *had never been ratified, and therefore had never gone into effect.*

But even if Harris had grasped this through the three-language tangle, he would have remained convinced that the Japanese were lying. For he was certain that Captain Fabius had shown him a ratified copy of the convention last October.

It was one more case when Harris's information was wrong. The convention had never been ratified (one can only guess what Captain Fabius told Harris) and it had been superseded within three months by another treaty signed January 30, 1856, which struck out articles 12 and 13, and which was itself yet to be ratified.

The Governors were taken by surprise and they floundered. They correctly asserted that articles 12 and 13 were not in effect, but they confused the issue by trying to defend granting those rights solely to the Dutch. *They then took new ground. The Dutch had been in Japan more than two hundred years; that these were old matters and had no relation to the present state of affairs.*

All this contributed to Harris's exasperation and to his conviction, always ready, that he was being lied to. Unfortunately, his nearly ungovernable temper made him quick to say so. The Governors did not like being called liars, and their retainers were infuriated. The meeting degenerated into angry recrimination.

One can only conjecture what a less stormy approach might have gained, whether a man with better control over his temper and less prone to call an adversary a liar might not have surmised the existence of a later treaty and ferreted out the truth with fewer bruised feelings and less bitterness. What if, like Dr. Wood of the *San Jacinto,* he had "smoked comfortable pipes of mild tobacco, and drank small cups of sweet sake," and calmly asked to see what superseded the signed treaty at hand?

Four o'clock having arrived, I left them to meet again to-morrow at the same hour. The Goyosho passed the word to Hambei, who promptly notified the block leaders that an escort for the Governors would be required again the next morning.

Returning to their temple, Harris and Heusken might have done well to follow the ceremony performed that day in houses all around them in Kakisaki, in Shimoda, in the quarters within the Governors' compound at Naka, and throughout Japan. People took parched beans, one for each year of their lives, and threw them about their homes, crying: "Welcome, good luck! Out, devils!" Lion dancers—that is, men wearing heads made to suggest that frolicsome, peony-loving creature the Japanese call lion—went through the streets, performing their ancient dance in front of houses, and when suitably rewarded, trooping through a house, tossing more beans with the same cry: "Welcome, good luck! Out, devils!"

This was Setsubun. To the Japanese, tomorrow would be the first day of spring. By a calendar even older than the one they used, it would be the first day of the new year. It was an eminently suitable time to chase out bad luck and welcome good.

The Governors and their staff came to the Goyosho early the next morning, to prepare for the meeting. Harris and Heusken came by boat.

Friday, February 27, 1857. At the Goyosho at noon. The Governors opened the business by traveling over the same ground as yesterday (on my last proposition) for nearly two hours, not one new idea or argument being started.

On this day Harris offered an "unofficial" explanation of why it was essential that American merchants be given the privilege of residence in Japan, which was, after all, what he was fighting for. America had more whalers than any other nation in the world, he said, and the North Pacific was their best grounds. Previously, when they needed supplies they had to go all the way back to the Hawaiian Islands, which was why Perry had arranged that Hakodate be opened to them. But the Japanese could not supply all their needs. Therefore, it was necessary that American merchants be permitted there to stock such necessities as sails, iron chains, and beef.

Arrangements had already been made to have a plentiful supply of beef at Hakodate, the Governors answered, and why could not the Japanese buy such things as sails and chains from American merchant ships and offer them for sale through Japanese merchants at Hakodate? Why was it necessary that American merchants settle there?

At which point Harris seems to have lost interest in this argument. He shifted back to his insistence that Americans must be granted those same privileges which he was so certain had recently been granted the Dutch. The obfuscated quarrel continued.

Harris placed two new demands that day. *I next claimed the right to have purchases made for me by any person I might employ, and that*

A beggar who recites incantations to drive
away evil on the night before Setsubun
(*a book illustration by Jichosai*)

payment should be made directly to the seller without the interference of any Japanese official.

The Governors said they would issue him paper money (when the Great Council authorized issuing him "moderate" amounts of coin they evidently meant quite small amounts). Harris balked. He knew that the Shogunate's paper money commanded little respect among merchants: they wanted hard cash. With paper money he would still be forced to negotiate his purchases through the Goyosho; he would be no better off than he was.

I also claimed that the limits of seven ri and five ri at Shimoda and Hakodate did not apply to me as Consul General, but that the whole Empire of Japan was included in my Consulate.

The last was a claim that a Western negotiator would have laughed at, pointing out that (as Secretary Marcy had been informed from Paris) Harris was trying to act like a minister plenipotentiary instead of the consul he was. But the Governors were not familiar with the Laws of Nations that Harris so often referred to and so seldom cited, and they argued only from the wording of Perry's treaty. It stated that its provisions were to be obeyed by the citizens and subjects of each nation—by "all persons, high and low," was the way the Japanese read it—without exception, and they were not prepared to make an exception in the case of the Consul General, despite their great respect for him.

There was less falsehood in their replies to this point than there was to the preceding one, but this arose from the want of opportunity rather than the want of inclination.

It must have been at this meeting that the Governors, raising the currency question again, reduced their request for a discount to cover recoining from twenty-five to fifteen per cent. Harris told them their demand was unreasonable and repeated his offer of five per cent.

At last I told them I had something of great importance to communicate confidentially, and to them alone. To my great surprise the room was at once cleared of all but the two Governors and Moriyama Takichiro. I then read to them an extract from a letter to me from the Secretary of State, which was to the effect that, if the Japanese sought to evade the Treaty, the President would not hesitate to ask Congress to give him power to use such arguments as they could not resist. . . .

What Harris must have read was this paragraph from his instructions of October 4, 1855:

> While it is our policy and purpose to endeavor, by a conciliatory course, to induce the Japanese to accede to a fair construction of the

Treaty, or to enter into a new one for the purpose of preventing any misunderstanding in regard to our rights, if this disposition should not be promptly and fully reciprocated on their part, the President would not hesitate to ask for authority to adopt other measures. The expense which we have already incurred for the purpose of opening an intercourse with Japan, our national interests and our national character require, that we should not allow the main object of the existing treaty to be thwarted by a strained or unwarrantable construction. You may therefore intimate to the Japanese authorities that, if our reasonable expectations should be disappointed, we will be sure to demand, in a way which they cannot resist, privileges which we are entitled to. . . .

Probably Harris stopped there, though Marcy had gone on in conclusion:

I hope you will succeed not only in securing a liberal construction of the present treaty, but in procuring greater privileges than can be claimed under it.

The fluttering was fearful—the effect strong. They thanked me for the confidence I had placed in them by reading that part of the Secretary's letter, and asked if they might communicate the same to their Government. I told them they could do so. They then asked me to give them a written translation of the paragraph so that they might make a correct translation. This I declined, but I told them I would have it translated and that Moriyama might use that paper in my presence to translate it to them, but that the paper must be returned to me. This ended our proceedings for the day at half-past four P.M.

Having tossed his bombshell, Harris left, leaving the Japanese to sweat over the weekend. Shimoda boatmen carried him back to Kakisaki.

Saturday, February 28, 1857. At home all day, and very glad to rest after the vexing labors of the last three days.

His rest was interrupted by a visit from Moriyama. The day before, during the long wrangling over the rights Harris was sure the Dutch had acquired, the Governors had questioned the correctness of his translation. *I suddenly asked them to give me a copy of [the] 12th and 13th Articles according to their version, which they promised to do—apparently for the moment forgetting their denial of any knowledge of such a Convention only yesterday.* (Apparently Harris considered the Governors not only liars but dolts.) Moriyama now delivered a Dutch translation of those articles. Heusken compared them with Harris's copy and found them identical. So, said Harris, there was no longer any room for argument.

But Moriyama thought there was. The interpreting on the Japanese side had not been good yesterday, he said (evidently he had not interpreted except for the private session), and he would like to explain the Governors' position. And he repeated the argument that the articles in question only confirmed to the Dutch rights they had long held. He got nowhere. Harris repeated his assertion that the articles gave the Dutch entirely new privileges, which therefore accrued to the Americans. Moriyama also brought up the currency question, and got nowhere with it.

Nevertheless, it was a quite amiable conversation, for Moriyama's touch with this unpredictable foreigner was surer than any of his colleague's. He told Harris about his promotion and about his change of name. Harris took the opportunity to broach the idea of a trade treaty. It would come, Moriyama replied, it would come, but the time was not ripe.

On this same last day of February, Donker Curtius in Nagasaki delivered a long report to one of the staff of the Governor of that place, the Governor himself being ill. The Dutchman's subject was the war in China.

He spoke of the troubled relations between the foreign powers and China since the Opium War of 1839–1842. He told of the trifling incident over the ship *Arrow* that had led to the present outbreak. He described the destruction of Canton from the shelling by British warships. The Chinese had brought all this upon themselves, he said, because of their arrogance and hostility toward foreigners.

Curtius may not have had all his facts straight. He was unaware of how the war was going at the moment.

Sandwith Drinker's firm had lost another of its ships: the steamer *Queen* had been captured between Hong Kong and Macao by the Chinese passengers aboard. And the truth was that the British were on the defensive in the whole of the Canton area. As Captain Bell had already written to Harris, the commander in India had refused to send reinforcements on the grounds that he had no troops to spare. When news of what had happened reached London, Parliament was the scene of bitter attacks on John Bowring: accusations that there had been "a preconceived design to pick a quarrel with the Chinese"; that his letters to the Chinese commissioner had been "menacing, disrespectful, irritating and arrogant" and that he had made no attempt to come to an agreement; that he "had violated international law and had acted contrary to his instructions from the government." Men as different as Gladstone and Disraeli condemned him. The government won a narrow victory in the House of Lords but lost a narrower one in the Commons. Parliament was dissolved and elections scheduled. It was clear that something had to be done about Bowring, yet the government, having had to defend him, could not admit error by replacing him. They contrived a greater humiliation: to leave him where he was but to send out a new man, the Earl of Elgin, to supersede him as Plenipotentiary to China. Sir John would remain as nothing more than the Governor of Hong Kong.

Curtius knew none of this, but all his points were well taken, for the outcome of the war was inevitable. Eventually the Chinese would be crushed.

The basic mistake that China made, he said, was first to refuse what in the end it would have to concede. Every time it finally approved what it had first refused, it lost prestige. Every time a foreign nation won what it had once been denied, it gained prestige. "If you consider this point well, it will be a good lesson to you in formulating your foreign policy."

His government, he went on, had asked him to make certain points to the Japanese, with the hope that they would be considered carefully.

First, an international treaty was a matter of great importance. It could not cover details, but it should aim at promoting friendly relations, and this meant a great deal more than receiving foreign envoys with proper courtesy and decorum. Friendly relations could not be achieved by trying to narrow each provision of a treaty or by delaying replies or by postponing action on diplomatic affairs.

Second, there was the style of the letters written to foreigners. It was common opinion among Europeans that the Japanese were wise and considerate in dealing with foreigners, that Japan was the most civilized country in the East and should not be mentioned in the same breath with China. Nevertheless, government letters to foreigners were written as superior to inferior, and were bound to give offense.

The United States, Britain, and Russia were all complaining of the troublesome interpretations of their treaties by Japanese authorities. There was no doubt that France would soon seek to open relations. These were the four great nations of the world. Japan must achieve friendly and impartial relations with them. Nothing would gratify the Netherlands more than Japan's success in that. It was necessary that Japan move with the times.

The Nagasaki official thanked the Dutch representative for his concern and his recommendations, and asked that he continue in the future to speak without reserve.

And because Donker Curtius did not object to "spies" and scribes, his words were fully and faithfully transcribed and sent quickly on their way to the heads of the government in Edo.

Chapter 9

MARCH, 1857

On Sunday, March 1, Harris probably reviewed the situation. The Japanese had conceded much, yet they were stubbornly resisting some of his demands. But this was the month that Commodore Armstrong had promised to send a ship. A man-of-war in the harbor would be a powerful argument. With it, Harris felt confident he could get what he wanted. Probably he could even get a trade treaty. It was only a question of time: could he get it before the British or the Russians or the French arrived in force to wrest the honor from him?

Meanwhile there was another conference scheduled for tomorrow. Headman Hambei had been directed to provide the usual escort for the Governors and to send two *kago* with eight bearers to bring the foreigners from Gyokusenji.

Whoever ordered the *kago* had correctly forecast the weather. Monday brought rain, and winds so strong that extra bearers were sent to carry the *kago*.

Only Governor Okada appeared for the meeting. Inoue was ill. Flu had hit the area and it threatened to become epidemic. The doctors were already strained and weary, and the priests of Shinto shrines, Buddhist temples, and temples of the mountain religion were reciting their prayers and incantations.

Harris announced that he had compared with Moriyama his own and the Japanese versions of articles 12 and 13 in the Dutch convention. They had found no difference between them. In view of that, was the Governor now ready to accept his demands?

Okada, still trying to defend articles that had been struck out of the treaty, reiterated that Harris misunderstood their true import: they merely confirmed old arrangements. His answer, therefore, was no.

Harris said there was no misunderstanding on his part, and repeated his demands.

At this point Okada took a new tack. With a weekend to consider the situation, the Governors and their staff had decided that a new approach was essential.

We have met several times, he said, and we are still as far apart as ever. We are rambling endlessly in our talks and getting nowhere. He thought it best that Harris put his propositions in writing, including his plan to station American merchants in Hakodate.

Harris objected. He wanted to make no formal proposal concerning merchants (he had in mind much broader rights of residence) and he said he doubted that he could make himself completely understood in writing. It would be better to continue their discussions, with opportunity for questions and answers. Then he took a curious position: *once I had placed my name to a paper, it could not be modified and that I wished to leave a door open by which we might arrive at a solution of the questions.*

But Okada persisted. There had already been many misunderstandings due to interpretation of the spoken word. *It was finally agreed that Mr. Heusken, as from himself, would give them an unsigned paper containing the substance of my demands, the paper to be sent to the Governor's residence in the morning of to-morrow . . .*

Asking Harris to put all his propositions in writing was one new tactic. The other was to hold fewer meetings. Together they were intended to cope with one of the Governors' tribulations, Harris's fits of temper. Not only did these self-controlled gentlemen find such displays personally repugnant, not only did they halt any attempt at negotiation, but they were undermining the position of the Governors with their own staff. Many of these men took Harris's outbursts as insults to their chiefs. First they boiled with rage against Harris. Then they began to despise the Governors for accepting his abuse.

Harris seems to have been quite blind to the situation he was creating. To him the shoe was on the other foot. *I am really ill, yet I am forced day after day to listen to useless debates, on points that have been exhausted, and are only varied by some new phase of falsehood!*

New tactics were not all that Okada had to offer. It seems likely that it was at this session that he announced a major concession in an attempt to settle the currency problem. From a first demand for a twenty-five-per-cent discount, from last Friday's fifteen per cent, he abruptly lowered their request to six per cent.

It was, as Harris noted, a great step in his favor but he was in no mood to meet it with any concession on his part. *I refused to advance from the five per cent.*

Probing to see whether the Japanese were prepared to make any other concessions, he pressed for those privileges he claimed were due him as an official, despite Perry's treaty: the right to buy directly from the merchants and to travel freely throughout the country. In accepting the stationing of a U. S. official, he argued, Japan had accepted the obligation of treating him by international standards. This was the foot-in-the-door approach he used so often and which always perturbed the Japanese, and as usual he talked of the prerogatives of a minister, not of a consul.

Okada replied that of course the Japanese did not know the customs of other countries when they negotiated with Perry. That was why they had written into the treaty that it applied to all, irrespective of position. Officials would be treated with politeness but they must obey the treaty. (This was the kind of rigidity that Donker Curtius had warned against.)

Insistence on this would disrupt friendly relations, Harris answered. It was his old threat of war. Then in a somewhat mellower mood, possibly occasioned by weariness, he insisted on his sincerity and understanding. It was just that these long delays were so exasperating.

Okada asked that he forgive them their slowness. Theirs was a government which dealt with everything in the light of precedents. These matters were too important for quick decisions, because they would establish new precedents.

Finally all the Japanese except the Governor and Moriyama left the room, and Moriyama was handed a Dutch translation of that passage from the Marcy letter that Harris had read on Friday. Moriyama read it to the Governor in Japanese. Either scribes sat outside and took it down, or Okada and Moriyama had good memories, for the Japanese came up with a faithful translation and sent it off to Edo so that the Great Council could ponder its implications.

Back at the temple, it took Harris little time to set down his propositions or for Heusken to put them into Dutch—they had been over the ground so often. Next morning they were delivered to Naka compound as an unsigned memorandum from Heusken.

Four days later, on March 7, Heusken called at Naka compound to inquire after Inoue's health and to ask when "his" memorandum would be answered. He was told that Harris's good wishes would be conveyed to

Inoue at once and that a reply to the note could be expected in a day or two.

It was Hatsuuma, the festival to celebrate the beginning of planting, the beginning of the farmers' year. It came on the first day of the Horse after Setsubun, or according to that old, old calendar, the first day of the Horse of the New Year. The day was sacred to Inari, the goddess of rice and fertility, and at her many shrines, one in every home and many along the streets and roads, she was offered sake and food with prayers for a bountiful harvest.

Since Inari is also the special goddess of fishermen and merchants, the day was observed in Shimoda as much as in the farm villages. Appropriately, the town's largest Inari shrine was in Suzaki Block, the fishermen's block, but the festivities centered at the house of Wataya Kichibei. There, in the morning, drums were beat to mark the day. Ten bales of rice were cooked with red beans, and the chief priest of the town shrine came to offer this most auspicious of dishes at the Inari shrine of Kichibei's house. The town's important men were invited to a banquet, but red and white balls of rice and beans were given to all who appeared at the gate. Children thronged there, even from the outlying villages.

The establishment of Wataya Kichibei (*a print deleting all neighboring houses*)

In Kakisaki the customary offering to Inari was sake and fish and bean-curd cake fried in oil, but those who had reached an unlucky age served rice and red beans to their friends and neighbors in an effort to ward off the bad fortune of the coming year. Women especially dreaded the ages of nineteen, thirty-three, and thirty-seven. Men feared the years when they were twenty-five, forty-two, and sixty-one.

(Heusken had just turned twenty-five. Did anyone tell him it was an unlucky year? But, of course, by Japanese reckoning he was now twenty-six. It was his twenty-fifth year that had brought him to Japan.)

Sunday, March 8, 1857. A cannon from the Signal Hill announced a foreign ship at noon to-day, and caused emotions of sincere pleasure. That must be an understatement. The cannon shot set off real excitement at Gyokusenji. Surely it meant that Commodore Armstrong had sent the promised ship, and it could not have come more opportunely. That happy thought lasted only until Harris could scramble to an eminence and get a look at the ship. She was a merchantman. *On ascending a height near the Consulate I saw the blessed Stars and Stripes flying from a barque, which was standing towards the inner harbor, having a signal for a pilot flying, and the pilot was seen pulling off to her, but as the pilot neared her, she filled away, stood off until she was fairly in Edo Bay, and then stood southward.*

What does it mean? It was like the Flying Dutchman.

Monday, March 9, 1857. At nine this morning the barque again made her appearance and anchored in the outer harbor. Mr. Heusken went on board, and when he returned he brought with him Captain Homer of the Barque Messenger Bird, from Boston via the Sandwich Islands and Guam. Mr. Edward F. Hall, the supra-cargo, presented a letter of introduction written by the Hon. David L. Gregg, U. S. Commissioner to the Sandwich Islands. Captain Homer has his wife and two children on board—one an infant born at sea off the Caroline Islands.

Mr. Hall having come via San Francisco, I got newspapers up to the 8th of November, or six months later than my last dates. So, Mr. Buchanan is President. . . . as the newspapers were only from the 20th of October to the 8th of November, there is a large hiatus in details, and Mr. Hall being only eighteen years of age could not give me many particulars. Mr. Hall informs me that he has an assorted cargo and wishes to trade here, and that he shall then proceed to Hakodate and thence to the Amur River, at which last place he is to establish himself in business as a ship chandler. I told him I was still negotiating with the Japanese about the currency, and told him he could depend on not losing over six per cent. on the money he should expend here, which gave him great satisfaction.

It was while Captain Homer and young Mr. Hall were visiting at the temple that Moriyama and Dr. Ito arrived with the Governors' answer to the memorandum. "Please read it," said Moriyama, "and if you have any questions we are ready to answer them."

He was busy with his countrymen who had just arrived, Harris replied. Later he would have the letter translated and would study it. And he invited Moriyama and the doctor in to meet the Americans.

Moriyama asked what news the ship brought from home.

Nothing significant, said Harris, except the election of a new President, named Buchanan.

Moriyama and the doctor remembered the name Buchanan. Captain Buchanan had commanded the steamship *Susquehanna*, and as leader of Perry's first landing party, had been the first member of the expedition to set foot on Japanese soil. He was also Wells Williams's favorite among the captains, most of whom ranked very low in Williams's estimation: "all, except Buchanan, spent their thoughts in criticizing what he [Perry] did and wishing they were going home."

Americans who lived at Gyokusenji: Mrs. William C. Reed, described here
as a red-headed woman of thirty-five, holding her five-year-old daughter by the
hand while her nine-year-old son romps ahead with a pet, probably a goat
(*a painting by an unknown artist*)

The captain and the new President belonged to the same family, Harris told the Japanese, and he produced two letters which had arrived on the *Messenger Bird*, one addressed to Moriyama and the other to interpreter Hori Tatsunosuke. Both were from William C. Reed, one of those traders who in the spring of 1855 had lived at Gyokusenji with their families while their ship carried some of the stranded Russians from the *Diana*. "Neither letter was sealed," wrote Moriyama. "I read the one addressed to me. It said that an acquaintance of Reed's would be coming soon to Shimoda and asked me to take care of him. It also asked me to convey best regards to Mr. Aihara Isaburo." Obviously, Moriyama read Hori's letter too, for he noted that "it was even shorter and had nothing particular to say." Anyway, Hori wasn't in Shimoda any more.

"We ended our talks and came home," Moriyama continued, "and I reported both letters to the Lord of Shinano."

When Heusken was able to translate the Governors' letter and Harris to read it, it gave no great satisfaction.

—On the exchange of coins, the Consul General's proposal was acceptable, except that five per cent was not a large enough discount. Would Harris please increase that?

—Concerning the provisional treaty with the Netherlands, they had been informed by Edo that negotiations were still in progress and that only a few articles had been agreed on.

—They had no objection to Harris's proposals concerning punishment for criminal offenses, and they were ready to open Nagasaki, both based on the treaty with the Russians.

—As for bartering with ships who had no cash to spare, they had no objection since this was already covered by the existing treaty, but in accordance with that treaty they would not accept merchandise unless it was something they wanted.

—As for Harris's request that he be allowed to buy direct from merchants without the intervention of Japanese officials, they would like to decide each case as it arose.

—But they could not accept his contention that he was not bound by the treaty limits of seven *ri* at Shimoda and five *ri* at Hakodate. Whatever the situation in other countries, they were convinced that it was no basis for setting aside the provisions of the treaty which both sides had pledged to observe strictly. Nor could enforcement of the treaty be modified by the rank or status of certain persons.

—The Governors appreciated the kindness that led His Excellency to suggest bringing metalsmiths from America to recast coins, but the mint was a government operation and therefore his proposal could not be accepted.

In short, the Governors had considered his memorandum for one week without altering their position a whit.

Early the next morning Heusken was at Naka compound, requesting a conference with the Governors at noon. Harris wanted the *Messenger Bird* to carry out some word of progress. He knew that a settlement of the rate of exchange would be hailed by merchants in China and at home.

Inoue and Okada both appeared. *Told them the arrival of a ship required a settlement of the currency question. They stuck at the six, and I at the five per cent.*

The Governors did not seem to appreciate the need for haste. If Harris would not advance from five per cent, they said, they would have to consult Edo, and that would take at least ten days.

Harris railed at his. It cost money to keep a ship in port, he said; but the Governors couldn't see that this was their problem. Finally he agreed to wait ten days.

Then they got into an involved discussion on how to weigh coin against coin, and the relative content of alloy in the money of their two nations. At four o'clock a weary Harris called a halt, suggesting that they meet at eleven tomorrow to get an earlier start.

The Japanese agreed but said that Inoue was still not feeling well. Perhaps only Okada would be able to come.

On his way home Harris visited the *Messenger Bird . . . saw Mrs. Homer, a nice person indeed, with a bouncing baby in her arms. This home sight almost made me homesick.*

Ill or not, Inoue did appear the next day. The argument over the discount rate resumed.

I refused to advance from the five per cent. The Governor, the Prince of Shinano, rose from his seat and came to me; and, while standing, begged me as a personal favor to him to yield the one per cent. of difference; that they were most anxious to have the matter settled, but that it was impossible for them to go further than they had done, and (mark this) that, if they took the coin of the Americans at less than six per cent., the Government would lose by the operation of re-coinage. Contrast this with their solemn assurance that it cost twenty-five per cent. to coin the money of Japan. The mendacity of these men passes all human belief.

Unfortunately, the two sides were playing the game by different rules, and neither understood the other's.

The Japanese had come down from twenty-five per cent to six per cent; surely Harris could meet them by coming up from five per cent to six per cent. By Japanese rules one does not demand total surrender, one does not force the other side to lose face.

Inoue's personal plea was one that scarcely any Japanese could have resisted, and his men were outraged that it was met with scorn.

Harris, on the other hand, was outraged that Inoue had put government business on a personal basis. But with the *Messenger Bird* in port and Mr. Hall eager to trade, the pressure was on Harris. He offered to split the difference: make it five and one half per cent. The Governors held firm. Finally he gave in. *I proposed that this ship should settle at the six per cent., but that it should not be used as a precedent.*

Chafing, he changed the subject. Regarding the treaty with the Netherlands, he said, as he understood the Governors, they now claimed that after entering a provisional treaty their government had changed its policy and that the matter was still pending.

That was correct, the Governors replied.

Harris said it was a downright lie.

They roundly declared the Dutch Convention did not exist, that it was a false report. I told them with some sternness that I had seen it with my own eyes, on board the Dutch Frigate Diana [Medusa] in October last. They then said it had not been ratified. This I also stopped by saying that it did bear the ratification of the Japanese Government. This point was asserted and re-asserted by them time and time again and as often met by a plain statement of the truth by me.

Scenes like this reflect not only the bias Harris had brought to Japan and the temper he had never been able to control, but also his solitary situation. Had he had a companion of maturity, whose judgment he respected and who could reason with him, he might not have put himself in such untenable positions.

Again Harris threatened war, this time speaking not only for his country but for another as well. If his country informed the Netherlands that the Japanese were refusing to honor their treaty, a treaty the whole world knew about, the Dutch would send warships against Japan at once. And if the United States was not granted the privileges given the Dutch, she would do likewise. "With a single warship and a single cannon we can stop you."

The Governors told him to write to the Dutch "Kapitan" and ask him for the truth.

The Dutch "Kapitan," stormed Harris, was a mere merchant; it was beneath the Consul General's dignity to communicate with him—a remarkable statement since it was chiefly a Consul General's duty to deal with merchants.

The Consul General had great status; the Japanese were to remember that. He was privileged to buy direct from shopkeepers and he could travel freely without bothering with restrictions imposed on ordinary people.

The Governors said they would consider his buying his own necessaries, but they would never agree to his traveling outside the specified limits.

From now on he would go freely where he chose when he chose—the Governors would keep it in mind. He would go to Edo, he would go to Hakodate, he would go wherever the situation demanded. And if he were prevented, it would mean war.

Harris had completely lost his temper. His words were ugly. His actions were uglier still, for it must have been then that he picked up his smoking pot, filled with powdered ash to damp the sparks from a pipe, and flung it across the room against the sliding doors. A cloud of ashes filled the room. Had the Governors sprung to their feet, Harris might have been killed on the spot. They kept their seats, Okada immobile, Inoue brushing the ashes from his sleeves, quieting his retainers, commanding them to take their hands from their swords.

This scene is not in the record. The Governors would never report it, Harris would not boast of it. But later the story would leak out and circumstances point to its happening at this meeting.

In any event, Harris had ended the session. *I closed a very stormy interview . . .*

He cooled off by going out to the ship, *and after chatting for an hour went home.*

Captain and Mrs. Homer and Mr. Hall are to breakfast with me on Friday noon.

Did he consider writing to Donker Curtius as the Governors had suggested? If he did he rejected the idea, for now he had taken a stand. Yet letters were passing between Nagasaki and Shimoda, for in January, Curtius had offered to pay the expense of post, and the Governor at Nagasaki had recommended that the letters be routed through Edo, presumably so the government could read them. Probably Heusken had opened a correspondence with his countryman.

On this same day Shimoda and the villages received a circular giving advance notice that a foreign ship having arrived at Shimoda port, the Lord of Odawara was sending a force of a hundred and ninety men "to safeguard the foreigners." As usual they would be billeted on Kakisaki. Meantime, the Goyosho ordered Hambei to tighten the patrol in and around the town while the ship was in the harbor.

Of course, Hambei, and the headmen of the villages as well, had concerns besides the foreign ship.

Hambei received a request from the provincial magistrate for Izu that two or three ironsmiths be sent to assist in casting 1250-pound cannon.

(The reverbatory furnace in question, one of the Shogunate's major armament works, had once been located on the outskirts of Shimoda. In 1854
some of Perry's men had invaded its precincts to see what was going on,
and the whole thing had hastily been moved to provincial headquarters far
up the peninsula.) Hambei sent three men.

And a gambling case was uncovered at the village of Nashimoto on the
peninsula's central highway. It involved a *ko,* or "mutual assistance association," organized at the village temple to assist farmer Nisuke, who had been
ill since May of last year. The Shogunate was rough on such *ko,* because
each one was a gambling operation.

It worked something like this. Let us suppose that Nisuke needed ten
ryo to pay the debts that had accumulated during his illness, and that
twenty friends and neighbors joined the *ko,* each contributing two *bu* (four
bu equaled one *ryo*) in cash or rice, which was paid over to Nisuke; he in
turn agreed to repay twelve *ryo,* two *bu,* including interest, over a period of
ten years at the rate of two and a half *bu* every six months.

So far there was nothing to object to. The trouble was that each
semi-annual meeting of the *ko* members turned into a lottery. At the first
meeting each man made a secret bid on a piece of paper. The man who bid
lowest was the winner. He received not only Nisuke's payment of two and a
half *bu,* but the amount that he bid from all the other members. Once a
man had won he could no longer bid, and at subsequent meetings the
winner took Nisuke's payment, plus the same amount (two and a half *bu*)
from each man who had already won, plus the amount he had bid from
every other member. It was an exciting game, especially toward the end as
the winnings grew bigger and bigger. It involved both luck and judgment
but it was gambling, and every man in the country knew that gambling was
prohibited.

In this case, however, the Governors' police could see extenuating
circumstances because it was clear that Nisuke was indeed seriously ill and
needed help. Hambei was summoned to the Goyosho and given to understand that a petition for leniency from him and the headmen of all the
villages near Nashimoto would be considered favorably.

The petition was presented the next day. "We throw ourselves on your
mercy," it read in part. "Those sentenced to confinement are now penitent
for their sins. They have aged parents dependent on them, and their parents
have asked us to entreat your office to release them.

"We, all the officers of the town and villages concerned, appeal for
your pity. We shall be happy if you can deal leniently with them."

That probably would have been the end of it, except that one of the investigators discovered that a *ronin,* having slipped secretly into the Governors' seven-*ri* area, had been hiding at the Nashimoto temple, where the *ko* met. He was at once suspected of being the man who had threatened Heusken.

The priest of the temple was involved in hiding the *ronin* and was also involved in the *ko,* and the priest, the *ronin,* and all the members of the *ko* were at once suspected of a conspiracy against Harris and Heusken. It was a little far-fetched, but the police were always nervous about the safety of the foreign official at Gyokusenji.

Fortunately for their necks, all those charged were able to establish alibis. The local men were allowed to go home, and the *ronin* was summarily ejected from the area.

On Friday, March 13, Harris held his breakfast party. In the afternoon he and his guests walked up the hills behind the temple to a place where they could look out across the Bay of Edo and see Oshima, that forbidden island. No doubt Harris wanted Captain Homer's judgment as to whether it lay within seven *ri,* but since the captain's opinion is not quoted, it was probably equivocal at best. Nevertheless, *Day fine, and pass it most agreeably. Company leave at five* P.M.

In the evening write letter to the Governors on the two points, which I support with a few of the strongest arguments . . .

The two points were the rights which he insisted accrued to Americans because of the Netherlands Convention, and his own rights as Consul General. He repeated at length his contention that the Netherlands Convention had been "promptly ratified and exchanged" (thus continuing his assertion that the Governors were lying to him) and that the Dutch "thereby acquired the rights of permanent residence in Japan."

But, he argued legalistically, even if the convention had not been ratified, even if it had been superseded and articles 12 and 13 struck out (even if the Governors were not lying to him, as he knew they were), it would make no difference: the convention stated that articles 12 and 13 were to go into effect, whether ratification had taken place or not, on January 1, 1856. Therefore, the Dutch had actually held these rights even if they later gave them up, and once they had held them, even temporarily, they accrued to the United States.

It was essential that Americans have these rights so they could establish themselves at Hakodate and Shimoda to provide whalers with "salted provisions, cables, anchors, canvas, cordage, and a great variety of other articles which are not produced in Japan" (thus ignoring the Governors' proposal that the Japanese import these items and sell them through their own merchants, and, of course, ignoring Perry's treaty, which stated that ships' necessities should be supplied "as far as the Japanese have them").

As to his second point, he repeated that the Consul General must be given "all the rights which attach to his office under the 'Laws of Nations.' Among these rights freedom of action is amongst the most prominent; to subject him to restraint, to keep him under the supervision of the Japanese Authorities is to degrade him in the eyes of the people of Japan and to offer an indignity to his Government." He wanted "the right to purchase where he pleased, and to settle for his purchases without any interference of the Authorities," but this was of minor importance compared with freedom to travel: "he was appointed not for the Port of Shimoda alone, but for the whole Empire of Japan" (a possibility the Japanese had never entertained when they signed the treaty), and must therefore be free to travel throughout the empire.

He closed, as was becoming increasingly his habit, with a cold threat: "candor compels me to say, as I now say to Your Excellencies, that a refusal of these two points will endanger the good feeling now happily existing and may lead to results that I am sure Your Excellencies would deplore as deeply as I should lament."

Next day a reluctant Moriyama was ordered to call on Harris and try to persuade him to settle the currency issue at six per cent permanently, not just for the *Messenger Bird.* Moriyama was not happy about going alone. He suggested that Dr. Ito might go with him, but the Governors said no, another person might make Harris suspicious and spoil the talks. He could explain the doctor's presence by saying it was an English lesson for him, Moriyama suggested hopefully, but it was pointed out that Ito had had an English lesson only yesterday and it would not look reasonable for him to return so quickly. No, he had better go alone.

He had an indication of the reception he would get when he met one of the interpreters on the beach below Gyokusenji. Harris was upset, the man said, and intended to file a protest because someone from the *Messenger Bird* had tried to buy an umbrella in Shimoda and had been told by the shopkeeper that he could not get it until tomorrow and at the Goyosho bazaar.

Harris was not the only one upset. Both the Goyosho and the town office were in an uproar over the case of the paper umbrella. For the visiting foreigner, far from being thwarted, and despite the fact that it was a fair day without a sign of rain, had gone on to another shop, that of Bunzo of Tonokoji Block, and had picked up an umbrella and walked out, leaving a little money. Bunzo had promptly reported the incident, and the fuss began.

The Goyosho had issued an order on the previous day that shops were not to display goods: all sales were to be made at the official bazaar. Obviously, Bunzo had not complied with the order, putting not only himself but also Hambei on the spot. Both were embroiled with the Goyosho for five days, and it ended with Hambei's being slapped with a fine, three *bu*. Hambei was mortified. It was not the money, which the merchants' association quite properly provided, but the humiliation of being fined and the implication that he could not keep his town under control.

As for Harris, he must have had second thoughts when he later learned that the shopper had flagrantly violated the treaty regulation that all purchases be made through the Goyosho, for as far as the record shows he never made any protest.

Still, as Moriyama glumly realized when he heard the news from the interpreter, the Consul General was at present in a bad mood, and he climbed Gyokusenji's steps without hope of accomplishing anything. He found Harris alone. Heusken was off with young Hall, acting as his interpreter while he tried to sell his goods.

Moriyama did his best. He had come alone, he said, because both Governor Inoue and Executive Officer Matsumura were bedded with a fever (the flu again), but a decision had to be reached. And he did not hesitate to put the whole thing on a personal basis, despite Inoue's failure with the same gambit. The impasse reflected unfavorably on his own skill as interpreter, he said, and might well jeopardize his career.

Harris could work this vein too. So concerned was he about the relations between their two countries, he sighed, that he had lost much weight: look at him now, though he was stout when he arrived. Personally he would like to meet Moriyama's request, but the subject gravely affected his nation's interests. However, he announced, if the Governors would concede his two points, he would concede the six per cent.

It was only for his government that he was asking, Moriyama said. For himself he would never ask a personal favor even though he might have to starve to death or face all kinds of torture.

Moriyama's difficulties struck home, Harris replied, and aroused such sympathy he felt his heart would break. "Please do not continue," and he placed his hands on his bosom in a grand gesture of compassion.

With the scene turned into high comedy, Moriyama was beaten. Harris's performance had topped his, and there was nothing to do but with-draw. His own histrionics, he reported more in sorrow than in anger, had not even got him an offer of tea or wine.

That evening Kakisaki was again turned upside down as the soldiery of Odawara arrived. Again the householders yielded their best rooms, hulled rice, and ran errands, while the sailors of boats in the harbor took a back seat.

Economically it was a windfall for the village, but for the samurai from Odawara the timing was unfortunate. Influenza was rampant. On the same day that the *Messenger Bird* arrived, there were three deaths in Kakisaki and undoubtedly more in Shimoda and the other villages.

Harris was ill, too, but not from the flu. He had an attack of bleeding ulcers.

Sunday, March 15, 1857. I have never been so ill for seven years as I am to-day; vomited a quantity of fresh blood.

But next day he again received Moriyama, who again, and again reluctantly, had come alone. He had wheedled permission to bring Dr. Ito; unfortunately, the doctor could not be found.

His visit was very close to a replay of the call two days earlier. Again he met an interpreter on the beach road, hurrying to the Goyosho. This time it was Namura Tsunenosuke, bearing Harris's letter to the Governors on his two points. Heusken had finally got it translated into Dutch, though he was spending most of his time with the visitors from the *Messenger Bird*. The young man always found it a relief to get away from Gyokusenji.

The conversation with Harris was about the same as the earlier one, too, except that it lacked comedy touches. Harris mentioned the letter he had just dispatched. Reading it, he said, the Governors would have no choice but to agree with him, but again he suggested a deal, the discount rate for his two demands. He was reminded that he himself had said a few days earlier that these issues were quite unrelated.

Moriyama got no tea, no wine, and no agreement, though he was treated to plentiful threats of war if the Japanese did not give in, and quickly too. And after the war, Harris gibed, there would be no negotiations over a discount rate.

In New York City on this same date, Commodore Perry was writing to encourage Harris. "Although there is no certainty of your receiving this letter within any presumable time," he wrote, he wanted Harris to know that he was thinking of him and of his mission "of strengthening our friendly relations with Japan . . ."

In Hong Kong, John Bowring was adding another letter to the accumulation of Harris's undelivered mail. He wrote of the war in China, optimistically as usual, but he took pains to emphasize that "Japan, of course, occupies much of my thoughts." He did not yet know that he was being superseded.

And in Edo, the Great Council, having pondered Donker Curtius's sobering report on the fate of Canton, was preparing to issue new instructions to those branches of the government dealing with foreign policy, including the Governors of Nagasaki, Shimoda, and Hakodate. The directive bore the stamp of Lord Hotta's thinking. More and more he was assuming the dominant role. Men had noticed that Lord Abe's health seemed to be failing, and that his grip on government affairs was weakening.

The Dutch Kapitan has made a statement concerning an attack made by the English on Canton. We have given careful consideration to this and it seems that the matters raised by the Dutch, though not immediate, are becoming more and more urgent. It is not insisted that we should reach an agreement that would accomplish all the foreign demands, but it is a fact that our present manner of dealing with foreigners is generally recognized, even among our own people, to be unsuited to existing conditions. Thus if we continue adding to the anger of the foreigners it is even possible that Japan might suffer the fate of Canton. . . .

Any attempt on our part to cling to tradition, making difficulties over the merest trifles and so eventually provoking the foreigners to anger, would be impolitic in the extreme. Should there once be the sound of a single cannon-shot, then it will already be too late to turn back. The position is such, therefore, that we must adopt a realistic policy, handling affairs in the same way at each of the three ports of Nagasaki, Shimoda, and Hakodate and so acting with respect to all questions of protocol in negotiations and the exchange of documents [treaties] as to convince the foreigners of our sincerity.

Urgent problems are already pressing upon us one after another—the published [newspaper] reports about English intentions, the demands of the American consul, and now the demands of the Dutch. It is evident that the policy we have pursued so far cannot long be maintained. Therefore while we are still in safety we must make a long-term plan . . . With these objects in mind, you are accordingly to give full and careful consideration to the question of future . . . policy and after investigation are to submit an early report.

The Governors of Shimoda could be forgiven a sense of frustration when they received this directive. Its talk of new policies may have had a hollow sound, while the call for new recommendations was rubbing salt in an old wound—the Governors had not been able to get Edo to take action on recommendations they had already made regarding Harris. Delay, they had learned, was costly. Every week of delay made Harris's demands harder and his temper shorter.

In fairness to Lord Hotta, it should be said that his directive was probably aimed not so much at the Governors of the ports as at the die-hards in Edo. It was another attempt to brush away old bias and to face reality. If he could convert a few more men, Hotta must have thought, he would be free to move.

Even if Harris had not been ill and the atmosphere at Gyokusenji somber, Heusken would have enjoyed having some company nearer his own age. The eighteen-year-old Hall was callow in comparison with the dashing officers of the *Olivuzza*, but that gave Heusken a chance to play man of the world.

Hall's business was not brisk, as Heusken noted:

> The Japanese show no enthusiasm to buy. From a cargo made up of all kinds of things, they would buy only weapons, woolens, and cotton fabrics. But once they were quoted the price of these commodities, they claimed the prices to be exorbitant and they will buy nothing at all. The *Messenger Bird* is the first [ship] to take advantage of the change in the rate of exchange of the dollar which allows only six per cent and weighs the dollar against Japanese *ichibus*. The Japanese expected that since we now pay one third of what we formerly paid, the price of American goods would go down at the same rate, for they did not understand that they used to charge three times over and that American goods were always selling according to the just value of the dollar.

Harris wasn't so sure about that last statement. On at least this one point he agreed with the Japanese: *Mr. Hall cannot sell anything to the Japanese, and no wonder, for his prices are most exorbitant.*

In contrast, Hall saw a good bit that he wanted to buy, while the merchants of Shimoda were exposed to that most dedicated of shoppers, the lady tourist. Mrs. Homer and her older child made several forays on the bazaar, all noted in Hambei's diary, for although foreign men were becoming commonplace, a foreign woman and child still attracted a curious crowd.

Hall's slow sales may have discouraged him, but there were compensations. A session of haggling over prices would be followed by the heady entertainment of bath-watching, to which Heusken certainly introduced him, and no doubt the merchants of Shimoda gave the merchant from America a party in hopes of lubricating the channels of business. In one evening at Hamadaya this eighteen-year-old was endowed with memories to carry through a lifetime: of haunting songs of love, of hot sake that quickened his pounding pulse, of girls whose red lips and dark eyes glowed against their whitened skin in candle-thrown shadows, whose soft, scented flesh clung to his.

> . . . love for him
> filling my whole body, an unbearable
> longing and passion.

(It was a passage from "Raven at Dawn.")

> Cut off from the world
> by the protective bedding, reluctantly
> the lovers rise and she
> smooths and smooths his rumpled sidelocks.

Despite all this, Hall's prices remained high, and that was what brought Moriyama back to Gyokusenji on the nineteenth, in company with both Wakana and Matsumura, the latter risen from sickbed. Heusken came out to meet them at the gate. Harris was sick, he said (and no doubt he was, after his attack of four days earlier: *I have been and still am very ill,* he wrote on this date). It would be impossible to talk with him, but they could leave a message.

The officers of the *Messenger Bird* said they had no money to pay for the goods and provisions they were buying, Moriyama explained. Of course, barter was authorized but the things offered from the ship were priced so inordinately high that the Japanese were reluctant to accept them. What was to be done?

Heusken left to talk with Harris. The Consul General was in no position to intervene in commercial transactions, he reported when he came back, but if the goods offered by the American were priced too high they could be refused. The Japanese were under no obligation to accept goods at unreasonable prices, and refusal could not be called an infraction of the treaty.

While Hall was having trouble selling, Captain Homer was having problems of his own. The *Messenger Bird* lost an anchor and chain—the anchor about two thousand pounds, with sixteen fathoms of chain, value if new $225, as Harris jotted it down. The captain offered to pay salvage, and the Goyosho ordered the fishermen of Shimoda, whose province included salvage operations, to go to work.

They sent out a fishing boat with a crew of eight and two small boats. Using grappling hooks in rain and a west wind, they worked for two days without success, and then were ordered to double the force. Two days later the anchor and chain were recovered.

If the salvage was paid at the usual Japanese rate of ten per cent for underwater recovery, the fishermen involved received something in the neighborhood of sixty-five silver *bu*. The money was divided about the same way as fishing proceeds and was a burst of good fortune for several families of Suzaki Block.

This unusual prosperity had at least one unhappy consequence. One of the men, Chuzaburo, ran away with an out-of-town woman who had been working at a dockside bar. It was generally believed that his sudden affluence had deranged him. Of course, with spring coming on, that sort of thing could be expected.

It was the coming of spring that caused the Goyosho to direct Hambei to find new quarters for the transient workmen who were still repairing the typhoon damage. They had been living in a temple barracks, but warm weather made the men complain that these accommodations were close and depressing.

The headman found time to negotiate a pay raise for the townspeople who worked at government offices and the jail; then he organized a delegation to call on the Governors to express appreciation.

He coped with a steady flow of visitors. Some came on official business, either from Edo or from the provincial headquarters. Some were sent by daimyo to see firsthand how the foreigners were being controlled and how they were behaving. All had to be handled with deference, met along the road, given satisfactory quarters in the bulging town, their whims catered to (a lamp lent to one man, a new bathtub sent to another's quarters), and then politely seen off. (Among the new arrivals there were some familiar names, like Matsumura and Ito, and one guesses that these were sons of the executive officer and the doctor, come to join the English classes at Gyokusenji.)

And from Gyokusenji there was the usual stream of orders, to be placed with the most reliable shops and then followed up to make certain nothing went amiss: underwear to be mended, razors to be sharpened, pots and pans to be repaired.

But surely Hambei's most important function in the life of his town at this juncture was to lead the elders and townsfolk in night-long services at the shrine, prayers and exorcism to banish the epidemic sweeping the area.

All the villages around Shimoda held their own services. Naka, having the Governors' compound in its midst, sent respectful notification that it might be difficult to sleep: "We beg to report that since many of our villagers have colds and fever we will hold a meeting for exorcism again tonight. Please be advised that bells, drums, and trumpet shells will be used."

On the day after Heusken had stopped them at the gate, Moriyama and Matsumura returned to find Harris much improved, though he complained that his stomach was out of order. Learning that Heusken was away with Hall, they agreed to Harris's suggestion that they return the next day at noon and started to leave, but the Consul General pressed them to stay.

Today he was genial and talkative. He was also flushed from drink, and Moriyama guessed it was the alcohol that had wrought the transformation. Today the wine bottle was passed. This was Harris the good host, the entertaining conversationalist, showing the bullets and gunpowder he had bought from the *Messenger Bird,* even giving a can of gunpowder to Moriyama as he and Matsumura left.

The next day brought the vernal equinox. Either that or Harris's own prescription seems to have worked.

Saturday, March 21, 1857. Better to-day. Weather fine. Wheat grows beautifully. Japanese busy in planting potatoes, etc. I have a camellia tree in my yard which is some twenty feet high. It is now in full flower, and has perhaps thousands of flowers out—the finest sight of the kind I ever saw.

The people of the village around him were aware of the day. They converged on the cemetery around the temple to clean the graves of their ancestors, and went home to eat rice dumplings. Old women gathered before the altar in the chapel to recite the invocation to Buddha.

And according to Moriyama's diary, spring crept into the talk at Gyokusenji that afternoon, when Wakana, Matsumura, and Moriyama called again. First Matsumura tried to discuss the discount rate, but Harris would have none of it: this was a question he would debate only with the Governors. And when Matsumura tried to raise the question of the *Messenger Bird's* high prices, Harris asked with some sarcasm why a highly placed government official should concern himself with mundane commercial transactions. Wakana explained that they were not personally concerned, but when the merchants asked why the prices were so high, the officials wanted to be able to give reasonable answers.

The Consul General delivered one of his little lectures. Commerce was nothing to look down on, he said. It was essential to national well-being. But governments should stand above it. If a government became involved in commerce, it would lose its own high position. In all the world, he added, only the governments of the Netherlands and Japan directly engaged in trade. (Adam Smith would have applauded.)

Changing the subject, he brought out a tinplate box. It contained seeds of a hundred different American flowers, he said, and he wanted to give half to the Governors. As for the half he would keep, he had no place to plant them. He wanted to rent a garden plot near the temple. The officials promised to look into it (as indeed they did: next day Yoheiji was ordered to send someone to the Goyosho who was familiar with the farmland around Gyokusenji).

And now Harris, who had just castigated the Japanese for their government's involvement in trade, tried to do a little trading on behalf of his own. He had among his papers a copy of a memorandum to Secretary of State Marcy from Secretary of War Jefferson Davis, quoting prices on guns available from government arsenals: rifles, carbines, muskets, pistols; cannon were priced by the pound.

He had a friend, Harris said, who wanted to sell guns to Japan, guns of all sizes. This friend wanted to buy copper from Japan, more than a million pounds of it, which he would be glad to pay for in either silver dollars or in guns. He didn't want the Japanese to think he was trying to do business on his own account. He was just speaking for his friend, but he hoped they would give his friend's offer favorable consideration.

Probably it never occurred to him that this kind of deception, practiced by him, brought angry charges of mendacity.

The executive officers were noncommittal. They said they would reply later.

Incidentally, Harris said, he wanted to buy a complete set of men's formal clothing to send home to the United States.

The Japanese said they would look into the matter.

And when some of the issues they had been debating so long were settled, Harris went on, he hoped they would find him a woman. As they could see, he was an old man and sick, and he needed a woman who would take care of him. He would treat her carefully.

Truly spring had come.

Wakana pointed to his colleague. Matsumura, he said, was in charge of women. Together they tried to laugh off the matter as they took their leave.

Three days later the Japanese were back at Gyokusenji. The butler Assam told them Harris was sick abed again. They found Heusken assisting with the ship's business at the Goyosho, and asked him what they should do. They had word regarding the Consul General's request for a garden, and they would like to make some representation in regard to his letter of the two demands. If Heusken could represent the Consul, they would like a conference tomorrow. Otherwise they would postpone talks until he had recovered. They would send an interpreter to the temple tomorrow morning to learn the answer.

The answer was a *note verbale* from Harris: he would receive no one for talks until he had received a reply to his letter.

Matsumura and Moriyama went to Gyokusenji themselves and spoke with Heusken. It was difficult, they said, to answer Harris's letter without a chance to talk it over with him. Heusken checked and confirmed Harris's decision. He would talk with no one until he had received a written reply. Harris's mood had switched again.

With negotiations stalemated once more, Moriyama sat down and wrote a secret report to Inoue. He was upset. Matsumura and Wakana had ample opportunity to urge their views but he felt that his opinions were never listened to with the same attention, though when it came to negotiating with foreigners in general and Harris in particular his own experience was greater than that of anyone else at Shimoda.

What's more, he did not like the way the negotiations were tending. He considered that Governor Okada's views were far too liberal. Okada thought they were being too stringent in restricting Harris to the seven-*ri* area; he even advocated permitting Americans to lease land and construct buildings. Inoue favored a tougher line, and he was backed in this by practically the whole staff, including Matsumura and Wakana, but it seemed to Moriyama that Inoue was too prone to make concessions to Okada in order to get agreement.

Moriyama pointed out Harris's inconsistency. It was inconsistent to threaten war and then offer arms for sale. "His favorite phrase is 'a war may break out,'" Moriyama wrote, "but you need not take it seriously."

But there remained, Moriyama went on, the danger of war from another power. "Harris talks often of Bowring, whom he expects to come to Japan soon. We cannot relax our guard even for a moment."

As to Harris's demands:

> You need not permit him to travel beyond seven *ri* from Shimoda, but you had better let him buy directly. Any attempt to tax his purchases or to make him use paper money, which the merchants distrust and discount, will anger him and lead to serious problems for our officials and our country.

Regarding the claims that he bases on the Netherlands treaty, I think there must have been a misunderstanding between him and Captain Fabius last autumn. . . . But it is going to be extremely difficult to change his mind on this.

It seems to me that he intends to introduce the issues of trade, additional ports, and authorization for foreigners to live permanently in Japan. There is no doubt he wants to work out a new treaty on the same basis as the one with Siam.

Therefore, I think it is important that you refuse him permission to go up to Edo. Recent indications are that he will not again propose such a visit, but he is a double-dealer and no one can predict his actions.

If he is permitted to go to Edo, he will bring up the problems of trade and additional ports. If he is not satisfied with Japan's answer, he may refuse to leave the city, and any action you may take then will be too late. It is in the interests of the state to turn down his proposals before they produce ill effects. . . .

I dare express my humble opinions to you, even though it is rude to do so, because I have long received your favors and I am very grateful for them. I am honored that you trust me to conduct negotiations with the American. I hope to see everything settled peaceably.

Please keep what I have written today secret.

Moriyama's counsel did not sway the decision. Okada's views prevailed. Two weeks earlier the Governors had sent to the Great Council a translation of Harris's "Heusken memorandum," with their comments. They had received no response. Now, faced with Harris's blunt letter concerning his "two demands," they sent another message advocating complete capitulation: permitting American merchants to reside at Hakodate and Shimoda, with the right to lease land and construct buildings; permitting Harris to have coins and to buy direct; and permitting him to travel beyond seven *ri*. Only on the last point did they admit some hesitancy; they believed that the Japanese position was correct. But Harris's threats of war had worked. Probably they were mere intimidation, the Governors indicated, but they also thought they dare not run that risk.

The twenty-eighth of March by Harris's calendar was the third day of the Third Month by the Japanese calendar. It was one of the Japanese holidays that Harris had jotted down in his commonplace book, and the flag flew from the consulate's staff.

It was commonly called the Doll Festival and in almost every home dolls were lovingly unpacked and set out in the best room—dolls to whom the daughters of the house played hostess. At a wealthy house like merchant Wataya Kichibei's the display was costly and ornate: five tiers covered with scarlet cloth; at the top a prince and princess on a dais before a golden screen; ranged below them maids of honor serving festive sake, court musicians playing tiny drums and flute, noble guardsmen armed with bows and arrows, and attendants and servants, with furniture and *nori-mono* in lacquer and gold. At a poor farmer's, the dolls were likely simple ones of wood and paper. But everywhere around Shimoda, visitors noted, all the little figures, even the prince and princess, seemed to look like fishermen.

A doll maker (*a book illustration by Jichosai*)

This was the girls' day, a day on which they were made to feel as important as the doll-princess on the top tier, but also a day to remind them of their duties as women. These were summed up in a treatise called *The Greater Learning for Women,* which covered very thoroughly the subject of what a woman should and should not be. Here are a few excerpts to give the general idea:

Seeing that it is a girl's destiny, on reaching womanhood, to go to a new home, and live in submission to her father-in-law and mother-in-law, it is even more incumbent upon her than it is on a boy to receive with all reverence her parents' instructions. Should her parents, through excess of tenderness, allow her to grow up self-willed, she will infallibly show herself capricious in her husband's house, and thus alienate his affection, while, if her father-in-law be a man of correct principles, the girl will find the yoke of these principles intolerable. She will hate and decry her father-in-law, and the end of these domestic dissensions will be her dismissal from her husband's house, and the covering of herself with ignominy. . . .

. . . Even if thy father-in-law and mother-in-law be pleased to hate and vilify thee, be not angry with them, and murmur not! . . .

A woman . . . must look to her husband as her lord, and must serve him with all worship and reverence, not despising or thinking lightly of him. The great lifelong duty of a woman is obedience. . . . A woman should look on her husband as if he were Heaven itself. . . .

Let her never even dream of jealousy. If her husband be dissolute, she must expostulate with him, but never either nurse or vent her anger. . . . Never set thyself up against thy husband with harsh features and a boisterous voice!

A woman must be ever on the alert, and keep a strict watch over her own conduct. In the morning she must rise early, and at night go late to rest. Instead of sleeping in the middle of the day, she must be intent on the duties of her household, and must not weary of weaving, sewing, and spinning. Of tea and wine she must not drink overmuch, nor must she feed her eyes and ears with theatrical performances, ditties, and ballads. To temples (whether Shinto or Buddhist) and other like places, where there is a great concourse of people, she should go but sparingly till she has reached the age of forty.

. . . Without her husband's permission, she must go nowhere, neither should she make any gifts on her own responsibility.

The five worst maladies that afflict the female mind are: indocility, discontent, slander, jealousy, and silliness. Without any doubt, these five maladies infest seven or eight out of every ten women, and it is from these that arises the inferiority of women to men. A woman should cure them by self-inspection and self-reproach. The worst of them all, and the parent of the other four, is silliness. Woman's nature is passive. This passiveness, being of the nature of the night, is dark. Hence, as viewed from the standard of man's nature, the foolishness of woman fails to understand the duties that lie before her very eyes, perceives not the actions that will bring down blame upon her own head, and comprehends not even the things that will bring down calamities on the heads of her husband and children. . . . Such is the stupidity of her character that it is incumbent on her, in every particular, to distrust herself and to obey her husband. . . .

Parents! Teach the foregoing maxims to your daughters from their tenderest years! Copy them out from time to time, that they may read and never forget them! Better than the garments and divers vessels which the fathers of the present day so lavishly bestow upon their daughters when giving them away in marriage, were it to teach them thoroughly these precepts which would guard them as a precious jewel throughout their lives. How true is that ancient saying: "A man knoweth how to spend a million pieces of money in marrying off his daughter, but knoweth not how to spend a hundred thousand in bringing up his child!" Such as have daughters must lay this well to heart!

It probably goes without saying that these precepts were directed to the samurai classes, and were to some degree flouted in a town which seemed to take perverse pride in its cold west wind and shrewish women. Nevertheless, *The Greater Learning for Women* set the standards for the age, which were by no means ignored even in a village like Kakisaki. A pity that no one ever translated it for Townsend Harris; he would have found that some of its judgments fit very well in the section on women in his commonplace book.

Neither Harris nor Heusken made any mention of the festival, and probably neither noticed one of the local customs: broken dolls were brought to the village shrine this day for proper last rites and interment.

The day was more than just a girls' festival. It was the second great holiday of the year, and it was necessary for the Shimoda town clerk to issue his annual prohibition against bamboo firecrackers.

Town and village officials made the obligatory "gratitude calls" on the Governors, and in turn received the calls of their own people. In several cases there was particular cause for congratulation, for only the day before, a number of officials from the town and the villages, having duly presented themselves in formal dress as ordered, had received government citations for their work two years earlier. In the face of double disaster—foreign intrusion and the tidal wave—these men had kept their heads and performed with credit.

The festivities, however, were curtailed by rain and driving wind from the north, and were sobered by the epidemic which still hung over the area. Gennosuke of Kakisaki had returned home from receiving his citation to find that his father was dying.

And holiday or not, business continued. A few days earlier a considerable committee had been appointed to receive payment from the *Messenger Bird,* for in the end Mr. Hall had been unable to sell anywhere near as much as he wanted to buy (Hambei recorded that it took only two men to carry what the Japanese bought from the ship to the Goyosho), and therefore had been forced to part with some of his silver dollars.

Instead of over three thousand three hundred dollars which they would have demanded under the old rates, he paid them about one thousand one hundred and fifty dollars; this saving of over two thousand dollars is owing to my action.

It must have been an impressive scene as the first payment was made under the new regulations. The Japanese wanted to be sure it was done correctly, and so there were present three officials from the Goyosho, three town officials, three interpreters, the three top officers of the ship, and Heusken.

The Goyosho commemorated the holiday by paying the merchants who had sold the goods, after withholding the tax on sales to foreigners.

Late in the day Hambei received word that the ship was preparing to sail. Arrangements were made for a pilot and pilot boat. Wakana and Matsumura had provided a letter to the executive officers at Hakodate with word of the new currency agreement and the six-per-cent-discount rate.

There is nothing in Harris's journal to indicate that he was sorry to see these Americans leave. They had been a disappointment to him on two counts.

He had thought to restock his larder, but: *Get a portion only of my supplies from the Messenger Bird, the remainder is stowed either quite forward or quite below a large quantity of cargo.* As a former trader and supercargo he was shocked at this inefficiency. *This is bad management. A vessel on such a voyage should have her cargo so stowed that any portion of it may easily be got at, so as to be ready for trade, however small, at any port.*

He was even more disgruntled the next day. *Pay my bill to Mr. Hall in silver at very high prices, and in return he wished to pay me in gold, which entails a loss of seventy-five per cent. to me here in Japan, as their ratio of gold as to silver is only three and one seventh to one, instead of sixteen to one, as with us.* Harris was speaking of the tonnage and certification fees he had collected as consul, but his concern was personal because the fees he collected were to be applied against his salary. The amount was only $10.10, but in the process of converting the gold to silver *bu*, its purchasing power would have shrunk to about $3.50 and the loss would have been Harris's. Hall, of course, was trying to save his silver dollars for trade with the Japanese, but Harris was not about to be taken in by such tricks. *It*

* This statement is in error. The Japanese ratio of gold to silver ran about five or six to one. This is demonstrated by a statement later in his journal, dated November 7, 1857, that he was buying gold from the Japanese at 34½ cents per dollar, indicating a ratio of 5.52 to one.

takes, this New Yorker growled, *a New England man to do such things.*

And even on a holiday the task of coping with Harris went on. Forced to make a written reply to Harris's letter, the Governors and their men drafted the only response they could. They said they appreciated the importance of the issues he had raised, they said the government was now pondering them, and they asked him to wait for a decision from Edo.

Superintendent Wakiya and Moriyama delivered the note. As usual, Harris refused to discuss the issues at hand, but he was willing to chat, and he elicited from Moriyama the opinion that *taking ten persons in authority, three would be in favor of opening the country at once, two would be in favor but with delay, three would refuse so long as force is not used, but would yield to such a demonstration without fighting, and two would fight to the last.*

This was a fair assessment, and it might have indicated to Harris that he was dealing with a government which faced serious problems no matter what position it took, and serious difficulties in arriving at any position, and that under the circumstances "a full share of patience," as Commodore Perry had suggested, might be a virtue. The thought does not seem to have crossed his mind.

Moriyama says the Prince of Shinano wishes to call on me tomorrow. I request the Prince to excuse me on Sunday, but that I shall be very happy to see him on any other day of the week.

The visitors left, Heusken translated the note, and Harris bristled again. In reply he wrote two angry letters, one to the Governors and one to the Great Council.

To the Governors he expressed "surprise":

> Your Excellencies have repeatedly and in the most earnest manner assured me that you had full powers to act on all matters I might propose and that you would give prompt answers. . . . This further delay . . . bears the appearance of a wish to procrastinate the subject indefinitely. . . . I am hourly expecting a U.S. man-of-war to arrive here . . . delay of a definitive answer will be considered by me as tantamount to a refusal. . . .

This letter was fired off at once, but Harris must have had second thoughts about what he had written to the Great Council; that was held up.

The Governors, understandably upset by the tone of Harris's letter, wrote another note immediately:

> . . . You say that our delay in answering you is a telltale sign of our intention to shelve your proposals or to deny them, but such is not the

case. We acknowledge the extreme importance of your representations, and that is why we are unable to reply before we know our government's decision. We will continue to try to present your proposals to the government in their true light and we will press for an early decision. We ask you again to wait for a little while.

Moriyama delivered this message Monday morning, and he tried to point out to Harris that it was to his advantage to exercise a little patience, for if he forced a swift reply, it was likely to be negative.

Inoue was in the neighborhood on an inspection tour, he added, and would like to take the opportunity to call. Harris said he would be welcome.

Moriyama reported to Inoue in Kakisaki, where he was having a word with the commander of the Odawara contingent, which was preparing to leave now that the ship had sailed. A circular had gone out alerting the villages along the route to ready bearers and horses. Tomorrow the train would file out of the village, carrying the flu back to Odawara.

Inoue's call at Gyokusenji was another attempt to smooth the American's ruffled feathers. Like most of their social visits this one went well. Harris was especially pleased at being able to make the party a small one. *The Prince . . . was attended by a very large train, but only a Vice-Governor* [Wakana] *and the interpreters* [including Moriyama, whom Harris persisted in regarding as merely an interpreter] *were admitted to my private rooms. I have completely broken up the system of having a cloud of secretaries and spies crowding into my private rooms. All are delighted except the writers and spies. Gave the Prince a Colt's revolver, one of three that was put into the case of arms I purchased for the Kings of Siam in lieu of discount.* He neglected to mention that Inoue gave him a set of ten lacquered cake trays.

Without broaching business, the Governor tried to soften the American with an analogy he knew would be understood. Japan, he said, was like an unsophisticated maiden. She was amazed at seeing how geisha girls disport themselves. She would become accustomed to such behavior but it would take a little time. She could not become a playgirl in one bound.

Harris could use the same technique. He reached for the legend of Rip Van Winkle. Japan, he said, was like a man who two hundred years ago was second to none in wisdom and valor. Then he went to sleep, and while he slept others worked hard, inventing steamships and other machines. He still slept, though others were trying hard to waken him. And he threw in another simile: Japan could run like a tiger, but chose to keep its feet in fetters.

We are not told Inoue's reaction, but Moriyama confessed in a letter to a confidant in Edo that he was enormously impressed: "To repeat his similes to the uninformed or thick-headed might lay me open to suspicion, but I want you to hear them because they stirred me so."

The month of March had slipped away. It had brought no Commodore Armstrong, no naval vessel. And in Hong Kong, Captain Bell was writing to Harris that there seemed no imminent possibility of one.

Chapter 10

APRIL, 1857

The first of April brought rain driven by a north wind. The few people in the muddy streets of Shimoda hunched against the drenching gusts and scurried between puddles. Governor Okada canceled a scheduled inspection tour.

About midday a ship entered the harbor in evident distress. Well before she reached anchorage, trained eyes at the shipping exchange had identified her: she belonged to Tarojiro of Edo and her captain was Matsugoro, who hailed from a seacoast village not far from Shimoda. Her flags announced that she carried a cargo of rice belonging to Lord Nambu of Morioka. Though Morioka lay far to the north and the rice was bound for Edo, it was not unusual for such a ship to appear at Shimoda. It was often easier to sail across the Sea of Sagami and then double back to Edo than to sail into the Bay of Edo directly.

As soon as she was recognized, runners were on their way: to Kahei, owner of the ships' inn Nakamuraya, who always played host to Tarojiro's ships; to Hanjuro, who was their agent in Shimoda; and to Nagano Matabei, who would serve as ship inspector. Very soon the three of them, clutching umbrellas and huddled under reed mats in an attempt to keep dry, were being sculled across the choppy waters of the harbor. Not much later they were back at the shipping exchange with Captain Matsugoro to file the necessary reports. The story was common enough. Caught in the same storm which was now soaking Shimoda, the vessel had shipped water and seemed in danger of capsizing. The captain had ordered thirty *koku* (more than a hundred and fifty bushels) of rice thrown overboard to save the ship. Some of the rest of the rice was wet. Much of the cargo would

314

have to be unloaded and probably sold on the spot to prevent complete loss. Notice of the salvage operation was rushed to the chief fisherman of Shimoda and to the headmen of Kakisaki and Suzaki. Tomorrow morning, if the rain had stopped, the fishermen of the town and the two villages were to begin unloading, with officials from each place standing witness.

One of the elders of Shimoda called at the Goyosho to report the circumstances. It was routine that Goyosho officers would conduct an investigation. Such investigations seldom uncovered any wrongdoing, but a cargo of rice belonging to a major daimyo was too important to be treated lightly, and, besides, it was almost taken for granted that sailors were thieves.

There were known to be exceptions. The cemetery of Daianji, one of the temples ranged behind Shimoda, contains the graves of sixteen men. They committed suicide when they lost their cargo of massive timbers sent by one of the daimyo of Kyushu to rebuild the Western Palace of Edo Castle, which had burned. Since the mission was so important, three of the lord's samurai were on board. When the ship was caught in a great storm and seemed in imminent danger of sinking, the captain pleaded with the samurai for permission to jettison the timbers in order to save the ship. The samurai, deciding that human lives were more valuable than the cargo, gave their approval, and so the ship was able to reach Shimoda. There the samurai, considering that they had been responsible for the cargo, consigned by their lord to the Shogun, committed suicide by *seppuku*, ripping open their bellies with their short swords. The captain, realizing that the samurai had acted on his advice, followed them, and the rest of the sailors said: "How can we continue to live after the samurai and our captain have committed suicide?" So they also prepared to die. Among them was a fifteen-year-old apprentice named Shichizo. The others told him that he was too young to die, that he should go on to Edo to report what had happened. But Shichizo said: "I am fifteen and a man and it would be shameful of me to be alone in saving my life. I know how to do *seppuku*." And so every one of them died by his own hand.

But this had happened a long time ago, in 1688. No one knew of a similar incident since, and it must be confessed that those men, though they were greatly honored, were considered to represent an antiquated morality.

Nowadays shippers were accustomed to having their cargo shrink en route; they expected that some rice would disappear from each bag or some sake from each barrel. Petty thievery was considered a sailor's prerogative, and it was taken for granted that captains cheated and stole. There was the

315

story of the ship that was consigned a cargo consisting only of stone Buddhist statues—the crew was so infuriated that there was nothing of value to steal that they knocked the noses off all the statues.

Most of Japan knew an old saw indicating, probably unjustly, that the people of Echigo Province were so greedy and devious that it was risky to do business with them. "Behind the man from Echigo," it went, "even grass does not grow." Harbor towns like Shimoda had their own variant on this saying. For "the man from Echigo" they substituted "the captain of a ship."

Not that the government took all this lightly. The penalty for theft of cargo was death and every shipwreck was investigated for fraud. But very seldom was fraud discovered.

That night Captain Matsugoro and his chief officer and ship's pilot, Zenemon, with the help of Kahei and Hanjuro, celebrated their escape from the storm in a room at Hamadaya. Perhaps they asked for the girl called Okichi and the song "Raven at Dawn" that she sang so well.

> Ah, now mingled with my
> sorrow, the sound of that samisen
> from the second floor: some time ago it was,
> Tokijiro stayed on with me, day and night;
> embracing each other all the time in
> night dress, talking together with such joy—
> but tonight what contrast! I know not even
> where he may be—we two, who
> can never become man and wife— Oh,
> what a pitiless, floating world!
> Ah, for the man I love, my life
> I'd gladly give—what could I regret,
> leaving this evanescent life?

Most of Matsugoro's crew did their own celebrating in the bars and noodle houses of Shimoda. There was only one man left to stand watch on the ship, kept company by a couple of Shimoda's fishermen posted as guards.

Next morning the rain had stopped and unloading began. The wet rice was lifted from the hold, lowered into boats, and carried ashore. Standing witness for Kakisaki was Chuemon, worrying as usual, keeping tally as each soaked bale came out of the ship.

Midmorning there was something more exciting to watch. A Western-style schooner sailed into the harbor, the original Kimizawa ship, the one built for the Russians at Heda and returned by them to the Japanese only last autumn. She had come down from Edo on a training cruise. Unloading of the rice-ship slowed as the men admired the schooner's grace.

Then they set to it again and the bags of wet grain piled up on shore. It was late in the afternoon when suddenly work was halted. Officers from the Goyosho went out to the ship, climbed down into the hold with ship inspector Matabei. They emerged frowning. Matsugoro, Zenemon, and the crew were ordered into boats, taken ashore. The ship was put in the custody of the town's chief fisherman. The Goyosho issued a series of summonses. For hidden in the hull of the ship, discovered quite accidentally by the fishermen-stevedores of Shimoda, Kakisaki, and Suzaki, were thirty *koku* of rice. It was the same amount that Matsugoro claimed had been thrown overboard to save the ship.

At about the same time—at four in the afternoon, as Moriyama recorded it—a letter was delivered to Moriyama at Naka compound by one of the interpreters assigned to Gyokusenji. Heusken had given instructions, the interpreter said, that the letter should be delivered at once to the Governors. Moriyama saw that it was addressed to the Great Council.

It was the letter that Harris had drafted on March 28, along with his letter to the Governors and written in the same mood of wrath and frustration. Apparently he had had second thoughts about whether this note should be dispatched. He had held it up for five days. *I have delayed writing this letter so long in the hope of bringing things to a quiet close here* was the half-apologetic note in his journal as he sent it forward.

It was an angry letter. He was angry at being told to handle his business at Shimoda, angry that the President's letter had not got him an invitation to Edo.

"A letter written by the head of a great nation and addressed to the sovereign of another nation is no ordinary communication; it is to be treated with honor and respect, to neglect it is to cast a slight on the high writer and on the nation he represents. It will be my duty to inform my Government that although more than five months have elapsed since I informed you that I was the bearer of a letter from the President of the United States addressed to the Emperor of Japan, yet you have not taken any notice of it."

From this it was clear, he wrote, that the amity promised by Japan in the Perry treaty "is but of little value. . . .

"It is not for me to indicate the course the President will adopt under the present circumstances, but I have no doubt that it will be such as will be calculated to vindicate his honor and that of his country."

317

ヲロシヤ国
船手組ノ印十文字也

As for dealing with the Shimoda Governors, "they can only hear what I have to say and report to the government at Edo." To "open the important matters with which I am charged . . . to persons not having powers corresponding with my own would be derogatory to my Government.

"Over six months have elapsed since I opened some matters of minor importance with the Governors of Shimoda, yet from the necessity of their making constant reference to Edo no conclusions have been arrived at." Clearly, he indicated, it was essential to negotiate at Edo.

日本出来ノ呉船
二本柱ノ船ッヒテナ

The first Kimizawa ship, built for
the Russians at Heda in 1855, and
shown here flying a Russian flag
(*a painting by an unknown artist*)

As for "my personal offer to communicate valuable information to the
Government of Japan"—his "personal knowledge of the intentions of the
English Government in relation to this Empire"—"I have no right to complain that you decline accepting my most friendly offer on my terms, but
that does not bind me to make the communication on yours." His friendship
for Japan was great enough for him to talk at Edo but not at Shimoda. "Self
respect forbids my opening the subject at any other place [than the capi-
tal]."

"I am daily expecting the arrival here of an American man-of-war; by her I must write to my Government an account of the action of the Government of Japan. I most earnestly hope that you will by prompt action make due amends for the acts of which I complain . . ."

There is no doubt that this letter made it all the more difficult for the government to invite him to Edo: it would be giving in to threats. Hotta had already decided to let him come to the capital; the question was when. A letter like this gave additional arguments to those, and they were many, who advocated indefinite postponement, even reconsideration.

As soon as the letter was delivered to Moriyama, he took it to Governor Inoue. After they had sent Harris's first letter, back in October, to Edo without reading it, the Governors had been instructed to read and translate any future letters. Inoue unsealed this one himself and went over it with Moriyama. "Then he ordered us to make a close study of it," Moriyama wrote, "and we did so."

The next day Harris was planting a little garden on the temple grounds, helped by a handyman sent from Shimoda, when he received word that the Governors wished to see him at the Goyosho.

They wish to know the contents of my letter to Council of State. Sorry, but it would be improper in me to disclose it.

Why was he sending a letter directly to Edo when the government had requested very clearly that he deal with them? Because they had demonstrated that they could decide nothing, and therefore the government's letter was unacceptable. He added that he would like a quick answer to the questions they had been discussing so that he could report to his government by the warship which would arrive soon.

The Governors said they could not promise a quick answer.

It was a brief, cold meeting. There had been one point of agreement: Harris asked for another garden plot, and was told he would get it.

Back at Naka compound, the Governors fired off to Edo a translation of Harris's letter, with an accompanying note: "We have repeatedly asked him to negotiate with us, but he refuses."

At Gyokusenji, gardening was not the only seasonal activity. The temple was undergoing a thorough spring cleaning and renovation. Hambei's diary is peppered with references to laborers dispatched: cleaning men, carpenters, joiners, tinkers, men to repaper the sliding doors, others to re-cover the tatami mats.

The latter found their way into Harris's journal: *Men employed to re-cover the mats that have become worn or soiled. These mats may properly be called mattresses. They are made on a frame and composed of layers of* mats, the coarsest at the bottom, until they are about two inches thick. The ordinary exterior cover has quite the appearance of Chinese matting. They make a very good bed. Since Harris and Heusken persisted in walking on this bed with their shoes on, it took them only about as many months to wear out the mats as it took the Japanese years.

The two of them also indulged in a little male adornment. Harris ordered two gold watch chains, and on being informed that in Japan gold was too tightly controlled to be frittered away in such a manner, provided three gold coins to be melted down and reworked.

In the meantime Harris and Heusken kept busy bringing their files up to date, making duplicates of dispatches, preparing the quarterly reports required by the distant government in Washington. Everything was to be ready when Commodore Armstrong arrived, and surely he would arrive soon.

Monday, April 6, 1857. Moriyama calls about garden spot. Have given me the piece asked for, about one eighth of an acre.

It turned out that the land in question was one of the scattered plots belonging to Juemon, who lived below Gyokusenji and doubled as farmer and fisherman. When approached by Moriyama and Saito, who entered the picture as a real estate specialist, Juemon allowed as how he could rent the land for six *bu* (about two dollars), but he pointed out that he had already planted it in sweet potatoes and he thought he ought to get two *bu* more to move them.

When Moriyama and Saito moved on to Gyokusenji to close the deal, Harris threw everything into confusion by announcing that six *bu* was too cheap. It is the only case on record when he thought he was being undercharged. He would, he said, pay ten *bu*, including the consideration for moving the sweet potatoes. He would also pay ten *bu* next year, if he were around to use it—he wasn't sure he would still be living in Shimoda.

This contretemps was hustled to the Governors. They ruled that Juemon was to get no more than the six *bu* plus two he had asked for. Paying rent of ten *bu* would set an undesirable example: "it might cause the lowly farmers to grow impudent and make unreasonable demands when the government needed some land in the future."

Next day Moriyama summoned Juemon and told him the arrangements, and then took him to the temple and introduced him to Harris. Harris asked that Juemon take care of the garden, including the little plot near the temple, and they agreed on a daily wage of five hundred copper coins (about ten cents to Harris) when he worked, though of course he would not need to work every day. And then Harris, who was not about to accede to the Governors even when they tried to save him some money, got his own way by announcing that if the crops were good he would give Juemon a bonus of two *bu*—but if not satisfied, he would cut the wages. Moriyama told Juemon to do his best and dismissed him. There was no need for concern: Juemon had sons and daughters he had trained to be good weeders.

Moriyama was about to leave when Harris asked him to stay for a chat, *as he is quite alone and therefore more communicative.* They were intimates, said Harris, and he hoped that Moriyama would give him some candid answers. Moriyama assured him that he would speak without concealment.

Harris had some questions about the Great Council: what really was their status?

Moriyama assured him that as the government's supreme administrators they were "immensely venerable persons, as venerable as the heavens," of a position so high that he himself could not talk with them directly. When Harris appeared skeptical, Moriyama acted it out, assuming, as he put it, "an awestruck air." Allowing for the thespian in him, he was not exaggerating: one had to reach the rank held by Inoue and Okada before he was entitled to audience with the Great Council.

Harris was still dubious. *I put down the information I get from time to time from [the] Japanese. I know there is much falsehood, but I cannot at the time separate the true from the false.*

He wrote also that Moriyama said *that I must not hurry them too much.* According to Moriyama's diary the advice was much more explicit. "If you go to extremes," he told Harris, "you will arouse grudges. If functionaries—people of rank like mine—come to resent the way you handle things, they will go badly. When a man, however powerful, forces his way, he cannot win the respect of others. Usually I am in no position to say such things to you, a man of erudition and discretion, but you told me to be candid, so I take this liberty."

And according to Moriyama, Harris, relaxing, admitted: "I think your remarks are quite reasonable. I am impatient by birth. When things go against me I explode like gunpowder, but that is only momentary. I try to keep myself under control. However, my stubbornness is not in my own interest but in the interest of my country." His look, Moriyama added, "seemed to show that he was speaking his mind, but he is cunning and it is difficult to know what he is really thinking."

Moriyama reiterated that if Shimoda were an isolated case it would be easy to reach decisions, but everything done here had to be done with consideration for its effect on the rest of the country. (They were setting precedents, and precedents were not to be set lightly.)

Japanese and Americans were different, he said. Japanese had cool-water natures while Americans had hot-water natures. He hoped that Harris would not force the Edo government into hot water.

All his representations, Harris said, were based on the treaty.

For their part, Moriyama replied, the Governors were extremely careful not to misinterpret the treaty.

Ah, but what he was concerned about, answered Harris, was not the treaty's words but its spirit.

"It is logical," Moriyama countered, "to understand the words first and then explore their significance. The 'spirit' fills every corner of the room, but if handled violently it vanishes in an instant. So let us act with circumspection and without haste."

When he was about to leave, Moriyama concludes, Harris offered him liquor, telling him to feel at home always and to help himself as he wished. Moriyama reports that he refused the drink, and perhaps he did on this date: many of the Governors' staff took a cruise on the Kimizawa ship that day, and Moriyama may have been in a hurry to join them.

It had been an interesting talk, but any effect of Moriyama's sound advice was negated when, on the same day, one of the interpreters *told Mr. Heusken that all the buildings at Deshima had been sold to the Dutch.* The interpreter was both misguided and misinformed but the erroneous statement was to Harris one more confirmation of Japanese "mendacity."

Anyway, Harris had Juemon's field and Juemon's help. He began using them the next day. *Wednesday, April 8, 1857. Plant four rows of Irish potatoes in my new garden. The seed grew at Hakodate. A peach tree in my compound just begins to bloom. The blossom is very double, and of the color and size of the "Cinnamon Rose" of the United States. Cherry trees in full bloom, but no fruit comes from the peach or cherry blooms. Why, I cannot say. My grand camellia is still in fine bloom.*

Spring blossoms were something that the crew of Tarojiro's ship would have given a great deal to be free to gaze upon. For six days they had been grilled by a team of the Goyosho's police inspectors. Several merchants of the town were questioned too, on suspicion of collusion. Other officials went over the ship, finally ordered that she be completely unloaded for stem-to-stern examination, a job requiring that additional stevedores be requisitioned. Chuemon and the two witnesses from Suzaki were summoned almost daily to repeat their stories of the first day's unloading. Chuemon was certain that the investigators doubted him and were trying to catch him in some inconsistency. He couldn't sleep for worrying.

Yoheiji missed Chuemon's help, for these were busy days at the village office. It was the time for submitting the annual census.

It was more than a count of people. It listed every family, showing by male and female those who had been born and those who had died, those who had come from other villages and those who had moved away. It showed how much land each family had and how much rice it was expected to produce, and how much land they rented and from whom; for town families it showed whether they owned a house or a shop, or from whom they rented. It showed whatever penalties a village or a town had imposed on its members. But more than that, it certified that each member of each family was a bona-fide parishioner of a Buddhist temple and therefore no Christian.

These were the days when all through the Shogun's domains village and town scribes, or sometimes the headman himself, were making up the new lists, one copy to go forward to the government, one copy to keep on file. When the lists were ready, the local priests came in one by one, and each placed his seal by the name of each of his parishioners. When such a list was complete, signed and sealed by the headman and elders, it constituted a guarantee that there were no Christians in that community.

But while the census was based on the fact that every Japanese was required to be a parishioner of a Buddhist temple, almost every Japanese was loyal to Shinto gods as well: farmers looked to them for abundant crops, fishermen for big catches, merchants for satisfying profits, and every man venerated the guardian deity of his own village or town. The Shogunate's governors for shrines and temples were careful not to neglect the Shinto cults, and at just this time the villages of Izu Province were notified that a team of instructors from the bureau of religion was heading their way to instruct Shinto priests and check on the well-being of shrines. This was official business, all were reminded: men and horses and accommodations would be provided to the party without recompense—call it taxes. Headmen took note of the schedule and their obligations.

It was time, too, now that winter was past and the hard work of growing rice had not yet begun, to repair the roads. Each village mustered men to work on its own, filling in the washouts left by winter storms, hauling in crushed rock if resurfacing was necessary, and cutting back the underbrush that threatened to choke the narrower paths. But of mutual concern was the highway that ran from Shimoda up the middle of the peninsula, connecting with the Tokaido Road at Mishima. This was their most important land link with the rest of the country, and their section of it was in bad shape.

In meeting this problem, Hambei naturally took the lead, summoning the headmen of all the villages to confer. The several sessions were long and hard. It was necessary to determine what had to be done, and what the cost would be, and what the town and each village should contribute.

They ended up petitioning the Governors for help. The road had been badly damaged by the tidal wave of 1854, they pointed out, and further injured by last autumn's typhoon, until now in rainy weather it was almost impassable (a condition the Governors must have been aware of, since they traveled the road when they went from their compound into Shimoda). The villages had done their best but the job was beyond them: a major reconstruction was necessary. The farmers could not provide the labor because rice-planting would soon begin, and therefore it would be necessary to hire workmen. The town and villages could raise no more than two thirds of the cost, "for we are not so rich." They begged the Governors to provide the remaining one third. Evidently the Governors came through, for not much later the reconstruction of the road went forward.

The day after his long chat with Harris, Moriyama received a letter from the executive officer of the finance bureau in Edo. The governors of finance, including Kawaji and Mizuno (who served on the committee to study foreign trade), were not hesitating to send him secret instructions and to ask for private reports.

Probably the Shimoda Governors were aware of this. Inoue, at least, must have acquiesced, for his views on how to handle Harris were close to the rather hard line advocated by his brother, Kawaji, and by Mizuno.

Moriyama replied the next day, bundling up a lengthy report on negotiations over the past two weeks, including his private conversation with Harris, and sending it off with a covering letter. He acknowledged receiving secret instructions "on the treatment of the difficult problems occurring in Shimoda," problems which sometimes, he confessed, seemed too much for him:

> But when I feel that way, I remember the honor paid an incompetent person like myself in being trusted to treat such important matters, and the kindness and warm words with which you received me in Edo—they give me strength.
>
> Every time we talk with the American his attitude changes. His true intentions are beyond conjecture. But I will do my best to guide the negotiations in a direction favorable to Japan.

Further evidence that Moriyama was serving two sets of masters came a couple of days later. Moriyama noted in his diary that he had received a letter from Mizuno "written in his own hand." He was obviously pleased by this mark of esteem.

He doesn't tell us what Mizuno wrote or how he answered, but by that time Harris's disturbing letter would have reached Edo, and Mizuno would have been among the first to read it. Perhaps it raised questions that Mizuno wanted to put to his man on the scene.

Mizuno (*a drawing by Kobayashi Donge*)

At any rate, Mizuno, Kawaji, and the rest of the finance people lost no time in stating their opposition to most of Harris's demands, pretty much along the line that Moriyama was advocating: they were willing to let Harris have Japanese coins and do his own buying, but they opposed letting him travel beyond Shimoda's seven-*ri* limits except in some emergency like the wreck of an American vessel, and they opposed even more vehemently the residence of American merchants in Japan, pointing out that this proposal went far beyond Perry's treaty.

Certainly Harris's letter spurred Lord Hotta to issue another directive on the touchy subjects of foreign relations and foreign trade. It called for more study and more recommendations, and it posed just those questions that most of his staff wanted to avoid:

I. Dealing with foreigners

It seems that the American consul is inclined to regard the Shimoda *bugyo* [Governors] as of little consequence. How can it be possible, then, for the discussions between them to be brought to a successful conclusion? Is it not more likely that in the course of further negotiations Harris will become more and more incensed and make all kinds of unreasonable demands, until we are in the end forced to accept terms many times worse than those now under discussion? Indeed, he has never been satisfied with the present arrangements for discussions. Is it not possible, therefore, that he may report home accordingly and that as his dissatisfaction mounts we may be drawn into considerable difficulties?

Since the consul has recently sent us yet another letter, we might send him a friendly and carefully-reasoned letter in reply, thus taking steps to complete the negotiations by an exchange of correspondence. Alternatively, we might send one of the original *ōsetsu gakari* [the officials appointed to negotiate with Perry in 1854] to him as a special envoy. What do you think of this?

It having been decided that we shall open trade, do you consider it desirable that we, for our own part, should initiate discussions with the American consul, the Dutch Kapitan, and the others? And if by our so doing their resentment is evaporated, ought we to discuss other matters as well and reach agreement with them? . . .

Both Russia and America have asked that we substitute some other port for Shimoda; and if they continue to urge this strongly hereafter, it seems likely that we will find ourselves in a position where we have no choice but to open some other port. Do you know of any port that would be suitable [to propose] in such an eventuality?

Hitherto it has been our general practice to reject all foreign requests, both the important and the unimportant; then, when they have been repeated and become demands, we have been forced to grant them. . . . This seems to be our accustomed procedure. It is due to the fact that the situation here is difficult and we have no choice but to act in this way, but the Dutch have already told us that such action is harmful to our national prestige, and it is certainly not wise to give the impression that our actions are being forced on us by foreigners. Moreover, if other countries are made aware that this is our practice, they will simply seek means of enforcing their demands by threat. If that happens, will it not be detrimental to our interests both at home and abroad? Would it not better serve our interests, in the long run, that instead of leaving the problem until it is too late we should from the beginning make up our minds what it is that we are unable to refuse?

II. Plans for trade

With regard to the opening of trade, for the Bakufu [Shogunate] to open trade when the English come and demand it, might seem proper for purposes of discussion and negotiation, but it might be thought that this, too, would be for Japan to have her action forced on her by others and thus be harmful to her prestige. Would it not therefore be better for the Bakufu first to make a public announcement, though only within Japan, that such is its intention? The Dutch have urged trade plans upon us with every argument at their disposal. The American consul has told us that there is a matter of the utmost importance which he wishes to report at once. In the past year we have been repeatedly informed that the Englishman Bowring will come to Japan and published [newspaper] reports from that country have been forwarded to us. I do not know how true it may be, but I suspect that this is because all countries have agreed that they will first try the effect of threats against us, using America and Holland to influence us by these means, and that if this fails the English will use a show of force to intimidate us. If this is the truth of the situation, it would not seem to be a wise plan to wait for the arrival of the English. While this is no more than a suspicion, I am anxious that you should give it consideration. Then again, if we refuse the requests of America and Holland and complete an agreement at the request of the English, will this not give the first two countries grounds for questioning Japan's good faith and making yet more presumptuous demands?

. . . The Bakufu having decided that, whatever the course we pursue, trade must be opened, it is my wish that you shall without a moment's delay complete an investigation of the main questions involved, such as how trade is to be handled, what goods are to be used in it, and at which ports it is to be conducted. . . . if we on our side have neither plan nor purpose, we will find ourselves in the end unable to do anything but accept foreign proposals as they stand. This would put our national strength in lasting jeopardy. Is it not necessary, then, that we prepare an overall plan? . . .

The products of the territories of the feudal lords will also be considerable. I want you also to give consideration to the circulation of these goods and to the fact that once the Bakufu opens trade, discontent will be caused unless the lords, too, receive similar benefit to alleviate the poverty they have felt for many years. . . .

It probably would have had a salutary effect on Townsend Harris, brooding in Shimoda, had he been able to read this directive. He would have realized that the Japanese knew perfectly well that he was after a trade treaty, and that they were quite aware of the British threat which was his big secret. He could have seen that the government was seriously preparing to open trade.

He could not have known that there had been even more radical proposals from the *ometsuke* and *metsuke:* that men be sent abroad to study foreign ways so that Japan might initiate trade with her own ships.

He would, of course, have found no reference to inviting him to Edo. The tone of his own letter had made that so impossible for the present that this directive did not even mention the possibility; it suggested alternatives instead. But the recommendations that Hotta had called for earlier concerning such a visit were now coming in to the Great Council.

As usual the committee on foreign trade split.

The *ometsuke* and *metsuke* said again that he should be invited, and soon. As for the treatment to be accorded him, "the simpler the better." They thought it would be easier on everybody if he came by ship. He could be put up at a temple in Shinagawa, on the outskirts of Edo, where he would land, and meetings could be held at Lord Hotta's mansion. (They pointed out that if the conference hall were any less handsome than Shimoda's Goyosho, Harris would be sure to think he was being treated impolitely.)

And then, getting into the spirit of things, they roughed out the ceremony of his whole visit: who should greet him on his arrival, and call on him later; when he should meet the Great Council, the dress on that occasion ("it should be plain"), and when during the visit tea and cakes should be served, when sake, and when dinner; when he should be permitted to visit the castle and by what gate he should enter, what rooms should be used for the audience (they thought he should be allowed to sit on a chair to make a distinction between him and the Dutch Kapitan, who had always stood), and how the inevitable gifts should be presented to him; what officials should be charged with housekeeping at his temple; the necessity that a doctor be standing by (the precarious state of his health was well known by then); and who should see him off when he left.

Predictably, the finance officials took a dimmer view of the whole business. They advocated delay and they found a reason for it: Harris could scarcely be trusted when he spoke of the importance of his own position, they pointed out; it would be natural for him to exaggerate. They recommended that Donker Curtius in Nagasaki be questioned concerning Harris's rank.

About the only point on which they agreed with the *ometsuke* and *metsuke* was that he should be treated as informally as possible. "Politeness does not always mean friendship," they added disarmingly, "and, as you know, Western peoples seem to love simplicity."

Since they had to give some kind of answer to Hotta's directive, they suggested that Harris could be accorded treatment "two degrees" higher than that given a Dutch Kapitan. They agreed with their *ometsuke* and *metsuke* colleagues that he should stay at a temple in the suburbs.

But they "dared to express" all their old misgivings—not only that receiving Harris would set a precedent which all other nations would rush to take advantage of, but that Harris himself had already demonstrated that once in Edo he would be arrogant, arbitrary, and tricky; he should not be received until a plan had been devised to blunt his tactics. "We are seriously anxious about receiving him," they concluded. "We think it best if matters could be settled at Shimoda."

Since other officials had already put themselves on record as opposing any concessions to Harris (especially an invitation to Edo) until the country was prepared for war, Lord Hotta had, as usual, a variety of opinions to choose from. There seemed little hope of reconciling them, and he found himself in disagreement with the majority. His was not an enviable position.

Easter Sunday, April 12, 1857. I have kept a very good account of the festivals of the church since my arrival here. It has served to bring up many pleasant recollections and association of ideas in my mind. The day is a lovely one; the fields around me are green with the waving wheat, or finely decorated with flowers. An abundance of violets grows about here. Thermometer 69 °.

While Harris was celebrating Easter, a balmy day in the midst of a cold and backward spring, the two Governors were conferring together at Naka compound. There still were no instructions from Edo. The problem was how to stall. The not surprising decision was to send Moriyama with some words of reassurance.

It was also suggested that he might try to settle the question of the wages Harris was to pay Sukezo and Takizo. Everyone agreed that Harris's offer of one *ryo* (about $1.40) a month was too low, and agreed that he should be told so, explaining that it was out of line with the wages they paid their own servants. But they also agreed that they would not beg. After giving Harris the facts and their opinion, they would accept his decision. On this question at least, they would maintain some dignity—nobody could lose by it save Sukezo and Takizo.

Of course, Moriyama could not undertake his errands until Monday, by which day the weather had reverted to unpleasant: *A strong wind and driving rain from the S. W. . . .*

*Moriyama calls on me, nominally to see me, but in reality to settle the
wages of my two Japanese boys . . .*

At first Harris declined to see his visitor on the grounds that no
appointment had been made, but he relented. He was probably glad for the
diversion, since the record shows that a carpenter and four cleaning men
were underfoot at Gyokusenji that day.

As expected, he led off by asking whether word had been received
from Edo, and when Moriyama apologetically admitted it had not, he
professed great surprise. He was daily expecting the ship by which he must
report to his government—how was he to cope with the situation?

Moriyama confessed that he must ask the Consul General to wait.

It was most embarrassing, said Harris. He could only hope that the
instructions from Edo arrived before the ship. —But today his heart did not
seem to be in this performance, and he changed the subject. He was very
much afraid, he said, that his American seeds were not going to grow
because they had been so long aboard the steamship. He would be much
obliged to get some Japanese vegetable seeds.

Moriyama said he would arrange that, and was inspired by the success
with which Harris and Inoue had exchanged figures of speech a couple of
weeks earlier to coin one of his own. Negotiations, he said, were something
like seeds: they could not germinate on rock, which he likened to the
current situation in Japan, but when the rock by time and hard work had
been changed into soil, the seeds could be productive. Patience would do it.

Unfortunately, the simile did not appeal to Harris. It only brought
forth a recital of the government's dilatoriness, and it took Moriyama some
time to calm him and bring up the subject of the boys' wages.

Harris said he had heard that a manservant received nine *ryo* a year
plus food and clothing. The wage for a boy should be less, he thought.

Moriyama pointed out that in Japanese households a manservant could
work in his underwear in the summer, thus saving kimono. This was not
possible at Gyokusenji, and the boys paid as much as adults for food and
the public baths.

The Governors also kept several young servants, he went on, and paid
them six *ryo* a year plus food, clothing, and an appropriate allowance for
lessons in reading and calligraphy and the martial arts, such as swordsmanship, gunnery, and horsemanship.

Harris laughed. There was no need, he thought, of farmers' sons
practicing swordsmanship. He did not understand that these boys' lives
were vastly different as *ashigaru*. They had the right to use a family name
and to wear two swords. They were considered samurai now and though

they were on the lowest rung of the ladder and their appointments were temporary, they were expected to behave like samurai.

Anyway, Harris and Moriyama figured it all out—the cost of food and clothing and incidentals—and agreed on a wage of one and a half *ryo* (six *bu*) a month, or about two dollars. (*The Vice-Governor last December wanted me to pay them sixteen dollars per month,* wrote Harris; maybe— but the Japanese record shows that in January, Wakana had asked three or four *ryo* a month, about four to five and a half dollars.)

Having settled this problem (probably to the satisfaction of both the Governors and the boys, who also received their rice stipend as *ashigaru*), Moriyama became expansive. He told Harris that *Japan will be opened to foreigners within the year,* that *the Japanese are now negotiating a commercial treaty with the Dutch,* and that the *Diana's* guns *have been taken to Edo; that eight or nine of them are to be mounted on a corvette they have built on the Western model. The corvette is 120 feet keel.* It sounds very much as though on this day Moriyama accepted a drink.

Speaking of the *Diana's* guns reminded Harris that he had been wanting to broach the subject of salutes to visiting ships. From now on, he said, he would arrange that American ships on entering the harbor would fly the Japanese flag and fire a twenty-one-gun salute. He hoped the Japanese would reciprocate from the shore. Would Moriyama sound out the Governors? Harris did not want to make a formal proposal in writing unless he knew it would be accepted (if he put it in writing and was refused, he would have one more failure to report to Washington).

Moriyama said he would consult the Governors and let the Consul General know.

Next day, perhaps emboldened by Moriyama's success in setting the boys' wages, Vice-Superintendent Kikuna called. To break the ice he brought a Japanese dictionary *and promises in a few days to bring me some school books, works of fiction and history.* He also brought the accounts for Harris's first seven months at Shimoda.

The total looks alarming, as it is 2,087,009 of their coins, but luckily that is fully liquidated with the sum of $447. Harris did not, however, choose to pay up just yet. He would first go over the bills very carefully.

Presentation of this account set Harris to surveying his financial status. He had experienced a long drought when he had no assured income—it had been more than seven years from the day he sailed out of New York to begin his unsuccessful career as a trader in Asia until he took up his post at Shimoda—and he found genuine pleasure in the prospect of accumulating a nest egg for retirement. Judging from the several entries in his journal during this month, he covered a good many sheets of paper with figures.

My servants (i.e., the Chinese) are the heaviest item of my expenses here, as their wages amount to more than $700 per annum, that is for four men, and I also give them their food and lodging, while for five Japanese I pay $132 per annum and they board themselves.

. . . In my account for the last seven months are many things that I shall not have to renew, such as furniture, norimono, horse, etc., etc., all of which amount to $144,—so that leaves about $300 as my expenses for seven months. But my bread, tea, sugar, spices, pickles, coffee, etc., etc., are all brought here and are a very considerable item. . . . had I not brought them to terms about the currency, I should have found my salary insufficient for my support.

A few days later he sharpened his pencil and went over the whole thing again.

I have been overlooking my accounts from the Japanese, which they have now rendered to me for the first time. Although they charge me double prices for everything they furnish to me,* yet my bills to them for food, fuel, lights, etc., etc., will not exceed $500 per annum. . . . Mr. Heusken pays me $365 per annum for his board, washing, etc., which reduces my expenses to less than $1,500 per annum. Clothing, books, and the wine I must use when I have guests will probably leave the full outlay about $1,750 per annum.

My servants consist of a butler, cook and his mate, washman, two house boys, one water carrier, one sweeper, one gardener, one groom,—in all ten persons, and not one that I can do without.

A couple of days later: *In my previous statements of my expenses of living here, I have entirely omitted rent. As yet I have not paid any, but when I shall occupy a house specially built for me, I shall of course have to pay it. This item will probably bring the total to a little over two thousand dollars per annum.*

Since his salary was five thousand dollars he would be able to save about three thousand dollars a year. He was fortunate, as may be judged by the remarks of his friend Charles Huffnagle, Consul General at Calcutta, in a letter probably then lying in Hong Kong waiting a ship to Shimoda. Congress had set the salary of his post at five thousand dollars, and he was bitter:

---

* But two paragraphs later he noted: *I am well supplied with fine pheasants at about sixteen cents each, and so large that one makes an ample dinner for Mr. Heusken and myself.*

This will be a capital berth for somebody; the expenses of office are not over $3600 and this will leave $1400 to the Consul General per annum—his passage out and home he must pay out of this of course; and Spence will board and lodge him respectably in a two pair back for say $1500

Hunter & Co. supply him with a buggy @ 150	900
say servants, washing and clothing, etc., etc., etc.,	600
	$3000

So if by possibility he can live for $3000 and does not care ever to see a friend or to buy a bottle of wine or beer he can serve his Country without losing more say than $2000 a year at any rate.

I have under [these] circumstances earnestly prayed for immediate relief and I only hope my successor may be some stump orator—some tobacco-eating greedy abolitionist for it would serve him just right. . . .

When you write tell us of anything new and pretty which your Consul Generalship may have taken a fancy to and always believe me,

Sincerely yours,
Charles Huffnagle

A glance back at Harris's figures shows that he had not figured the expense of "anything new and pretty."

Harris's feeler about the exchange of salutes triggered another disagreement between the Governors. In conveying the proposal, Moriyama made clear his disapproval of it. Inoue was inclined to agree with him, but he was otherwise persuaded by Okada, who was always willing to give a little on minor issues if it would make for an easier relationship with foreigners. Besides, he enjoyed the sound of the cannon, as he had remarked to Harris in their very first interview.

The Governors had just instructed Moriyama to tell Harris that they approved of the idea of exchanging salutes, though they could speak only for Shimoda, when Executive Officer Wakana joined them and offered a dissent. The firing of salutes, he argued, was a foreign practice. If the Governors followed it, they would be creating a whole new ceremonial based on foreign ideas. "How much better to answer a salute in our established manner. Specifically, send an executive officer and his entourage on board with our greetings. This means that we exchange courtesies the most natural way, the American side with its manners and our side with our own."

Inoue changed his mind again. Okada was not convinced but he agreed to let Moriyama try to sell this alternative to Harris. And Moriyama

334

was left to nurse a peeve: why had his recommendation failed to sway the Governors even though they had accepted the same idea from Wakana?

Harris was not happy. He would not insist, he told Moriyama, but the exchange of salutes was a well-nigh universal practice which created a bond of good feeling. "Siam returns our salutes, but China refuses to"—and China's behavior, as the Japanese did not need to be told, was a shining example of how not to deal with foreigners.

I told him that I was anxious that the Japanese should take their place among the civilized nations of the world, and that all these small things were so many steps in that direction. Thus he labored to convince Moriyama that firing guns was more civilized than speaking words of greeting, and he asked that the question be put to the Governors again.

It was another wide-ranging conversation that afternoon.

Moriyama transmitted a request from the Governors for books used to teach military and naval science at West Point and Annapolis, and Harris said he was sure he could get them. Harris wanted Japanese books, and Moriyama, unlike Kikuna, was not at all sure he could get those.

Histories, he said, were banned from circulation among the people and were therefore unavailable. Schoolbooks were restricted to the teachings of Confucius and Mencius and were the same as used in China. And since poetry-making was the privilege of the nobility, books of poems were denied to the rank and file like himself (this was fantasy, but he was still smarting from Wakana's opinion being valued more highly than his).

But when Harris produced a British book and read from it in Japanese a poem usually attributed to an unlucky statesman of the ninth century, Sugawara Michizane—

> *Kokoro dani*
> *Makoto no michi ni*
> *Kanai naba*
> *Inorazu totemo*
> *Kamiya mamoran.*

—Moriyama, understandably startled, said he would see what he could do about books.

The transliteration to the English alphabet in either of the books Harris might have picked up is much more eccentric than that given above, so that Harris's Japanese was probably difficult to follow. But the poem was, and is, so familiar that any Japanese given the first two or three words would instantly recognize it. The translation in Harris's book read:

> Upright in heart be thou, and pure,
> So shall the blessing of God
> Through eternity be upon thee;
> Clamorous prayers shall not avail,
> But truly a clear conscience,
> That worships and fears in silence.

But it has been translated less windily as:

> Unsought in prayer
> The gods will guard
> The pure in heart.

Moriyama then finished his errands by telling Harris it would not be possible to pay the craftsman who was making his gold watch chains by giving him the gold left over. Such a man could not have gold in his possession, for gold and silver were strictly controlled by the government mints and except for money could be used only to decorate weapons. The Consul General would please pay the artisan in the usual way (the fee for making the two chains was two *bu,* or about seventy cents), and the extra gold would be turned in to the mint for reimbursement.

Harris said if that was the way it had to be done, very well, and then, according to Moriyama, pressed him to stay on for a drink. As usual, Moriyama insists that he declined, but as usual he found himself with a glass in his hand.

The drinks seem to have loosened both their tongues.

Moriyama *said that he wished to ask me a question, and that he wanted me to consider it as a dream,—i.e., to forget it. The query was: "Suppose the Governors of Shimoda should wish to make a commercial treaty with you, what would you do?" I replied that I should first ask to see their full powers, and if those were satisfactory, that I would then show them mine, and after that we would go to work at a treaty at once. He said if that was so, that they had misunderstood me, that they supposed that I would only negotiate at Edo and with the High Council.*

I told him that they had confounded two things; that what I had to say confidentially as from my Government could only be said at Edo, so also the President's letter could only be delivered by me at Edo and in the imperial presence, etc.

That negotiations were a different thing; that I was ready to negotiate with any person of proper rank who could show me the requisite full powers, etc., etc.

It is not surprising that the Japanese should have had a different

336

understanding: in February, Harris had gone out of his way to tell the Governors that he would negotiate important matters only at Edo, though there were minor issues relating to Perry's treaty that he was willing to discuss at Shimoda; and he had emphatically repeated this stand in his latest letter to the Great Council.

Since Moriyama had asked his question "as in a dream," he did not mention it in his diary. And on the other hand, Harris did not record rambling on at some length about the warship that wasn't there. He supposed it had been delayed by a visit to Siam to exchange the ratifications of his treaty, but it would surely arrive soon. In the meantime the Japanese seemed somehow to have got the idea that in pressing for a reply to his proposals he was acting for selfish reasons, his own and his country's. The fact was, he said, that the earlier the Japanese replied, the better for their own country. In demanding answers (affirmative, of course), he was acting out of kindness to Japan, and it grieved him that the Japanese did not understand this.

Of course his own country would never take action against Japan, but she had better watch out for Britain and France. Bowring might come tomorrow, or he might not come for six months—there was no way of knowing, it was a military secret. What was certain was that he would come. Britain, he went on, was angry over Russia's incursion into Manchuria and was certain the Russians planned to invade China and then attack India. The British believed that by taking Hokkaido and Sakhalin from Japan, they could confront the Russians in the north and stop them there. That was why the British wanted to pick a fight with Japan.

He was asking the Japanese to consider these facts carefully. That was what he meant when he spoke of his kindness toward Japan.

Moriyama thanked the Consul General for his kindness and went home to muse on his inconsistency.

Harris was left to regret that he had revealed to Moriyama practically all of the "secrets" he was holding out as bait to get to Edo (though as long as the Japanese did not realize that, he had not lost much). There may have been no connection between his drinking that afternoon, and his dwelling on the fact that Commodore Armstrong had sent no ship, and his brooding over the possibility that John Bowring might appear any day and steal the credit for all that he, Harris, had accomplished—there may have been no connection between these things and his *violent attack of cholera morbus* the next day. Perhaps that was due to something he ate, but he was very ill and for three or four days after had *an almost constant relax.*

The attack intensified his worries about his health. *I am much con-*

cerned at the non-arrival of the <u>San Jacinto</u>. *Commodore Armstrong promised to be here in March, and now more than one half of April has slipped away. My last letters from the United States were dated March 17, 1856. More than thirteen months ago. How much may have happened in that time. My health is not good. . . .*

I wish the frigate would arrive that I could have some medical advice.

In this frame of mind, he might have derived a wry laugh had he been able to read a circular then making the rounds. It announced that Goyosho officials would be inspecting all of the ninety-odd villages within the seven-*ri* area "where foreigners make merry these days."

However poor Harris's health, it was robust compared with that of the crew of Tarojiro's ship. They had been clapped into jail, and there, since under the law the only valid proof of guilt was the confession of the accused, they were being encouraged to confess. This involved torture, not as wildly barbarous as the West's rack or the boot, but just as efficient. It came in four degrees.

The first was scourging. The prisoner's handcuffs were removed and his upper clothing stripped off. His arms were twisted behind his back, pulled up to his shoulders and tied, and prison underlings (members of that outcast group who were confined to their homes at New Year's) in front of and behind him held tight the ends of this rope so that he could not move no matter how great the pain. Then the warders beat his back and shoulders with scourges of split bamboo bound with hemp. When blood flowed, the underlings sprinkled fine sand in the wounds to stop the blood and the beating went on. At intervals, questions were put to the accused. The scourging was stopped at about one hundred and fifty blows or when the officer judged the man could take no more.

The next stage was called "hugging the stone." The prisoner, bound as before, was made to kneel on sharp bars laid in front of a pillar to which he was tied. Then slabs of Izu stone, so conveniently at hand here at Shimoda, each weighing about one hundred pounds, were laid on his lap. Most men fainted after the fifth stone.

The third stage, undertaken after several days to rest and recover from the second, was called "the lobster." The arms were twisted behind the back, the legs were tied together and pulled up to the chin, and front and back were pulled together as tightly as possible. Within half an hour the body became red and cold perspiration flowed; within another hour the color changed to purple, and then to green, and then all color drained away. This was the sign that death was approaching, and so the ropes were loosened. But few men were able to hold out so long.

For the indomitables there was one final stage. The arms of the accused were pinioned behind his back and he was suspended from the wrists.

So far not even the first stage had been used on the sailors. They were being given time to contemplate the prospects while word was awaited from the owner of the ship, Tarojiro of Edo, and from the stewards of Lord Nambu, whose rice was the cargo. But confinement, questioning, and lesser ways of inflicting pain were taking their toll.

This took place in the new jail at Naka, not far from the Governors' compound. The location gave rise to yet another petition from the officials of that village. They pointed out that the jail had been built close to the house of farmer Rokubei. Ever since, he and his family had been troubled by the traffic. Village officials had several times persuaded him not to make a complaint, but recently the number of thugs passing his premises to communicate with their friends within (by bribing the guards, no doubt) had become so great that Rokubei and his family could not go out of their house at night. They were thoroughly frightened, and Rokubei earnestly wished to move his house to another part of the village. "As he is very poor," the headman and elders wrote, "he cannot find the money for moving. We hereby apply for a loan of ten *ryo* to be repaid in one year. We throw ourselves on your mercy, with the hope that your kind help will be given to this poor farmer." The record does not show what action was taken on this petition, but one hopes it was granted.

Monday, April 20, 1857. A miserable wet day. . . . It was spring by the calendar but the sea was still treacherous. A circular was being sped from village to village along the seacoast, announcing that a ship of Osaka, laden with yarn, cotton, and other goods, was missing since March 24. Any village which had any information of it was ordered to report by express messenger.

Despite the miserable weather, Harris felt sufficiently recovered from his latest illness to send word asking the Governors to confer with him the next day. *I wish to engross the Articles already settled with them, and have them make their translation, as the last is always a work of much time, and thus I shall be able to expedite the whole matter the more promptly when I get a decision on the "two points."*

After obtaining the Governors' agreement on this, Harris brought up two matters on which he had received instructions from the Secretary of State before he left the United States.

They involved Americans who had preceded him to Japan: first, the traders Reed and Dougherty, most of whose party had lived at Gyokusenji while their ship carried some of the *Diana's* crew back to Russia; and second, Lieutenant John Rodgers and his U. S. Navy surveying expedition, which, over vehement Japanese protests, had been charting the coasts of Japan at the same time.

Reed and Dougherty were the leaders of what Secretary Marcy called "the somewhat premature adventure of our enterprising countrymen." Word of Perry's treaty was no sooner published than they "embarked for Hakodate . . . for the purpose of settling there and supplying the wants of the whale-ships which were expected to touch at that port." Their ship came first to Shimoda to trade, and it was while they were installed at Gyokusenji that the then Governor had informed them that as soon as their ship returned they must re-embark "as they would not be allowed to reside at either Shimoda or Hakodate." They protested, and Lieutenant Rodgers, who was on the scene, added his protest, but they had to leave Shimoda, and at Hakodate they were not even permitted to land until they agreed in advance to leave in a short time.

It was a matter of interpreting the treaty. When it referred to "ship-wrecked men, and other citizens of the United States, temporarily living at Shimoda and Hakodate," the Japanese considered that it meant people living there for a short time until they could conveniently leave. And there is no doubt that that was the basis on which Perry negotiated: on this issue the official narrative of his expedition stated that "it was perfectly plain that the Japanese meant to be distinctly understood as prohibiting, absolutely, at least for the present, the *permanent* residence of Americans, with their families, in Japan."

Now, however, the United States government chose to consider that "temporarily" meant "indefinitely," and that Reed, Dougherty, and their associates were quite within their rights when they attempted to settle "indefinitely" at Hakodate and open a business there. This was another example of the foot-in-the-door approach which had made the Japanese wary.

The other matter also related to the treaty. Lieutenant Rodgers had reported to Washington that the Japanese version of article 7 included the italicized words which were not in the American version:

It is agreed that ships of the United States resorting to the ports open to them shall be permitted to exchange gold and silver coin and articles of goods for other articles of goods, *such as may be necessary for them,* under such regulations as shall be temporarily established by the Japanese government for that purpose. . . .

Lieutenant Rodgers, it may be noted, had no interpreters with him and conversations at Shimoda were carried on through Hori Tatsunosuke (the Japanese interpreter to whom Reed had written the letter delivered in March by the *Messenger Bird*), who was wrestling English with the help of the Noah Webster dictionary which was one of Perry's gifts to the Japanese. Obviously, therefore, Rodgers was in no position to know precisely what the Japanese were saying on any topic. Something like the phrase in question did appear in another article.

Nevertheless, article 7 was the foot in the door toward trade, and the United States, as Marcy made clear, took a dim view of any attempt to restrict it. It was the Secretary's blunt stand on these two matters that Harris had read to the Governors a couple of months earlier and which had produced such a "fearful fluttering."

No doubt the reason Harris had not brought up these questions sooner was that he hoped to solve them by laying claim to the new rights he thought, erroneously, the Dutch had secured at Deshima. But a satisfactory answer to that was very slow in coming, and meantime, if a Navy ship appeared, he could scarcely avoid sending home a report on these two topics. The Secretary had instructed him to "lose no time" in taking them up.

On this day at the Goyosho, neither issue led to argument because Harris contented himself with serving notice that he intended to write a letter on these subjects and that he expected a letter in reply.

He had something else on his mind today and he asked that the room be cleared for a secret session. The Governors excused all their men except Moriyama and Dr. Ito, and then Harris again tried to peddle American arms. As Moriyama recorded it, Harris said:

> In the United States there is a big merchant who controls the supply of all weapons. When I was leaving my country, he handed me a list of weapons that could be sold if your country should need them, with their prices. I will give you this list translated into Dutch. If you want any of these weapons, I will report it to that merchant.

Evidently Harris had received no response to his earlier conversation with Matsumura and Wakana at Gyokusenji. He felt it necessary to speak to the Governors. He had asked for a secret session, he told them, because he would not want Britain and France to know that Japan was getting weapons from the United States.

The Governors did not appear eager to buy. If his client wanted copper, they answered, they had little to sell. And the new rate of exchange had proved very disadvantageous when they were dealing with the *Messenger Bird*. If that handicap continued, there could be no trade between the two countries.

Harris delivered his little Adam Smith lecture again. "You had better leave trade to the merchants," he said. "Let the government stand aside except to collect taxes from the merchants." It was a position he would have found awkward had he admitted that his own government was trying to sell munitions.

He brought up another subject that afternoon but did not press it. *I found the matter of salutes . . . is a perplexing matter to them, so I let it rest where it is for the present.* He told the Governors he felt good because there had been no disputes that afternoon, and went home.

But there had been a dispute and a serious one, though no doubt it was argued with civility. It was between Inoue and Okada on the "perplexing matter" of salutes. Each now considered it a matter of principle. They had labored to present a show of unity despite their differences, but now they split openly. Each wrote a letter to the Great Council.

Inoue wrote:

> . . . I think it is a matter of course that the customs of Japan are different from the West. If she accepts other nations' customs at their request she will be compelled to change all of hers to theirs, and this will mean loss of dignity. I know that we must consider the danger of war which the American official repeatedly insinuates, but giving in to his request will weaken us in future negotiations.
>
> As the opinions of the Lord of Bingo and myself differ on this point, I have stated my views to you spontaneously. I would be very happy if you would give me your direction immediately.

Okada wrote:

> . . . At the two ports opened for the United States we must as a matter of course revise some of our regulations. Of course we must maintain our dignity, but when one of America's requests would not seriously affect Japan, it would be generous of us to accept it. I believe that returning their salutes could never mean loss of dignity. We could refuse this request if we had never permitted foreign ships to fire salutes in our ports, but we have, and clearly this practice is grounded in friendship. This may seem unimportant to us but it is important to them. The American has been expressing displeasure over our attitude in negotiations. If we could accept this request it would please him and soften his stubbornness; it would ease future negotiations. . . .

I have stated my opinion spontaneously, for it differs from the Lord of Shinano's. I would be very happy if you would give me your direction immediately.

Okada probably thought he had made a strong case, quite in line with the Great Council's directive of a month earlier ("Any attempt on our part to cling to tradition, making difficulties over the merest trifles and so eventually provoking the foreigners to anger, would be impolitic in the extreme"). But it was Inoue's letter which was endorsed back to Shimoda; the Great Council's order: "You must withhold the firing of salutes by our side."

Okada was the junior. In dealing with the American he had consistently advocated a more liberal approach than his senior. Now he had made an issue of their differences and had been rebuffed. His position at Shimoda began to look very shaky.

The weather continued cold and damp, but Harris did more gardening. *Wednesday, April 22, 1857. The seeds I brought from the United States will, as I fear, prove to be a total failure. I put eighteen sorts in the ground on the 3rd inst., but only some few peas have as yet come up. It will be a sad drawback to my comforts if they should fail. To-day put in the ground a few grains of corn, watermelons, cucumbers and eggplant seeds procured from the Japanese. Twenty grains of corn and seven watermelon seeds were all I could procure! They said all their seeds were planted.*

His canary pleased him by hatching a new brood and then disappointed him by abandoning her nest. *I cannot account for her unnatural conduct. I separated her and the male the moment she commenced to incubate, and have not only kept him out of sight but out of hearing. I can only suppose I have fed her too high. She had a yolk of egg every day.*

He brooded over his slow progress with the Japanese. *I cannot see what it is that keeps away Commodore Armstrong. If I had a vessel of war here, I should have speedy answers to my demands on the two points, but I feel sure they will not be settled so long as no ship-of-war comes here.*

Lacking the Navy to enforce his demands, he resorted to canceling the English lessons he had been giving. Of Dr. Ito he wrote: *I found him very apt. He has been absent for some weeks to visit his sick father at Edo, and to-day came to renew his lessons. I did not give him anything but a letter to the Governors, in which I told them that I should be very happy to give instruction in English, after I had been permitted the full exercise of my rights as Consul, but, so long as I was denied any of those rights, I must decline the lessons.*

The Governors probably took his letter philosophically. They were used to this kind of behavior by now.

Monday, April 27, 1857. The rhododendron, althea, is now in beautiful flower, colors chiefly pink. I have planted some of them in the cemetery where the four Americans are buried.

On the same day Moriyama called with the Japanese version of the four articles agreed on. He brought Dr. Ito: there was more than one way to get an English lesson. There was the probably inevitable row over wording.

According to Moriyama, there was agreement on the first three articles but some difficulty over the fourth. According to Harris, there was *a cunning attempt to interpolate words of different meaning. Moriyama says very coolly that "it is a very different thing to say a thing or to write it"* (a point to which most writers would probably say amen!). *In other words, they are always at liberty to deny anything they have said or promised, so long as it is not in writing.*

Heusken complained that the Japanese did not use good Dutch. Harris charged them with *duplicity and constant efforts to vary the substance.*

One would think the translation of a paper to be a simple process, he wrote. But no expert has ever found it so, especially when one of the languages is Japanese. Yet despite Harris's fulminations, the difficulties could not have been serious, for it took conferences on only two days to bring agreement on the wording of the four articles.

I feel sure that what I have accomplished will give satisfaction. I have settled the currency so that one dollar goes as far almost as three did when Commodore Perry left the question. I have opened the Port of Nagasaki to American ships wanting supplies.

Americans are only to be amenable to American authority for offenses committed in Japan.

American ships in distress and who have no money can pay for all necessary supplies by barter.

The great point of residence of Americans is still pending; and, although it may not now be admitted, yet I have placed it on a footing which must ultimately secure it. The consular rights and franchises stand on the same ground as the rights of residence.

I have fought the battles; and although I may not recieve the victory, yet victory will come and will be owing to my labors.

He had more potatoes planted in Juemon's field. *Those planted on the 8th inst. are coming up. The Japanese say the season is unusually backward and the weather colder than they ever knew in April. . . . The Seville orange trees in front of my house do not show a single leaf as yet.*

Perhaps he sputtered to keep warm. *As a specimen of the cool mendacity of the Japanese, even about things that are tangible to the sight, I note the following: the Island of Oshima is in plain sight of Shimoda and some twelve or fifteen miles distant from us, so that it comes within the limits of seven ri, or sixteen and five-eighths miles as settled for the Americans. Yet the Governors coolly tell me that Oshima is twenty-five ri, or fifty-nine and three-eights miles distant from Shimoda!!* (This passage implies language problems on even the simplest matters: for as we know, Oshima is twenty-five *miles* rather than twenty-five *ri* from Shimoda, but still well outside the seven-*ri* limit.)

He closed his journal for the month on a gloomy note. *My health is very unsatisfactory. I am unable to cure my acid stomach arising from indigestion. I have reduced my food to bread, rice and the flesh meat we get here, having left off butter, oil, fruit, and all vegetables except potatoes. Still my indisposition continues and I am constantly growing thinner and thinner. I walk every day from six to eight miles. Perhaps the machine is wearing out, and these are premonitions of the approaching end.*

Far to the north, Elisha E. Rice, after some months of misadventure on the China coast, had just arrived at Hakodate on a whaler and announced to the Governor that he was the U.S. commercial agent for that port. He was a big bear of a man, "a larger man than the Commodore by a *head and shoulders,*" as Captain Bell had written to Harris in yet another undelivered letter; "what will the poor Japanese think when they see him?"

What they thought was that they were being put upon, for the treaty did not authorize a United States official at Hakodate, a fact that seems to have been of no concern to the State Department when it issued his credentials. But the Governor and his men found Mr. Rice a difficult man to say no to, and they finally agreed to let him stay "temporarily" and installed him in a temple.

Back at Kakisaki, Yoheiji noted in his diary that Kichiemon's boat had brought in the season's first haul of bonito. Raw and cold though it was, it was spring.

Chapter 11

MAY, 1857

May in Japan is often the loveliest month of the year, a gentle and a fragrant month. The air is balmy. Fields of winter wheat turn golden. The salmon-pink of wild azaleas brightens the mountain slopes. Williams's Chinese teacher Lo had remarked on those azaleas, going on to commend his friend Dr. Morrow for assiduously collecting and preserving botanical specimens, "showing himself worthy to be a disciple of Confucius."

The May of 1857 was a notable exception. The raw wind from the northeast that had swept through April sullenly persisted, bringing dull skies, rain, and chill. It is not surprising that the lonely American at Gyokusenji felt unwell. For most of the month he had an acid stomach and a disposition to match. His view of Japan and the Japanese was correspondingly jaundiced.

Yet the month began well. *Friday, May 1, 1857. May Day! A fine day indeed. Thermometer, 69°. Mr. Heusken brought me a bunch of violets which gave out a fine fragrance. Generally the flowers here have but little perfume.*

And there was a visit from Moriyama, who brought the Governors' reply to the questions he had raised concerning Lieutenant Rodgers and the Messrs. Reed and Dougherty. Moriyama was alone again (he had tried to talk Governor Inoue into letting him bring Dr. Ito, and failing there, had approached Governor Okada with the same request, only to get the same answer); and since he was alone he and Harris had a relaxed chat.

Moriyama had brought with him something Harris had asked for—a table of *hiragana*, the cursive syllabary of forty-seven symbols by which Japanese can be written. Moriyama read the table and Harris added phonetic approximations in roman letters. The sign for *mi* launched a discussion. A character with this sound appeared in the date of letters that Harris had received from the Japanese; what, he asked, did it mean?

It signified the year, Moriyama explained. The current year was the Year of *Mi*, the Year of the Serpent. And he gave Harris a little discourse on the system of zodiacal signs, the cycles of years, of days, of hours. Later Harris put what he had learned in his journal. For a first lesson, it was good.

By the Western calendar, he told Moriyama, today was the day of the flower festival. "He recited the American flower festival poem," Moriyama wrote in *his* journal, "and explained its meaning. He looked very tranquil."

But after Moriyama left and Heusken had a chance to translate the Governors' letter, the Consul General was not so tranquil. *It is all of a piece with their falsehood and duplicity. I do not think that any Japanese ever*

Dr. James Morrow (*detail from a scroll painting by an unknown artist*)

347

The table of *hiragana* brought by Moriyama (*from Harris's letters and papers*)

tells the truth, if it can possibly be avoided. He prefers using falsehood when the simple truth would answer just as well.

In the matters now at hand, the terms "truth" and "falsehood" were not even pertinent. The issues were questions of interpretation. The Governors' reply simply restated what had been the Japanese position all along.

To Lieutenant Rodgers's statement that the Japanese version of article 7 of the treaty had a qualifying clause which the American version did not, they answered it was not so, and sent along their Dutch version of the article to prove it. (The curious thing is that the article which Harris had recently negotiated with the Governors spoke of American ships' "obtaining *necessary* supplies, or to repair damages"; he had inserted, where there had been none before, just such a restriction as Lieutenant Rodgers and Secretary Marcy had inveighed against.)

To the charge that they had refused permission to Reed and Dougherty to stay at Shimoda and at Hakodate "temporarily" (that is, to use Secretary Marcy's words, "for an indefinite time"), they replied that they had permitted the group to live at Shimoda longer than "temporarily" while their ship carried some of the stranded Russians to Kamchatka; at Hakodate, they were told they could come ashore temporarily, which the Governor there had said meant a few days or at the longest two months, adding that the fact that they had brought their families seemed to indicate they intended a much longer stay, which he would not permit. The actions at both places, wrote Governors Inoue and Okada, were in line with the Japanese interpretation of "temporary," an interpretation they would continue to act upon.

Next day Harris relieved his sense of outrage by dispatching to the Governors a long memorandum about the prices charged in the accounts submitted to him the previous month. He complained about the price of almost every item, from boar's meat to birdseed. "Everything," he wrote, "is overcharged."

This was a letter the Governors must have been dreading. They knew that his prices were padded and they were embarrassed about it. First, there was the ten-per-cent tax on his purchases; they had begged Edo to end this, but without success. Second, partly because of the tax and partly because Harris was still not permitted to make his own purchases, there was the red tape which entangled shopkeepers when they sold something to him: they had to sell through the Goyosho, they had to calculate the tax which the Goyosho would withhold, and their payment was delayed; as a result, some of them, especially those who disliked foreigners anyway, preferred not to be bothered; when they had to sell, they tacked on an aggravation fee.

But when Harris presented his case, he so clouded it with irrelevancies that he made it easy to answer.

On some items his complaints sound reasonable. He objected to paying eleven cents a dozen for eggs when he had "reason to believe" the Japanese paid only one half to three quarters of that. He objected to paying thirty-one cents apiece for chickens "lean, poor, and tough," so aged that they sometimes expired in his cages before his cook could get them into the frying pan.

But he chose to parade his merchant's lore by attacking the Japanese price structure. Pigs cost twice as much as they did in China. Charcoal cost more than potatoes: this was "unreasonable." Fish cost more than rice: "In all countries, fresh fish is never dearer than rice, yet here in Shimoda, which is placed on the seashore, and whose waters abound in fish, and where the price should be lower than rice," it was sometimes five times as expensive (it cost him from four to thirteen cents a pound). "A laboring man in

Shimoda is paid 288 *seni* [copper *mon*] for one day's work, yet it is pretended that fresh fish is worth 282 *seni* for one kattie." (A catty equals one and a third pounds.)

Chickens too: "In other parts of the world, a laboring man earns two fowls in one day, but here it appears he must work nearly three days to get one fowl."

Lo *(detail from a scroll painting by an unknown artist)*

These arguments were totally pointless. A laboring man in Shimoda ate fish, yes, not every day but often: a broiled morsel with his rice and pickles, or a tidbit in his soup—never a plate full of it as Harris did and never the choice, expensive fish that were sent to Gyokusenji.

But chickens?—except for the sophisticated officials from Edo on those rare occasions when they dined with Harris or on some foreign ship, it is doubtful that any resident of Shimoda ate the flesh of chickens. In Buddhist terms, it was a barbarism. Lo, complaining about the absence of meat in the Japanese diet, had noted that fowls "obtained a most venerable age." And

350

so they did: hens past laying and cocks that had lost their virility were simply turned loose, often in the shrine precincts, to forage for themselves until they could forage no longer—that is, until the carnivorous foreigners appeared on the scene.

Under the circumstances Harris's arguments scarcely made sense. They illustrated chiefly how little he had learned about his neighbors in eight months. In the Governors' list of things to worry about, the relative price of chicken in Shimoda as compared with that in Hong Kong or New York held a very low priority.

But this dreary month of May was a time for haggling over prices. Serious negotiations had come to a halt, immobilized by the tormenting silence from Edo and the split between the two Governors. For all his brave calls for long-range plans to open the country to foreign trade, Lord Hotta was unable to issue specific instructions to cope with the lone American at Shimoda.

In the strained atmosphere at Naka compound, the Governors could agree on one thing at least, that the government owed them an answer. They sent off a note which was about as testy as men of their rank could get in dealing with the Great Council.

They had sent to Edo, they wrote, a translation of the American official's letter, the one claiming the right of residence for merchants, and, for himself, the right to buy direct and to travel freely throughout Japan. They had sent their own recommendations on these questions. They had forwarded another letter of Harris's addressed to the Great Council, the one in which he protested their attitude toward the President's letter. But they had received no answers. The American had pressed for a reply over and over again, saying it was inconceivable to him that it took more than forty days to get an answer from their government. He had also said that he would sail to Edo to confront the government himself if he had not been answered by the time the American warship arrived.

"It is," they concluded, "almost impossible for us to persuade him to wait longer. We ask you to give us your directions concerning these matters as soon as possible." In Edo, Okada would be blamed for the bluntness of this letter. It would do little to enhance his position.

The Governors also sent off to Edo a copy of the four articles on which they and Harris had reached agreement, and a copy of their letter on the Reed–Dougherty and Rodgers matters.

And further taking advantage of the respite from negotiations with Harris to clean up some of their paper work, they answered two queries from the government:

One concerned a request for guidance from the Governors of Nagasaki concerning problems raised by foreigners at that port—how to handle their purchases (Inoue and Okada, citing their own experience, agreed with the Nagasaki Governors that it would be best to convert the foreigners' money and let them do their own buying); how to provide resting places when they went sightseeing (it was impossible to have an officially appointed rest house everywhere one was needed, they said; best let the foreigners stop at any suitable house or temple and serve them whatever food and drink happened to be available); and whether to let the foreigners enter the red-light district (since Shimoda had no officially designated district, the Governors thought perhaps this problem was outside their ken, but as, on the other hand, there were in fact some prostitutes in Shimoda, though unlicensed, they said they would investigate further and report again, thus opening prospects of an inquiry that their man Saito would relish).

And finally they sent in their reaction to Donker Curtius's advice about the war in China, which had been circulated for comment:

> What the report tells us is very reasonable. As the condition of the world has changed, Japan, like China, will be compelled to conclude treaties with many foreign countries. . . . If we stick to old customs and try to exclude foreigners, it will result in war. If we delay in accepting their requests until the last moment, it will bolster them in thinking that their threats will always overmaster us.

And they added, with feeling:

> They think we act too slowly. We believe we should decide matters related to foreign countries as quickly as possible.
>
> Other nations are displeased that Japan treats the Netherlands as an exception because we have traded with that country for two hundred years. Russia and America will request that we treat them exactly as we do the Netherlands. We think that the government should treat equally all countries where the languages are written sideways: it evidently will profit the future of Japan.

In the meantime other recommendations were flowing in to the Great Council. Notable were the replies from Lord Hotta's committee on foreign trade.

As usual the committee split. The *ometsuke* and *metsuke,* Iwase and his associates, foresaw advantages from trade:

> . . . By doing no more than cling to our ancient methods, while engaging in fruitless debate of impracticable plans, we give the impression of trying to impose restrictions on the foreigners. There may be those who

mistakenly believe that in present circumstances this is in some degree the seemly thing to do; but when the time comes, with the arrival of the foreigners, to conduct actual negotiations with them, all will fall to ruin. . . .

Turning our attention more closely to specific points, there is the question of the places at which trade is to be opened. Were Nagasaki to be the only place, it does not seem in the least likely that the foreigners would agree: they would press for Osaka as well, and that is in the immediate neighborhood of Kyoto. (It appears that the foreigners are generally aware that the aforesaid Osaka is one of our most important centers and a thriving commercial city.) The Bakufu [Shogunate] should, however, select instead of Osaka a place which would satisfy the foreigners, which would be to our advantage and which would, of course, be under Bakufu control. It should establish there a new guard-house to regulate the entry and departure of both Japanese and foreign ships and set up a large trade center . . . Trade goods from the different provinces . . . could be loaded there after examination, a suitable tax being imposed. . . . Similarly, foreign cargoes could be landed there, their value assessed in the presence of the officials and a suitable duty levied from the foreigners also. . . . the officials should in no way interfere in the purchase and exchange of goods. Thus the merchants of the different provinces would bring all such goods as are to the liking of the foreigners and the volume of our exports would naturally increase. And as it did so, from taxes alone the Bakufu would derive enormous profit. This is the universal rule throughout the world . . . Moreover, if the Bakufu were to announce widely throughout Japan that the products not only of Bakufu territories but also of the territories of feudal lords might be sent if desired to the above trade center . . . and . . . the officials there would arrange for them to be traded with the foreigners, then by these means the country and the government would both profit. The government would not be competing for profits with the common people and would benefit accordingly, while the system would not differ from that now generally in force throughout the world, so that the foreigners for their part would also gladly accept it.

. . . at no distant date the foreigners will assuredly come and insist on trade and the other privileges they have long desired. If the Bakufu announces its plans for trade only when that occasion arises, it will be said that these plans have been forced upon it by the foreigners. . . . This thought greatly troubles us.

It is very true, as you stated in your recent instructions to us, that once the ancestral laws have been revised, it will be essential for the Bakufu immediately to adopt a flexible policy appropriate to that change. The fact is that our people now desire the opening of trade. What is more, we believe, at a time like this when there is. hesitation and doubt, for the Bakufu to issue an announcement that it will soon open trade would be a means whereby it could bring the whole country under control and also lay the foundations of national wealth and military strength. . . . We append a proposed draft of a public announcement to be made by the Bakufu on this subject. Submitted with respect.

The draft said simply that trade would be granted to all friendly countries and that details would be announced later.

All this would have gladdened Townsend Harris's heart, but he would not have been so happy to read the report from the other half of Hotta's committee, the finance officials, including Kawaji and Mizuno:

. . . At first sight, trade seems to be of the utmost importance as profiting the government, while it is also, of course, to be regarded as a source of national wealth and military strength. Thus it would seem the utmost folly not to adopt a policy which brings profit to the government. This seems a strong argument. Yet if one considers the matter from the point of view of fundamentals, on the other hand, must one not agree that the only sound and far-sighted policy for the Bakufu to adopt would be to aim in all things at fully preserving the laws established by generations of Shogun for the good of all ages, at maintaining permanent peace and thereby saving the whole people from plunging into misery? Our country is unparalleled in the world in that it has both fertile soil and habits of simplicity. In this we differ from the foreigners, who love luxury though their lands are poor and barren. What is particularly important is the very grave danger of the propagation of Christianity, for if we become intimate with foreigners we shall come inevitably to be tainted by that creed. It was for this reason that the seclusion system was originally established, and if the Americans had not entered our waters there would certainly have been no talk of the desirability of trade with foreigners. This, we believe, is the true substance of our people's attitude. This being so, it is incumbent on the Bakufu to manifest its military strength by killing the men and destroying the ships of these cunning foreigners. Yet the change in world conditions and the vicissitudes of the time give us no choice but to announce a policy of peace and friendship towards foreigners. Thus we must never forget that our alternative to bringing war and unspeakable calamity on our country, which has known almost three hundred years of peace and tranquillity, is trade. We must conform to the wishes of the cunning foreigners and act in accordance with the treaty. We must take care not to give them pretext [for the use of force]. And while the

Bakufu is acting in this way, it is best that its ideas and its inner thoughts be rooted in the former system. . . .

It is desirable, therefore, that the Bakufu should open trade, as we recommended this winter. However, it must regard as the reason for so doing not the profit it might make but rather the fact that such action is inevitable. Its general plan should be first to open trade at Nagasaki, taking care that it attract no particular attention, and to provide necessities at Shimoda and Hakodate. It should then observe the results, meanwhile coming to a decision about whether to expand or reduce the privilege. This seems the best course, for by so doing men will not be alarmed and all will be accomplished peacefully. If, on the other hand, we act in such a way as to reveal a desire to acquire profits, we very much fear that it might quickly happen that we should soon go too far and find it difficult not to become barbarians ourselves. Of course, men of resolution will call our views the height of indecision and vacillation, but it seems to us better that the Bakufu's essential aim should be to do only that which it is forced into doing, rather than that it should fix its eyes only on profit, thereby destroying our national laws and bringing unforeseen calamity upon us. . . .

We report this as our opinion for your secret perusal.

Perhaps to these men the past seemed more golden than it really had been. Perhaps they were merely phrasing their recommendation so as to appease that powerful group which rallied around the Elderly Lord of Mito. Nevertheless, the dangers that the writers saw in the future were not to be brushed aside lightly. Their concern was genuine.

Faced with opinions so divergent, it was neither within Lord Hotta's nature nor within his power to take decisive or far-reaching action. He would continue to seek for consensus. Granting this, his handling of the situation seems ingenious. He decided to dispatch one man from each group to Nagasaki to make an on-the-spot study. From the *ometsuke* and *metsuke* he chose Iwase, his ablest troubleshooter in the field of foreign affairs. From the finance group he chose Mizuno, who was concurrently one of the Governors of Nagasaki. The two of them were directed to work with the other Governor, at present resident at the city.

They were to go by ship to save time. Three years earlier a mission including Kawaji, which had been delegated to meet and negotiate with the Russians, made their stately way to Nagasaki by land, consuming weeks, while Admiral Putiatin waited impatiently. Now there did not seem to be so much time.

On their way they were to stop at Shimoda to confer with the Governors there. Word of this was sent to Shimoda, and Headman Hambei was directed to arrange accommodations for the visitors. He selected temples for Iwase and Mizuno, and private homes for the thirteen lesser members of the party.

Rumors flew. Heusken heard that Moriyama had been drafted to join the mission and that his replacement had already arrived. If so, it would be a homecoming for Moriyama. He had a wife still living in Nagasaki, and a daughter growing up. (He had taken another wife and established another family when he was transferred to Edo.)

It may be that stopping at Shimoda was Iwase's idea. He had seen the hot-tempered American in action; perhaps he wanted a second chance to study him. As he was preparing to leave Edo, he and his associates sent another note to the Great Council:

> We think you had better inform the American official that you will invite him to Edo before long. We have tried to put off inviting him, and to refuse it if possible; our uncertain attitude has increased his displeasure. It would be an irretrievable loss of dignity if we should delay until we were forced to invite him. To procrastinate further may increase his anger. We understand that the American war with Mexico broke out for trifling reasons.

Uncertainty, procrastination, indecision—these were the government's great weaknesses, and they were aggravated by the steadily worsening health of Lord Abe. Lord Matsudaira Yoshinaga noticed and began to worry; he told his intimates that his friend's face had lost its healthy color.

In Shimoda, Townsend Harris was sure he knew how to get action from this government. What he needed was a man-of-war. The Japanese, he wrote, *have yielded nothing except from fear, and any future ameliorations of our intercourse will only take place after a demonstration of force on our part.* . . .

It is now eight months and three days since the San Jacinto *left here. Commodore Armstrong promised me he would be here again in six months. I am a prey to unceasing anxiety. I have not heard a word from Washington since I left the United States, say October, 1855.*

What can be the cause of this prolonged absence of an American man-of-war? Where are the English? Where the French? And, above all, where is the Russian Consul? He should have been here before this. I am only nine days distant from Hong Kong, yet I am more isolated than any American official in any part of the world.

I have important intelligence to send to my Government—intelligence that will give an immediate spur to our trade with Japan; yet here it remains, month after month, without my being able to communicate it to my Government, or enabling my countrymen to benefit by it. (He was speaking of the new conversion rate.)

I will not suppose this apparent neglect arises from indifference or idleness on the part of our naval commanders out here. I, therefore, am left a prey to all sorts of imaginations as to the detaining causes.

The chief detaining cause, the war in China, was running its aimless and irregular way. The British had not the power to attack, and the Chinese continued to make life unpleasant for them.

It was early this month that word reached Hong Kong that Lord Elgin had replaced John Bowring as Plenipotentiary to China. Sir John, diminished to Governor of Hong Kong, was forbidden to communicate with the Chinese government or to fulfill his long-cherished ambition of going to Japan. It was a stunning blow and he was bitterly resentful. His only satisfaction lay in the fact that the men who had attacked him so scathingly in Parliament had been soundly thrashed in the elections which followed.

But the English merchants were pleased by the news, certain it meant that the new High Commissioner would bring with him sufficient force to crush the Chinese once and for all.

They, too, would be disappointed, for almost as Harris was writing the lines above, and Bowring was summoning the strength to bear humiliation, India was exploding into rebellion. The Sepoy Mutiny flared on May 10, and all the force the British could summon in Asia had to be rushed to meet it. The war in China would have to wait. A British expedition to Japan would have to be put off even longer.

Isolated from all of this, ignorant of what the rest of the world was up to, the exile in Shimoda was left to complain about the weather. *We have had six days of the most unpleasant weather I have experienced since I arrived here.* He did not allow it to immobilize him. He was grimly taking exercise, long walks in the chill wind, under leaden skies, in a vain attempt to improve his health.

I have left off the use of tobacco, and have come down to plain boiled rice, fish and chicken,—but all is of no avail. I use a great deal of exercise, but it cannot reach my liver, and that is the source of my trouble. Oh, for a foreign ship to come here with a good doctor!!

Incidentally, some other Izu exiles made a break for freedom this month. Eight men sentenced to exile for life on Hachijo Island stole a fishing boat belonging to the island's headman and made their escape. Since three of them were gamblers and the rest farmers, none of them knew how to handle a boat. Their chance had come when they found two of the island's fishermen sleeping off a drunk on the beach. When the sleepers woke up they found themselves adrift. They were given a choice: sail the boat to a lonely spot on the mainland or be killed. They chose to live, and though some of the cutthroats were in favor of killing them anyway after they reached shore, the chief gambler said no, he never went back on his word. So the two crapulent sailors were left bound to the boat, where they were not discovered until the criminals had had plenty of time to get away. There is no record that they were recaptured.

Harris's exile was not of a kind to be solved by such primitive methods, and for the time being there was not much besides the weather and his health that demanded his attention.

I am collecting specimens of natural history, but they are but meagre, as the Japanese will not bring me one, on the national principle of conceal-ing everything.

He planted more of his American seeds, though he knew by now they would not germinate.

He fussed over his birds. *Out of three nests my pigeons have only raised one,—i.e., one pair. I had a fine nest of thirteen eggs, which would have hatched in three days, when the brood hen was almost murdered by a rascally tomcat; so the poor thing refused to go back to the "post of danger," and gave me another lesson on the folly of "counting our chickens before the eggs are hatched."*

I have recorded the shortcomings of my canary, and how she cruelly abandoned two nests of her callow young. She is now incubating a third nest of eggs, and I have put her on a low diet, and separated her from her mate, hoping by these measures to keep the "devil of concupiscence" out of her little body, until her young can feed themselves.

It was no use. Two weeks later he wrote: *My canary left her nest, leav-ing her eggs unhatched, although she had set for twenty days. On breaking the eggs I could not discover any sign of young in them; apparently the eggs were not impregnated by the cock bird.*

He did some shopping for souvenirs. Back in Macao on August 7 he had written: *Mrs. E. E. Spooner, wife of Mr. D. N. Spooner, of the house of Russell & Co., sent me seventy-five dollars to purchase articles of Japanese manufacture for her. I have before this received orders amounting to thousands of dollars for similar purposes, but this is the first one that was accompanied with money, and assuredly it will be the first one to be attended to.*

Now, nine months after his arrival, he attended. He went to the

Goyosho bazaar, a visit noted in Hambei's diary, and bought seventy-five dollars' worth of lacquerware.

He was not pleased with his purchases. *I think we have overrated the habit of the Japanese in making elaborately fine articles of any kind. The genius of their government seems to forbid any exercise of ingenuity in producing articles for the gratification of wealth and luxury.*

There is no way of knowing what quality of goods the merchants were offering at the Goyosho, but since at this date almost nothing was being made especially for export (in this part of Japan, that is; around Nagasaki it was a different story), we may assume that the items on sale there reflected Japanese taste. Harris, whose taste was bred in New York and fattened in China, was not equipped to appreciate the restraint and understatement of Japanese art. That appreciation would come to Westerners slowly.

Yet he was not quite sure of himself when he condemned the Japanese way. *Simplicity and frugality is the great maxim of this country, and it is enforced in a most surprising manner. It would be an endless task to attempt to put down all the acts of a Japanese that are regulated by authority. This is no country for modistes, tailors, jewelers and the whole army that batten on the imaginary wants of the West.* Might the Japanese be right in wanting to preserve those "habits of simplicity" that Kawaji and Mizuno had been talking about?

To continue with the catalogue of Harris's random activities during this month of May, he had the pigsty at Gyokusenji demolished and a new one built. And for himself: *I ordered a small belvedere to be erected on the top of a hill near the Consulate, so that I might enjoy the cool air during the hot season, and also have a view over the whole of the harbor.* He seemed surprised that the Japanese tried hard to please him, that they took pride in their work. *To-day they brought me some plans and elevations very neatly done, with estimates of the cost of the work. It seems to be a most important matter to them, as they have been a number of days about it and many persons were engaged on it. I was satisfied with their plans and accepted them. The price is fifteen dollars.* He did not seem to feel that he was being overcharged.

Japanese records show that Gyokusenji's residents were keeping a corps of tailors busy. No doubt the Chinese servants, frustrated at making so much money with so little to spend it on, had a part in this, but most of the effort went toward repairing the clothes of Harris and Heusken. It was more than a year and a half since they had left New York; their suits and linens and shoes were showing wear. (The shoes had to be dispatched to the village of *eta* up the valley. The *eta* were the lowest of all pariahs, lower by far than the outcast watchmen seen in the towns. Though physically indistinguishable from other Japanese, they were segregated into their own villages and were called on to perform tasks regarded as repulsive, such as slaughtering animals. Since shoes were made from the skins of animals, no respectable Japanese would degrade himself by working on them.)

Heusken's journal is still scanty but we are given a couple of bright glimpses of him: bringing that bouquet of wild violets to Harris, and getting a horse of his own.

Harris's comment was characteristically dour (*The Japanese brought a horse for Mr. Heusken to-day. It is dearer than mine, although not so good looking, but this is Japanese custom, always advance the price, but never lower it.*) but Heusken was jubilant. He delighted in his present affluence after the privations of his days as a young immigrant in New York, and he sketched a mocking portrait of himself as a man of means:

> May 21, 1857. Today I find myself the happy owner of a horse—a thoroughbred—a horse that cost me no less than 128,000 *casch** or $27.41. What an enormous amount for a thoroughbred horse! It looks as though my affairs are not going too badly. I started off in Japan by taking a valet. Here I am now, owner of a horse! If I go on this way why shouldn't I maintain my own carriage and ask in marriage the Emperor's only daughter? Satrap that I am. Oh! New York! Oh, days spent without dinner, and the fine chances I missed to sleep in the open air. Oh, black clothes, shining with old age. Oh, beloved shoes in which my heels and toes enjoyed perfect ventilation! Oh, trousers with holes worn in them! Where are you, old friends? Come and see his Very Serene Highness, Lord Heusken, parading on a horse. No, no, it is not a rented horse! That is an unworthy insinuation! No, gentlemen, there he is on his own horse, a horse that belongs to him and for which he has paid—or must pay, but that's the same thing—the enormous sum of one hundred and fifty francs.

Another event had nothing to do with Heusken directly, yet he must have learned of it quickly and just as quickly passed the word to Harris. In this month that Heusken acquired a horse, Saito took a mistress.

A letter to Saito from the headman of Naka village confirmed the arrangement:

> Sir:
> I am pleased to stand guarantee for a girl named Asa. She has been known by all of us since the time she was born in this village. She will serve as a maid in your house for one year at a salary of one *ryo*, three

---

* Heusken is using the Chinese term for the copper coins the Japanese called *mon*.

通弁官
安島之章

Heusken on his horse (*a Japanese drawing*)

bu. Of this amount, three *bu* have already been received in advance with thanks. Please pay her the balance in two installments in the Ninth and Twelfth Months.

Should something go wrong, such as flight by night, pilferage, or a long illness, I shall compensate for your loss and recommend a substitute in case you need one, in accordance with your instructions.

She will obey the laws and regulations and conform to the rules of etiquette in your home. If she does something inexcusable, she is to be dismissed.

Her family belongs to the Zen sect and I certify that they are parishioners of the temple Fukusenji of Hongo village. I am holding the certification issued by the temple and it will be submitted to you if you so request.

I hereby state that I am responsible for any troubles which Asa may cause you.

> Respectfully,
> Seizaemon
> Headman of Naka

This letter was written like an ordinary servant's contract, but the gossip around Naka was that the deal had been sweetened with two *ryo* extra.

It was in Saito's nature to let his acquaintances know of the delights that followed. What Heusken heard must have aroused even further the "devil of concupiscence" that was in him. Harris might write of "a craving for something I cannot define" but Heusken knew exactly what *he* craved. If Heusken had before this been badgering Harris to insist on women, his campaign must have been stepped up after Asa moved in with Saito.

The chances are that except as a matter of principle—that in Asia a Westerner was entitled to a native woman if he wanted one—Harris was more excited about something else: he had found a way to make money by capitalizing on the fact that the Japanese undervalued gold.

Purser Bradford of the *San Jacinto* had paid the Goyosho $283.50 in gold, accepted reluctantly by the Japanese and only with the promise that it would be redeemed in silver when the ship returned. In addition, having run out of both gold and silver, Bradford had written a draft on Harris to cover the balance of what the ship owed. The *San Jacinto* was now long overdue and the fifth day of the Fifth Month was approaching, which was not only a holiday but the first major accounting day of the year. The Japanese indicated they would like to settle these old accounts. Harris obliged, *but, instead of paying them a silver dollar for each gold dollar, I give them a silver ichibu for each dollar of gold.*

The Japanese were satisfied. Harris was elated: for one gold dollar he was paying roughly one third of a dollar in silver. *The amount of the accounts settled to-day was $452.50, but I paid it with $153.50, thus saving $299!!* "Saving" was a euphemism: he had *profited* by $299. And the possibilities seemed limitless; all he had to do was bring in silver and exchange it with the Japanese for gold.

For the purpose of ascertaining whether gold is really as cheap in Japan as the Japanese pretend, I ordered two mustard spoons to be made of pure, unalloyed gold. They wished me to give them coin to make the spoons from. This I declined, as it would defeat the object I have in view.

After some days, a formal message was sent to me by the Governors, stating that, by the laws of Japan, gold could only be used to ornament their swords, and that its use by the people in any other form was absolutely prohibited. A greater falsehood was never uttered. It is true that the Japanese use but few ornaments, or indeed articles of luxury of any kind; but gold is used in weaving brocades, in decorating saddles, in making a small chain which secures a small basket which contains a cloth with which they wipe perspiration from their faces, and for women's ornaments.

It probably goes without saying that Harris was wrong. He had seen ornaments of gold but they were not newly made. Two years earlier the government had strictly prohibited all such use of the metal.

I told the messenger to say to the Governors that I knew that gold was used for many purposes besides swords; but, even if that was not the case, it was nothing to me, as I was not a Japanese, nor bound by Japanese law. This was a position so outrageous that it could have been scarcely credible even to him. At any rate, he added corroborative detail intended to give artistic verisimilitude to an otherwise bold and unconvincing demand: he told the Governors he could not use silver spoons in his mustard because the silver contained copper and the reaction of the copper to the mustard was injurious to his health.

Wednesday, May 13, 1857. . . . Moriyama comes to say that Bingo-no-kami has received orders to go to Edo and that he is to leave early to-morrow morning; that he is unable to call in person to take leave of me, and begs me to excuse his apparent neglect. I send him messages wishing him a pleasant journey to Edo and a favorable reception on his arrival.

Okada's summons no doubt demanded haste, for he no sooner reached Edo than he was handed orders relieving him as Governor of Shimoda and reassigning him as Governor of the construction bureau, a favorite dumping ground for officials who had fallen out of favor. The new Governor of Shimoda was a man named Nakamura, who had been serving as a comp-

Nakamura Dewa-no-kami (*a drawing by Aleksandr Mozhaiskii*)

troller in the finance bureau under Kawaji and Mizuno, and with them had been a member of Lord Hotta's committee on foreign trade.

Nakamura had had a long association with Kawaji. When Kawaji was a leading member of the delegation that had negotiated with the Russians at Nagasaki early in 1854, Nakamura was secretary to that delegation. He served in the same capacity when much the same group went to Shimoda late that same year for more talks with Admiral Putiatin (this time Kawaji came equipped with incense against the bad smell of foreigners). At Shimoda, Nakamura and Moriyama had done much of the actual negotiating while the senior delegates held themselves aloof. He had experienced the tidal wave, had escorted the Russian admiral when he traveled between Shimoda and Heda, had been present when the Americans arrived to exchange ratifications of Perry's treaty. Thus he had had considerable experience with the Russians, who respected him; he had some knowledge of Americans; and he was familiar with Shimoda. He was known as an amiable man, his new assignment was a significant promotion, and he had Kawaji to thank for it. It could be expected that Inoue would find him easy to work with, which would be a change from Okada.

One of Nakamura's last acts in his old position was to sign the paper from the finance wing of the foreign trade committee, giving the Great Council their reactions to Donker Curtius's report on the war in China.

They recalled how the war had started over the *Arrow* incident:

> It is a living example to show that a serious situation often develops out of a petty thing. As Your Excellencies say, if we ire the foreigners for small reasons it reflects nothing but incompetence on our part. Now that the ancestral law is revised, it is up to us to change our treatment of foreigners in accord with the revised law. We must be guided by sincerity—not feigned but real sincerity—to attain peace and amity in our relations with them. Once we have concluded a treaty with them, we can no longer treat them as barbarians even though they really are barbarians.

At Shimoda, where Nakamura would soon have a chance to test these generous sentiments, the barbarian at Gyokusenji was noting that bad weather notwithstanding, the season advanced in its course.

Monday, May 11, 1857. . . . Saw the first land crab to-day since last October. I suppose I may put this down as a proof that the summer has now actually commenced.

The large Camellia Japonica in my compound, which first showed its blossoms on the 5th of January, is now going out of bloom. It has been a splendid sight and has, I have no doubt, produced some thousands of roses!

Tuesday, May 19, 1857. . . . The wheat in the vicinity begins to assume a golden hue, and will soon be ready for harvesting.

He might have recorded, but did not, one more sign that spring would not be denied. The Governor sent him a present of fresh plums, the first to appear on the market. With his acid stomach he probably dared not try them and left them for Heusken to enjoy.

The unseasonable, blustery winds made one springtime sport more exciting: *For the last few weeks I have seen the only attempt of Japanese boys at amusement of any kind. They have no games, no plays, do not congregate together, have no hoops, no skip ropes, no marbles, no tops, and, I fear, nothing else; but I have been relieved by the sight and sound of kites lately. I say sound of kites; they affix some thin slips of bamboo on the back of the kite, which give out a sound like the Æolian harp; and, the kite being made to plunge violently, gives out the sound constantly.*

Of course, Japanese boys *did* congregate and they *did* have their games *; Harris noticed them as little as he did the rest of his neighbors.

---

* One of Perry's officers had watched "a dozen or more children playing the game of blind man's bluff, precisely as it is played with us."

But in the spring kite-flying was conspicuous. Even men took a hand at it. It reached a climax on the third major holiday of the year, which Harris saluted by having his flag run up.

Wednesday, May 27, 1857. To-day being the fifth day of the Fifth Month is a great festival among the Japanese, and is attended to by abstaining from labor, putting on their best clothes, and by flying their musical kites, which sometimes remind you of a distant organ.

I do not see any special religious attendance. I must say that I never was in a country so abounding with priests, temples, miya [shrines], statues, etc., etc., where there was so great indifference on religious subjects as there is in Japan. I believe all the higher classes are in reality atheists.

He could not see, of course, how deeply simple religion entered into the daily life and work of the people around him. As for this holiday, it was not a religious festival—Harris might as well have looked for the churches at home to be filled on May Day. The girls had had their day back in the Third Month, now it was the boys' turn. This was a day to celebrate what was masculine.

Households brought out warrior dolls clad in suits of lacquered armor, and people remembered how in the thirteenth century, when the country faced invasion from the Mongol hordes of Kublai Khan, an Imperial prince had gone to pray at a great shrine on the fifth day of the Fifth Month, just when the iris were in full bloom, and having prayed, went out to face the enemy on the beaches; and how a furious storm had risen and destroyed the enemy's ships and soldiers. And people said it was because he had prayed on the fifth day of the Fifth Month, when the iris was in bloom. It was, naturally, the flower of this festival. Its long pointed leaves suggested a sword, and a phallus. (An iris which failed to bloom by this day was inexcusably tardy; there was a proverb about being too late, "as late as the iris which blooms on the sixth day.")

People decorated their houses with the flowers, inside and out, and some said that if one threw a bundle of them high on the thatched roof, an efficacious medicine would drip down from the roof. Everyone bathed in a bath with iris leaves in it, which was said to be a great protection against venereal disease, and drank sake flavored with iris petals. Here the girls got into the act, for a sip of this drink was considered especially good for them.

As the festival approached, boys surged through the streets, armed with swords made of plaited iris leaves, slashing at each other in mock battles. And any woman passing by was likely to get smacked across the rump with those green swords. This could hurt, and it made the ladies indignant and afraid to go out, and so it had become customary for

Shimoda town officials to issue a circular each year prohibiting this game, especially in the bathhouses, where rumps were bare and even more vulnerable. It was a difficult order to enforce. It was the season for rowdyism.

It was customary for festivities to begin at the fifth hour, about nine in the morning by Harris's watch, assuming it was still anywhere near on time. As might have been expected this disagreeable spring, it rained on and off, but the day's formalities proceeded even if the fun was damped.

Not all labor could be suspended, of course. In Shimoda one of the elders rose early and went to the jail to witness the inspection of the handcuffs on the crew of Tarojiro's ship, a ritual performed every four or five days, and then hurried home to change into formal clothes for the gathering of town officials. It was summer clothing they wore, ordained from this day. Harris and Heusken had been amused to learn that *The Japanese have fixed days for their change of clothing. The law settles the matter beforehand, and no inclemency of weather can postpone the change.* But contrary to what the foreigners thought, a man had wide latitude in color. Town secretary and chronicler Hirai Heijiro had made a point of it: blue, light yellow, dark red, brown, or the light green of spring verdure called *chigusa* —all these were acceptable, "according to the taste of the wearer."

In the town and in each village, officials congratulated each other, and then set out to Naka to extend their greetings to the Governor and his chief assistants, a somewhat simpler procedure than it would have been a few weeks earlier, for today there was but one Governor on hand. Then each delegation adjourned to the house of its own headman for iris-scented sake and a feast. Hirai Heijiro set down the traditional menu for Shimoda, and an elaborate one it was, but he added his usual disclaimer: "It is not that these dishes should always be served; rather that one should serve whatever happens to be on hand."

Most other people celebrated with rice cakes stuffed with sweet bean paste and wrapped in oak leaves. Proud parents carried baby boys to present them to the god of the local shrine.

It was at the town shrine of Shimoda that catastrophe ensued. A Goyosho official, Inspector Yamashita Kanzaemon, brought his infant son to the shrine, and while he and his wife and the older children and the nurse who was holding the baby were bowed before the shrine, a carpenter named Isoemon and three of his apprentices, who were flying a huge kite in the shrine precincts, *plunged* their kite so that, whistling, it plummeted toward the shrine, and the tail of the kite brushed across the baby.

The child was only scratched but he set up a howl, and the nurse howled too, and Goyosho constables who were patrolling the shrine at once arrested Isoemon and his apprentices and confiscated the kite.

It was particularly embarrassing for the town officials because Yamashita was assigned to oversee town affairs and was a man they had to deal with daily. But he maintained his calm and said that since he was involved he would not participate in judging the offenders but would leave it to his colleagues. They promptly sentenced Isoemon to house arrest for thirty days and the apprentices to have the term of their apprenticeship extended for thirty days.

Hambei and the town elders quickly saw the flaw in this: Isoemon, though shamed and inconvenienced by being confined to his house, would benefit by the extension of his apprentices' term of service. Next day the headman and three of the elders went to Yamashita to offer their personal apologies, and they obtained his permission to handle the case themselves. They at once ordered Isoemon and all three apprentices to house arrest for fifty days, and decreed that in the future there should be no flying of kites, whether large or small, at the shrine. Which was a great blow to the kite-flyers of Shimoda.

Isoemon could, of course, continue to work in his shop at home. One of his current jobs was to build a new bathtub for Harris, and this went forward without delay. Harris had evidently grown tired of folding himself into Gyokusenji's little tub, which was deep but was meant for a Japanese to soak in with his legs pulled up. Harris wanted a tub he could stretch out in, as he had wanted a *kago* he could stretch out in. The measurements of the new tub that Isoemon built have come down to us: two feet nine inches deep, three feet one and a half inches wide, five feet eight inches long. Harris was five feet eight inches tall; he could certainly stretch out in that tub.

On the day before the holiday Harris had received a reply to his complaints of high prices. It was a coolly factual rebuttal: eggs had never been sold as cheaply at Shimoda as the Consul General contended they were, though they became cheaper in the summer, as he would note from his bills; the price of rice had naturally risen because the crop was damaged in last autumn's typhoon; charcoal was dear because it had become scarcer all around Shimoda, and its price had no relationship to that of potatoes; potatoes brought from Hakodate were naturally more expensive because of the freight charge; the price of fish depended on the kind of fish and varied widely—it had nothing to do with the price of rice; the poor quality of the chickens was admitted—farmers raised only a few and did not want to sell young birds, but the merchants would be instructed to deliver the best available; pigs were no doubt more expensive than in China, but since they had never been bred here until they were demanded by foreigners, the farmers had little experience with them and found them costly to raise. To conclude, all the articles sent to the consulate had been priced according to the current market—a statement fuzzy enough to avoid untruth. And seizing the opportunity to needle their foreign mentor, the writers (probably including a mischievous Moriyama) explained that prices depended on whether harvests were good or bad and on the interplay of supply and demand, principles which Goyosho specialists would be glad to explain at greater length verbally should His Excellency the Consul General desire.

It is plainly and unequivocally a full support of the Goyosho rascality in all of its ramifications.

They do not regard the promise they gave me last August as worth the breath it cost them to utter it. However, to lie is, for a Japanese, simply to speak.

And he began to draft his indignant answer. He would, he thundered, demand repayment of all overcharges "from the Supreme Government of Japan."

After the fifth-day festival Moriyama called with news it gave him much pleasure to deliver: *Bingo-no-kami is not to return to Shimoda, having been appointed "Superintendent of Repairs" at Edo. His successor is not a kami, but will be made one before he comes here. He is said to be a mild and amiable man. If so, I am glad to change Bingo-no-kami for him, as the former is anything but a friend to foreigners, and besides he is the most inveterate liar I ever met with.*

This was a rather remarkable misjudgment. Harris had lost his strongest advocate at Shimoda, and he was pleased about it.

Moriyama had reason to be pleased. He was Inoue's man and had never liked Okada. A couple of days later he brought more details of Okada's comeuppance. *Moriyama says that in reality Bingo-no-kami is in disgrace, as his new appointment is two grades lower than the post of Governor; that his salary is a mere trifle compared with what he enjoyed here, and that he is now excluded from all knowledge of foreign affairs, nor can he even have interviews with the members of the High Council. . . .*

Moriyama was being carried away. Okada had lost no rank by his transfer, though he had lost prestige. He had lost the special allowance given to a Governor of Shimoda, which reduced his salary by one third, but not to *a mere trifle*. In his new position he would not be consulted on foreign affairs, but he had not lost his right of audience with the Great Council.

The causes of this disgrace are said to be various; but the chief one was that he did not agree better with me, the Government apparently holding him responsible for all my complaints, and for my recalcitrations against their various attempts to restrain me and deprive me of my just rights. . . .

It is easier to believe that Okada was shifted because he agreed too much with Harris. There had been clashes of personality too, as Harris knew: *Bingo-no-kami did not carry his honors meekly. He was (to the Japanese) haughty and overbearing, and did not practice the usual Japanese sauviter in modo—hence he had made many small enemies, who no doubt did all in their power to prejudice him with the Government at Edo.*

On the same day that Moriyama was delivering the news, the new Governor, as he was winding up his affairs in Edo, received word that the Great Council had awarded him three crested jackets on the occasion of his leaving his post as comptroller. There is no record of Okada's receiving any award on leaving his post at Shimoda.

The weather is very bad indeed, almost constant rain and a raw unpleasant wind from the northeast.

The Japanese say that "the oldest inhabitant" does not recollect such a miserable May as this is. Still, by the end of the month the wheat harvest was in full swing in all the villages—in coastal villages like Kakisaki and Suzaki, in upriver villages like Hongo and Naka.

At Naka the songs and chatter of the harvesters in the fields around the jail may have drifted over its walls and reached some of the seamen of Tarojiro's ship through the pain and despair that gripped them. They had not yet confessed.

The cargo of rice, a part of which they were accused of stealing, had, a few days earlier, been turned over to officers of Lord Nambu who had come down from Edo to accept it—minus, of course, that share of it paid to the fishermen of Shimoda, Kakisaki, and Suzaki for the stevedoring they had done, and minus the gifts which had to be distributed to various officials (all of which amounted to considerably more than the crew had allegedly tried to steal), and minus the rice which had been so wet it had had to be sold on the spot. What was left was reloaded on the same ship, manned by a new captain and crew recruited by Tarojiro, and sent on to its original destination, Edo.

The old captain and crew were past caring what happened to the rice. They had endured almost two months of confinement, bound and handcuffed. They had been grilled again and again. All but the youngest, a lad of fourteen, had been whipped, and more than once.

The inquisition had fallen heaviest on those judged most guilty, Captain Matsugoro, Pilot Zenemon, and the senior crewmen. By the closing days of May their bodies had absorbed about all the punishment they could. Shimoda town officials were receiving almost daily orders to send a physician to the jail. (It was a long walk, but doctors were privileged to use *kago*.) Nevertheless, the amenities were kept up: barbers, too, were regularly summoned to shave the prisoners and trim their topknots.

Early in the morning of the thirtieth there was a call for a physician. Dr. Asaoka Kyoan responded. At nine in the evening there was an emergency call; Kyoan was not at home, so Dr. Teian was summoned. The town officials had scarcely gathered for work the next morning when they were hit by a flurry of orders from the jail: a town official was to report at once, three laborers were required, a coffin was to be delivered. Zenemon was past confessing. As Hambei tactfully put it in his diary, "he had died of illness."

The town arranged that the body be buried at the temple in Naka. But then shipping agent Hanjuro, acting on instructions from Tarojiro, petitioned for permission to return the body to Zenemon's village, only a few miles distant, so that his family and neighbors could perform the last rites and bury him in the family plot.

Hanjuro and a town elder waited all day for the prison officer's decision. At last it came. He could not approve the petition as it stood in view of the seriousness of the case, but on the other hand, it seemed too cruel to hustle the body from the prison to the grave. He would, under the circumstances, take the special action of "abandoning" the body so that the petitioner might remove it and hold a funeral..

In the meantime there had been two other emergency calls for physicians. Four others of the crew were "very sick" and had asked, as was their privilege, to be temporarily released into the custody of townspeople so that they might receive treatment. Since the town would be responsible for them, it was up to the town to initiate the petition. Working late on the last evening in May, Hambei had it drawn up so that it could be submitted early in the morning.

In Edo, on this last day of May, Lord Abe failed to report for his daily duty at the castle. He had become too ill to work.

And at Gyokusenji, Townsend Harris summed up an almost cheerless month: *I have walked this month, for exercise, over three hundred and fifty miles. I have entirely quit the use of tobacco in all its forms. I have brought down my diet to plain boiled rice and a little fowl. I tried fish for some days, but that was worse than the fowls. I cannot eat bread, either fresh or of the American biscuit. I have taken any quantity of blue pill, but all is of no avail. I suffer horribly from acid stomach and am getting leaner day by day. What is very singular is that my appetite is uncommonly good; but, my digestion being so much out of order, my food does not do me much good. . . .*

Where, oh, where is Commodore Armstrong? I am sick and weary of looking out for him.

Chapter 12

JUNE, 1857

Having dismissed Okada to satisfy his critics, the Great Council was now free to adopt his ideas. It finally acted on the Governors' recommendations of late March. An endorsement to that letter was handed to the new Governor, Nakamura, who had now acquired a title appropriate to his loftier status: he was Dewa-no-kami, the Lord of Dewa.

The endorsement could not be called a model of clear-cut decision making. On only one point was it unequivocal. The Consul General and his attendants could have Japanese coins, and with them they could make direct purchase of their necessities. However, the Governors were to exercise great care that Harris did not abuse the privilege: that he did not hoard, that the things he purchased were for the consulate alone, that he resold nothing to ships which might call at Shimoda.

As for permitting American merchants to reside at Shimoda and Hakodate, and allowing Harris freedom to go beyond Shimoda's seven-*ri* limits, the Governors were exhorted to "exhaust themselves" in opposition. But the Great Council did not flatly reject these demands, and it seems clear enough that before Nakamura left Edo he had a conversation, most likely with Lord Hotta, in which he was instructed to come to terms with the Consul General. Somehow this choleric American must be mollified. "Trifles" must not be allowed to build into reasons for war.

If possible, Harris should be persuaded to give up or postpone his demand to come to Edo. What a relief it would be if he would deliver the President's letter in Shimoda, and confide his "very important matters" there, and negotiate whatever he had in mind at that inconspicuous port. What a relief if the government were not—just now at least—forced into another showdown with all those powerful forces so hostile to greater foreign intercourse. If all this could be achieved, wonderful, but in any case Nakamura was directed to get a settlement.

With this clear in his mind, the Lord of Dewa said goodbye to his family, and with his attendants set out for Shimoda.

Waiting there, the man he was deputed to make content had found something new to be indignant about. He had been lied to again.

Monday, June 1, 1857. The Japanese have said that strawberries grew around here, and that, as soon as they were ripe, I should have a good supply of them. At last they brought me some ichigo, or strawberries. They prove to be a kind of raspberry, of a pale straw color and of an insipid taste, quite without aroma or flavor; and these are their promised strawberries.

(They must have been the same berries about which Dr. James Morrow had written, almost exactly three years earlier: "I found a new and fine variety of rasp berry, of which the fruit is delicious.")

Harris could almost do better himself. *I have found in the woods a fruit of the size, shape, color, leaf, etc., etc., of the real strawberry, but the fruit is not edible, having a decidedly unpleasant flavor.* It was well for him that he found these wild strawberries unpalatable: they are poisonous.

Spring flowers, too, let him down. *Generally speaking . . . wild flowers are not abundant here, and scarcely none are cultivated, and but few have any scent.*

How much I miss that Queen of Flowers, the Rose that is now in full bloom in New York; I should not be sorry to have a few sprigs of champacka, from Penang, the tuberose from Macao, or the jessamine from Calcutta, to please my sense of smell.

Quite ignorant of all the floral excitement they were missing by not living in the tropics or in New York State, a number of the villagers of Kakisaki gathered that same evening at Yoheiji's house for some excitement of their own, the lottery of their Kompira Association. For a year each of them had contributed a few copper *mon* each month. Now the winner would take all, and with that as his purse, would make a pilgrimage to the far-off shrine called Kompira. He would go up the length of Izu to the famous Tokaido Road, down that bustling highway to the country's greatest commercial city, Osaka, and across the Inland Sea to the island of Shikoku —a long journey and surely the great event of his life.

At the mountain which was his goal he would worship a god with special power to protect seafarers—which explains why Kakisaki and most other villages that drew their living from the sea turned their affection on Kompira instead of on the even more venerable shrines at Ise.

The winner that night was Masujiro—the second son of Juemon, who owned Harris's garden and tended it. Sometimes Masujiro helped his father. As a second son he had grown used to short shrift, and when his name was called he could not believe his luck. When he went to bed that night he buried his head and wept for joy.

The next day Yoheiji began to prepare the application for Masujiro's travel permit. It was, by coincidence, the same day that Harris, after another of his rambling conversations with Moriyama, wrote in his journal: *A man wishing to perform a pilgrimage must procure a passport for that purpose, which runs from one to eight months, according to distance.* Perhaps the news of Masujiro's good luck had reached Harris.

That day, June 2, was cloudy and the wind was from the north, but Harris took his boat across the harbor and walked southwest from Shimoda toward the tip of the peninsula. *It is of the same character as the other parts seen. Every possible spot is cultivated, and as many inhabitants as can be, supported. I find that what I considered as jungle on the steep hillsides, is actually all planted. Trees, bamboos, rushes, etc., etc. All are renewed as they are cut off for use. No spot is neglected. I have never seen a person that had the appearance of want marked on his countenance. The children all have faces like "full moons," and the men and women are quite fleshy enough. No one can for a moment suppose (after seeing the people) that they are not well fed.* This was, he might have added, quite different from what he had seen in China and India.

The next day was fair and he must have itched to get out for another walk, but first he sent off a letter to Governor Inoue, continuing the argument over "temporary residence" which had been raised by the case of Reed and Dougherty.

He had, he wrote, so fully explained "the right of American citizens to reside at Shimoda and Hakodate" in his letter of March 13 that he found it unnecessary to restate it. (That was the letter which based the right on the nonexistent articles in the Dutch treaty and on the implied need for American merchants at Hakodate to meet the whalers' requirements.) But he could not let pass, he went on, the Governors' interpretation of "temporary residence" as meaning "five to seven days, or at the utmost one or two months." A damaged ship, he theorized, might require six or eight months to make repairs, or even more "in a small place, like Shimoda, which does not of itself possess what may be necessary for such repairs, and consequently the materials must be brought from other places."

(Since it had taken the Russians, at Heda, a place smaller than Shimoda, only a little more than three months to build a schooner from scratch, the Japanese were not likely to take this argument seriously. And though the Governors had not told Harris, they had laid in a substantial stock of copper plate, the item most needed in ship repair; evidently they did not intend to inform him of this, lest he renew his pressure on them to sell copper.)

"So also as regards Americans coming to trade," Harris went on, "it may be necessary to send to many distant places to procure the articles they wish to obtain, and to force them to leave before they can complete their purchases would also be an infraction of the treaty." The Perry treaty did not authorize "trade" in this sense, and Harris knew it; this was the old foot-in-the-door technique again.

His letter on the way, he walked up the river valley and along the road to Matsuzaki under a warm sun and a blue sky. The wheat had been harvested and the paddy fields were now flooded. In some, men plowed behind oxen, in others the soft wet earth was being turned with long hoes. Fertilizer was being trampled into the mud—grass cut from the hills, seaweed, fish scraps, night soil collected from the town and villages. The land was being made ready for rice.

These sights did not get into his journal but another did. *Visited a new hot spring. It is arranged as a bath house like those before described, but the water is much warmer and more strongly impregnated with sulphur. I found a woman in the bath with her child. She was not in the least discomposed, but gave me the usual "Ohio" (good-morning) with a smiling face. Her skin was very fair, nearly as white as a Circassian.*

On my return homewards I called on the Prince of Shinano and passed a very agreeable hour with him. He presented me with some superior tobacco from Edo, but, happily, I do not now use it.

In visiting Inoue at his residence, Harris passed close by the jail. The physicians of Shimoda were making frequent calls there these days in response to urgent summonses. Still pending was the application of the four crewmen to be released into the custody of the town so that they might obtain nursing care. The day after Harris passed by, a prison official again called for a doctor, indicating that his report would have much to do with whether the application was approved. Hambei sent Shimoda's most highly regarded physician, Asaoka Kyoan.

The doctor's report was persuasive, and next day three of the men were released. Hambei himself went to the jail to get them, taking with him shipping agent Hanjuro and ship inspector Nagano Matabei. A written oath was deposited, pledging that the town officials would be wholly responsible for the men while they were in the town's custody, and then the three were gently carried to the ships' inn of Kahei. Release had come too late for the fourth man. Hanjuro made arrangements for his burial at the temple in Naka.

On June 6, not long after a runner had puffed into town with the day's dispatches, Hambei was summoned to the Goyosho. He was told, first, that Mizuno and Iwase had decided not to stop at Shimoda—the arrangements that had been made for them could be canceled; and, second, that the new Governor, Nakamura, Lord of Dewa, would arrive tomorrow.

The headman at once mustered two of the town elders, who set out to meet Nakamura at Nashimoto village, where he would be spending that night.

The next day all the other town officials assembled—the elders; the chiefs of the ship inspectors, of the shipping agents, of the fishermen, of the innkeepers, and of the merchants; the town treasurer, and the leader of each block. Led by Hambei they moved out toward Tachino, the village just upriver from Naka. There they would greet the new Governor and escort him the rest of his way. The men of Shimoda were reinforced by the contingents from the villages, who buzzed greetings among themselves but were largely ignored by the townsmen—one must not become too familiar with rustics.

Nakamura must have been moved by the deference he was paid that day, for he was a warm and open man, and he could remember very well how he had come to Shimoda two and a half years earlier as a relatively minor figure, when the reception was for others. Thus in midafternoon he was escorted to Naka compound and to the quarters and offices which were now his within the white walls.

He might have been expected to rest after his tiring journey. Instead he went almost immediately into conference with Inoue. Very soon after that, one of the interpreters set out for Gyokusenji to request that Harris confer with the Governors next morning, and a message was dispatched to Hambei directing that the Goyosho be cleaned for the meeting.

An elder, two block leaders, and two forerunners went out the next morning to greet the Governors, who emerged from their compound about ten o'clock and traveled on horseback to the Goyosho. Their early arrival gave time for Nakamura to meet the staff for more conferences before the American arrived.

Harris and Heusken, who came by boat, arrived at noon and went into their first meeting with the new Governor, the "mild and amiable man," with his easy manner and his husky voice.

To judge by Harris's journal for this date, Nakamura's amiability was even greater than could have been hoped for. Harris is exultant. *I have at*

*last carried every point triumphantly with the Japanese, and have got
everything conceded that I have been negotiating for since last September.*

That was not what happened. Harris may have scented victory when
he went home that afternoon, but as yet he was in no position to claim it. A
comparison with Japanese records shows that this entry is misdated. Its first
words confirm this: *I omitted to enter the arrival here of the new Governor
. . . ,* a statement which makes it sound as though Nakamura had come to
Shimoda some time ago instead of the previous afternoon. In point of fact,
the journal for most of the rest of the month was obviously written some
time later from notes and from memory. The chronology is badly off and
there is a good bit left unsaid.

After introductions and greetings, the meeting went like this:

> INOUE: We have had a number of conversations but we have not
> reached an understanding. The Lord of Dewa has been sent here under
> special orders so that we may negotiate frankly and fully. We hope that
> you will meet us in this spirit.
>
> HARRIS: I appreciate your views fully. I shall hereafter speak very
> frankly.
>
> INOUE: No doubt you have been expecting an answer to your recent
> letter to the Great Council, but there was some anxiety that the
> Council's views could not be expressed in a letter. They were imparted
> to the Lord of Dewa. This is a letter to you from the Great Council. I
> now deliver it to you.

Since they seemed about to embark on serious talks, Harris asked that
the Governors' entourage leave the room. Then he examined the Great
Council's letter and, the Japanese noted, "his color changed and he seemed
to become suspicious." Why, he asked, were there no signatures?

In official letters of this sort, the scribe wrote the names of the senders
and generally each of them brushed a kind of monogram under his name.
These monograms, which Harris had found on his previous letter from the
Council, were missing on this one.

Nakamura explained that because of haste the monograms had been
overlooked, but that their absence did not alter the validity of the document. Harris said that he wanted them anyway, and the Governors agreed
to send the letter back to Edo to get them. For the moment, although not
accepting the letter, Harris agreed to listen to it, and so, through Moriyama
and Heusken it was read to him. It was characteristically brief:

> We have received from the Governors of Shimoda your letter which
> was sent on the seventh day of the Third Month of the fourth year of

Ansei. It is natural that we should make a response but we think that a letter cannot bring about full understanding between us. So we have given detailed instructions to Nakamura, Lord of Dewa, and we send him to you. We hope that you will talk with him sincerely.

INOUE: Please tell us, as requested in this letter, what you have wished to tell the Great Council in Edo. When you speak to us it is the same as speaking to the government.

As for your going to Edo, it is not that we forbid it, but the time is not ripe. It is not long since the opening of the ports and the alteration of laws which were in force for more than two hundred years. The people are apprehensive, and if you were to insist on going to Edo, there is no telling what disturbances might result. Until that danger passes, the government cannot consent to your visiting Edo.

HARRIS: What I wish to say is of the greatest importance to the country and therefore can be told only to the Great Council. However, if you will present a letter investing you with plenary powers, we can compare it with a similar letter I have from the President and we can then negotiate together.

INOUE: If we bring such a letter, will you tell us those "important matters"?

HARRIS: I am governed in this matter by the President's order and our laws, and I am obliged to go to Edo. I appreciate your good will however; if you will produce the letter I shall negotiate with you.

It is clear from the Japanese record that they did not get Harris's point. The fog generated by double interpretation had blotted the distinction that Harris was making between confiding his "important matters," which were little more than bait to enable him to get to Edo and there present the President's letter to the Shogun, and negotiating, which to him meant drawing up a new treaty.

Such a misunderstanding cannot be blamed entirely on Moriyama. By now Heusken had worked with Moriyama more than nine months. He should have learned how to make himself clear, and he must share fully any blame for misinterpretation. As a matter of fact, there is nothing to indicate that Harris went out of his way to make himself clear; a little misunderstanding here was to his advantage.

At any rate, the Governors thought that Harris had agreed to tell all at Shimoda, and encouraged, they pressed on.

INOUE: We would like to tell you the instructions we have received concerning your demands.

HARRIS: We have discussed these matters several times and I do not see the need of discussing them again. It will be sufficient if you will send me a note stating yes or no.

INOUE: We would like to write to you after we have verbally explained the circumstances.

HARRIS: We have discussed them repeatedly and all the arguments have been exhausted. It would be intolerable to spend several more days on them. I hope you will reply to all three points by letter.

INOUE: It is impossible to express ourselves fully by letter. Unless we can first tell you our real views and explain the facts in detail, we cannot reply by letter. The facts of the situation would otherwise be misunderstood, and the friendship between the two countries broken. Do you wish this to happen?

HARRIS: If it is so important, I shall listen.

He learned then that the Japanese would agree to let him buy directly and that they would exchange Japanese for American coins so that he could do so, provided he understood that this permission was granted to him and his attendants only.

Harris agreed that he would never buy for other persons, nor take coins or goods out of the country. One bothersome issue was resolved, and Inoue tackled another.

INOUE: The government knows that you are a high official, and it therefore does not intend to forbid you permanently from traveling about. But only a short time has elapsed since the opening of the ports and there is much unrest. If some ruffians were to injure you, peace between the two countries might be destroyed. We hope, therefore, that you will not insist on travel for a short time.

HARRIS: I refer not only to Edo, or Kyoto, or Osaka when I say I have the right to go freely anywhere I please.

INOUE: Even though you have the right, what will you do about the possibility of danger should you travel freely? Did not the letter from your President which Perry presented state that there would be no interference in the governing of our country? Were you to travel about, and were unrest and disturbance of the peace to ensue, this would constitute interference with the governing of our country. The tendency which you have to destroy our friendship does not conform with your stated principle of fair dealing. We hope that you will not press this matter until conditions make it permissible.

HARRIS: I will consent to nothing which injures my rights.

INOUE: We do not propose to restrict your rights in any way; we are merely hoping that you will not exercise your rights for the present.

HARRIS: If your government will recognize my rights, I will agree not

to exercise them for the time being; but it must be understood beforehand that whenever a vessel is in need I shall go to the place.

INOUE: Exceptions will apply, of course, to cases of shipwreck and
other extraordinary occasions.

And another knotty issue was resolved.

> INOUE: With regard to your desire that American merchants be
> allowed to live in Shimoda and Hakodate, this is a matter we would like
> to postpone for a short time. An agent of your country, named Rice, has
> recently arrived in Hakodate with the purpose of taking charge of
> distressed seamen and to help your vessels and nationals. He asks
> permission to bring in from America such necessary articles as cannot be
> procured in Japan. This is now being investigated, and until some
> decision is reached we hope to lay aside the question of merchants.

This was the first Harris had heard of Rice and clearly he was discon-
certed. He said that he knew nothing of this man, that "he must have come
of his own accord to take advantage of the Dutch treaty. The government
could not have sent him here without consulting me. I firmly believe that he
has not been sent by the American government."

The Japanese gently refused Harris's offer to go to Hakodate and
investigate if they would lend him a schooner, and they repeated that no
decision could be made about residence for American merchants until the
Rice matter was resolved.

Harris asked them to confirm in writing the decisions that had been
reached. As far as the record shows, no other matters were discussed, and at
about four o'clock he and Heusken left. He was discomfited by the news of
Rice, but he was close to winning his demands. With the arrival of the new
Governor, the Japanese clearly were in a mood to make a settlement.

The Governors, too, must have left the meeting highly satisfied. Harris
had agreed to restrict his travel, and they had the distinct impression that
he had relinquished, or at least modified, his demand to go to Edo. They
believed that if they produced full powers, Harris would say what he had to
say at Shimoda.

They wrote a hasty letter to the Great Council reporting this, and
asking that the councillors place their monograms on the letter that Harris
had questioned. They even suggested the wording of the authority they
requested: "You are invested with full powers to negotiate with the foreigners at Shimoda."

At four the next morning, in total darkness and driving rain, a police
official named Kawakami, whose chief duty was bearing important docu-

ments to and from Edo, started another trip to the capital. One of Shimoda's elders sloshed through the mud to Naka to see him off.

Through the downpour, sometime later in the day, the Governors sent to Harris the memorandum he had requested, summarizing the decisions of yesterday's meeting.

The cloudburst continued. Following a cold and rainy spring, the true rainy season now was due, but this was too much. By midafternoon the river was out of its channel. By evening the wharf and street at Suzaki Block was half destroyed and closed to traffic. In the fishermen's houses muddy water eddied over the floors. The riverlet that purled through the gay quarters had flooded the streets along its banks and was swirling into the entryways of restaurants and teahouses.

Clearly it was incumbent on the officials of the flooded town to extend their sympathy to the Governors, who, a mile upriver, were not suffering at all. Hambei and his men tried, but they could not cross the river.

The rain ended during the night, the clouds blew over, and at dawn the sun began to dry things out. The headman and the elders made their visits that morning, to the Goyosho in the town and to the compound at Naka.

There was another caller at Naka that day. Heusken appeared and asked for Moriyama. To him he handed back the Governors' memorandum. The Consul General, he said, was abrogating the agreements.

About a week later the Governors sent to the Great Council an explanation of this surprising act:

> For some time the Consul General has been asking us to find two girls to serve him and his interpreter, basing his request on the grounds that there is no one to attend them if they become ill. We have politely refused and tried to avoid discussing the issue. A few days ago he very forcefully repeated his request and asked for an immediate reply. Since this is a private concern and we are in the midst of official negotiations, we replied that we would consider the matter when our negotiations were concluded. At this he became very angry.

In returning the memorandum, the Governors went on, Heusken stated that mutual compromise had made agreement possible, and that the Consul General on his part had accepted many Japanese proposals. It seemed only natural, then, that the Japanese should accept his request for women. It was difficult to understand why this request had not been granted when it was first placed. Delay could only mean that the Japanese intended to deny it. In the face of such insincerity, the Consul General had no choice but to nullify the agreement.

With that [wrote the Governors] Mr. Heusken left, leaving the document behind.

Having received Moriyama's report of the interview, we considered the matter in earnest. Certainly it is not desirable to offer Japanese girls to them. Moreover, there are no licensed quarters in Shimoda from which to draw such women. We had to consider, too, the question of establishing a precedent for the officials of other nations who will come here. Nevertheless, we are in the midst of negotiations which must be carried forward. As we discussed the problem, it seemed to us that sooner or later we would have to provide maids.

On the following day Mr. Heusken came again to our office on behalf of Mr. Harris, who, he reported, was unwell. If we would comply with the request for maids, he would take back our memorandum. He urged us to accede immediately.

We have been specifically instructed in Edo to show good will in negotiating with the American official. Failure to settle this problem could jeopardize all our agreements, including the restriction he has accepted on his travel.

Therefore, we have sent a girl to the Consul General under the title of nurse, with the approval of those concerned. The girl was formerly employed to attend seamen when they drank. Similar arrangements will be made for the interpreter.

Since it would be most troublesome if such accommodations are requested each time a foreign ship makes port here, we have made it clear that this arrangement is for the Consul General and his interpreter only. The American official has assured us that he would keep it secret, because it would embarrass him if it became public.

(It goes without saying that none of this got into the journals of Harris or Heusken.)

Having been told that girls would be provided, Heusken accepted return of the Governors' memorandum. At Gyokusenji, Harris prepared to send to the Governors his own version of the articles agreed on.

As we know, Vice-Superintendent Kikuna was in charge of miscellaneous affairs for the consulate. Miscellaneous affairs in any headquarters are by definition those that nobody else wants to handle. It was thus that the opium affair had fallen to him. Now he was designated to procure women.

On the day after Heusken's second visit to the Governors' office, at about eight o'clock in the evening, Kikuna and his assistant, Uchino, appeared at the town office and announced that girls had been selected to serve the Americans. A man was dispatched to summon them.

The next day Hambei chronicled developments:

It has been decided that Kichi,* the daughter of Ichizo * of Sakashita Block, be sent to Gyokusenji to serve the American official. Assistant Inspector Uchino Ryuzo-sama † brought a *kago* with sliding doors which was borrowed from Inspector Yamashita Kanzaemon-sama. Kichi went in this, accompanied by Uchino-sama, Kikuna Sennojo-sama, Moriyama Takichiro-sama, and interpreters Namura Tsunenosuke-sama and Tateishi Tokujuro-sama. At Gyokusenji she was delivered to the American official, who said that she was needed that night but could return home in the morning. She was so informed and at about sunset the officials left.

And so Okichi was plucked from the night life of Shimoda, from the gay parties in the restaurants, from the willow-lined street which was her world. She was no longer available to sing "Raven at Dawn."

> "Here now, it's time
> to appear, time to appear on display!
> When you're ready and made up—
> hurry, hurry!" Thus
> the madame loudly grumbles, and
> they all rush downstairs and the rooms
> are silent, after the sound of so many steps
> upon the stairs.

This is how it ended, the campaign for women which, despite those passages to the contrary in Harris's journal, seems to have begun even before he and Heusken disembarked from the *San Jacinto*.

And this is how it began, the story that has become one of the national legends of Japan, a story of Japanese womanhood sacrificed to a foreigner's lust for the sake of her country.

It is a legend which very nearly missed being born. It was created almost single-handedly by a man named Muramatsu Shunsui, a physician, amateur historian, and would-be novelist, who came to live in Shimoda thirty-eight years after these events, and who, almost accidentally as he told it, found references to the woman Okichi in some old and discarded documents. Today it seems practically impossible to cut through the many layers of Dr. Muramatsu's romantic fantasy to the facts of the story, but it is worth attempting.

There is clear indication in documents which have survived that Okichi

* Writing as an official, the headman does not use honorifics in referring to common people: thus Okichi becomes merely Kichi and no -*san* is added to Ichizo.
† The honorific -*sama* signifies greater respect than the more familiar -*san*.

was not happy with her assignment, and that she accepted only after pressure had been applied from the town fathers (Dr. Muramatsu says from the Governors' staff, especially Executive Officer Isa Shinjiro; this seems improbable—first, because the Governors' men could easily delegate such an onerous task to the town officials, and, second, because, of the three executive officers, Isa was the one whose work did not concern the Americans—but it was a touch that served Muramatsu's purposes: by the time he was writing, the Shogun's government had ceased to exist; its memory had been vilified and its men, though many of them had stepped into posts in the new government, had become likely candidates for any villain's role; and besides, the more Muramatsu implicated government officials, the more clearly Okichi emerged as a national heroine).

Okichi (*a photograph considered to be of Okichi at twenty-eight*)

Admittedly, the accounts of Okichi's popularity in the preceding chapters of this book are based on what Muramatsu wrote. But surely the authorities would choose a girl considered desirable, for having given in on the issue of providing a woman, they would not likely have jeopardized everything by sending someone unattractive.

Dr. Muramatsu says that Heusken specifically asked for Okichi for Harris and a girl named Ofuku for himself. Presumably he based this on what he heard from townsfolk—unless it is one of his several fictional embellishments. One story goes that Harris saw Okichi on the street fresh from her afternoon bath and found her comely. (Of course, he might have seen her *in* the bath.) There is not much to reinforce this tale, except that it may explain why, if Okichi was reluctant, it was insisted that she go. After all, Shimoda was rich in women who attended seamen when they drank.

Okichi went first to Gyokusenji the evening of June 13. On the fifteenth she received her "preparation money," twenty-five *ryo*. This was about thirty-four dollars to Harris. In this one payment she received more than the average workman of Shimoda made in a year, considerably more than the eighteen *ryo* a year that Takizo and Sukezo got. It is impossible not to wonder whether Harris bargained as hard over Okichi's wages as he did over those of the two boys. But the twenty-five *ryo* was to be only the beginning, as shown by a document signed this same day:

> Kichi, a daughter of Kiwa, widow of the late Ichizo, of Sakashita Block, Shimoda, and Fuku, daughter of the widow living at Heikichi's, of Yajigawa Block, Shimoda, are being sent to serve the American official and his interpreter living at Gyokusenji in Kakisaki.
>
> Kichi will be paid a yearly wage of one hundred twenty *ryo*, so that she will receive ten *ryo* every month from the American official, while Fuku is entitled to a yearly wage of ninety *ryo*, so that she will receive seven *ryo* two *bu* every month from the interpreter.
>
> As a special allowance, Kichi will receive twenty-five *ryo* and Fuku, twenty *ryo* from the American official and his interpreter respectively.
>
> We hereby acknowledge receipt of twenty-five *ryo* as the special allowance from the American official to Kichi.
>
> (signed with fingerprints)
>
> Moto, the elder sister of Kichi
> Kiwa, mother of Kichi

It was not, however, until the eighteenth that Heusken's girl was sent to him. One can imagine the torment the young man endured alone in his room while a few feet away Okichi shared Harris's bed.

Hambei wrote:

> Kikuna-sama, Uchino-sama, Yamaguchi-sama, and Namura-sama, the interpreter, came from the Goyosho to take Fuku, a daughter of Tsuji, a widow living at Heikichi's, of Yajigawa Block, to Gyokusenji as maid for Heusken. Heusken was highly pleased, saying all but the girl could leave right away. Later Heikichi was summoned to the Goyosho to receive the twenty *ryo* paid by Heusken as an allowance.

No *kago* was provided for Ofuku. She walked, and no one has suggested that she went reluctantly. It is said that she and Heusken had met before. Her widowed mother was living with Heikichi, a paperer, evidently without the formality of a wedding. Muramatsu says he saw an invoice showing that it was Heikichi who repapered the sliding doors at Gyokusenji in April. He adds (and here it is impossible to say whether one is dealing with a particular that Muramatsu uncovered or one he invented) that Heikichi brought the girl to help him, and seeing her busy with paper and paste, Heusken was smitten. Others have written, probably more accurately, that Ofuku carried Heikichi's lunch to him.

Why did she go to Gyokusenji later than Okichi? The indefatigable Muramatsu says he found the answer to that too: her period came at just the wrong time. And he quotes an old comic poem:

> With smiles, a messenger is sent
> To postpone the wedding date.

By the time Ofuku reported, Okichi was no longer there. After three nights' duty she had been instructed to stay home to cure a sore or skin eruption, something Harris found repellent if not suspect.

In the meantime negotiations at the Goyosho had gone so smoothly that two more meetings, on June 16 and 17, had brought agreement.

Dr. Muramatsu credits Okichi for this. He claims that the triumph of getting her and her calming influence had made Harris a more reasonable man. But an examination of the record shows that things went smoothly

Harris, with Heusken, conferring with Governors Inoue and
Nakamura at the Goyosho, with Moriyama in the middle acting as interpreter
(*a drawing by Heusken from his journal*)

because Nakamura gave in to Harris's demands. Inoue must have sat dazed as Nakamura relinquished position after position that he and Okada had fought for, no doubt citing always those instructions from Edo that they must get along with this difficult foreigner. If Okada had been jettisoned for any reason other than a personality clash with Inoue, if it had ever been suggested that he was too soft with Harris, those who maneuvered him out were paid back in full. Significantly, Moriyama's diary suddenly dries up. It is as though he no longer had the heart to record what was happening.

And so it was June 17, not June 8, that Harris was thinking of when he wrote that exultant entry in his journal.

I have at last carried every point triumphantly with the Japanese, and have got everything conceded that I have been negotiating for since last September. Among my papers will be found a copy of the Convention which contains the following provisions:

1st   Opens the Port of Nagasaki to American ships:

2nd   Gives the right of permanent residence to Americans at Shimoda and Hakodate, and the right to appoint a Vice-Consul at the latter port;

3rd   Settles the currency, so that where we paid $100 we now pay only $34.50; *

4th   Americans to be exclusively under the control of their Consuls and to be tried by American law;

5th   Concedes the right of the Consul General to go where he pleases in Japan,† and to be furnished with Japanese money to enable him in person, or by his servants, to make his purchases without the intervention of any Japanese official. . . .

Am I elated by this success? Not a whit. I know my dear countrymen but too well to expect any praise for what I have done, and I shall esteem myself lucky if I am not removed from office, not for what I have done, but because I have not made a commercial treaty that would open Japan as freely as England is open to us.

Besides, it is so easy to criticize, and so agreeable to condemn. It is much more pleasant to write imbecile, ass or fool, than to say able, discreet and competent.

The day after agreement was reached, the Governors wrote to the Great Council to explain its terms. The way was now cleared, they added, to hear from Harris those matters of importance which he had been pressing to announce at Edo.

---

* He had finally agreed to a six-per-cent charge for conversion.

† He had, of course, agreed to delay the use of this right except in cases of emergency, shipwreck, etc.

In Edo, by this time, Kawakami had been handed, with great formality, the precious document bearing the Shogun's vermilion seal which conferred on the Governors of Shimoda the full powers they had requested. It was not an authority which was given lightly. It was issued in this case on the Governors' assurance that if they had it, Harris would relax his pressure to come to Edo and would reveal at Shimoda those "important matters."

Kawakami had also had returned to him the Great Council's letter to Harris, now bearing the monograms of all the councillors, and with these two documents he was on his way back to Shimoda.

The names and monograms of Lord Abe (left) and Lord Hotta
(*from Harris's letters and papers*)

It must have seemed to the Great Council that things were going better in Shimoda. But they had worries enough in Edo. Not the least was Lord Abe's illness, which appeared more serious every day. The Shogun, kept advised by the councillors, expressed his concern by sending a personal message and gifts to the sick man.

On June 15 Lord Matsudaira Yoshinaga, to whom Abe was not only friend but also almost indispensable ally, sent his own physician to make an examination. Returning, the doctor reported that the patient was seriously ill; it was a question whether he could survive the heat of the coming summer. Shocked, Yoshinaga asked Abe to call in a physician of the "Dutch" school of medicine. Perhaps the sick man would have liked to follow this advice, but he answered that there was a law on the books which forbade the practice of Western medicine by official doctors, and as a member of the Great Council he could not evade that law.

Tokugawa Nariaki, too, was disturbed by what he learned of Abe's illness, which seems to have been a disease of the liver or kidneys. Nariaki had heard that sunfish were good for a man so stricken, and he rushed an order to Mito that the fishermen there should provide a steady supply of fresh sunfish at Edo.

In Shimoda, where advance notices of Kawakami's return had already been received, people went about their business, paying little attention to the new domestic arrangements at Gyokusenji. Farmers were occupied from dawn to dark with the hardest work of the year. The fields which had produced their crop of wheat were now flooded and plowed, and the rice seedlings had been taken from the seed beds. There was a song for this, as there was for most jobs:

> When I uproot this seedling,
> where will they live, the locusts?
> —in the cut grass,
> in the pampas grass,
> in the tips of the miscanthus reeds—
> where will they live?

Now farm families were knee-deep in the flooded fields, backs bent, transplanting the seedlings to the hospitable mud. It was hard work but there were compensations: neighbors worked together, helping each other; there was chance for gossiping and for flirting, and there were songs to speed the day.

> Floating weeds upon the water,
> lovely things: their form
> I'd like to dye and place
> upon my patterned robe.
> * * *
> In a pipeful of tobacco
> I'd like to stuff my thoughts of him,
> and have my love smoke on them.

Yet one was nonetheless dog-tired at sundown.

Townsmen were not as busy as farmers but there were matters to keep them occupied.

Officials at the Goyosho called for a representative from the town and each of the villages to report concerning the current campaign for contributions to the Mishima shrine. The shrine's solicitor was in town again, pursuing the calling that his father and grandfather had before him, going from door to door, sermonizing the householders and selling charms.

There were many such campaigns during the year for many different shrines and temples throughout the land. The Governors' men kept an eye on them. Giving was all very well, of course, and most families would feel lost without the year's talisman from their favorite shrine or temple, but charity could not be permitted to get out of hand—not to the point where it might interfere with the ability to pay taxes.

Another set of officials at the Goyosho summoned the wardens and woodcutters of the Shogun's forests. For several days they went into the woods with government inspectors, selecting trees to be felled for the building of, as Hambei put it, "long and slender ships." The Shogunate was pushing ahead with its program of constructing Kimizawa schooners.

And one more important item of business: the town was notified that its petition for a reduction in the tax on *tengusa* had been granted. The *tengusa* plant was one of the sea's most valuable crops. There were great beds of it off the coasts of Izu, its red fronds gesticulating in the currents. From it came (and still comes today) agar-agar, which is the basis of, among other things, all the jellied sweets the Japanese are fond of.

Long ago the government had started leasing the harvest rights, as well as taxing the crop. Reduction of the tax would permit more of the profits to stay in Shimoda. The first man to learn that the petition had been granted was not Headman Hambei but merchant Wataya Kichibei. It was an indication of the esteem in which the Goyosho held Kichibei. For years his house had held the *tengusa* rights for a long stretch of coast southeast from Shimoda (these rights had just been renewed in March), as landlord Heiemon of Kakisaki held the contract for the area around Suzaki and Sotoura. A man wealthy enough to bid for and get *tengusa* rights was almost certain to become wealthier.

The *tengusa* season was well under way. It began early in May, as soon as the water was warm enough to dive in, and closed in mid-November when it became too cold again. Shirahama, a couple of miles up the coast from Sotoura, was blessed with the finest beds of all, and at Shirahama's shrine the gods were officially thanked three times a year: one festival opened the season, another closed it, and the third and largest celebrated the completed season.

Harris had found some *tengusa* early in the month after his walk up the valley and his visit to Inoue. *On my walk home I picked up (on the beach) some pure white fuci. I find nothing in my books analogous to this. It was not an isolated specimen, as abundance of it was found. It is quite as white as the best quality of the celebrated "Edible Bird's Nests."*

What Harris found and could not identify from his books was deep red *tengusa* bleached white by the sun. Had his walks taken him to the right places he would have seen this process going on, seen vast stretches of beach covered with *tengusa* and women turning it so that the sun would blanch it evenly.

Harris had found a few fronds that had broken off and washed ashore. Almost all the crop was gathered by women divers, it having been learned long ago that women beat men at this work: they stood the cold better and were longer-winded.

There were two classes of divers, deep and shallow. A deep diver worked with a man, often her husband, who sat in a boat. Holding a stone of thirty pounds or so to sink her quickly to the bottom, she worked waters as deep as fifteen or sixteen fathoms, stayed under as long as three or four minutes. While she gathered *tengusa* the man pulled up the stone by a rope attached to it; when she had filled the net hung around her neck she tugged the rope tied to the net and the man helped pull her and her pickings to the surface. It might take from thirty minutes to two hours to fill the boat; when she became too cold she climbed into the boat to warm herself over a fire pot. A strong diver could go out and fill a boat three times a day.

> Having to work as a diving girl,
> you soon lose your femininity;
> but granting that, suppose your husband lacks
> ability—how can you quit?

A shallow diver stayed closer to land, in five to eight fathoms of water. She worked alone from a barrel floating on the surface, diving to fill her net, placing what she collected in the barrel. When she became chilled she swam to the shore. Little groups of such women could be found under the pines or among the crags which gave shelter from the wind, naked, warming themselves at a fire.

> Why do you worry that
> your skin's so dark?
> Just give up working

Women divers (*a print by Utamaro*)

Gathering seaweed at ebb tide at Kakisaki (*a drawing by Aleksandr Mozhaiskii*)

as a diving girl and
you'll get white soon enough!

When the *tengusa* was brought to the collection point it was washed in some fresh-water stream that wound across the beach, sorted for grade, and weighed for payment. A diver was well paid.

Then the crop was spread in the sun to bleach, for until it turned white the agar-agar could not be extracted. Bleached and dried, it was pounded to break off the calcium deposits made by shellfish, and then it was sent to Shimoda for shipment. Here Wataya Kichibei came into the picture in his second role: he was a major agent in shipping the *tengusa* to Osaka, whose merchants distributed it to cold mountain areas where it could be frozen as a necessary part of the process of making agar-agar.

Tengusa does not grow inside Shimoda bay and Harris's journal gives no indication that he ever found an explanation for the white fuci. But he had seen the residents of Kakisaki gathering the various green and brown edible seaplants for their own use and for sale. *The quantity . . . collected at Shimoda is quite large, and it appears to form one of their articles of export to Edo.*

These were the days when the villagers of Kakisaki wondered how to stretch the days and their strength to do all that had to be done: to transplant rice, to catch fish, to gather seaweed. Nor were these all their chores.

394

The day for boat cleaning came around. The fishing boats of the village were beached at high tide, raised on blocks, and fires of dry pampas grass built beneath them. The heat and smoke made the barnacles drop off and killed the marine worms that were constantly menacing the hulls. In those days, before paint and tar came into use, this was a job that had to be done every month or so; it was almost always going on at the Shimoda shipyards, where it was done commercially; at Kakisaki it was a community enterprise, performed on days designated by the headman.

Unfavorable winds brought into port a Nagasaki ship, loaded with

Gathering seaweed (*a print by Hiroshige*)

cannon bought from the Dutch and bound for Edo. She anchored near Kakisaki, and each day her crew came ashore for a bath and a rest at Gonzo's home, which was a ships' inn. After five days she tried to sail; fishing boats from Shimoda, Kakisaki, and Suzaki were mobilized to tow her into deep water, but at the harbor's mouth the wind switched from southerly to northerly and a hard rain began. The ship was driven toward the opposite shore and there she anchored again. Two Kakisaki seamen were assigned to guard duty on her.

In the meantime a waterlogged ship made port at Sotoura, loaded with rice and lumber from the port of Shingu in Kii Province. She was too badly damaged to proceed, and the unloading of her cargo began. The shipowner arrived and called for faster work; ten men were drafted from Kakisaki, and the working hours of everyone in the village were lengthened to make up for them.

It was on June 19 that Moriyama delivered to Harris a draft of the convention that had been agreed on, as the Japanese understood it. He also brought a couple of letters from Elisha Rice, forwarded through Edo. The Governors had held them a few days, perhaps fearing that something in them might upset their negotiations with Harris, but now the talks seemed completed.

They were the first letters Harris had received since he reached Shimoda. He wrote of them under the incorrect date of June 23, his chronology still askew: *Today I received an official and also a private letter from Mr. "E. E. Rice, U. S. Commercial Agent at Hakodate," announcing his arrival at that place, and that he had "hoisted his flag." His private letter to me is a curiosity in composition and orthography.* This was no doubt true: these letters have not survived, but others sent by Rice have and they are difficult to decipher. He was not a learned man.

But it was not so much the letters' style as their content that upset Harris. *He writes me that two ships under the American flag are there from Hong Kong, and that the supercargo Mr. Lühdorf has some things for me, which Mr. Rice promises to forward to me, if they are landed at Hakodate, but he does not say one word about letters.*

This is most tantalizing. I am now more than ten months in Japan, and have not as yet received a single letter from the United States. As no direct communication is allowed by sea between Shimoda and Hakodate by Japanese junks, my supplies might as well be at Hong Kong as there. I have been out of flour, bread, butter, lard, bacon, hams, sweet oil, and in fact out of every kind of foreign supply for more than two months. I am living on rice, fish and very poor poultry, as no game of any kind has been brought to me for the last three months.

My health is miserable, my appetite is gone, and I am so shrunk away that I look as though a "Vice-Consul had been cut out of me." Where, oh! where is Commodore Armstrong?

He was even more upset when he read the Japanese draft of the convention. His meeting with the Governors next day was a long harsh wrangle over wording. Again and again he accused them of bad faith, of breaching their promises, and, finally, of allowing themselves to be misled by their scheming interpreters, a charge that must have called for a good deal of self-control on Moriyama's part when he had to interpret it. Harris threatened to nullify everything he had agreed to, and of course he threatened war. He got red in the face, he tore papers and flung them to the floor, he started up as if to walk out.

His assertion was that the Japanese were seeking to destroy the agreement by changes in wording, though he seems at times to have admitted that in most cases he was objecting to phrasing he had previously accepted and initialed. In a journal entry he implies that the difficulties were all of language, repeating his disparagement of the Japanese interpreters. . . . *the wording of the Articles . . . is a work of much difficulty, as the Dutch of the Japanese interpreters is that of the ship captains and traders used some two hundred and fifty years ago. They have not been taught a single new word in the interim, so they are quite ignorant of all the terms used in treaties, conventions, etc., etc. This, joined to their excessive jealously and fear of being cheated, makes it excessively difficult to manage such a matter as the present one. They even wanted the words in the Dutch version to stand in the exact order they stood in the Japanese!! Owing to the difference of grammatical structure this would have rendered it perfect gibberish.*

We cannot be certain what difficulties arose over wording, for most of the working papers of these negotiations have not survived. But Harris's blanket indictment of the Japanese interpreters' Dutch does not stand up. The statement that the Japanese had not learned a single new word in two hundred and fifty years is patent nonsense, but, further, Harris's papers today include certain letters which the Japanese wrote to him in Dutch, such as their reply to his complaint of high prices. The Dutch of this letter is good, in a rather stately style not at all suggestive of a merchant's patois. On this subject Harris had to rely on what Heusken told him. Certainly the young man stood to increase his own importance by enlarging on the difficulties of his work.

As to Harris's reference to *all the terms used in treaties, conventions, etc., etc.,* one must remember that the Japanese had by this time negotiated at least half a dozen compacts with four different powers, and there comes to mind an incident which took place in Siam after a familiar pattern of events: Harris had suffered severe gastric problems, he had several times lost his temper, and he had labeled the Siamese all liars.

The King of Siam wished to insert in Harris's treaty the preamble of the existing treaty between Siam and the United States, negotiated a few years earlier by Edmund Roberts. Harris objected, saying that it was *not good English, being ungrammatical, and that it would be laughed at.* There was, in fact, nothing wrong with Roberts's English except that it was not Harris's. Harris was inordinately jealous of his own phrase-making.

Finally, and most important, the difficulties at Shimoda were not merely over wording. They involved substance.

To cite the article most fought over, the Japanese draft was to the effect that American merchants were to be permitted to reside at Shimoda and Hakodate to provide goods not produced in Japan but required by American whaling vessels. That was exactly what Harris had said he wanted all along.

But now he demanded that every restrictive word and phrase be deleted. He insisted on striking out the references to merchants, to goods not produced in Japan, and to whaling vessels—and confronted with another of Harris's bursts of temper, the Governors gave in.

The article in question (the second), as finally written, is so loose as to approach non sequitur:

> It being known that American ships coming to the ports of Shimoda and Hakodate cannot have their wants supplied by the Japanese, it is agreed that American citizens may permanently reside at Shimoda and Hakodate, and the Government of the United States may appoint a vice-consul to reside at Hakodate.

Why this battle? Harris made clear in his journal what he emphatically did not make clear to the Japanese: *No class of Americans is named in the second Article, so that missionaries may actually come and reside in Japan.*

Heusken's diary is more revealing:

> The establishment of a right of permanent residence already constitutes half a treaty of commerce, and since any American citizen will be able to avail himself of it, it will not be long until American missionaries arrive in Japan. The Japanese will not expect that, but it will be explained to them later that a missionary is a citizen just as much

as a merchant or a ship's captain. Women, excluded so far from Japan, will be able to use that title; but the Japanese plenipotentiaries have affixed their signatures to the treaty, and unless they fail to honor the treaty, which would bring upon them numberless calamities, they will be powerless to oppose it.

Great victory!

In looking back, one cannot help feeling that Harris's display of anger on June 20 was feigned: having discovered that the Japanese were appalled by his temper, he used it as a weapon to obtain concessions he could not get by reasoned argument. Is it any wonder the Japanese had a *fear of being cheated?* There is no doubt that Harris believed the end justified the means. There is no doubt that this is a dangerous belief.

There were, however, still a few days before the convention was signed and the foreigners could celebrate their triumph. Harris and the Governors met for a calmer discussion on June 22 (in the course of which they decided to date their pact back to June 17, the day on which they had reached agreement in substance, or thought they had—a circumstance that evidently slipped Harris's mind when he later wrote that it had been signed on the seventeenth), and then there was the labor of preparing final copies in Dutch, Japanese, and English.

This was tedious and exasperating work, and the weather did not make it easier. The rainy season was upon Japan. The rain would make the rice grow, but in the meantime everything within sight or touch seemed to drip or ooze or sweat. The tatami mats were dank, papers were sodden, bedding was clammy. Harris and Heusken found that their woolen suits and leather shoes felt always damp, and then discovered that suits and shoes and books sprouted green mold overnight. Each hot and sultry day was followed by another just as oppressive. People grew snappish.

Yet these were happy days for Heusken, for each evening Ofuku reported to Gyokusenji. Harris's was a different story. In the rainy season only the young enjoy making love. We do not know when Okichi advised that her abscess was healed, though on June 24 Hambei noted in his diary that while both girls reported for duty, Okichi was told to go home again. Because of the rain she spent the night at Shinzaemon's, just below the temple gate; it had been arranged that the girls would go to his house and wait there until called up to the temple.

There are little signs that Ofuku was lightening the atmosphere at Gyokusenji. We read that, evidently for the first time, a masseur was summoned to the temple. This happened on only the second evening that the girl reported; she must have surmised at once that what the crotchety old man required was a relaxing massage. Ihei, who was blind, as those who took up this profession usually were, was called from Shimoda. He kneaded Heusken as well, and for having come so far, was tipped liberally, further evidence of Ofuku's influence.

She was also being rewarded with gifts, her first being two tea containers and "thirty-three pieces of something like nails." (Hambei was at a loss for the right word; the things must have been pins.) At the Goyosho, Kikuna deliberated and decided that she could keep them. We do not hear of any gifts to Okichi.

There are those who state that Harris grew as fond of Ofuku as he might have of a daughter-in-law. This seems reasonable, for we know that he was susceptible to honorary nieces. Fatherly affection for this bright child must have come easier to Harris than passion for his ripe party girl, who had resented being ordered there and probably showed it.

On June 26 Headman Hambei and two elders signed a pledge that Okichi's duty and pay having been set, "this settles everything about her service at Gyokusenji, and from now on no one will complain about the matter." It certainly sounds as though there had been complaints before.

And on the same day, June 26, the labors of Heusken, Moriyama, Dr. Ito, and scribes being finished, the Governors and Harris met at the Goyosho and signed the Convention of Shimoda.

Then everyone relaxed a bit. Harris told the Japanese what he had learned from Rice's letters: that indisputably Rice had a bona-fide appointment as commercial agent, and that there was a war in China. The latter was old stuff to the Japanese but they listened politely as Harris gave them a colorful but inaccurate (if they understood him correctly) story of the fighting at Canton. It was entirely a British action, he told them. Either Rice did not tell him or Harris suppressed word of the American attacks on the Barrier Forts.

The convention out of the way, the Japanese announced that they were ready to push ahead on negotiating those "secret matters." They decided to exchange Dutch translations of their plenary powers and, if those proved mutually satisfactory, to meet five days later to confirm formally their acceptance of each other's credentials—agreeing that on an occasion of such dignity they should meet in formal dress and act with the utmost decorum.

Next day the Governors sent to the Great Council a summary of their convention, with an indication that they may have had a few qualms about it: Inoue, they wrote, would like to come to Edo and explain further.

In another letter they passed on the information they had from Harris about Rice's status and the war in China, and in a third document they requested that one Governor be stationed in Edo unless things again became critical at Shimoda; Inoue would come up to the capital now and they would trade places in the second month of next year. With the signing of the convention, they indicated, things should return to normal at Shimoda.

A transaction of the sort they hoped would become normal took place the next day. A group of Goyosho officials accompanied by a delegation of elders from Shimoda came to Gyokusenji to collect payment at last on the account that had been running since Harris's arrival. It was their second trip. They had appeared by appointment two days earlier, been kept waiting at the gate, and then told to come back "day after tomorrow." Harris evidently had decided not to pay until he had the Governors' signatures on the convention.

Under the wrong date, Harris wrote as follows: *To-day I paid the Japanese my account for my household expenses, including some articles of furniture, a horse, saddle, etc., etc., a norimono, together with the Government bill for my flagstaff material, the accounts of my Chinese servants, and also for seventy-five dollars of lacquer articles purchased for Mrs. S. N. Spooner. The accounts begin about the 30th August, 1856, and end May 22, 1857. The total presents the alarming amount of 3,476,594. But these are Japanese seni, and I settled the whole for $699.*

Had I paid the accounts on the basis admitted by Commodore Perry, the amount would have been $2,173, so that $1,474 was saved by my arrangement of the currency with the Japanese.

The fact is that he could not have paid $2,173. He had carried ashore $2,450. What with the amount just paid to the Japanese, the thousand-dollar loan to the Russians, Heusken's salary,* wages and holiday cumshaw to the Chinese, and the purchases from Mr. Hall, the cashbox was all but empty. Heusken had a quarter's salary coming due in three days, and the Chinese, their monthly wages. Harris would not be able to pay them. And for food and necessities, he had no choice but to ask the Japanese for credit. It was embarrassing. *Where, oh! where is Commodore Armstrong?*

That same day, the bill collectors having left, Moriyama delivered a Dutch translation of the Governors' credentials. Heusken put it into Eng-

---

* Heusken had received little cash. The salary posted as paid to him was $1,125, but Harris had advanced him $750 in New York. When one deducts this, his mess bill on the *San Jacinto*, the dollar a day for meals at Gyokusenji, laundry, etc. ($270), and purchases such as horse and saddle, it can be seen that twenty-one months after leaving New York, Heusken had accumulated little if any money.

lish. It read just as the Governors had asked that it should and bore the Shogun's vermilion seal.

INOUE, LORD OF SHINANO

&

NAKAMURA, LORD OF DEWA

Ye are appointed and invested with Full Powers to negociate in Shimoda on everything concerning foreign affairs.
In the fifth year of Ansei, *Mi,* Fifth Month.

Harris thought this over, and two days later sent the Governors a letter. Their powers, he wrote, were not full. The document in question

undoubtedly confers on you the power to negotiate upon any subject, but it does not give you power to conclude anything. . . .

Another omission exists in your Powers; it is that they are general and not specific. It is due to the dignity of my Government that your Powers should be direct, authorizing you to negotiate and conclude with the representative of the United States of America.

Whenever your Powers are so much enlarged as to cover these two points, it will give me great pleasure to enter into negociations with you.

It took the Governors no time at all to make a reply. Moriyama delivered it the next day. The word used, *torihakarai,* they wrote, covered both negotiation and decision. "Thus our powers are not in the least incomplete."

And there the matter stood at month's end, as the Governors reported to the Great Council:

The American official has puzzled us with further demands and we have answered him anew. We shall try our best to persuade him to complete the checking of credentials as soon as possible so that talks may proceed and we may hear his explanation of what he terms the "important matters" and question him about them if necessary. However, we are still in the dark as to what foreign practice lies behind the American move. . . .

In Kakisaki the planting of rice was going forward, and the crippled ship from Shingu was being unloaded. The Nagasaki ship, with its cannon, had at last been able to sail. A dead dog washed up on the beach; since no Kakisaki man would touch the carrion for fear of defilement, Yoheiji sent for *eta* outcasts from their village up the valley to bury it.

On the last day of the month one of Kikuna's assistants summoned Okichi and Ofuku and read them a set of instructions:

1. They must not engage in any secret deal with either Americans or Japanese.

2. They must report any gifts received from the Americans. They must never transfer such gifts to others.

3. They must tell the foreigners nothing about any Japanese official or about anything that happened at the Goyosho, and they must tell outsiders nothing of what went on at Gyokusenji.

4. They must tell the Americans nothing about Japanese money or the prices of things.

5. They must report any delay in menstruation.

6. When unable to go to Gyokusenji because of illness, they must report it.

7. While with the Americans they must be polite and careful in their conduct and refrain from useless chatter. They must turn to the Japanese interpreter if they have something special to tell the Americans.

8. While at home they must behave themselves.

9. Their kin must never visit them at Gyokusenji.

10. They must not converse with the houseboys at Gyokusenji, or with the Chinese servants or any of the other employees.

Having heard these commandments—and the men at the Goyosho seem to have thought of everything—the girls placed their fingerprints on the document to pledge obedience. (Dr. Muramatsu says that Okichi could write and was insulted by this procedure.)

Kikuna hoped that this situation was now under control.

Chapter 13

JULY, 1857

The rainy season dragged on. Knowing that it brought out the meanness in people, Hambei was not surprised that he had to cope with a police case.

Iwakichi, a stonecutter who had a long record of unfilial conduct, was hauled in again on the same charge. Few crimes were more repugnant: Executive Officer Isa Shinjiro, a man of gentle dignity who had a considerable reputation as a calligrapher, had painted a scroll which read: "Filial piety is the beginning of morality." Confronted with Iwakichi, Goyosho police prefects were exasperated. They interrogated him, released him, then changed their minds, summoned him again, and put him in the town's custody pending further action.

The air was sometimes chill, sometimes sweltering, but always heavy with dampness. It weighed especially on the dyspeptic man at Gyokusenji.

On the last day of June another letter had been added to the many waiting somewhere to be delivered to him. The friend he had appointed to act in his stead when he was named consul at Ningpo, missionary D. J. Macgowan, wrote from Shanghai. Like so many of Harris's friends, the Macgowans had provided him with an honorary niece. "Poor child," Macgowan wrote, "she has suffered much from the ague, and it is on her account that I have made this trip from Ningpo. She is much better in consequence."

It was a warm and sympathetic letter and it would have done Harris good to read it, but it lay in China waiting for the day that Commodore Armstrong would dispatch a ship. "It seems to me that you have been cruelly treated and the public interests neglected"; it began, "for it must now be nearly a year since you have had communication with the outside world. But for your exuberance of spirits you would sink under the exile you endure." *Saturday, July 4, 1857. I never felt more miserable and wretched than on this day. Ill in health and in want of everything but low spirits, of which I have an abundant supply.*

If Okichi was supposed to have therapeutic value, she had failed. Harris did not even want to see her; he told officials he was too ill. (There are hints that, waiting at home, she was still giving Kikuna headaches. Town officials were required to submit an oath that neither the girls nor their families would make any objections about their service. The point was clear: however bitter any complaints, they were not to be transmitted to the Goyosho.)

Ofuku appeared every evening and left the next morning. Hambei was not yet bored with chronicling her goings and comings:

> Fuku, on her way to work, came about four o'clock in the evening to report that she found nothing unusual at Gyokusenji last night.

> Fuku returned from Gyokusenji about nine in the morning. Her elder sister Shime reported on her behalf that there was nothing at all unusual.

> Fuku, accompanied by her elder sister Shime, returned home from Gyokusenji around eight this morning. There was nothing unusual there,

Calligraphy by Isa Shinjiro: "Filial piety is the beginning of morality"

405

she reported. At the Goyosho she submitted a package containing a piece of white crepe, seventeen by fourteen inches, eleven triangular pieces of pink silk, and several small pieces of cloth which she was given when leaving Gyokusenji this morning. It is said that on Kikuna-sama's orders the package will be transferred to Fuku later.

She had been given scraps from the tailoring of underwear for the occupants of the temple. Several Shimoda tailors had been kept busy making up drawers in white, pink, and black silk; one exhausted his own stock of material and had had to appeal through the town office for a loan of cloth from a competitor.

Around four in the evening Fuku went to Gyokusenji.

It sounds as though she was reporting in time for dinner. Perhaps one of the gentlemen found this wearing or perhaps the question arose of paying for her meals. At any rate, Hambei recorded a couple of days later that "from now on Fuku is to take up her duty at eight in the evening," and he added, remembering that she was called a nurse, "to give her master medicine."

Despite Harris's lament that he had *never felt more miserable and wretched* than on the Fourth of July, Moriyama found him much improved when he called to offer congratulations on that day. Indeed, Moriyama reported when he returned to Naka compound, the Consul General was "almost completely well," and had asked for a conference with the Governors two days hence.

Their conversation had been punctuated by the boom of guns, for Harris had arranged to have a salute fired *in honor of the day by the Japanese,—I paying the expense, which was less than two dollars.* He and Moriyama got the full benefit since the cannon were set up just below Gyokusenji. Heusken presided: "The Consul being ill, I go in my dress uniform, accompanied by a servant who carries the flag of the United States, to the beach where the two cannons are placed. The American flag receives a twenty-one-gun salute in honor of the eighty-second anniversary of the independence of the United States."

If the salute was intended to impress the local residents, it failed, for no one told them what it was all about. Yoheiji attended with two of the elders, Gennosuke and Kosaburo, bringing six men to assist, but he put the whole thing down as test firing. The shooting evidently took Hambei by surprise; he had it investigated and recorded that the guns had been borrowed by the American and were returned about four o'clock, by boat across the harbor and by wagon drawn by six men (the Kakisaki men) to the Goyosho.

Now that the convention was signed, it was time for a few amenities. Harris presented to Nakamura the last of his three "engraved, richly gilt, ivory-handled" pistols (he had previously given one to Okada and one to Inoue). And he gave each of the Governors a feathered fan and some liqueurs.

He also decided that he could now, without loss of dignity, resume his tutoring in English, and so Dr. Ito Kansai, Tateishi Tokujuro, and the two young men whose fathers were officials at Shimoda again began reporting to the temple for their lessons.

"This being the case," the Governors wrote to the Great Council, "we must pay tuition. We previously sent a length of silk as entrance fee. We believe it should not fall on the students to pay their own tuition. So we propose to send, with your approval, items from our office valued at twenty *ryo* [about $27.60] per student per year, following the example set at Nagasaki. The gifts will be sent not all at once but in installments." And being seasoned administrators, they added: "This special payment will be included in our supplementary budget request."

They were also worrying about those pure gold mustard spoons that Harris needed, and they wrote to the Great Council on this topic as well. Since silver spoons were so bad for the Consul General's health, they asked permission to buy out of their own pockets some of the American gold coins on hand in the treasury and to have these made into spoons by the Shogunate goldsmith in Edo. Then they would make Harris a present of the spoons. They could hardly be expected to know that a gift would anger the recipient. The Great Council approved, with the usual reminder that no precedent was being established.

As requested, the Governors met Harris at the Goyosho on the sixth. There they handed over the Great Council's letter, now bearing the monograms of all five councillors, including that of the ill Lord Abe. It was their handling of this letter that gave Harris his opening. They had previously notified him that it would be handed to him at their next interview. Heusken tells the story:

> He answered that the state of his health did not allow him to leave his house and he consequently requested them to give me the letter, whereupon the Governors answered that Japanese etiquette demanded that the letter bearing the signatures of the Great Council be handed to the Consul-General himself by the Governors or the Vice-Governors.
>
> That incident afforded him an excellent argument to hasten his trip to Edo.
>
> "What!" he said, "you yourselves refuse to hand my secretary a letter

signed by the legislative power * of this Empire and you demand that it be delivered only to the person to whom it is addressed? While I, bearer of a letter signed by the Chief Executive of a powerful nation addressed to the Sovereign of this Empire, am refused permission to hand it to the person to whom it is addressed? I demand that I may deliver the letter of the President to His Majesty, the Emperor of Japan, in person, and I can give it to no one else. I repeat to you at the same time that your refusal is a great indignity to the illustrious writer, to the United States, and to myself, their representative.

"I cannot compel you to grant what I demand, but it is up to me to inform my government of the manner in which the President's letter is treated here and it will be up to my government to react."

It was this speech which punctured the Governors' dream that by making bold concessions in writing the convention, they had bought Harris's agreement to waive his trip to Edo and to settle things at Shimoda. It seemed to them that Harris had broken his word. Suddenly it seemed to them that they had been swindled and made dupes.

When Harris spoke of his government's "reacting" he did not veil his threats. Citing the recent war with Mexico as an object lesson, he suggested that it might be necessary to humiliate Japan before all the world by sending battleships to chasten her.

The Governors burned at this but they hid their feelings and kept the conference going. They argued that Harris was a plenipotentiary, as they were: since the President and the Shogun could not meet personally, Harris had been designated to deliver the letter, while the Japanese, recognizing its importance, had invested them, the Governors, with full dignity and authority to receive it. Harris's journeying to Edo in these uneasy times could cause political turmoil. And they pointed out that Perry had delivered *his* President's letter † to the envoys sent to confer with him.

Harris's brief account of the meeting is misleading as well as misdated: *The Governors now produce an imperial mandate under the "Seal and Signature Royal," commanding them to receive the President's letter and bring it to Edo, and they are quite dumbfounded that I refuse to yield to the mandate.*

---

* The Great Council was of course not a legislative body any more than it was a regency; in it resided the most important decision-making and executive powers of the government. But, as is probably evident by now, the Shogunate was a government of councils and bureaus that operated by consultation and search for consensus.

† By the time Perry delivered President Fillmore's letter, Pierce was president; Harris's letter was written by Pierce and Buchanan now was president.

The "imperial mandate," if by that Harris meant the vermilion-seal grant of full powers, made no reference to the President's letter. Neither did the Great Council's letter, which was simply a request that he negotiate with the Governors.

And what "dumbfounded" the Governors was what appeared to be Harris's about-face now that the convention had been signed. They had asked for full powers because they thought that if they produced them he would reveal his "important matters." Now not only was he haggling over those powers but he was saying that regardless of them he would deliver the President's letter only in Edo and only to the Shogun, and would discuss his important matters only after that was done.

They debated for four hours that day (including a long digression in which Harris probed that loophole he had carved in the convention for the benefit of missionaries, though he did not yet point it out to the Governors, and elicited a statement that the Japanese government had no intention of persecuting foreign Christians—as long as they did not propagate their faith).

They came back the next day for more of the same. By the end of it, Inoue had said that he would go to Edo to get a decision concerning Harris's trip to the capital.

The Governors went home to survey their troubles. Several accusations could be leveled against them:

—That they had been tricked by Harris into obtaining plenary powers so that he could open discussion of a commercial treaty. (They had realized in the past two days that that was all he would discuss with them, and they had shied away; they did not want to discuss such a treaty and they knew their government would not permit them to.)

—That they had not stature enough, did not command sufficient respect from Harris, to make him live up to his promises.

—That the present situation was based on misunderstanding which reflected ineptitude and inadequacy on their part; that they had requested full powers without careful consideration, almost under false pretenses. The Shogun's vermilion seal was not issued casually. They could be accused of regarding it too lightly.

The Governors were in a very difficult position. Their dismay was great.

At Gyokusenji the author of their troubles made an effort to communicate with the "civilized" world. *I have now abandoned all hopes of seeing Commodore Armstrong, and I accordingly have made an effort to send some letters through the Japanese to Hakodate, hoping Mr. Rice may be able to forward them. . . . My letters were very short and very guarded, as I do not doubt the Japanese will open them.*

He sent a number of personal letters to friends, a plea for a ship to Commodore Armstrong, and an order for a hundred catties of oolong tea to Armstrong & Lawrence (one hundred catties was a hundred and thirty-three pounds; clearly, he had not been converted to the green tea of Japan).

He wrote to Commissioner Peter Parker and to all the United States consuls in Asia to let them know about his convention. And feeling that he had something to crow about, he finally wrote to Dutch envoy Donker Curtius at Nagasaki to give him the same news.

He also sent a bleak little dispatch to the Secretary of State, pointing out that he had been unable to draw any salary since he arrived in Shimoda. "The money that I brought to Japan is now exhausted," he concluded, "and I am reduced to the mortifying necessity of asking credit from the Japanese for my daily supplies."

All but the letter to Curtius he bundled up with two letters for Rice, one official and one personal. With his official letter, he sent a copy of his convention, pointing out that it authorized a vice-consul at Hakodate effective July 4, 1858:

> . . . it will be necessary to have your commission changed to that of *Vice Consul*, as the Japanese are very particular as to title.
>
> In the interim, I think you may fairly claim to remain at Hakodate under the Treaty of Kanagawa, which provides for the temporary residence of American citizens at Shimoda and Hakodate.
>
> I could not get from the Japanese Commissioners any formal promise that you should not be ordered away from Hakodate, but *it was understood* that you would not be disturbed, but not recognized in your official capacity.

The private letter said more—on most subjects:

> My dear Sir:
>
> Many thanks for your letter of May 17th; it is the first letter I have received since I have been in Japan. I have not heard from the Department since October, 1855, nor from China since last August. A bark from Boston, bound to the Amur River, came here in March, and by her I got a newspaper of November 8th, 1856, and learned the election of Mr. Buchanan; all but that is a blank to me. In pity to me give me what news you can from the U. S., from Europe, and from China. I will remain eternally your debtor. My official letter will show

you how your matters stand. Do not let them force you away, but claim to write to me and hear in reply before you leave. If you manage them quietly, I think they will let you remain. I am living very comfortably except my total isolation from everything civilized. I cannot give you any information in the chapter of women. Copper cannot be had here; the Japanese say they have no surplus beyond what they give the Dutch under their old contract. I do not know what the Dutch pay for copper nor the amount they get. I dare not enter into any particulars, *as I do not know who may read my letter before it reaches you,* but as soon as one of our men of war come here (if they ever come) I will visit you and then we can fully talk together.

(There followed a list of his letters and instructions concerning them. One letter was to Lühdorf, who had brought Harris's boxes and crates to Hakodate.)

I have offered Mr. Lühdorf $100 if he will bring my things here but if he cannot I have requested him to deliver them to you. *Please give him a receipt for the packages and the number of letters he may deliver to you.* I have particular reasons for asking this. I am surprised he should say I used him ill. I opened my house to him and he was constantly dining with me, in fact, the last dinner he ate at Shimoda was at my table, and he left me apparently well satisfied; he did not ask me to do anything for him, altho' I told him to command my services in any way I could serve him. I am astounded at his conduct.

The Governors of Shimoda have promised to write to the Governor of Hakodate to assist you in shipping my articles to me, should they be landed at Hakodate.

They will have to go to Edo as no trade between Shimoda and Hakodate is permitted except via Edo.

Pray let me hear from you soon.

Lühdorf had long since sailed from Hakodate, leaving Harris's freight. Since Rice's letters to Harris have not survived, we have no way of knowing Lühdorf's complaints against Harris. It will be remembered that Lühdorf had not been successful in trying to sell the Japanese a cargo of rifles, and perhaps this left him bitter. It seems, however, that Harris did not get along very well with any of the merchant traders who called at Shimoda; his parting with Captain Homer and Mr. Hall of the *Messenger Bird* had been strained, though he had been happy to see them arrive.

Most of the other American consuls in Asia got on very well with traders (most of the consuls were themselves merchants with whom the public business came in a poor second) but were frequently at odds with the Navy. With Harris the opposite was true. Having aspired to a professional career, he had been a merchant reluctantly (which may explain why he failed at it), and he seems to have felt superior to the traders who came to Shimoda, a feeling they no doubt sensed. But naval officers he regarded as professional men and government officials, like himself. To them he was truly cordial.

Elisha Rice—who would soon fit the norm by having good relationships with traders and bad with the Navy—was in the meantime getting along very nicely, if not exactly quietly, at Hakodate. The Japanese kept him under constant surveillance and sent a report to Edo every ten days, but they found little to complain about. The big man was unpretentious, gregarious, free and easy—in short, very unlike Townsend Harris.

He visited the Governors' riding ground, where he proved himself a good equestrian. He wanted to join the children at their folk dances, though the Governors' men dissuaded him. He tried to teach a tobacconist to make cigarettes. He encountered a man with a sore foot and gave him medical treatment.

He got a cow and milked her himself. He butchered pigs and gave pork to the Governor and his staff. He learned of an oven the Japanese had made to bake bread for shipwrecked sailors and had it moved at his own expense to his temple. He found the temple overrun with mice and asked permission to keep a cat; when the Japanese approved he promptly asked for two—his only act resembling a diplomat's.

He asked for a woman, but the Japanese reported that when they turned him down he merely looked shamefaced and said he hadn't been serious.

His first attempt at commerce fizzled but left no hard feelings. He asked for a sample of tea and then startled the Japanese by ordering more than 190,000 pounds of it for export, saying he assumed the price would go down for such a large quantity. Not at all, the Governors' men assured him: in Japan supply and demand were in such delicate balance that the larger the quantity, the higher the price—but not to worry, he wouldn't be permitted to buy the tea anyway.

He gave the Governor a set of a dozen drills used in shipbuilding, and when the Governor in return gave him lacquerware, eggs, and vegetables, he pleased his hosts by pronouncing the lacquerware the most beautiful he had ever seen anywhere.

And he kept asking about a ship to Shimoda so that he could send Harris's things to him.

Back at Shimoda, Inoue was preparing to go to Edo to face the music.

He must try to justify his and Nakamura's actions, and to wrest from the Great Council a decision on Harris's demand to present the President's letter to the Shogun. Inoue had hoped to be rotated to the capital, to spend the better part of a year with his family, in the center of things again. He had hoped to carry back a proud report of achievement. It had not worked out that way.

Jointly the Governors sent off a letter to the Great Council summarizing the situation and stating that Inoue would provide details, and their men passed the word to the town office about what was needed for the journey—supplies for the merchants to assemble and manpower for the first day (a new contingent would be drafted each night along the way).

In early-morning darkness on July 9 Nakamura dispatched by courier a brief confirming note: Inoue would leave today, accompanied by Moriyama and one servant. It sounded like a small party but that was to overlook the dozens of attendants and the great boxes of luggage.

A hundred and ninety-four men from the villages around Shimoda had been summoned to get that party on the road. In good military fashion they had been ordered to report the night before and had spent a futile night of waiting.

While the sky was still black a group led by an elder of Shimoda, with a representative of each of the villages, set out for the last village on the highway which was under the Governors' control; there they would provide the final send-off.

A little later all the other officials of the town and villages began assembling. They planted themselves, with due regard for precedence, along the road just outside Naka compound.

At dawn order emerged from confusion, the long procession filed out of the gateway, and along the road Hambei and the others kneeled and bowed to the ground.

The entry in Harris's journal sounds a trifle smug: *Shinano-no-kami started to-day for Edo for the purpose of reporting my refusal to deliver the letter of the President anywhere but at Edo, or to anyone but the Emperor. They assure me that it is quite preposterous to even think of an audience of His Majesty, as the laws of Japan forbid it. As it happens, they also told me that the Council of State could not write to any foreigners (the laws forbidding it); and, as the Council has written to me, I am shrewdly inclined to think that they will be found equally pliable in the matter of an audience.*

With Inoue gone and everything in abeyance until he brought back a decision, there was little for Harris to do but to brood on Commodore Armstrong's neglect and his own ill health, which invariably made the latter worse.

I do not make any entries of my walks and wanderings. In fact, I am too miserable to go out. I have a horse, but I do not use him, as it is impossible for any but a Japanese to use their saddles, and mine is snugly lying at Hakodate, thanks to Commodore Armstrong.

He did keep up his weather observations: *Tuesday, July 14, 1857. This has really been a shocking day—to make a poor pun. We had twelve shocks of earthquake—the first and sharpest one occurred at two A.M. and lasted about two minutes. It shook my bed so violently that it made it creak. Happily but little damage was done. Eleven shocks followed at intervals during the day, the last occurring at seven and a half P.M.*

I could not perceive any sensible effect on the barometer or thermometer, nor did an ordinary pocket compass show any particular perturbation, beyond what would be produced by a jar of similar force produced by any other means.

Yoheiji recorded the same tremors much more offhandedly—"small quakes all day"—but then he had other things on his mind.

There had been a great to-do over recompense for the salvage and stevedoring work on that ship from Shingu which lay at Sotoura. The first offer from shipowner Sanjuro had been rejected as a matter of course—it was much too small—and Yoheiji had sent a delegation to negotiate. They had done very well, substantially increasing the village's reward, and the evening of the next day, when Sanjuro returned to his inn at Kakisaki, he delivered eighteen *koku*, more than ninety bushels, of wet rice, which was distributed to the villagers at once.

Then the owner of the cargo arrived on the scene and all the negotiations had to be gone over with him. Just when everything seemed settled, the other villages that were entitled to share in the spoils complained that Kakisaki was taking more than its fair share. This led to more conferences at Sotoura and brought the Shimoda shipping agents into the picture as umpires. Predictably, Yoheiji was indignant at their handling of the investigation. They hadn't even visited the vessel, he sputtered, but had handled the whole thing from their office at Shimoda, and he wrote darkly of petitioning the Goyosho if the shipping agents didn't mend their ways.

The Shingu ship was not his only problem. Shichibei, assigned to Gyokusenji as sailor to scull the foreigners across the harbor whenever they wished, fell ill, and a substitute had to be found from the village's overworked labor pool. Yoheiji ended by giving double duty to Chugoro, who had the job of carrying drinking water to the temple.

Then Kosuke, Harris's "sweeper," became sick. Fortunately, Gyokusenji sent word that they required no substitute; his illness did not appear serious, just a rainy-season cold, and they would get along till he returned.

On a happier note, stonemasons started building a foundation for a new public notice board, something the village had been petitioning the Governors for ever since Yoheiji became headman. Now they could hope for bright new signs bearing the government's strictures and exhortations. Of course, everyone knew them by heart, but it was agreed that the old board, weatherworn and nearly illegible, gave the village a shabby and neglected air.

The rice, Yoheiji could write, was all transplanted. As the end of the job had come in sight the days had become sweltering, and the villagers had decided to finish in one great spurt by working all night under a full moon. So all through the night lanterns had bobbed among the paddy fields as old men brought seedlings to be planted, and tea and rice-balls to keep the planters going. Songs had echoed off the hills. Harris in his bed, Heusken and Ofuku in theirs, must have heard them.

> When your lover's watching,
> oh, show him how well
> you can work,
> your hands moving so swiftly.

Everyone took the next day off. It was usual to declare a holiday when the rice was all planted. This one was doubly earned because of the night's work.

In the afternoon the farmers on the hill held a party. Every man got as drunk as he liked, and those who felt like showing off sang and danced. It was noisy and bawdy and a great success.

The families along the shore held their own party. They hadn't planted as much rice as the farmers but they found an excuse to celebrate. They made their party a send-off for Masujiro, about to leave on his pilgrimage to Kompira. They toasted the young man until he was horizontal.

Yoheiji was pleased. Parties relieved tensions. Everyone would be better friends tomorrow.

There was one more traveler to see off, a personage important in the village. Buntatsu, priest of Daijo-in, the temple of the mountain religion, was leaving for Kyoto.

415

Shugendo priests (*a book illustration by Kokan*)

In the mountain religion—Shugendo—a priest's rank was based on the number of times he had carried out ascetic retreat in the mountains. Shugendo was weak in doctrine and paid not much attention to sacred writings. It was a direct and practical religion, and it placed great emphasis on ascetic practice.

There were two kinds of mountain priests. There were those like the man Harris had met on one of his first walks back in October and had described as *one of a class whose vow binds him to ascend all mountains he can meet with*. These men were constant pilgrims, wandering from one sacred mountain to another, living on alms or on the gifts of persons who might call them into their homes to use their arts of divination or exorcism against some evil that had taken hold there.

Other priests of Shugendo were like Buntatsu and his father before him. They were those who had settled in one place and founded a temple like Daijo-in. They ministered to a parish and entered deeply into the life of that community. Very often, again like Buntatsu and his father, such a priest married a woman who possessed the occult powers of a medium and then man and wife worked as a team. The wife, entering into a trance, revealed those spirits of evil which were causing sickness or misfortune; the priest used his mystic powers to combat them.

Buntatsu's parishioners might do all that was required of them merely by climbing certain mountains—especially those that had a sacred character—on a pilgrimage that was half holiday, half ritual. Indeed, Buntatsu might climb those mountains as a proxy for his people, and bring back to them the protective charms earned by the climb.

But much more was expected of him. He was obligated to withdraw deep into the mountains for periods of self-denial and contemplation, for a basic tenet of Shugendo was that by such practices man could eliminate his evil passions and penetrate to the true wisdom. Such retreats were not without their dangers: it was considered that in the mountains there were poisonous vapors, perhaps the breath of sinister spirits; against such vapors the Shugendo priest wore a distinctive cap.

Buntatsu had now completed the number of retreats required for advancement, and he was traveling to Kyoto for formal elevation to the next rank. His younger brother was accompanying him. It was an auspicious occasion and they were escorted out of the village with formality.

Hambei in Shimoda was keeping busy too.

The case of Iwakichi, the unfilial stonecutter, had come up. He was brought before two Goyosho officials, who took turns in remonstration while he bent before them. Wearing the awesome authority of the government, they gave him a tongue-lashing to remember all his days. Their finding read: "Iwakichi is not only at odds with his parents but is dissolute in conduct. Moreover, he is a heavy drinker and fails to fulfill his duty. He is due to be severely punished, but he has fervently pledged himself reborn, asking for leniency, and the authorities will keep pending the judgment on him. He shall be put in the custody of his kin until he proves to have truly reformed."

"All gratefully listened to the remonstration," according to Hambei, and then Iwakichi put his thumbprint to his oath, and the representatives of his kinfolk and of his neighborhood group submitted a pledge to keep close watch on him, and the stonecutter was released for one more chance.

The town office faced the usual budget of work relating to the American at Gyokusenji. There was a steady stream of orders: for sake, and for ducks; to replace the hoops on buckets; to build new chicken coops; for scarlet crepe to mend the foreign flag; for camphor. The camphor was supplied from the pharmacy Nagasakiya; the apothecary supposed it was for the Consul General, who, he understood, was usually ill.

Again, some tatami had to be re-covered (would foreigners never learn to take off their shoes?) and again Heikichi was called to repaper doors. This time he went without his little helper, but perhaps because of her he insisted on using the very best paper.

It did not make things in general any easier when the Goyosho ordered that the townspeople, if approached by any of the foreigners in town to shop, should speak only through a Japanese interpreter (it sounds as though Heusken's Japanese was becoming fluent enough to be trouble-some), and if no interpreter was present, should answer "I don't know" to all questions, and most particularly those about prices.

Hambei knew his people and he had serious doubts about how effec-tive this order would be. Old Unsho, for example, the artist who could paint holding his brush in his mouth, had never been known to admit ignorance on any topic in his life, and Hambei doubted that he could be trained to now.

Those Chinese continued to upset the economy. The butler Assam, while shopping for sweet bean-cakes, spotted three goldfish in the confec-tioner's shop and insisted on buying them at a hundred coppers each. And on another occasion he encountered a young fellow doing the lion dance in the street and gave him one *shu* to dance for him. The lad was accustomed

A stonecutter (*a book illustration by Jichosai*)

to receiving a few *mon,* and Assam had given him the equivalent of four hundred, a man's daily wages. Hambei wrote in his diary that the street artist danced one *shu's* worth, but this seems doubtful. He would have dropped in his tracks before he could dance that much, even though, as the Governor of Hakodate had explained to Rice, in Japan the price went up as the quantity increased.

Ominously, Tago village reported another vagrant *ronin,* this time from Satsuma Province. It was the kind of report which always made the Goyosho's constabulary look grave as they wondered about the safety of the unguarded foreigners at Kakisaki.

Meantime, Inoue and Moriyama were on the road to Edo. Moriyama, who had for several weeks been remiss about keeping his diary, now jotted down notes to mark their progress.

Their first night was spent at Yugashima, halfway up the peninsula and across the Amagi mountains. It is a hot-spring village, which was a blessing, for midday had brought heavy rains which soaked the travelers and made the mountain road treacherous and wearying.

There followed other lessons on the folly of traveling in the rainy season. After their night at Yugashima, the party marched in steady rain all day before reaching the town of Mishima on the Tokaido Road.

Next day they followed the Tokaido up and over the Hakone mountains and through the mountain barrier station, with the castle town of Odawara as their goal for the night. But just short of Odawara they found a bridge out and a mountain stream turned into a muddy torrent, and they were forced to halt at the village of Yumoto. There were compensations, for Yumoto is another hot-spring resort, but they had to wait there two full days.

On the sixth day of their journey they made the hour's trip into Odawara, only to be halted again because the river on the other side of town was flooded and unfordable. They spent all next day in Odawara, giving Inoue more time to worry over the reception he would meet in Edo.

By the time the highway authorities decreed the ford open he was more than impatient, and he set a hard pace until they reached the capital. It had taken them nine days to make a trip that had been scheduled for five. Nevertheless, they had reason to congratulate themselves on their timing. The night that they arrived in Edo the whole area they had traveled was lashed by the worst storm of the season.

Yoheiji wrote:

Rain began at eight P.M. and at midnight became heavy with a strong northerly wind. At dawn a ship in the harbor was discovered in danger of sinking and we mobilized thirty-five men and two fishing boats as a rescue party. We wanted to report it to the Goyosho but could not because the river was too high to wade. At the estuary at Shimoda several large boats are in distress.

At daybreak the house of Fujibei partially collapsed and protruded into the road. A little later Juemon's house collapsed and blocked the road there.

Hambei wrote:

At midnight the storm gathered force. At six in the morning all officials gathered at the town office. They intended to go to Naka village for a sympathy visit to the Governor but had to cancel the plan because of the flood. They made a round of visits within the town. At nine o'clock the flood receded and the headman and elders were able to get to Naka.

All day long, reports of shipwrecks came in. A ship from Totomi lost one of its crew and jettisoned its cargo of rice and beans. A ship from Edo lost a man and drifted helplessly onto the shore. The ship from Shingu at Sotoura, already damaged, was almost completely wrecked, as was another ship which had anchored there. Three boats were dashed onto an island at the mouth of the harbor. And the fishing boat of Genzo, out after bonito, was swamped while the crew struggled to bring it home. Most of the men were able to cling to the capsized boat until they were rescued, but Genzo had the hard duty of calling on Kichizo's wife to tell her that beyond doubt her man had drowned.

Again there was flood damage to clean up. It was soon discovered that a number of animals had perished in the storm. Hambei summoned the head of the *eta* village and ordered him to send men to clear them away.

And again the officials of Shimoda and the villages had to submit reports of damage. Governor Nakamura made an inspection tour.

Assam came bustling in from Gyokusenji with a broken umbrella. The cook, he said, had tried to go out in the storm to see whether his chickens were being washed away. He had no sooner got outside the door than he had been blown back in with his umbrella inside out. It must be repaired at once.

The town clerk gravely accepted the battered umbrella but assured Assam that there was no need for great haste. For quite suddenly, with the storm's end, the rainy season was over. The air was no longer sodden. Cicadas shrilled in every tree. It was summer.

As if to confirm it, there was a new moon and a new month. People

Fording the river at Odawara (*a print by Hiroshige*)

turned a leaf on their calendars and bade a relieved farewell to the second
Fifth Month of the year. (This was one of those years when an extra month
had to be inserted into the calendar. Twelve months of twenty-nine or
thirty days based on the phases of the moon simply did not make a full
year, and consequently every third or fourth or fifth year a thirteenth month
was inserted to bring New Year's back close to where it should be. This year
there had been two Fifth Months, both unpleasant, and folks were glad to
welcome the Sixth.)

On the first day of the new month the flag went up at Gyokusenji as
usual, and town and village officials visited Naka compound and the
quarters of the principal functionaries who lived in Shimoda to extend the
greetings of the season.

It was also the day of a minor and light-hearted festival. Convivial
bands puffed up the steep path to the summit of Shimoda Fuji, carrying
kegs of sake. At the top, with the panorama of the town and the harbor
beneath their feet, they broke open their sake, gave the god of the mountain
in his little shrine the first drink, and themselves the rest. It is taken for
granted that the god got roaring drunk that day, but he did not fall down
the mountain, as did some of those who toasted him.

In the town a major festival was approaching, that of the shrine dedicated to the god of the sea, who was entitled to particular deference in a place like Shimoda.

This year, however, there was a cloud over the festival. The Governors' office had received notice of a period of official mourning because of the death of a former Keeper of the Privy Seal of the Emperor's court at Kyoto. However powerless the Emperor's officials, their ceremonial rank was high. The Shogunate solemnly decreed mourning when one of them died. And so all noise-making was banned, and particularly the playing of musical instruments. A festival without noise and music is an impossibility.

"The festival, usually held the fourth through the seventh days, is ordered suspended this year except for the fourth day," Hambei wrote. "And even for this fourth day, the Governors' office is in no position to permit drumbeating and the parade of the god's vehicle because as yet no notice has been received from Edo that the period of mourning is over." Hambei and one of the elders went to the Goyosho to say that the parade would be postponed to the tenth day of the month. The official in charge told Hambei he would assign two extra patrol officers to keep order.

The youths of each block held strangely sober "services to wait the day." The day arrived and the vehicle was moved, but quietly, to its temporary sanctuary. On the next day the drum-carts, silent, were pulled past the shrine as the headman and town dignitaries watched.

Heusken joined them to see the sight. Perhaps he was restless after the excitement he and Harris had suffered through three days earlier. *Thursday, July 23, 1857. The cannon from the lookout hill was fired at noon to-day, and it caused such joy as can only be felt by those who have been living isolated, as I have been, for the past eleven months.*

That the signal cannon really was fired this day is confirmed by the diaries of Hambei, who recorded that the Goyosho ordered him to alert a pilot and make ready a boat for the boarding party, and of Yoheiji, who noted that Chuemon, ever edgy on such an occasion, climbed a hill, sighted the vessel, and reported to the guard station on the shore.

Chuemon was not, however, the first to the summit. *Mr. Heusken ran like a deer to the top of the signal hill . . .*

Heusken told it more dramatically, though he addled the date:

Today there is a cannon shot from atop the lookout mountain. This shot makes me thrill with joy; finally, after four months we shall see again the inhabitants of the civilized world. After two years without letters, I imagine an immense packet. I shall soon see my mother's handwriting. I shall know how she is, whether or not she is now happy

—if she can ever be happy in this world, poor dear soul! I shall hear from my friends. I shall soon know what is happening in the world. I leap from my chair; I dance and I sing; in spite of the heat of the vertical sun I climb at a gallop a neighboring mountain; I run to a certain promontory that juts into the sea and that affords an unlimited vantage point. Standing on the edge of the precipice I follow the line of the horizon, and penetrating the fog that floats over the waves, I discover far, far away the triple masts of a large ship. I return to inform the Consul of the happy results of my hike.

He started again for Vandalia Point (the most southern point) to watch her approach.

I climb again mountains and hills and scramble down again all day long . . .

At four P.M. he returned quite down-hearted. The ship had disappeared in the blue haze at a little after one o'clock and had not reappeared; she appeared to be standing about northeast. We are now in doubt what it can mean, but think she must be bound here, else why approach so near?

Friday, July 24, 1857. Up at daylight and off to the east hills that command a view of the Bay of Edo and the South Pacific.

Alas! No ship could be seen; whoever she was, it was clear she was not bound to Shimoda. I never had anything to try my philosophy so hardly as this.

I am inclined to think she was not the Flying Dutchman (as suggested nationally by Mr. Heusken) but simply a whaler, fishing along the coast. I wish the "blubber hunter" had kept a few miles further from land and spared us the excitement of hope and the bitter disappointment that followed.

A muted festival at Shimoda could scarcely compensate for all that, but Heusken was there.

On the seventh day of the Sixth Month (to Harris it was July 27), which ought to have brought the climax of the festival, officials could only permit a parade, and that short and quiet, by the youths of Ise Block, who this year had chief responsibility for the celebration.

The day was not without excitement, however. Suzaki Block's most celebrated fisherman, the wildly unpredictable Tokuzo, got into trouble again.

Tokuzo had a gift for trouble. The only thing that saved him was that he also had a gift for getting out of it. He loved to gamble, and on one occasion the police had found a gambling session in progress at his home. This was a serious offense but somehow he wriggled out of it, probably because the authorities saw little profit in prosecuting a town hero. But they set a watchman at his door to prevent a recurrence. On a wintry night the watchman was drenched from above by a bucketful of icy water. Somebody at the Goyosho must have been amused: the watchman was removed and nothing was done about his cold bath.

Tokuzo had a nickname. He was called Gokan-taba, which was the name for a string of copper coins. Stringing them through the hole in their centers was about the only way to make a pile of them manageable. Tokuzo liked to think he was called that because of his flair for settling disputes, his ability to put things in order. Sometimes he did show such a talent, but the nickname referred rather to his tendency to get all unstrung when fishing was bad.

Ordinarily he was a cheerful man, and he was a born storyteller. He had been known to spin one of Japan's great epic yarns for two days and two nights on a fishing boat far out at sea. And when foul weather kept the boats tied up, it was his house where fishermen gathered to while away the day with gossip and the nonsense they talked to keep their spirits up, while they tried not to remember an old song.

> Fine weather's still far off, far off:
> the offshore wind is strong.
> What's fearsome is the west wind that
> follows the offshore wind.

But when that killing west wind blew steadily and for days on end the boats could not go out, or when they went out and day after day brought back no fish, Tokuzo would fall into a black mood. He would become unnerved and irritable. His friends said that at times like those he went crazy, and that was why they called him Gokan-taba.

Today was a festival day and he was in a good mood, a little too good, for he had started drinking early. When the heat of the day got to him, he became quite disconnected. And so it was that when he was beset by necessity to relieve himself, the post he chose to water turned out to be a Goyosho constable.

He was apprehended on the spot and penned outside the town office —outside so that his worried friends and admirers could douse him with bucket after bucket of water. And his luck held, for when he was sufficiently sober to apologize, he was magnanimously forgiven (it was not the kind of case on which an officer of the Shogunate would relish submitting a report to Edo), and he was released into the custody of the leaders of his block, who promptly organized a party to celebrate.

The next morning's courier brought good news. Hambei was summoned to the Goyosho and told that the mourning was lifted. The festival proper might take place the next day. The youths of Ise Block paraded through the whole town to let everyone know, and got into only one fight along the way. Messengers were sent with invitations to all the villages.

Goyosho patrol officers were on hand by six the next morning. Town and village officials gathered by seven. At eight the vehicle of the god began its rowdy journey through the streets to the lusty tempos of the drum-carts. All day long the god and his attendants twisted through the town. In Shinden Block they were treated to sake. In Doshin Block the dancers and the drummers left the procession to sing and clap their way through the Goyosho and then went on to the quarters of Executive Officers Wakana and Matsumura and Superintendent Wakiya and finally to the tenements of the constabulary. It was late that night before weary town officials and even wearier patrol officers could tell each other that it was safely over.

Funeral at Shimoda: in the barrel-like coffin, the corpse was seated upright, legs drawn up (*an engraving from a drawing by Wilhelm Heine*)

The festival had brought no joy to the house of Kichizo. A circular had been received from Tago village stating that a man's body had washed ashore there, clothed in a cotton loincloth and a dappled bellyband. The men of his crew, his neighbors, had set off at once to bring the body home. Against a background of song and pounding rhythm to celebrate the god of the sea, a priest recited the service for one whom the sea had claimed, and Kichizo was buried beside his father and his grandfather, fishermen before him as his son and grandson would be fishermen after.

A fisherman was buried at Gyokusenji, too, but with a difference. Kyuemon had died in his bed with his family about him, full of years and honors. He was chief of Kakisaki's fishermen and an elder of his village. His son said that he was a victim of the storm, for he had gone out as soon as the worst had passed to inspect the damage and organize relief parties. He had tried to do too much, and he had collapsed.

The suddenness of Kyuemon's death embarrassed Yoheiji. A man was not supposed to die in office. The village oligarchy was supposed to be farsighted enough to replace a man before that happened, so that there would be no break in the continuity of government. When Yoheiji heard, his first act was to rush word to the Goyosho that Kyuemon had resigned. Then the headman dressed properly and went to the home to offer his condolences.

Next morning he sent Kosaburo to report the truth. For several moments the Goyosho official directed his gaze at a point somewhere above Kosaburo's head and then, without acknowledging that he had heard any mention of death, directed that a successor to Kyuemon be named immediately.

The men who were Kyuemon's neighbors were released from salvage work on the ships at Sotoura to take up their funeral duties. And again there was a ceremony outside Harris's rooms to remind him of the evanescence of life. It did not, however, produce in him any Buddhistic sense of resignation. He continued to stir things up.

It seems that both he and Heusken had been won over by the comfort of the Japanese kimono, or at least by the cool cotton robe of summer—strictly for wear at home, of course. (Is this additional testimony to Ofuku's brightening presence?) At any rate, the Consul General raised a fuss because a summer kimono he had ordered for himself was not made immediately, so that Kikuna, who had been advised that the foreigners' tailoring fell within his province, took the material away from one tailor and gave it to another, while Hambei warned the first man not to repeat such a blunder.

And though Harris had been drinking the water from Chuemon's well for eleven months, he now decided he didn't like it. He said he wanted his water brought from the spring at Buzan hill, about a mile away, or from the one at the temple Daianji, behind Shimoda and two miles distant. When informed of this, Chugoro, who had been in charge of the water supply, rebelled and announced that he no longer wanted the job. Yoheiji had to ask Gennosuke to find a successor. Harris continued to use his patented water filter from London, a brown earthenware vessel whose middle section was filled with charcoal.

Harris and Heusken together decided that their horses, which had been kept at the stable of the guard station on the shore, ought to be closer to Gyokusenji. Perhaps they learned from Ofuku, who was quite familiar with Shinzaemon's house by now since she stopped there every day before climbing the steps to the temple, that Shinzaemon had a sizable stable. They placed their request before the Goyosho, and the Goyosho passed the word to the village. Yoheiji and Gennosuke talked it over with Shinzaemon; he was one of the village elders and he exercised his right to grumble, saying he didn't want to stable the foreigners' horses any more than he wanted to provide a waiting room for their mistresses, but he didn't have much choice and the two horses were brought up. Shinzaemon promptly shifted the responsibility for them to his retired father. The rent, Heusken noted, was four hundred *mon,* or about eight cents, a month for each horse. The grooms, who were nominated by the Goyosho because it was considered that no farmer could take proper care of such fine horses, cost more: about $2.75 each a month, including their food.

Shinzaemon found himself even more deeply involved with the foreigners when he was appointed to tend their garden. Juemon, with one son off on a long pilgrimage and his house nearly destroyed by the latest storm, no longer had the time.

A month having passed since Okichi and Ofuku first reported to Gyokusenji, each received wages. Ofuku got the seven *ryo* two *bu* (say $10.35) called for by her contract, but Okichi's receipt is for only seven *ryo* instead of the ten she was supposed to receive. Since she was not reporting these days, perhaps Harris had negotiated stand-by pay.

Yoheiji and the elders conferred over Kyuemon's successor and decided it should be Yahei, fisherman and farmer. After permitting him a day to protest his lack of qualification, they wrung his consent from him. Chuemon carried the nomination to the Goyosho.

The salvage and stevedoring operations at Sotoura had been keeping as many as thirty men busy, and the village had hired eight *tengusa* divers to clear the bottom of the bay of the ships' fittings and cargo that had sunk there. Only after that work was nearly finished did the village have manpower enough to begin clearing away the landslides of the recent storm.

On the day for dragnet fishing, Kakisaki's fishermen netted, along with a satisfactory haul of smaller fish, two large *tai,* which were at once bundled up in seaweed and matting and carried by Chuemon to Naka as a gift to the Governor. Two days later a call from the compound's kitchen official was answered by Kosaburo, who was presented with one hundred *hiki* of silver, equivalent to a thousand copper *mon*. "We gratefully accepted the money," Yoheiji wrote.

In Edo, Inoue was encountering the criticism he had expected. He gathered that there were few men in the government who did not think they could have done a better job. There was only grudging acceptance of the convention, chiefly on the basis that since it was done, it could not be undone.

He prepared a report and handed it directly to Lord Hotta. He described the course of the stalemated negotiations and how each side now insisted it could not budge without violating its government's directives.

He went on to give his own views. He insisted that to invite Harris to Edo would be "to invite national disaster." The American would insist on presenting the President's letter to the Shogun, and then would immediately open negotiations for trade and additional ports. The Shogunate, however unready, would be forced to accede. Other nations would follow suit. Better delay, he advised, and tell Harris that the country was still uneasy about foreigners; better delay until the government had completed its investigation and come to a decision on foreign trade. Then negotiations could be opened at Shimoda.

Inoue hoped that his firsthand experience would give weight to his views. He lobbied for them at every opportunity.

In the meantime, there was pleasure in being at home, with his family, though he learned that his brother Kawaji was profoundly depressed by the course of events. Kawaji felt that his recommendations had been more often ignored than followed. In his frustration he had brooded about resigning, only to tell himself that he must continue to work for his country as long as he could. His pessimism was deepened by Lord Abe's illness; Inoue learned with dismay how serious it was. Several physicians had given up hope, Kawaji said, and the two men wondered aloud why this had to happen when Abe's knowledge and experience and skill at conciliation were so desperately needed. One day Kawaji told Inoue that he had received from Lord Tokugawa Nariaki a Mito family prescription, with the request that it be forwarded to the sick man. Inoue saw tears in his brother's eyes.

Chapter 14

AUGUST, 1857

Lord Hotta promptly circulated Inoue's report, asking for comments and recommendations. They soon began to come in.

The views of the officials who constituted the Tribunal were markedly conservative. They declared that to let Harris come to Edo would only bolster his confidence that he could get anything he demanded.

He insists, they went on, that he is a plenipotentiary with the authority to make decisions on all affairs, but assuredly he has no authority to make decisions contrary to the laws and systems of his country; yet that is what he is demanding that the Governors of Shimoda do. The Shimoda Governors are entrusted with the negotiation of foreign affairs, but they are not empowered to make major policy decisions about opening trade or changing ports, for such decisions are vital to the future of Japan.

We should wait, they argued, until Mizuno and Iwase have completed their study at Nagasaki, and we should come to a decision after serious and unhurried consideration. Only then should we negotiate with the American, and only at Shimoda. It was a solid vote for Inoue's views.

The two wings of Lord Hotta's committee achieved a certain amount of harmony. Despite their divergent views on the desirability of trade, they agreed that there should be no negotiations with Harris about a trade treaty until Mizuno and Iwase had completed their inquiry and the government had been able to develop an overall policy.

Toward such a policy, the *ometsuke* and *metsuke* had a couple of thoughts to contribute. They considered that it was unnecessary to conduct an elaborate study of what items in what quantities could be exported, adding, with more than a touch of scorn, that it was best to leave such questions to merchants; they were experts at making money. As for a new port, they again expressed misgivings about Osaka: it was too close to Kyoto and it was a city of rich merchants, administered by only a Governor who would be unable to manage all the problems that would arise. They believed that the new port should be near Edo, within the Shogunate's own territories, where it could be effectively managed. "How about Yokohama?" they asked.

But the committee split, as they had in the past, on the question of inviting Harris to Edo.

The finance chiefs said that to let the Consul General come to Edo and confront the heads of government would demean the Great Council, make meaningless the vermilion-seal powers issued to the Shimoda Governors, and demonstrate to the foreigner that he could get his way by threats. They insisted that the Governors must be admonished to try harder; they repeated the arguments that the Governors had already used with notable lack of success, but they contributed one new idea: if Harris persisted, he should be told that the government would send a letter explaining its position to the United States government and would wait for a reply before receiving the President's letter. As a delaying tactic, this had merit.

The *ometsuke* and *metsuke* agreed that it would be better if things could be settled at Shimoda. But they doubted it was possible, and they recommended that the Governors, if they found themselves unable to handle Harris, be empowered to invite him to the capital. There the Great Council, even while it parried discussion of a trade treaty, could receive the President's letter, could accord the Consul General the courtesies that seemed so important to him, and could flatter him by listening to what he had to say. Then, they wrote to Hotta, "you can explain our situation from the bottom of your heart."

In their view the government had nothing to lose and much to gain by this.

> Harris may hold a grudge now, but if you treat him with broad-mindedness and without vanity, if you question him about trade and the change of ports in a confidential manner as though you are seeking his advice on our relations with all foreign countries, he will as a matter of course come to compromise with you. Everyone has been aware that sincerity and friendliness were necessary, but the manner of negotiating has been such that the heart and the words were different.

To continue the same kind of treatment would lead to a critical situation, they insisted, and they suggested that Harris's threats, his frequent references to the war with Mexico, might not be baseless (perhaps America as a nation might be as hot-tempered as its envoy).

We regret to state [they understated] that the government's military preparations cannot be called complete. If the worst should happen, as the American official threatens, both government and people would have to bow to foreign orders. This would give a great opportunity to those who want to start a civil war. Examples of this can be seen in history. We, therefore, worried and fearful lest our country pursue such follies, present the results of our discussion.

A couple of other reports came in to the Great Council. Since both Nagasaki Governors were in Nagasaki, no quick reply could be expected from them, but the Hakodate Governor who was on duty in Edo had something to say.

He observed that Harris had become more and more impolite and abusive. But he had a slap for the Shimoda Governors too. He could see "that we, the Japanese side, do not always act with sincerity. At times we resort to artifice and stratagem, and the official, knowing this, makes use of it to counterattack."

He thought it doubtful that Harris would agree to put off his Edo trip for even a few months, and he doubted that Mizuno and Iwase would bring back a solution for every problem:

I hope you will consider that the President of the United States is acting out of friendship in sending a message. I hope you will make a fresh attempt to remove the official's misgivings. Those policies of ours on which we cannot make concessions should be made clear to him in frank discussion. If we can make him understand and accept our purposes, we should ask the United States to be a go-between in our dealings with other nations. We should also treat the Dutch respectfully and listen to their advice, for they have long been a friendly power. We must remember that our problem is not only with America, it is also with Britain and France.

And he expressed a familiar worry:

If we are forced into an emergency where we must capitulate, we will be responsible for bringing not only national disgrace but also destruction of our national law. I beseech you to give a swift opinion in line with these thoughts.

And, finally, the Great Council received the opinion of the honored doyen of government administrators, Tsutsui Masanori. Tsutsui had been the author of those long memorandums on the financial plight of the country and the samurai class. He was in semi-retirement now, but only a few months earlier he had been an *ometsuke* and member of the foreign trade committee. In 1854 and 1855 he had headed the delegation, including Kawaji, which had negotiated with the Russians. Kawaji had impressed the Russians, who spoke of his "sound mind, sharp-wittedness, astuteness, and experience . . . his cleverness in skillful dialectics." But Tsutsui had charmed them. "Such old men exist everywhere, in all nations," wrote one of the Russian officers. "Wrinkles surrounded his lips in rays. In his eyes, voice, in all features shone aged, intelligent, and affable goodness—the fruit of long life and of practical wisdom. Everybody who will see this little old man would want to select him as grandfather."

Tsutsui had been born in 1778, which made him eighty by Japanese count and almost as old as the United States. At eighty he had earned the right to be a little crusty. He reminded the councillors that it was he who had prepared the statement of the *ometsuke* and *metsuke* last year, recommending that Harris be permitted to come to Edo. He had thought the matter was settled, and now here it was all over again.

> I think that it is impossible to refuse his coming to Edo, because we have concluded a friendship treaty and we have permitted his residence. To postpone our answer may make him think Japan is acting against the treaty and drive us into the danger of war. If we should permit his trip only after being driven to such an extremity, we will lose all dignity. Reflecting on China's mistakes, we should permit him to come to Edo and to see high officials. This treatment will soften his heart.

At eighty a man has also earned the right to be a bit loquacious, and Tsutsui did run on. He had some ideas on how the journey should be managed, and what Harris was likely to ask for, including the right to bring in Christian priests and an American woman (the old man was out of touch: the woman problem was settled); he told the government that it ought to get its answers to these and other questions ready beforehand.

While all of the writers worried about Harris's conduct at the capital, for his rudeness and ungoverned temper were well known, Tsutsui—as one might expect of an old man—was the one most deeply concerned about etiquette. How could Harris be made to understand the class system on which Japanese society was based?—that, for example, when approached by a person of high station one must sit on the ground and bow; that ordinary officials could not request an interview with a lord; that meetings were held only at the request of high officials and then usually proceeded through intermediaries, so that even high officials did not often talk face to face. Harris must be made to understand that it would be almost impossible for him to talk with high officials directly—but how, Tsutsui fretted, how make this clear without offending him?

Inoue found something to make him uncomfortable in every one of these statements. Even the first, most conservative statement expressed concern lest he and Nakamura exceed their authority. The finance officials, including Inoue's brother, had urged that Inoue be admonished and had recited old arguments to use on Harris, as though the men at Shimoda were at fault for not making them sound convincing. The *ometsuke* and *metsuke* and the Governor of Hakodate implied that insincerity, even ineptitude, in negotiation had contributed to present difficulties. Old Tsutsui said that evidently the Governors of Shimoda were unable to make Harris believe what they told him.

Nor did the letters from Nagasaki, when they came, offer full-hearted support. Mizuno and Iwase held out no hope that their investigation would solve all problems. Additional study would be necessary and even then decisions would not be easy. Iwase suggested that he be allowed to go to Hong Kong to observe international trade in action.

Both he and Mizuno disapproved of the idea of suspending negotiations in the meantime. As a matter of fact, they asked permission to make a trade agreement with Donker Curtius: if they were successful it could serve as a basis for negotiating with other countries.

They also wrote informal letters which were long and chatty and transmitted the latest foreign news. They reported that the wars in China and India were growing more and more severe, speculated on the role of the Russians in abetting the Indian mutiny, and agreed that the British had their hands full for the moment and would not be coming to Japan this year. Iwase said that the policies of the Chinese would ruin their country, and Mizuno worried that once the British had taken care of China, they would come to Japan with a large fleet and a "firm and arrogant attitude."

They reported that England and America had begun to lay a telegraph cable between their two countries, that Russia had invented a new and more powerful artillery shell, and that France had developed an electric steamboat and had tested balloons.

The steam warship which Japan had ordered from Holland was to be delivered soon and was said to be a splendid ship. There were stories that the British had built a ship intended as a gift to Japan.

They both recommended that a schooner which had recently arrived at Nagasaki and been offered for sale be bought by the government. They suspected that it had secretly been ordered by a local daimyo, but they thought the government should step in and pre-empt it. "It will," Iwase wrote enthusiastically, "be the beginning of our prosperity."

Both always asked after Lord Abe's health. Both felt close to him, and were indebted to him for their appointments to high office. Iwase had begun as one of Abe's own retainers—a minor one, but Abe had spotted his ability and brought him into government service.

Iwase's letter of August 10 began: "What is the condition of Lord Abe? I have been deeply worried about his illness since last spring. Aware of the problems that weigh on our officials, I pray for his recovery. Please let me know how he is."

Iwase had no way of knowing that Abe had died four days earlier. He had been only thirty-nine years old.

There was gloom in the capital but no official mourning, for his death was not yet announced. He had died without a legal heir, and should that fact be recognized, his fief would have to be confiscated. He had had four sons but each had died while still a boy. When he realized he was dying he had asked and been granted permission to adopt a nephew, but the formalities were not complete. Until they were, the Shogunate chose not to recognize that he was dead.

So business continued as usual, and it was only the day after Abe's death that Hotta sent to the Shogun a summary of the various views on handling Harris. Each of the opinions deserved consideration, he said, but those of the *ometsuke* and *metsuke* and of the Governor of Hakodate appeared to have most merit. However, it was difficult to break a two-hundred-year-old tradition, and there was reason to fear that if Harris came to Edo he might behave too "freely," in accordance with Western customs, and therefore it seemed best to follow the line suggested by the finance chiefs: to admonish the Shimoda Governors to greater efforts, to try to keep Harris in Shimoda, and to sound him out on those important matters. It was an equivocal report, perhaps out of a wish not to excite the delicate Shogun, perhaps out of deference to the views of Abe, for it must have been prepared while he was still alive.

Lord Abe's passing had followed by only one day the death of Ishikawa, Nariaki's mouthpiece in Kyoto. Possibly he had been more than that: there are those who say that Abe had used Nariaki and Ishikawa as an unofficial line of communication with the Imperial court to explain Shogunate policy and to gain a measure of understanding and support. Certainly Abe had sought an entente with the court. Now Abe and Ishikawa both were dead and the government was more and more ignoring Nariaki. The bridges between Edo and Kyoto were tumbling down.

All this was depressing to men like Lords Matsudaira Yoshinaga and Shimazu Nariakira, who had looked to Abe as the greatest champion of reform and reconstruction within the Shogunate. The gloom in their mansions was deep.

Meanwhile, every day the time came nearer that some kind of decision would have to be made concerning the intransigent American and his demands.

Those busiest of writers, the *ometsuke* and *metsuke,* sent another memorandum to the Great Council: "It seems nothing has been done. It will increase the displeasure of the American official that the government gives him no answer. If an American ship sails in, by which he can report to his government, Japan must surely face difficulties."

Trying to blast away the tradition of seclusion, they invoked the founding spirit, the first and greatest Shogun of them all, Ieyasu. He had been no isolationist, they reminded the councillors. When a Dutch ship had reached Japan in 1600, he had brought its Dutch and English officers to the court and permitted them to stay in Japan. He had concluded a friendship treaty with Korea, he had opened communication with the Ryukyus. He had received letters and gifts from countries ringing the China Sea and from as far away as England and the Netherlands, and he had always sent letters and gifts in return. In a letter to Cambodia, he had written that the peoples of the countries around Japan were brothers to him. "We should revere him for his profundity in making Japan prosperous through friendly relations with foreign countries."

It was not until the third Shogun, the writers pointed out, that foreign trade appeared to have become only a veil for plots against Japan's social system and independence. It was the third Shogun who had made seclusion the national policy. The people had welcomed it, and as their prosperity increased, the inconvenience of being cut off from the rest of the world had disappeared. This action of the third Shogun was a demonstration that government policy must change with the times.

And now times had changed again. Now all foreign countries traded with each other, increasing their wealth and armaments. All expected Japan to emerge from her isolation.

> To refuse cannot benefit our country. The government has gone so far as to permit the American official's residence, yet there is still a lingering attachment to the old policy. This policy will arouse the doubt of learned persons both at home and abroad, for it is clear that we can never turn back to seclusion.
>
> We should follow the policy of the first Shogun. We should invite the

American official to Edo at once. If he can meet with the Shogun, if he is treated courteously and respectfully, he will change his stubborn attitude and become amenable.

If the government invites him only after being forced to, he will think he has won through his obstinacy. It would be unwise of the government to make him think so.

When the government decides to invite him, we will do our best to manage his trip. Even if he should behave rudely, the government should treat him as politely as possible; if his rudeness should pose serious problems we will do anything necessary to put a stop to it.

And having stated their case as eloquently as they knew how, they waited, like the others, as Edo lay baking under the August sun.

Around Shimoda, too, things moved slowly, to a tempo set by the drowsy hum of the cicadas.

In Kakisaki, Yoheiji and the elders were giving much attention to preparations for the forthcoming festival of their village. In July, after a series of long and involved discussions, they had decided that the festival instruments and the vehicle of their god should be renovated, and they had loaded them in a fishing boat which had carried them around the tip of Izu to Matsuzaki and a craftsman there; perhaps he gave them the best price or perhaps resentment against Shimoda was so strong that the villagers did not want Shimoda men handling the objects of their shrine. Now the repairs had been completed. Another boat was sent to Matsuzaki, and the next afternoon most of the people of Kakisaki assembled on the shore to greet it as it returned. With relief the instruments were installed in the shrine again.

In the meantime Gennosuke and Yahei had been summoned to the Goyosho and informed that Kyuemon, because he was "ill," was being relieved as an elder of the village and that Yahei was appointed to succeed him. With that little ceremony finished, the two men called at the residences of Governor Nakamura and other senior officials to report the new appointment and to present at each house a fan bearing Yahei's name and new title.

The time was drawing near when Priest Buntatsu of Daijo-in would be returning from Kyoto, confirmed in new and higher rank. Arrangements had to be made for his reception.

Late one evening the retired priest and his wife, Buntatsu's father and mother, arrived from Shirahama. That village was part of Daijo-in's parish and the old couple often visited there now that they had relinquished their duties. Obviously, they wished to be on hand to welcome and congratulate their son. This was understandable, but it caught Yoheiji and the elders by surprise, and hastily next morning they conferred with the elders of Sotoura to devise a proper greeting. The old priest and his wife commanded great deference, both because of their age and because, though retired, the aura of mystical power still surrounded them. When the village officials called to pay their respects, the old priest responded graciously but his wife seemed scarcely aware of what was happening. Yoheiji thought that she had aged very rapidly.

Two days later Buntatsu's younger brother appeared. Having notified the village that the priest would reach Rendaiji that afternoon, he returned there himself. Rendaiji village was scarcely an hour from Kakisaki, but the priest would spend the night there (and enjoy the hot springs) in order to give his people time to organize their welcome. Yoheiji sped word to Sotoura and Shirahama.

Next day Yoheiji recorded:

> Shinzaemon, the elder, representing the village officials, and the leaders of each neighborhood group, went to Rendaiji to greet the priest of Daijo-in. We mobilized two horses, each led by a man, and six young lads to escort him on his way back to Kakisaki. Ten officials from Shirahama and three from Sotoura, as well as all the farmers of our village, went out along the beach road to welcome him home.

After a day of rest from his travels, the priest called at the Goyosho to deliver to the Governors' religious affairs officer the document confirming his promotion. The elders of Kakisaki escorted him with pride. After completing the ceremony at the Goyosho, the priest announced that in commemoration of his visit to Kyoto and his advancement, he was changing his name from Buntatsu to Kentatsu. Yoheiji saw to it that a report of this went promptly to the Goyosho. There remained for Kentatsu to make a round of formal calls to report on his trip. These he took care of over several days. In August's heat there was no need to hurry.

The people of Kakisaki returned to mundane chores. Led by the owners of the ships' inns, the village undertook to clear its anchorage of hazards to ships. *Tengusa* divers hired from Suzaki and Sotoura located dangerous rocks and attached hooks and ropes; Kakisaki's seamen in fishing boats tugged the rocks out of the way. Sometimes village officials went out to oversee the operation. It was a pleasant way to pass hot summer days.

In Shimoda, Hambei passed out an assignment not so suitable for a hot summer day. On orders from the Goyosho he sent two top seamen and a town elder for instruction in gibbeting a criminal's head.

The headman also recorded another series of emergency calls for a physician from the jail, where the sailors of Tarojiro's ship were still undergoing interrogation. This time it was Captain Matsugoro and the apprentice lad Kikutaro who were ill. Then he wrote that Matsugoro had died. Tarojiro, who was still staying in Shimoda, was notified, and with one of the elders he reported to the jail to claim the body. The Goyosho was running out of defendants before they had a case to take to court.

By far the most exciting news of the month for the townspeople was a notice that a troupe of sumo wrestlers from Edo would stage a tourney in the town. The shrine would be the sponsor; the priest was busy organizing a committee. The boys of the town prepared to go out along the road to greet their ponderous heroes with more joy though less formality than ever their elders met government officials.

Gyokusenji and its inmates figure very little in Hambei's diary for these days. It was noted that Assam, after making several purchases from a tailor, gave seven coppers to a child he found in front of the shop. And on August 8 Hambei wrote that Okichi had recovered from the infection that had caused her to be furloughed, but that when this was reported to Harris he stated that he was ill and wanted her to wait at home for his recovery. A week later, when queried again, Harris gave much the same reply.

Harris's major excursions these lanquid days were from the temple to his belvedere, where he could sit watching the harbor entrance for ships that never came. We hear very little of life at Gyokusenji in August, except concerning Heusken's adventures with the horses.

> August 1, 1857. . . . The reason I haven't used my steed yet is that I have been expecting daily an English saddle from Hong Kong, for the Japanese saddles do not suit me at all. Tired of waiting, I have a cotton blanket, thickly quilted, made here. It is to be attached under the horse's belly, in the manner of our saddles. . . .
>
> I went horseback riding this afternoon. The roads are abominable. Every dozen steps you must go up or down. The roads are strewn with stones and holes. You can go only at a slow pace and there are only three paths, the longest of which does not exceed half a mile, where one can risk a trot or gallop. My improvised saddle is even more uncomfortable than the road and keeps sliding under the belly of the horse.
>
> August 2, 1857. After another ride, I discover that the Japanese, in order to tie the two ends of my so-called saddle, have used only one rope, which, as you might easily conceive, has cut into the back of my horse in a frightful manner. Since it is very hot, one or two months will have to pass, possibly, before I can use him again.
>
> August 8, 1857. The Consul was kind enough to loan me his horse,

while mine is incapacitated. To top off all my troubles that horse, while stepping down a steep grade (an ordinary thing on those abominable roads of Japan), slips and wrenches the muscles of his right shoulder. According to the opinion of the veterinary surgeon, he will be lame for the rest of his days. . . .

A veterinarian (*a book illustration by Jichosai*)

All this brought about Harris's first journal entry of the month: *Saturday, August 15, 1857. Mr. Heusken, having extemporized a saddle and bridle, has been riding for some time past. As he is somewhat inexperienced in riding, he has laid his horse up with a sore back and I lent him mine until he should recover. The second time he rode out with him a difference of opinion arose between Mr. Heusken and the horse,—the latter wishing to return and Mr. Heusken to go on. Then ensued a trial of force vs. obstinacy, which ended in the horse slipping his shoulder and thus disqualifying himself from ever being mounted again. I ordered the poor brute killed, but no one would perform the butcher's part. As I had parted with my last revolver, I could not shoot him, and I could not bring myself to cut his throat like a butcher. At last by great good luck I succeeded in giving him away!!*

Think of that! Ye Knackers of London and Masters of the Abbatoir at Montmartre and manufacturers of "real bologna" sausages in Germany! What a country it is for you, where it is considered a favor to accept a horse as a gift with full privilege to "look in his mouth."

Harris had run up against his neighbors' Buddhist scruples against taking life, and also, apparently, against a reluctance to tell him of the existence and role of the *eta*.

Back in Edo, the death of Lord Abe was formally announced on August 16, the matter of the heirship having been cleared up. He was buried on the twenty-second. Early in the morning a procession started from his mansion in the most ceremonious fashion, as though he were still alive and reporting for duty. But this time the retinue wound not to the castle but to a quiet temple in the suburbs. Only after entering the temple gates did the train become a funeral cortege. Under an opaline midsummer sky they buried the man who had worked and worried himself to an early death in his country's service. He had written, when Perry appeared:

> Day in and day out
> I am full of anxiety
> over the black shadow
> which the Black Ships
> cast on our country's future.

His days of anxiety were over but the black shadow remained. Mourning could not stop the conduct of necessary business at the castle. On the eighteenth the Great Council issued a set of orders to Inoue.

They were bewilderingly contradictory, as orders can be when a government is trying to placate all factions and, anyway, relies more on spoken than written orders. There is little doubt which order Lord Hotta told Inoue to act upon. That one began: "We have decided to permit the American Consul's trip to Edo. . . ."

It was as if Hotta had been waiting for Abe's death to make the decision that Abe had never approved.

Qualifications followed, of course. The invitation could not be extended at once, for laws had to be revised, and some officials still objected, and Harris had not been in Japan very long. If he insisted on making the trip at once, he was to be told that there was no intent to offend him or his country and that the Japanese government would send a letter to his government explaining the delay.

Inoue must probe to learn those important matters. If, as everyone supposed, they turned out to be the opening of trade and a change of ports, he was to be told that the government had already made a decision to proceed with these but that no discussion would be undertaken until its studies were complete. And such issues would be decided not by the Governors of Shimoda but by all the high officials of the government.

Inoue's reply was delivered the next day:

I told the Consul General that I would give him the final answer concerning his trip to Edo on my return. About forty days have passed since I left Shimoda, and I have heard that he is angry at the delay. I must give him an answer at our first meeting.

If we tell him that his trip will be permitted after he discloses his important matters, it will be impossible for him to postpone telling me about them. I think we should make him realize that he cannot come to Edo to present the President's letter directly to the Shogun without first revealing those important subjects he wishes to discuss.

If they are the beginning of trade and a change of ports, and he insists on opening negotiations, I will answer as I have been ordered, but to tell him only that both subjects are under investigation will certainly make him think the government is procrastinating and has no intention of negotiating. I will tell him that these matters are outside my province, but once the subject is broached I will have to give him at least a date for opening trade. If I can do this, it will be possible to conduct our meetings smoothly. Any other course will only increase his annoyance. His anger will disrupt our meetings; the embroilment will reflect on the dignity of the Japanese government and make it impossible for us to achieve our objectives.

Please give me your answer as soon as possible. Having received it, I will proceed to Shimoda by ship.

The government was moving now with dazzling speed. Copies of Inoue's memorandum went out at once, and with them a suggestion, probably Inoue's, that if a date had to be set for opening trade, it be eighteen months hence. Lights must have burned late in Edo offices that night, for the next day the comments came in.

The *ometsuke* and *metsuke* said they thought an eighteen-month delay was unreasonably long. This postponement would only offend the American official and increase the anxiety of the nation. Since Americans had already been granted permission to reside at Shimoda and Hakodate in the Sixth Month of next year, why not offer to open trade then? (And they added snappishly that the Shimoda Governors should be directed to pay attention to the orders given them and to heed their great responsibility.)

The finance officials said they had always believed that it would be best to avoid letting the American official come to Edo, for other nations would demand the same treatment, with evil results, but they realized that the decision was made. As for the eighteen-months proposal, they understood the argument, but if an arbitrary date was set and then it was necessary to make a postponement for some unavoidable reason, it would reflect unfavorably on the government: they hoped any deadline could be avoided.

The officials of the Tribunal advised against setting any date for any action: time was needed and delaying tactics were in order. The Governors could say that no negotiations could be opened until Mizuno and Iwase returned. They were sure that would satisfy the American.

On the following day Hotta called in Inoue and handed him an endorsement to his letter, which read:

> The problem of the Consul's trip must be handled as I have directed. The issue of the date for opening trade is not one to be decided between you and the Consul. But if you should be driven into a situation where you cannot help giving him an answer, the date must be at least eighteen months later.

He gave the Governor another order: return to Shimoda, confer with Nakamura about the government's decisions, and try to extract from the American what he means by "important matters." Hotta added verbally that the Governors were to be particularly careful in the forthcoming talks.

Hotta was moving almost impatiently now. On that same day—the anniversary of Harris's arrival at Shimoda—he directed the various bureaus to make plans for the American's trip to Edo. It was the second such order he had issued, but this one had a no-nonsense tone. He wanted immediate recommendations on the journey itself—route, accommodations, attendants, guards, and emergency arrangements—and on the stay in Edo: on the Consul's quarters and how to manage and guard them; on his food and his sightseeing; on the formalities of his reception at the castle; on the place for negotiations and the proper dress for them (in other words, just how ceremoniously Harris was to be treated); on the proper gifts to him from the Shogun and Great Council; on the manner of notifying the Emperor and the houses related to the Shogun; and on anything else that came to mind.

On the same date Hotta sent to Mizuno and Iwase some reference material which would be very pertinent to their talks with Donker Curtius: translations made at Shimoda, from Harris's book, of treaties between the

United States and Russia, France, and China, the latter including a schedule of taxes and custom duties.

On the following day, after attending Lord Abe's funeral, Inoue left for Shimoda on the schooner returned by the Russians. With him were his son, coming for a visit to his father's post, Moriyama, and a legendary figure of those times, Nakahama Manjiro.

When Manjiro was a fourteen-year-old in a seacoast village, some sailors coaxed him to come along on a short voyage, and he climbed aboard without his parents' knowledge. The boat was caught in a storm and disabled; it drifted for a week until it touched a small uninhabited island. He and the four other survivors were rescued by an American whaler and carried to Honolulu. The four were left there, but the captain had grown fond of Manjiro, and practically adopting him, took him home to Fairhaven, Massachusetts. In the next ten years the young man received an American education, signed on for a whaling cruise and rose to be first mate of his ship, joined the California gold rush, and finally made his way back to Japan, braving the danger that under the exclusion edict he might be executed. He was not executed; he was questioned at Nagasaki and then sent home to his village on the island of Shikoku.

His daimyo decided to utilize his knowledge and made him a low-ranking samurai to dignify the relationship. Then Perry arrived, and the Shogunate sent in haste for the one man in the realm with a thorough firsthand knowledge of these foreigners. Lord Abe and Kawaji had the idea of using him as an interpreter in dealing with Perry, but Nariaki prevented this. A man like Manjiro, the Elderly Lord asserted, could not help having divided loyalties, and so Manjiro never got close to the Americans, though later he was made curator of the gifts Perry had brought—the little railroad train, the telegraph set, and all the rest. He was used, too, as a teacher of navigation and seamanship, which was probably his position on the schooner, and he was very likely the instigator, through Kawaji, of at least one of the incidental orders Inoue was carrying back to Shimoda: whaling, it said, would be very profitable for Japan and would also provide training in seamanship; the Governors were to negotiate with Harris for a completely equipped whaler and Americans to teach its operation. The scheme never came to much. It turned out that Harris knew very little about whaling and showed no interest in getting the information they wanted.

It was only after the order was out to prepare for Harris's visit, only after Inoue had sailed, that old Tsutsui realized that the plan was to let Harris appear before the Shogun himself. He was horrified. He could be liberal enough on the subject of receiving Harris in the capital and paying him the respect due a foreign emissary, but to let him see the Shogun's person would ravish every canon of the creed of ceremony and etiquette the old man had lived by. It would, for him, rip the national fabric. For the first time he was ready to think about war as an alternative to the visit. It would be, he admitted, a very difficult decision, for the internal situation was most disturbed. The earthquakes and storms of recent years had caused great distress, and not a small number of people were restless and discontented. In such difficult times, if the United States sent battleships to attack Japan, perhaps the defenses around Edo might hold up, but in that case the ships could easily withdraw and attack elsewhere. To fortify the entire coastline would impoverish the country and lead in turn to further confusion and a breakdown of order which local officials could not check. The country would become as riotous as China. He was, he went on, acutely aware that Japan had not yet achieved wealth and military strength. It was best to concede enough to keep the foreigners from resorting to arms—if only that did not include reception by the Shogun. He worried the problem at great length, doggedly weighing each alternative, though like the good soldier he was he presented his ideas on how to conduct the ceremonies if the Great Council went through with its plan. Those were only rough ideas, he concluded. He could do better after further study.

Word had been received at Shimoda that Inoue was returning by sea. Hambei sent men to clean the Governor's residence, and Kakisaki men kept a watch for the ship (interrupting the search they had been ordered to make for a man who had fled Shimoda after poaching birds).

Unfortunately, Inoue's bad luck as a traveler continued. The schooner ran into head winds and took two days to make a trip that usually required but a few hours. It was not until the twenty-fourth that it was sighted off Shirahama. Kakisaki and Shimoda sent fishing boats to the harbor mouth to tow the vessel in, but it made port at Sotoura as darkness was falling, and Kosaburo, Gennosuke, and Yahei rushed there to escort Inoue to his residence.

Next morning the village contributed two fishing boats to the little fleet that towed the ship around the promontory and into the harbor, while Gennosuke again hiked to Naka to express Kakisaki's gratitude at the Governor's safe arrival. That eliminated Gennosuke from the delegation that made a round of visits to give thanks for the successful completion of the village's festival a few days earlier. There is no indication that Harris or Heusken had come to watch, though they could scarcely have been unaware of the noisy cavalcade that escorted the newly refurbished vehicle of the god in its procession along the shore and up the hill to the farmers' houses and back down again and finally with a tumultuous rush into the cleansing, purifying sea.

Inoue sent off to Edo a report of his arrival, and then set out with Moriyama to call on Harris. He apologized for appearing empty-handed, explaining that his gifts had not yet arrived. He hoped they would not be as badly delayed as he had been, and he explained how the weather had marred his trip both going and returning.

He told of Lord Abe's death, and how, before he died, Abe had asked him, Inoue, whether the American official had the spirit of *jin*—of benevolence, compassion, sympathy—and how he had answered that the American did indeed have such a spirit (probably telling himself that a little lie was forgivable if it would comfort the dying man).

Although his mission had been delayed by Abe's illness, he had given the government a full report, he told Harris, and had received instructions, and was ready to open talks at any time. But since tomorrow was the seventh day of the Seventh Month and a holiday, he suggested that they meet the day after, and they agreed on the hour of eleven.

The holiday festivities began at nightfall, for they celebrated the once-in-a-year meeting of the stars known in the West as Vega and Altair. Vega, the Weaver Princess, was the daughter of the Celestial Emperor, who chose for her husband Altair, the Herdsman Prince. Because the two fell so deeply in love that they quite neglected their duties, the angry Emperor punished them by decreeing that they must live apart, on opposite banks of the River of Heaven—the Milky Way—save for this one night of the year. On this night magpies flocked together and with their outstretched wings formed a bridge over the river so that the princess could cross to her prince.

Woe to any magpie found loitering on earth the day of the festival: children pelted it with stones to punish it for its truancy. Otherwise it was a gentle festival which called for love poems, written on colorful strips of paper and hung from branches of bamboo. It was appropriate to pray that one's daughters would become skilled at weaving and other household arts. In Edo, girls vied at such tricks as threading seven needles with one pass of the thread, but at Kakisaki humbler arts held sway: it was said that washing on this day made clothes cleaner than on any other day of the year. The young men's association entered into the spirit of things by cleaning wells.

It was a day for doing things by sevens. Kakisaki people liked to eat seven times and to swim in the sea seven times, saying this would make them strong. This year some of the men were unable to complete their

Sumo wrestlers *(a print by Shunsho)*

schedule, for another of the government's schooners put in at Sotoura. This one carried Inoue's baggage, including his gifts for Harris, and the men had to go help unload her.

The holiday weather was skittish, alternately sunny and showery, but it did not diminish the crowd at the sumo matches in Shimoda. The tournament was in full swing. Its sponsors had petitioned the Goyosho for permission to hold the event nearer the center of town than the shrine compound in order to attract more people. The petition granted, the arena had been constructed, the schedule approved, and the town elders had indited an oath that order would be maintained and gambling prohibited. The latter bit of nonsense having been solemnly proffered and solemnly accepted, the tourney had been opened with ancient ritual and a prayer by the shrine priest. It was now in the eighth day of its eleven-day run and the tension, and wagers, were mounting as the number of possible winners narrowed to three or four of the great-bellied contestants.

The weather worsened the next day, but in the morning Moriyama made his way through rain to deliver Inoue's gifts: for Harris, a set of porcelain sake bottles and cups and a pottery dish, and for Heusken, a length of fine silk to make a Japanese jacket (Inoue knew by now that Harris *did* drink and that Heusken was something of a dandy).

The gusty wind raised whitecaps in the harbor. The schooner that had brought Inoue was scheduled to sail back to Edo. Manjiro and the crew tried and gave up.

Harris's conference with the Governors was, like the weather, squally. Heusken described it:

> The Prince of Shinano begins by saying that, after many objections and difficulties, the High Council has finally agreed to receive the Consul-General in Edo. But, he added, you cannot hand the letter of the President to the Shogun himself; however, the High Council will accept it for him.
>
> The Consul answers that he must give the letter to the Shogun personally.
>
> The Governors reply that it cannot be done, that the Shogun never treats personally, but that all business goes through the Council of State . . .

Before going on, the Governors cleared the conference room of all their retinue except the executive officers and Moriyama. Then they told Harris that of the daimyo (as Heusken described them, "princes, independent, or at least halfway so"), eighteen were quite set against the Shogun's personally receiving the letter and "that to grant what the Consul General is asking for would create disturbances in the Empire. If the Consul is not satisfied with the last offer of the Council, then a letter will be written, addressed to the Secretary of State in Washington, in which the above-mentioned reasons will be set forth and the Consul will be asked to kindly forward said letter."

This proposition could not have been attractive to Harris but he put on a brave front: "The Consul answers that he will gladly forward any letter they will be pleased to entrust to him. 'But I can assure you,' he said, 'that it will be of no avail. I had always believed Japan to be a single united Empire and its government to have the power to command obedience.'"

Harris told the Governors what they already knew, that these formalities were of concern not only to his country but also to Russia, Britain, France, and the other powers. He tried to draw a comparison with China, which, he said, had brought its troubles on itself by refusing to receive foreign envoys in Peking, a comparison blunted by the fact that the Governors had already told him he could go to Edo. And he insisted that it would not be the first time a Shogun had received an ambassador. "The

Governors answer that they have leafed through all ancient documents and archives but have not been able to find any such occurrence." And they attempted without success to get Harris to reveal those "important matters."

The trip back to Kakisaki was uncomfortable whether by *kago* or by boat. It sounds as if Shimoda was being brushed by the edge of an early typhoon. The rain was heavy, and even within the harbor the water was so rough that when a Goyosho official came to Kakisaki with an order for the Kimizawa ship which had arrived yesterday at Sotoura and had by now been towed to Kakisaki's anchorage, Gennosuke and Hikoemon and four sailors had great difficulty getting him out to the ship and back. And then the weather was so bad that he stayed at Yoheiji's house that night.

The next day was clear but still so windy that a boat from the schooner was swamped when it was returning from shore, and one of its sailors drowned.

The day's conference achieved no more than yesterday's. The Governors, Heusken recorded,

> reiterate several times their request that the Consul be kind enough to inform them of that important business. "For," they add, "if you refuse, we may not be able to meet again in such a pleasant manner."
>
> The Consul, angered by that answer, asks whether they intend to threaten him? [and says] that threats make no impression on him. They could put him in a cage, [but] he will always remain faithful to the honor which he owes his country. It was explained to us later that these words: "We may not be able to see you again in such a pleasant manner" were not a threat but a Japanese idiom that refers to harakiri. In other words, the Governors will be forced to cut open their own stomachs and die if they cannot transmit a satisfactory answer to their government.

The two sides were still having difficulty understanding each other. Having talked themselves to a standstill, they agreed to a few days' adjournment to think things over.

Harris took advantage of the lull to prepare another packet of correspondence. *The Japanese inform me that all the American ships left Hakodate in June, so my letters sent there cannot go by them. I have made duplicates of all those letters and sent them to Nagasaki, writing to Mr. H. Donker Curtius, requesting him to forward them by one of his ships.* After more than a year he had finally decided to use a channel of correspondence that had been open to him all along.

As for Okichi, he decided to terminate the relationship. The Goyosho passed the word to Hambei that she was no longer needed.

It had been a brief affair. She had reported to Gyokusenji only three days and since then had been waiting for another call. Nor had it been as profitable as the girl had been told it would be. Since her initial payment of twenty-five *ryo* she had received only seven *ryo*, though she had been in Harris's service for two and a half months and her contract called for ten *ryo* a month.

Under the circumstances, Hambei felt perfectly justified in couching in the strongest possible terms the petition which the town office prepared for Okichi and her family.

To the Honorable Officials of the Goyosho:

When it was decided a while ago that Kichi be sent to Gyokusenji as personal maid to serve the American official there, your authorities explained the circumstances leading up to that decision.

However, since it was our first experience in offering a woman to serve a foreigner, not only Kichi herself but all of her relatives found it difficult to accept the decision. They asked for the best efforts of the authorities concerned to have her relieved of that duty, only to find that the town officials were being pressed hard to carry out the decision.

Kiwa, the aged mother, and Kichi, her daughter, at that time had no fixed work besides doing the laundry for the sailors who manned the ships operating to and from the Osaka area. In the hope, therefore, that, if Kichi was paid an appreciable wage for her services at Gyokusenji, she and her mother would be assured of a reasonable living, we defied the objections of her other kinfolk to accept the decision of your authorities, and Kichi assumed her duty at Gyokusenji.

At that time she had an abscess on her body, and after three nights of service she was ordered home to take care of it. In due course she was cured and a report to that effect was made to the authorities. It was then learned that the American was sick.

Thus she lost her job, but having sold herself to a foreigner, neither she nor her mother will be able to obtain work from her fellow Japanese, much less can she return to being washwoman for sailors.

Such being the case, we hereby beg your authorities as a special favor to help Kichi and we will be greatly obliged if they can meet our humble request.

(signed with fingerprints)
Kiwa, a widow, care of Ichizo
Sogoro, elder brother of Kichi

I hereby affirm that the above statement is true in all respects.

(signed)
Hambei, Headman, Shimoda Town

Okichi was, of course, not a washwoman for sailors. This was a euphemism. But how degraded Okichi must have felt. If she was the girl of spirit and standing we have supposed her to be, the experience with Harris must have been hard on her. It was not only that he was a repugnant foreigner and an old man to boot, not only that her vaunted right to choose her own customers had been shattered; she had dismally and publicly failed to please. If there had been any doubt that she, like her father, would end as an alcoholic, there could be doubt no longer.

Ofuku, in contrast, was doing very nicely. On August 23, for example, she turned in to the Goyosho "two large dollar coins" which Heusken had given her as she left Gyokusenji that morning. She was given the Japanese equivalent, one *ryo* and two *bu* in silver (she received it on the Seven-Seven holiday, which, since it celebrated romance and the feminine arts, seems appropriate).

On the next to the last day of August, Heusken gave her four silk drawers, colors unspecified, of the kind Shimoda tailors had been busily stitching up for the menfolk at Gyokusenji. It is hard to guess her reaction, since Japanese women did not wear panties. Officer Uchino of the Goyosho, who considered the case, decided that the garments could be released to Ofuku.

The day that Okichi's petition went forward was also the day that Hambei recorded the delivery of several items to Gyokusenji, including about two and a half ounces of opium. In his illness and depression Harris was relying on the drug for relief.

That was the same day that the crews of the wrecked ships at Sotoura held a mass for their shipmates who had drowned. Most of Kakisaki's elders attended.

And it was also the day that the sumo tournament ended in a blaze of excitement, following which the shrine priest, the headman, and several of the elders who had been co-sponsors reported that fact to the appropriate Goyosho officials (who knew it perfectly well, having been regularly in the audience), and expressed their gratitude for permission to hold the matches.

The following day the wrestlers, now that they had played the biggest town on Izu, split into two groups to work their way back up the peninsula along the mountain and the coastal roads, performing in villages as they went. They made their dignified exit from Shimoda to the cheers of a multitude of young boys and some old ones too.

That was the day the Governors sent back to Edo a report on their meetings with Harris so far. It was brief and gloomy.

On the same day in Edo, Lord Matsudaira Yoshinaga tried to take advantage of the decision to let Harris come to Edo: it seemed to offer an opportunity to raise the question of naming an heir to the Shogun. Yoshinaga visited Lord Hotta at his residence and referred to a rumor which was buzzing through the capital—that when the American visited the castle he would be received not by the Shogun but by two related princes (one of them being Keiki, a lord in his own right since he had been appointed head of one of the Tokugawa branch houses). And the reason, it was being whispered, was the Shogun's "illness." Was that true? Yoshinaga asked solicitously.

Not at all, Hotta replied. There was no basis for the rumor, and the firmness of his answer forestalled Yoshinaga's attempt to discuss with the head of the government the need of nominating an heir and the commendable qualities of candidate Keiki.

There was another conference at the Goyosho on the last day of the month. Since the previous meeting, Harris had done some thinking. Perhaps he was now convinced that he could push the Japanese no further, that the alternative to going to Edo soon on their terms was a long wait with the outcome in doubt, a wait during which another nation's emissaries might sail in to lift the honor he had struggled for. Certainly he had no wish to reveal to Washington an impasse—one that he had created without the approval of either the President or the Secretary of State, and was now unable to resolve; he wanted to send home none but optimistic reports of progress. At any rate, he offered a compromise. He made the Governors two proposals. Heusken described them:

> The first one is that, after having communicated the *important matters* to the Governors, he will go immediately to Edo and will deliver into the hands of the Shogun personally the President's letter.
> The Second Proposal: The Consul will go immediately to Edo and deliver the President's letter into the hands of the Premier in the presence of the Shogun. He will address the Shogun with a speech to which His Majesty will reply. (This last condition is also a part of the first proposal.) After the audience, the Consul will return to Shimoda and will then begin the important business with the Governors of that place.

The Governors thanked Harris and asked for a day to think it over. Back at their residence, they lost no time in dispatching a hurried note to the Great Council. They recommended accepting Harris's second proposal.

That was the way things stood as Harris made his usual end-of-the-month entry in his journal. *Monday, August 31, 1857. Health wretched. I weigh about 130 pounds. Weather report: thermometer, highest, 87°; low-est, 67°; mean, 77.7°. . . .*

But during the month certain events of interest had occurred on the China coast.

On August 8 Commodore Armstrong wrote to the Secretary of the Navy from Shanghai, referring to the arrival from Hong Kong of the sloop-of-war *Portsmouth,* veteran of the attack on the Barrier Forts, and to the fact that it had been necessary to put her into drydock: "I have much pleasure in informing the Department that it was found that her bottom had not sustained any material damage from worms.

"So soon as the *Portsmouth* is ready for sea I shall despatch her to Shimoda, Japan . . ."

On August 20 Commodore Armstrong issued orders to Captain Andrew H. Foote, commanding the *Portsmouth,* directing him—as soon as his ship was ready for sea—to proceed with her to Shimoda and Hakodate. On August 22 the *Portsmouth* sailed from Shanghai.

An American warship was on its way.

Chapter 15

SEPTEMBER, 1857

Taking up on the first day of September where they had left off on the last day of August, the Governors tried to get Harris to yield a little more.

> They are charmed, gratified, and happy [Heusken wrote] that the Consul should have been kind enough yesterday to make them such an important concession as to declare himself satisfied with delivering the letter into the hands of the Premier in the presence of the Shogun. But (there is always a *but* which Japanese diplomats add whenever they give a favorable answer), but they beg the Consul to be kind enough to add one thing to what he has proposed: instead of communicating to them the important matters after having been to Edo, he should do it before leaving for the latter place.

Harris said no.

The Governors sent their attendants out of the room, and Inoue pleaded. He would be driven to adversity by Harris's stubbornness. It might prevent their meeting again for friendly negotiations. He was repeating that he might have to commit suicide, and he was quite sincere. At this stage he was deeply depressed. He considered that he had lost every round to the American so far and he believed that he had to salvage something to justify the trust placed in him. He had staked his reputation on his ability to get Harris to talk before leaving for Edo. If he failed and the government made known its displeasure, he would likely choose *seppuku* as the way out.

Harris said he understood but he could not change his position. It was fruitless to try to postpone receiving the President's letter until he had revealed his important matters. Soon Japan would be compelled to receive the letter and, for her own sake, the sooner the better. Foreign battleships could come any day now. If the government was still making difficulties over the letter, it would be in deep trouble.

The Governors asked more time to consider, and the conference adjourned.

By now Harris understood what the Governors were saying when they spoke of suicide, but there is no indication that he understood how serious they were or why. In a dispatch to the State Department a few days later, he wrote:

> This remark had been made a number of times before, but I had always met it with some playful observation; on this occasion, however, I met it seriously. I said I hoped that remark would not be repeated to me, that while I should deeply regret any misfortune that might happen to either of the Governors, yet I could not be held responsible for it. That my duty was to my Government and to that alone; that I should endeavor to perform my duty faithfully, and that in so doing I could not regard any consequences to others, that the remark had the appearance of a wish on their part to cause me to neglect my public duty from private considerations.

How it looked to Japanese eyes is revealed in a secret letter from one of the Governors' staff to a friend in Edo:

> Saying that they could not present the situation to the government without committing *seppuku* in apology, the two Governors made a scandalous appeal to the American official to take pity on them.
>
> Hearing this, the American became more domineering, replying that their attitude was not that of plenipotentiaries. He said he was there by order of the President of the United States, charged with a state mission, and making every effort to fulfill his mission.
>
> "How could I justify abandoning an important state mission for the sake of being humane to you two?" he said. "It is up to you whether or not you commit *seppuku*." He being so merciless the Governors could only agree with him. It is the most unfortunate occurrence since the establishment of the Shimoda garrison. There has scarcely ever been so serious a stain on Japanese honor.

In retrospect, the Governors' request seems reasonable. One would almost take it for granted that before an emissary goes to a capital for important talks, he would reveal what it is he wants to talk about.

Had Harris been minister to the government of Japan it would have been a different story. A minister would rightfully be received by a nation's ruler before he took up his duties. But he was not a minister. Secretary Marcy certainly did not consider him a minister: he had censured, almost recalled, him for "strutting about" in Paris as though he were one. The

Japanese knew very well he was not a minister: they had only with great reluctance agreed to a consul, and a consul he was. His responsibilities related to his country's ships and commerce. He had the additional duties of delivering the President's letter and of negotiating a trade treaty if he could, but these did not entitle him to assume the mantle of minister in Japan any more than they had in Paris.

But if Harris was not being logical he was being tenacious, and it is not hard to understand why.

There was his deep distrust of the Japanese, the distrust that made him label them liars even though their record for telling the truth was better than his. It made him think they might learn his secrets and then refuse to let him go to Edo. He told the Governors as much, and they indignantly denied it.

His distrust was rooted in the bias that he had acquired in his years on the China coast, his conviction that he was dealing with inferiors who, lacking Christianity, democracy, and the steam engine, had to be taught proper Western ways of doing things. This made it difficult for him to be flexible, to alter a stand once he had taken it, to engage in the give and take natural between men who accept each other as equals. It was this that made him put most of his negotiations with the Japanese in the form of unalterable propositions which once made had to be accepted as they stood or would be withdrawn.

And, finally, though we cannot be sure of this, he must have sensed by now that his "important matters" had been magnified out of all proportion to their worth. They consisted of little more than his jaundiced view of British character and British intentions. He was so convinced of British perfidy that he still believed he had important secrets to impart, but what if the Japanese did not value his revelations as highly as he did? Might time have dulled his disclosures? Might the Japanese be better informed about recent developments than he? Might he have begun to suspect that the Japanese had made their own judgment of the various powers harassing them, and that what he had to say would not much alter that judgment?

Whatever he was thinking, his tactics were predictable.

Consulate General of the
United States of America
Shimoda, September 2, 1857

To Their Excellencies
Inoue, Prince of Shinano,
Nakamura, Prince of Dewa,
Governors of Shimoda, etc.

For the purpose of facilitating the delivery of a letter from the

President of the United States of America to His Majesty the Shogun, I made a proposition to Your Excellencies on the 8th of June, and on the 31st of August I made another proposition on the same subject.

(The proposition of June 8 was his offer to negotiate with the Governors if they had full powers. It was this offer and the Governors' misunderstanding of it that had led to their present difficulties.)

To my surprise and regret neither of these propositions have been accepted and yesterday Your Excellencies refused to receive a written copy of them, which I tendered to you.

The honor of my Country forbids me to permit the proposals to remain any longer before you after having been declined by you.

I therefore do now withdraw the two propositions above referred to, and being so withdrawn they can no longer be the subject of future discussion between us, but are to be considered as not having any existence.

I renew, etc.

When this letter was about to be sealed, Heusken tells us,

Moriyama Einosuke arrives, sent by the two Governors. He repeats yesterday's request, saying that Shinano-no-kami will, perhaps, share the fate of Bingo-no-kami if the Consul will not grant him that for which he is asking. For an answer he is handed the letter I have just sealed.

Around four in the afternoon, Moriyama returns saying that the Governors have not rejected at all the two proposals, that they have only begged the Consul to reconsider their wishes for a few more days and would only like him to change that last little clause; they cannot understand the importance the Consul seems to place in communicating the important matters to them afterwards.

The Consul answers that in reality he has been dissatisfied with himself ever since he made the concession to the Governors—that he would communicate his business to them prior to the delivery of the letter . . . that the Governors, by refusing yesterday to accept his proposal, have done him a true service, because he is now relieved of his promise and may retract it honorably . . . that from now on, the Governors are to consider his proposals as void—that he does not have any more proposals to make and that it is now up to the Governors to come forth with suggestions.

Moriyama went back to report.

The day was *Bon*. It was a time for remembering one's ancestors.

A week earlier, as part of the observance of the seventh day of the Seventh Month, families had visited the cemeteries to clean the graves.

Yesterday, the thirteenth day, as Harris and the Governors had struggled in conference, town and village officials had called at Naka Compound to deliver pre-*Bon* greetings. In the evening Harris and Heusken could scarcely have failed to watch as in the gathering darkness family after family came to Gyokusenji's cemetery. They brought white lanterns, lit them, and left them on their family graves to light their ancestors' way back from the spirit world to the homes they had known on earth. As night fell, the cemetery that arched around the temple glowed with dozens of soft white lights. The hillside was fragrant with incense.

Some families assumed that the spirits of their ancestors would come later in the night. Some believed that the spirits were with them as they walked home, and they lighted the path for them and pointed out stony places. Some carried home on their backs the spirits of aged parents or grandparents, talking with them as they went, giving them news of the family since last year, assuring them that they were remembered and loved.

At each house a little welcome-fire was set outside the gate and a tub of water placed at the doorway so that each traveler on the long journey might wash his feet before he entered. In the morning there would be grains of sand at the bottom of the tub, proof it had been used.

Each house was decorated with flowers and grasses, with lanterns and special ornaments. Each house offered food to the spirits, the fruits and vegetables of the season, with rice and dumplings and cakes.

Today hundreds of prayers were being offered. Heusken observed that the priests were busy all day,

> repeating: Amida, Amida, Amida, before the statues of Amida, of Canon and of Sesi.* A few candles cast only a flickering glow; in the temples, the altars strewn with flowers, the statues, the incense, everything made me believe I was in a Catholic church. A number of women came to make their devotions before the altars after first having pulled the cord of a small bell and made some small money offering. . . .
>
> It is noteworthy indeed that one always sees women at their devotions and so seldom men. Whatever may be the God to whom the temple is dedicated, be it the God of the Christians or the idols of the Heathen, women are the ones to crowd the places of worship. "The last at the cross and the first at the sepulchre."

Speaking of women, it was on this day that a grudging payment was made to Okichi. Five *ryo,* or half a month's pay, was delivered to her older

---

* Kannon and Seishi, or Dai-Seishi, are two Bodhisattvas (semi-Buddhas) who attend the Amida Buddha—Seishi on his right representing wisdom, and Kannon on his left representing mercy.

brother. It was credited to her overdue account, but it certainly was not considered in settlement of her petition. That was still pending.

Next day the schooner that had brought Inoue sailed back to Edo. There was so little breeze that the ship had to be tugged out of the harbor, the fishermen of Shimoda manning three boats, and those of Kakisaki, one.

And so Nakahama Manjiro, who had not been permitted to talk to Perry, left Shimoda without having been permitted to talk with Harris. It seems a pity. Both men might have been cheered by a meeting.

The schooner very likely carried the Governors' report of their latest meeting with Harris, and word that Harris had withdrawn his two proposals. "It seems to us," they wrote, "that he will never change his attitude, but we will perseveringly hold meetings in an effort to make him accept our requests."

Perhaps the ship's sailing reminded Heusken of another. He wrote that it was the anniversary of the *San Jacinto*'s departure. He was a day in error: it was really the anniversary of the day he and Harris had moved ashore; the *San Jacinto* had sailed the next day. His mistake can be laid to the day's excitement.

> Who would have guessed that a year would pass before we would receive any news? A Japanese government officer comes on behalf of the Governors to deliver us a package which has just arrived from Hakodate. Two letters from my mother, Praise God! She is happy and fully recovered; she is alive; and seven letters from Hong Kong. There remains a large package of letters and newspapers that the mail refused to take because it was too heavy. Important news from China! The letters Mr. Harris has received from Sir John Bowring, Plenipotentiary of Her British Majesty in China and Governor of Hong Kong, are most important.

Harris must have received on this date all four letters that Bowring had written. And so he had before him all the ammunition the British diplomat had been sending him, all those statements made to be quoted, chiseled for effect:

> We shall have an immense fleet in these seas.
> If I go [to Japan] I shall certainly go reasonably *determined*,—but *determined* in my reasonableness—with olive branches in both hands— but behind me—a becoming accompaniment.
> . . . if I had reason to know that I should have a becoming reception and a disposition to give me such a treaty as I could accept . . . I have no desire to be accompanied by so great a fleet as to cause alarms and apprehensions.

And he had, too, those needling asides to spur him on:

> I had rather welcome you becomingly in Edo than worship at your temple at Shimoda.
>
> You may be very useful in making straight the path for future negociators—[gloomy thought!] and useful *as* a negociator if you can persuade the Japanese that there may be *doings* behind your *sayings*.

Oh, where was Commodore Armstrong?

Even if Bowring's letters nettled Harris (who had no way of knowing that the writer was no longer Her Majesty's Plenipotentiary in China and had no chance of ever welcoming anybody to Edo), getting the letters made it a *Happy day!*—though what day it was he had forgotten by the time he wrote up his journal: he consigned this entry to the anniversary of the *San Jacinto*'s arrival instead of her departure.

Happy day! I get a package with a dozen newspapers and some China letters from Mr. Rice. He writes me that he will forward my packages about October next by a Japanese schooner (American model), which will leave about that time. What a relief to have this slight glimpse of the outer world, although I do not get any American letters. This day is the anniversary of my arrival in Japan. One year here, and not a single letter from America. My last letters were dated February, 1856. Eighteen months ago! How much may have happened in the meantime, whom among my old friends has death removed?

I suppose my letters must be packed up in a box which was not known to Mr. Rice, or he would have sent letters in place of newspapers. What has become of the American men-of-war of the East India Squadron?

The second thing that made the day memorable for Heusken was lunch.

> What powers are those of circumstances! For the past five or six months I have eaten nothing but poultry. Since we finally succeeded in securing a small pig in Shimoda, lunch today consisted of two dishes: one, pork chops (Pork! the food of the peasant), and the other, a roast pheasant, worthy of being chewed and digested by the Emperor of Japan himself. The Consul asks what I would like to be served, pheasant or pork. By Jove! Who would have believed it? I answer, and without any hesitation: "Pork, please." A lowly pig thus triumphs over a splendid pheasant. Truly, my taste is becoming plebeian.

With letters to read and reread, he may not have gone to the shore that evening to watch the closing ceremonies of *Bon*.

The beach was lighted by fires as neighborhood groups burned the

459

decorations brought from their houses. The fires would light the way for the spirits on their long journey back. There was a special farewell for any relative whose third *Bon* this was. The offerings of food and flowers were put on board a tiny boat, with a lantern and a bit of white wood bearing the spirit's posthumous Buddhist name. Then, as the full moon of the fifteenth day of the lunar month rose in the sky, family and neighbors in their boats escorted the little craft to the entrance of the harbor and saw it off, watching its glow recede into the darkness of the open sea.

Next day, September 4, there was another conference at the Goyosho.

Harris thanked the Governors for the letters delivered yesterday, and then asked about Moriyama, who had not made an appearance.

He was absent because of his bungling, the Governors replied. The letter which Harris had sent them indicated that their statements at the previous meeting had been misinterpreted. They had not rejected Harris's proposals. Since the fault was Moriyama's, he had not been permitted to attend today.

The responsibility was not Moriyama's, Harris answered, making it clear he blamed the Governors; Moriyama was a good interpreter, and his absence was a great inconvenience.

In Moriyama's place, Heusken wrote, were "two other interpreters who do not know, between them, as much Dutch as Moriyama alone," and he smelled a trick: "I believe, after all, that it is only a scheme of the Governors so that they might regain the refused proposals."

But Harris refused to discuss them and from then on was brusque and disdainful. He questioned the Governors' powers to either accept or reject his propositions; he was certain they had to run to Edo for every decision. From now on, if it was necessary to talk with Edo, he would do it himself.

The letters he had received yesterday contained important information which the Japanese government should know. He would reveal it as soon as the arrangements were set for his trip to Edo.

Another of the letters, he said, contained word that his government had awarded him thirty thousand *ryo* for his Siam treaty. Since no such letter has survived among Harris's papers, it is impossible to tell whether the blame for this misstatement lies with the letter, with Harris's habit of reporting wish for fact, or with the poor interpreters. The Senate, when they ratified the Siam treaty, passed a bill to award him ten thousand dollars—which would have been equal to about thirty thousand *bu*, or one fourth of thirty thousand *ryo*—but the bill died in the House (probably to help make up for this, the State Department in 1861 paid him $7298.62 as salary for the period from his appointment as Consul General until his arrival at Shimoda).

Harris also asked that his freight at Hakodate be forwarded to him by ship. The Governors said that the Governor of Hakodate had written that he was reluctant to send the goods by sea because of the danger of shipwreck. Harris replied that he was quite aware of the dangers of the sea, that the packages were obviously too heavy to be sent by courier, and that he wanted the stuff delivered without delay.

The Governors asked for another meeting tomorrow; they would have Moriyama present. Harris said he was too busy, and the day after tomorrow was Sunday, but he would meet with them on Monday.

It is clear that he left the Japanese seething. The anonymous informant who reported Inoue's suicide threat obviously was prejudiced but probably he reflected the majority view: "The two Governors were forsaken as imbecile by their fellow Japanese as a result of their talks with the American. Men of common sense ridiculed them, saying, 'How patient are those who serve as Governors.' . . . Please commit this letter to the flames."

They did hold another meeting on Monday, September 7, and Moriyama was back.

What's more, Harris was in a better mood. He had relented his position of the last meeting; he was willing to discuss his two proposals. He was even willing to let the Governors borrow—quite unofficially—a draft of his second proposal, but he demanded an answer on it by the day after tomorrow. They promised they would give it to him. And if they did not, he said, he would never negotiate with them on any subject again. Issuing ultimatums had become a habit.

> Upon our return to the consulate [Heusken wrote] we hear a cannon shot from the lookout mountain. In spite of the precedent of the whaler I climb said mountain in my slippers under a burning sun. When I reach the summit I am gratified to see in the distance a large ship coming from the south and headed for the port. With the help of a telescope I seem to see it flying the Russian flag. I run down the mountain at full gallop. I regret it is not an American ship because, since the negotiations for our trip to Edo are still pending, we might lose the glory of being the first embassy ever to be received by the Shogun in his capital and of breaking the ice that surrounds the chief of that Empire like another arctic pole, if another foreign mission arrives in this country.

It was a comfort to think that she was coming here, although we did not know what flag she wore,—at all events she was from a civilized land.

It was now one year and four days since I was left here by the San

461

Jacinto, and full six months had run beyond the time that Commodore Arm-strong had promised to visit me. That it was not the Commodore was clear, as it was a sailing ship. The wind fell provokingly light, and at seven P.M. the boom of a heavy gun came from the ship. Mr. Heusken volunteered to go to her, although she was some ten miles off.

Launching a fishing boat at Kakisaki
(*a woodcut from a drawing by Wilhelm Heine*)

The sun has already gone down and it casts a reddish glow on the summit of the mountains that rise towards the west. I can't restrain myself; I take a boat and ten oarsmen; this time I want to be sure of my ship and should I row all night long, I just have to catch up with it; this time the ship will not escape us!

It was after he had left the temple that the faithful Ofuku arrived. She was told she would not be needed that night and was bundled off home.

We have left the Bay of Shimoda; we are now on the open sea. It is very dark. For the past hour and a half we have rowed at random. Signs of discouragement are beginning to appear. I promise a tip to the oarsmen—in every country of the world a tip is effective—and the Japanese increase their efforts. One of them glimpses a light! Hurrah! We are saved. The moon is now slowly emerging from the clouds and casts a soft and welcome light around us. The steep coastlines and the

462

reefs are covered by turns with a fringe, gleaming like snow under the sun of the Alps: it comes from the waves breaking against the rocks. The mountains that form the promontory of Izu and the silvery waves of the Pacific Ocean stand out in the darkness. Near us a war frigate raises heavenwards her triple masts, and sways majestically upon the deep.

If we were still in the good old days one would think twice before boarding an unknown ship, but even if someone had assured me that this one was the famous *Flying Dutchman,* or a red pirate flying its grim flag adorned with the skull and bones, I would not have hesitated a moment to go aboard, so great was my desire to escape, were it only for a moment, my Patmos * or my St. Helena. Who can it be? Is it a Russian, a French, or English, or an American? But soon my uncertainty was dispelled, for I heard the familiar tune of "Yankee Doodle." A few moments later I was aboard the corvette *Portsmouth* and was greeted by Captain Foote and the officers. I am led into their quarters and there I spend two hours, the most pleasant two hours I have spent since the *Olivuzza* left. I can assure you that conversation did not lag. I did not need to draw upon stock phrases! "How warm it is today! We are going to have some rain," etc. We have so many questions to ask each other. I, poor ignoramus, who hardly knows whether the world still exists, and on the other hand, the officers of the *Portsmouth* who want to know in turn how things are going in Japan.

Heusken was not the only man who enjoyed a visit to the *Portsmouth* that night. When the consulate called for a boat, Yoheiji had exercised his prerogative and included himself and one of the interpreters in the party; probably the boat used was one of his two.

And so Yoheiji and the interpreter also climbed aboard the *Portsmouth,* and while Heusken and the officers talked in the wardroom the crew crowded around the Japanese. Unless there was a sailor who spoke Dutch, the language barrier must have been formidable—perhaps this is the reason that the headman's diary is not very informative. It says cagily that "we had talks on various subjects"—but no doubt they got through to each other to some degree. Yoheiji sounds self-satisfied, and no wonder: not even Hambei could boast such an adventure.

Finally I leave, carrying a huge package of letters and newspapers which I begin to read by the light of a Japanese lantern once I am back in the boat. At two in the morning I am back at the consulate.

---

* Patmos is an island of the Dodecanese group where St. John the Divine is believed to have suffered his exile and to have written the book of Revelation. [Note by the editors of Heusken's journal.]

The ship proves to be the United States Sloop-of-war <u>Portsmouth,</u> Captain A. H. Foote, eighteen days from Shanghai, where he <u>left</u> Commodore Armstrong in the San Jacinto, and where he <u>has been</u> nearly three months, at the distance of <u>seven days</u> steaming from me. The <u>Portsmouth</u> did not expect to visit Japan when she left Hong Kong, so that <u>all</u> my letters from home that have been received since April last are still at Hong Kong. She brought me letters from Captain Bell and the officers of the <u>San Jacinto</u> only. I was up all night eagerly reading the newspapers and the <u>few</u> letters she brought to me.

Captain Bell's letter:

San Jacinto, Shanghai
21st August 1857

My dear Mr. Harris:

I am exceedingly disappointed that we shall not make another visit to Japan, for it seems we are doomed to loiter in one or two ports of China for the balance of the cruise, a most vexatious and wearisome state of things. It is gratifying, however, to hear that the *Portsmouth*, Captain Foote, is on the point of looking in upon your banished mission at Shimoda. You will find Captain Foote communicative and agreeable . . .

Since Bell had written in a previous letter of Captain Foote's exploits in silencing the Barrier Forts, he did not mention them here. He naturally supposed that Harris had received the earlier correspondence, though it was still lying at Hakodate.

The home news you will glean from the papers at your leisure. The Journal of Commerce will inform you that our affair with the Chinese at the Barrier Forts was "fully settled at the time," and there remains nothing at issue between the two governments—only a few proposed amendments to the treaty. It is reported that Dr. Parker was removed * because of his want of sympathy for the Chinese and his avowed enmity to them, and that our future policy towards them is meant to be most conciliatory and winning; and that henceforth (after the adjustment of the present imbroglio) the same disposition and desire will characterize the British government in all of its intercourse with the Chinese. I understand that this change of policy on the part of the British is in consequence of the vast influence which Russia is acquiring and has already acquired in China through the Tartar race, and which insidiously pervades the Empire as well as all Asia. Before this new policy

* On taking office, President Buchanan had promptly appointed a new commissioner to China, William B. Reed.

can be inaugurated, a peace entirely honorable to Great Britain must be concluded; but the kindest and best disposed persons towards the Celestials, the missionaries included, agree in saying no honorable or lasting peace can be made until the Cantonese, in and around Canton, shall have been well thrashed, and the conceit wholly taken out of them —that John Bull or the European must now prove himself stronger than the Chinaman. . . .

Russia, not Britain, was the enemy of the United States, Bell went on:

I have no dread of British power; on the whole between them and us there exists a healthy commercial rivalry, which is not only good for us, but contributes to a common prosperity. . . . But I have dread of that unsocial Polar Power, which chills, benumbs, and dwarfs every state within its influence . . . You perceive that I am anti-Russian, most unqualifiedly.

We look with much solicitude for the next news from India; the last was very unsatisfactory. It would not at all surprise me if the state of things there were to demand the instant presence of all the British military and naval power in the East; for all her other interests in the East are more or less dependent on India, and are quite insignificant in comparison. In that case the Chinese affair would be postponed, I presume.

The Commodore having been quite ill for the last few months, from the natural effects of the climate on a frame already sinking under a weight of years, lives ashore at Russell & Company's, but is now improving as the weather cools.

Please present my kindest regards to your worthy Secretary, Mr. Heusken.

Believe me very cordially,
Yours very truly,

H. H. Bell

It was a letter which ruffled Harris's prejudices, but he must have read it more than once, since it was one of the few letters he had.

Next morning the *Portsmouth* moved into the outer harbor and anchored near the bluff the Americans had named Vandalia. "As soon as we had anchored," Captain Foote noted, "a large boat came alongside with four officials, high in rank, who, in the name of the Governor . . . gave us a courteous and cordial welcome. These representatives were inquisitive, and manifested a degree of intelligence and culture corresponding to their urbanity and courtesy." He added that they were clean, "a practice which their celestial neighbors . . . might advantageously adopt."

A flurry of orders issued from the Goyosho. Hambei was on the receiving end of many of them. A man was required to "wash and clean" the cannon on Buzan mountain after its firing yesterday (the Governors' artillerymen were above menial labor). Another man was needed in connection with reopening the guard station at Oura cove; he was to bring a scythe: the grass had grown high since the last warship visited Shimoda. And Ofuku's mother was sent word that her daughter need not report for duty as long as the foreign ship was in port.

The ship came up at noon and at two P.M. *the Captain came to see me. He was much pleased when I showed him the Convention of June 17th, and said that all would be surprised at my success. He told me that he had great difficulty in getting the Commodore's consent to come here, and I believe it was only obtained by some medical ruse, by which the ship was ordered here for the health of the crew. Captain Foote told me he had the most stringent orders not to enter the harbor of Shimoda; that he was to stay the shortest possible time here, and an ungracious addendum was made,—that he would probably have to bring me away.*

It appears that Commodore Armstrong has been occupied from December to June in protecting the British Colony of Hong Kong, thus enabling Admiral Seymour to employ more of his force in active hostilities against the Chinese. He found himself able to send a ship to Manila to inquire about some Americans who are imprisoned there under a charge of murder, and he was also able to send another to Singapore to inquire into,—what? A case of salvage!!! However, let him pass with this addition. I informed Captain Foote that all my dispatches from the Government were at Hakodate, where they had remained since last May, and that, as he was going there, I asked him to touch here on his return and give me my letters. It would seem as though the Commodore had foreseen this request, for he positively ordered Captain Foote on leaving Hakodate to stretch out one hundred and fifty miles from land, while his direct route would have carried him about twenty-five miles south of Shimoda.

Captain Foote invited me to visit his ship to-morrow to receive a salute and to dine with him. He then went over to the Goyosho to look at the lacquer ware, Mr. Heusken attending him as his interpreter. Employed until a late hour of the night on my correspondence.

Mr. Harris, our Consul-General, [Foote wrote] welcomed us with that emotion which the seclusion for a year from one's countrymen naturally inspires. Leaving the Consul's we strolled through the town of Shimoda, with its thousand small houses and numerous temples, followed by a crowd of men, women, and children, expressing in significant ways their gratification at our presence among them. . . . They are the best developed, most intelligent, healthy, and happy-looking people, we have seen on this side of the Cape of Good Hope. . . . The cleanliness of their houses far surpasses anything of the kind I have ever seen, the Quaker settlements in our country not excepted.

Crewmen came ashore, too, that afternoon, and the ship's purser began placing orders for provisions: casks of fresh water, fish, eggs, ducks, pheasants, some of those chickens Harris found so tough, all kinds of vegetables, barrels of soy sauce, "medicinal" sake and hard liquor. The next day was a busy one for Shimoda's merchants.

The villagers of Suzaki also hustled, for on orders from the Goyosho, where the next day's reception for the ship's officers was being planned, Hambei requisitioned many shrimp and five large *tai* fish.

Meanwhile the *Portsmouth*'s crew, having reconnoitered the town, zeroed in on its bars. Especially popular was Chiyokichi's, a dockside place in Daiku Block, conveniently close to the landing. Much sake was guzzled there despite great confusion as to how it was to be paid for. Silver dollars were offered but they meant nothing to Chiyokichi, who finally resorted to getting signatures on chits. These he carried hopefully to the town office, who forwarded them to the Goyosho. It would be surprising if many of the names were not fictitious but one hopes that Chiyokichi was paid anyway.

The officers, who could drink on the ship, descended on the bazaar, as Foote recorded:

We availed ourselves of this visit to Shimoda to make extensive purchases in the beautiful lacquered-ware of Japan. This, with sundry articles, was taken from the shops to the bazaar, where the officials, supervising the shop-keepers, almost equalled the latter in number. The purchases of the officers for themselves and friends amounted to more than $1,000. Goods exceeding $40,000 in value were displayed.

The officers were *delighted at only paying thirty-four and a half cents for what cost the San Jacinto officers one dollar. Mr. Heusken is constantly occupied with them, which retards my writing sadly.*

To Harris, one of the blessings of the *Portsmouth*'s visit was the opportunity to become solvent again.

Wednesday, September 9, 1857. The Purser of the Portsmouth has brought me $1,000 from Purser Bradford [of the San Jacinto], which I lent to the ship September 1, 1856, and which I have sadly wanted since. Captain Foote kindly offers to advance me as much money as I may want, taking my

*draft on my agents at Hong Kong, which is a great favor to me, and I gladly
accepted $500 . . . The Purser will also exchange the gold I took from the
Japanese, which had been paid to them by the Purser of the San Jacinto.*

*I told Captain Foote and his officers that I was deeply mortified that I
could not invite them to dine with me, as in reality all I had to offer them
was rice, fish and tough chickens. They begged me not to mention it, as
they had been fully prepared to find me suffering from privations, owing to
the manner in which I had been neglected. Went on board at two p.m., and
had my salute of thirteen guns from the heavy sixty-eight pounders, which
were loaded with full charges and not with the usual reduced charge which
is used for saluting. A pleasant dinner in the cabin, with Captain Foote and
his First Lieutenant Mr. Macomb, son of Major General Macomb, of
Plattsburg memory.***

Heusken, though he was given no salute to describe pridefully, may
have enjoyed the afternoon even more, for he had found a hero:

> Complete harmony seems to prevail among the officers of the *Ports-
> mouth*. Captain Foote is a charming man, simple, open, sincere, gener-
> ous, a true naval officer. At the dinner table he was telling us about his
> battles with the Chinese (I love to hear an old sea dog tell of his feats)
> and the capture of the Barrier Forts. He was commander-in-chief of the
> fleet after the departure of the Commodore.
>
> He related to us in such a candid and animated manner how he had
> bombarded the four fortresses, how he had landed at the head of two
> hundred eighty men and routed the Chinese who numbered more than
> twelve thousand able-bodied men, and how he had taken the fortresses
> armed with one hundred fifty cannon. There was one enormous cannon,
> twenty-three feet long.

*I am to go with Captain Foote and his officers to visit the Governor
to-morrow, and afterwards dine in the ward room. Returned home at five
p.m., and went to work and wrote to a very late hour.*

Town officials were out early the next morning to greet the Governors
on their way to the Goyosho. There, in the conference room, they received
seven officers from the ship, Harris, and Heusken. Tea and sweets and
tobacco were served but the ship's officers missed their chance to sample
Japanese food: Harris had declined the Governors' dinner in favor of one
on the *Portsmouth*. (Was it possible to cancel that order for shrimp and *tai*?)

"We were received with great courtesy and apparent cordiality," Foote
reported.

* Battle of Plattsburg, War of 1812.

. . . had a pleasant visit, wrote Harris.

It was more than a pleasant visit. Harris's appointment to meet the Governors for their answer to his second proposal was of course put off by the *Portsmouth's* arrival. But in this meeting, with Foote's assistance, he was able to score more points than he could have hoped to in the postponed meeting.

For in the midst of the chitchat—the polite inquiries about the health of the President, of Perry, and of his officers; the assertion by Inoue that someday the Japanese would go abroad; the opportunity taken to ask the price of a whaling vessel, since Harris didn't know—in the midst of all this, Captain Foote blandly informed the Japanese that he would return to Shimoda after visiting Hakodate, a lie obligingly rendered at Harris's request.

It worked. The Americans had no sooner left to board the *Portsmouth* than the Governors were framing an urgent message to Edo: the ship would be back in eight or nine days. They did not have to point out what this meant: Harris must be given an answer that satisfied him before then so he would not carry out his threat to go by warship to Edo.

Went on board ship at one P.M. and remained until five, having dined in the ward room. . . . I am pleased to learn that the [Siamese] Treaty is working admirably. Ships have already loaded for New York and San Francisco, and a large quantity of American tonnage is employed in the trade between Siam and China. Many of the finest American clippers have loaded in this manner at the Menam. Captain Foote has kindly permitted the Purser to supply me with flour, butter and pork from the ship's stores, I paying for them, and a great favor it is, in two senses: first, to be able to get them at all; and second, the price is only about half what they would have been at Hong Kong. I cannot find words to express my thanks to Captain Foote and the officers of the Portsmouth for the generous manner in which they have divided their own private stores to help me in my distressed situation. Captain Foote supplied me with a quarter box of superior tea, two jars of lard, and a bag of prepared hominy. From the ward room I received half a dozen fine Virginia hams and five smoked tongues. I had nothing to give them in return but barren thanks.

Mr. Heusken will be employed until noon to-morrow with them at the Goyosho, in settling their accounts; . . .

Hambei had passed the word: bills had to be in by tomorrow morning (did the message trickle down to Chiyokichi?). And on instructions from Kikuna he had ordered twenty-four fishing boats to be ready as tugs.

. . . as the ship must leave at daylight on Saturday morning, I have

but very little time to get my letters ready. I returned home at five P.M. and worked until a very late hour writing.

Considering the shortness of the *Portsmouth's* stay, Harris got out a good many letters:

—to Purser Bradford of the *San Jacinto,* acknowledging receipt of the thousand dollars and venting some indignation:

> I was compelled to ask credit from the Japanese in consequence of my being left here for more than one year without any communication with the American Squadron, which was only some nine days' steaming distance from me. I cannot permit my pen to express my feelings on this point as I might write under the impulse of feeling, what I might subsequently wish to recall, therefore I remain silent.

—to Baring Brothers, his London bankers, arguing about the way they had computed his salary for the first, broken quarter he had taken up his duties at Shimoda (he considered that they had shorted him about half a day's pay).

—to Russell & Company in both Shanghai and Hong Kong, with warm thanks for a considerate letter from them offering to be of help (did he remember his bitter letter to the State Department a few years earlier accusing this firm of trading in opium, part of his unsuccessful attempt to dislodge the company's partners from the China consulates?), and asking them to transmit $2500 to New York, not a small remission out of a year's salary of $5000.

—an order for groceries to Hunt & Company (flour, butter, lard, hams, bacon, tea, sugar, ale, saltpeter, and Calcutta sealing wax), indicating that the letters which had been forwarded from Hakodate included one from his old friend Sandwith Drinker, saying that he was now associated with that company.

—a letter for Captain Foote to carry to Mr. Rice, begging him to open the boxes waiting there, forward the letters and newspapers, and return the stores to Hong Kong (a request Rice was wise enough to disregard); sending, in answer to Rice's request, two sticks of State Department sealing wax ("and very miserable stuff it is, it burns like a candle but you cannot drop it on a letter") along with two sticks of his Calcutta wax; and defending his convention as against the Dutch treaty, or what he knew of it, because Rice had indicated that he thought the Dutch had done better (this was the second letter in less than a week to Rice on this subject, but the first had gone by Japanese courier and no telling when it might arrive); "I have not been ignorant of what the Dutch are doing," he wrote, though he most certainly had been, "and you may be assured that so far as it is in my power, they shall not make any treaty in advance of us."

—and, most important, a long dispatch to the Secretary of State with a résumé of the negotiations (including Inoue's suicide threat) and a flat assertion that he had achieved complete success:

> On the 7th of the present month the Governors requested me to meet them, and at this interview to my agreeable surprise, they yielded every point they had so strongly contested for eight months.
>
> They said they were ordered to inform me that I was to proceed to Edo with every honor, that on my arrival I was to have an immediate interview with the Prime Minister, and on the first ensuing fortunate day I should have a public audience of the Shogun, and at that audience I should deliver the President's letter.

Since nothing of the kind had occurred during the conference on the seventh, this dispatch has caused some confusion among those who have studied Harris's papers. It can only be considered a fabrication, a pastiche of what the Governors had told him and what he sensed they would finally yield. It was an account of what he confidently (especially since Captain Foote's helpful lie) anticipated would come true, not what had. It was quite in the pattern of Harris's sending only optimistic reports of progress to the State Department, lest they question his effectiveness.

Next morning, while Heusken helped the ship's officers settle their acounts at the Goyosho, Captain Foote paid a final call on Harris.

I gave him my pet dog Edo, as he could not get one of the kind here. I sent a fine Japanese sword to Captain Bell and some crepes to Commodore Armstrong. Captain Foote had several orders for Captain Bell, which I was anxious to pay for, but Captain Foote would not permit it. I have some Japanese blades that are now being mounted, and I promised to send one to Captain Foote. I also gave him some trifling articles, and much regret that I had nothing for him or his officers that was worthy of their acceptance.

Mr. Heusken returned at noon and we went to work on our correspondence, and continued so occupied until midnight.

The Governors were to have visited the ship that afternoon but, as Foote wrote, "a strong wind and heavy sea, in the exposed harbor of Shimoda, necessarily prevented."

Had the *Portsmouth* been anchored in the inner harbor the Governors could have come aboard. Captain Foote was more than a little annoyed by Commodore Armstrong's orders. In preparing his report he pointedly stated that he had anchored in the outer harbor "by your directions," and went on to take issue with the Commodore, and, incidentally, with Harris:

The inner harbor of Shimoda is too small to admit of more than five or six vessels obtaining a good anchorage. For this number I regard the harbor to be as safe as many ports in other parts of the world where vessels lie during all seasons of the year. The outer harbor I consider wholly unsafe, as a heavy swell is continually setting in from westward, besides its being quite as difficult getting to sea from under Vandalia Bluff as from the inner harbor itself.

Shimoda Fuji 680 ft.　　　　　　　　　　　　　　　　　　*Suzaki*

Shimoda harbor entrance (*detail from a map prepared by Perry's expedition*)

Saturday, September 12, 1857. Mr. Heusken finished his copying at four A.M. *and, having made up our mail, he went on board the* Portsmouth *at five* A.M.

> I have been writing all night [Heusken set down in his journal] and still have been able to write only three of my personal letters. . . . What with dinners, helping the officers at the Bazaar and writing letters to the government I have had almost no time to think of my own affairs. After nine months an occasion appears to write letters—I have a mountain of them before me to be answered—but I can't do it.

In the final paragraph of this entry he reveals a matter that had been festering between him and Harris:

> Captain Foote promised me to use his influence with the government on my behalf and to request that my salary be paid to me starting on the day that I left New York.

Heusken had sailed from New York anticipating a journey of two or three months. What with the eccentricities of the *San Jacinto* and the mission to Siam, it had stretched to nine, during which he received no salary, though he served as secretary in Bangkok and though he had to pay his mess bill on the ship, and room and board while it was laid up for repairs at Hong Kong. Harris had written asking the State Department to begin Heusken's salary in March, 1856, when the *San Jacinto* arrived at

Penang and the young man took up his duties. Heusken wanted more than that.

When Captain Foote wrote of the difficulty of getting to sea from under Vandalia Bluff, he knew what he was talking about. The *Portsmouth* was scheduled to sail at daylight. It could not. Harris wrote that the wind was too light. Actually, though light, it was too heavy. Yoheiji, watching, saw that even with the twenty-four tugboats from Shimoda the wind was too strong.

The delay enabled Harris to send off one more letter: he had quite forgotten to set down what he had gathered about coal deposits in Japan— the only subject in which Commodore Armstrong had expressed any interest. He wrote a hasty note and sent Assam out with it, Yoheiji providing a small boat.

The delay in sailing made Kikuna nervous. He asked for another twenty-four tugs and then, as they were assembling, hastily canceled the order. He could see that the ship was under way.

At three in the afternoon, "the wind suddenly veering with a fresh breeze to the east, we ran out of the harbor without waiting for a pilot." At sea, Captain Foote would set down his impressions of the Japanese:

> They readily admit our superiority, and seem to be strongly impressed with the power of our country. The frequent presence of this power is therefore imperative, with this people, to the establishment of trade and the introduction of Christianity. The missionary and the commercial interest are equally benefitted by naval protection. For, as Christianity and commerce are carried into heathen and uncivilized lands, their supervision and defense necessarily follow.

This was the mission so many Americans regarded as their sacred trust. The captain might have been quoting Harris, who would certainly have uttered a hearty "Amen." The oftener the Navy appeared, the better, though this short call had left him exhausted.

The visit of the ship has thrown me into a state of intense excitement, as may well be imagined. I have not had three hours of consecutive sleep since the signal was fired announcing her approach.

The inevitable followed. As the *Portsmouth* beat her way up the coast toward Hakodate, Harris took to his bed, *wretchedly ill.* (There is no indication that he had consulted the ship's doctor.) By the time the *Portsmouth* reached Hakodate after five days' passage, he was feeling *a little better,* and he was additionally cheered when he received a package of

Singapore newspapers from Donker Curtius. Perhaps they made him realize that he was not so cut off from the world as he had imagined.

These newspapers gave him his first solid news of the mutiny raging in India. He read it with "deep interest," for, as he wrote to Curtius in thanking him, he "passed a part of the year 1855 at the principal places of the revolt, and became acquainted with a number of gentlemen who have fallen victims to the infuriated Sepoys."

It was now the seventeenth of September. And what had been happening in Edo in response to the urgent dispatches from the Governors' compound at Shimoda?

As the first gloomy reports had come in from Shimoda, even the conservatives of the Tribunal had come around to the view that there was no hope of getting Harris to reveal his "important matters" before he was received in Edo, and that pressing him to do so only increased his choler.

Nevertheless, the only action which could be agreed on was to send the Governors a brief, chill note expressing disappointment at their failure and directing them to suspend talks until they received further orders. (The finance officials apparently took it upon themselves to rush down a secret message saying not to let Harris know that negotiations were broken off; that would only make matters worse.)

But when word reached Edo that Harris had agreed to present the President's letter to the head of the Great Council, and then that an American warship had appeared, the impasse was broken. The talk was no longer on whether Harris should come, but when he should come and with what degree of honor.

How to notify him was a troublesome detail. Should it be by letter from the Great Council, and, if so, should it be the briefest of announcements or something longer, letting him know that this was the government's own decision, not the result of pressure from Harris? Should it be by letter from the Governors? Or should the Governors handle it verbally? This issue brought the unusual spectacle of the *ometsuke* and *metsuke* concurring with the Tribunal: this event was not so important, they agreed; a letter from the Great Council would enlarge it out of all proportion and set a vexing precedent.

On one point everyone agreed: Harris must be notified quickly to forestall his sudden appearance at Edo on that warship.

And so, while Harris's post-*Portsmouth* illness gave the Japanese a little time, an order was drafted and sent down from Edo. The Governors were told they could leave the "matters of importance" in abeyance now. The important thing was to nail down Harris's agreement to present the letter to the Great Council in the Shogun's presence.

The details of Harris's reception were to be worked out with him, keeping things as simple as possible. He was to be treated as an ambassador —and here the Great Council overrode the Governors—because although he was only a consul he was the bearer of the President's letter. A word of caution was added: while Harris would have to be informed in a general way of arrangements for his travel and accommodations, the Governors were to be chary of giving him details—whatever they told him he was certain to ask for more.

He was to come toward the end of the Ninth Month (which on Harris's calendar meant the first half of November). He was to be warned that Japan had her own ways of receiving persons of high position, and that they might differ from what he was used to. He was to be told that Edo still suffered from the earthquake of two years earlier, so that although he was being invited, an invitation to the Dutch Kapitan was being deferred.

At the same time the Great Council published their decision in notices to the Emperor, to the daimyo, and to the families related to the Shogun.

The first outburst was not long in coming.

It is said that when Tokugawa Nariaki first read the notice he exploded. This, he cried, was leading the people of a sacred land to bow in front of a dog. But his reaction was couched in slightly more temperate terms when it was delivered to the Great Council.

The situation having been permitted to develop as it had, he implied,

> the invitation seems inevitable, but your faintheartedness is bound to make him more presumptuous. You have no idea what is written in that letter of the President, but once you receive it you cannot return it. If it is objectionable it may precipitate a serious crisis, even jeopardizing the Shogunate. . . . You must proceed cautiously so as not to stain the unsullied honor of the Tokugawa.
>
> Above all to allow a Barbarian to come near the person of the Shogun is very dangerous, and duty forbids me to remain silent in the circumstances, even if this memorandum be left unnoticed.

The last phrase was not mere rhetoric. With Lord Abe's death, Nariaki's influence had faded. Abe's tactics of keeping him informed, of mollifying him by soliciting his opinions, went by the board. Hotta could not see the point of asking a hostile critic for advice he had no intention of using. The Great Council now did not want to be bothered. On September 11, Nariaki's resignation as advisor had been ceremonially accepted.

While the Great Council's decision was still on its way to Shimoda, while the Governors were still on tenterhooks, the Japanese turned a month on their calendar. Friday, September 18, was to everyone in Shimoda except Harris and Heusken the first day of the Eighth Month. The flag was run up the consular flagstaff.

There had been a Goyosho conference scheduled for that day, but only Heusken showed up. Harris, he reported, was too ill to come. Governor Nakamura received him, probably with distaste. The Governors, bred in a society where age was paid deference, must have found the arrogant young man at least as trying as the irascible old one.

Concerning the trip to Edo, said Heusken, the Consul General wanted an answer within ten days. He should have received an answer by now, but considering the circumstances he would wait ten days more. If he had no answer by then, he would report that fact to his government by warship. Once he took such a step he would never touch on the matter again: his government would handle it directly. Heusken did not have to say how Harris expected his government to handle it; he merely added that the consequences would be disastrous for Japan.

Nakamura told him that they were expecting word from Edo.

Another thing, said Heusken: the Consul General had recently read a report that the Japanese government had concluded a treaty with the Dutch. Though it was clearly written in the Treaty of Kanagawa that rights granted to other nations would be granted to the United States at once, Harris had received no word of this treaty from the Japanese. Why?

He did not deny having heard of the Dutch treaty, Nakamura replied, but the Governors had received no official notice of it and therefore could not inform the Consul General. They had no intention of concealing the treaty. He said they would make inquiries, and in the meantime, he asked ingenuously, would Harris let them read his report?

Heusken had one more complaint, an old one: slow delivery of things they ordered. It was, he said, a serious inconvenience. He asked the Governor to order the officials in charge to hurry things up. (The official in charge was Kikuna, who had his hands full.)

He would direct the officials to do their best, Nakamura replied, but as Heusken could see for himself, Shimoda people were extremely independent. Their casual attitude toward government procurement was a trial to the Governors themselves.

What about those gold mustard spoons that Harris had ordered four months earlier?

But, answered the Governor, they had been made as requested, and had been presented as a gift, and had been refused.

And thus we learn that Harris, never one to admit that he had been outflanked, had refused the gift and demanded that the spoons be sold to him. Couldn't this be done, Heusken asked, seeing that they were necessary to protect the Consul's health? He did not attempt to explain how they would protect the Consul's health more if he bought them than if he accepted them as a gift. The Governor said he thought they had done all that was required of them.

They adjourned, and another worried report sped up to Edo: if the American carried out his threat to report to his government, all past negotiations would come to naught and future ones be made impossible; please furnish directions as soon as possible.

Heusken was back the next day. This time Inoue chose to receive him. It was a decision he must have regretted, for he was greeted by a tirade.

The Consul General, said Heusken, was most surprised to learn that the Governors did not know of the treaty with the Dutch, though several months had passed and all foreign countries knew about it. As for lending them his report on a treaty their own government had concluded, he found this request grotesque and the answer was no. If the Governors were really plenipotentiaries, they must be informed of such vital matters. If they really did not know of it, he would no longer regard them as plenipotentiaries and would no longer negotiate with them. "We therefore ask again, whether you know that the treaty has been concluded. The Consul General has sent me today to learn the truth."

By the time this speech had been translated, there must have been more than one arm in the room tensed to pull a sword. And again Inoue was cast in the role of scapegoat.

He was, of course, seriously embarrassed at not having a copy of the treaty. It was a slip on someone's part, perhaps in the Governors' own Edo office, which was understaffed because both Governors were in Shimoda.

The Governor of Hakodate had the treaty, and Rice had already obtained a copy and sent it on to the State Department, along with some sharp criticism of Harris's convention because it did not open Japan to American trade, and a request that if he, Rice, was not able to trade, he be given the same salary as Harris, "for I have all the work to do"—quite true, as far as consular affairs were concerned.

It was an unhappy mistake that Shimoda had no copy, though not so inexplicable as it might at first seem. In the first place, the treaty had not been ratified, though Harris thought it had been. In the second place, Mizuno and Iwase were still negotiating supplementary articles which were to become an integral part of the compact. And in the third place, it contained nothing very pertinent to Shimoda or to Americans.

The treaty itself was concerned almost entirely with removing onerous local restrictions under which the Dutch had lived and worked for some two centuries (restrictions which Commodore Perry had insured would never be applied to Americans). The Dutch could now, for example, leave their little island without an escort, and they could row and fish in Nagasaki bay, though without landing along the shore. And as for those articles 12 and 13 of the previous convention, which had so excited Harris, they were omitted, just as the Governors had told him they were.

Inoue, as he struggled to maintain some dignity in the face of the young man's abuse, could say only that last year he and Okada had discussed with Harris the negotiations then going on with the Dutch: of course they were aware that a treaty was in the making. They had not received a formal report on it or a copy of it. He had written to Edo to ask for one. As soon as it arrived it would be shown to Harris.

There followed more wrangling over the gold spoons: accusations that the Governors were exhibiting bad faith and duplicity, and ignoring the Consul General's requests.

Heusken repeated that he and Harris were suffering terrible inconveniences because of slow delivery of goods, and announced that they would pay for nothing more until everything ordered had been delivered. He left after reiterating that they must have an answer concerning the trip to Edo within ten days from yesterday, or they would never negotiate with the Governors again.

It had been an unpleasant meeting, painful to Inoue, and providing more ammunition to the hot-headed gossips around him.

That same day the Governors sent off to Edo one more plea for haste. "We think," they wrote, "that we must take any means to keep him from breaking off negotiations." They had not long to wait. It must have been the next day, or at the latest the day after, that they received the Great Council's message. One can imagine them savoring the relief it brought, making plans, finally sending word to Harris on September 22 that they would like to meet with him the following day.

Harris had been writing letters. One went to the Great Council, asking for a copy of the Dutch treaty and giving them an unsolicited lesson in etiquette: he had taken umbrage at their laconic style of correspondence. "In the various letters that I have written to Edo since my arrival at

Shimoda, I have invariably concluded them with the formula that politeness and good breeding required, having used words to the following effect.
'I avail myself of the present occasion to assure Your Excellencies of my
distinguished consideration.'" This, he said, was "the invariable custom of
the Western World" in writing diplomatic letters, but he had "observed
with regret" that none of the letters he had received from the Great Council
"contain this or any other expression of respect."

Unless they mended their ways, he would omit his formula in future
letters. "I have set the example of courtesy, and if you refuse to follow it,
and thereby our correspondence shall not be closed with the usual kind
expressions, the fault will rest with Your Excellencies and not with me."

He also wrote to Donker Curtius, congratulating him on his convention
and would he please send a copy of it. He had asked the Japanese for a
copy, he said, but they could not be trusted to give him one "exactly
correct." And more than six months after Governor Okada had asked him
to, he inquired of the Dutch envoy whether articles 12 and 13 of the 1855
convention had been ratified. "All the evidence I have ever obtained on the
subject goes to prove that the articles were ratified, and so strong is that
evidence that I have no doubt of its substantial correctness."

He sent word that the United States Navy's Asian squadron was to be
reinforced, and that an American company had been formed to inaugurate
steamship service from California to China, touching at Hakodate and
Nagasaki. He closed by asking a free exchange of correspondence:

> As my Government desires no special privileges in Japan, I have no
> secrets to guard, and shall therefore feel myself at liberty to communi-
> cate to you all negociations that I may accomplish with the Japanese
> Government. In these views I do not doubt your Government partici-
> pates; the only emulation between us is as to who can do the most to
> open this interesting country to the world.

It was an affable letter, and it marked a change in tune from that day
in March when he had scornfully told the Governors that the Dutchman
was a mere merchant with whom he could not condescend to communicate
officially. Perhaps reading the newspapers had taught him that Curtius did
in fact outrank him.

On September 23 Yoheiji found nothing worth entering in his diary
save that the day was a fine one. But Townsend Harris had a triumph to
record (though he misdated it by one day).

*Tuesday, September 22, 1857. At the Goyosho this morning at eleven
o'clock. The Governors informed me that they had received letters from*

Edo relating to the President's letter; that after many anxious consultations it was finally settled that I am to go to Edo, in the most honorable manner; and, after my arrival, I am to have an audience of the Shogun, and then present the letter of the President!

It was all to the good at this point that Harris did *not* have with him a man like S. Wells Williams who understood Chinese and Japanese. For the word the Japanese were using for audience was *hairei,* meaning to pay homage. Had he known, what a fuss Harris would have kicked up over that!

Since Harris's trip would be the very first of its kind, Inoue explained, there were many details to be discussed and decided. And he proceeded to discuss.

Harris of course pressed for speed. He reiterated that the sooner he went, the better for Japan. The Governors replied that they were well aware that Harris was anxious to make haste. Inoue would leave soon for Edo to help make plans. When he returned he would know the date set for Harris's departure.

They talked about the journey. If a schedule were set beforehand, Harris said, it would be impossible to adhere to it in case of sickness or bad weather, so he proposed to stop and stay overnight according to circumstances. The Japanese knew perfectly well that, as for any official trip, they were going to make advance arrangements and stick to them if humanly possible, but they agreed with Harris in principle: Inoue knew from experience that a schedule could be upset. The Governor added that it would be necessary to keep on traveling if it rained, and Harris said he wouldn't want to do that, but since no one knew whether or not it would rain, the issue was left unresolved.

Harris said that he and Heusken would need new horses to replace the ones Heusken had put out of action. The Governors, fearful that the two might forge ahead of their party, jeopardizing security arrangements and upsetting the schedule, tried to persuade him not to use horses, but gave in when Harris assured them that he would stay with his escort and that being able to shift from *norimono* to horseback to foot was essential to relieve the tedium of travel.

They tried to persuade him to use one of their *norimono* instead of his enormous one, but he insisted he could not: when he had used one of theirs recently to come to the Goyosho in the rain, he had had to double up his legs, so that even that short trip was painful.

They would be taking the east-coast road up Izu, Inoue said. There were few relay stations and the temples where they would stop would be humble ones, for which he wanted to apologize in advance, but the road was more level and considerably shorter than the middle route over Mount Amagi. It would be possible to reach Edo on the seventh day.

Harris had heard the trip could be made in five days.

It could, Inoue replied, but that meant starting in the morning while the stars were still out and traveling after the lamps had been lit at night, and Harris quickly agreed to seven days. Even that, Inoue told him, meant setting out about seven in the morning and keeping at it till around four in the afternoon. Harris reminded them he would not travel on Sunday.

As for Edo, Inoue went on, the city had suffered from a series of storms, earthquakes, and floods. Things were still unsettled and a certain informality might be unavoidable. Quite understandable, said Harris, but he would not stay at any place that looked inferior. He did not expect the Japanese to follow European custom and accommodate him at the castle or at the mansion of some member of the royal family, but neither would he stay at an ordinary hotel.

He agreed to go by *norimono* when he visited the castle and the residences of high officials, and he suggested that for these trips his own was too large and that the Japanese might lend him one. He acknowledged the need for an escort on visits, but asked that he be permitted to go sightseeing with only an interpreter; the escort, he said, made him feel uncomfortably like a prisoner. But he gave in on this point when the Governors pointed out that Edo was such a complicated place that no stranger could find his way about.

He sensed, it would seem, that the Governors were worried about his behaving with too much Western "informality":

> You Japanese may not be interested in shopping, but we foreigners love to look at things on display. But even if I drop in to shops selling lacquer or porcelain or clothing, I will not be so unmindful as to buy there. I will have things delivered to my hotel and I will pay for them later in Shimoda. I realize that I shall make this trip not only as Consul General but also as deputy of the President, and I will never act heedlessly.

They again reviewed the ceremony of audience that Harris had described before. He would wear, he said, his dress uniform with all its gold braid. And he indicated that by Western custom a banquet was in order after the audience.

At last there came the moment when Harris realized that he really was going to Edo, that the Japanese had suggested nothing he could not accept, had made no *objectionable proposition . . . which would throw the respon-*

sibility of the non-delivery of the letter on me . . .—nothing of the kind occurred. His premature dispatch to the Secretary of State had come true.

"Today for the first time," he told the Governors, "I feel as though the clouds and fog all have lifted."

Inoue answered that he too had been gravely troubled and now was greatly relieved. For the past two or three days, he said, he had been suffering from a cold and slight fever. He would leave for Edo as soon as he felt well enough.

For a change, the Governors could report to Edo agreement instead of conflict. They could even enclose Harris's written concurrence in the plans they had discussed.

Three days after the Goyosho conference the word went out that Inoue would leave for Edo the next day. With him would be his son, and Moriyama, and Dr. Ito Kansai, who had at last finished translating most of the book of treaties borrowed from Harris last October.

The villages were to provide two hundred and fifty men and six *kago* for the first day's travel. This time the levy fell light on Kakisaki—only eight men—but since Inoue was taking the coastal road he had recommended for Harris's trip, the coastal village of Shirahama was required to provide a hundred men. There would be little *tengusa* gathered there that day.

There was the usual uproar at Hongo that night, but as usual the long train wound out on schedule the next morning. It passed Kakisaki with little formality. Yoheiji and Gennosuke were standing by at Shirahama for the formal send-off, while Chuemon and Shozaemon accompanied the party another six or eight miles.

Monday, September 28, 1857. Shinano-no-kami, with Moriyama Einosuke, started yesterday for Edo. The Commissary of Shimoda came to-day to take orders for procuring the men I shall want, and preparing their dresses.

I shall not take any of my Chinese with me, as the Japanese have a great dislike to the Chinese, and I do not wish to be associated in their minds with the Chinese or any other people. I shall, therefore, only be accompanied by Mr. Heusken and my two Japanese house servants from my family. My own train will consist of some forty porters bearing my luggage, cooking utensils, bedding, etc., etc., and by the following, who will all have the arms of the United States on their dresses, as the coat-of-arms is worn by the Japanese,—viz.,

20 norimono bearers	1 sword
12 guardsmen	2 swords
2 standard bearers	2 swords

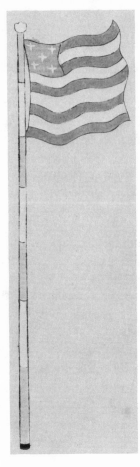

The American flag carried by Harris
(*a Japanese drawing*)

The United States seal embroidered
on Harris's livery (*a Japanese drawing*)

2 *shoe and fan bearers*	2 *swords*
2 *grooms*	1 *sword*
2 *quinine* [*Gokenin,* squad leaders], *or*	
commanders of the foregoing.	

All except the grooms and norimono bearers are to have silk dresses.

I am to be attended by the Vice-Governor of Shimoda, the Mayor of Kakisaki, the Commissary of Shimoda, and by the private secretary of Dewa-no-kami. They will have, together, a tail of some one hundred and fifty or more men, so that the whole train will form a body of not far from two hundred and fifty.

When Harris wrote *Vice-Governor of Shimoda* he meant Executive Officer Wakana Miosaburo. By *Mayor of Kakisaki* he meant Superintendent Wakiya Usaburo, and by *Commissary of Shimoda,* Vice-Superintendent

Kikuna Sennojo. These men would be responsible for his journey. All were veterans of the past year's ordeal. This undertaking offered at least the reward of a stay in Edo.

Two days later Harris was able to write his month-end entry on an unaccustomed bright note.

Wednesday, September 30,1857. My health is much improved. I attribute this to my improved diet, as I am now well supplied with delicate China pork, my sow having littered thirteen pigs on the fifth of August last. I have no doubt that the agreeable termination of the vexed question of the reception of the President's letter has also been of great service to me, as it has removed an immense pressure from my mind. I cannot help hoping that I shall be able to do something satisfactory in the way of a commercial treaty before I leave Edo.

It is doubtful that the pork was doing his tormented digestive tract much good, though it contributed to a renewed interest in food. The improvement in his health was due to his happier frame of mind.

Also on this last day of September, Hambei sent out a circular to all the villages. It was time, he reminded them, to apply for permission to harvest the early rice, and he enclosed a sample petition. If all the villages followed the sample, and no doubt they did, each of them pleaded for tax relief on the grounds that it, most particularly, was ill-favored in the matter of irrigation.

Chapter 16

OCTOBER, 1857

十
六

A NOTICE FROM THE GREAT COUNCIL

Before the Kan'ei period [1624–1643] foreign envoys were often received in audience, but later the practice was discontinued on the ground that foreign influence was harmful to the State.

But now an American official stationed in Shimoda, Izu Province, has applied to visit the Court bearing a Presidential message. Since the Japanese officials assigned to deal with him are most ignorant, faint-hearted, and negligent, they have played into the envoy's hands. Therefore the Shogun is reluctantly permitting the American to come to Edo.

It is common practice throughout the world that when two nations have concluded a treaty, they exchange envoys. Such an envoy often seduces the public with false reports, propagates an evil religion, damages the national polity, and finally, seizing some opportunity, starts a war which ravages the country and reduces its territories. All this is certainly undesirable, but since it is common practice the American will soon be received in audience.

This notification is published for the information of all concerned.

This is not exactly the way the government's notice was worded. It is a rewrite by some wit within the bureaucracy. It appeared in a clandestine publication under the name of Tengu, a *tengu* being an egotistic, know-it-all, long-nosed goblin. Actually, Tengu must have been many men, for he spoke with many voices. He was on all sides of every issue, with opinions as diverse and contradictory as they were irreverent.

There were few subjects of moment on which Tengu had nothing to say. He criticized the Shogun's reading habits (too much Chinese literature, not enough Japanese), and he forecast the price of eggs (going up, so

485

A *tengu* writing (*a book illustration by Hokusai*)

better buy chickens this winter). He ridiculed the idea of keeping foreigners in remote places—even if allowed to visit the castle he doubted that they would commit incendiarism or purloin treasures. He mocked Lord Hotta's committee on foreign trade with a set of fatuous recommendations signed with a pun which could be read "The Lose-All Commission."

Tengu's wit and comment enjoyed a wide if surreptitious circulation from desk to desk. There was no lack of material for each issue. Harris's impending visit had the capital on edge, and rumors whipped around the city like the falling leaves of this autumn season. Schemes and plots were rampant; everyone of importance was trying either to promote or uncover one.

It was a worrisome time for Lord Hotta and the Great Council. They had many problems, and not the least was the strong, even violent, opposition to receiving Harris, some of it from important places.

Nariaki's reaction had been predictable. Nor was it a great surprise when the Lord of Owari seconded him, putting two of the Three Houses, the senior Tokugawa branch families, in opposition. For all their exalted position, the Three Houses had little function in the government; their advice could be brushed aside.

Much more serious was the blistering denunciation which came from that room of the castle called the Antechamber. (Each lord, according to his rank and status, was assigned to a certain room of the castle; though the lords were seldom assembled at the castle save for the monthly ceremonies of audience with the Shogun, they formed cliques and friendships based on their assignment.) Of all the rooms, the Antechamber was the only one whose lords had a regular advisory role in the Shogunate; they were major Inside Daimyo; they should have been a citadel of support for the government. Yet they wrote that the reception of Harris would be a national disaster, that it could only lead to receiving the envoys of other nations, and that all this was contrary to the policies of the Tokugawa. They said that the Great Council, who were responsible for maintaining the dignity of the nation, were disgracing it instead. They asked that the invitation be withdrawn. Their attitude was a clear indication that in his preoccupation with foreign affairs, Lord Hotta had lost control of the machinery of government.

At his castle in Hikone, word of the Antechamber's attack reached Lord Ii Naosuke as he was preparing to return to Edo for his next period of duty in the capital. His preponderant power made him the leader of the Antechamber, but these opinions were not his. They were those of the lords now on duty in Edo, men who were his friends. He would have to try to change their minds when he could talk with them.

On the other hand, Hotta drew a much more encouraging response from a quarter which might least have been expected to give it—the Great Corridor. This was the chamber of the Three Houses, other major houses of the Tokugawa family, and a few especially honored Outside Daimyo. Of the Three Houses, Nariaki and the Lord of Owari were already lined up in opposition. But Nariaki's influence had waned. Most of the lords of the Great Corridor looked for leadership to Matsudaira Yoshinaga and Shimazu Nariakira, and they were among the staunchest supporters of opening the country. What made their support a mixed blessing was that they were also leaders of the campaign to "reform" the Shogunate.

On October 5 several of the lords of the Great Corridor held a conference. They discussed Harris's impending visit, which was on everybody's mind, but they went beyond that to something basic. What they wanted was to be consulted in advance of such important decisions in foreign affairs, not merely notified after the decisions had been made.

This was no small demand. It amounted to asking that the government be reshaped, for since the time of Icyasu these lords had been excluded from decision-making (except as some rare individual might make his opinion felt by force of personality).

A second demand was "improvement" in the system under which a daimyo was obliged to spend every other year in Edo and to leave his wife and children there as hostages when he went home. By improvement, these lords meant that instead of spending every other year in the capital they should serve every third to fifth year. They pointed out that this would ease the financial plight of the lords, since the expense of living in Edo was enormous. They did not point out what was obvious,—that it would loosen the grip of the Tokugawa on the daimyo. (Matsudaira Yoshinaga had in fact threatened to take home his wife and children, reform or not.)

What made these discussions critical was Lord Abe's death. As long as he was alive the Outside Lords had a powerful advocate within the Great Council, for he had believed that just such changes were essential if the Shogunate were to survive. Abe's death had not changed their plan. They still must get, as the first step, a strong and able Shogun who shared their views—Nariaki's son Keiki. But without Abe, this would be much more difficult. Nobody knew where Hotta stood.

One decision of the October 5 meeting was to make a direct approach to Hotta, perhaps as much to cultivate him as to learn the government's position. A couple of days later two of the lords called on Hotta at his mansion and listened while "in strict confidence" he ticked off the reasons for inviting Harris: the American's insistence that he had something to say to the Great Council which would benefit Japan; the fact that it was universal practice for the head of state to receive an envoy; and Harris's repeated threats that if he were not received he would withdraw and turn the matter over to his country's Navy.

The two who had seen Hotta promptly called another meeting. After hearing their report, these lords of the Great Corridor decided to forward their views on the matter to the government. It was a chance not only to assert themselves but also to make another approach to Hotta.

They did not go out of their way to offend Nariaki by praising the decision to receive Harris, though clearly they accepted it as a case of sound judgment. But they were concerned, they wrote, that Harris carry away an impression of military strength and preparedness. He must, therefore, be guarded with great care by trained and disciplined soldiers, who would not only insure his safety but would also make certain that he had no opportunity to act rudely or indiscreetly.

What worried them, they went on, was that in spite of the fact that the government had ordered vigorous military training and rearmament when the first Black Ships arrived, there were many daimyo who were not training seriously because they had grown used to a peaceful and elegant life, and there was waste, confusion, and lack of coordination in the rearming effort. Things would get worse instead of better if the Harris visit went smoothly, for the sense of crisis would disappear and men would slacken their efforts even further. Therefore, the government must issue and enforce sound military regulations. Twin programs of military preparedness and polite treatment of foreign nations would insure Japan the respect of the rest of the world.

Yoshinaga was delegated to deliver this opinion to Hotta, and this time he did not hesitate to urge the necessity of the Shogun's adopting an heir and the desirability of that heir's being Keiki. Hotta was noncommittal.

Yoshinaga did not stop at this. He went from conference to conference, trying to plumb the views of the Great Council. About all he learned was that the councillors seemed to be full of apprehension concerning Harris's visit, but this made him hopeful that the atmosphere of urgency and crisis would make it possible to push through some favorable action on Keiki. No other decision, he reasoned, would have such a calming and stabilizing effect on the country.

To Hotta the issue of an heir seemed untimely if not irrelevant. He was preoccupied with foreign problems. The great powers crowding in on Japan threatened her independence, her very existence, as they threatened China's. Impoverished samurai, an empty treasury, Nariaki's intransigence, the schemes of Yoshinaga and Nariakira—these were problems certainly, but to Hotta the first necessity was to create a new foreign policy. He had no feeling, as Abe had had, for the restive new forces within Japan. Assuredly he lacked Abe's conviction that the way to save the Shogunate was to invite its traditional enemies to share its power.

When it came to foreigners, Harris was not, of course, his only concern. In Nagasaki, Mizuno and Iwase had completed a new trade agreement with Donker Curtius. It represented a compromise: it comforted Mizuno by preserving the old system of government-to-government trade, but it satisfied Iwase by opening the door to private trade between merchants, under government supervision, without limit on volume. Moreover, it was the first treaty to prohibit the opium trade in Japan.

Then Russia's Admiral Putiatin had sailed in, and Mizuno and Iwase had seized the opportunity, without waiting for approval from Edo, to negotiate the same kind of agreement with him. In reporting what they had done they reminded the government that in 1854 Tsutsui and Kawaji had promised the Russians that they should be first in line if the Japanese ever decided to trade. Moreover, treaties with both Holland and Russia would set a pattern for other nations and should make it easier to negotiate with Harris.

Harris was the major problem. His imminent appearance at the castle would be a milestone on the new road Hotta had laid out for his country— if it went well. "The people of Edo are uneasy," said one report, "and as they are traditionally short-tempered we worry about incidents like that in Shimoda when Heusken was threatened by a swordsman."

A mountain of paper was piling up. Every branch of the government that had a hand in the visit submitted plans and recommendations which the Great Council sifted, approving or rejecting or calling for more study.

Most of the big questions were answered by this time. He would travel by land, for if he came by ship, the Shimoda Governors had said, he would certainly demand to visit Oshima. At Edo, since there was no temple conveniently located, and since he could not be quartered at an inn, where, the Governors had warned, "waitress-prostitutes would exert an unwholesome influence on the party," it was decided that he would be put up at the recently renovated building of the Institute for Foreign Studies. The institute had been founded, in Kawaji's words, "to study the West, to learn its military power, its strengths and its weaknesses, its virtues and its vices." It seemed appropriate that Harris be housed there, and though the institute's scholars would be temporarily displaced, they would be compensated by the chance to study their subject matter at first hand. (Tengu had suggested building a special hotel for foreigners: "rooms for rent to barbarians.") Harris would be permitted to do some sightseeing (and Tengu, cognizant of Harris's behavior in Shimoda, advised that a bathhouse featuring the current fad, baths in barley tea, would be a suitable attraction).

But many details could not be settled because as yet unanswered was the perplexing question of just what degree of honor to accord him. So much hinged on that: the ceremonies of audience, the dress of those attending, the presents he would be given, the dinner he would be served —it went on and on.

There were those who said he should be treated like the Koreans, who had come as representatives of a sovereign nation. There were others who said that the treatment accorded to the Ryukyuans was more suitable; they had come not as equals but as vassals. (Tengu broke into the argument to say that it was quite improper to use that word *hairei* to describe this audience; no reasonable government would be so discourteous as to use this term.)

The Great Council had decided that he would be treated as an envoy but, after all, he held the rank of only Consul General. Surely some distinction should be made between ranks. But what?

The trouble was that there was no precedent. And so there were conferences which produced no agreement, and more confusion as a result, and in the end, said Tengu, everything was left to Moriyama.

A committee—the Commissioners for the Visit—including Tsutsui and Kawaji was appointed to supervise the arrangements, and Inoue was made responsible for the details, and almost at once there were signs of bureaucratic infighting. The Great Council had to issue a rather sharply worded directive telling everyone to stop fussing and get on with the job. And eventually they did, though the date had to be set back almost a month so that things could be made ready.

It was decided that the Shogun should sit to receive Harris. Those in attendance would wear *nagabakama,* the long trousers-like garment which trailed out behind the feet and was the next-to-most-formal uniform of the court. A dinner menu was drawn up which was a nice compromise between what the Koreans had been served (too elaborate) and what the Ryukyuans had got (too simple), and it was settled that Harris should be given fifteen kimono appropriate to the season, a standard item of presentation from the Shogun.

Orders went to the construction bureaus. Okada, though frozen out of the negotiations, was handed many of these responsibilities. The Institute for Foreign Studies was to be redecorated and furnished with specially built beds, chairs, and tables. Bamboo screens would be borrowed from another part of the castle if those where Harris would be were soiled.

It was ruled that traffic should be stopped when he traveled to the castle but might be permitted when he went sightseeing, so that he could see the everyday life of Edo.

All concerned were reminded that everything must be managed with the greatest care: "As old customs and regulations are being changed, the matter is attended with difficulty. You must neglect nothing. You are to be alert and firm against disorder."

491

Nagabakama (*a print by Shun-ei*)

And at last the Great Council was able to report to the Shogun the particulars of the audience: the ceremonies, those who would attend, the dress of the Shogun and the others. Perhaps it would be a little overelaborate, the Council wrote, "but it is certain that the American envoy will quickly report to the world on all that takes place, and this is a good opportunity to demonstrate our prosperity and our culture."

Back in Shimoda the author of all this excitement had celebrated another birthday on a day that had begun rainy but, clearing early, had turned fine.

Sunday, October 4, 1857. My birthday. I am fifty-three years old. My lease is rapidly running to its close. God grant that the short remainder of it may be usefully and honorably employed. My health is better than it was a month ago, but far, very far from being as good as it was this time last year. Shall I ever see New York and my dear American friends again? Doubtful, but God's will be done, I can say truly and heartily.

Among the Japanese around him, things were relatively quiet. The heat of summer was past, its humid haze erased by autumn's winy sparkle. The paddy fields were dry now, the rice was turning golden. And with these genial days there came a lull, the lull that preceded the rice harvest.

The full moon of the Eighth Month came around, considered the most radiant moon of the year. In its honor the families clustered above and below Gyokusenji set out offerings: a little pyramid of rice dumplings, another of boiled taro, and a vase of autumn grasses. Sliding open the doors of their houses so that the moon's first beams would find the tribute, they prepared to stay up late to drink a little, to remember a suitable verse or compose a new one, but mostly just to gaze upon the moon. Unfortunately, the night turned out to be cloudy. Perhaps someone remembered an old poem addressed to the heavens on another such evening:

> And hast Thou clouded o'er,
> This night,
> The moon of the year?

But the heavens' misbehavior did not spoil the fun of the children, who crept through the darkness to filch the dumplings and the taro while their parents pretended not to see.

It was a good time of year for weddings. The town clerk of Shimoda, consulting the record of annual events compiled by his predecessor Hirai Heijiro, read:

> It has long been a custom in this district, on the occasion of a matrimonial celebration, for young men to throw stones at the paper doors of the house where the marriage is taking place, by way of participating in the auspicious event. Small children, too, indulge in the same kind of frolic when the wedding procession goes through the town introducing the bride to relatives. The result often is that some people in the happy wedding party are hurt, which is outrageous. Therefore, a circular is issued each year prohibiting such harmful conduct.

493

And so, though happily this misconduct seemed to be dying out, the clerk drew up the usual circular to go out to each block leader: "Concerning the subject of stone-throwing on the occasion of weddings . . ."

Weddings were not the only subject of conversation. Harris had a new horse and *having extemporized a saddle, bridle, etc., etc.,* began to ride. Heusken's horse had recovered. *Mr. Heusken's performances on horseback, and my riding,* wrote Harris, making a nice distinction between them, *have raised us to a pinnacle of glory among the Japanese. . . .*

The Japanese are no horsemen; both hands are employed in holding the reins; they have no martingale, the horse therefore carries his head very high with his nose stuck out straight. They therefore have no command over him. Usually the groom leads the horse by a third rein put on for that purpose. The Governors were very fearful for my safety; they assured me that the Japanese horses were so vicious, that my life would be in danger if I attempted to ride in any different manner from their mode.

The Governors' fears were not entirely groundless, as Heusken let us know:

Yesterday I nearly killed myself. While I was riding a horse on these miserable roads of Japan, my steed stumbled, fell, and I was projected over his head to the ground. I made a complete somersault and landed head first on the rocks strewn on the road. I might have wrenched my back or fractured my skull in those acrobatics! I jumped back on my horse and came back to the consulate, to the great surprise of the inhabitants of Kakisaki, with blood dripping in great drops from my hat. It seems that a sharp stone on which I had fallen had made a rather deep cut. It was precisely at the same spot where the Catholic clergy wear the tonsure. "Wretched you," I thought, thinking of my tonsured skull. "They are going to mistake you for a Jesuit or a Franciscan in disguise, and if they don't cut off your head immediately, the alarmed authorities of Japan will lock you up in a cage for the rest of your days!"

Harris had his problems, too, though he did not mention them. His horse always reared and bucked at a certain spot on the beach road; the inhabitants thereabout rushed to watch when they saw him coming: they were certain the horse was being frightened by some local spirit.

But Harris was never thrown, as far as we know, and he continued to ride, though *alas! Shimoda is no place for equestrian exercises. It is all up and down; no roads, but mere footpaths; and, in a great many places, these are so steep that a regular staircase is made of stone steps, and at a giddy angle, particularly when you look down. . . . In 1848 Lieutenant-Colonel May, of the U.S. Horse Artillery, rode his horse up the stone steps and into the hall of Barnum's Hotel [at] Baltimore, and then rode him down again. The feat was considered so wonderful that it was glorified in the newspapers from the Rio Grande to the St. Croix. If Colonel May could see the staircase I ride up and down, he would decline hearing his exploit mentioned again.*

Among the villagers, Shinzaemon was not so impressed that he considered it a privilege to house their horses. He asked for the return of his stable. Yoheiji talked with him and persuaded him there was no chance of that, but he and the elders did submit a petition to the Goyosho asking that the farmer be permitted to use his building during the rice harvest. That was not far off, for the headman recorded that in answer to their application, permission had been granted to harvest the early rice which some farmers grew along the footpaths between fields.

If Shinzaemon was unable to oust the foreigners' horses, he could draw some consolation from the fact that during the middle part of October, at least, his house was uncluttered by the foreigners' ladies. Okichi was long gone, of course; it was just at this time that she received a settlement of thirty *ryo* in answer to her petition. Kikuna had succeeded in prying that amount (about forty-one dollars) from Harris, a feat no doubt made easier by Harris's feeling well supplied with cash after the visit of the *Portsmouth*. Of the thirty *ryo*, the receipt shows that twelve were at once returned to town officials in repayment of two advances. Clearly, Okichi was indulging in woeful extravagance.

As for Ofuku, she was absent because she was ill. Hambei and two of the elders reported this to the Goyosho on October 8, adding, in compliance with the directive concerning the girls, that her menses were two months in arrears. Ofuku's private life was a matter of public concern.

Saturday, October 10, 1857. I am every day called on to see something the Japanese are preparing for my journey, or to give some new directions. One item Harris must have supervised with great care: some Shimoda tailor was stitching up a new American flag of good Japanese silk. The ensign which had flown from Gyokusenji's staff, and whose shoddy manufacture had excited some of his earliest grumbling, was by now far too tattered to carry in the ceremonial procession to Edo.

Saturday, October 17, 1857. . . . I have been almost daily occupied in seeing to clothing, etc., etc., preparing for my people. He was alert to every detail.

His standard bearer would wear *a long kabiya, or gown made of brown and white calico, of a particular pattern, and open at the sides like a herald's coat, from the hip downward.*

His guards, each wearing *two swords,* would be *clothed in silk dresses,* with *the arms of the United States on the right and left breast of their upper garment.*

The *norimono* bearers—*picked men (twelve for me and eight for Mr. Heusken), and very tall for Japanese*—would be *dressed in dark blue, with the arms of the United States on the back.* . . . *The coat of arms is very neatly done, and the motto E pluribus unum, the eagle, arrows, and olive branch quite perfect.*

I *am informed that the news of my visit has spread like wildfire over the country and, as they express it, "millions will go to Edo to see the grand entry of the American Ambassador." They will call me that name instead of Plenipotentiary, as the former has the grandest sound to their ears. They tell me that printed accounts of me, illustrated by drawings, are circulated by thousands. These are not in the form of newspapers, but are analogous to the "broad sheets and little books" that preceded that mighty engine,—the newspaper.*

While Harris was thus happily occupied, things were happening at the opposite ends of Japan.

In Nagasaki on October 16 the Dutch and Japanese ratified their January treaty and signed the additional articles on trade. These did not obtain all the concessions that more aggressive nations were after but clearly Donker Curtius was one up on Harris.

A few days later Admiral Putiatin and the Japanese signed their trade treaty, which put the Russians, too, ahead of the Americans. Mizuno was able to write to Kawaji that Japanese and foreigners were now mingling in Nagasaki:

> In many places, foreigners, mostly Dutch, are found on the street, and in some cases they even appear to enjoy their company with the local people. The latter, for their part, do not seem to abhor the foreigners, even the women and children going shoulder to shoulder with them. All this change has taken place during the past couple of years. I cannot imagine what may develop in years to come.

At Hakodate, far to the north, Elisha Rice was carrying on his own competition with Harris. On October 10 he wrote to the State Department reporting that after a flare-up when the *Portsmouth* was there, the problem of supplying beef to ships was now settled, and complaining again of the Dutch advantage in trade. The solution he advocated had a familiar ring: a "show of force." "And as I think this [trade] properly comes under my department, I respectfully ask that one ship [he meant warship, of course] be directed to render me such assistance as may be advisable . . ."

October 18 was the first day of the Ninth Month. It was the day for putting on the lined kimono of the autumn months, for packing away the unlined garments of summer. From Kakisaki, Kosaburo made the required courtesy calls at Naka compound and at the Goyosho. To the regular first-of-the-month greetings, he added felicitations to those who would be making the trip to Edo with the American official.

October 19 brought a couple of happy events to the foreigners. First, as Hambei reported to the Goyosho, Ofuku returned to work. She had recovered, and her menses had resumed. Second, a government ship put in. This would not attract the attention of Harris or Heusken, but Yoheiji was ordered to send four men to the beach next day to carry freight to Gyokusenji.

Tuesday, October 20, 1857. At last, and fourteen months after my arrival in Japan, I have received my letters and supplies from Hakodate, from which place they were conveyed in a schooner to Edo, and from thence were sent to me in a Japanese junk. Thank God for them. I find letters from my kind and sincere friend N. Dougherty of the following dates: July 22nd, August 16th, September 22nd, October 15th, November 12th, November 26th, all 1856, and March 18, 1857. From my other dear and valued friend, General Wetmore, I have letters dated June 9th, July 21st, and November 10th, 1856.

I received in all twenty-eight letters, but not one word from the Department of State about my Treaty with Siam, or one word in answer to some of mine that it was important to me to receive answers.

All the letters from the Department were printed circulars, except one dated August, 1856, and relating to a debt contracted by two Americans, Reed and Dougherty, with the Japanese.

Reed and Dougherty, while Lieutenant Rodger's warship was in the harbor to back them up, had demanded goods on credit and sailed away leaving notes totaling about two thousand dollars. Moriyama had already approached Harris about this back in April, though Harris did not consider the matter of sufficient importance to advise the State Department of it or even to note it in his journal.

But the Department had learned of it from Lieutenant Rodgers, and directed Harris to "inquire into the business in order that the Japanese officials may see that an interest is taken by this Government in the scrupulous discharge by citizens of the United States of the obligations which they may contract in Japan." Harris was given a special fund of $3000 to pay the notes. (Harris did nothing about the matter before his Edo trip, and what with one thing and another it was the following summer before he reported to Washington. Although the notes were drawn in dollars, he considered it proper to apply the conversion rate he had negotiated two years later, settling claims amounting to $2490 with $859.05.)

The State Department mail was a disappointment to both men. For Heusken, there was nothing on the subject of his being paid any salary for the months before his arrival in Japan. For Harris, not only was there no word of praise or advice of reward for his Siam treaty, but he learned from other letters that he had almost been fired.

Saturday, October 24, 1857. I find that the President was strongly inclined to reward my services in making a commercial treaty with Siam, by removing me from my office of Consul General at Japan. It appears that the Treaty reached Washington on the 17th of September, 1856, and on the same day the New York Times published what it said was the actual Treaty. The President held that it was I and I alone that communicated it to the Times, and was for my instant removal. This was only prevented by the friendship of Governor Marcy and the untiring labors of my kind friend General Wetmore.

The President appeared to think the best mode of proceeding would be to punish me first, and then call on me for my defence. This mode of procedure is quite common among Oriental despots, but I am inclined to think that the Western rule is to hold every man innocent until he is proved to be guilty. Had the President, in his ardent desire to punish the guilty, given orders to compare the publication in the Times with the official copy in the State Department, he would at once have seen that the Times's version could not have emanated from me, nor from anyone who had an opportunity of copying the Treaty!!! . . . I wonder the Times correspondent was so inexact, as he could easily have procured an accurate copy. . . . Everyone who has had anything to do with Oriental Courts knows that the idea of secrecy as attached to negotiations is absurd. . . .

It seems a good guess that President Pierce, who had harbored serious reservations about Harris in the first place, had been thoroughly disenchanted with his appointee by those reports from Paris.

Considerably let down, Harris set about to answer his official mail. He began with somewhat ambiguous congratulations to Lewis Cass, the new Secretary of State: "I earnestly hope the appointment may prove as agreeable to you, Sir, as it is satisfactory to the People of the United States," adding, "Your letter is the first I have received since I arrived in Japan."

He reported that the fund set up to pay Heusken's salary was exhausted, and repeated his request of July, 1856, that his young secretary's salary begin March 1 of that year.

He also asked a little something for himself. He reminded the Department that regulations provided that consuls who were not permitted to engage in trade might be allowed the actual expense of their office rent, not to exceed ten per cent of their official salary. He had set aside one of the best rooms of his house as an office, he wrote, and had fitted it up in a proper manner. "I respectfully ask to be allowed a reasonable sum as rent for the same. As the office is a part of my domicile, I cannot show any vouchers for express payment for rent, but I think that two hundred dollars per annum would be an equitable allowance." He could not show any vouchers because the Japanese were giving him Gyokusenji rent-free.

Executive Officer Wakana, who was to escort Harris to Edo, called on him one day with a question about, as Wakana put it, a small but ticklish detail: would Harris present the President's letter in a box or would he take it out of the box first? Inoue, working in Edo, would like to know.

Harris was sorry, but he could discuss a matter relating to the presentation of the President's letter only with a minister of the government.

Wakana was irked. Inoue, he said, had full responsibility for smooth management of Harris's trip and audience. Though this was a small matter, if he could not know in advance, he would be "troubled, inconvenienced, and blamed." If Harris had any consideration for the Governor, he would answer the question.

Harris replied that he would not, but he relented enough to say that in Western countries, generally speaking, the most ceremonious treatment would be to present such a letter in its box.

WAKANA: Would the box be locked?

HARRIS: I cannot answer your question.

Giving up, Wakana shifted to another issue that had been irritating the Japanese for more than a year. The two of them always wore shoes, he said. "I think you should wear different ones inside and outside."

Of course they would wear new shoes when they visited the castle, Harris said (though they never had done so when they conferred at the Goyosho). They had brought dress pumps with gold buckles for this occasion.

After he left, Wakana told one of the interpreters to ask Heusken later about that letter box. Heusken confided that it appeared to have no lock.

Yoheiji, meantime, had been informed by the Goyosho that servant Kosuke was to remain on duty at Gyokusenji while the foreigners were in Edo. As for the Chinese, the headman arranged with Heizo, the barber, to keep a close watch on them. They often came to his shop. Like the men of Kakisaki, they gathered there to gossip, wreathed in the friendly scents of steaming cloths and perfumed oils, surrounded by posters of favorite *sumo* wrestlers. Assam had grown chummy with the barber: just a few days earlier he had given Heizo's mother a silver *bu*. Yoheiji had at once submitted a written report to the Goyosho. The officers there decided that the old lady could keep the money.

Heizo and the Chinese being on such close terms naturally gave rise to talk. Yoheiji had to investigate gossip that a Suzaki man working in the shop was secretly selling a bird to the American. The headman, who was always inclined to find an unpleasant rumor unfounded, determined that there was nothing to it.

Yoheiji found another matter not so easy to dismiss, though he tried valiantly.

It began on October 24, when the Goyosho patrol officers, checking on rumors, summoned the headman and elders to a meeting at Daijo-in, the temple of the mountain religion, below Gyokusenji. The purpose of the gathering was to examine Tami, wife of the retired priest and mother of the incumbent. She was old and ill, and her mind was clouded. It seemed clear that the rumors were true: Tami was bewitched.

Had she been an ordinary old woman of the village no one would have been concerned. Senility was not so rare that each case called for investigation by the Governors' staff. But Tami was not an ordinary woman. She was the wife of a priest who possessed mystic powers. She herself was the medium through which the demonic world revealed itself. If she was bewitched, then awesome sinister spirits were at work.

The officers questioned her gently, warily. She asserted that she was being treated by Okamura Bunkei, a physician of Sotoura, and that she wanted him present.

The meeting shifted to the house of one of the elders of Sotoura, and Bunkei was summoned. He insisted that he knew nothing of the patient, and the officials decided that in order to learn who was telling the truth the two must confront each other. They were brought face to face at Yoheiji's house and at once began to quarrel.

The officers decreed that the whole matter would have to be carefully probed. They left for Shimoda, taking Bunkei with them for detention in the town, and ordering that Tami be well cared for.

Next day a runner brought word that the two principals were again to face each other. Tami and her kinfolk were to report to the Shimoda town office. Kosaburo escorted them. As soon as the woman and the doctor were in the same room a wrangle developed. The meeting was cut short and the inquiry rescheduled. Tami was ordered home; Bunkei was kept in custody.

The following day was the ninth day of the Ninth Month, the Chrysanthemum Festival, last of the five great holidays of the year.

There were the usual courtesy calls, and in Shimoda the usual gifts from the town officials to the Governors and their chief aides, and to the harbor master from Uraga—two packages of sugar, perhaps, or two towels. The town had gifts for its own, too: a packet of copper coins, formally wrapped, for the headman, and another for the chief of the fishermen. After all these obligations were taken care of, Headman Hambei entertained the other town officers, serving sake flavored with chrysanthemums. If the headman followed the example of the Shogun, who on this day received all the daimyo present in Edo, he sent each guest home with a little package of ginger. That was an old custom, borrowed from the Chinese. It may have sprung from the notion that ginger's warmth would help to face the winter. Chrysanthemums and ginger: these were the symbols of this autumn holiday. (This was also the last day for going barefoot, summer-style: from tomorrow people who dressed with decorum would wear *tabi* socks.)

The holiday brought a respite from the investigation, but the next day brought another summons. Tami, her husband, and their son were to report again the following morning.

But morning found the retired priest seriously ill. It had all been too much for him. The son asked permission to report in his father's stead, and Yahei hurried to Shimoda to obtain it. At midmorning Tami, her son, their kinfolk, Yoheiji, and most of the village elders appeared at the town office. This time Tami was interrogated by a senior investigator. He confirmed that she was bewitched—there was no question about it.

The next day two officials called at Daijo-in. Yoheiji, hopeful as always, thought that as they talked to Tami she showed signs of coming to her senses. On this inconclusive note the story trails off. Tami was bewitched, Bunkei was locked up, accused of bewitching her, and evidently no one knew what to do next. The investigating officers turned their attention to a bitter dispute over money and property rights between two farmers of a village up the coast past Shirahama, who were summoned to Kakisaki so the Goyosho men would not have to travel so far. For the next several days Yoheiji's diary is filled with that case. Presumably Tami's condition neither bettered nor worsened, and in the meantime, Bunkei, like the remaining sailors of Tarojiro's ship, moldered in jail.

On October 27 Harris wrote a letter to Commodore Perry, answering one he had received on the twentieth. He told of his forthcoming trip to Edo, and of the concessions he had obtained by his convention—including extraterritoriality, which Perry had refused to inflict on the Japanese.

I am much obliged to you for your good advice. It was both sound and well-timed advice, and I have found every one of your opinions as to the course the Japanese would pursue with me, prove true to the letter.

The question is whether Perry would have recognized his ideas as put into action by Harris.

I have just obtained a copy of your *Expedition to Japan and the China Seas* [the official report of Perry's expedition], and have read it with intense interest. I hope it is no vanity in me to say that no one, at present, can so well appreciate and do justice to your work as I can. You seem at once, and almost intuitively, to have adopted the best of all courses with the Japanese. I am sure no other course would have resulted so well. I have seen quite a number of Japanese who saw you when you were at Shimoda, and they all make eager inquiries after you. Moriyama Einosuke is at Shimoda, and has not forgotten the art of lying.

As if determined not to make a liar out of Harris, Moriyama arrived in Shimoda that same evening, having made a grueling four-day dash from Edo with the latest plans, decisions, and questions concerning the trip.

Wednesday, October 28, 1857. Moriyama appeared at my house this morning, having just returned from Edo. He brought a message from Dewa-no-kami, requesting to meet me at the Goyosho at noon to-day. Moriyama brought me a box containing files of the Singapore Free Press, Illustrated London News, *and* Java Bode, *which were forwarded to me from Nagasaki on the 14th of August by Mr. H. Donker Curtius by sea, and had (of course) passed by Shimoda and been taken to Edo. Moriyama informed [me] that it was true that publications had been made concerning my visit, and added that the Government had suppressed them, as they contained so many mis-statements. On going to the Goyosho, Dewa-no-kami showed me various ground plans of the buildings where my audience was to take place, and explained their views of the ceremonies to be had, etc., etc. I accepted the whole program with one exception. They proposed that, after my audience was over and I had retired, I should return to the Audience Chamber, not as the representative of the President, but in my private capacity; that, instead of proceeding to the place I formerly occupied, I should stop at the place where I made my first bow; that the Shogun would then address me, to which I was not to reply, but simply bow and retire.*

It struck me that there was some petty scheme of glorifying themselves at my expense in this proposition, and I avoided it by saying that I could not divest myself of my character of Plenipotentiary which had been conferred on me by the President, and that, so long as the President pleased, I must maintain that character. They were evidently chagrined at this and tried to persuade me to alter my decision, assuring me that it was meant as a personal honor to me, etc., etc. I replied that I was gratified for the intention; and that, if the Shogun wished to see me at a private audience, I would cheerfully attend him, but that it must always be in my official character.

Harris and Heusken, in one of the publications concerning Harris's visit that has survived. Captions, from right to left: "Official of America Doinsento Haruris, aged sixty-one. Official interpreter. Gifts bestowed on them [from the Shogunate], fifteen mirrors, fifteen ceremonial garments" (*a print by an unknown artist*)

Despite the claim in his journal, Harris entered demurrers on a couple of other points as well. He was, as Heusken commented, highly suspicious about the place the Japanese wanted him to leave his *norimono* and continue on foot when he visited the castle, very likely because the plan indicated that Inoue was to alight from his own *norimono* at the same place. He was assured that no one but the heads of the Three Houses was ever permitted to ride up to the entrance, and he finally acceded to the plan, though he warned the Japanese that the British and French in the future would not be so amenable.

On another matter he did not give in. The Japanese had intended that he and Heusken should sit alone at the dinner he had requested. Harris said that unless there was company at the table he could not eat.

Would he be willing to eat if Inoue joined him?

It was not that he objected to dining with Inoue, he said, but this case was different. He wished it were possible to dine with the Shogun, but he was willing to concede that this was impossible. Under the circumstances he thought Lord Hotta should sit with him.

My departure is fixed for Monday, November 23rd. They proposed Friday, November 20th, but as that would cause me to pass Sunday among the hills, I declined it and fixed on Monday, which will cause me to pass my Sunday at Kawasaki, a town about fifteen miles from Edo . . .

By Western custom, Harris said, he would bear the expense of the trip, and he would appreciate knowing the details.

Nakamura assured him that since all the men and horses would be provided by order of the Shogun (that is, drafted from the villages along the way), there was no need to pay them. And all the expenses of the entire party in Edo would be borne by the Japanese government. There would remain only the hotels along the way to pay for. Harris offered no argument against this violation of Western custom.

There was one other matter. Earlier Harris had noted: *I have selected a variety of such things as I have that will probably be acceptable as presents to the Shogun and the Ministers at Edo.* Now he told the Governor that since it was not the practice in the West to exchange gifts between the heads of state on such an occasion, he had no gift for the Shogun from the President. "But as I understand the Shogun will be giving me presents, I would like to reciprocate as an individual." He had in mind some wines and liqueurs; two books of natural history profusely illustrated; a telescope; a barometer; a "rich astral lamp, three rich cut globes, extra chimneys, etc., etc."; two "very rich cut-glass decanters"; five patent locks; and a box of sardines preserved in oil. Did Nakamura think there was anything inappropriate in that list?

Nakamura thought it would be just as well to eliminate the sardines.*

They parted amicably.

After only two days in Shimoda, Moriyama left early in the morning of the thirtieth for a fast trip back to the capital. He therefore missed Harris's party, which was surely less lively without him.

Friday, October 30, 1857. To-day is the anniversary of the first visit paid to me by the Governors of Shimoda; . . . To mark the occasion, Harris invited Nakamura to dinner.

"Today the Governor with several of his staff inspected the observation post on Buzan hill," Yoheiji recorded. "Then they dropped in to the guard

---

* Harris acceded to Nakamura's suggestion with respect to the Shogun, but he later included some of his sardines (he must have been overstocked on this item) in his gifts to the Commissioners for the Visit—all of which he included in his expense account.

station at Kakisaki, and finally visited Gyokusenji, where they had conversations with the American."

. . . Dewa-no-kami . . . visited me attended by one of the Vice-Governors [Wakana], the Mayor or Prefect of Kakisaki [Wakiya], the Commissary of Shimoda [Kikuna] and his private secretary, besides a large train of officers, guards, etc., etc., but the above were all that were admitted into my private rooms. After an hour of pleasant chat we sat down to a very good dinner provided in our style, and they did full honor to my cheer, both solids and fluids.

As soon as this was done, the dishes were removed and I gave them a second one in Japanese style. Still they ate, but nature has its limits; they did what they could, but fell far short of their first performance. They left me at five P.M., full of fun and good cheer. Their conduct at table would have passed in any society of New York, Paris or London.

An enormous umbrella has been added to the paraphernalia of my tail for Edo.

Saturday, October 31,1857. I am truly grateful for improved health. I begin to recover a little of my lost flesh.

In Edo, right up to the end of October, it had seemed to Yoshinaga that things were going very well in his campaign to have Keiki appointed heir. Then he was startled by the news that Matsudaira Tadakata had been reappointed to the Great Council. Previously a member, he had been dismissed by Lord Abe a year before on the grounds that he had intrigued with Ii Naosuke and others against Abe and Nariaki; there was no doubt that Nariaki had pressed for his dismissal.

"A man of dark and conspiring nature," Yoshinaga called Tadakata. His reappointment could only mean greater influence for Naosuke, greater hostility toward Nariaki and his son Keiki. It was a development that was most unpleasant to Yoshinaga, and he set about to see what he could do to counteract it.

Chapter 17

NOVEMBER, 1857

November 1: Moriyama had not yet reached Edo but couriers had. They had brought word of Harris's refusal to take dinner alone or to present himself for a second audience with the Shogun.

To the Commissioners for the Visit, and then to the Great Council, Inoue outlined the arguments he would use with Harris. "As soon as he arrives at his quarters in Edo," Inoue wrote, "I shall visit him to extend greetings, and I shall take the opportunity to explain the honors being tendered him." He would emphasize that the dinner and the second audience were honors in Japanese eyes, and he would remind Harris that he had said he would follow Japanese customs as long as they did not impair his dignity. "Of course, if he still refuses," Inoue admitted, "there is nothing we can do but accept his decision. The dinner then will be carried to his quarters."

Inoue had a concession which he hoped would help: the original plan had been altered to permit Harris to go eighty steps farther into the castle grounds before dismounting from his *norimono*—eighty steps farther than Inoue would ride. The Governor had rightly guessed that Harris was upset at the first plan's calling for them both to dismount at the same point.

It seems scarcely possible that Inoue, after his experience over the past year, really hoped to change Harris's mind. But he would try. He would do his best. He was exhausting himself doing his best.

He must have been the busiest man in Edo. The Commission for the Visit was too large and unwieldy a body for administration. Most of the burden fell on Inoue, as he later told Harris: *He spoke of his anxious days and sleepless nights; that care and anxiety had taken away his appetite, so that he had become lean in his person; and that his blood had frequently gushed from his nose from his great agitation;* . . . All this is quite believable when one looks at the sheer volume of his paper work, and certainly it has not all survived.

He had thought that other agencies of the government, like his brother's finance bureau, would assist him. When they did not, he had to submit urgent requests that more of the Shimoda staff be assigned to his group in Edo. Then he had to request allowances to cover their expenses in journeying to the capital; some were approved, some disapproved, and most he was told to absorb within his own mangled budget.

Citing Harris's poor health, he recommended that Ito Kansai be assigned as his physician in Edo, noting that the doctor had called on Harris when he was ill in Shimoda (the first time we hear of this).

He asked permission for Wakana to wear formal dress when accompanying Harris to Lord Hotta's mansion and to the castle, and to take two samurai with him. The dress was approved, the samurai were not. Then another request had to go forward, asking that the Shogunate's keeper of the wardrobe lend the formal clothes to Wakana for the occasion.

He had to ask that Wakana be permitted to use a *kago* throughout the trip. The executive officer had been suffering from piles, he told the Great Council, and recently they were especially severe. It would be appreciated if he could be permitted to ride. The Great Council granted such permission for one month.

And, looking ahead, Inoue and the commissioners recommended that as soon as Harris had had his audience he be hurried back to Shimoda, there to reveal his "important matters" to the Governors. It would not do to let Harris stay in Edo and conduct negotiations, they argued, for negotiations should be opened only after careful preparation which must follow consideration of the President's message. They made this recommendation twice without drawing any response from Lord Hotta, an unsettling indication that he did not agree: perhaps he wanted any negotiations conducted where he could keep a finger on them. The *ometsuke* and *metsuke* were on record that the Great Council should solicit Harris's opinions on world affairs. As Inoue well knew, it would be no problem to get Harris to talk; a problem would arise only if they wanted to keep him from talking.

Inoue was not, of course, the only man coping with the forthcoming visit. The Governors of Edo had the primary responsibility for guarding Harris. Okada's men in the construction bureau were rushing essential remodeling and repairs. The government's chief scholar, Hayashi, who had been chief of the delegation that negotiated with Perry and now was one of the Commissioners for the Visit, rendered opinions on ceremony and protocol.

Hayashi also took up a problem not immediately related to the visit: Harris's demand that the government's letters to him be closed with honorific phrases. The issue had come as a surprise to him, he confessed, because he and the other officials read Harris's letters in translation and therefore had no way of knowing what honorifics the American was using. There was no need for the Japanese to follow a foreign style of writing letters, he said, but the Japanese had long used complimentary closings and certainly an appropriate one should be used in a letter to a foreigner. It was the kind of issue which the Chinese usually met with stiff-backed intransigence; the Japanese were more adaptable.

The crest of Hayashi Daigaku-no-kami

All of these papers—Inoue's recommendations and requests, the Edo Governors' plans, the construction bureau's reports, the advice from Hayashi—all flowed to the Great Council. In matters as critical as these, it took the Great Council to make a decision.

Nor were these the only communications the Council had to handle. We may note a jarring message from the Lord of Sendai, the most powerful Outside Lord north of Edo, the man who had often sent retainers to check firsthand the situation at Shimoda. He would not be faithful to his duty, this influential daimyo wrote, if he did not protest the Shogun's receiving Harris. It would be an act of exceeding rashness; the Shogun's dignity would be irretrievably lost, even among the Emperor's court in Kyoto:

Many others hold this same opinion, though they hesitate to tell you so.
It is impossible for us to treat America on the same basis as Korea and

Ryukyu, for these are countries with whom we have maintained friendly relations for a very long time. Besides, America is a Christian country and that religion may spread if you permit the envoy's visit.

Once you permit the American to visit the Edo court, you will have to grant the same privilege to the envoys of other countries, and the government will reveal its real condition to foreigners. Two centuries of peace have made the spirit of the people weak.

He was grateful, the Lord of Sendai continued, that the government had assigned him to guard the west coast of the northern island of Hokkaido, for through this stern duty his subordinates had regained a spirit of fortitude. He clearly implied that the men of other daimyo lacked just that: the country was soft, a fact which should not be advertised to foreigners.

Another response to the announcement of Harris's visit must have disturbed the Great Council at least as much, for different reasons. It came from the lords of the Great Hall, the third-ranking chamber at the castle. They joined the chorus asking for greater military preparedness, and then had the audacity to ask for an advance report on what the Shogun would reply to Harris, a request of such daring that it would have been unthinkable at the height of the Shogunate's power.

Harris probably would have been shocked to know how powerful and widespread was the opposition to his visit. Perhaps he would have been puzzled that it could be expressed so openly. This did not correspond with his notion of Japan as a monolithic despotism.

He had, of course, only a foggy idea of how Japan was governed. Certainly he would have been surprised to learn that there was under way a struggle for control of the Shogunate just as bitter and divisive as the struggle over how to face foreigners like himself. He would have found it hard to follow its convolutions, hard to follow, for instance, the devious twisting of a man like Nariaki, who desperately wanted his son to be the next Shogun and was himself the greatest obstacle in his son's path to power.

Just now the Elderly Lord, having been rebuffed by Edo, was muddying the waters with new overtures to Kyoto: he presented a sword to the Emperor, who was already displaying disquieting assertiveness.

Behavior like this caused Matsudaira Yoshinaga to take over leadership of the forces trying to make Keiki the Shogun's heir. He assured Hotta that father and son were entirely different, and he offered to see to it that if Keiki were chosen, Nariaki would be kept at Mito, safely out of things. To his ally Shimazu Nariakira, he made it clear that if Keiki were made heir, Nariaki's every move would have to be watched.

Calling on Hotta early in November, Yoshinaga finally got the head of the Great Council to express an opinion: if it were necessary to select an heir, he supposed the eleven-year-old Lord of Kii, one of the Three Houses, would be most suitable. He was young enough to be the Shogun's son and he was more closely related than any other candidate.

In ordinary times that would be true, Yoshinaga replied, but the present times were not ordinary. The nation was faced with grave crisis and that was why men like himself were urging an heir who could assist the Shogun in meeting his heavy responsibilities. Keiki was such a man. At twenty he was wise and mature. He commanded the respect of the daimyo. His appointment would strengthen the Shogunate.

Hotta promised to give the matter close attention.

Pleading the case with Hotta was not the whole campaign, of course. Overtures were made to other councillors by men close to them. Nariakira tried an approach to the inner court, the Shogun's private realm, run by the women who surrounded him. Nariakira thought he had established a bridgehead to this matriarchal enclave when he made his daughter the Shogun's bride. He learned that her influence was nil. Enmity for Nariaki made the inner court hostile territory.

Yoshinaga tried to bribe the new councillor, Tadakata, whom he believed to be bribable, but who on this occasion, at least, refused to live down to his reputation. He would say only that he could not focus on the problem of the heir because the troublesome American was keeping him so busy.

Oblivious of all this, still tucked away in Shimoda, the troublesome American was happily puttering with preparations for his trip, enjoying the return of relatively good health after the release from strain.

He wrote a letter to be delivered by Assam to the commander of any American man-of-war that might appear in his absence. He asked that a letter stating the circumstances of the visit be sent to him in Edo.

> You can write freely to me, as letters properly closed are no longer opened by the Japanese. I shall feel greatly obliged by any items of news you can send me, as well as for one or two of your latest newspapers. I earnestly hope you will remain at Shimoda until you can hear from me, as I shall have important dispatches to forward by you.

He had some recommendations about an anchorage, assurance that at this time of year there need be no fear of hurricanes or gales, the usual advertisement of the new rate of exchange, and a request that "you will not take your ship up the Gulf of Edo as it might embarrass me in my negotiations with the Japanese."

However, there was one place he did want the ship to go.

> You would confer a benefit on our interests here by ascertaining the longitude of the west coast of the Island of Oshima, or Volcano Island, which lies due east from your anchorage, in the Gulf. I wish to ascertain if it does not come within the limit of 7 ri or 16½ statute miles from Center Island in Shimoda Harbor. You will readily identify the island by observing the steam that ascends from it, which is always seen in fine weather.

Nothing had changed his assumption that the Japanese were liars.

He wrote a similar letter for any merchant vessel that might sail in, without the request about Oshima and without any request that the captain wait for dispatches. He really didn't trust traders.

He didn't trust his Chinese servants, either, as he made clear in a letter to Governor Nakamura. After requesting that they "be supplied with all necessary food, fuel, etc., for themselves, as well as food for my pigs, fowls, pigeons, etc., etc.," he asked that two officers be assigned to keep order at Gyokusenji. "My servants have strict orders to conduct themselves well during my absence and I will punish them on my return if they behave badly. I send a warrant under my seal authorising any Japanese officer to arrest any of my servants that may try to leave Shimoda during my absence."

He settled accounts with Kikuna and surveyed his finances, growing steadily more cheerful: *I paid . . . the Goyosho for my bills with them for four months, amounting to 754 ichibus, or $260; but this covers a good deal of carpenter's work and other extras. My bills with the Japanese for supplies will be about $700 per annum. To this add supplies from Hong Kong, say $500, servants $650, gives a total of $1,850 per annum, less $365 per annum paid by Mr. Heusken as his share of household expenses,—leaving my outlay about $1,500 per annum. But, at the rate of exchange against the United States, which varies from thirty to forty-five per cent., I can remit to New York some $6,000 per annum as my savings out of a salary of $5,000! Besides, I have made a little sum of about $2,500 by taking from the Japanese foreign gold at the rate at which they took it,—i.e., 34½ cents per dollar. This I send to Hong Kong to be disposed of by remittance to New York or for sale, as may be most for my interest.*

As far as his impending trip was concerned, the Japanese were busy shuttling men and messages between Edo and Shimoda, but Harris was little involved in their preparations. The record reveals nothing more exciting for him than a visit from Wakana, who acted on orders from Inoue and the commissioners to tell him that should he meet any daimyo or officials on the road, he need not greet them. Harris protested a little. Some of the glamour would be lost if roadside ceremony were dispensed with. Of course, he considered his rank higher than that of anyone he might meet, so that he expected to receive, not pay, the courtesies. On the other hand, Inoue and the commissioners knew that it was unthinkable that any daimyo would acknowledge the Consul General from America as a superior. A good deal of effort went into seeing that Harris would encounter no one of importance on the road, but in case such a confrontation should occur, it was decreed that the two parties should pass with stony indifference.

It was Wakana who would bear the brunt of any such meeting. Worry about such contingencies was no doubt aggravating his condition. One hotheaded defender of Japan's honor, one flashing sword, could spell disaster—probably for Harris, certainly for Wakana, very possibly for Japan. Harris, who steadfastly refused to believe that he was in any danger, was unconcerned.

Wednesday, November 4, 1857. A beautiful day. Thermometer, 70°. Rode down towards Cape Izu as far as was possible on horseback, and over roads that would startle any English steeplechaser. The country looks far more beautiful than it did at this time last year, as the typhoon of September 22, 1856, destroyed nearly all [the] vegetation. Rice crop is about one-third harvested and looks very well. Buckwheat in full bloom.

It may be that harvesting had not yet begun at Kakisaki. The crop inspection had not yet taken place. On the seventh Yoheiji received word that it would be conducted on the ninth. Each village was to send men to the Goyosho that morning to guide the examiners. Yoheiji put a notice on the bulletin board, and on the appointed morning Chuemon and Mohei reported, but it began to rain and the survey was put off to the next day, and then to the day after. So it did not take place until the eleventh. In the morning the inspectors visited the fields of Shimoda and Okagata, and then they came to Kakisaki, where they were given lunch. After that they sampled Yoheiji's fields and on their way home they checked two more.

There was nothing to hold up the harvest now except that many families found themselves short-handed. Heusken's diary gives a clue.

November 13, 1857. It seems that the Japanese do everything they must do at the same time, prescribed by law. They take their breakfast, lunch, and dinner all exactly at the same hour. They change clothes four times a year on the same day. One day everybody is busy drying fish; another day is to dry fabrics woven by the women. Apparently they go even further, for today everybody without exception has a cold, certainly by order of the government.

To the village it was not that amusing. Priest Bimo recorded a startling number of deaths during the first half of the month. An epidemic, probably influenza again, was sweeping the area. It was not easy to get in the harvest when many were sick.

In Edo, decisions had been made regarding the streets Harris would travel when he arrived in the city, when he visited Lord Hotta, and when he went to the castle. The Great Council then issued instructions, as notable for what they did not require as for what they did:

> When, in the near future, the American ambassador visits Edo, it will not be necessary to repair the mansions along the road; the temporary board fences may be left as they are. Each householder is to keep his portion of the road swept clean. It will likewise not be necessary to set out the ornamental firemen's buckets before the houses, nor to place guards there. Travelers may be allowed to pass along as usual. Guards should be placed at the guardhouses to suppress any disorder, if required to do so by the officers in attendance on the ambassador.
>
> As for sightseers, they may stand at designated spots along the road, but are not to be allowed to crowd together at the upper-story windows of tenement houses and like places. As much as possible, all encounters of persons on horseback are to be avoided.
>
> Great care must be taken by the officials to avoid all noise and confusion on the way. Hence, to avoid mistakes, careful directions must be given to even the lowest official. The foregoing is to be made known to all officers in charge.

The Governors of Edo promptly issued implementing orders to the headmen of the towns, or neighborhoods, which made up the city. These orders and the headmen's responses produced some instructions more explicit:

> It is prohibited to erect bleachers along the American's route.
> It is prohibited to watch the procession from roofs, the tops of walls, or fire-towers.
> Shopkeepers along the way are to admit only the usual number of customers. [Since it was conceded that this might be difficult to enforce, shopkeepers were directed to hang curtains or bamboo screens outside their second-floor windows to discourage customers from crowding in to use those vantage points.]
> Shops are prohibited from displaying swords, spears, halberds, suits of

armor, or other weapons; also maps, books in Dutch, and erotic pictures.

If the American wishes to buy something he is not to be permitted to haggle over price.

Public bathhouses may remain open but naked bathers will not be allowed to watch the procession either from the front of the house or from second-story windows.

Fish and vegetable markets usually held on streets to be traveled will be moved elsewhere for the day.

Buildings ravaged by the 1855 earthquake and still unrepaired are to be hidden behind board fences.

Beggars are to be kept out of the American's sight. [It was Danzae-mon, hereditary chief of all beggars and outcasts, who would implement this order.]

Toilets are to be prepared along the way so that the American need suffer no inconvenience.

Similar instructions went out to the officials responsible for the highways between Shimoda and Edo. Bearers and horses were to be provided. The roads were to be cleaned and bridges repaired if necessary. Houses and fences need not be decorated but each householder was to sweep the road in front of his place. At overnight stops, officials and men were to stand by and alternate places of refuge made ready in case of fire or other emergency.

On the fifteenth of November, Inoue issued the schedule of the trip:

	MIDDAY STOP	OVERNIGHT STOP	DISTANCE
Monday, November 23	Mitsukuri	Nashimoto	15 miles
Tuesday, November 24	Mount Amagi	Yugashima	16 miles
Wednesday, November 25	Ohito	Mishima	20 miles
Thursday, November 26	Hakone	Odawara	20 miles
Friday, November 27	Oiso	Fujisawa	21 miles
Saturday, November 28	Hodagaya	Kawasaki	20 miles
Sunday, November 29	rest at Kawasaki		
Monday, November 30	Shinagawa	Edo	14 miles

Inoue had changed his mind about using the coastal route, perhaps after traveling it himself. The party would take the central road up Izu, over the Amagi mountains.

The first day the train would wind along the river which waters the Shimoda valley, through brown fields where the last of the rice was being cut and threshed. At midday they would halt and climb stone steps to a Shinto shrine set among the cedars. Below them the river divided: Harris could look up the valley and the road which led west to Matsuzaki, as well as up the valley and the road he would travel, twisting northward. One of the villages at his feet would be Shiibara, where the *eta* of this valley lived, but no one would tell him that.

The elders of Shimoda who had been accompanying them would take their leave here, presenting their name cards, their compliments, and their good wishes for the journey ahead. After a little prompting, Harris would show his appreciation with some cash for their trouble.

In the afternoon the train would push up the narrowing valley, the road rising, the river diminishing to a thread. They would cross a mountain and begin the descent into another valley, moving now through forest: *some noble cypress and camphor trees,* Harris would write, noticing espe-

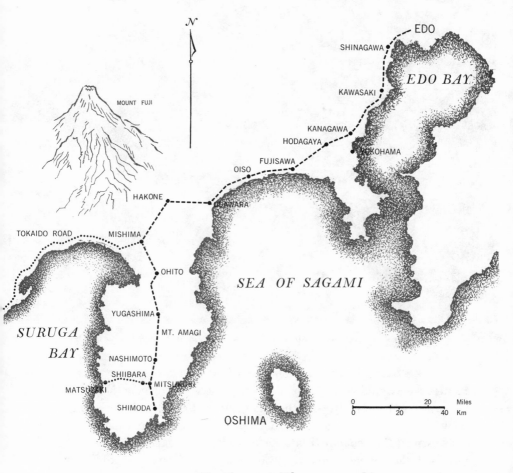

Harris's route to Edo.

cially one enormous camphor many hundred years old. Heusken would be less happy in their shadows. He would call the scene "gloomy and monotonous," until a waterfall came into view: "I love waterfalls!"

They would stop for the night at a temple on an eminence commanding *a most beautiful view of the hills and valley, and of the village which lay some one hundred and fifty feet abruptly below us.* It was the same temple where the "mutual assistance association" for the sick farmer had been organized, and whose priest, for a time at least, had been suspected of harboring a *ronin* who was plotting against the Americans.

Harris's procession on its way to Edo (*a painting by an unknown Japanese artist*)

". . . a lane lined with magnificent pines leads the weary traveler to it," Heusken would write. Then out of the packs would come the two chairs, the table, and the mattresses they had felt compelled to bring along. And their cook, who had been trained for five weeks by the Chinese cook at Gyokusenji (*His cookery is inferior to Delmonico's, but much more to my taste than the Japanese cuisine*), would take over the temple's kitchen.

Kikuna would come to apologize for the accommodations, but there

516

would be no need: "These good Japanese!" Heusken would exclaim. "They are full of attentions. They have built a bathroom expressly for us!" And when he had looked about him—"Two hundred feet below one sees a lovely little brook cascading its clear and limpid waters from stone to stone and flowing into the sea a couple of leagues in the distance"—he would forget his weariness and, of all things, go for a walk.

> After having crossed two hills and a stream I see two soldiers running after me, while two others, out of breath, run to me from another direction. The poor fellows are exhausted; they have had a hard time catching up with me. They tell me that the Vice-Governor, having arrived at the temple, wants to pay his respects to the Ambassador and that I am needed to interpret what he has to say. . . . I retrace my steps and find the Ambassador and the Vice-Governor trying to outdo each other, gesticulating, speaking respectively English and Japanese to the interpreter who understands only Dutch and his native tongue.

So he would rescue them, and transfer their compliments one to the other, and then he would take a *cold* bath, which would surely amaze the Japanese even more than his walk. And after dinner he would read himself to sleep with "a few strophes of Corneille."

The second day would take them over Amagi, the cluster of volcanic peaks that dominate the middle of Izu. It would be rough going: they would realize how cut off they had been from the rest of Japan. Both the old man and the young one would retreat from their horses to their *norimono*. "We climb steep paths above deep chasms," Heusken would write. "Sometimes there are steps hewn out of the rock like a genuine staircase, because the path follows an almost vertical grade." (Harris, a less poetic observer, would say that the angle was sometimes thirty-five degrees.)

"The paths are so narrow that four men cannot walk there abreast and the curves of the route are so sharp that our *norimono* can hardly negotiate them." Harris's huge palanquin had a twenty-two-foot pole. There would be times when he was hanging over an abyss as his straining bearers tortuously jockeyed the zigzags.

At the summit they would break out of the forest of cypress, pine, and camphor with their clinging orchids, and they would find a small inn with a dazzling view of the peninsula and the ocean on either side. There would lie Shimoda, there tantalizing Oshima.

> Wherever we go it seems that a kind genie supplies the Japanese with food and drink. In a wink, without us knowing from where it

comes, they are supplied with all kinds of victuals, and take their dinners, suppers or lunches as comfortably as they would at home.

Of the descent they would, as they frequently did, disagree: to Harris, *not quite so abrupt as the ascent was;* to Heusken,

> even worse than the way up. It seems an abyss is opening under our very steps ready to swallow us; and then the sharp outcropping of rock pushing through what little sand and turf there is on the road offers no foothold for a horse's hoof.

The young man would choose to walk—a decision he would regret, for in the mud of the spring-soaked path he would ruin a precious pair of shoes and again he would be forced to place himself "under torture, seeing my limbs crippled or my muscles stiffened, in a word, enclosing myself in my *norimono.*"

As soon as the worst was past, the two of them would emerge from their cages and on horseback reach the hot-spring village of Yugashima, where they would spend the night. They would turn off the main road toward their temple. A vista would open before them: thirty miles north-west would be Fuji.

It is grand beyond description; viewed from this place the mountain is entirely isolated and appears to shoot up in a perfect and glorious cone, some ten thousand feet * *high; while its actual height is exaggerated by the absence of any neighboring hills by which to contrast its altitude. It was covered with snow, and in the bright sun (about four P.M.) it appeared like frosted silver. In its majestic solitude it appeared even more striking to me than the celebrated Dwhalgiri † of the Himalayas, which I saw in January, 1855.*

For Heusken it would be almost too much.

> As we near the valley and emerge from the clouds that hover over the summit of Amagi, the countryside begins to unfold; valleys of ravishing beauty upon which the sun casts a gentle glow appear before our eyes. Rounding a mountain, I sight through the foliage of a few pine trees a white peak that gleams in the sun. In an instant I realize that I am looking at Fujiyama. Never in my life will I forget the sight of that mountain as I saw it today for the first time, and I don't think anything in the world will ever equal its beauty.

---

* Actually, 12,397 feet.

† Dhauagiri, in Nepal, 26,790 feet high, the world's sixth highest mountain, once thought the highest, and as of this writing, the only one of the world's ten highest mountains which has not been climbed.

There were mountains higher than Fuji. There were the Alps and the Himalayas.

But here, in the midst of a smiling countryside covered with abundant crops—with pine groves and giant camphor trees that seem to vie in longevity with the very soil where they were born, making shade with their majestic foliage for some *miya*, or chapel, dedicated to the ancient Gods of the Empire, and as a backdrop for this theater of plenty and serenity—the pure outline of the unique Fujiyama rises like two symmetrical lines toward the sky, whose pale blue seemed dark, compared to the immaculate snows of the mountain that reflected, like another Kohinoor, the rays of the setting sun.

In spite of myself I pulled the reins of my horse and, carried away by an outburst of enthusiasm [which must at once have dampened Harris's delight] I took off my hat and cried: "Great, glorious Fujiyama!" Glory forever to the mountain of mountains of the Pacific Sea, which alone raises its venerable brow covered with eternal snow amidst the verdant countryside of Nippon! Jealous of its beauty, it will not suffer a rival which might lessen its splendor. Its crown of snow stands out alone above the highest mountains of Nippon, and Amagi, which we have just passed after a most difficult day, seems only a small hill, hardly worth mentioning.

Ah! Why don't I have about twenty of the friends of my younger days around me! The surrounding hills would soon repeat the echo of a thrice repeated *hip, hip, hip, hurrah* in honor of the sublime Fujiyama.

Never, anywhere, have I seen that mountain as beautiful as it appears from here. A few steps from this point we reach a temple, the Temple of Yugashima, where we are to spend the night. From the windows of my room I can enjoy an excellent vista of my favorite mountain. I draw a sketch of it, and I can assure you that it is a detestable sketch, one that resembles anything but Fujiyama.

Their third day's journey would bring them at last to Japan's great highway, the Tokaido, and to the post station town of Mishima. Their road would cross a fertile plain *covered with a heavy crop of rice, of which the harvest had just commenced; . . .* Harris would be reminded of *the golden wheat fields of old Ontario.*

After their noon stop at Ohito the Consul General would forget his promise to stay with his escort. Impatiently he and Heusken would forge ahead. Kikuna would stick with them and fall from his horse in the effort, fortunately wounding nothing but his pride. (Heusken, who was an expert on such matters, would be unkind enough to say that it was Kikuna's fault, not the horse's.) Two soldiers and the standard bearer would manage somehow to keep pace on foot, with, as Heusken would put it, "an emulation worthy of praise" (worthy of a handsome tip, too, but it is doubtful that they got it).

They would reach Mishima in midafternoon, with time enough to visit the town's famed shrine, or at least its precincts, the main hall having been destroyed by the 1855 earthquake. Harris would make a contribution toward its reconstruction and be thanked by a covey of priests, and his name would be written on a board in strange-looking characters and put up with thousands of others along the entrance lane (joining those of his neighbors back at Kakisaki, for their small shrine was considered a branch of this great one, and they had already contributed their bit).

That night they would experience their first *honjin,* or, as Harris would put it, a *rest house for persons of the highest rank, such as the princes, etc.* They would be pampered and they would like it, and be delighted by the garden in the rear: *dwarf trees, miniature mountains and other rock work; diminutive ponds with bridges over which nothing grosser than a fairy could walk, etc., etc.*

At seven-thirty next morning they would begin the trek over the Hakone mountains. Now they would be on *the great road of Japan; it is from thirty to forty feet wide and is bordered by very noble cypress, pine, fir and camphor trees. Many of the cypresses are of extraordinary size.* The typhoon Harris had experienced the autumn before had made *sad ravages among these fine trees. I found marks of its effects almost every hundred yards.*

Soon they would begin *to ascend the spurs of Hakone. The road up the mountain is paved with flat stones; and, from the total absence of wheel carriages, or of horses that are shod with iron, the stones are quite polished and so slippery that it is dangerous riding a horse over them.*

Harris would take to his *norimono,* but Heusken would prefer to climb afoot in the company of Superintendent Wakiya and Inspector Aihara, with whom he would carry on

> a conversation in Japanese which lasts for a long time because it takes me about ten times longer to express a thought in Japanese (than in my native tongue) and after all my pains I often fail to make myself understood at all. But the satisfaction I feel from speaking Japanese is so gratifying to me that I keep on talking, and if my words do not sound too clear I throw in a word of Latin or Greek to the great edification of my audience.
>
> I also take pleasure in quoting to them a few verses by Racine or

Corneille and I have myself the pleasure of making the mountain of Hakone echo the imprecations of Camille.

(Camille, like the heroine of "Raven at Dawn," was a girl whom his Japanese companions could take to heart; one hopes he told them her story.)

Over the summit of the mountain they would find the village of Hakone by the deep blue waters of a lake reflecting the image of Fuji. At the far end of this village they would stop before the barrier station, confronting officers whose ancient instructions were to search each traveler: to prevent weapons' being carried into Edo, or women and children who were hostages, out of it. "This barrier is placed in a defile so that, since the surrounding mountains are very high and steep, anyone who wishes to go to Edo is compelled to go through this very passage." With a wind cold from the snows of Fuji whipping up whitecaps on the lake, whistling through the defile, and chilling those in it, the stage would be set for another of those tests of will power Harris so loved to chronicle.

Here the Vice-Governor of Shimoda, after a vast deal of circumlocution, informed me that, when the great Princes of the Empire passed here, the door of the norimono was opened and an officer looked into it, without stopping the bearers; that it was a mere ceremony, but the ancient laws required it, etc., etc.

I replied that, as I was not a Japanese subject, and being as I was the diplomatic representative of the United States, I was free from any such search; that they knew what was in my norimono, and could inform the officers at the pass that there was nothing forbidden in it. The Vice-Governor tried for some time to change my determination, and at last proposed that I should ride through on horseback, and then permit the search of the empty norimono. I decidedly declined this, telling him that it was the search under any form that I objected to. He then said that we must stop until he could send to Edo for instructions, which would only take five days. I told him I should not wait five days nor five hours; that if the search was insisted on I should at once return to Shimoda. The poor Vice-Governor was in great tribulation and finally went to the guard house, and after a delay of two hours returned with word that it was all settled and that I should pass unmolested.

Here Harris would end his story, unable to mention the compromise he had accepted: that while his own *norimono* was to pass unopened, the Japanese reserved the right to open Heusken's.

He was even less able to record the story's anticlimax, but Heusken couldn't bear not to tell. For the firm stand, the right so rightly asserted, would come to naught:

> Upon arriving at the barrier, Takizo, Mr. Harris's valet, opened the door of his *norimono* and closed it immediately. Mr. Harris was furious, believing with reason that the Japanese had broken their given word; but it appears, after all, that the only person responsible for this was Takizo, who, having heard Sukezo being ordered to open the door of my *norimono* and knowing that everyone has to submit to this custom, and being ignorant of the rights of general extraterritoriality of ambassadors, believed that he was subject to the order as well and obeyed it.

They would be late now, and long before they reached Odawara and their *honjin* it would be dark. Perhaps as well, for the pageantry of the night would help put out of mind the contretemps at the barrier. . . . *I was not sorry for the delay, as the effect of my train with an immense number of flambeaux made from bamboos presented a curious and novel appearance, as it wound and turned in the descents of the mountain, making a figure like the tail of an imaginary fiery dragon. Beyond the walls of the town I was met by the officials, with an army of lanterns of all imaginable sizes, shapes and colors, all decorated with the arms of the owner.*

They would make a leisurely eight-thirty start the next morning. Izu and the mountains were behind them. Now the Tokaido, "perfectly tended, smoothly leveled," traversed the fertile, densely populated plain that extended to Edo and beyond.

> On both sides of the road, as far as the eye can reach, one sees rice fields in which countless flocks of storks walk with measured tread, heedless of everyone, or take wing to settle again in the next field, now running, then flying, or running and flying at the same time. Great numbers of wild geese streak across the sky, and their honks, although not at all melodious, please me because they are familiar to me and remind me of other times and other places.

They would travel an empty road as the government had ordered: no encounters, no trouble. But in the villages there would be silent throngs of sightseers.

> In all the places through which we pass, a deputation of the authorities comes to meet us and escorts us through the place, acting, so to speak, as a guard of honor. Before the entrance to the place the deputation is lined up in order; they pay the usual compliments, bowing their foreheads to the ground, which they repeat when they leave us.

Crossing the Hakone mountains at night *(a print by Hiroshige)*

The officials are accompanied by policemen armed with iron rods. In this way an open passage is always made in the middle of the road. Before the houses the people are gathered in groups in order to let us pass. They are all sitting in good order, not uttering one word, hands towards the ground as a sign of the deepest respect. Not only the ground floors but also the second floors are packed with people assembled here to watch us pass. . . . Undoubtedly they may have paid an enormous price for a window overlooking the street . . .

Some people, walking ahead of our procession continually shouted: "*Shita ni iro, shita ni iro,*" kneel down, kneel down, and all the common people, men, women, and children, knelt down and remained in an attitude of the deepest respect until we had passed. I traveled from Shimoda to Shinagawa, a journey of seven days, amidst a kneeling population, while our heralds continually repeated the "*shita ni iro,*" kneel down, even in the remotest parts of the forests or on the tops of mountains where there was no one, as if the trees and plants should pay homage to the Embassy of the Republic Par Excellence.

The acid in this remark would show that certain things were getting under the young man's skin. "The sight of all these human beings, as good as I am or even better, on their knees began to disgust me."

Ferryboats on the Banyu River (*a print by Hiroshige*)

Harris's journal, in contrast, would indicate obeisance accepted as to the manner born. *The people were perfectly well behaved, no crowding on me, no shouting or noise of any kind. As I passed, all knelt and cast their eyes down (as though they were not worthy even to look at me). Only those of a certain rank were allowed to salute me, which was done by "knocking head" or bringing the forehead actually to the ground.*

"*Shita ni iro, shita ni iro*": to Harris the heralds' cry *sounded quite musical.*

They would travel the same road, these two, but they would see many things differently. One imagines them quite civilly disagreeing over dinner in the evening. They had to get along, but each of them, later alone with his journal, would make his own point of view triumphant.

On this fifth day of their journey they would have a new experience. They would be forded across the Banyu River,* *now some 200 yards wide, but in the rains of May and June it is over one mile wide. The land on either side is a mere bed of sand, and the river is filled with quicksands. These sands [and] the great width of the river during the floods, joined to the very low banks, render the bridging of the stream very difficult.* And so a small army of coolies would already have been mobilized to carry *kago,* baggage, and men through the river.

As I mounted my horse after being ferried over the Banyugawa, my vicious brute of a horse both bit and kicked me. The little finger of my left hand was very painful and I ordered some leeches to be applied. The doctor approached with great trepidation, while large drops of perspiration stood on his forehead. I asked what ailed him; he said that he had never approached any person of such exalted rank before, and he was terrified at the idea of drawing blood from me. He was told to forget all about rank, and to apply his remedy as quickly as possible. The leeches are very small and of course not very efficient. Excellent leeches are found in every part of the tropical East. A tank like those of Pulo Penang would be a pretty fortune to a man if he had it in New York. . . . My surgeon, having finished his labor, retired a proud and happy man; happy that he had pleased me, and proud that he had been called on to attend a person occupying my position.

Shortly afterward they would halt for the night at Fujisawa.

Their next day's journey would bring them to the shores of Edo bay, with a midday rest at Kanagawa (a bit farther than Hodagaya and the only change in their original schedule). From their inn they would *look across*

---

* The lower reaches of the Sagami River.

Fujisawa (*a print by Hiroshige*)

the bay to Yokohama, the place where Perry had anchored his fleet and negotiated his treaty. Harris would be *much surprised by the sight of three ships of European build and rig, which with two schooners were lying about midway between Kanagawa and Yokohama*—evidence that despite some mistakes Japan was aiming to build a navy. (One of the vessels had been contributed by Satsuma, another was Mito's *The Rising Sun*—"The Nuisance": since she was so difficult to sail, she was usually moored here, quietly collecting barnacles.) Farther up the bay would be visible Japan's first steamship, the little paddle-wheel *Kanko Maru,* a gift from the King of the Netherlands. Harris would be attracted to this place and regret leaving it to push on toward Kawasaki, where he was to pass Sunday.

Like the owner of every other designated *honjin* along the way, the innkeeper at Kawasaki would have been terribly busy. The day before, he would have sent a message to Fujisawa, listing the provisions that he had been ordered to lay in to feed the foreigners:

> three pounds of wild boar meat
> five pounds of pork
> forty eggs
> one young cock and one young hen

>two ducks
>sole, *tai,* and lobster
>persimmons, pears, and ginkgo nuts

and the inevitable oil in which Harris liked his food cooked. A hasty postscript would add that in accordance with a late message advising that the American also enjoyed quail, snipe, teal, oysters, tangerines, grapes, and turnips, a supply of these items had been carefully chosen.

What, alas, the keeper of the *honjin* would not have done, for he could not afford to, was refurbish his inn. His family had fallen on bad times; his inn was shabby and in disrepair. And so when Harris would arrive and look it over, he would flatly refuse to stay there. *Doors and windows would not close, the paper in many places broken, so that the wind played freely through the rooms, while an air of dirty slovenliness reigned over the whole. This was the first instance of a dirty house I had ever seen in Japan, and it struck me all the more forcibly as I was to pass Sunday here; . . . so, after much grave remonstrance on the part of the Vice-Governor, Mr. Heusken sallied out to look at the hotels of the place.*

Kikuna and a small entourage of Kawasaki village officials would go

Kanagawa (*a print by Hiroshige*)

with him, leaving Wakana to fret over his inability to convince Harris that his position required him to stay in a *honjin.*

The scouting party would soon find "a little white pavilion, detached from the main house (a public tavern), with two apartments on the first floor" looking out on *a pretty garden* and past to "the environs of the town and the rice fields where the storks were strolling peacefully."

The Vice-Governor implored me not to think of going to a tavern, but, rather than I should do so, he would give up his quarters and go to the tavern himself. I told him I could not think of disturbing him; and, as to my dignity, that was my affair, and I would take good care of it. So to the hotel Mannenya, or "the felicity of ten thousand years," I went, and a very good change it was, for I had a bright, clean and comfortable house in place of the dark, dirty and uncomfortable honjin. . . .

My cook served me up some very delicate teal and delicious quail for my dinner (the food being transferred to the *Mannenya* with the guests). For the rest, it is happier not to speculate on the gloom and humiliation that would settle over the *honjin.* Harris would not realize it, but he would have witnessed evidence of the decay of the old regime. For most of those whose destinies were tied to it, times were hard. The old amenities were crumbling away.

Sunday, November 29, 1857. The first Sunday in Advent. I read the whole service for this day with Mr. Heusken as my clerk and congregation. I experienced some peculiar feelings on this occasion. It was beyond doubt the first time that ever a Christian service on the Sabbath was read audibly in this place, which is only thirteen miles from Edo, and this, too, while the law punishing such an act with death is still in force! (Since the Japanese had assured him that they had no intention of hindering foreigners in the practice of their religion as long as they did not proselyte, he would not be placing himself in grave danger.)

The next day they would enter Edo. Harris would write: *I am the first diplomatic representative that has ever been received in this city; and, whether I succeed or fail in my intended negotiations, it is a great fact that will always remain, showing that at last I have forced this singular people to acknowledge the rights of embassy. I feel no little pride, too, in carrying the American Flag through that part of Japan, between the extremity of Cape Izu and into the very castle of the City of Edo.*

After the midday stop at Shinagawa, he would choose, *after much deliberation,* to proceed uncomfortably. *My wish was to go into Edo on horseback, and the Vice-Governor eagerly encouraged that idea. This excited my suspicions; and, after much difficulty, I discovered that none but the*

528

Daimyo, or Princes of the highest rank, can enter Edo in their norimono; all below that rank enter the city on horseback or on foot. This fact, coupled with the Japanese idea of seclusion and respectability being equivalent terms, determined me very reluctantly to proceed in my norimono.

Heusken, who would handle the involved conversation, would not be at all certain that that decision was sound, but once the Consul General's suspicions were excited, it was difficult to allay them.

The procession would be re-formed now. Kikuna, who had led it so far, would move back and Executive Officer Wakana would take the lead: *the whole cavalcade was nearly half a mile long. We proceeded with slow and stately step . . .*

Heusken would itemize it:

> Wakana Miosaburo, in a *norimono* surrounded by four soldiers, and preceded by a man carrying his pike; then came another one carrying his bows and arrows, two others carrying his travel chests, etc., etc. Then came Mr. Harris, in his *norimono*, surrounded by ten guards, and preceded by the flag of the United States. The *norimono* was carried alternately by twelve men; then came his umbrella-bearer, his shoe-bearer, his horse led by the bridle by a stable boy, and a man carrying a basket for the horse. Then came my *norimono* in which I was suffering all kinds of tortures, not knowing what to do with my legs, then three guards, one of whom was my valet, one my shoe-bearer and one my umbrella-bearer, and then my horse led by the bridle by my stable boy, a man carrying the basket of my horse. Then the *kago* of the Japanese interpreter. The interpreter himself, Namura Tsunenosuke, walked beside the door of my *norimono; . . .*

Next followed a long retinue bearing packages containing my bedding, chairs, food, trunks, and packages containing presents; . . . The packages containing my bedding, clothing, etc., were covered with black cotton cloth with the arms of the United States neatly put on them. The other packages were neatly put up and had a little pennon with the United States arms flying from a short bamboo, which was placed upright on each package. Then would come the men and *kago* of Aihara Isaburo, who was in charge of all this baggage; the *kago* of Wakiya Usaburo, with his men; the chests of armor and clothing belonging to the Japanese; the *kago* of Kikuna, and his retinue; the *kago* of Saito, supervisor of the lower ranks, "one hundred thirty men, not overlooking the cook, a man who is in Japan more indispensable than the air we breath"; and, at the tail, to keep an eye on everything, the chief constable in his *kago*.

From Shinagawa *the people no longer knelt, nor did they avert their eyes*—a demonstration of the untrammeled spirit for which the people of Edo were celebrated. As a matter of fact, Heusken would note that "when we passed they stooped down one over the other in order to glance into our *norimono*. . . . All seemed happy that the gates of Edo had been opened to foreigners; . . ." (More likely they were delighted by the chance to watch a parade featuring two barbarians.)

The number admitted into the streets through which I passed formed a rank of five deep on each side of the way. Every cross-street . . . seemed a solid mass of men and women. . . . I calculated the number of persons . . . at one hundred and eighty-five thousand. . . . The most perfect order was maintained from Shinagawa to my lodgings,—a distance of over seven miles. Not a shout or a cry was heard. The silence of such a vast multitude had something appalling [in] it. Lord Byron called a silent woman sleeping thunder. . . .

In this manner I went on passing over seven bridges, the fifth was the Nippon Bashi, or Bridge of Japan. It is from this bridge that all distances are reckoned in this country. . . . after a while we reached a broad moat on the opposite [side] of which rose a stone wall varying from twenty to forty feet in height according to the make of the ground.

Harris would be carried along these outer works of the castle for a mile or more, and then his bearers, in a final burst of honor, would break into a full run, rush him through a gate, across a court, and into an entryway. He would have arrived. Inoue and Moriyama would be there to greet him.

That is the way his trip would go. But it was yet to come. Harris was still in Shimoda, still preparing, still anticipating.

Wednesday, November 18, 1857. I have got everything packed up and ready for my journey to Edo, which is to begin on Monday next, the 23rd. Visited the Prince of Dewa . . . to take leave of him before my setting out, according to Japanese custom. The Governor gave me a copy of a Treaty made with the Dutch in January, 1856. It is only a recapitulation of the substance of the Dutch Convention of November, 1855, except it withdraws the right of the Dutch to lease the grounds and buy the buildings at Deshima.

That is all he had to say. For almost a year he had been calling the Japanese liars over this issue. It had clouded his relationship with them and marred his negotiations. Yet there is here no acknowledgment that he was wrong, and there is nowhere in the record any indication that he offered a word of apology.

A couple of days later: *Friday, November 20, 1857. Went to the Goyosho at the special request of the Governor, who gave me copies of Additional Articles made with the Dutch, October 16, 1857, and with the Russians on the 24th of the same month.* The Japanese were certainly not slow with these. Copies must have been rushed to Shimoda as soon as they were received from Nagasaki.

The only points of importance in these Articles are those contained in my Convention of June 17th. This is a singular statement, for both Dutch and Russians had achieved trade treaties, which the convention of June 17 certainly was not.

In addition, the Dutch had obtained the right to worship as Christians. Harris heaped special scorn on this article: *A curious Article is inserted in the Dutch papers,—viz., "The Dutch shall have the right to exercise their own, or the Christian religion, in the buildings occupied by them at Deshima." It would appear from this Article that the "Dutch religion" is not the Christian religion.*

He amplified the same theme in transmitting copies to the State Department. He dismissed the opening of trade with the statement that "no advantage to commerce can accrue from these documents"; he ridiculed the article granting freedom to worship; he found, as he usually found in other men's treaties, "many obscurities of expression and errors of language." One wonders what they made of this dispatch back in Washington.

Heusken had less to pack than Harris and was properly grateful. "I thank Heaven that I can always carry my belongings, movable or immovable, on my person," for the alternative, he wrote tartly, was to entrust them to the Chinese.

At the last moment he purchased a parting gift for Ofuku. A rush order for a *haori* jacket of silk crepe with a scarlet lining and black velveteen trim was given to the tailor shop Tachinoya, who promised to have it ready in three days, by the Saturday evening preceding the Monday of departure.

In those last few days Ofuku received her final monthly salary of seven *ryo*, two *bu*, with an additional ten *ryo* in parting. No doubt Heusken slipped the *haori* around her shoulders himself, but the money was relayed to her, as usual, by Headman Hambei and two elders, who reported to the Goyosho that she had been pleased to receive it. They also acknowledged that her service at Gyokusenji was terminated and asserted that no one had any complaints.

It is clear that Heusken was ending the affair. He had no reason to suppose it would be long before he was back in Shimoda, but he had a roving eye and perhaps Ofuku's girlish devotion had begun to cloy.

The day before departure, Sunday, November 22, was gray. There was a drizzle of rain as Ofuku walked for the last time homeward along the beach. The weather must have suited her mood.

Later in the morning Yoheiji and Gennosuke reported to the Goyosho for the last of many conferences concerning the trip. On the way they crossed with a messenger headed for Gyokusenji.

This morning I received a package from Mr. J. H. Donker Curtius, Dutch Commissioner at Nagasaki, in answer to my letter of August 27th. He sends me copies of the Dutch and Russian negotiations of October last, and a copy of the Overland Mail of August 10th. All of which are very acceptable. Harris speedily discovered, though he never noted it in his journal, that these texts were identical with those delivered by the Japanese, who evidently could be trusted to give him accurate copies. Perhaps Curtius also informed him that at the Shogunate's request a Dutch scientist named van Meerdervoort had come out from Holland to expand the course of studies at the naval school; he was lecturing on medicine and surgery, physics, chemistry, geology, and mineralogy.

Toward evening the rain stopped and the sky began to clear. At dusk Mohei and six men started for Okagata to join the others assembling to move the caravan out.

Dawn flooding over the hills brought a clear and sparkling day. Between six and seven o'clock the yard of the temple filled with a crowd of soldiers, bearers, and attendants. Yoheiji and the village elders came in a body, save only Mohei, still busy at Okagata, and Gennosuke, who had gone on to Tachino for the leave-taking there.

The Chinese cook, having risen while it was still dark to prepare breakfast, sat now in the open doorway of the kitchen, observing the commotion and anticipating an extended vacation. Assam and the laundryman rolled and strapped the two mattresses; Kosuke hovered over the bearers who came to take possession of them. Takizo and Sukezo, their faces pursed with importance, bustled from temple to baggage chests with last-minute packing.

> Kikuna Sennojo comes on behalf of the Governor to tell the Ambassador—that's how we now style the Consul-General—that everything is ready and that he has been appointed to head the party and to see that everything proceeds in good order as far as Edo.

The packing was finished, the temple yard was cleared. The entourage formed in the lane between the houses below the temple. As Harris and

Heusken came through the gate, Yoheiji and the elders bowed to the ground. A suitable distance apart, Kosuke, too, knelt with his head low.

At eight this morning I start on my journey to Edo. I went on horseback; the morning was very fine, and the idea of the importance of my journey and the success that had crowned my efforts to reach Edo, gave me a fine flow of spirits.

Yoheiji watched the little procession move past the shrine, and then turned to the work at hand. Two officials from the Goyosho were ready to move into the tenement just vacated by Takizo and Sukezo. They would keep an eye on the Chinese as Harris had requested. Yoheiji named a man to help them get settled and two others to serve them while they stayed there.

He was relieved that the departure of the Americans had gone smoothly. He glanced at the sky. It was a good day, the sun warm, the air brisk. With luck there might be many more like this, but the winds were becoming westerly and the nights were chill. It would not be long before the gales of winter would be upon them and ships would be scurrying for haven. The ships' inns would be busy again and country girls would come over the mountains to help entertain the sailors. Some ships would limp in damaged, and the work of salvage would keep the village busy. Some ships would not make it.

He checked once more to be sure that the officials from the Goyosho were being properly moved in, and started home. The American's procession was moving along the road that skirted the harbor.

"Upon arriving in front of the Governor's palace . . . where the Japanese retinue which is to accompany us to Edo is waiting, we dismount and greet the Vice-Governor of Shimoda, Wakana Miosaburo, who had left his *norimono* and come to greet us." The contingent from Gyokusenji fell in at the head of the longer train, and the procession was formed as it would move to Edo.

Far in front were the heralds, *three lads each bearing a wand of bamboo with strips of paper attached to the top*. It was they who would cry out to the people to bow down.

At the head of the column was Kikuna on horseback, followed by a soldier bearing his pike, and by his attendants and his *norimono* and his bearers.

Next . . . came the American Flag guarded by two of my guards. Then I came on horseback with six guards, next my norimono with its twelve bearers and their headman; bearers of my shoes, etc., etc. The etc., etc. in-

533

cluded Takizo and, as Heusken noted, "a man armed with a huge umbrella."

Then came the only man in the procession who saw something amusing in it all, "his Excellency, the Most Serene Mr. de Heusken on his steed, followed by two samurai," his *norimono* and its bearers, his shoe bearer, his umbrella bearer, and his man Sukezo.

Here it lay, stretched along the road under the bright sun, the pomp and panoply that would carry Townsend Harris to Edo.

Kikuna glanced back. All was ready. He raised his hand and his horse stepped out. In front, the heralds darted forward. "*Shita ni iro! Shita ni iro!*" Kneel down! Kneel down!

Chapter 18

DECEMBER, 1857–
JUNE, 1859

In Edo, Harris had his audience with the Shogun and he presented the President's letter, his chief instrument in obtaining this audience; the letter was, as the Japanese had suspected, a request for a commercial treaty. He appeared, as he had vowed he would, for just one audience and he refused the dinner served to him at the castle. Nor was he hustled out of the capital. He was invited to the mansion of Lord Hotta, and there he lectured on world affairs. "His eloquence was like a rushing torrent,"

Harris being presented at Edo Castle. From left to right: an *ometsuke* (Toki Tamba-no-kami, one of the Commissioners of the Visit), Governor of Shimoda (Inoue Shinano-no-kami), Harris, Heusken, an interpreter (probably Moriyama) (*a painting by an unknown artist*)

according to one of those present. He was on his way to making a trade treaty.

That he would achieve this became inevitable when the Dutch and Russians succeeded in making commerical treaties before him. The kind of treaty he would make became inevitable when Lord Hotta appointed the men who would negotiate with him: Iwase and Inoue. His choice of Iwase over Mizuno meant that Hotta had relinquished the old idea of foreign trade as a government monopoly, which it had been for more than two centuries with the Dutch. It was Mizuno who had managed to keep this concept alive in the treaties with the Netherlands and Russia; it was Iwase who had opened the gates to private trade, merchant to merchant. In negotiating with Harris, Mizuno would be out of the picture. Hotta was willing to accede to the Western idea of trade in which governments acted only to set the rules and tax the profits.

This does not mean that Harris achieved his treaty overnight. He had to work for it. As was to be expected, he argued that the United States had no aggressive intentions but that England would not hesitate to wrest Japan's northern islands from her in order to check Russia. Therefore, it was in Japan's interest to negotiate a moderate treaty with the Americans to thwart the exorbitant demands of the British. They were the villains in his scenario.

As the *ometsuke* and *metsuke* had suggested, the Japanese let him talk, and talk, and talk. They let him explain and cajole and argue. They let him cast himself in the role of teacher: teacher is an honored role in Japan.

Thursday, December 17, 1857. . . . I may be said to be now engaged in teaching the elements of political economy to the Japanese and in giving them information as to the working of commercial regulations in the West.

. . . I am sometimes employed for hours in trying to convey a very simple idea. It requires an incalculable amount of patience to prevent my throwing the matter up in despair. . . .

Monday, December 21, 1857. . . . The chief point of their inquiries related to the object of sending Ministers to foreign countries; their duties, their rights under the laws of nations. . . . The Commissioners asked questions also respecting commerce, and what I meant by trade being carried on without the interference of government officers. . . . They said they were in the dark on all these points and therefore were like children; therefore I must have patience with them. They added that they placed the fullest confidence in all my statements.

There was a good deal the Japanese did not know about Western commercial practices. But there was a great deal they did know (they had

had an able tutor in Donker Curtius) which they inquired about again and again. Then they sat patiently listening as Harris held forth.

They believed that the more they let him talk, the more they let him think he was teaching them, the more flattered and therefore amenable he would be, and the more responsible he would feel for making a treaty that was fair.

But more important, the arguments he presented were being heard not only by Iwase and Inoue, not only by the Commissioners for the Visit, and not only by the Great Council, to whom they were always swiftly relayed. They were being passed on to every daimyo, whether on duty in Edo or at home in his territories. There was hope that what he had to say might help persuade a few more of these men that foreign trade would be good for Japan.

Inoue told him *that the position of the Government was most difficult; that they were enlightened, and knew that what I had recommended was truly for the best interests of Japan, but their conviction alone was not sufficient,—they had to convince the brothers of the Tykoon,* the Daimyo, the military, and [the] literary classes of the wisdom of following my advice; that the Minister and his colleagues had labored constantly night and day to secure the consent of the persons referred to; . . .*

To a limited extent their strategy may have worked. Perhaps the case that Harris presented was of some help to Ii Naosuke in changing the views of the lords of the Antechamber. At any rate, with Naosuke back in Edo, this powerful chamber submitted much more moderate advice.

And so the Japanese let Harris talk and they let him wait and worry. Harris soon found that his being in Edo was not enough to make things move swiftly. Every issue was conveyed to the Great Council and was weighed and deliberated by the whole machinery of government. Harris's every proposal, whether wise or foolish (and his journal reveals that he made his share of demands which were neither discerning nor practicable), was met by counter-proposals, some wise and some foolish. Every argument that any member of the government could dream up was given its hearing. There could be no unseemly haste in making this treaty. Every aspect of every issue had to be debated over and over again. It was important that this be done. Harris seems never to have realized that the Japanese negotiators were playing to the gallery as much as they were parleying with him.

---

* The Japanese had decided to call the Shogun the Taikun in dealing with foreigners, feeling that "Taikun" had more impressive connotations; as "tycoon" the word entered the English language. By the Shogun's brothers they meant the lords of the Three Houses, including the retired Nariaki—an unlikely convert to a trade treaty.

It took Harris a long time to realize the power of the forces opposed to his treaty. The men who sat opposite him tried to tell him. He thought they were lying as part of their strategy of negotiation.

They told him that most of the daimyo were set against the kind of treaty he proposed and that the Shogunate had not the power to ignore them.

They told him they had discovered a plot against him (*what they intended to do to me I could not learn,* he wrote with unintended whimsy). He thought they had fabricated the story to make him give up his demand that foreign ministers be permitted to reside in Edo, which was indeed one of the issues that most excited the treaty's opponents. But the plot was real and it was one of many.

On the same day that the commission gave him this bit of news, January 25, the government dispatched to Kyoto emissaries led by the Shogunate's chief scholar, Hayashi, to explain to the Emperor's court the demands made by Harris and the circumstances which made it necessary to accept them: the great changes which had taken place in the world since Japan had gone into seclusion, and the country's military weakness.

As the Shogun's representative, Hayashi must have traveled to Kyoto with confidence. He was soon shaken. Most of the courtiers with whom he had to deal were not even modestly aware of what was going on in the world: the Shogunate's policy of keeping them in ignorance had accomplished that. Moreover, they had been infected by the virus spread by men like Nariaki. They rallied to the cry of "Expel the barbarians!"—pawns in a campaign partly sincere and partly concocted to embarrass the Shogunate.

In dealing with these courtiers, hot-blooded with a new sense of power, Hayashi was helpless. He could not make them understand, for example, that opening ports to the barbarians did not mean ceding territory to them. His accounts of the foreigners' military superiority infuriated his audience. They professed to be offended that a man of such "low" rank had been sent to confer with them. For two and a half centuries the Imperial court had docilely done as the Tokugawa Shogunate bid, but it was docile no longer.

Back in nervous Edo everyone heard rumors that Harris would be assassinated. Matsudaira Yoshinaga seized on them as an excuse for another call on Hotta. Citing the rumors, he urged Keiki's appointment as heir to the Shogun *before* settling the American affair: tensions would be at once relieved. He emphasized the impressive list of daimyo supporting Keiki and he assured Hotta that they would accept Shogunate policy if it came from a man they had confidence in.

The chances are that Hotta would have been quite willing to trade the appointment of Keiki for approval of the American treaty, but he was not his own master. Behind him loomed Ii Naosuke, around whom had coalesced all the forces unalterably opposed to reconstructing the Shogunate. He was the natural leader of those who held power and had no wish to share it. To them Keiki was a threat. They fought his appointment.

But it is unfair to imply that they were motivated primarily by self-interest. Their candidate was the young Lord of Kii and there were plausible arguments in his favor. The boy was more closely related to the Shogun than Keiki, and his age made his adoption as a son more reasonable. It was more logical to choose an heir from the Three Houses than to dip into the second echelon of eligibles and name Keiki. Most important, the boy from Kii was the Shogun's choice: the Shogun, though not brilliant, could understand that to adopt Keiki, a grown man, vigorous and popular, would amount to abdication; and the women who surrounded and dominated the Shogun had seen to it that he shared their animosity toward Nariaki and consequently toward his son.

To Ii Naosuke there was really no question. If the Shogun had a preference, it must be honored. And the venomous antagonism between Naosuke and Nariaki made this a preference easy to support.

The question of an heir had not been settled in mid-February when the treaty was near completion. At that stage it was submitted to the daimyo for their opinions.

Ash Wednesday, February 17, 1858. The Commissioners, instead of meeting me at noon, as they had appointed, did not arrive until near five P.M. *They commenced by giving me a history of my negotiations from the day of my audience up to the ninth inst., repeating many parts three or four times and constantly referring to the Daimyo and their opposition to any change in the ancient customs of the land, by permitting the residence of foreigners in Japan, etc., etc. This lasted for more than an hour, without their giving me any information as to what they desired. I plainly saw that there was a hitch somewhere. Then they proceeded to say that on the eleventh inst. the Treaty, as it then stood, had been submitted to the Daimyo and instantly the whole Castle was in an uproar.*

Some of the most violent declared that they would sacrifice their lives before they would permit such great changes to be made. (Nariaki, who was not much for martyrdom, had snapped that Hotta and Matsudaira Tadakata should be ordered to commit *seppuku* and Harris's head cut off.) *The Council of State had labored incessantly to enlighten these men; had pointed out to them not only the policy, but necessity there was to make the Treaty if they would avert the ruin of the Kingdom, etc. They had brought over some, but others still remained obstinate; that the Government could not at once sign such a treaty, except at the expense of bloodshed; that they were sure the President did not wish to bring any such evil on Japan, etc., etc.*

I at last discovered that they wished to delay the signing of the Treaty until a member of the Council of State could proceed as "Ambassador to the Spiritual Emperor" at Kyoto and get his approval; that the moment that approval was received the Daimyo must withdraw their opposition; that they were content to take the Treaty substantially as it stood, having only some slight verbal alterations to suggest, and solemnly pledged their faith that the Treaty should be executed as soon as the Ambassador returned from Miako [Kyoto], which would require about two months. Having concluded this extraordinary conversation, I asked them what they would do if the Mikado refused his assent. They replied in a prompt and decided manner, that the Government had determined not to receive any objections from the Mikado. I asked what is the use then of delaying the Treaty for what appears to be a mere ceremony. They replied that it was this solemn ceremony that gave value to it; and, as I understood, it being known that the Mikado [had been] thus gravely appealed to, his decision would be final, and that all excitement would subside at once.

Considering the way things were going with Hayashi's mission in Kyoto, the commissioners' statement that the Shogunate "had determined not to receive any objections from the Mikado" sounds either brave or naïve. But Lord Hotta himself was to go to Kyoto, and to the men speaking to Harris it was no doubt inconceivable that the head of the Great Council would not get whatever he asked for.

Thursday, February 18, 1858. . . . I made the following suggestion to Shinano. Let us proceed and complete the Treaty as soon as possible and have it engrossed and ready for signature. Then, let the Council of State, or the Minister for Foreign Affairs, write me a letter saying that the Commissioners appointed to negotiate with me a commercial treaty between the United States and Japan had completed their labors, and that the Treaty was now ready for signature, but, for certain important reasons, the signing of the Treaty must be postponed for sixty days, on or before the expiration of which time the Treaty, as it now stood, should be signed.

Thereupon I would return to Shimoda to prepare my dispatches for my Government; that at the end of fifty days (if not before) the Government should send their steamer to Shimoda for the purpose of bringing me again to Edo, for the purpose of executing the Treaty. The Prince was much

pleased with the idea, and told me he would communicate it to the Govern-
ment at once and speak to me about it to-morrow. I do not see what I can
do better under the peculiar circumstances in which I am placed. If I can
get the written promise of the Government, that the Treaty (not a treaty)
shall be signed by a certain day, I do not see but it is as binding on them as
the signature of the Commissioners to the Treaty itself.

Friday, February 19, 1858. . . . Did not meet the Commissioners until
nearly five P.M. They informed me that the proposition I made to Shinano-
no-kami yesterday was accepted by the Government; and that the letter
pledging the faith of the Government that the Treaty should be executed
within sixty days from this date would be signed by Hotta, Prince of
Bitchu, Minister for Foreign Affairs; and that the steamer should be sent to
Shimoda ten days before that time to bring me to Edo.

By the end of February the treaty was finished. It permitted full trade.
It authorized a United States envoy to reside at the capital, Edo (something
not yet achieved with respect to China), and reciprocally, a Japanese at
Washington. In addition to Hakodate and Nagasaki, it opened the ports of
Kanagawa (adjacent to Edo) on July 4, 1859, Niigata (on Japan's west
coast) on January 1, 1860, and Hyogo (near Osaka) on January 1, 1863;
Shimoda would be closed. It opened Edo to residence by all Americans on
January 1, 1862, and Osaka on January 1, 1863. It gave Americans free
exercise of their religion. It was to go into effect on July 4, 1859, a date
patriotically selected by Harris.

It was a complete victory for the Consul General from the United
States. But the work, the worry, and the waiting had told on him. Early in
March he became ill and asked to be returned to Shimoda at once. He was
so weak that Heusken had to carry him from his *norimono* to the launch
which took them to the government steamer. The commissioners, alarmed
at Harris's condition, sent along a doctor on the ship, though not Ito Kansai.

On the same day, March 6, Lord Hotta set out for Kyoto. He considered that ten days would be ample to accomplish his purpose. As the
Shogunate's first officer, he represented its full power. He believed his
arguments irresistible and to help present them he was taking two of his
ablest men, Kawaji and Iwase, both veterans in foreign affairs. He knew
that his opponents had strong connections with the Imperial court, but on
the scene to counteract this was the secretary of Ii Naosuke, who had court
connections of his own. As insurance Hotta was taking plentiful amounts of
gold: the Emperor's courtiers were chronically hard up, and what reason
failed to accomplish, bribery was expected to. The commissioners had

Dr. Asaoka Kyoan (*a drawing by Aleksandr Mozhaiskii*)

confided this to Harris: *I am told that large sums of money have already [been] distributed among the officers of the Mikado, and that still larger sums will be applied in the same manner.*

Back at Gyokusenji, Harris's illness rapidly became critical. Governor Nakamura asked if he would not see the doctor who had accompanied him from Edo. He refused, but on March 10 when he became delirious Heusken took it upon himself to summon the doctor, who on Nakamura's orders moved into the temple with Shimoda's Dr. Asaoka Kyoan. (Yoheiji was ordered to send in their meals.) We can read today the bulletins they sent to the Governor. It seems evident that Harris had typhoid fever. For most of three or four days he alternated between coma and delirium, and both doctors thought he was dying: ". . . they say again," Heusken wrote on March 11,

> that it is impossible to save him. I try to speak to him but do not succeed in reaching him. Then as loud as I can, "Mr. Harris, you are very ill," but he does not understand me. Then I repeat several times, "Mr. Harris,

would you not pray, pray to God?" He replies, "Pay you?" "Oh, P-R-A-Y." "Oh, yes! I will pray to God bye and bye," and he goes back to sleep. I cannot make him understand anything. What am I to do? I am entirely alone here. My God! This is a terrible thing. . . .

This evening I succeeded with difficulty in making myself understood a little. I explained his plight to him and asked him if he would not like to pray a little with me. He replied, "Yes, Mr. Heusken." Then I took the book and read him some prayers. He gave most of the responses and the Amens in a very distinct voice and with nods of his head without my assistance. I said the Lord's Prayer again and again. This was most comforting to me, and inspired by the circumstances, I read the prayers as movingly and convincingly as I could.

. . . I could not restrain my tears. "Heusken," he said, "wipe your nose not so near my face."

The Governor sent gifts of sugar and eggs. Every day he or Wakana or both came to the temple to ask the patient's condition. Daily dispatches were sent to Edo. There the worried commissioners made plans to summon Elisha Rice from Hakodate in the event of Harris's death. The Great Council dispatched Dr. Ito Kansai posthaste, and sent a solicitous message and gifts.

By the time they arrived, Heusken, the doctors on hand, and Harris's own will to live had pulled him through. He was reverting to his normal intransigence—not that he had ever been a docile patient.

Tuesday, March 16, 1858. The Vice-Governor pays him a visit. He is much better, but refuses to take any more medicine.

Wednesday, March 17, 1858. He eats nothing today. All he does is smoke opium.

It was the next day that Wakana brought the Great Council's letter and the gifts. Because of them he was preceded by heralds shouting the familiar cry of "*Shita ni iro*," and those along the road knelt. The gifts were a set of gold-lacquered boxes and more eggs. The letter said:

An urgent message from the Governor of Shimoda advises that you have been ill since your return to Shimoda and that in recent days your condition has become increasingly grave. It has been decided to send Dr. Ito Kansai to you as speedily as possible to insure that you will be well cared for, and the things on the attached list are being presented to you with our good wishes. We earnestly hope for your recovery.

But as delivered to Harris, this letter, having been put into Dutch by Moriyama and English by Heusken, read somewhat differently. The

Shogun's name was injected, and it must have been by Moriyama—perhaps at the direction of Governor Nakamura, perhaps in connivance with Heusken, perhaps on his own because he knew how it would delight Harris:

> His Majesty the Tycoon has been informed from a letter of the Governor of Shimoda, that Your Excellency's indisposition since your return at Shimoda, continues the same and that you are at present very seriously ill. Therefore doctor Ito Kansai has been sent with haste, so it is desirable, you should take good care of yourself.
>
> As a friendly salutation a present is sent to you, as mentioned on the list, it is repeatedly desired you should always take good care of yourself.

Just how much this little ploy delighted Harris can be judged by the yarns he later spun about his illness. A few months after his recovery he wrote to Mrs. Drinker:

> The Emperor and Council of State manifested the utmost solicitude during my illness. His Majesty daily sent me very Kind Messages, with presents of fruit, and little delicacies to tempt my appetite; he also sent

The Great Council's letter (*opposite*) to Harris concerning his illness. Dated the 29th day of the First Month of the fifth year of Ansei, Uma [Year of the Horse] [14 March 1858], it bears the names and monograms (*above*) of the men who then composed the great Council: from right to left, Matsudaira Iga-no-kami, Kuze Yamato-no-kami, Naito Kii-no-kami, Wakisaka Nakatsukasa-daiyu (*from Harris's letters and papers*)

544

two of his best Physicians to attend me. The Doctors sent a daily report of my situation to the Court, and on the receipt of a Bulletin, stating that I could not recover, the Emperor issued peremptory orders to the Physicians to cure me, adding, that the *safety of their heads* depended on my recovery!—

And a page or two later, describing his mortifying shortage of cash: "I am in debt, to my servants, and was disturbed in what were supposed to be my dying moments, by their murmurs for 'their pay'—can you imagine anything more unpleasant?" In later accounts he added another fanciful detail: the "little delicacies" sent by the Shogun had been prepared by the Shogun's wife with her own hands.

By his illness Harris accomplished one thing previously declared impossible. On the same day that the Great Council's letter and the "Shogun's" gift arrived, the first milk was delivered to Gyokusenji. It came from Shirahama, and Yoheiji received orders that about a cup and a half were to be supplied to the American daily. Later it appeared more practical to move a source of supply nearer to the point of consumption: a cow and her calf were installed in a cowshed built at Gyokusenji.

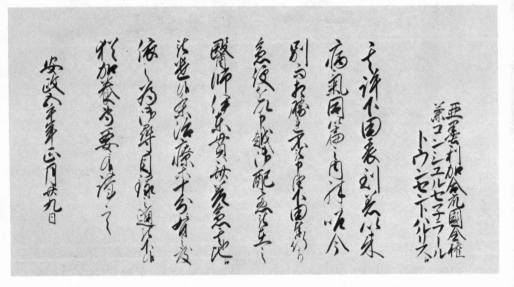

By early April, Harris felt strong enough to return to Edo. He asked for the steamer to come and get him.

Governor Nakamura said that in the doctor's opinion it was dangerous for him to travel; he should wait another month. Harris said he could not: he must be in Edo by April 18, for Lord Hotta had agreed to sign the treaty by that date. The Governor admitted that Hotta had not yet returned from Kyoto. Harris insisted he must go anyway.

The Institute for Foreign Studies, Harris's
quarters at Edo (*a painting by Aoda Denzan*)

On the morning of April 18 the steamer brought Harris and Heusken to Shinagawa, and though it was Sunday, Harris was willing to disembark and enter his *norimono* for the final leg of the journey. Heusken, who this time had his way and rode a horse into the city, wrote that at the Institute for Foreign Studies, Moriyama welcomed them and gave them "presents from the government, lovely potted flowers, a dwarf cherry tree, a double camellia, etc., all magnificent."

For the moment that was all the government had to offer. The next morning Inoue brought a letter from Hotta in Kyoto, saying that he could not keep his promise to sign the treaty on the appointed date.

There was little to do but wait. Four days later Donker Curtius arrived in Edo. His company made the period of waiting both more pleasant—the two parties of foreigners exchanged visits and dinners and went sightseeing together—and more disturbing—for Curtius, who was also received by the Shogun, let it be known that he was willing to make a treaty which, though going further than the one he had concluded at Nagasaki, would still be acceptable to the daimyo. The contest between the two envoys was not yet over: which would have the honor of opening Japan wide to Western-style commerce?

On the first of June, Hotta returned from Kyoto, a beaten man. Neither his arguments nor his gold had worked. He had been insulted and his life threatened. He had heard Harris's Shimoda convention labeled an outrage and the new treaty, a surrender of national dignity. He had been told that the daimyo were to be consulted again before another request to the court, and that if this meant the foreigners might attack, the nation was to be girded for war.

Beyond that, he had learned that the issue of the Shogun's heir had become inextricably linked with that of the treaty. For when Keiki's advocates sensed that their cause was lost in Edo, they had turned to Kyoto. Shimazu Nariakira had sent letters to two of the court's high officials, arguing that the government was weak for lack of a strong Shogun and that Keiki was the man for the job. At first the court had been reluctant to mix in a purely political struggle, but then they reasoned that if Shogunate weakness led to disasters like Harris's treaty, a strong Shogun was necessary. Hotta's own advisors, Kawaji and Iwase, favored Keiki and even indicated a desire to see Yoshinaga made Chief Councillor, a position above the Great Council, usually filled only in emergency. Hotta came back to Edo convinced that that was the only way to get the treaty approved.

He found that he was no longer in control. During his three months' absence a coup had been hatched. Three days after his return, not Yoshinaga but Ii Naosuke was named Chief Councillor. Naosuke at once made it clear that he would run the government with dictatorial firmness. Keiki's chance of becoming the next Shogun was gone. Within a few weeks the young Lord of Kii was named heir. The plans of moderates like Yoshinaga and Nariakira to "reform" the Shogunate were blocked; from then on more radical leaders would come to the fore with more drastic solutions.

Again Iwase and Inoue visited Harris to ask a delay in signing the

547

treaty. Harris finally agreed to another postponement of three months, until September, with the promise that the Japanese would sign no other treaty for at least thirty days after signing his. By extracting this pledge he had taken care of Mr. Donker Curtius, and he and Heusken went back to Shimoda to wait.

He did not have to wait until September. On July 23 the steamship *Mississippi,* which had been one of Perry's fleet and now was back in Asian waters, arrived by way of Nagasaki with all kinds of news. Some of this Harris rushed to Lord Hotta:

An American steam warship (*a painting by an unknown artist*)

The arrival of the steamer *Mississippi* enables me to communicate some important communications to Your Excellency.

The mutiny of the Sepoy troops in India has been put down. The Chinese, having been defeated by the French and English forces . . . were compelled to submit to the terms dictated by the English and French, and consequently the China war is ended. This leaves the English and French at liberty to direct their attention to Japan.

I am informed that an English fleet of thirty to forty vessels may be expected to arrive in the Bay of Edo at any hour, and that the French fleet will accompany the English. This is very serious news and calls for immediate action on the part of the Government of Japan.

If the Treaty made by me and the Japanese Commissioners is not signed before these fleets arrive, it is not to be expected that they will be contented with a similar one. On the contrary, proud of their recent triumphs in India and China, they will demand much larger freedom for the English in Japan.

I urgently press on Your Excellency the very great importance of having the Treaty signed without the loss of a single day. The neglect of this warning may cause serious misfortunes.

Admiral Putiatin arrived at Nagasaki on the 8th of the Japanese Sixth Month.

The Russian admiral had hurried to Japan for the same reason as the Americans—to advise the Japanese that the English and French would soon follow. And like Harris he meant to use this news to spur the Japanese into signing a new treaty.

Two days after the *Mississippi,* another American steamship, the *Powhatan,* also a veteran of Perry's expedition, arrived at Shimoda. She bore Commodore Tattnall, who had relieved Armstrong. President Buchanan had not only strengthened the Asian fleet but also installed a new team. The first to go, as Harris already knew, had been the bellicose missionary, Peter Parker; among the letters brought by the *Powhatan* was one from the new commissioner to China, William B. Reed, who could report that he had signed a "very satisfactory" treaty with the Chinese (in China the Americans were still riding the coattails of the English).

There were other letters more personal. Both Captain Foote and Captain Bell wrote, the latter ending his letter with discouraging news from home:

> Utah is declared to be in rebellion, and troops are marching against Brigham Young, who declares he will exterminate them. Kansas troubles are more vexed than ever and civil war rages there, backed by their respective friends elsewhere. . . . The elements appear to be rife for the disruption of the Union.

There was a morose note from John Bowring, now discredited and inconsequential though still Governor of Hong Kong.

There were two of Sandwith Drinker's newsy, peppery letters, but from others the melancholy word that the writer had died in January of diarrhea, which meant dysentery, the kind of disease which struck down so many foreigners those days on the China coast. There was the farewell letter of Mrs. Drinker, who with Kate and the other children had already left for home.

Harris gave himself little time to brood over this sad news. The next evening he and Heusken boarded the *Powhatan* just as Admiral Putiatin was arriving from Nagasaki. Wakana and his party came on board the *Powhatan* shortly after midnight and the next morning, July 27, the steamer moved into Edo Bay.

An officer of the *Powhatan* was busy noting the details for the *New York Herald:*

> Almost in the mouth of the Bay we passed the populous city of Uraga, . . . off which were anchored hundreds of junks, awaiting examination before continuing on to Edo. Uraga is, it seems, a kind of custom house for all ports situated along the shores of the extensive bay.
>
> We steamed swiftly through these junks without pretending to stop for the several government boats which threw themselves in our way, for our friend, the Vice-Governor, stood upon the port wheelhouse, waved his fan and shouted loudly, "Amerikin! Kanagawa!" and so we passed on. The old fellow had been drinking sherry with the Commodore, champagne with the Captain, and constantia in the wardroom, so that he shouted with unusual energy; and, as the officials in the boats readily recognized him as their superior, they waved their fans in return and motioned us ahead. This was a great trip for our Japanese friends, who could not tire of admiring the working of the engine and of commenting upon our great speed.
>
> Shortly after passing Uraga we sighted Kanagawa, and an hour later found ourselves safely at anchor half way between that city and another called Yokohama . . . The Vice-Governor and suite now went on shore, and one of the latter continued on to Edo with a letter . . .

The letter was a note from Harris to Hotta announcing his arrival, enclosing a copy of his letter of the twenty-fourth, and adding that "the news brought by Commodore Tattnall more than confirms all the matters" reported in it: "the French will be here within five days. Admiral Putiatin will be at Kanagawa tomorrow."

Ii Naosuke and the Great Council went into emergency session. In view of all that had happened, could the treaty be signed without Imperial assent? Hotta had nothing to say. Matsudaira Tadakata advocated signing the treaty at once and spoke with contempt of the Kyoto court. Iwase and Inoue dwelt on the terrible dangers of delay. Only Naosuke and a junior councillor maintained that the Emperor's approval should first be obtained. Naosuke was confident that given time he could obtain that approval and he knew the Shogunate's vulnerability if it now acted without it. But the opinion of the men around him was overwhelmingly for signing. He retired to think alone. Then he summoned Inoue and Iwase and instructed them to use all their powers in urging Harris to agree to a delay, but if they failed in this, then to sign the treaty.

For Harris on the *Powhatan* time dragged through the afternoon of July 27 and all the next day. About midnight that night the little Japanese steamer anchored nearby. In the morning it was learned that it had brought Inoue and Iwase.

The two commissioners, with their suite and the indispensable Moriyama, were welcomed aboard the warship with a salute of seventeen guns. "After this," wrote another of the *Powhatan's* officers to the *New York Journal of Commerce*, "the band struck up 'Hail Columbia,' 'The Star-Spangled Banner,' and various popular American tunes, which did not seem to draw the attention of the Japanese, who either have no ear for music, or else are ignorant of harmony."

The visitors were shown over the ship and were entertained at lunch. At last the two commissioners and Moriyama withdrew with Harris and Heusken to the commodore's cabin.

Inoue and Iwase, already convinced that the treaty must be signed, were scarcely the men to exhaust themselves in trying to delay signature. Their performance was perfunctory and Harris seems to have sensed it. He evidently assured them that the English were coming with "several tens" of warships, and to their argument that signing the treaty now "would cause a very great excitement," he replied, as he reported to Secretary of State Cass: "I had merely informed them of the approaching danger and had given them my candid advice as to the best course they could pursue . . ."

Iwase asked for assurance that the English and French would accept the American treaty. This Harris could scarcely give, but he wrote to the Great Council:

> I have this morning heard from Their Excellencies the Prince of Shinano and the Prince of Higo * the welcome you gave to my friendly letter of the 24th instant.
>
> I would now state to Your Excellencies that I have no doubt that all the foreign powers that may come to Japan to negotiate treaties will willingly accept that already made with my Government.
>
> Should any difficulties arise in any future negotiations, I will, at the request of the Government of Japan, act as a friendly mediator, and in such character will use my best exertions to induce such powers as may be negotiating to accept the Treaty already made.

The Japanese returned to their own ship to translate and consider this letter. Soon they were back on the *Powhatan*. Shortly thereafter, late in the afternoon of July 29, 1858, the treaty was signed.

"We all collected on the poop," wrote the *Herald's* correspondent, "to

* Iwase's title had been changed from Iga-no-kami to Higo-no-kami.

witness the grand finale. Our heavy guns were loaded with full charges, the American and Japanese flags hoisted side by side at the fore, and a salute of twenty-one guns fired at intervals of a few seconds."

"The Shogun will hear your guns in Edo and know that the Treaty is signed," Inoue is quoted as saying. And then several more bottles of champagne were opened.

The festivities concluded, the Japanese steamed for Edo. The next morning the *Powhatan* was under way toward Shimoda. "As we again passed the smoking peak of Oshima, we met the Russian frigate *Askold*, bearing the flag of Admiral Count Putiatin, who was bound to Kanagawa upon a similar errand—treaty making."

Harris was quite correct in assuming that the other powers would accept his treaty. It contained all they could have asked for and more. Similar pacts were signed with the Dutch on August 18 and with the Russians on August 19. In the meantime Lord Elgin had appeared, not with "thirty or forty vessels" but with two steam frigates and a small gunboat plus the handsome yacht which was a gift from Queen Victoria. He signed his treaty on August 26, Harris having loaned him the services of Heusken. The French arrived on September 25 and signed their treaty on October 7.

But it took a member of the Great Council dispatched to Kyoto by Ii Naosuke until late November to get the Emperor's grudging approval of Harris's treaty, and to get it, damaging concessions had to be made: that despite the treaty, the Shogunate would try to prevent the opening of Hyogo and Osaka, so close to Kyoto, and that the Imperial court would be consulted on foreign affairs.

Even so, the Imperial statement was an unsatisfactory document. It opened: "The treaty providing for friendship and trade with foreigners and other matters is a blemish on our Empire and a stain on our divine land. . . . we must assuredly keep aloof from foreigners and revert to the sound rule of seclusion as formerly laid down in our national laws." However, it went on: "The Emperor fully understands that in the circumstances the Bakufu could have done no other than it did; and he will therefore exercise forbearance on this occasion."

In considering Harris's treaty, it must be placed in the context of its time.

That it would be an unequal treaty was to be taken for granted. Neither the United States nor any other Western power was willing to treat with the Japanese as equals.

It is therefore unfair to criticize the inclusion of extraterritoriality. No Western nation would have signed a commerical treaty without it, and the

Japanese welcomed it as an easy solution to the thorny problem of controlling the barbarians. It was only later, when they became more knowledgeable about international relations, that they realized they had compromised their sovereignty: then they became exercised about what this meant in terms of national prestige.

It is unfair as well to criticize a tariff schedule's being built into the treaty. This infringement on sovereignty was common practice in dealing with Asian nations. The United States's treaty with China established a tariff and so did Harris's treaty with Siam.

In negotiating the tariff, the Japanese expressed a preference for a flat twelve and a half per cent on both imports and exports; Harris tried to talk them out of export duties and failed, but he persuaded them to reduce export duties to five per cent and to accept a varied scale on imports:

—Five per cent on ships' supplies which whalers required and which then were the only significant items of American trade;

—Thirty-five per cent on all intoxicating liquors, which Harris abhorred as a man often abhors his own weakness, and which the United States didn't export anyway;

—Twenty per cent on all other items.

Harris displayed pride in his handiwork when he wrote to the Secretary of State reporting that the treaty was signed: ". . . the tariff is arranged with a view first to secure an income to the Japanese Government, and second to enable our whaling ships in the North Pacific Ocean to obtain their supplies on reasonable terms."

He thought he had been ingenious: American trade was taxed at five per cent, whereas the Japanese were to derive most of their revenue from a twenty-per-cent tax on British manufactures and thirty-five per cent on French wines. (This was in an age when customs duties paid the entire cost of operating the United States government and created a surplus in the treasury.)

It did not occur to him that more than one could play this game, but Lord Elgin promptly reduced the import duties on most British goods to five per cent, and the French tried, though at first without success, to reduce the duties on liquors to the same nominal figure. Harris protested; he thought they were being unfair. Within a few years the tariff on all items was hammered down to a merely nominal five per cent, scarcely enough to pay the costs of collecting it.

What made these inequalities—extraterritoriality and a built-in tariff —so onerous for Japan was Harris's ineptitude in drafting his treaty. He intended that the Japanese should be able to amend the treaty itself in 1872 and the tariff in 1864. "I constantly told the Japanese commissioners," Harris later wrote, "that before the time came around for revising the treaties they would have gained such experience as would enable them intelligently to deal with this matter themselves; remarking that, while ten years was an important part of a man's life, it was as nothing in the life of a nation."

Unfortunately, what his treaty actually said was that its provisions should "be subject to revision" by mutual consent of the two governments. Neither the treaty nor the tariff had any termination date. The envoys who followed Harris happily seized on the same phraseology, with the result that for almost forty years Japan was clamped into a series of unequal treaties, none of which she could either revise or terminate without the consent of all the other governments with whom she had signed treaties, for each treaty contained a most-favored-nation clause.

Harris cannot be blamed for the revisions other nations made in the tariff schedule, and no one can say for certain that given the chance, the Japanese could later have obtained better terms. But Harris must be blamed for denying them any such chance.

In retrospect it can be argued that being limited to a purely nominal tariff forced Japan to greater efficiencies and faster modernization. But this is hindsight, and it was not available to a proud nation struggling for equality in a world of nations hostile, or scornful, or patronizing. It was not until 1894, when Japan had developed military and naval muscle sufficient to command respect, that she was able to obtain treaty revision, and even then she was not able to obtain complete control over her tariffs or to wipe out all other infringements on her sovereignty.

His treaty signed and on the way to Washington for ratification, Harris waited at Shimoda for the date when it would go into effect.

In those days he had a steady stream of visitors. Both Lord Elgin and the French envoy, Baron Gros, had stopped by on their way to make their treaties; it is reasonable to assume that Harris found the visit of the French more enjoyable. American warships appeared more frequently, and Elisha Rice came down from Hakodate for a long visit.

But neither the triumph of his treaty nor frequent visitors could cure Harris's dyspepsia and fits of depression. In April, 1859, he wrote to Secretary Cass that the *Mississippi* was in port, that the ship's physician had imperatively recommended "a change of scene and a relaxation from labor," specifically a visit to China on the ship, and that he was departing at once to follow the doctor's advice.

Heusken was left in charge of the consulate. Takizo was taken along, Harris promising Governor Nakamura that he would not take the young man out of the country, which would violate Japanese law, but would leave him at Nagasaki to await the ship's return. He broke his promise and took Takizo on to China, with consequent embarrassment to the Governors of both Shimoda and Nagasaki.

When Harris reached China he learned that he had been elevated from Consul-General to Minister. He would move to Edo, establish the legation there. The *Mississippi* brought him back to Shimoda in late June. He and Heusken closed the consulate, and taking with them Takizo, Sukezo, and Kosuke as well as the Chinese servants, they sailed from Shimoda for the last time.

555

Chapter 19

E P I L O G U E

十
九

With Harris's departure from Shimoda, the Governors left also. The almost new rest house for foreigners was sold and dismantled. The Goyosho was turned over to deputies of the provincial magistrate for Izu. Naka compound was emptied of officials, the buildings removed, the land released. Unfortunately, the rich paddy fields had been filled in with rock and gravel to create a building site; the land now was infertile and could not be irrigated.

The government advised merchants that if they wished to move to one of the open ports—Kanagawa, Nagasaki, or Hakodate—they would be given letters of introduction.

And Shimoda drifted back into obscurity—still beautiful, but sleepy, dull, and poor.

When Gyokusenji reverted to its parishioners, turmoil erupted. There were those who insisted that the temple must be destroyed and replaced. It had been profaned by foreigners who walked its floors in their dirty shoes, drank milk and ate meat within its walls, butchered animals and stained the holy precincts with their blood. To these people their temple stank of the barbarians. The priest's quarters were fetid with the grease from their cooking.

There was a more moderate group which insisted that the halls could be cleaned and purged to restore their sanctity. To destroy and build anew would take a long time and they did not want to wait. For three years they had been denied the use of their temple: they had had no proper setting for services in memory of the dead.

Even when Priest Bimo had died he could not be given a proper funeral. (He died just at the time that Harris left for China; Heusken sent

556

Sukezo with a memorial gift of seven *ryo*, two *bu*, an amount curiously reminiscent of Ofuku's monthly wage. There were many in Kakisaki who attributed the priest's demise to the fact that he had recently permitted some foreigner to photograph him.*) Now the hundredth-day anniversary of his death was approaching and there was a great desire that the important memorial service of this day be conducted in the temple. And the *Bon* season was close at hand; people wanted those services in their temple.

There was another very compelling reason to save the temple. In answer to the village's petition, the Governors allotted one hundred *ryo* as compensation for its three years' use by Harris. A hundred *ryo*, carefully spent, would renovate the existing building but it would not construct a new one.

So the moderates won, as they had in Shimoda when there were those who wanted to burn Wataya Kichibei's bench because Perry's men had sat on it. The whole village turned out, and after a meticulous cleaning of the main hall the people restored to their places the sacred image and the altar (they were in such a hurry that without noticing they set the base of the altar upside down), and then they brought back their ancestral tablets.

There was still much to do—plastering, papering, re-covering the tatami—and the priest's quarters were as yet quite unusable. This work was done gradually over the next months. Naturally, squabbles developed over how the hundred *ryo* was being spent, but they passed. At last, in the Twelfth Month, a new priest having been installed—the young man who had entered the priesthood through falling from a tree—a proper funeral was held for the old priest.

The temple still stands today much as it did then. It has a roof of tile instead of thatch, there are new quarters for the priest, the tenement where first the guards and then Takizo and Sukezo lived has been torn down. But one can see the rooms where Harris and Heusken lived, even the hole cut for the pipe of the recalcitrant Philadelphia stove.

The end of the story of the sailors of Tarojiro's ship can be guessed from a brief report submitted by Hambei and an elder to the Goyosho on October 13, 1859. It reported that a search had been conducted for "the six missing crewmen," but in vain, and the deadline having passed, the hunt was being abandoned. Something about this suggests that their escape was

---

* There was deep-rooted superstition about having one's portrait made: the soul might leave one's body to take up residence in the "new self," causing the fatal "shadow sickness." Photography, which produced so exact an image, was considered even more dangerous than portrait painting. Priest Bimo's photograph can still be seen at Gyokusenji.

connived at by the authorities. There had been enough punishment and enough death.

We have a few more facts in the story of the bewitched Tami. Her husband, the retired priest of the temple of the mountain religion, died early in 1858, broken, one suspects, by the scandal surrounding his wife. The villagers of Kakisaki, Sotoura, and Suzaki submitted a series of petitions for the release of Bunkei, the ill-fated doctor; none was granted and in September, 1858, he died in prison. Presumably Tami herself drifted through senility to a natural death.

The lives of Okichi and Ofuku must be dealt with too.

I have told the story of Okichi's brief affair with Harris as I believe contemporary records clearly show it to have happened. Others have used the same facts to argue that there was no affair at all, that all the machinations were Heusken's, who in order to get a girl for himself had to make it appear that Harris demanded one. (This is frequently coupled with the postulate that Harris, as a Christian gentleman, could not possibly have wanted a mistress—an argument that seems weightier to some Japanese than it does to most Americans.)

This can be made to sound reasonably convincing until later events are considered. The records show that Harris took another mistress, Osayo, who served him from August, 1858, shortly after he returned from Edo with his signed treaty, until mid-January, 1859.

In view of the experience with Okichi, it is a relief to note that the letter of contract from the Shimoda town office to the Goyosho characterizes Osayo as a "mild-tempered girl, whose parents and other relatives have no objection to her serving the American." Furthermore, her monthly salary was set at seven *ryo*, two *bu*, and her "preparation money" at twenty *ryo*, the same as Ofuku's had been. Evidently Harris had decided that his rank did not entitle his woman to any more money than his secretary's. No doubt Osayo's duties were less strenuous.

At his temple residence in Edo, Harris requested, and government officials arranged, a liaison with Orin, an eighteen-year-old maid at the temple. She returned from her first assignation with an initial gift of twenty-five *ryo*, though we do not know her monthly salary. She served for about three months and according to the record received many farewell gifts: Harris mellowed as his stay in Japan lengthened.

The fact that calling these women "nurses" was mere subterfuge is revealed in a letter which Harris wrote to Elisha Rice after Rice complained that women were not available at Hakodate. This was written in Edo on February 1, 1858, while Harris was still negotiating his treaty:

The question of women was a delicate one to manage. You are aware that it could not be noticed officially, but I immediately brought it to the private notice of the Government here, and fully pointed out the danger of serious difficulties arising if they persisted in their previous course of conduct. They have sent orders to Hakodate that you shall be supplied with female attendance "for fear of sickness," and they promise me a decision about the sailors in five days from this time. I have no doubt they will settle it in a satisfactory manner. [They did.]

Heusken, naturally, was more active than his aging chief. He had a brief fling with a girl named Okiyo and a long relationship with a sensual creature named Omatsu. That tireless researcher Dr. Muramatsu says that Omatsu was not exactly beautiful but that she had a way with men. "A certain old woman told me things that Omatsu had secretly told her close friends, but I don't consider it proper to write about such things," the doctor wrote primly. The length of time that she stayed with Heusken—almost one year—is good evidence of her accomplishments, as is the fact that when Heusken was loaned to Lord Elgin as interpreter he tried to take Omatsu with him to Edo on the British warship. Of course, once he moved to Edo, the young man found that the girls there had charm enough and more.

The legend that Dr. Muramatsu created about Okichi gives the later years of these girls some interest.

The life of Okichi, who was well on her way to alcoholism at seventeen when she went to Gyokusenji, was a disaster. She seems to have migrated to the new port for foreigners on Edo Bay: witnesses are quoted as having heard her singing "Raven at Dawn" in the streets of the new town's entertainment quarters. She returned to Shimoda, tried to rehabilitate herself as a hairdresser, but slid back to drink. Friends set her up as the operator of a brothel named Anchoku-ro, (Anchoku meaning "cheap and honest") which was profitable at first, but in her drunkenness she so mismanaged the place that it was soon bankrupt.

By then she was becoming ugly, ravaged by drink and syphilis. She had a stroke which crippled her, and thereafter she dragged herself around the town, repulsive but still mettlesome, a beggar scornful of charity, the natural butt of taunts and target for small boys' stones. It is probably this period which gave rise to the notion that she had been persecuted by the townspeople when she became the foreigner's mistress. She lived until she was nearly fifty and ended in the river, whether by suicide or accident it is difficult to say. At first no one would claim her remains, but at last the compassionate priest of Hofukuji brought her body to his temple for burial. It was an act which proves that charity is rewarded, for today her tomb is one of Shimoda's great attractions for tourists and their offerings are a boon to that priest's descendants.

It was this depressing story that Dr. Muramatsu romanticized to create his probably imperishable legend of a woman sacrificed for her country.

It was necessary, of course, that he endow her with talents and accomplishments which no doubt far exceeded those she really possessed. Then we are told of a true love between her and an honest young carpenter, and how the villains of the Goyosho smashed this love, bribing the young carpenter by making him an *ashigaru* and persuading him to leave town. We are told how her life was ruined by the scorn the townsfolk heaped on her for giving herself to the barbarian. We are told that she faithfully served Harris for years, that it was she who nursed him through his illness, that it was she who obtained milk for him.

It is a tale with all the elements to pluck the heartstrings. Every Japanese knows it. It has spawned novels and plays, movie after movie, song after song.

> . . . Sleeves wet with weeping,
> bosom torn with cares
> and sad regrets.
> The past will ne'er return:
> will drinking bring forgetfulness?
> Forget and drink—
> besides that, only to
> pluck the samisen with
> muffled fingertips.
> Once more I hear the raven's
> cry at dawn: that memory. . . .
> Night deepens on Shimoda's waterfront.
> Tears falling, drop
> like red camellias.

It is a moving story, and who can begrudge people a story that means so much to them? But it is not a true story.

Beyond question there were those in Shimoda who despised Okichi for becoming a foreigner's woman. But her alleged martyrdom crumbles when one checks the stories of the other girls. Muramatsu does not even attempt to make martyrs of them. He reports that he was able to find little concerning Okiyo or Omatsu, but that Osayo made two creditable alliances, first with the local gambling chief and then with a curio shopowner; unhappily she was both times widowed. As for Ofuku, she made a good marriage into a respected family of Kakisaki, and lived out her life as a matron of the village, hard-working and well liked. She is buried in Gyokusenji's cemetery.

Of all the men who came to make treaties with Japan, Harris was the only one who stayed to make his work.

Having closed out Gyokusenji, he went first to Kanagawa to open a consulate there. He appointed a merchant as acting consul and saw him established in a temple. On the Fourth of July, 1859, as scheduled in the treaty, the American flag was raised and saluted by the guns of the *Mississippi*. (The British treaty was already in force: Lord Elgin, who was not amused by Harris's choice of the Fourth of July, had made his treaty effective July 1.)

However, Harris was angered to find that the Japanese were constructing the buildings and wharves for foreign trade not at Kanagawa but at Yokohama, across the harbor. He saw it as an attempt to create another Deshima, as at Nagasaki, a foreigners' town sequestered from the Japanese. He protested, and all the other envoys protested, but the decision was Ii Naosuke's and he, to quote a contemporary chronicle, "being no longer afraid of anybody or anything, opened resolutely at Yokohama in Musashi a port and a town; erected factories for the Russians, English, Dutch, Americans, and French, and built shops and native houses and drove a brisk trade. A brothel quarter was also set apart beautified as much as possible, pleasure gardens full of artificial scenery, of fountains, and of the flowers which flourish each season. . . ."

Naosuke knew that to put the foreigners in Kanagawa, astride the Tokaido Road so heavily traveled by daimyo, would be to invite trouble. He assumed that most of the foreigners would be arrogant boors, and he knew that most samurai were arrogant, and that therefore the less chance of confrontation, the better. Events proved him right.

This was an argument the Japanese won. The foreign envoys kept protesting, but the foreign traders, impatient to do business, moved into Yokohama and in the end the consulates had to move from Kanagawa to join them.

"The vessels of all sizes of the five barbarians came and anchored in number in the port; the sight was most beautiful and incomparable, and the place became the busiest port of all Kanto; * nay, it was enough to make any traveler wonder."

From Kanagawa, Harris moved on to Edo, where he established his legation at a temple called Zempukuji, which might be translated "the Temple of Peace and Happiness." For Harris it was never that. To start things off, on July 4, 1859, Heusken had declared his independence by walking out, as Harris reported to Secretary Cass, "without giving me a single day to provide a substitute.

Zempukuji (*an engraving by Gauchard*)

"I have strong suspicions," Harris went on, "as to the means that were used to induce Mr. H. to act in a manner so contrary to the rules of propriety and integrity, and to leave this Legation at a most important juncture, and in a manner so well calculated to embarrass and injure the interests of the United States"; but Harris never amplified this remark, and the circumstances surrounding the incident remain a mystery today. Probably they were not complicated. Heusken was by far the ablest interpreter in Japan; as Harris's only assistant he had shouldered great responsibility; and he was being miserably underpaid, something Harris had never tried very

* Edo and the surrounding district.

hard to rectify. Harris had just received a major advancement; Heusken had received none. The two men, so different in age and contrary in temperament, had finally come to open rupture.

Two weeks later Heusken was back. Harris wrote a very lame explanation of the affair (it had all been a misunderstanding, he said), but more important, he insisted that Heusken's salary be raised to twenty-five hundred dollars. This was done and Heusken stayed on, though at Zempu-kuji he moved into a house of his own. The following months were happy ones for him. He had earned esteem. He made many friends among the other legations. He was probably the most popular member of the foreign community. He was often a guest, and he entertained with excellent dinners in return.

But there were troublesome issues to be dealt with.

Foreign trade in these opening years did not prove to be the bonanza that Harris had promised. Under the pressure of the foreign exporters' demands, the prices of items like tea and silk rocketed—"from 100 to 300 per cent," Harris reported, pointing out that "A change so great and so sudden could not fail to press heavily on all official persons of fixed and limited incomes . . ." On the other hand, imports of cheap cotton textiles threatened domestic industries. The Shogunate fought to obstruct and limit foreign trade, and found itself frustrated. As he had time and again in Shimoda, Harris threatened war.

And as Ii Naosuke had anticipated, the behavior of the foreigners was exacerbating. "Unfortunately," wrote Harris, "a portion of them are neither prudent nor discreet, and they are numerous enough to imperil the safety of the orderly and well-disposed, and seriously endanger the amicable relations that have been established with so much difficulty and labor with this government."

With all of this, anti-foreign feeling in Japan did not die down, as Harris had been so sure it would—it increased. Those who had always opposed opening the country turned to violence. At Yokohama several foreigners were murdered. Consuls advised their nationals to remain indoors after dark, or if they went out, to go with guards and weapons.

Clearly, Japan had been pushed too far too fast. Nevertheless, on February 9, 1860, a large party of Japanese officials embarked on the *Powhatan* and on their own *Kanrin Maru*, the new steamship purchased from the Dutch, to journey to the United States to exchange ratifications of the treaty at Washington. Their adventures and their reactions, the enthusiasm with which they were hailed in San Francisco, Washington, Baltimore, Philadelphia, and New York, the mutual curiosity and excitement, make a fascinating story in itself. In New York, Walt Whitman was among the crowd and went home to write "A Broadway Pageant":

> Over the Western sea hither from Niphon come,
> Courteous, the swart-cheek'd two-sworded envoys,
> Leaning back in their open barouches, bare-headed, impassive,
> Ride to-day through Manhattan. . . .
> Comrade Americanos! to us, then at last the Orient comes. . . .

—Whitman was really writing a paean to America:

> I chant the new empire grander than any before, as in a vision it comes
>   to me, . . .
>   . . . Libertad of the world! . . .

Invigorating thought, and no doubt it helped some Americans to forget for a bit their gathering crisis. The visit of the Japanese coincided with the nomination of Abraham Lincoln for the Presidency, the split in the Democratic Party, the increasing certainty of civil war.

In Edo, Harris's troubles mounted. The new government under Ii Naosuke proved much less amenable than the old. Hotta had been almost immediately dismissed, primarily because of his pro-Keiki views, and then disgraced as a scapegoat for the treaty's ever having been negotiated. Matsudaira Tadakata, who had busily campaigned for Naosuke's appointment as Chief Councillor but was suspected of being even more interested in acquiring power for himself, was dropped as well. The new councillors replacing them were men who could be trusted to give Naosuke no opposition.

Kawaji had been demoted at the same time that Hotta was dismissed, and a year later he was relieved of all duties and retired in disgrace; he used some of his unaccustomed leisure to study Dutch with Moriyama. Iwase and Inoue, who had been retained long enough to bear the brunt of the negotiations with the Russians, British, and French, suffered much the same fate. Iwase was retired and punished at the same time as Kawaji; he died not much later. Inoue was treated a little less roughly: he was first transferred to the construction bureau (the same ignoble fate that Okada had suffered), and then when a fire in Edo Castle and the need for reconstruction made that post important, he was quickly shifted out of it to become superintendent of naval forces; this was a fine ringing title but the job was a cul-de-sac of frustration, for the Shogun's navy was practically nonexistent.

With the wholesale ouster of men like these, the whole complexion of the government changed. Naosuke's belief that it was necessary open trade and diplomatic relations with foreigners did not mean that he liked them. Harris and the other envoys were constantly complaining that they were treated with discourtesy.

Nor could the foreigners get along together. Especially there was bad feeling between Harris and Rutherford Alcock, the British envoy. Alcock bitterly resented the statements that Harris had made about the British during his negotiations with the Japanese. To quote one man, the two "quarreled like old women."

Worst of all was the violence in the streets. Harris finally came to realize that the Japanese who had negotiated with him were not lying when they told him of the fanatic opposition to opening the country.

On March 24, 1860, foreigners and Japanese alike were thrown into panic. By the Japanese calendar it was the third day of the Third Month, a festival day which brought each daimyo in Edo to the castle to pay his respects to the Shogun.

It was spring, but the day was anything but springlike. The morning had begun with driving sleet and rain, and that had given way to heavy snow whirled by a cold and cutting wind. A few paces distant all was blurred and indistinct.

In midmorning the gate of Ii Naosuke's mansion opened and his escort of fifty or sixty samurai began to emerge, bundled in raincoats, sword hilts in bags to keep them from getting wet. It was only a few hundred yards to the nearest gate of the castle. As the procession approached the gate, some of a nondescript group loitering there darted forward and attacked the advance guard. Others compounded the confusion by attacking the rear. Then within seconds men rushed at the Chief Councillor's *norimono*. A pistol was shot at it, three or four swords thrust fiercely into it. The door was opened, the body pulled out. A man slashed off the head, screamed in triumph, and dashed away into the storm. Ii Naosuke was dead.

The head was quickly recovered and sent to the Ii mansion as the head not of Naosuke but of one of his retainers: the government issued word that the Chief Councillor had been attacked and wounded. For weeks formal messengers were sent from the castle to inquire about the patient's condition. Nearly a month later his resignation was accepted, and finally his death was announced. But everyone in the streets knew what had happened. Kosuke obtained leave from Harris to walk all the way back to Kakisaki and assure his family that he was safe though Edo was in turmoil.

All save one of the conspirators proved to be *ronin* from Mito, men who had been vassals of Naosuke's archenemy, Nariaki. For days it seemed that open warfare would erupt between Hikone and Mito. Somehow it was averted. All the assassins but one had been killed on the spot, had died by their own hand, or had been captured and executed. In their last statement they had solemnly denied all hostility to the Shogunate:

> Our conduct does not indicate the slightest enmity to the Bakufu. We swear before Heaven and Earth, gods and men, that our action proceeds entirely from our hope of seeing the Shogunate resume its proper form, and abide by the holy and wise will of the Emperor. We hope to see our national glory manifested in the expulsion of foreigners from the land.

In the autumn of that same year, on the evening of the fifteenth day of the Eighth Month, Nariaki, who was confined to his mansion at Mito, attended the traditional moon-viewing party, eating and drinking in apparent good health. Stopping to use the toilet on his way to bed, he emerged mortally stricken. There are those who believe he was stabbed there by a *ronin* of Hikone who had got inside the mansion disguised as a gardener. Certainly such a revenge would have had its element of justice. In any event, there is still, today, deep bitterness between the people of Hikone and those of Mito.

In the midst of this terror, of murders in Yokohama and assassinations in Edo, Harris showed a personal courage which explains more than anything else the high regard the Japanese came to have for him.

On December 6, 1860, he wrote to Kate Drinker:

> You must not believe any of the "raw head and bloody bones" stories of our living here in constant dread of assassination—these tales are principally concocted at Shanghai and belong to a class of stories that are called *bunders,* at that place.
>
> I sleep in a house with twenty doors, not one of which is bolted or barred, and I can honestly say that in my house or in the streets of this City, I feel that I am safer than I should be in the City of New York.—During all the time I have lived in this country I have never lost the value of a Shilling.

Yet on New Year's Day, 1861, he sent Heusken to the British legation with a warning passed from the Great Council: a band of several hundred Mito *ronin* were plotting to set fire to the foreign settlement at Yokohama and at the same time to attack each of the legations in Edo and murder its inmates.

"Nothing changed in the position of foreigners for the week following," wrote Alcock. "The alarm spread by the Government of an impending attack continued, though with the usual vagueness and uncertainty as to

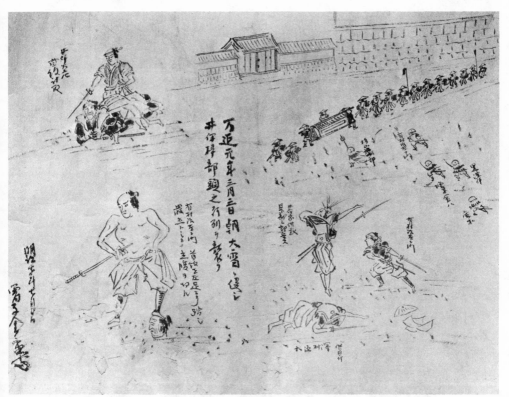

The assassination of Ii Naosuke (*sketches by Masuko Kanehito*)

the true source and degree of danger; and in this unpleasant state of suspense the days passed . . ."

On January 15 Heusken spent most of the day at the Prussian legation. He had assisted the Prussian envoy, Count Eulenberg, in protracted negotiations toward a treaty, which was at last ready to be signed. He dined with Eulenberg, and then about nine o'clock mounted his horse to return to Zempukuji.

In a dispatch to Secretary Cass, Harris wrote:

He was attended by three mounted officers and four footmen bearing lanterns; one of the mounted officers preceded Mr. Heusken and the other two followed close behind him. While proceeding in this manner the party was suddenly attacked on both sides; the horses of the officers were struck and cut; the lanterns struck out and Mr. Heusken wounded on both sides of his body; he put his horse into a gallop and rode about two hundred yards, when he called out to the officers, that he was wounded and that he was dying, and then fell from his horse. The assassins, seven in number, instantly fled, and easily escaped in the dark streets.

Mr. Heusken was brought to this Legation about half past nine o'clock. I immediately procured surgical aid from the Prussian and English Legations, and he received every possible assistance that skill and kindness could supply, but all was in vain, his wounds were mortal, and he died at half past twelve o'clock on the morning of the sixteenth.

Officials of the government called at once to express condolence and their horror at the tragedy, and to assure Harris "that no exertions of the Government should be wanting to arrest and punish the perpetrators of this fearful crime, and tendering me any assistance I might desire."

Heusken's funeral (*a woodcut by an unnamed artist*)

The funeral was held on the eighteenth. The cortege was led by the commissioners for foreign affairs with a long train of their retainers. There followed all the members of the diplomatic and consular corps, the band from a Prussian frigate, and marines and naval officers from Dutch and Prussian men-of-war.

Just before the procession started its passage of about a mile to the temple where Heusken would be buried, a Japanese official, fearing that Harris would be attacked, asked him not to join them.

I answered that I considered it as a sacred duty to attend, and that I should do so regardless of any danger, and I warned him that if anything happened to me under such circumstances, that his Government would be held responsible. I informed my colleagues of this communication and they all resolved to accompany me.

There was no difficulty, and Heusken was laid to rest.

I am at a loss to assign any special motive, that could have influenced the assassins of Mr. Heusken. He was kind and amiable in his temper; he never used any violence towards the Japanese, and from speaking their language, he appeared to be a universal favorite. . . .

On my first arrival here, the authorities informed me that the streets were very unsafe at night; that they never went out themselves except in the case of necessity, and then they were always attended by a large train with many lanterns.

I have constantly warned Mr. Heusken of the danger he was incurring and prayed him not to expose himself in the manner he did.

For more than four months, he was in the habit of visiting the Prussian Legation, almost nightly, and would return home from eight to eleven o'clock at night. I fear that it was this long continued and regular exposure of himself to danger that led to his untimely death.

I am suffering deeply from this sudden and awful catastrophe. Mr. Heusken was associated with me over five years, and he was the companion of my long solitude at Shimoda.

Our relations were rather those of father and son, than *chef* and *employe*.

For the other envoys in Edo, Heusken's murder was the breaking point. Led by Alcock, whose own interpreter had been assassinated just a year earlier, they decided to withdraw from Edo to Yokohama, where they had ships and men to protect them. Harris refused to go with them. He insisted that Heusken had placed himself in jeopardy, and that though the Japanese government must bear the responsibility for his death, it was making serious efforts to protect the foreigners and to honor the treaties. He thought that withdrawal might be the first step toward war. In a letter to Alcock he wrote these lines—words he never could have written at Shimoda, but now he had seen more and he understood more:

I had hoped that the pages of future history might record the great fact that in one spot in the Eastern world the advent of Christian civilization did not bring with it its usual attendants of rapine and bloodshed; this fond hope, I fear, is to be disappointed.

I would sooner see all the Treaties with this country torn up, and Japan return to its old state of isolation, than witness the horrors of war inflicted on this peaceful people and happy land.

Alcock retorted that war was more likely if they stayed in Edo. The debate was acrimonious and it deepened the rancor between them.

So Harris remained alone in Edo for several weeks. To the Japanese he was demonstrating the spirit of a samurai. They could pay no higher compliment.

He succeeded in obtaining from the Shogunate a payment of ten thousand dollars for Heusken's mother. He erected a granite monument over Heusken's grave—and was again criticized, for while the marker that the British had placed over the grave of their interpreter read that he had been "murdered by Japanese assassins," Harris refused to follow this example. The inscription for Heusken reads simply:

SACRED

to the Memory of

HENRY C. J. HEUSKEN,

Interpreter to the

AMERICAN LEGATION

in Japan.

BORN AT AMSTERDAM,

January 20, 1832.

DIED AT YEDO,

January 16, 1861.

Perry's former interpreter, A.L.C. Portman, was hired as replacement, and Harris's judgment in first choosing Heusken was vindicated, for Portman got along with Harris a good deal less well than Heusken had done.

Harris was tired now, and as usual was convinced that his health was rapidly failing and that death was imminent. With the election of a Republican President he asked to be replaced. The new Secretary of State, William H. Seward, requested that he remain at his post, but Harris was insistent. His successor, Robert H. Pruyn, relieved him in 1862.

It is perhaps unfortunate that this narrative has been concerned with Harris's first year or two in Japan, when all of the prejudices of his time and his class and all of the bias he had acquired in China, in addition to ill health, loneliness, and the conviction that his government had deserted him, combined to make him behave as he did.

In his later years, in Edo, he showed a sympathetic understanding of the Japanese which was lacking earlier. This knowledge came slowly, and he continued on occasion to threaten war. Nevertheless, the doubts he had expressed on his arrival in Shimoda—*Grim reflections—ominous of change*

A. L. C. Portman (*detail from a scroll painting attributed to Takagawa Bunsen*)

—*undoubted beginning of the end. Query,—if for the real good of Japan?* —began to reassert themselves as his ambitions were achieved and his frustrations subsided.

He left with the task in Japan only begun. Had he stayed he might have prevented some of the difficulties that arose from his treaty and those modeled after it. But this is a doubtful proposition, for among Edo's small diplomatic corps he failed to assume the leadership which his experience, his seniority, and his rank demanded of him. Perhaps because he was still lonely and ill and homesick, perhaps because he realized that inevitably the British would be the paramount foreign power in Japan for years to come, he was more than willing to abdicate primacy to Alcock, a man whose record in Japan makes Harris's glow in comparison. With Harris gone, Alcock's dominance was undisputed, and for the Japanese there was nothing to cheer about in that.

On the other side of the Pacific, America was preoccupied and exhausted by its Civil War. Its magnificent clipper ships were doomed by steam; its whalers, by the discovery of oil in Pennsylvania. Its people lost for a while much of their interest in the rest of the world, and some of their confidence that they could remake it.

They experienced, too, a sense of disappointment with Japan. Despite the conviction of Harris and most Americans that Japan need only be exposed to Christianity and democracy for them to sweep the country, and despite the desperate fears of men like Nariaki that this was only too true, neither of these creeds took root amid the alien corn. And so Americans were disillusioned with the Japanese, whom they had considered so promising. (It was not until after World War II, when they were once again the most important foreigners in Japan, and were able to do a little remodeling according to their own tastes, that a new love affair developed.)

Harris returned to the tragic violence of the Civil War. In Japan there were even more years of violence.

Of the officials whose careers we have followed, Inoue was the most active in this turbulent era. Having been pushed into the empty job of naval chief, he waited out the change in government that followed Ii Naosuke and then promoted a plan for building a real navy. When political power shifted, he was once again placed on the commission for foreign affairs. During the next few years he was appointed Governor of Edo, the highest post open to a man of less than daimyo status; was dismissed and sentenced to house arrest for concessions wrung from the Shogunate by the British; was reprieved and for the third time appointed to the foreign affairs commission; and finally was reappointed a Governor of Edo. In this post he was responsible for the security of the city, but as the Shogunate steadily weakened, the city was no longer governable. Gangs of bandits roamed the streets. Most of them were politically inspired, the men of feudal lords now in all but open revolt. They robbed rich merchants to get "funds for action"; they sought to create chaos. A man of Inoue's character could not help feeling personally responsible. Despite a recurring fever he began to lead street patrols himself. Early in 1868 he fell ill and on January 19 he died. In his last delirium he talked only of his duty to protect the citizens of Edo.

His brother Kawaji had survived disgrace to serve again on the commission for foreign affairs, but he resigned in despair when he realized that his ideas for rebuilding the Shogunate could never be adopted.

He lived to see Keiki become Shogun, but if there had been any chance back in 1856 and 1857 that Keiki and the men who supported him could transform the Shogunate into a truly national government, that chance was gone by 1867 when he came to the office. A year later he resigned his authority to the Emperor. There was a brief, not very bloody, revolution, and the rule of the Tokugawa was ended.

Kawaji remained faithful to the end. One of his last poems, reflecting his despondency over the disintegration of the Shogunate and the death of his younger brother, he signed "Hereditary Vassal of the Tokugawa." On April 6, 1868, he was told—erroneously—that Edo Castle had fallen to the forces from Kyoto. The next morning he committed suicide. Since all Tokugawa followers were confined to their homes and the enemy was approaching the city, there were few at his funeral.

It is probably not surprising that of all the Japanese officials we have watched, it was Moriyama who fared best. He became an advisor to one of Yokohama's great silk merchants and made a tidy fortune.

Some of the men of the old regime followed Keiki into retirement on his own estates. Some found it easy to transfer their allegiance and serve the new oligarchy as they had served the Shogunate.

The new government had no more legitimacy than the one it replaced, but it behaved as if it had. It was astute enough to use the symbol and the person of the Emperor to establish rule over the whole land. The feudal fiefs were abolished, the daimyo pensioned off, Edo renamed Tokyo. The cry of "Expel the barbarians!" which had been so cleverly used to gain power was quickly forgotten as new men with new energy charted the most amazing modernization that any nation has ever accomplished.

Yet Shimoda, isolated beyond the mountains of Izu, remained for decades a drowsy backwater, cherishing thoughts of the past, of the days when it held center stage in the drama of Japan's re-entry into the world.

In this now quiet scene Yoheiji's wife died at fifty, as the god Fudo had foretold, but Yoheiji lived to a ripe old age, as the god had also predicted. In his late years he set down reminiscences of his days as headman: the visits of the Black Ships of Perry and the Russians, the great tidal wave and the loss of the *Diana*, the typhoon of 1856, the quarrels with Shimoda, the tribulations when Gyokusenji was the American consulate.

With Harris's departure from Japan, Kosuke came home to Kakisaki, but he remained what he had always been, a quiet man, keeping his memories to himself.

Not so Sukezo. When he returned to Naka he played the role of a celebrity. He loved to talk about the days when he served the Americans. He was an obliging spinner of yarns, tailoring his stories to his audience, telling what the listener at hand wanted to hear. He had no competition from Takizo, who went to Manchuria to seek his fortune.

573

Townsend Harris lived in New York for fifteen years, despite his dyspepsia, a clubman called by his juniors "the old Tycoon." He was always eager to talk about Japan. He lived to grieve over his treaty and those it spawned, treaties he had expected would be revised long since.

In 1875 a young man, returned from Japan after four years of teaching there, called on him at his club. They talked for a long time. There was much that Harris wanted to know. But, the young man wrote, "his main question, put to me in a form varied and repeated, was 'What do the Japanese think of me?'"

A BRIEF CHRONOLOGY
OF EVENTS RELATED
TO THIS STORY

Tokugawa Shogunate founded	1603
Check-point established at Shimoda	1616
Foreigners expelled, Japanese forbidden to go abroad	1624–1641
Check-point moved from Shimoda to Uraga	1720
Townsend Harris born in upstate New York	*1804*
Henry Heusken born in Amsterdam	*1832*
Lord Abe appointed to the Great Council	1843
The Free Academy (now The City College) founded in New York	
largely through the efforts of Townsend Harris	*1847*
Harris's mother dies	*1847*
Harris resigns from the Board of Education	*1848*
Harris sails from New York on a trading expedition	*1849*
Ranald MacDonald ventures into Japan	1848–1849
Perry expedition opens Japan	1853–1854
Perry treaty signed	March, 1854
Tidal wave almost destroys Shimoda	December, 1854
Lord Hotta appointed to the Great Council	1855
Harris appointed Consul General to Japan	*1855*
Harris negotiates a commercial treaty with Siam	*1856*
Harris arrives at Shimoda	*August, 1856*
Typhoon hits Shimoda	September, 1856
Shogun Iesada married	January, 1857
Okada dismissed, Nakamura appointed, as Governor of Shimoda	May, 1857
Convention of Shimoda signed	June, 1857
Lord Abe dies	August, 1857
Harris travels to Edo	*November, 1857*
Harris completes negotiation of a commercial treaty	*February, 1858*
Harris is critically ill at Shimoda	*March, 1858*
Lord Hotta attempts to obtain Emperor's approval	
of Harris's treaty	March–June, 1858
Lord Ii Naosuke appointed Chief Councillor	June, 1858
Harris's commercial treaty signed	*July, 1858*
Lord Hotta dismissed from the Great Council	August, 1858
Commercial treaties signed with the Netherlands,	
Russia, England, and France	August–September, 1858

A Brief Chronology of Events Related to This Story

Harris, on a holiday in China, learns of his appointment as Minister to Japan	*April–June, 1859*
Shimoda closed as a port for foreigners	July, 1859
Harris establishes the U.S. legation in Edo	*July, 1859*
Japanese mission sails to exchange treaty ratifications in Washington	February, 1860
Lord Ii Naosuke assassinated	March, 1860
Lord Tokugawa Nariaki dies	September, 1860
Henry Heusken assassinated	*January, 1861*
Harris relieved, returns to New York	*1862*
Keiki becomes fifteenth and last Tokugawa Shogun	1866
Inoue dies	January, 1868
Kawaji commits suicide	April, 1868
Tokugawa Shogunate ends	1868
Townsend Harris dies in New York City	*1878*

POSTSCRIPT

Shimoda Story is not fiction. It is as historically accurate as I could make it given my own limitations and the structure I chose for the book. The story of Townsend Harris and his negotiations, and the circumstances of Japanese history which bore upon those negotiations, are drawn from standard materials—official documents and authoritative interpretations—in Japanese and English. The local events in Shimoda, Kakisaki, and the other villages are based on the wealth of material surviving from those years—diaries, directives, and that encyclopedia of Shimoda life, Hirai Heijiro's record of annual events.

However, in dealing with these purely local events I have occasionally permitted myself some liberty. I have fleshed out certain incidents where the headmen's diaries are too laconic or too discreet to tell the whole story. (An example of this is the story of the young priest of Mida-do. We know from Yoheiji's diary that a scandal in the young man's past came to light and caused great concern, and that the case was resolved as I have indicated, but Yoheiji does not tell us the nature of the scandal. The young priest's story as I have told it is my invention, but it is based on the possibilities within the situation, the law of the land, and the Shimoda milieu, and it is an attempt to illuminate all these.) I have also transposed some incidents in time, events which I wanted to include but which occurred a little later than the fifteen-month period which was my special concern. (Again I cite the case of the young priest, which actually occurred in October, 1859, instead of November, 1856.) Such transpositions are revealed in my citations of source materials.

Since the story of Harris's relations with Okichi will be of concern to some people, I must emphasize that I have taken no liberties in treating that material. As stated in the text, the story of Okichi's life before she served Harris is based largely on Muramatsu's book; admittedly this is questionable source material but no better exists. My story of the relations between Harris and Okichi is based on documents whose authenticity is not open to doubt. Others have the privilege of believing that these documents do not mean what they say, but long and intensive study has convinced me that they do.

Japanese names and terms are a problem in a book like this. As to names, I have tried to adopt a consistent and modern romanization and I have edited other materials in English to conform. Most notably, perhaps, this applies to Harris's journal; here I plead that I have only continued what the editor of the journal, Dr. Mario E. Cosenza, began: he changed Harris's spelling "Simoda" to today's more usual "Shimoda" and I think he would have gone further had he had more help with the Japanese language. With regard to terms and titles, I have most often tried to find a reasonable English equivalent. For those who know the Japanese terms, a cross reference is provided in the index.

I do not read Japanese and, besides, it takes—even in Japan—a scholar with special training to read the Japanese of the Tokugawa period. In a very few instances I was fortunate that documents I needed had been well translated. In most cases, I had translations made for me. I make no claim that these translations as I have edited them are literal; they should be considered paraphrasing but I have taken precautions to insure that they do not violate the meaning.

I am fortunate that my friend Dr. Richard Lane consented to translate the folk songs I have used and, more especially, the ballad "Raven at Dawn" (*Akegarasu*), from which I have quoted at several points. Concerning this ballad I would like to pass on some of the information given me by Dr. Lane: In the year 1769 a young man named Inosuke and the Yoshiwara courtesan Miyoshino committed love-suicide together. Three years later the event was memorialized when Tsuruga Wakasanojo wrote *Akegarasu* in the form of *joruri* known as *shinnai*, which was usually devoted to emotional tales of love and love-suicide in the Yoshiwara. (In the nineteenth century, *shinnai* minstrels were banned from the Yoshiwara for inciting too many love-suicides with their plaintive ballads.) *Shinnai* has never been considered one of the more elevated types of Japanese music, but it mirrors the fin-de-siècle sentiments of the more romantic of the Edo populace in the second half of the eighteenth century.

In trying to list all those who have assisted me in writing this book, I am faced with a formidable task. I must begin with the late Dr. Cosenza, who not only edited Harris's complete journal for publication but thereafter spent years in painstaking research and writing about the man and his work. Dr. Cosenza provided both valuable information and encouragement, and it saddened me that I could not agree with his eulogistic view of Harris.

Among the first with whom I discussed this project was Professor John W. Hall, then of the University of Michigan, now of Yale. He gave me important suggestions and, in particular, an introduction to Mr. Madoka Kanai,* research scholar at the Historiographical Institute of Tokyo University. From first to last, Mr. Kanai and his colleague, Mr. Minoru Tada, have given me unsparingly their guidance and assistance, without which this book could not have been written.

As I was on my way to Japan, Professor Robert A. Wilson of the University of California at Los Angeles kindly gave me a typescript of Heusken's journal as edited by him and Mrs. Jeannette van der Corput. Having this long before it was published was a great boon.

Early in my stay in Japan I met Professor Seiichi Sakata of the National Diet Library, who has made a study of Harris. I am grateful to him and to his colleagues, my old friend Mr. Makoto Kuwabara, Mr. Hiroshi Ueno, and Mr. Sadao Nakano. Mr. Nakano in particular helped me to use the facilities of the library.

* Hereafter in this postscript Japanese names are in Western style, given name first.

Professor Ken'ichiro Shoda of Waseda University, one of the coauthors of the study *Izu Shimoda*, regularly provided clarification of matters that puzzled me in my study of Shimoda and the economics of the period. I was assisted with other problems, and always graciously, by Professors Tsunekichi Yoshida and Shiro Konishi of Tokyo University, Takashi Ishii of Tohoku University, Yoshio Sakata of Kyoto University, and Motoi Kimura of Meiji University.

I was fortunate that my stay in Japan coincided in part with that of Professor W. G. Beasley of the University of London. He was generous in helping me, and his fine book *Select Documents on Japanese Foreign Policy, 1853–1858* not only provided those few scholarly translations available in my field but has been in steady use as a reference.

I should also mention Professor E. S. Crawcour of Australian National University; but for his suggestion concerning the translation of documents I might still be floundering.

This seems the point to name Miss Junko Asai and Mr. Uki Odate, who provided the transcriptions into modern Japanese which made possible the translation of a very large number of documents.

Among the many who assisted me as translators and interpreters I must name Mr. Tanejiro Kamei, Mrs. Mariko Sato, Mrs. May A. Hashimoto, Mr. Kinjiro Otsuka, Mrs. Shizuyo Fukuda, Mr. Roy Yamaguchi, Mr. Shozo Tokunaga, Mr. Shigeo Tsuyuki, Mr. Kaoru Watanabe, Mr. Tsujio Endo, Mr. Hirotaka Hatakeyama, and Mr. Takeo Yamaoka.

Mrs. C. M. van Buitenan of the University of Chicago translated for me the long letter in Dutch which is the reply from the Governors to Harris's complaints of high prices.

The Reverend Father Wilhelm Schiffer, S. J., of Sophia University, Tokyo, gave me a resume of the lengthy chapter on Shimoda from Lühdorf's book, a little-known item which was brought to my attention by Mr. Paul Blum.

I lived in and around Shimoda for two years, trying to learn all I could about the town and its people, to sense its atmosphere, to understand its history. I shall always be grateful for the kindness I was shown and the help I was given; I came away richer by many friends. I cannot name here all the individuals of Shimoda, Kakisaki, and the surrounding area to whom I am indebted; most of them are listed among those I interviewed. But I must speak of two men. The first is Mr. Hajime Mori, who edited and published *Kurofune* (Black Ships) for almost two decades before he was forced to stop by the tensions which were leading to the war in the Pacific; he died before I came to Shimoda to work and so I could not learn from him as I would have liked to, but his magazine is a gold mine of local lore. The second is Mr. Hideo Matsumoto, who from my arrival until his untimely death was my guide and guarantor to the people of the town.

After I returned from Japan, a great many questions arose as I set to work with the material I had gathered. In this situation I opened a correspondence with my Shimoda friends; Mr. Tatsuo Matsumoto and members of the Shimoda local history club did extensive research and responded with full and complete answers.

Mr. Matsumoto has graciously said that I stimulated the formation of their club; if so, this gives me one more happy association with Shimoda. I should add that I am indebted to Mrs. Shigeto Fujimoto of Huntley, Illinois, and to Dr. and Mrs. Gen'ichi Kobayashi of Elgin, Illinois, for their assistance in corresponding with Mr. Matsumoto. And in speaking of local friends I must name Mrs. Donald Hardy, who typed the manuscript, most of it several times, and gave needed encouragement during the long period when she and I were the only ones reading it.

At home I turned to American scholars for help and was never refused. At my own university, the University of Chicago, I was lucky to meet and form an enduring friendship with Professor Joseph M. Kitagawa, and I have relied heavily on his knowledge and insights. In the university's library Professor James Morita gave unstinting assistance with difficult source materials. At the library of the University of Michigan, Professor Yukihisa Suzuki provided skilled bibliographic help.

I am grateful also to Professors Ardath W. Burks of Rutgers, Allan B. Cole of The Fletcher School of Law and Diplomacy, Tufts University, Hyman Kublin of Brooklyn College, George A. Lensen of Florida State University, Henry Rosovsky of Harvard, and Thomas C. Smith of Stanford.

My friends Richard S. Baum, M.D., and Lee Gladstone, M.D., gave me helpful medical opinions on Townsend Harris's ailments and illnesses.

Harris's papers are, appropriately, preserved in the library of The City College, New York. In my use of these papers I was assisted with unfailing kindness and efficiency by Mrs. Wolf Franck, the archivist, and by her successor, Mrs. K. M. Dailey.

For help in obtaining illustrations I am indebted to Miss Margaret Gentles of the Art Institute of Chicago, Mr. Karl Kup of the New York Public Library, Mrs. Yoshiko Mori of Shimoda, Mr. Kunio Hariu of Tokyo University's Historiographical Institute, Mr. Charles Mitchell of Tokyo, Mr. Harry Hess of New York City, and many of those already mentioned—including Professors Kanai, Tada, Wilson, and Lensen. Particular thanks go to Mr. Fumio Kitaoka, who remade his woodblock print, *Namako-kabe*, especially for this book.

When my manuscript finally reached a state in which it could be read I sought a wide range of critical opinion. I am grateful to all the following for taking time to read and comment on my work: Professors Marius B. Jansen of Princeton University, Conrad Totman of Northwestern University, and Dr. Richard Lane; Mr. Paul Blum and Mr. Don Brown; Professor Allen Tuttle of Valparaiso University, Mr. and Mrs. Kenneth G. Hecht, and Mr. Emerson Crocker. I have profited greatly from all their corrections and suggestions. The faults that remain must be blamed on me alone.

Finally, I want to say how very fortunate I feel that my editor is Albert Erskine and that I can rely on his sensitivity, judgment, and patience.

OLIVER STATLER

NOTES

The following notes identify source materials. To avoid making these notes unduly long I have made certain omissions. First, I have seldom documented general historical background which I assume is familiar to readers interested in my sources. Second, I have not given citations for material drawn from Harris's journal (always italicized), Heusken's journal, the journals of the headmen of Shimoda and Kakisaki, and the petitions of Naka village (if identified as such), when the exact or approximate date seems evident from the text. (Unless otherwise noted, the material concerning local events in Shimoda and Kakisaki has been drawn from the journals of the respective headmen; when other sources have been used as well, the headmen's journals are cited without specifying the entries.)

Dates according to the Japanese calendar are given in this fashion: 11–IV–A4, meaning the eleventh day of the Fourth Month of the year Ansei 4; the date by the Gregorian calendar follows in parentheses. In some cases, documents show only the month, not the day. There was an intercalary Fifth Month in Ansei 4; this month is designated Vx.

Certain works are identified in the notes by the initials preceding their listing in the bibliography. In other cases abbreviated titles are used.

Volume numbers are given in Roman numerals and page numbers are given in Arabic numerals, except that in citing Harris's papers and letterbooks and the *Dai Nihon Komonjo, Bakumatsu Gaikoku Kankei Monjo*, the Arabic numerals are document numbers rather than page numbers.

Chapter 1: August 21, 1856

3 sign in Dutch: Hawks I, 404
6–7 early history of Shimoda: IzuS, 237–39
12 Black Ship verse: Nitobe, 1
12 notice of Perry visit: MTOK, 27–28
12 Wataya Kichibei's bench: *ibid.*, 32–33
14–15 Saito's visit: BGKM XIV, 161
14–15 government's worry: *Ishin shi*, 204
15 instructions to Governors: BGKM XII, 131
15–16 Aihara's visit: *ibid.*, XIV, 162;

Miller, 639–40 (summary)
16–17 Chuemon: interview Masuda
17 government directive: MTOK, 51–52
18–19 foreigners use Gyokusenji: Hawks I, note 390–92; Cole YS, 15–16, 57; Lensen RJE, 105; Lühdorf; Kawaji diary, 185
20 Naka compound: interview Tanaka
21 report to Great Council: BGKM XIV, 170
22 Hamadaya: MTOK, 55

Chapter 2: August 22–September 4, 1856

24–26 Aihara's visit: BGKM XIV, 168

26–28 Harris's background: Crow, 30–40, 43–44; Griffis TH, 3–13; THJ, 277, 432 (note 515)

28 Marcy: Learned, 157

28 letter to Marcy, 1854: Marcy folios 43798–9

28 letter to Marcy, 10 Oct 1853: National Archives, record group 59

28 Americans in opium trade: Dennett, 115–22

28 letter re Perry: Marcy, folios 46854–5

28 Perry, move slowly in Japan: Hawks II, 185–87; Treat I, 25, 31

29 Brodhead: DES I, letter Brodhead, 17 Mar 1855

30 Harris's appearance: HL&P I (passport)

30 Heusken: HHJJ, xi–xii; Patterson

30 Heusken quotes: HHJJ, 4, 99

30–31 Siam assignment: INS, No. 1, 12 Sep 1855

31 Harris quotes: THJ, 17, 34, 48

31 letter to Wetmore: Marcy, folios 47754–5

32 Harris quote: THJ, 34

32 letter to Wetmore: Marcy, folios 47764–5

32–33 letter to Harris: Marcy, folio 47766

33 Drinker letters: HL&P I, 23, 25

33–34 Macgowan letter: *ibid.*, 31

34 *San Jacinto:* Bennett, 110–21: THJ, 76

34 Siam, departure: Moffat, 82–87

35 Harris anti-British: Griffis TH, 4

35 Bowring: Bartle, 297

35 U.S. policy in China: Dennett, 303–5

35 British opinion: Beasley GB, 87

35–36 letter to Marcy: Marcy, folios 48441–3

36–37 Williams: FWW, 39, 54, 93–100

37–38 Williams in Japan: SWW, 47–70, 99–227

38 Harris never sought Williams: DES–CHI, Nos. 12–22, 1856 (Williams must have been in the Canton area; on June 30, 1856, Peter Parker left

Macao on the Navy sloop *Levant* for a tour of the ports north of Canton, up to Shanghai, hoping eventually to get to Peking to talk treaty revision; but Parker's dispatches make it clear that Williams did not accompany him.)

38 Perry recommends Williams: FWW, 235–36

38 Williams undecided: FWW, 238–39

38 Drinker re Parker: HL&P I, 25

38 voyage to Japan: THJ, 190–4; USN–1

39–40 mountain religion (Shugendo): Earhart, 264, 316, 392–93, 496–500

40 Lo quotes: Hawks II, 397, 403–4

40 regulations: *ibid.* I, 479–81

41 Yoheiji's boats: KSI&FB

42 bazaar: Wood, 305–6

43 Aihara's visit: BGKM XIV, 169

43 Williams quote: SWW, 165

44 Perry describes Shimoda: Hawks I, 402–4

44–45 Perry describes Ryosenji: *ibid.*, 409

47 Aihara's visit: BGKM XIV, 176

48 Goyosho: Wood, 309–10

48 seating arrangement: MTOK, 60–61

49–50 Goyosho meeting: BGKM XIV, 178

50 menu: MTOK, 61–62

50 gifts of chickens: HHJJ, 86

51 Wood re Moriyama: Wood, 311

52 travel time to Edo: *ibid.*, 309

52 Williams re Moriyama: SWW, 120

52–54 MacDonald: MacDonald—birth, 92; Japanese seamen, 120–23; signs on whaler, 137–38; leaves ship, 150–51; lands Japan, 153–59; reaches Nagasaki, meets Moriyama, 207–8; description of Moriyama, 209–10; interrogations, 210–11, 214–21; teaches English, 225–27

54 Moriyama's interpreting: Sakamaki, 47

54 *Preble, Lagoda* deserters: *ibid.*, 50–55; MacDonald, 195–97, 246–47

54 MacDonald re Moriyama: MacDonald, 263–64

54 Moriyama's temperament: SWW, 211; interview Furusho
54–55 Williams quote: *ibid.,* 150
55 order to Inoue: BGKM XIV, 179
57–58 Goyosho meeting: *ibid.,* 181
57 Japanese knew, obligated to accept Harris: *Ishin shi,* 204–7
58–59 Goyosho meeting: Japanese report of meeting: BGKM XIV, 183; Miller, 640–41 (summary)
59–61 meeting on *San Jacinto:* BGKM XIV, 189
62 priest moves: interview Murakami
62 maxims: Lombard, 105

63 Governor unable to visit ship: BGKM XIV, 194
63 invitation to Goyosho: *ibid.,* 203
64 letter to Baring Brothers: HLB I, 63
64 letter to Russell & Co.: *ibid.,* 62
64–65 letter to Armstrong & Lawrence: *ibid.,* 61
65–67 Goyosho meeting: BGKM XIV, 210; Wood, 308, 313–16
65 gifts to Americans: HHJJ, 86
67 letter to Minister of Foreign Affairs: HLB I, 56
68 letter to Comm. Armstrong: USN–1
68–69 reception on *San Jacinto:* Wood, 317–18

Chapter 3: September 5–30, 1856

72 report to Great Council: BGKM XIV, 222
73–74 Gyokusenji becomes residence: TH Saka, letter 1, sheet 3
74 uniform: HL&P II, 7; Moffat, 66
75 Okubo's mistress: KJ, 18, 19–IV–A1 (14, 15 May 1854)
76–77 Moriyama calls: BGKM XIV, 227
77 Japanese holidays: HCB, 6
78–79 Moriyama calls: BGKM XIV, 236
79–81 Wakana calls: *ibid.,* 245
82 letter to Great Council: *ibid.,* 234
82–83 letter to Inoue: HLB I, 68
83 engineer re coal: HL&P I, 42
83–92 Shimoda festival: interviews Kada Manzo, Matsumoto, Saito, Shazawa, Usui
92–95 Moriyama, Wakiya call: BGKM XIV, 258
93 Takizo, Sukezo were *ashigaru: ibid.* XVI, 104; Kuro–2, 125
93 conditions, Naka village: NP, X, XI–A3 (29 Oct–26 Dec 1856)
96 informant's letter: BGKM XIV, 299
96 Great Council order: *Ishin shi,* 215
97 committee recommendations: BGKM XIV, 298
97–98 Great Council order: *ibid.,* 270
98 public order: *ibid.,* 271
99–100 order to Iwase: *ibid.,* 272

100–1 Iwase's voyage: Hibata, 545–46
102 orders to Kii and Awa: Tokutomi, 39
102 message to Imperial Court: BGKM XIV, 284: XV, 53
103 reply to Lo: Hawks II, 398–99
104 Hotta order: BGKM XIV, 213
104–5 Hotta order: *ibid.,* 277
106 Mt. Takane: interviews Kada Manzo, Tiba
107 Aihara calls: BGKM XIV, 269
107 treaty (article 7): Hawks I, 379
107 regulations (article 9): *ibid.,* 480
107–8 weather observations: HLB I, 87; THJ, 284 (note 350)
109 wickedness, Izu coast: Adachi, 500
109–10 shipping regulations: Hibata, 549–53
110–11 salvage operations, dispute: Hamada
111–12 *yamagoshi:* interview Tasaka
112 noodle houses: interview Funada
112–14 letter to Governor: HLB I, 69
114 Rodgers: Cole YS, 16, 109–10
115 "Laws of Nations": Martens, 112, 155–56
115–16 Bowring letter: HL&P I, 43
116–18 committee memorial: BGKM XIV, 278
118 Wetmore quote: Marcy, folio 45752

Chapter 4: October, 1856

119 body at Suzaki: KC, 6–IX–A3 (4 Oct)

119 Owari lumber, retainers: KC, 8, 17–IX–A3 (6, 15 Oct)

119 report, reconstruction: KC, 7–IX–A3 (5 Oct)

119 dispute: Hamada

120–22 Fabius at Goyosho: BGKM XV, 4

121–22 letter, King of Holland: William II, 110–14

122 Japanese visit *Medusa:* BGKM XV, 5

122 drafts, salary: HLB I, 70, 71, 72

122–23 order, Armstrong & Lawrence: *ibid.,* 66

123 shopping list: Murakami, 117–18

124–26 harvest inspection: Hirai, book 6

126–28 Hirai Heijiro: IzuS, 318–20

128 Unsho: Hawks II, 406

128 Lo: *ibid.,* 404–5

128–29 austerity pledge: KC, X–A3 (29 Oct–27 Nov)

129 festival visit canceled: KC, 20–IX–A3 (18 Oct)

129 Chrysanthemum festival: Erskine, 109

129 *General Pierce,* letter-writing: THJ, 240–41

129–30 dispatch: DES I, No. 16, 9 Oct 1856

130–31 letter, *norimono,* horse: BGKM XV, 40

131–32 letter, currency exchange: *ibid.,* 14

132 Harris letter, currency exchange: HLB I, 75

132 Japanese will discuss 3 for 1: Great Council endorsement, BGKM XV, 14

132–33 letter, Shimoda unsuitable, British plans: *ibid.,* 15

133 Lühdorf: Lühdorf, 121, 123–24, 132, 134–36, 138, 141–42, 144–50, 185–87

133 Lühdorf re Bowring: BGKM XV, 15

133–36 Kakisaki-Shimoda dispute: Hamada

136 Iwase's farewell party: MTOK, 248

137 hospitality to foreigners: KC, 15–IX–A3 (13 Oct)

137 Iwase credited, boar: MTOK, 246

137 Lühdorf, boar: Lühdorf, 171

137 Councillor alerted to go to Shimoda: BGKM XV, 26

137 British warship, Nagasaki: Beasley GB, 162–63; YRH No. 36, 32

137–38 Great Council order: BGKM XV, 29

138 *Arrow* incident, war: Hurd 11–12, 17, 21–32

138 American involvement: (letter Capt. Bell, 10 Jan 1857) HL&P I, 54

138 American consul joins attack on Canton: Dennett, 283

138 note Parker's belligerence: *ibid.,* 281–90

139 *The Rising Sun:* Hibata, 543

139–40 Abe's handling of Nariaki: *Ishin shi,* 33–34

140 Nariaki's loyalty to Shogunate: Ishii, No. 8, 26

141 Nariaki's background: Totman "Struggle," 52–53, 57–59, 61

141–42 Nariaki's letter to Great Council: Tokutomi, 21–22

142 Kawaji re Government policy: Yamamoto, 102

142 visit Nariaki: *Ishin shi,* 195–96

142–44 letter to Yoshinaga: *Sakumu kiji* II, 3–6

145 letter to Abe: Tokutomi, 23

146–47 letter to Ishikawa: *ibid.,* 27

147 U.S. imports, exports: *Historical Statistics,* 545

148 Kawaji to Kyoto: Tokutomi, 31

148–49 tangerine boats: interview Kada Manzo

149–50 Kakisaki-Shimoda dispute: Hamada

150 shipwreck: KC, 17–IX–A3 (15 Oct)

152 Williams quotes: SWW, 218, 219

152–53 Kawaji, Russian's greeting: Kawaji diary, 165

154–55 Harris letter: HLB I, 76

155 Wakana calls: BGKM XV, 59

155 forward Harris letter: *ibid.,* 44

Chapter 5: November, 1856

Chapter 6: December, 1856

Chapter 7: January, 1857

nenpyo, 18, 19–XII–A3 (13, 14 Jan)
223 Nariaki's opposition: Ishii, No. 8, 23
224 Atsu's furniture taken away: Ishii, No. 8, 27
224 Iwase promoted: BGKM XV, 141
225 Harris appoints Heusken vice-consul: HLB I, 103
225–26 meeting at Goyosho: BGKM XV, 137
226 Royal Asiatic Society: HL&P I, 53
226 Bowring letter: *ibid.*, 52
226–27 course of war: Bartle, 305
227 Canton burned: Hurd, 33–34; Bartle, 303–4
227 Williams: FWW, 238–39, 242
227–28 Drinker letter: HL&P I, 62
227–28 bread poisoned: Hurd, 35–36; Bartle, 304; MacNair, 249; FWW, 243
228 Lady Bowring's death: Bartle, 313; Bowring, 25
228 letter to Minister of Foreign Affairs: HLB I, 101; BGKM XV, 139
229 Kyuhachi: Ishii Shinichi, 84
229 mustaches: Preble, 125–26
229 Tateishi translates, Ito checks, Harris letter: BGKM XV, 139
229–30 send Harris letter to Great Council: *ibid.*, 140
231 Harris's drinking: IzuS, 741; McMaster, "Alcock and Harris," 352
231–34 Wakana calls: BGKM XV, 145
231 Heusken threatened: THJ, 293
232 Tachino version: MTOK, 240–41
234–35 Wakana calls: BGKM XV, 146
234–35 Harris quotes: THJ, 295–96
235–36 Goyosho meeting: BGKM XV, 148; THJ, 297–99
237 notice, Okada's trip: BGKM XV, 151
237 reports of meetings transmitted: *ibid.*, 152
237 call for bearers: KC, 22–XII–A3 (17 Jan)

237 Harris's "knowledge of Eastern character": INS, No. 2, 13 Sep 1855
238 taxes on sales to foreigners: KC, 22–XII–A3 (17 Jan)
238 Heusken's birthday: Patterson, 3
239 duty roster: KJ, 1–XII–A4 (15 Jan 1858)
239 farmer in debt: KJ, 4–XII–A4 (18 Jan 1858)
239 cleaning out soot: Hirai, book 7
239 housecleaning: IzuS, 630
239–40 dispute, calendars: Uragaya, XII–A3 (27 Dec 1856–25 Jan 1857)
239–40 Tottori ship: KJ, 6–10–XII–A4 (20–24 Jan 1858)
241 make no *mochi* day of Ox: Hirai, book 7
241 Kakisaki, *mochi*: IzuS, 630
241 Tachino, *mochi*: interview Nakada
241–42 decorate with pine and bamboo: IzuS, 630
242 tree stump for fire: *ibid.*
242 year-end duties at Goyosho: KJ, 30–XII–A5 (2 Feb 1859)
242 old man tours streets: interviews Kada Manzo
242 first water from well: IzuS, 631
242–43 Shimoda officials gather: Hirai, book 3
244 watchmen banned from streets: Hirai, book 7; Simmons, 147–48
245 shipwreck: KC, 1–I–A4 (26 Jan)
245 work symbolically begun, boats purified, crews entertained: IzuS, 631
245–46 Governor to receive 6th day: KC, 2–I–A4 (27 Jan)
246 decorations removed: *ibid.*, 632
246 bamboo for flood-time: Hirai, book 3
246 Buddhist priests first appear: IzuS, 631
246 stricture against gambling: Hirai, book 3

Chapter 8: February, 1857

247–48 holiday: IzuS, 633; Erskine, 29–31
247 official aspects: Hirai, book 3

248 11th day conference: *ibid.*
248 reward from Tottori: KJ, 11–I–A5 24 Feb 1858)

248–50 reading of code: Asakawa, 266–68
248–49 code: Simmons, 177–216
250 storehouse opening: IzuS, 633
250 midmonth: *ibid.*, 633–34
250–51 17th day conference: KC, 15–I–A4 (9 Feb)
251 ship's inn conference: interviews Takeshi, Kokubo, Suzuki Kumetaro; KJ, 20–I–A5 (5 Mar 1858)
251 loan repayment: KC, 8–II–A4 (3 Mar)
251–52 Perry, Williams advocate resthouse: SWW, 209
252–53 harbor filled, sumo, girls: interviews Takeshi, Kokubo, Suzuki Kumetaro (see 393–94)
253 Perry's men defeated at sumo: KJ, 3–IV–A1 (29 Apr 1854)
253 rice, daughter: interview Mori Kikuro
253–54 Oko: MTOK, 6–9
254 ballad: from "Raven at Dawn"
256 Great Council order: BGKM XV, 178
256 finance bureau resists 3 for 1 rate: *ibid.*, 159
257 Great Council letter to Harris: *ibid.*, 177
257 English lessons: *ibid.*, 181; THJ, 349
257 Abe quote: Brinkley, 666
258 Governors, Nagasaki, Hakodate, opinion: BGKM XV, 174
258 Tribunal opinion: *ibid.*, 228
258 committee opinion: *ibid.*, 187
258–59 ometsuke, metsuke opinion: *ibid.*, 91, 173, 188
259 finance opinion: *ibid.*, 189
260 *ometsuke, metsuke* discouragement: *ibid.*, 173
260 Hotta vexed: *Sakumu Kiji* II, 103–4
260 Hotta directive: BGKM XV, 179
260 advance notices, Okada arrival: KC, 23–I–A4 (17 Feb)
261 Takane festival: interviews Kada Manzo, Tiba
261–62 method of rescue: interview Kada Manzo
262 Matsumura, Moriyama call: MOR, 26–I–A4 (20 Feb)
262–63 Okada calls: *ibid.*, 27–I–A4 (21 Feb)
263–65 funeral: interview Kada Manzo
266–68 Governors' reception: MOR, 1–II–A4 (24 Feb)

269 gobangoshi: a corruption of *goban-sho-shu,* Shogunal guards
271–73 Goyosho meeting: BGKM XV, 199
272 Martens quote: Martens, 112
273 translation, Great Council letter: DES I, No. 13, 11 Sep 1857, enclosure 2
273–78 Goyosho meeting: *Hotta Masayoshi,* Chapter 2, 57–61; MOR, 3–II–A4 (26 Feb)

To follow the exact course of the negotiations over the next several days would likely be wearisome and probably is impossible. The Japanese record is incomplete. The single entry in Heusken's Journal is of little help because of the young man's habit of summarizing the events of a considerable period under one date. Harris's record is inaccurate: he not only describes some meetings on the wrong dates, he even describes more meetings than actually occurred, as is quite clear from the Governors' formal record, from Moriyama's diary, and from Headman Hambei's diary (the latter recorded as a matter of importance every occasion that the Governors came to the Goyosho); therefore Harris's version of what was discussed at the various meetings is certainly filled with error. However, it is possible to plot the general course and tenor of the talks, and this I have tried to do.

274 Harris's instructions: INS, No. 2, 13 Sep 1855 (see also note on page 294)
275–76 opening Nagasaki: BGKM XV, 206
275–76 Perry re Nagasaki: Hawks I, 364
276 treaty (article 7): *ibid.*, 379
276 Japanese accept extraterritoriality: Murdoch, 640–41
276 Williams re extraterritoriality: SWW, vii
276 U.S. extraterritoriality in China: Dennett, 319–20
278 Wood quote: Wood, 316
278 Setsubun: IzuS, 634; Erskine, 38–43
278–81 Goyosho meeting: BGKM XV, 201; MOR, 4–II–A4 (27 Feb)

280 paper money: BGKM XV, 206
280 treaty (article 1): Hawks I, 378
280–81 instructions: INS, No. 6, 4 Oct 1855
281–82 Moriyama calls: MOR, 5–II–A4 (28 Feb)

282–83 Curtius report: BGKM XV, 202
282 war in China: Bell letter, HL&P I, 54; Drinker letter, *ibid.*, 62; Bartle, 305; Hurd, 33–38
282–83 reaction in England: Bartle, 306–8; Hurd, 53–82

Chapter 9: *March 1857*

284 Armstrong promised ship: THJ, 347
284–86 Goyosho meeting: BGKM XV, 206; MOR, 7–II–A4 (2 Mar)
285 Governors' men outraged: BGKM XVII, 56; Kuro–4, 56
286 6% discount: THJ, 327. Harris makes the date of this offer Friday, March 6, a date on which I think no conference took place. There is no Japanese record of a conference on that date and Moriyama's diary states that on March 7 Heusken called to inquire about Inoue, who was ill, and to ask when Harris would get an answer to his written proposals, questions which seem unlikely had there been a conference the day before which was attended by Inoue. Japanese records indicate that there were no conferences between March 2 and March 10, and I believe this was the case.
286 Marcy statement sent to Edo: BGKM XV, 210
286 Heusken delivers memorandum: MOR, 8–II–A4 (3 Mar)
286–87 Heusken calls: *ibid.*, 12–II–A4 (7 Mar)
287 Hatsuuma: IzuS, 634; interview Kada Manzo; Erskine, 41
288–90 Moriyama and Ito call: MOR, 14–II–A4 (9 Mar)
289 Williams quote: SWW, 222
290 Governors' letter: MOR, 14–II–A4 (9 Mar)
290 Heusken calls: *ibid.*, 15–II–A4 (10 Mar)
291 Goyosho meeting: *ibid.*
291–93 Goyosho meeting: THJ, 327; MOR, 16–II–A4 (11 Mar)

293 throws smoking pot: Kuro–4, 56
293 letters Nagasaki-Shimoda: BGKM XV, 164
293 Odawara force: KC, 16–II–A4 (11 Mar)
294–95 gambling case: NP, 15–II–A4 (10 Mar); *ko:* Embree, 138–40
295–96 letter to Governors: HLB I, 106
296–98 Moriyama calls: MOR, 19–II–A4 (14 Mar)
298 deaths in Kakisaki: interview Murakami (Gyokusenji records)
298 Moriyama calls: MOR, 21–II–A4 (16 Mar)
298 Perry letter: HL&P I, 57
298–99 Bowring letter: *ibid.*, 58
299 Abe's health: Watanabe, 503
299 Great Council instructions: BSD, 130–31
301 Moriyama, Wakana, Matsumura call: MOR, 24–II–A4 (19 Mar)
301 lost anchor, chain: HCB, 8
302 salvage rate: Fujita, 46–47
302 division of money: interview Kada Manzo
302 pay raise: KC, 30–II–A4 (25 Mar)
303 Moriyama, Matsumura call: MOR, 25–II–A4 (20 Mar)
303 vernal equinox (*Higan*): IzuS, 634
303–4 Moriyama, Wakana, Matsumura call: MOR, 26–II–A4 (21 Mar)
304 order re farmland: KC, 27–II–A4 (22 Mar)
304 armament price list: HL&P II, 19; INS, No. 5, 2 Oct 1855
304–5 Japanese return: MOR, 29–II–A4 (24 Mar)
305 Matsumura, Moriyama call: *ibid.*, 30–II–A4 (25 Mar)

305–6 Moriyama's secret report: BGKM XV, 221

305 Moriyama considers Okada too liberal: MOR, 29–II–A4 (24 Mar)

306 memorandum sent to Great Council: BGKM XV, 211, 212

306 Governors advocate capitulation: *ibid.*, 235

306–7 doll festival: Casal, 36–60

307 dolls look like fishermen: Kuro–1 [p. iii]

307–9 *Great Learning for Women:* Chamberlain, 502–8

309 broken dolls to shrine: IzuS, 634

309 firecrackers prohibited: Hirai, book 4

309 holiday calls: *ibid.*

309 citations to officials: KC, 1–III–A4 (26 Mar)

309 Gennosuke's father dies: interview Murakami (Gyokusenji records)

310 letter to Hakodate: BGKM XV, 236

310 fee of $10.10: Harris, government account book, 20

311 Moriyama, Wakiya bring letter: BGKM XV, 247; MOR, 3–III–A4 (28 Mar)

311 Perry letter: HL&P I, 51

311 letter to Governors: HLB II, 1

312–13 Governors' reply: MOR, 5–III–A4 (30 Mar)

312–13 Moriyama, Inoue call: *ibid.*

312 order bearers and horses: KC, 6–III–A4 (31 Mar)

312 Inoue gives cake trays: BGKM XV, 247

313 Moriyama quote: *ibid.*

313 Bell letter: HL&P I, 61

Chapter 10: April, 1857

315 notice, salvage operation: KC, 8–III–A4 (2 Apr)

315–16 sailors considered thieves, break noses off statues: interview Kada Manzo

315 Daianji suicides: interview Osawa

316 punishment for theft, investigation for fraud: Hibata, 552

316–17 Kimizawa ship: KC, 8–III–A4 (2 Apr)

317 30 *koku* of rice hidden: KJ, 10–V–A6 (10 Jun 1859)

317 Harris letter delivered: BGKM XV, 247

317–20 Harris letter: HLB II, 2

320 letter makes it more difficult to invite him to Edo: *Ishin shi*, 257

320 Inoue receives letter: MOR, 8–III–A4 (2 Apr)

320 Goyosho meeting: BGKM XV, 241

320 Governors transmit Harris letter: *ibid.*, 242

321 gold watch chains: MOR, 21–III–A4 (15 Apr)

321–23 garden; Harris, Moriyama chat:

MOR, 12, 13–III–A4 (6, 7 Apr); BGKM XV, 247

323–24 ship investigation: KC, 14, 17–III–A4 (8, 11 Apr)

324 annual census: Hirai, book 3; KC, 21–III–A5 (4 May 1858), 17–III–A6 (19 Apr 1859)

324 Shinto instructors: *ibid.*, 22, 27–III–A4 (16, 21 Apr)

324–25 road repair: *ibid.*, 3, 18, 25–III–A4 (28 Mar, 12, 19 Apr); NP, III–A4 (26 Mar–23 Apr)

325 Moriyama's instructions from finance bureau: BGKM XV, 246

325 Moriyama sends report: *ibid.*, 246, 247

326 Mizuno letter: MOR, 17–III–A4 (11 Apr)

326 finance officials oppose Harris demands: BGKM XV, 272

327–28 Hotta directive: BSD, 131–34

329 propose Japanese go abroad: *Ishin shi*, 237

329 *ometsuke, metsuke* opinion: BGKM XV, 330

329–30 finance opinion: *ibid.*, 274, 276

330 others' opinion: *ibid.*, 228
330 Governors confer: MOR, 18–III–A4 (12 Apr)
331–32 Moriyama calls: *ibid.*, 19–III–A4 (13 Apr)
332 Wakana asked 4 *ryo*: BGKM XV, 145
332 boys' rice stipend: *ibid.*, XVI, 104; Kuro–2, 125
333–34 Huffnagle letter: HL&P I, 45
334–37 disagreement re salutes, Moriyama calls: MOR, 21–III–A4 (15 Apr)
335 British book: it could have been either the book by Busk (page 215) or by McFarlane (pages 318–19); while Harris notes (HLB I, 85) that he gave both to Captain Possiet, they were such standard items that he may well have had more than one copy; they contain the same translation.
336 shorter translation: Brinkley, 66
338 inspection: KC, 2–IV–A4 (25 Apr)

338–39 confession required, torture: Hall, J. C. ("Note on Torture")
339 Osaka ship: KC, 24–III–A4 (18 Apr)
339–42 Goyosho meeting: MOR, 27–III–A4 (21 Apr)
339–41 instructions: INS, No. 6, 4 Oct 1855
340–41 treaty: Hawks I, 378
340 quote, expedition narrative: *ibid.*, 377
340 Rodgers report: INS, *op. cit.*
341 Rodgers, Hori: Cole YS, 13
342 Inoue letter: BGKM XV, 258
342–43 Okada letter: *ibid.*, 259
343 Great Council directive: BSD, 130–31
343 cancels English lessons: HLB II, 14
344 Moriyama calls: MOR, 4–IV–A4 (27 Apr)
345 Rice arrives: HL&P I, 54, 60, 62, 63
345 Bell quote: *ibid.*, 54

Chapter 11: May, 1857

346 Lo quote: Hawks II, 404
346–47 Moriyama calls: MOR, 8–IV–A4 (1 May)
348–49 Governors' letter: BGKM XV, 294; MOR *ibid.*
348 Harris article (5): THJ, 572
349–50 letter re prices: HL&P I, 65
350 Lo quote: Hawks II, 398
351 Governors to Great Council: BGKM XV, 295
351 transmitted Harris's letter: *ibid.*, 214
351 Governors' recommendations: *ibid.*, 235
351 transmitted another Harris letter: *ibid.*, 238
351 transmit articles agreed on: *ibid.*, 292, 293
351 copy, letter re Reed-Dougherty, Rodgers: *ibid.*, 294
352 answer re Nagasaki: *ibid.*, 319
352 reaction, Curtius advice: *ibid.*, 320
352–54 *ometsuke*, *metsuke* recommendation: BSD, 134–36
354–55 finance recommendation: *ibid.*, 137–39

355 team to Nagasaki: BGKM XV, 302
355 earlier mission to Russians: Lensen Push, 324–25; Lensen RJE, 39–40
356 Moriyama background: interviews Furusho, Hattori, Nishi, Nohtomi
356 Iwase, associates to Great Council: BGKM XV, 329
356 Abe's health: Watanabe, 503
357 war in China: MacNair, 251
357 Bowring learns replaced: Bartle, 309–11
357 Sepoy mutiny: Collier, 12, 33–41
357–58 Izu exiles: KC, 16–V–A4 (7 June); interviews Takeshi, Ueda
359 Kawaji, Mizuno quote: BSD, 137
360–62 letter to Saito: NP, 12–IV–A4 (5 May)
362 gossip in Naka: MTOK, 150
362 first accounting day: Erskine, 148
363 Harris wrong re gold: Griffis TH, note 155
363 silver spoons injure health: BGKM XVI, 101
363 Okada reassigned: *ibid.*, XV, 309
363–64 Nakamura: Lensen RJE (see in-

dex); incense: Kawaji diary, 176;
Nakamura, Moriyama negotiate: Kawaji, *op. cit.*, 117, 123, 131–32
365 finance officials' reaction: BGKM XVI,
35
365 note childrens' game: Preble, 210
366–67 holiday: Casal, 61–78; Hirai, book
4; IzuS, 635; Erskine, 73–77

368 bathtub: MTOK, 264–65
368 Harris's height: HL&P I (passport)
368–69 reply to complaint re prices:
ibid., II, 68
369 answer re prices: HLB II, 15
370 Nakamura's award: BGKM XVI, 15
371 Abe too ill to work: Watanabe, 503

Chapter 12: June, 1857

373 Great Council endorsement: BGKM
XV, 235
374 Morrow quote: Morrow, 192
374–75 Kompira lottery: KJ, 10–V–A3
(12 Jun 1856), 30–V–A5 (10 Jul
1858)
375–76 Letter re residence: HLB II, 16
375 build schooner in 3 months: Lensen
RJE, 104, 109, 135
376 copper plate: BGKM XV, 267
377–81 Goyosho meeting: *ibid.*, XVI, 10;
Miller, 642–44
378–79 Great Council letter: BGKM XVI,
11
381 Governors to Great Council: *ibid.*,
12
382 memorandum to Harris: *ibid.*, 15
382 Heusken returns memorandum: *ibid.*,
31
382–83 report to Great Council: *ibid.*;
YRH No. 32, 66–67
383 Harris memorandum to Governors:
BGKM XVI, 18
383–87 Okichi sent to Harris, Ofuku to
Heusken: SJ; Murakami, 93–106,
125–26, 128; Uragaya, 22–V–A4
(13 Jun); YRH No. 32, 67–68;
MTOK, 92–4, 103–10, 70–71
387–88 Nakamura gave in to Harris:
BGKM XVI, 25, 26, 28, 30
388 Governors to Great Council: *ibid.*,
30
389 Kawakami receives document: *ibid.*,
17
389–90 Abe's illness: Watanabe, 503–4
391 Mishima shrine: Hirai, book 8
391–94 *tengusa*: IzuS, 558–60; interviews
Fujii, Hara, Kada Manzo, Marumiya

395 boat cleaning: KJ, 21–V–A3 (23 Jun
1856); interview Kada Manzo;
Norbeck, 20
395–96 Nagasaki ship: KC, 2–V–A4
(24 May)
396 Moriyama delivers draft: BGKM
XVI, 32
396 letters from Rice: *ibid.*, 53; HLB II,
20
397 Goyosho meeting: BGKM XVI, 33
398 Harris quote, Siam treaty: THJ, 152
398 Japanese draft: BGKM XVI, 32
398 article 2: THJ, 571
399 Goyosho meeting: BGKM XVI, 51
399 girls wait at Shinzaemon's: MTOK,
112–3; interview Izumi
400 pledge re Okichi: Uragaya, 5–Vx–A4
(26 Jun)
400 Goyosho meeting: BGKM XVI, 58
400 summary of convention to Great
Council: *ibid.*, 59
400–1 information from Harris: *ibid.*,
60
401 one Governor to stay in Edo: *ibid.*,
61
401 carried ashore $2450: HLB I, 60
401 note advanced Heusken $750:
ibid., 8
401 note Heusken mess bill on San
Jacinto: *ibid.*, 47
402 translation, Governors' powers:
HL&P II, 69
402 Harris letter to Governors: HLB II,
17; BGKM XVI, 63
402 Governors reply: *ibid.*, 64
402 report to Great Council: *ibid.*, 65
402–3 instruction to girls: SJ; Murakami,
100–2

Chapter 13: July, 1857

Chapter 14: August, 1857

Chapter 15: September, 1857

that the letters arrived October 20. What Harris wrote may have been due to a slip of memory or it might have been intentional so that he would not have to admit to Bowring that he had received his letters before the *Portsmouth* arrived but had failed to answer by her.

458–59 Bowring quotes (in order): HL&P I, 58, 43, 58, 43, 43

459–60 *Bon:* IzuS, 636–37

460–61 Goyosho meeting: BGKM XVI, 236

460 Congress, Siam treaty award: HL&P I, 55; Crow, 306

460–61 1861 payment of $7298.62: HLB V, 113, 114; DES III, No. 42, 18 Oct 1861

461 secret, anonymous letter: BGKM XVII, 56

461 Goyosho meeting: *ibid.*, XVI, 245

464–65 Bell letter: HL&P I, 71

465 Foote quote: Foote, 129–30

466–67 Foote quote: *ibid.*, 130–31

467 Chiyokichi: IzuS, 290

467 Foote quote: Foote, 132

468–69 Goyosho reception: *ibid.*, 131–32; BGKM XVII, 9

468 Foote quote: USN–6

469 Governors' message to Edo: BGKM XVII, 10

470 letter to Bradford: HLB II, 39

470 letter to Baring Brothers: *ibid.*, 45

470 letters to Russell & Co.: *ibid.*, 41, 42

470 order to Hunt & Co.: *ibid.*, 75

470 letter from Drinker: HL&P II, 62

470–71 letters to Rice: HLB II, 44, 38

471 dispatch: DES I, No. 13, 11 Sep 1857

471 Foote quote re Governors: Foote, 132

471–72 Foote quote: USN–6

472–73 Harris asked Heusken's salary begin March, 1856: DES I, No. 10, 3 Jul 1856

473 *Portsmouth* delayed: USN–6

473 report on coal: Harris-Foote

473 Foote quotes: USN–6; Foote, 131–32

474 letter to Curtius: HLB II, 49

474 Tribunal opinion: BGKM XVI, 249

474 order to suspend talks: *ibid.*, 246

474 finance officials' secret message: *ibid.*, XVII, 6

474 how to notify Harris: *ibid.*, 22, 26, 27, 28, 29, 30, 31, 32, 33, 45

474–75 orders to Governors: *ibid.*, 37, 21

475 decision published: *ibid.*, 19, 20

475 Nariaki's reaction: Kumada, 472; BGKM XVII, 34

475 Nariaki resigns: Tokutomi, 21; Murdoch, 621

476–77 Goyosho meeting: BGKM XVII, 66

477 report to Edo: *ibid.*, 67

477–78 Goyosho meeting: *ibid.*, 70

477 Rice to State Department: DES–HAK, 10 Sep 1857

478 Netherlands treaty: Gubbins, 250–55

478 plea for haste: BGKM XVII, 72

478–79 letter to Great Council: HLB II, 48

479 letter to Curtius: *ibid.*, 49

479–82 Goyosho meeting: BGKM XVII, 79

481 Harris quote: *ibid.*, 84

482 Governors' report, Harris's concurrence: *ibid.*

482 levy 250 men: KC, NC, 9–VIII–A4 (26 Sep)

484 harvest of early rice: KC, 13–VIII–A4 (30 Sep)

Chapter 16: October, 1857

485 Tengu's "Notice": BGKM XVIII, 254

487 reaction, Lord of Owari: *ibid.*, XVII, 177

487 Castle chambers: Hall, J. W., 24–25;

Totman *Politics*, 35–36

487 Antechamber opinion: BGKM XVII, 178

487–88 October 5 conference, Great Corridor lords: Ishii, No. 8, 21

488 lords call on Hotta, forward views: *Sakumu Kiji* II, 145–46

488–89 Great Corridor opinion: BGKM XVII, 192

489 Yoshinaga visits Hotta: Ishii, No. 8, 25; *Sakumu Kiji* II, 146–47

489–90 trade treaty with Dutch: BSD, 130, 149–55

490 trade treaty with Russians: *ibid.*, 146; Lensen *Push*, 348–50

490 "Edo people uneasy": BGKM XVII, 97

490 Harris to travel by land, inn not suitable at Edo: *ibid.*, 5; YRH No. 37, 16

490 use Institute for Foreign Studies: BGKM XVII, 97

490 Kawaji quote: Yamamoto, 103

490 Tengu: BGKM XVIII, 254

491 treat like Koreans: *ibid.*, XVII, 44

491 treat like Ryukyuans: *ibid.*, 73

491 envoy, but only consul general: *ibid.*, 47, 48

491 Tengu: *ibid.*, XVIII, 254

491 Commissioners of the Visit: *ibid.*, XVII, 36

491 Great Council directive: *ibid.*, 106

491 date set back: *ibid.*, XVIII, 254

491 Shogun to sit: *ibid.*, XVII, 74

491 wear *nagabakama*: *ibid.*, 159

491 dinner menu: *ibid.*, 164

491 gifts to Harris: *ibid.*, 82, 83, 209

491 renovation, furnishings: *ibid.*, 112, 167, supplements 1, 2, 3

491 traffic: *ibid.*, 123

491 manage with great care: *ibid.*, 110; For Rel 1879, 622

492 report to Shogun: BGKM XVII, 99

493 full moon, Eighth Month: IzuS, 637; Erskine, 112–16; Chamberlain, 441

493 poem: Blyth, 385

493–94 wedding rowdyism: Hirai, book 6; Hall, J. C., 773

494 Harris's horse reared: interview Suzuki Suketaro

495 Okichi settlement: MTOK, 204–5

495 Ofuku ill: Murakami, 126–27

495 flag: THJ, 573–75

496 Dutch treaty ratified, trade articles signed: Treat, 30; BSD, 130, 149

496 Russian treaty signed: Lensen *Push*, 350

496 Mizuno quote: YRH No. 37, 39–40

496 Rice to State Department: DES–HAK, 10 Oct 1857

497 1st day, Ninth Month: Hirai, book 6

497 Ofuku returns: Murakami, 127

497–98 Reed, Dougherty debt: INS, No. 7, 19 Aug 1856; MOR, 3–IV–A4 (26 Apr); DES II, No. 22, 31 Jul 1858

498 congratulates Cass: HLB II, 65

498 Heusken's salary: *ibid.*, 71

499 requests rent allowance: *ibid.*, 72

499 Wakana calls: BGKM XVII, 198

501 holiday: Hirai, book 6; Erskine, 109–11

501 last day, barefoot: Hirai, book 6

501–2 letter to Perry: Harris-Perry

502 Moriyama to Shimoda: MOR, 10–IX–A4 (27 Oct)

502–4 Goyosho meeting: BGKM XVII, 209

504 Harris's proposed gifts: THJ, 482

504 note sardines to Commissioners: *ibid.*, 504

504 note gifts on expense account: HL&P II, 72

504 Moriyama to Edo: MOR, 13–IX–A4 (30 Oct)

505 Yoshinaga considers things going well: Kumada, 560–62

505 Matsudaira Tadakata's appointment shocks Yoshinaga: *ibid.*, 562–63

505 Nariaki had pressed for Tadakata's dismissal: Totman "Struggle," 62

Chapter 17: November, 1857

506 Inoue to Commissioners: BGKM XVII, 219

506 Inoue to Great Council: *ibid.*, 220

506–7 burden on Inoue: *ibid.*, 249; THJ, 451

507 additional staff from Shimoda: BGKM XVII, 249

507 requests for allowances: *ibid.*, 170, 251
507 Ito assigned as physician: *ibid.*, 200
507 Wakana: *ibid.*, 132, 257, 254
507 return Harris to Shimoda: *ibid.*, 162, 248
507 *ometsuke, metsuke* opinion: *ibid.*, XVI, 173, XVII, 46
508 Hayashi re closing letters: *ibid.*, XVIII, 8
508–9 opinion, Lord of Sendai: *ibid.*, XVII, 260
509 lords of Great Hall: *ibid.*, 224; Ishii, No. 8, 21; Konishi, *Nihon Zenshi*, 48
509 Nariaki, sword to Emperor: Tokutomi, 20
509 Emperor's assertiveness: *Ishin shi*, 6–13
509–10 Yoshinaga: Ishii, No. 8, 23–24; Kumada, 565–66, 577–79; Totman, "Struggle," 69–70
510 attempt to bribe Tadakata: Kumada, 568–72, 576, 583–84; Totman "Struggle," 70
510–11 letter for Navy ship: HLB II, 55
511 letter for merchant ship: *ibid.*, 56
511 letter re Chinese servants: *ibid.*, III, 4

511–12 Wakana calls: BGKM XVII, 221
512 crop inspection: KC, 21–IX–A4 (7 Nov)
513 deaths in Kakisaki: interview Murakami (Gyokusenji records)
513 streets Harris will travel: For Rel 1879, 622
513 Great Council instructions: *ibid.*; BGKM XVII, 206
513–14 implementing orders, responses: *ibid.*, XVIII, 10, 11, 12
514 instructions, highways: For Rel 1879, 623; BGKM XVII, 207, 208
514 itinerary: THJ, note 446
516 Harris quote re Delmonico's: *ibid.*, 430
526 *The Rising Sun:* Hibata, 543
526–27 innkeeper's message: BGKM XVIII, 14
529 Harris quote re retinue: THJ, 412–13
529 order of march: BGKM XVIII, 61
531 dispatch: DES I, No. 25, 20 Nov 1857
531 *haori* for Ofuku: IzuS, 288
531 Ofuku, final payment: Murakami, 128
532 Meerdervoort: Meerdervoort, 211–21

Chapter 18: December, 1857–June, 1859

535 Harris's lecture: BSD, 159–65
535–36 "eloquence" quote: Gubbins, 289
536 Harris re England, Russia: BSD, *loc. cit.*; Murdoch, 637–38
538 Harris quote re plot: THJ, 509
538 Yoshinaga visits Hotta: Kumada, 585–86; Ishii, No. 8, 25
539 Nariaki re Hotta, Harris: Akimoto, 147; Ishii, No. 9, 37; Kumada, 510
541 Harris becomes ill: HHJJ, 194–95
541 send doctor on ship: *ibid.*, 196
542 Harris quote re bribes: THJ, 549
542–43 Harris illness: HHJJ, 196–201
542 doctors' bulletins: Miller, 644–46
543 plan to summon Rice: *ibid.*, 646–48
544 Moriyama-Heusken translation: HL&P II, 71
544–45 letter to Mrs. Drinker: TH Saka, letter 3, sheet 1

545 delicacies, Shogun's wife: Griffis TH, 312–13
546–47 return to Edo, wait: HHJJ, 201–9
547 Curtius offers acceptable treaty: HHJJ, 210; Murdoch, 654
547 Keiki's advocates turn to Kyoto: Totman "Struggle," 70
547–48 postponement: THJ, 561
548–49 letter to Hotta: HLB III, 69
549 Putiatin to Japan: Lensen *Push,* 350–51
549 Reed letter: HL&P I, 91
549 Bell letter: *ibid.*, 85
549 Bowring letter: *ibid.*, 89
549 Drinker letters: *ibid.*, 69, 70 (While these letters were written before the *Portsmouth* sailed to Shimoda, Captain Bell, in the letter cited

Chapter 19: Epilogue

Notes

564 Iwase: Kawaji, *Kawaji,* 633; Kawaji, *Inoue,* 9–10; BSD, 333

564 Inoue: Kawaji, *Inoue,* 9–10; BSD, 333

565 bad feeling, Harris and Alcock: McMaster "Alcock and Harris," 350–54

565 "quarreled like old women": Pruyn, quoted in Treat, 208

565 Naosuke assassinated: Murdoch, 699–701

565 Kosuke walks home: interview Terakawa

566 assassins' statement: Murdoch, 701

566 Nariaki assassinated (?): *Tokyo Shimbun*

566 letter to Kate Drinker: TH Saka, letter 7

566 warning to Alcock: Alcock II, 31–32

566–67 Alcock quote: *ibid.,* 39

567–69 Heusken assassinated: Patterson, 9–10

567–69 Harris quote: DES III, No. 3, 22 Jan 1861 (quoted HHJJ 223–26)

569 Harris to Alcock: enclosure, DES III, No. 8, 13 Feb 1861

570 Harris criticized for Heusken's monument: HHJJ, 230

570 monument, interpreter for British: Alcock II, 47

570 Heusken's monument: MacCauley, 2

570 Portman hired: DES III, No. 5, 23 Jan 1861

570 Harris, Portman do not get along: Kuro–2, 126

570 Harris's recall: TH Saka, letter 8; DES III, No. 29, 10 Jul 1861; HLB V, 133; INS, No. 24, 21 Oct 1861; DES III, No. 6, 18 Feb 1862; INS, No. 25, 19 Nov 1861; DES III, No. 15, 26 Apr 1862

571 abdicates primacy to Alcock: McMaster, "Alcock and Harris," 320

572 Americans' disappointment with Japan: Cole D, 148

572 Inoue: Kawaji, *Inoue,* 10–15

572–73 Kawaji: Kawaji, *Kawaji,* 690–703

573 Moriyama: interview Nishi

573 Yoheiji: Hamada

573 Kosuke: interview Terakawa

573 Sukezo: MTOK, 117–18

574 Harris: Griffis TH, 328–30

574 Harris quote: Griffis "Japan," 5

A LIST OF
MATERIALS USED

The bracketed symbols and abbreviations
are those used in the notes.

Primary Sources

Ansei Nenpyō (Chronology of the Ansei period, covering 1854–57). 10 manuscript volumes. Naikaku Bunko, Tōkyō.

[BSD] Beasley, W. G., translator and editor. *Select Documents on Japanese Foreign Policy, 1853–1868*. London: Oxford University Press, 1955.

[BGKM] *Dai Nihon Komonjo, Bakumatsu Gaikoku Kankei Monjo* (Ancient documents of Japan, official documents of the late Tokugawa era concerning foreign relations), Vols. XII, XIV–XVIII. Tōkyō: Tōkyō Daigaku Shiryō Hensansho, 1920–5.

[DES] *Despatches from United States Ministers to Japan.*
Vol. I: March 17, 1855–June 29, 1858
Vol. II: July 1, 1858–December 31, 1859
Vol. III: January 3, 1860–May 6, 1862
(National Archives Microcopy 133, Rolls 1, 2, 3)

[DES-CHI] *Despatches from United States Ministers to China. Vol. XII, March 13, 1856–August 28, 1856.* National Archives Microcopy 92, Rol 13.

[DES-HAK] *Despatches from United States Consuls in Hakodate, 1856–1878. Vol. I, July 15, 1856–December 31, 1869.* National Archives Microcopy T113, Roll T1. (Communications from commercial agent [later consul] E. E. Rice are included.)

[INS] *Diplomatic Instructions of the Department of State, 1801–1906, Japan. Vol. I, September 12, 1855–June 29, 1872.* National Archives Microcopy 77, Roll 104. (These instructions are also found among Harris's "letters and papers.")

Foote, Andrew H. "Visit to Simoda and Hakodadi in Japan," *Journal of the Shanghai Literary and Scientific Society* (title later changed to *Journal of the North-China Branch of the Royal Asiatic Society*), I (June, 1858), 129–37.

[For Rel 1879] *Papers relating to the Foreign Relations of the United States, transmitted to Congress, with the annual message of the President, December 1, 1879.* Washington: Government Printing Office, 1879.

Hamada Yoheiji. *Kairiku Ansei Ki* (Notes on land and sea affairs in the Ansei period). 1 manuscript volume. Collection of Gyokusenji. Recollections by the former headman of Kakisaki. Mentions the visit of a Russian ship in 1895 and that the Russians questioned Yoheiji about the loss of the *Diana* as a result of the tidal wave of 1854, as well as other events when he was headman; one gets the impression that this interview led Yoheiji, then eighty-four years old, to set down his recollections.

[THJ] Harris, Townsend. *The Complete Journal of Townsend Harris.* Edited by Mario E. Cosenza. Rutland and Tōkyō: Tuttle, 1959.

[TH Saka] ———. *Some Unpublished Letters of Townsend Harris.* Edited by Shio Sakanishi. New York: Japan Reference Library, 1941. Unpaged.

[HLB] ———. Private letter books. 5 manuscript volumes containing copies of the official and business letters that Harris wrote. Archives, the library of The City College, New York.

[HL&P] ———. Letters and papers. 2 manuscript volumes containing much of the correspondence that Harris received.

Archives, the library of The City College, New York.

[HCB] ———. Commonplace book. 1 manuscript volume. Archives, the library of The City College, New York.

———. Government account book. Archives, the library of The City College, New York.

[Harris-Foote] ———. Letter to Andrew H. Foote, Captain USN, commanding *Portsmouth*, Shimoda, 12 September 1857. New York Public Library, Manuscript Division.

[Harris-Perry] ———. Letter to Commodore Matthew C. Perry, Shimoda, 27 October 1857. Published in the *New York Herald*, 12 December 1858, and in the *New York Daily Tribune*, 13 December 1858.

Hawks, Francis L. *Narrative of the Expedition of an American Squadron to the China Seas and Japan performed in the years 1852, 1853, and 1854, under the command of Commodore M. C. Perry, United States Navy*. 3 vols. Washington: published by order of the Congress of the United States, 1856.

[HHJJ] Heusken, Henry. *Japan Journal 1855–1861*. Translated and edited by Jeannette C. van der Corput and Robert A. Wilson. New Brunswick: Rutgers University Press, 1964.

Hirai Heijirō. *Shimoda Nenjū-gyōji* (Record of annual events at Shimoda). 87 manuscript volumes. Collection of Shimoda town office.

Ishin Shiryō Kōyō (A summary of historical documents on the Restoration), Vol. II. Tōkyō: Tōkyō Daigaku Shuppankai, 1966.

[KJ] Kakisaki, headman's official journal of village affairs. 8 manuscript volumes, in the collection of Gyokusenji, cover the following periods:

(a) from the 1st day, Fourth Month, Ansei 1 (27 April 1854) through the 24th day, Sixth Month, Ansei 1 (18 July 1854) (this covers the period when the Perry expedition visited Shimoda)

(b) from the 15th day, Fourth Month, Ansei 3 (18 May 1856) through the 14th day, Eighth Month, Ansei 3 (12 September 1856)

(c) from the 2d day, Fifth Month intercalary, Ansei 4 (24 June 1857) through the 7th day, Eleventh Month, Ansei 5 (11 December 1858)

(d) from the 27th day, Twelfth Month, Ansei 5 (30 January 1859) through the 29th day, Fifth Month, Ansei 6 (29 June 1859)

(e) from the 20th day, Sixth Month, Ansei 6 (19 July 1859) through the 4th day, Twelfth Month, Ansei 6 (27 December 1859)

[KC] Kakisaki village circulars. 5 manuscript volumes. Copies of circulars and other directives received by the headman of Kakisaki from the 25th day, Eighth Month, Ansei 3 (23 September 1856) through the 16th day, Twelfth Month, Ansei 4 (30 January, 1858). Collection of Gyokusenji.

[KSI&FB] Kakisaki village, reports of ships' inns and fishing boats, submitted to Governor of Uraga and/or provincial magistrate for Izu, in 1819, 1822, 1825, 1830, 1831, 1834. 1 manuscript volume. Private collection.

Kawaji Saemon-no-jō Toshiakira. Diary during negotiations with the Russians at Shimoda (1854–55). *Dai Nihon Komonjo, Bakumatsu Gaikoku Kankei Monjo*, supplement, I, 113–93. Tōkyō: Tōkyō Daigaku Shiryō Hensansho, 1913.

Lühdorf, Fr. Aug. *Acht Monate in Japan*. Bremen: Drud und Berlag von Heinrich Strad, 1857. (Chapter "Simoda," pp. 114–89.)

Marcy, William L. Papers. Library of Congress.

[MOR] Moriyama Takichirō. Diary from the 26th day, First Month, Ansei 4 (20 February 1857) to the 23rd day, Eleventh Month, Ansei 4 (7 January 1858). 1 manuscript volume, copy. Shiryō hensansho, Tōkyō University.

[NC] Naka village circulars. Copies of circulars and other directives received by the headman of Naka, Ninth through Twelfth Months, Ansei 3 (29 September 1856–25 January 1857). 1 manuscript volume. Nakamura kōmin-kan (community center).

[NP] Naka village petitions submitted to the Governors of Shimoda, Ansei 3 and 4 (1856–57). 1 manuscript volume. Mori Hajime collection.

New York Herald, 16 November 1858, p. 1.

New York Journal of Commerce, 25 November 1858, p. 3.

Sakumu Kiji (Records of Matsudaira Yoshinaga with connecting narrative, July 1853 to August 1858). 4 volumes (*Nihon Shiseki Kyōkai Sōsho.*) Tōkyō: Nihon Shiseki Kyōkai, 1920–21.

[SJ] Shimoda, headman's official journal of town affairs (*Machi kaisho nikki*). Manuscript volumes from the collection of the Shimoda town office:
(a) from the 5th day, Ninth Month, Ansei 2 (15 October 1855) through the 15th day, Tenth Month, Ansei 2 (24 November 1855)
(b) from the 1st day, First Month, Ansei 4 (26 January 1857) through the 26th day, Third Month, Ansei 4 (20 April 1857)
(c) from the 18th day, Fourth Month, Ansei 4 (11 May 1857) through the 28th day, Fourth Month, Ansei 4 (21 May 1857)
(d) from the 10th day, Fifth Month, Ansei 5 (20 June 1858) through the 10th day, Eighth Month, Ansei 5 (16 September 1858)
(e) miscellaneous reports to government headquarters
From the collection of Gyokusenji: 2 manuscript volumes covering from the 1st day, Fifth Month, Ansei 4 (23 May 1857) through the 1st day, Eighth Month, Ansei 4 (18 September 1857)

[USN] U.S. Department of the Navy correspondence, National Archives, record group 45 (all dispatches below are from Commodore James Armstrong to the Secretary of the Navy):
[1] Dispatch No. 25, Shimoda, 3 September 1856
[2] Dispatch No. 26, Shimoda, 3 September 1856
[3] Dispatch No. 76, Shanghai, 8 August 1857
[4] Commodore Armstrong to Commander Andrew H. Foote, commanding U.S.S. *Portsmouth,* Shanghai, 20 August 1857
[5] Dispatch No. 77, Shanghai, 1 September 1857
[6] Commander Foote, U.S.S. *Portsmouth,* to Commodore Armstrong, Hakodate, 9 October 1857

Uragaya Kōsuke (Chūbei). Extracts from the diary of this shipping agent and elder of Shimoda, for Ansei 4. 1 manuscript volume. Collection of Nakamura Chūbei.

William II, King of Holland. "Correspondence between William II. of Holland and the Shōgun of Japan. A.D. 1844." *Transactions of the Asiatic Society of Japan,* Vol. XXXIV, Part IV, pp. 99–132.

[SWW] Williams, S. Wells. "A Journal of the Perry Expedition to Japan," *Transactions of the Asiatic Society of Japan,* Vol. XXXVII, Part II (1910).

Wood, William Maxwell. *Fankwei; or, The San Jacinto in the seas of India, China, and Japan.* New York: Harper, 1859.

Zoku Tokugawa Jikki (Records of the Tokugawa family, second series). Tōkyō: Kokushi Taikei Kankōkai, 1935.

Interviews and Correspondence

SHIMODA AND VICINITY:
Andō Benshin
Aoshima Chijō
Asaoka Akira
Chiba Sunjō

Dōke Tamotsu
Emoto Fuminori
Fujii Noboru
Funada Fusako
Hara Iwao

Hidakaya Denbei
Hirai Heijirō
Hirai Masaharu
Hirata Eiko
Hirata Jihei
Imai Mitsuko
Izumi Kichi
Kada Manzō
Kada Nao
Kamemura Masakichi
Katō Buntarō
Kikuchi Denjirō
Kiyota Gen'ichi
Kokubo Tsunekichi
Maeda Fukutarō
Marumiya Chūichi
Mashita Yoshiko
Masuda Chūemon
Matsumoto Hideo
Matsumoto Myōbun
Matsumoto Onokichi
Matsumoto Tama
Matsumoto Tatsuo
Misuda Tome
Mori Kikurō
Mori Yoshiko
Murakami Setsuko
Murashima Mansaku
Murashima Yusan
Murata Umeo
Murayama Shōbei
Murayama Tokishige
Murayama Toku
Nagase Shime
Naitō Sesui
Nakada Kōichi
Nakamura Chūbei
Noguchi Gonhei
Ogawa Ei
Ogawa Toriji
Ōsawa Shinkō
Ōta Ikurō
Ōta Sadako
Ozeki Daihachi

Saitō Seiji
Sakano Kichitarō
Sakurada Shigeru
Sasaki Dentarō
Sasamoto Chō
Sawamura Sato
Sawamura Seizō
Seino Akio
Shazawa Noboru
Shimizu Nami
Shinji Eikichi
Sugie Isamu
Suzuki Kiyoshi
Suzuki Kumetarō
Suzuki Sadao
Suzuki Suketarō
Takahashi Satoshi
Takaishi Genshō
Takeoka Norio
Takeshi Fukutarō
Tamura Jun
Tanaka Ken'ichi
Tanaka Rokuichirō
Terakawa Otokichi
Torii Kikujirō
Tsuboi Takeno
Tsuchiya Chū'ichi
Tsuchiya Denbei
Tsuchiya Gonji
Tsuchiya Kaname
Tsuchiya Yoshitarō
Tsuchiya Yutarō
Ueda Shōjirō
Uematsu Tadao
Usui Iku
Usui Kunio
Usui Muneo
Usui Taisuke
Usui Takehiko
Watanabe Hanako
Watanabe Tamotsu
Yamada Kenji
Yamashita Sajihei
Yanagida Kane

Interviews and Correspondence

Yashiro Torakichi
Yokoyama Hideo
Yokoyama Tsunekichi

OTHER LOCALITIES:
Akimoto Shunkichi, Tōkyō
Azabu Shōkai, Tōkyō
Chiba Teruya, Sakura
Clarke, Mrs. Earl Perry,
Washington, D.C.
Curtius, Marie Donker,
Yokohama
Furushō Miya, Fujisawa
Harris, Florence, Bethesda,
Maryland
Hattori Yuriko, Tōkyō
Hayakawa Sessue, Tōkyō
Ii Naoyoshi, Hikone
Iizuka Dentarō, Shizuoka

Ishiguro Keishichi, Tōkyō
Itō Kahichi, Chita Peninsula
Kimura Ki, Tōkyō
Mizuno Ryuen, Chita Peninsula
Mochizuki Hanjūrō, Okitsu
Morita Isuke, Chita Peninsula
Moriyama Shōma, Tōkyō
Nishi Seiho, Tōkyō
Nomura Yōzō, Yokohama
Nōtomi Jirō, Tōkyō
Shinomaru Yorihiko, Sakura
Suyama Genzō, Chita Peninsula
Suematsu Osamu, Hikone
Takeuchi Saichi, Chita
Peninsula
Tasaka Chōjirō, Tōkyō
Tsuchiya Motoichi, Shizuoka
Washizu Sekijō, Chita Peninsula

Selected References

Adachi Kuwatarō (ed.). *Nanzu Fūdoshi* (Local legends and miscellaneous notes of Southern Izu). Tōkyō: Hakubunkan, 1914.

Alcock, Rutherford. *The Capital of the Tycoon: A Narrative of Three Years' Residence in Japan.* 2 vols. London: Longman, Green, 1863.

Akimoto Shunkichi. *Lord Ii Naosuke and New Japan.* Translated and adapted from *Ii Tairō to Kaikō* by Nakamura Katsumaru. Tōkyō: Japan Times, 1909.

Asakawa, K. "Notes on Village Government in Japan after 1600," *Journal of the American Oriental Society,* Vol. XXX, Part 3 (1910), pp. 259–300, with notes in Vol. XXXI, Part 2 (1911), pp. 151–216.

Bartle, G. F. "Sir John Bowring and the *Arrow* War in China," *Bulletin of the John Rylands Library, Manchester,* XLIII (1960–1), 293–316.

Beardsley, Richard K., Hall, John W., and Ward, Robert E. *Village Japan.* Chicago: University of Chicago Press, 1959.

[Beasley GB] Beasley, W. G. *Great Britain and the Opening of Japan, 1834–1858.* London: Luzac, 1951.

Bennett, Frank M. *The Steam Navy of the United States.* Pittsburgh: Warren & Co., 1896.

Blyth, R. H. *Haiku,* Vol. III, Summer–Autumn. Tōkyō: Hokuseidō, 1952.

Bowring, John. *Autobiographical Recollections of Sir John Bowring, with a brief memoir by Lewin B. Bowring.* Arranged and edited by Lewin B. Bowring. London: King, 1877.

Brinkley, Frank. *A History of the Japanese People from the Earliest Times to the End of the Meiji Era,* with the collaboration of Baron Kikuchi. New York: Encyclopaedia Britannica, 1914.

Brooke, John Mercer. *Brooke Journals.* (*Collected Documents of the Japanese Mission to America,* Vol. V.) Edited by George M. Brooke, Jr. Translated by Eiichi Kyooka. Tōkyō: Association for Japan–U.S. Amity & Trade Centennial, 1961.

Busk, Mary Margaret. *Manners and Customs of the Japanese, in the Nineteenth*

Century. From the accounts of recent Dutch residents in Japan, and from the German work of Dr. PH. Fr. Von Siebold. New York: Harper, 1841. (Published anonymously; other editions bore the title *Japan and the Japanese*.)

Casal, U. A. *The Five Sacred Festivals of Ancient Japan, Their Symbolism and Historical Development*. Tōkyō: Sophia University in cooperation with Charles E. Tuttle Company, 1967.

Chamberlain, Basil Hall. *Things Japanese, being notes on various subjects connected with Japan for the use of travellers and others*. Fifth edition revised. London: Kelly & Walsh, 1905.

Clement, E. W. "The Tokugawa Princes of Mito." *Transactions of the Asiatic Society of Japan*, Vol. XVIII, Part I, pp. 1–24.

[Cole D] Cole, Allan B. "The Dynamics of American Expansion toward Japan, 1791–1860." Unpublished Ph.D. dissertation, University of Chicago, 1940.

[Cole YS] ———. (ed.). *Yankee Surveyors in the Shogun's Seas*. Princeton: Princeton University Press, 1947.

Collier, Richard. *The Great Indian Mutiny*. New York: Dutton, 1964.

Crow, Carl. *Harris of Japan*. London: Hamish Hamilton, 1939.

Dennett, Tyler. *Americans in Eastern Asia*. New York: Barnes & Noble, 1963.

Dore, R. P. *Education in Tokugawa Japan*. Berkeley and Los Angeles: University of California Press, 1965.

Earhart, H. Byron. "A Religious Study of the Mount Haguro Sect of Shugendō: An Example of Japanese Mountain Religion." Unpublished Ph.D. dissertation, University of Chicago, 1965.

Embree, John F. *Suye Mura, a Japanese Village*. Chicago: University of Chicago Press, 1939.

Erskine, William Hugh. *Japanese Festival and Calendar Lore*. Tōkyō: Kyōbunkan, 1933.

Fairbank, John K., Reischauer, Edwin O., and Craig, Albert M. *East Asia: The Modern Transformation*. Boston: Houghton Mifflin, 1965.

Fujita Akira. "Edo Jidai no Kaiun Jigyō" (Marine transportation of the Edo period), *Nihon Kōtsū Shiron* (History of traffic in Japan), pp. 34–62. Compiled by Nihon Rekishi Chiri Gakkai. Tōkyō: Nihon Gakujutsu Fukyūkai, 1916.

Griffin, Eldon. *Clippers and Consuls, American Consular and Commercial Relations with Eastern Asia, 1845–1860*. Ann Arbor: Edwards, 1938.

[Griffis TH] Griffis, William Elliot. *Townsend Harris, First American Envoy in Japan*. Boston and New York: Houghton, Mifflin, 1895.

———. "Japan at the Time of Townsend Harris." *Japan—A Comparison*, pp. 5–29. New York: Japan Society, 1923.

Gubbins, J. H. *The Progress of Japan 1853–1871*. Oxford: Clarendon, 1911.

Hall, J. C. "The Tokugawa Legislation, IV." *Transactions of the Asiatic Society of Japan*, Vol. XLI, Part V, pp. 683–804, and following unpaged "Note on Torture."

Hall, John Whitney. *Tanuma Okitsugu, 1719–1788, Forerunner of Modern Japan*. ("Harvard-Yenching Institute Monograph Series," Vol. XIV.) Cambridge: Harvard University Press, 1955.

Hibata Sekko. *Edo Jidai no Kōtsū Bunka* (Traffic culture of the Edo period). Tōkyō: Tōkō Shoin, 1931.

Historical Statistics of the United States, Colonial Times to 1957. Washington: U. S. Department of Commerce, 1960.

Honjō Eijirō. *Economic Theory and History of Japan in the Tokugawa Period*. Tōkyō: Maruzen, 1943.

———. *The Social and Economic History of Japan*. Kyōto: Institute for Research in Economic History of Japan, 1935.

Hotta Masayoshi. Compiled by Chiba-ken Naimubu (Chiba Prefectural Office, Department of Internal Affairs). Tōkyō: Shōbundō, 1922.

House, E. H. "The Martyrdom of an Empire," *The Atlantic Monthly*, XLVII (May, 1881), 610–23.

Hurd, Douglas. *The Arrow War, an Anglo-Chinese Confusion, 1856–1860*. London: Collins, 1967.

Selected References

Huyssen de Kattendyke, W. J. C. *Le Japon en 1857.* Paris: Librarie Fischbacher, 1924.

Ishii Shin'ichi. *Bakumatsu Shimoda Kaikō Shi* (History of the opening of Shimoda in the late Tokugawa period). Shimoda: Kamo-gun Kyōiku Kai, 1925.

[Ishii] Ishii Takashi. "Bakuhan Kankei no Hendō o Chūshin to Suru Kaei Ansei Nenkan no Seikyoku" (The political situation in the Kaei-Ansei period, with focus on the change in the relationship between the Bakufu and the fiefs), *Nihonshi Kenkyū,* No. 8 (June, 1948), pp. 11–31, and No. 9 (October, 1948), pp. 31–41.

Ishin Shi (A history of the Restoration), Vol. II. Edited by Ishin Shiryō Hensankai. Tōkyō: Monbushō, 1942.

[IzuS] *Izu Shimoda.* Compiled by Chihōshi Kenkyūjo, Meiji Daigaku. Tōkyō, 1962.

Kaempfer, Engelbert. *The History of Japan, together with a description of the Kingdom of Siam, 1690–92.* Translated by J. G. Scheuchzer. 3 volumes. Glasgow: MacLehose, 1906.

Kaneko Hisakazu. *Manjirō, The Man Who Discovered America.* Tōkyō: Hokuseidō, 1954.

Kawaji Kandō. *Kawaji Toshiakira no Shōgai* (The life of Kawaji Toshiakira). Tōkyō: Yoshikawa Kōbunkan, 1903.

———. *Inoue Kiyonao Ryakuden* (A short biography of Inoue Kiyonao). Supplement 2, pp. 4–15, to *Kawaji Toshiakira no Shōgai.*

Kelly, Walter K. *Proverbs of All Nations.* London: Diprose & Bateman (no date).

Konishi Shirō. *Nihon Zenshi* (Complete history of Japan), Vol. III, *Kindai I.* Tōkyō: Tōkyō Daigaku Shuppankai, 1962.

Kumada Sōjirō. *Sakura Shidan* (Episodes in the history of Sakura). Tōkyō: Ryōsho Kankōkai, 1917.

[Kuro] *Kurofune Dansō* (A collection of essays from *Kurofune* [Black Ships], a magazine published at Shimoda by Mori Hajime from 1924 to 1939). Shimoda: Shimoda Bunka Kyōkai, 1947.
[1] Kimura Ki. "Jo" (Preface), unpaged.
[2] Kubota Kohan. "Harisu no Kyūji

Nishiyama Rōjin no Danwa" (Conversation with old Nishiyama, Harris's valet [Sukezō]), pp. 125–26.
[3] Muramatsu Shunsui. "Kurofune Kanwa" (Sidelights on the Black Ships), pp. 10–17.
[4] Shimooka Renjō. "Shimooka Renjō ō Omoidebanashi—Harisu no Ōtai" (Recollections of Shimooka Renjō—the reception of Harris), pp. 55–56.
[5] Suzuki Toranosuke. "Harisu no Gyokusenji Taizai Kikan to Tōjin Okichi wa Ikunichikan Harisu ni Jishitaka" (How long did Harris stay at Gyokusenji and how many days did Okichi serve him?), pp. 200–25.

Learned, Henry Bartlett. "William Learned Marcy, Secretary of State March 7, 1853 to March 6, 1857," in Bemis, Samuel Flagg (ed.), *The American Secretaries of State and Their Diplomacy,* Vol. VI. New York: Knopf, 1928.

Lee, Edwin Borden. *The Political Career of Ii Naosuke.* Ph.D. dissertation, Columbia University, 1960. Ann Arbor: University Microfilms.

[Lensen Push] Lensen, George Alexander. *The Russian Push Toward Japan.* Princeton: Princeton University Press, 1959.

[Lensen RJE] ———. *Russia's Japan Expedition of 1852 to 1855.* Gainesville: University of Florida Press, 1955.

Lombard, Frank Alanson. *Pre-Meiji Education in Japan.* Tōkyō: Kyōbunkan, 1914.

MacCauley, Clay. *The Heusken Memorial.* Tōkyō: printed by the author for private circulation, 1917.

MacDonald, Ranald. *Ranald MacDonald.* Edited and annotated from the original manuscripts by William S. Lewis and Naojirō Murakami. Spokane: The Eastern Washington State Historical Society, 1923.

MacFarlane, Charles. *Japan: an account, geographical and historical, from the earliest period at which the islands composing this Empire were known to Europeans, down to the present time, and the expedition fitted out in the United States, etc.* Hartford: Andrus, 1856.

McMaster, John. "Alcock and Harris, For-

eign Diplomacy in Bakumatsu Japan."
Monumenta Nipponica, Vol. XXII, Nos.
3–4 (1967), pp. 305–67.
———. "The Japanese Gold Rush of
1859." *The Journal of Asian Studies*,
Vol. XIX, No. 3 (May, 1960), pp. 273–
87.

MacNair, H. F. *Modern Chinese History,
Selected Readings.* Shanghai: Commercial Press, 1927.

Martens, G. F. Von. *The Law of Nations:
being the science of national law, covenants, power, &c. founded upon the
treaties and customs of modern nations
in Europe.* Translated from the French
by William Cobbett. Fourth edition.
London: William Cobbett, 1829. (Townsend Harris's copy of this work is preserved in the Aoi Bunko, Shizuoka City.)

Matsueda Teruo (ed.). *Shin Nanzu
Fūdoshi* (New compilation of local legends and miscellaneous notes of Southern Izu). Shimoda: Kamo-gun Kyōiku
Kenkyūkai, 1957.

Meerdervoort, J. L. C. Pompe van. "On the
Study of the Natural Sciences in Japan."
*Journal of the North-China Branch of
the Royal Asiatic Society,* II (May,
1859), 211–21.

Merk, Frederick, with the collaboration of
Lois Bannister Merk. *Manifest Destiny
and Mission in American History.* New
York: Knopf, 1963.

Miller, Hunter (ed.). *Treaties and Other
International Acts of the United States
of America,* Vol. VII. Washington: U. S.
Government Printing Office, 1942.

Moffat, Abbot Low. *Mongkut, the King of
Siam.* Ithaca: Cornell University Press,
1961.

Morris, Roland S. *Townsend Harris, A
Chapter in American Diplomacy.* New
York: Japan Society, no date.

Morrow, James. *A Scientist with Perry in
Japan, The Journal of Dr. James Morrow.* Edited by Allan B. Cole. Chapel
Hill: University of North Carolina Press,
1947.

Murakami Bunki. *Kaikoku Shiseki, Gyokusenji Konjaku Monogatari* (The past and
present of Gyokusenji, a historic site related to the opening of the country).

Shimoda: printed by the author for
private circulation, fourth edition, 1940.

[MTOK] Muramatsu Shunsui. *Jitsuwa
Tōjin Okichi* (True story of foreigner's
woman Okichi). Tōkyō: Heibonsha,
1930.

Murdoch, James. *A History of Japan,* Vol.
III, *The Tokugawa Epoch, 1652–1868,*
revised and edited by Joseph H. Longford. London: Kegan Paul, 1926.

Neumann, William L. *American Encounters Japan, from Perry to MacArthur.*
Baltimore: Johns Hopkins Press, 1963.

Nitobe Inazō. *The Intercourse Between the
United States and Japan.* Baltimore:
Johns Hopkins Press, 1891.

Norbeck, Edward. *Takashima, A Japanese
Fishing Community.* Salt Lake City:
University of Utah Press, 1954.

Patterson, Richard S. *Henry C. J. Heusken,
Interpreter to the First American Consular and Diplomatic Posts in Japan.*
Washington: American Foreign Service
Association, 1948. (Reprinted from *The
American Foreign Service Journal,* Vol.
XXIV, No. 7 [July, 1947], with the addition of notes.)

Preble, George Henry. *The Opening of
Japan, A Diary of Discovery in the Far
East, 1853–1856.* Edited by Boleslaw
Szczesniak. Norman: University of Oklahoma Press, 1962.

Sakamaki Shunzō. "Japan and the United
States, 1790–1853." *Transactions of the
Asiatic Society of Japan,* Second Series,
Vol. XVIII (1939).

Sansom, George. *A History of Japan,* Vol.
3: 1615–1867. Stanford: Stanford University Press, 1963.

———. *The Western World and Japan.*
New York: Knopf, 1951.

Satoh, Henry. *Agitated Japan, The Life of
Baron Ii Kamon-no-kami Naosuke*
(based on *Kaikoku Shimatsu* by Shimada
Saburō). Revised by William Elliot
Griffis. Tōkyō: Maruya, 1896.

———. *Lord Hotta, The Pioneer Diplomat
of Japan.* Tōkyō: Hakubunkan, 1908.

Satow, Ernest Mason (translator). *Japan
1854–1864, or Genji Yume Monogatari*
(by Baba Bunyei). Tōkyō: Naigai Shuppan Kyokai, 1903.

Selected References

Simmons, D. B. "Notes on Land Tenure and Local Institutions in Old Japan." Edited by John H. Wigmore. *Transactions of the Asiatic Society of Japan*, Vol. XIX, Part I, pp. 37–270.

Smith, Thomas C. *The Agrarian Origins of Modern Japan*. Stanford: Stanford University Press, 1959.

Takekoshi Yosoburō. *The Economic Aspects of the History of the Civilization of Japan*. 3 vols. New York: Macmillan, 1930.

Taylor, Archer and Bartlett, Jere Whiting. *A Dictionary of American Proverbs and Proverbial Phrases, 1820–1880*. Cambridge: Harvard University Press, 1958.

Tokutomi Iichirō. *Kinsei Nihon Kokumin Shi* (A history of the Japanese people in the early modern period), Vol. XXXVI. Tōkyō: Kinsei Nihon Kokuminshi Kankōkai, 1965.

Tōkyō Shimbun, March 3, 1966, p. 6.

Totman, Conrad D. *Politics in the Tokugawa Bakufu*. ("Harvard East Asian Series," 30.) Cambridge: Harvard University Press, 1967.

———. "The Struggle for Control of the Shogunate (1853–1858)," *Papers on Japan*, I, 42–88. Cambridge: East Asian Research Center, Harvard University, 1961.

Tōyama Shigeki. *Meiji Ishin* (The Meiji Restoration). Tōkyō: Iwanami Shoten, 1951.

Treat, Payson J. *Diplomatic Relations between the United States and Japan, 1853–1895*, Vol. I (1853–1875). Gloucester: Peter Smith, 1963.

Trewartha, Glenn Thomas. *Japan, A Physical, Cultural and Regional Geography*. Madison: University of Wisconsin Press, 1945.

Warinner, Emily V. *Voyager to Destiny*. Indianapolis-New York: Bobbs-Merrill, 1956.

Watanabe Shūjirō. *Abe Masahiro Jiseki* (The record of Abe Masahiro), Vol. II. Tōkyō: printed by the author for private circulation, 1910.

Webb, Herschel F. "The Mito Theory of State," *Researches in the Social Sciences on Japan*, edited by John E. Lane (Columbia University East Asian Institute Studies, No. 4). New York: East Asian Institute of Columbia University, 1957.

[FWW] Williams, Frederick Wells. *The Life and Letters of Samuel Wells Williams, LL.D.* New York & London: Putnam's, 1889.

Yamamoto Shirō. "Kawaji Toshiakira, Toku ni Sono Gaikoku Shisō Nitsuite" (Kawaji Toshiakira, his thought concerning foreign countries), *Historia* (journal of the historical society of Ōsaka), No. 11 (February, 1955), pp. 97–105.

[YRH] Yoshida Tsunekichi. "Bakumatsu Gaikō Shijō ni Okeru Gaijin Kyūsokujo Oyobi Baita Settai no Mondai" (Problems concerning rest-houses and prostitutes for foreigners in the diplomatic history of the late Tokugawa period), *Kokushigaku*, No. 32 (October, 1937), pp. 41–71, No. 35 (August, 1938), pp. 19–37, No. 36 (December, 1938), pp. 9–42, No. 37 (March, 1939), pp. 15–46.

———. *Ii Naosuke*. (*Jimbutsu Sōsho*, No. 113). Tōkyō: Yoshikawa Kōbunkan, 1963.

———. *Tōjin Okichi, Bakumatsu Gaikō Hishi* (Foreigner's woman Okichi, the story behind late Tokugawa period diplomacy). Tōkyō: Chūō Kōronsha, 1966.

———. "Tōjin Orin, Zenpukuji ni Okeru Harris no Josei" (Tōjin Orin, Harris's woman at Zempukuji), *Nihon Rekishi*, No. 220 (September, 1966), pp. 73–81.

INDEX

Index

About the Author

Oliver Statler first went to Japan in 1947 when he began seven years as a civil service employee of the U.S. Army. That ended, he remained in Japan for four more years of study and writing—years that produced *Modern Japanese Prints: An Art Reborn,* monographs on several artists including Azechi Umetaro, Munakata Shiko, and Saito Kiyoshi, and weekly art reviews for the English-language newspaper *Asahi Evening News.* When in 1958 he returned home to the Chicago area he carried the first draft of *Japanese Inn.*

Returning to Japan in 1961, he settled in Shimoda for two years to get to know the setting for this book. While on the spot he wrote the text for *The Black Ship Scroll,* which reproduced an anonymous Japanese artist's hand scroll with its mostly unflattering views of Commodore Perry's visit to Shimoda.

His interest turned next to the ancient Buddhist pilgrimage that circles the island of Shikoku. The result, in 1983, was *Japanese Pilgrimage.*

Since 1976, Statler has lived and worked in Honolulu, where he is adjunct professor of Asian studies at the University of Hawaii.